The MERCHANT *of* MANCHAC

Manchac 23 Jany 1777

Mr. Oliver Pollock

Dear Sir

Your favour of 6th Instant is now before me, the Contents of which have observed; I am Much oblig'd to Mr. Proffit for having mentioned to you that I had a number of Illinois Stag'd Skins on hand; But as they have Been Remited to me in payement at the rate of bbls p lb, Can't think as yeat to Let them go for Less; then what they Cost me, I Shall be down with them myself in the cource of the Insueing month and if something more Can be had for them then 35 tbls; you Shall have the refusal

I am much oblig'd to you for your kind offer, & Should with pleasure have Dailte with you, But have found an occation of Supplying myself hear, on such Reasonable terms that I Could not Defer supplying myself Prettey plaintifully for the Sale of the Insueing year; with out; it is much more Large then I ever found it at Manchac; this with my Best Respects to you & Mrs. Pollock is the needfull from

Dear Sir
yours &c

The MERCHANT *of* MANCHAC

The Letterbooks of John Fitzpatrick, 1768-1790

Edited with an Introduction by
MARGARET FISHER DALRYMPLE

Published for the Baton Rouge Bicentennial Corporation by the
 LOUISIANA STATE UNIVERSITY PRESS
 Baton Rouge and London

Copyright © 1978 by Louisiana State University Press
All rights reserved
Manufactured in the United States of America

Design: Dwight Agner
Composition: Heritage Printers, Inc.
Printing: Heritage Printers, Inc.
Binding: The Delmar Companies

LIBRARY OF CONGRESS CATALOGING IN PUBLICATION DATA

Fitzpatrick, John, ca. 1737–1791.
   The merchant of Manchac.

  Bibliography: p.
  Includes index.
   1. Louisiana—History—To 1803—Sources.　2. Fitzpatrick, John, ca. 1737–1791.　3. Pioneers—Louisiana—Biography.　4. Merchants—Louisiana—Biography.
I. Dalrymple, Margaret Fisher.　II. Title.
F373.F57　　1978　　　　976.3′03′0924　　　　77-28801
ISBN 0–8071–0268–7

For MAX SAVELLE,
who has so generously shared
with so many
the joys of scholarship
and a civilized life

CONTENTS

	Preface	ix
	Acknowledgments	xi
	Introduction	3
Part One	1768–1769	35
Part Two	1770–1775	81
Part Three	1776–1778	199
Part Four	1779–1790	309
Appendix I	The Succession of John Fitzpatrick	425
Appendix II	Glossary of Eighteenth-Century Mercantile Terms	433
	Bibliography	437
	Index	445

LIST OF MAPS

following page 164

Louisiana and British West Florida, 1776
Settlement of Manchac, 1772
Mississippi River from Bayou Manchac to Pointe Coupée, 1778
Mississippi River from Thompson's Creek to Buffalo Creek, 1778

PREFACE

THE LETTERBOOKS of John Fitzpatrick, which repose in manuscript form in the Manuscripts and Archives Division of the New York Public Library, comprise a rare source of firsthand information about colonial Louisiana and the period of British ascendancy on the Gulf Coast, and provide insight into the mind of a true pioneer, a man who did not win, but who endured. Although the task of editing them has been a rewarding one, the letterbooks present an editor with several problems. First, they were written by several hands, sometimes Fitzpatrick's own and sometimes those of men he occasionally employed as clerks to write his letters and accounts and to make the copies which are preserved in the letterbooks. These hands vary in legibility and their owners in literacy. Consequently, the letters display a considerable variety of notions about spelling and punctuation, and are written in styles which vary from a trained eighteenth-century clerical hand to Fitzpatrick's own heavy scrawl. Second, the physical condition of the letterbooks has presented problems, as many pages have faded and others are torn or badly damaged by acid migration.

It is therefore appropriate to make an explanation of the editorial policy employed in transcribing the letters. The transcription is as exact as the physical condition of the letters allows, preserving the spelling and punctuation of the originals. Where necessary for comprehension or ease of reading, omitted words, letters, or punctuation marks have been added in brackets, and where additional comment or explanation has seemed desirable, it has been added either as a bracketed and italicized insertion in the text or as a footnote. Words or passages which were illegible have been indicated, and questionable readings are followed by an appropriate symbol: [?]. Occasionally, a word or passage has been legible, but its meaning remains an enigma to the editor. In such cases, the exact transcription will permit the reader to employ his own knowledge or imagination in rendering clear what has hitherto been obscure. Usually, the symbols and abbreviations employed in the manuscript have been preserved. There are two exceptions: the symbols used for *per* and *at* have been spelled out into full words. A number of letters written in Fitzpatrick's highly idiosyncratic French have been translated into modern English, and all letters so treated are identified.

Each letter has been given a standardized heading, indicating the person to whom it was written and the place of his residence, if known. Likewise, the date and place from which the letter was written are given in standardized form. The salutations and complimentary closings characteristic of the eighteenth-century epistolary style have been omitted, and elision marks have been inserted at the end of each letter to point out the deletion of the closing. Accounts and other financial information are transcribed exactly as written; where necessary, explanations are provided in footnotes. A few letters have been rearranged into strict chronological order to make it easier for the reader to follow the continuity of Fitzpatrick's story.

While the letterbooks themselves bear no clear chronological divisions, the text has been arbitrarily divided for the convenience of the reader into four sections which reflect the fluctuations of Fitzpatrick's fortunes. Part One contains the letters written between 1768 and 1769, during his residence in New Orleans and his stay in Mobile after his expulsion from Spanish Louisiana. Part Two contains the letters written from Fitzpatrick's arrival in Manchac in February, 1770, until the end of 1775, years during which he established himself as a frontier merchant and began to enjoy a degree of prosperity. Part Three, containing letters written between 1776 and 1778, reflects the turmoil wrought by the American Revolution; and Part Four, from 1779 to 1790, reflects the changes in West Florida brought by the Spanish conquest and Fitzpatrick's efforts to recoup his wartime losses.

Eighteenth-century merchants dealt in a number of products unfamiliar to many modern readers, and their business was transacted in terms equally obscure. To assist the reader through these linguistic brambles, a glossary of mercantile terms is included at the end of the book.

ACKNOWLEDGMENTS

FEW PROJECTS of this type are ever completed without the assistance and encouragement of many people, and the scholar always remains their grateful debtor. I wish first of all to acknowledge my gratitude to the Baton Rouge Bicentennial Corporation, which has provided funds to help defray the cost of publication. A member of the commission, Mrs. Jo Ann Samuel, saw the project through from its inception, and her unflagging support is greatly appreciated. To Charles East, former director of the LSU Press, I owe my introduction to John Fitzpatrick; the support and advice which both he and his successor, Leslie E. Phillabaum, provided have been of great assistance to me, and I gratefully thank them. I am also grateful to the administration of Louisiana State University, which granted me a sabbatical leave during which this book was completed.

The staffs of a number of libraries and special collections have been of enormous assistance in helping me locate and use materials needed in this project. They include the staffs of the Louisiana State University Library, Louisiana State University School of Geoscience Map Library, the Louisiana State Museum Archives and Library, the Louisiana State Land Office, the Department of History and Archives of the Baton Rouge Catholic Life Center, the Louisiana Division of the New Orleans Public Library, the New Orleans Notarial Archives, the Louisiana Division of the Louisiana State Library, the St. Louis Cathedral Archives, the East Baton Rouge Parish Clerk of Court's Office, and the Louisiana State Archives and Records Commission. All these people, dedicated custodians of the historical heritage of Louisiana, have earned my sincere thanks for their assistance. Finally, I wish to thank Jared W. Bradley, who shared his knowledge of early Louisiana history and its sources and thereby directed me to materials I might not otherwise have found.

Despite all efforts to eliminate them, some errors may unfortunately remain. For these, I accept full responsibility.

Last, but by no means least, I wish to thank my husband Nick, who not only graciously endured my long preoccupation with

John Fitzpatrick, that demanding other man in my life, but sustained my labors with his customary encouragement, good humor, and love. Without him, such work might still be possible, but it would be not nearly as pleasant.

The MERCHANT *of* MANCHAC

INTRODUCTION

WHEN JOHN FITZPATRICK came to the Mississippi Valley in the early 1760s, the region was just emerging from a long period of international dispute, warfare, and political change. For nearly fifty years, the trans-Appalachian West had been a subject of bitter contention between Britain and France. Rich in natural resources (particularly furs, minerals, and fertile land), populated by Indians who provided potential markets for European manufactures, and drained by an arterial system of rivers that promoted both commerce and conquest, the Mississippi Valley was regarded by both sides as the essential heart of a great American empire. The ultimate showdown between the rival domains came with the outbreak of the Seven Years' War in 1756, and by the time the peace treaties were signed in 1763 Britain had virtually driven France off the North American continent. France surrendered all claims to its territory on the east side of the Mississippi River, with the sole exception of a small area surrounding New Orleans, and Spain, which had entered the war as an ally of France, ceded Florida to Britain for the return of Havana, which had fallen to the British in 1762. France, in its turn, ceded Louisiana, its vast colony on the western side of the Mississippi, to Spain, partly to console its unfortunate ally for the loss of Florida and partly because it could no longer afford to maintain that relatively unprofitable colony.

Even before the war was over, ambitious and energetic British merchants, farmers, and hunters began to move across the Appalachians into the Ohio Valley, the Illinois country, and the Gulf Coast. To most observers of the period, it seemed there were great fortunes to be made in these new British colonies, and many men came prepared to endure the rigors of frontier life in the hope of eventually acquiring wealth. Among these men was John Fitzpatrick. Like many others on the frontier, Fitzpatrick left most of his past behind him. Of his early life, he has revealed only that he was born in Waterford, Ireland, about 1737, and that he was Roman Catholic.[1] The date of his arrival in America is unknown. During the Seven Years' War he spent three and a half years in

1/Declaration of John Fitzpatrick, December, 1784, Survey of Federal Archives, *Archives of the Spanish Government of West Florida: Transcriptions and Translations* (19 vols.; Baton Rouge, 1937), I, 28–34.

military service as a colonial ranger with Major Robert Rogers. By 1762 Fitzpatrick was in Illinois, employed as a trader by the firm of Oakes and Godderd (or Goddard). In August of 1763 he was captured by Indians and held prisoner for some time before making his escape. In 1764 he visited West Florida for the first time when he came to Mobile. By the end of that year he was in Montréal where he transacted business with a local merchant named Laurent Ermantinger. By November of 1765 he was back in Illinois, a partner of a man named Francis Lavering. At some time previously, perhaps after leaving Montréal and before arriving in Illinois, Fitzpatrick and Lavering had traded at Michilimackinac, at the northern end of Lake Michigan.[2]

It is not known when Fitzpatrick first arrived in New Orleans. The letterbooks begin in 1768, and the earliest documents pertaining to Fitzpatrick's activities preserved among the New Orleans Superior Council records also date from 1768. However, from the context of the letters, we may assume that he resided there for some time previously, for in the earliest letters he discussed a well-established mercantile business with close ties to business firms in Mobile and Pensacola.

New Orleans, when John Fitzpatrick first lived there, was the largest town in the Mississippi Valley. A census ordered by Governor O'Reilly in 1769 counted 3,190 people, 1,225 of whom were slaves, and 468 houses.[3] Most buildings were constructed of wood, and many none too solidly. The major buildings which survive from the colonial period, including St. Louis Cathedral, the flanking Cabildo and Presbytère, and most of the residential buildings, date from the Spanish period. In 1768, the town had a rougher appearance. Life there was also sometimes rough; the numerous regulations concerning gambling, taverns, undisciplined slaves, and adulterated alcohols indicate that the town still retained many of the characteristics of a frontier settlement.

New Orleans was also the economic hub of the lower Mississippi Valley. It was from New Orleans that European goods were distributed throughout the colony, and to New Orleans that local products were sent for export. When the Seven Years' War was ended, the fur trade became one of the dominant economic activities of the town, as peace returned to the hunting grounds and the hunters again began sending their pelts down the Mississippi for shipment to Europe. In 1764, the Custom House recorded the exportation of 700,080 skins of all types, equalling about one hundred thousand British pounds sterling.[4]

Throughout North America, the mechanics of the fur trade differed little from one region to another. Pack-trains of horses or

2/John Fitzpatrick to Laurent Ermantinger, August 24, 1775, March 8, 1784, in Fitzpatrick Letterbooks. See this volume, pp. 196, 408.

3/François-Xavier Martin, *The History of Louisiana from the Earliest Period* (New Orleans, 1882), 206.

4/George Johnstone to Pownall, May 4, 1765, in Public Record Office, Colonial Office (PRO, CO), 5/574, p. 338.

convoys of canoes left the frontier settlements for the wilderness laden with such "Indian goods" as blankets, cloth, hardware, arms and ammunition, trinkets, and such alcoholic beverages as rum and brandy. Once in the Indian country, the traders would haggle for skins taken by the Indians during their hunts of the previous winter. Often, they remained in the wilderness through several seasons, trading and doing some hunting of their own, until their goods were exhausted, when they returned to civilization to dispose of the pelts.[5] Usually, the hunters and traders gave a first lien on the gross profits of their enterprise to the merchants who outfitted them. If the profits from the sale of the pelts did not equal the debt, the unpaid balance became a junior lien on future ventures, and the next year's outfit assumed a senior lien.[6] Through misfortune or mismanagement, some traders were never able to pay off their unpaid balances, and the accumulating interest caused their debts to grow greater each year. The vastness of the country and the difficulties of collecting unpaid debts plagued all merchants who engaged in the fur trade, as can be seen by John Fitzpatrick's efforts to bring his various debtors to payment.

The great staple of the fur trade was beaver, prized by European hatmakers as the source of fiber for lustrous, high-quality felt; however, martin, mink, and other furs also fetched high prices. In the Southwest, furs were somewhat less important than deer hides, which were sent to Europe to be processed into fine-grade leathers. The natural outlet for the fur trade of the vast country between the Appalachians and the Rocky Mountains was the Mississippi River, and in the last third of the eighteenth century hundreds of tons of skins came down from the Great Lakes region, the Illinois country, and the Missouri Valley.[7] Other branches of the fur trade developed in Natchitoches, along the Louisiana–Texas frontier, in Arkansas, and along the upper reaches of the river valleys of Alabama. Almost all the furs eventually came to New Orleans, and it was from New Orleans that the goods used in the trade passed through the first of the many hands that ultimately would bring them to the Indian lodges of the Great Lakes and the western rivers.

Besides the fur trade, agriculture was the other principal economic activity in colonial Louisiana. The most important agricultural export of the region was indigo, which flourished throughout the lower Mississippi Valley and was the major cash crop in Louisiana and eventually of the British plantations along the lower Mississippi River. Although some contemporary experts believed that Louisiana indigo was inferior to that grown in Central America and on some of the West Indian islands, the dye usually found a ready market in European textile centers and in

5/Max Savelle, *A History of Colonial America* (Rev. ed.; New York, 1964), 437.

6/Stanley Faye, "The Arkansas Post of Louisiana: Spanish Domination," *Louisiana Historical Quarterly*, XXVII (1944), 637–38.

7/John G. Clark, *New Orleans, 1718–1812: An Economic History* (Baton Rouge, 1970), 193.

a good year brought as much as a dollar a pound, and occasionally more. Its production, however, required a large capital outlay for equipment and a considerable labor force, so it was a crop mostly limited to large and prosperous plantations.[8] Less affluent planters and all sorts of small farmers depended on tobacco to augment their incomes. This crop had the advantage of being easily cultivated throughout the region, of requiring little labor in its processing, and of being easily transported. Another valuable product was lumber, and many men along the river derived considerable incomes from the production of barrel staves and construction lumber for the West Indies, and of the lumber, pitch, and tar used by local shipyards.[9] Corn and rice were also important crops, although they were grown mostly for domestic consumption.[10] Cotton and sugar had not yet assumed the importance they were to hold in the nineteenth century.

Transportation throughout the region was mainly concentrated along the waterways, since land travel was often hampered by heavy vegetation, swamps, and other natural obstacles. There was a road or trail that extended north from New Orleans along the east bank of the Mississippi River, although it does not seem to have been heavily traveled, and after 1763 a road developed between Baton Rouge and Natchez. From New Orleans a road ran back to Bayou St. John, the town's outlet to Lake Pontchartrain, and still another south along the riverbank to the plantations below the town. A trail was developed by the British along the north bank of Bayou Manchac, or the Iberville River, as the British called it, joining the head of navigation on the bayou, near the Amite River, with the British settlement at Manchac on the bank of the Mississippi.[11]

Water routes were much more frequently used, particularly for transportation of goods. The Mississippi River was, of course, the main channel for all movement. Ocean-going ships coming from the Gulf of Mexico or ports along the Gulf Coast landed first at the Balize, a fortified port at the mouth of the river. From there they could begin the laborious voyage upriver to New Orleans, or else transfer their cargoes and passengers to smaller ships for that part of the journey. New Orleans could also be reached by sailing through the Rigolets and Lake Pontchartrain, a route which many captains preferred, since it allowed them to avoid the strong currents and treacherous sandbars of the river. The route through Lake Pontchartrain and adjoining Lake Maurepas was also heavily used by British boats coming from Pensacola and Mobile. By traveling from Lake Maurepas up the Amite River to Bayou Manchac, and then up that stream to the head of navigation, a portage of about ten miles brought them to the Mississippi

8/Jack D. L. Holmes, "Indigo in Colonial Louisiana," *Louisiana History*, VIII (1967), 335–42.

9/Clark, *New Orleans, 1718–1812*, 29.

10/For a fuller discussion of the economy of colonial Louisiana and its environs, see Nancy M. Miller Surrey, *The Commerce of Louisiana During the French Regime, 1699–1763* (New York, 1916); Clark, *New Orleans, 1718–1812*; and the monumental work of Marcel Giraud, *L'Histoire de la Louisiane française* (4 vols.; Paris, 1953–75).

11/Frederick Stephen Ellis, "American Activity in Louisiana and West Florida during the Revolutionary War," *St. Tammany Historical Society Gazette*, I (1975), 4.

River. By this route the voyage from Pensacola to the Manchac settlement was accomplished in about eight to ten days, as opposed to the seven or eight weeks usually required to go by the Mississippi River.¹² The voyage from New Orleans to Mobile, going either through Lake Pontchartrain or down the river, took about four days.¹³

Traffic on the river between New Orleans and the Illinois country was quite heavy. Most boats from the Illinois, laden with furs, flour, and various local products, began the trip downriver about the beginning of February, when the water was high and the current at its fastest, about five miles per hour. The period of flood not only permitted faster travel, but the high water covered many of the sandbars that otherwise obstructed river traffic and helped discourage attacks from Indians along the river. Depending on weather and other conditions, the trip from the Illinois to New Orleans could be made in from twelve to twenty-five days. Most traffic from New Orleans to the Illinois left in convoys between August and November, when the river was lowest and the current slowest, about three miles per hour. The journey upriver was infinitely more difficult, since instead of drifting on the current the boats had to be rowed against it, or else "warped" along the shore, a laborious method of locomotion by which boats were hauled up the river with no help but the leverage obtained by pulling the tow ropes around trees along the bank. This trip, which required a sizable crew on each boat, took three or four months.¹⁴

The most common boat on the river was the "canoe" or "pirogue," a dugout, frequently made of cypress, about forty to fifty feet long and three to five feet wide, able to carry thirty men and with a freight capacity ranging up to five tons. It was normally propelled by oars but could also use sail when the wind was favorable. Large rafts called flatboats or "flatts" were used for the downriver trip; they could drift with the current, were able to carry large loads of cargo, and were easily constructed from the plentiful timber of the upriver country. Other small boats, constructed from local timber, plied the river and the lakes; they were propelled by oars, sails, or both, and were called, by French and English alike, *batteaux*.¹⁵

When the Peace of Paris gave Britain access to the Mississippi Valley and the Gulf Coast, British colonial administrators expected to share in the wealth which they believed flowed through New Orleans. Many believed that the prosperity of the new southwestern colony of West Florida depended upon participation in Louisiana's commerce. As West Florida governor George Johnstone reported in 1764, "the disposition of all seems to Lead them

Introduction

12/Memorial of Thomas Hutchins, 1779, PRO, CO 5/595, p. 318.
13/Surrey, *The Commerce of Louisiana During the French Regime*, 75.
14/*Ibid.*, 46, 75.
15/*Ibid.*, 57–64.

to Return [to the east coast] if the Spanish Commerce is not Open'd."[16] There was hope that the Spanish government would permit legal trade between Louisiana and West Florida, for this would provide the fastest returns of wealth to Britain. Governor Johnstone explained late in 1765 that "The fact is so that our Trade does not Yet admit of a direct intercourse of returns to Britain & unless the Spanish Commerce is open'd on a generous footing can we expect it (such returns) will take place soon."[17]

It was, in fact, the supposedly great commercial potential of Louisiana that drew many Englishmen to the southwestern area, and trade patterns there were established far more rapidly than the land itself was settled and placed under cultivation. British manufactured goods and foodstuffs from the northeastern colonies poured into the region through the Ohio Valley and by sea around Florida to the newly-British Gulf Coast ports at Mobile and Pensacola, and into New Orleans, the economic nucleus of the entire region.

This intercolonial commerce was one of the economic anomalies of the seventeenth and eighteenth centuries. In principle, the mercantilist imperial governments in Europe normally closed their overseas colonies to all foreign trade, reserving the use of their markets and products for themselves. In practice, local scarcities and surpluses were often relieved by recourse to a neighboring foreign colony, and temporary instances of local intercolonial trade can be found throughout the colonial period. In some cases, this clandestine trade evolved into a permanent commercial institution.

In America, such secret trade with the Spanish colonies became an important source of revenue for several nations. Spain, from almost the very beginning of its colonial establishment, lacked adequate native manufactures to supply its farflung overseas empire, and as Spanish colonial populations grew in numbers and wealth the problems of supply became ever more critical. The proximity of the colonies of more productive nations provided constant opportunity for clandestine trade, which supplemented the inadequate supplies sent from the mother country, and at times even supplanted them. Spanish colonial officials, recognizing that this trade was essential to the prosperity and sometimes the very survival of their colonies, tended to ignore or even protect foreign traders, and the entire commercial process, although absolutely illegal, became a recognized and highly valued branch of the overseas commerce of several nations.

Spanish Louisiana was no exception to this situation, either in the crushing scarcity of all types of manufactured goods and of basic foodstuffs which existed in the colony at the end of the war,

16/Johnstone to Pownall, February 19, 1764, PRO, CO 5/574, p. 230.

17/Johnstone to Secretary of the Board of Trade, December 29, 1765, PRO, CO 5/574, p. 953.

or in the ease with which clandestine trade could be carried on. British merchants, with over a century of smuggling experience in the Spanish Caribbean colonies behind them, were ready and eager to fill this need and soon became the principal suppliers of Louisiana. They were for several years spectacularly successful. British merchants, protected by "flags of truce," began to appear in French New Orleans during the late 1750s, bringing dry goods and foodstuffs which had become scarce in the colony. British control of the seas had raised the prices of various goods to such unprecedented levels that a shipowner, equipped with a commission from one of the British colonial governors and a few French prisoners, could make an extremely profitable voyage.[18] The scarcities in Louisiana, which at this time was dependent on outside sources for most of the major necessities of life, were so acute that all such ships, no matter how flimsy the pretext for their visit, were welcomed and quickly found buyers for their cargoes. Even after the war ended and Louisiana was transferred to Spanish control, British merchants continued to play an important role in the economic life of the colony. Many of the British mercantile houses which came to dominate the trade of the Gulf Coast had already been established, and numerous independent merchants like John Fitzpatrick had located themselves in New Orleans. By the time Alexander O'Reilly arrived as governor in 1769, the English seemed to dominate Louisiana's economy: "I found the English entirely in possession of the commerce of this colony. They had merchants among the Germans and stores in this city, and I can assure you that they got nine-tenths of all the ready money spent there. The commerce of France accepted the products of the colony in payment for goods, but the English, selling more cheaply, got all the silver."[19]

The overwhelming presence of the British was not, however, the most serious of the economic problems which afflicted Louisiana during the late 1760s. The vast and poorly populated colony had languished during the French regime under an inefficient and often venal administration, underdeveloped agriculture, and a constant lack of sound currency. By the time the French ceded the colony to Spain in 1763, Louisiana's monetary problems had become critical.

These problems were almost as old as the colony itself. Because the French government was burdened with heavy indebtedness and always reluctant to divert precious metals from the economy of the metropolis, Louisiana during the French regime had experienced a chronic scarcity of coins, whether of gold, silver, or copper. What little specie came into the colony, whether brought by colonists or government officials or as the result of

Introduction

18/This trade by "flags of truce," or *parlementaires* as the French called them, was a long-established feature of the colonial wars of the seventeenth and eighteenth centuries. The colonies were usually unwilling to expend public funds to hire ships for the exchange of military prisoners, so private ships were used instead, and the owners permitted to compensate themselves for the cost of the voyage by carrying on trade in the enemy port where the prisoners were delivered. See Abraham P. Nasatir and James R. Mills, *Commerce and Contraband in New Orleans during the French and Indian War: A Documentary Study of the Texel and Three Brothers Affairs* (Cincinnati, 1968), 6–7, 166–67.

19/Governor Alexander O'Reilly to Arriago, October 17, 1769, in Lawrence Kinnaird (ed.), *Spain in the Mississippi Valley, 1765–1794*, in *Annual Report of the American Historical Association for 1945*, (Washington, D.C., 1946–49), Vols. II–IV Pt. 1, pp. 104–105.

foreign trade, soon vanished to pay for imports. In an attempt to remedy this deficiency, the colonial administration periodically flooded Louisiana with paper currency of greatly fluctuating values. In addition to paper money, the colonists also attempted to fill the gap with bills of exchange, French treasury notes, storehouse receipts, and contracts. In such monetary confusion, many transactions were carried out on a barter basis.

By the time Governor Ulloa arrived in 1766, French paper currency circulated at a discount of nearly 50 percent. The Spanish troops refused to accept this virtually worthless money, as did foreign creditors and everyone paid from the royal exchequer. Lack of confidence in the currency also crippled the colony's commerce, since everything had to be bought on credit and creditors would not accept the local currency as payment for debts. The commercial stagnation which Fitzpatrick describes in his early letters threatened to destroy the economy of the colony.

Governor Ulloa's efforts to shore up the colonial currency met with little success. First, he offered to assume the expenses of the colony, including the debts of the previous colonial administration. The specie he brought with him was quickly expended, and the coins rapidly disappeared in recognition of their value over currency. Ulloa was then forced to seek additional funds, as the paper currency fell into total discredit and the colony's economy seemed utterly dependent on generous subsidies of Spanish specie. His letters from Louisiana constantly repeat his requests for additional funds, but the money that was sent was always inadequate. An allotment of sixty thousand pesos arrived from Cuba at the end of August, 1767; by mid-September it was gone, but the creditors of the colonial government had still not all been paid. By December the colonial exchequer ceased to pay anyone, including soldiers and officials. An allotment of one hundred thousand pesos which arrived in July, 1768, was also insufficient to pay the obligations of the exchequer.[20]

When Governor O'Reilly arrived in Louisiana in August, 1769, he had orders to reorganize the colony's administration and economy. The leaders of the revolt of 1768, which had driven Governor Ulloa out of the colony, were arrested and tried. Some were exiled, others executed by firing squad. O'Reilly then proceeded to reorganize the provincial government to conform with other local institutions in the Spanish empire, and he introduced measures to assimilate the colony into the legal, military, and fiscal branches of the empire.

It was as apparent to O'Reilly as it had been to Ulloa that the economy of the colony was in dire straits, and so he sought measures to develop a viable commercial system to support it. Direct

20/For further information about Louisiana's monetary crisis, see Ulloa's letters to Don Antonio María Bucareli, 1767–68, in Kinnaird (ed.), *Spain in the Mississippi Valley*, Pt. 1; John Preston Moore, *Revolt in Louisiana: The Spanish Occupation, 1766–1770* (Baton Rouge, 1976), 33, 113–23; and Jack D. L. Holmes, "Some Economic Problems of the Spanish Governors of Louisiana," *Hispanic American Historical Review*, XLII (1962), 521–43.

trade was permitted with Cuba and French St. Domingue, and efforts were made to find markets for local products. Because the Spanish government not only opposed smuggling in principle, but also recognized that foreign merchants presented serious competition to their efforts to encourage the development of domestic trade, the activities of foreign merchants, particularly the British, were ended or severely curbed. The commercial decree of March, 1768, which confined the carrying trade to Spanish vessels, was enforced. Then, on September 2, 1769, O'Reilly ordered all English merchants, including John Fitzpatrick, to leave the colony after disposing of their present stock of goods.[21] After O'Reilly's departure, however, British smuggling resumed, and by the time it was disrupted by the American Revolution in 1777 it dominated the commerce of Louisiana. But by then, John Fitzpatrick's residence in New Orleans was long over.

When Fitzpatrick learned that he would have to leave Louisiana, he tried frantically and unsuccessfully to terminate his affairs in New Orleans. This proved impossible. Specie was still scarce, and many of his debtors were even more overextended than he. Finally, he was obliged to entrust the settlement of all his business affairs to local friends who remained in the city.

Fitzpatrick left New Orleans on September 21, 1769, and went to Mobile, by this time a growing British commercial center. He made arrangements there to supply himself with an assortment of goods with which to open a store at Manchac, a small British settlement at the confluence of the Mississippi and Bayou Manchac. At the same time, he engaged a schooner, owned by William Marshall of Pensacola, to carry him and his goods up the Mississippi to his new home. Fitzpatrick disembarked in New Orleans in order to collect some unpaid debts but was arrested by Spanish soldiers and imprisoned for thirty-six hours. He was released only by promising to leave town immediately. By February 15 he had arrived in Manchac, where he lived for the rest of his life.

To the British leaders of West Florida in the 1760s, Manchac seemed a site of great strategic and commercial potential. The area was little known to the British when they first moved into West Florida in 1762, but surveys and explorations of their new acquisitions soon convinced them that it was necessary to find a way to circumvent Spanish control of the mouth of the Mississippi, and the water route offered by Lakes Pontchartrain and Maurepas, the Amite River, and Bayou Manchac seemed to promise a convenient way to bypass New Orleans and maintain constant communication between the British ports on the Gulf Coast and the upper parts of the Mississippi River.

21/Clark, *New Orleans, 1718–1812*, 171–73.

The great obstacle in this route was Bayou Manchac, or the Iberville River, as the British called it. Not a river at all, Bayou Manchac was a shallow, slow-moving stream, a typical distributary of the lower Mississippi. Over its first five or six miles the stream carried water only when the Mississippi was high enough to flow through the notch in its natural levee that formed an outlet to the bayou. In low water the bayou's dry bed lay about fifteen feet above the surface of the river, and the lower section of the stream near the Amite River, although filled with water throughout the year, was choked with debris.[22]

Late in 1763, Major Robert Farmar, commander of the British post at Mobile, sent a small force under the command of Lieutenant James Campbell accompanied by fifty slaves to open the channel of the bayou and create a permanent connection with the Mississippi River.[23] The men spent about six months clearing the stream, and by early 1764 Governor Johnstone was preparing to establish a post at Point Iberville which he hoped would eventually contain at least a regiment, for he believed that "There is no place of so much Consequence, to this Province, as that Settlement now the Iberville is open'd, & which will command the whole Trade of the Mississippi."[24] Soon, a number of German and French families from Louisiana applied for permission to move to Manchac, attracted by British promises of free land and protection and disturbed by the desperate state of finances in the Spanish colony. A few British merchants also moved to the settlement. James Campbell, who supervised the clearing project, predicted that "If the Spaniards govern at New Orleans in a short Time that [Manchac] will become a flourishing Settlement."[25]

A survey of Bayou Manchac was made by Philip Pittman in the spring of 1765, and General Thomas Gage, commander-in-chief of the British army in America, decided that an all-water route between the bayou and Lakes Pontchartrain and Maurepas was essential to the security of West Florida.[26] A small post called Fort Bute was established at the top of the bayou by part of the 34th Regiment, but in August a party of about fifty Indians raided the little settlement, broke open the stores and powder magazine, took or destroyed all the arms, killed the livestock, and stole the Indian gifts that were stored there. The British fled down the river to New Orleans.[27] In October, Governor Johnstone ordered the post reestablished, and a small stockade was built. The principal purpose of the post was to keep the channel of the bayou open, to protect the settlement at Manchac and British trade on the Mississippi and the lakes, and to serve as an outpost against the Indians.[28] There were plans to make Fort Bute a major mili-

22/Fred B. Kniffen, "Bayou Manchac: A Physiographic Interpretation," *Geographical Review*, XXV (1935), 462–63. The stream was permanently separated from the Mississippi in 1814 when Andrew Jackson ordered a dam built to block water communication between the two waterways. Subsequent levee construction has furthered the separation.

23/Douglas Stewart Brown, "The Iberville Canal Project: Its Relation to Anglo-French Commercial Rivalry in the Mississippi Valley, 1763–1775," *Mississippi Valley Historical Review*, XXXII (1946), 491–516.

24/Johnstone to Pownall, February 19, 1764, PRO, CO 5/574, p. 248.

25/Campbell to Johnstone, December 12, 1764, PRO, CO 5/574, p. 327.

26/Philip Pittman, *The Present State of the European Settlements on the Mississippi; With a Geographical Description of that River; illustrated by Plans and Draughts* (London, 1770. Reprinted, with introduction by Frank Heywood Hodder; Cleveland, 1906), Introduction; Clarence W. Alvord, *The Mississippi Valley in British Politics: A Study of the Trade, Land Speculation, and Experiments in Imperialism culminating in the American Revolution* (Cleveland, 1917), I, 306.

27/Archibald Robertson to Johnstone, September 2, 1765, PRO, CO 5/574, pp. 889–92.

28/By His Excellency George Johnstone... Orders and Instructions for the Officer appointed to Command at Fort Bute, October 2, 1765, PRO, CO 5/574, pp. 909–11.

tary base, capable of garrisoning over three hundred men and of overwhelming New Orleans if the need ever arose.²⁹

Bayou Manchac, however, again became choked with debris. By the autumn of 1766 it was no longer navigable along its entire length and the surface of the Mississippi lay twenty-four feet below its bed.³⁰ For the rest of the colonial period the little stream was navigable only along its last dozen miles, and it was necessary to carry cargoes in carts or by horseback along a road which was constructed between Manchac and the head of navigation.

In 1768 all but three companies of troops were withdrawn from West Florida, and those remaining were concentrated around Pensacola and Mobile. The Mississippi posts at Natchez and Fort Bute seemed less important for the security of the colony and so were abandoned. John Bradley, a merchant, occupied Fort Panmure at Natchez with the intention of creating a trading post there, and Fort Bute was dismantled "as there were no inhabitants of considerable property" settled there who required its protection.³¹ However, the little settlement at Manchac continued to grow, for it soon developed into a center for contraband trade between West Florida and Spanish Louisiana. Although John Fitzpatrick described the settlement as being "distitute of inhabitants" when he arrived there early in 1770, several other merchants had already established themselves in the vicinity. Isaac Monsanto, a Sephardic Jew expelled from New Orleans at the same time Fitzpatrick was, had a store at Manchac, as did Thomas Bentley, a Virginian who later became a prominent trader in Illinois.

As Fitzpatrick's letters describe, the years between 1770 and 1776 were busy and prosperous ones for the merchants of Manchac. A regular trade developed from Mobile and Pensacola through Lakes Pontchartrain and Maurepas and up the Amite River to "the forks," where the bayou ran into the Amite. From the forks, boats could travel up Bayou Manchac only about twelve miles. There, cargoes were unloaded and carried by horseback along a road which followed the north bank of the bayou to Manchac, where they were loaded aboard the *batteaux* that would carry them up the river, or else were sold locally. The fur trade followed the same pattern in reverse. Because of the irregularity of arrivals and departures of boats from Manchac and from the forks, warehouse facilities were constructed in both places to store furs and the various goods that constituted the trade of the lower Mississippi Valley.

During the years before the American Revolution disrupted the development of West Florida, a number of travelers passed

29/To the Right Honorable the Lords Commissioners . . . The Humble Representation of the Council, November 22, 1766, quoted in Clinton N. Howard, *British Development of West Florida, 1763–1769* (Berkeley and Los Angeles, 1947), 113.
30/Thomas Hutchins, *An Historical Narrative and Topographical Description of Louisiana, and West-Florida*, ed. Joseph G. Tregle, Jr. (Facsimile ed.; Gainesville, Fla., 1968), 60–61.
31/Joseph Barton Starr, "Tories, Dons, and Rebels: The American Revolution in British West Florida" (Ph.D. dissertation, Florida State University, 1971), 51.

through Manchac and left descriptions of the settlement and the surrounding country. Edward Mease, who visited the village in 1770, noted that vestiges of Fort Bute were still visible, but that the settlement itself had few inhabitants and only "mean dwellings."[32]

Rufus Putnam, a merchant, passed through Manchac in 1773 and observed "Several tollarable Houses, & very good gardens, but no Soldiers." Putnam also noted that during the dry season the water in the bayou fell so low "that many thousand fish ware Dead and made a Very Disagreeable Smell."[33]

By the time William Bartram visited Manchac in the autumn of 1777, the settlement had grown into a well-established village. There were numerous buildings, and a few were "large and commodious, particularly the ware-houses of Messrs. Swanson & Co. Indian traders and merchants." Bartram described the banks of the Mississippi at Manchac as being about fifty feet above the surface of the water (he visited the village in autumn, low-water time). There were visible remnants of a levee in front of the buildings of the town, but by 1777 it had partly crumbled as the river encroached on the bluff, and some of the inhabitants seemed in danger of being swallowed by the river.[34] The levee building project with which Fitzpatrick occupied himself in 1779 was apparently badly needed for the safety of the settlement, which during the spring floods must have been very close to the level of the river. Bartram also recorded that the Spanish had a small fort and garrison on the point of land just south of the bayou, close to the bank of the river. The Spanish fort, named San Gabriel de Manchack, communicated with the village by a slender wooden bridge across the bayou and was so close that it lay "not a bow shot from the habitations of Manchac."[35]

Throughout the West Florida period, the colonial government gave intermittent attention to the situation of Manchac and its strategic and economic potential, and many observers criticized the decision to abandon the fort. Thomas Hutchins, who was employed as a surveyor and engineer for the British army in West Florida, passed through Manchac in late 1766 and probably again in 1772. When he was asked to evaluate British and Spanish defenses in the lower Mississippi Valley in the early 1770s, Hutchins commented that "This place, if attended to, might be of consequence to the commerce of West-Florida; for it may with reason be supposed, that the inhabitants and traders who reside at Point Coupée, at Natchitoches, Attacappa, the Natchez, on the East Side of the Mississippi above and below the Natchez, at the Illinois, and St. Vincents on the Ouabasche, would rather trade at this place than at New Orleans, if they could have as good re-

32/Mease, "Narrative of a Journey through several parts of the Province of West Florida in the Year 1770 and 1771," PRO, CO 5/538, p. 364.

33/Albert C. Bates (ed.), *The Two Putnams, Israel and Rufus, in the Havana Expedition 1762 and in the Mississippi River Exploration 1772–73 with some account of The Company of Military Adventurers* (Hartford, Conn., 1931), 174, 245.

34/The Mississippi has since eaten away the entire area on which the village of Manchac stood.

35/William Bartram, *Travels through North & South Carolina, Georgia, East & West Florida, the Cherokee Country, the Extensive Territories of the Muscogulges, or Creek Confederacy, and the Country of the Chactaws*, ed. Francis Harper (New Haven, 1958), 270–71.

turns for their peltry and the produce of their country; for it makes a difference of ten days in their voyage, which is no inconsiderable saving of labour, money, and time." The only disadvantage of the place was the lack of navigation through the bayou to allow constant communication with Pensacola, but this seemed a minor drawback, for the ten-mile-long carriage road between the Mississippi River and the height of navigation on the bayou seemed an adequate substitute.[36]

New Orleans merchant James Jones, who was vitally interested in the development of West Florida, believed that many inhabitants of Louisiana could be induced to migrate into West Florida if sufficient security were available there. The abandonment of Fort Bute was a serious mistake, he maintained, for "Nothing could have been more adverse on this occasion for the miserable People of that Colony [Louisiana], or for the interest of this, than our want of an Establishment on the River Mississippi—Had such been the case, I can affirm with confidence there would have been a Migration of at least one half the Inhabitants to Our Side of the River—Even at this moment there are numbers who wou'd gladly fly to such an assylum, upon the most inconsiderable establishment of a Post any where on this side of Point Coupee."[37]

In response to such criticism, the provincial government generated occasional discussion about the development of Manchac. After Lieutenant Governor Montfort Browne traveled to Natchez in 1768, he recommended to the Earl of Hillsborough that a town be laid out at Fort Bute. Such a town, he predicted, could deflect the immense fur trade which at that time centered in New Orleans.[38] By 1771, plans for such a town had been drawn up. Located on the Mississippi River just above Manchac, it was to be called Harwich and was expected to become an entrepôt for supplying the upper country with British manufactures and goods for the Indian trade. There was some discussion of the possibility of cutting a channel between the Mississippi and Bayou Manchac to allow year-round water communication, and the possibility of eventually transferring the provincial capital from Pensacola to Harwich was also considered.[39] Despite such optimism, however, the town was never built. The site was apparently swampy and periodically inundated by floods from the Mississippi River.

In 1775 the Manchac area was again the subject of official consideration. The West Florida Council debated the establishment of a town at the confluence of the Amite and Bayou Manchac, to be called Dartmouth. The provincial council agreed that the town be established and described the division of lots, but no settlement in the area was undertaken until several years later, when the Spanish governor of Louisiana ordered a post established there

36/Hutchins, *An Historical Narrative*, 42–44.

37/James Jones to Frederick Haldimand, March 14, 1770, General Frederick Haldimand Papers, British Museum, Additional Manuscripts 21729 (microfilm in Department of Archives and Manuscripts, Louisiana State University).

38/Browne to Earl of Hillsborough, July 6, 1768, PRO, CO 5/577, pp. 5–6.

39/Peter Chester to Earl of Hillsborough, September 20, 1771, July 13, 1772, PRO, CO 5/578, p. 309, 5/579, p. 135.

to protect that approach to the island of Orleans from the British. At the same time that the establishment of Dartmouth was being discussed, the West Florida Council again considered the establishment of a town above Manchac. Several petitions for land in that area were received, but the council decided not to grant any land until the town was laid out.[40] Before any further action was taken, the disorders of the Revolutionary War halted the development of the Manchac area.

For John Fitzpatrick and his neighbors, these discussions seemed remote from the daily business of trade and farming. Life at Manchac must have been fairly placid. The settlement was isolated, and the terrain of the surrounding country discouraged casual visits around the neighborhood. The humid climate, the fevers bred in the nearby swamps, and the frequent scarcity of fresh food and of such luxuries as wine and books brought to Manchac the same hardships endured in any other frontier community—endemic diseases, loneliness, boredom, and discomfort.

In 1772 this life was disrupted by a local upheaval which caused great bitterness in the community and left Fitzpatrick threatening to leave Manchac. In October, 1771, a former artillery lieutenant named John Thomas had arrived at Manchac with an appointment as deputy superintendent of Indians for the Small Tribes. These Indians, chiefly Tonicas, eked out a meager existence on both sides of the Mississippi, having been driven out of their earlier homes on the coastal plain by more powerful tribes. Thomas had previously served at Fort Bute from 1765 to 1767 as part of the construction crew. He had been granted one thousand acres at Manchac in February, 1768, and by the end of that year was in New York, attempting to stimulate official interest in the Manchac area. In 1769 Thomas had sailed for England and returned early in 1771 with his appointment as deputy superintendent, which directed him to prevent abuses in the Indian trade and to counteract Spanish influence with the Small Tribes.[41]

Thomas had a tendency toward visionary and impractical ideas, as well as a dictatorial personality, and his tenure as deputy superintendent was fraught with difficulties. He accused both French and Spanish of attempting to gain the affection of English Indian allies, he was criticized for interfering with Spanish Indians, and he rapidly exhausted his limited budget.[42] By the spring of 1772, Thomas's superiors in Pensacola were thoroughly disgusted with his performance. Even more disgusted were the British merchants and traders on the river and at Manchac. As a deputy superintendent of Indians, and as a duly appointed justice of the peace, Thomas had been given authority to concern him-

40/Council minutes, November 13, 1775, PRO, CO 5/592, pp. 285–88.

41/Robert R. Rea, "Redcoats and Redskins on the Lower Mississippi, 1763–1776: The Career of Lt. John Thomas," *Louisiana History*, XI (1970), 5–33; John Richard Alden, *John Stuart and the Southern Colonial Frontier: A Study of Indian Relations, War, Trade, and Land Problems in the Southern Wilderness, 1754–1775* (Ann Arbor, 1944), 318–19.

42/Alden, *John Stuart and the Southern Colonial Frontier*, 330–31.

self with the activities of Indian traders and with civil matters in Manchac, but he seems to have assumed responsibilities far beyond those granted him. Moreover, the men with whom he had to deal were accustomed to running the settlement for their own convenience. The military barracks in the former fort were used by some of the merchants as storehouses, and the occupants refused to vacate the area to Thomas, who was forced to spend a sizable portion of his small budget refurnishing quarters for himself and his family. Other inhabitants, among them John Fitzpatrick, apparently used wood from the fort as firewood, rather than cut wood on their own land.[43] When drunken Indians broke into Thomas's house one night, the deputy accused Fitzpatrick of having supplied them with drink, a crime the merchant not only acknowledged but swore to do again whenever the Indians wished to trade.[44]

Thomas announced that he intended to control British trade on the lower Mississippi, forbidding any commercial activity without his permission or any departures from Manchac without his passport. Much of the trade conducted in the village was with French and Spanish residents of Louisiana and therefore technically illegal (although tolerated by both colonial governments), and Thomas's attempt to stop it aroused the hostility of the Manchac merchants. When a Monsieur Morell landed at Manchac with the intention of paying a debt he owed Fitzpatrick, Thomas ordered him to leave. Fitzpatrick insisted that Morell first settle his account, whereupon Thomas sent to the nearby Spanish fort for guards, who arrested Morell for illegal trade with a foreign colony.[45] On another occasion, a Mr. Hamilton from Opelousas came ashore to pay a debt to Fitzpatrick, and Thomas refused to allow him to return to his raft until he paid a twenty-dollar "debt" to an Indian.[46]

Thomas was openly disdainful of all the merchants, whom he regarded as "all dram shop keepers . . . and insulting vagabonds." John Fitzpatrick, however, received his most violent abuse, and the hatred of Thomas which Fitzpatrick expresses in his letters was amply returned by the deputy. Thomas accused Fitzpatrick of beating Indians, of cheating them, of kidnapping a Spanish trader, and of challenging him to a fight but backing down when he offered to accept. Thomas publicly declared he would ruin Fitzpatrick by any means he could find, and the harassment which Fitzpatrick describes was part of Thomas's method.[47]

By March of 1772 the merchants of Manchac were sufficiently outraged by Thomas's conduct to petition the provincial council to have him removed, describing in detail instances of his "absolute and despotic command."[48] Fitzpatrick was not among the

43/Thomas to John Stuart, March 12, 1772, PRO, CO 5/579, p. 66.
44/Rea, "Redcoats and Redskins," 21.
45/Affidavit of John Fitzpatrick, February 12, 1772, PRO, CO 5/589, pp. 354–55.
46/Petition of residents of Manchac, March 9, 1772, PRO, CO 5/579, pp. 55–60.
47/Rea, "Redcoats and Redskins," 22–24.
48/Petition of residents of Manchac, March 9, 1772, PRO, CO 5/579, pp. 55–60.

eight signers, who were Jacob and Manuel Monsanto, Charles Blanchard, James Kelly, Jacob Leonard, George Harrison, William Escott, and Joseph Pavie. Fitzpatrick made his complaints separately, first in a sworn affidavit taken when he visited Mobile in February, then in a letter to Philip Livingston, who sat on the West Florida Council and was apparently an acquaintance.[49] Louisiana governor Unzaga also protested Thomas's actions, threatening to arrest him if he ever set foot on Spanish soil.

In response to these complaints and on the recommendation of the council, Thomas's commission as a justice of the peace was rescinded and his appointment as deputy superintendent of Indians terminated in early April. Indian supplies at Fort Bute were transferred to Fitzpatrick's keeping. On April 22, Thomas was attacked by George Harrison, Thomas Topham, and several others, and in the ensuing struggle Thomas killed Harrison. A few days later Thomas Bentley and two companions drove the Thomas family out of their house and confined them to "a little stinking henhouse." Thomas was accused of having murdered Harrison, and at the end of May he was sent to Pensacola for trial. The jury there acquitted him, giving a verdict of excusable self-defense.[50]

Thomas returned to Manchac late in 1773 and continued his efforts to win the support of the Mississippi Indians. His presence had no further effect on the Manchac merchants, who, as before, carried on business with all comers. Thomas died there about June, 1776, and was succeeded by Henry Stuart, brother of Indian superintendent John Stuart.[51]

During these years, the province of West Florida experienced its greatest growth under British government. The Proclamation of 1763 promised land in the new colonies to veterans of the war, acreage to be allotted in proportion to rank. Field officers could receive up to 5,000 acres, captains up to 3,000, non-commissioned officers 200 acres, and private persons 50.[52] In practice, many grants were larger. People with influential connections were sometimes given very large grants which they held purely for speculation, and private persons often applied in family groups, thereby acquiring a substantial holding from a number of adjoining grants.

This generous land policy, together with the anticipated development of trade with the Spanish colonies, attracted many people to West Florida. Agents for London merchants began planning investments in the province, potential sites for dockyards and stores were quickly occupied, and land speculators, retired military people, and civilians optimistically invested in land

---

49/See this volume, p. 116.

50/Chester to Hillsborough, October 27, 1772, PRO, CO 5/579, pp. 241–45; Rea, "Redcoats and Redskins," 24–29.

51/Rea, "Redcoats and Redskins," 34–35.

52/Henry P. Dart (ed.), "British Proclamation of October 7, 1763, Creating the Government of West Florida," *Louisiana Historical Quarterly*, XIII (1930), 612.

that promised to become the source of valuable semitropical products like indigo and sugar. A land rush began in 1764, with the granting of lands surrounding Pensacola and Mobile Bay. It was soon evident that this area was not particularly fertile, and that the sandy soil covering much of it would not grow most of the crops the British needed; thus by late 1767 two new movements of settlement began. One moved north into the upper valleys of the Tombigbee and Alabama rivers, and the other involved the settlement of the fertile lands between Bayou Manchac and Natchez. In the next five years, this second movement became a boom, with settlers from the seaboard colonies moving down the Mississippi or else coming by sea through New Orleans, and other older settlers in the colony giving up their claims along the seacoast and petitioning for other lands in the Natchez area.[53]

Like his neighbors, John Fitzpatrick was subject to land hunger. In 1776 he requested a friend in Pensacola, John Stephenson, who was an attorney and member of the provincial council, to prepare a petition for a land grant based upon Fitzpatrick's military service during the Seven Years' War. He had apparently already occupied a piece of land along the Mississippi just north of Manchac; John Thomas mentioned that Fitzpatrick "owned" some land near the settlement,[54] and Fitzpatrick himself mentioned farming activities in his correspondence. The petition was never presented, however, but Fitzpatrick continued to occupy his plantation until he was given legal title to it in 1786, by a grant from Spanish Governor Miró.[55]

As the land was occupied, patterns of settlement and cultivation began to emerge. The main towns in West Florida were Pensacola and Mobile, both filled with new buildings constructed by the British and both largely involved in widespread commercial activities. The Pensacola area was not particularly suited to agriculture, but the lands around Mobile Bay and stretching north along the Tombigbee and Alabama rivers were divided into plantations and farms. Along the north shores of Lakes Pontchartrain and Maurepas a few settlers made tar and pitch and cut lumber, while scattered farms along the Amite and Comite rivers produced mainly lumber and rice.[56] North of Bayou Manchac, most of the land was divided into plantations, some of them numbering several thousand acres. Baton Rouge, or New Richmond as the British called it, was the center of a small but flourishing plantation society. Growing from a tiny collection of miserable huts in 1763, by 1782 the district of Baton Rouge contained 169 people, mostly planters and their slaves.[57] North of Baton Rouge there were some British plantations along Thompson's Creek and Bayou Sara, and several others opposite the French

Introduction

53/Howard, *British Development of West Florida*, 17–19, 36.

54/Thomas to John Stuart, March 12, 1772, PRO, CO 5/579, p. 66.

55/"An Act for the Relief of Josiah Barker," February 9, 1833, No. 802, Acts of Congress Pertaining to Louisiana, p. 358, Louisiana State Land Office, Baton Rouge.

56/Hutchins, *An Historical Narrative*, 61–62.

57/Rose Meyers, *A History of Baton Rouge, 1699–1812* (Baton Rouge, 1976), 64; Baton Rouge Census Document, Department of Archives and Manuscripts, Louisiana State University (original in the Archives of the Indies, Seville).

settlement at Pointe Coupée. This area, which included plantations and farms stretching for about twenty miles along the west bank of the Mississippi and including the west side of False River, was first settled by the French early in the century and contained by this time about two thousand white residents and about seven thousand slaves. Its major products were tobacco, indigo, and poultry.[58]

From Pointe Coupée north there was little settlement until Natchez. A few British traders came there in the early 1760s, and the British government granted numerous tracts of land, many very large, to private individuals between 1768 and 1780. The reputed fertility of the land and the healthful climate made the Natchez district very attractive. After 1775, waves of immigrants, many of them refugees from the unrest in the British colonies along the Atlantic seaboard, began to transform the area into the flourishing plantation center it was to become in the next century.[59] By 1776, the town consisted of between ten and twenty log cabins and frame houses, all clustered at the edge of the Mississippi "under the Hill." Among them were the four small mercantile establishments of Hanchett and Newman, Thomas Barber, John Blommart, and James Willing, all of whom had dealings with John Fitzpatrick. In the whole Natchez region there were about 78 families, few of whom had been there longer than four years.[60] The area prospered. Wealthy inhabitants established credits in London, Pensacola, and Jamaica and despite their isolation were able to enjoy many of the comforts of civilized life.[61] The last general Spanish census of the area, taken in 1788, counted 2,679 people in the Natchez district, about two thousand of whom were white.[62]

Above Natchez were a few small British settlements, mainly populated by traders, located at Petit Gulf, Grand Gulf, Walnut Hills (present Vicksburg), and at Ozarks, opposite the mouth of the Arkansas River and also called Concord. Between Concord and the settlements of British Illinois, the country was virtually empty of white men other than transient hunters and traders.

The main basis of the economy of West Florida throughout the British period was trade, and even men who were occupied in developing plantations usually engaged in some kind of commercial activity. Merchants on the borders of West Florida, like John Fitzpatrick, openly sold goods and slaves to residents of Louisiana. Mercantile houses in Pensacola and Mobile kept representatives in New Orleans, and goods were freely carried in and out of the city. Other British merchants carried on a brisk trade along the Mississippi River. Ships loaded in London were consigned

58/Pittman, *The Present State of the European Settlements*, 72.

59/Clark, *New Orleans, 1718–1812*, 184.

60/Charles S. Sydnor, *A Gentleman of the Old Natchez Region: Benjamin L. C. Wailes* (Durham, N.C., 1938), 3–4.

61/J. F. H. Claiborne, *Mississippi, As a Province, Territory and State, with Biographical Notices of Eminent Citizens* (Jackson, Miss., 1880), 116.

62/Martin, *The History of Louisiana*, 251; Marcus L. Hanson, "The Population of the American Outlying Regions in 1790," *Annual Report of the American Historical Association for 1931* (Washington, D.C., 1932), I, 405.

to British merchants at Manchac. They sailed by New Orleans and then slowly ascended the river, stopping frequently to give local planters an opportunity to purchase goods at prices far lower than those offered in New Orleans. This trade, which began in 1764, by 1766 controlled most of the commerce along the river between New Orleans and Manchac, and continued until 1777, when many of the British river traders were arrested and expelled from the colony by Governor Gálvez.[63]

The flourishing state of British smuggling earned the enmity of many Louisiana merchants and planters. Requests were made throughout the British period that the Spanish colonial government find a way to remove the British traders and the competition they presented to Louisiana merchants. One Louisianian, François Marie Reggio of New Orleans, complained in 1771 that the British were encompassing the fur trade of the colony. He felt that the English traders were taking advantage of the "decadence" of Louisiana's economy to extend their commerce "to a degree of superiority so marked, that all the pelts which previously appeared in this capitol, now come there only in their barges and boats."[64]

Such complaints, however, did not constitute a real threat to the British merchants. Many, like James Jones, who with his brother Evan was one of the most successful British merchants resident in New Orleans, were confident that "they [the Spanish] will be able to impose none [trade restrictions] that can impede us from carrying on a very lucrative Trade in the River."[65]

It must be observed that much of the prosperity engendered by this commerce was illusory. Most goods were purchased on credit and sold the same way, so that the economy of the frontier was in reality based upon a great chain of indebtedness. A poor crop or a bad year of hunting meant that none of the intermediaries between the original importer and the final purchaser could be paid. Moreover, the capacity of the local population to absorb all the goods available was limited. The market was often glutted with merchandise brought by British traders through Pensacola and New Orleans, by French and Spanish merchants, and by New Yorkers and Pennsylvanians, and in the end no one made much money. The frequent complaints that Fitzpatrick made about the slowness of his trade reflected a general problem faced by most merchants in the area. The "pretty fortune" that Fitzpatrick claimed in 1777 included numerous outstanding debts, uncollected notes and bonds, and pelts and local products stored in the anticipation of finding a profitable future market. This commercial network was exceedingly fragile and depended for its survival

63/Martin, *The History of Louisiana*, 196, 217.

64/François Marie Reggio to Monseigneur, November 22, 1771, Reggio Family Papers, Department of Archives and Manuscripts, Louisiana State University.

65/James Jones to Haldimand, March 14, 1770, British Museum, Additional Manuscripts 21729.

on local tranquillity and friendly relations with the Spanish. Unfortunately for Fitzpatrick and his neighbors, the tranquillity of the early 1770s did not last.

These years were a time of hard work and optimism for John Fitzpatrick. In 1770 he built himself a house, having found no habitable buildings in the settlement when he arrived. In May of 1770 he hired a clerk, Gregory French, who remained with him for several years and was responsible for much of the correspondence copied into the letterbooks. Fitzpatrick made yearly trips to New Orleans for the purpose of collecting debts or delivering skins and local produce, and experienced no further harassment from the Spanish. He also made occasional trips to Mobile and Pensacola, and in early 1774 traveled as far north as Grand Gulf, a small trading settlement about fifty miles above Natchez, where he attempted to collect some long overdue debts. As Fitzpatrick's letters indicate, his range of operation was very wide. He acted as an agent for several large mercantile firms in Pensacola and Mobile; he had ties with merchants in New Orleans, with merchants and farmers across the river in Spanish Louisiana and throughout the Amite–Manchac–Mississippi region of West Florida, and with merchants and planters in Natchez; and he supplied hunters and Indian traders operating out of Natchez, Concord, Grand Gulf, and from as far away as Illinois.

At some unknown date after his arrival at Manchac, Fitzpatrick was joined by Madame Blain, with whom he had lived in New Orleans. Born Marie Jeanne Nivet and apparently a native of New Orleans, Madame Blain had been deserted by her husband. In 1765 she petitioned the New Orleans Superior Council for authorization to recover 2,400 livres from an estate, stating that she was unable to obtain permission from her husband, who had been absent for over fourteen years.[66] The circumstances of her removal from New Orleans are unknown, but she was living in Manchac by the time John Thomas arrived there as deputy superintendent, for he mentioned her in his accusations of Fitzpatrick.[67] Fitzpatrick first referred to her as his wife in 1776,[68] so we may assume that her previous marriage was either annulled or else she was declared a widow. However, a search of marriage records in both the St. Louis Cathedral in New Orleans and the marriage register of St. Gabriel Parish, in which Manchac was located, did not reveal any record of a marriage between John Fitzpatrick and Marie Nivet Blain.[69] Nevertheless, their marriage was considered valid by local civil authorities, as Fitzpatrick named his wife as his sole heir when he wrote his will in 1787, and the numerous records dealing with Fitzpatrick's estate after his death

66/Petition, September 10, 1765, New Orleans Superior Council Records, Archives and Manuscripts Collections, Louisiana State Museum, New Orleans.

67/Rea, "Redcoats and Redskins,' 24–29.

68/See this volume, p. 209.

69/Many of the records of St. Louis Cathedral were lost in a fire in 1788, including registers of baptisms and marriages during the years when Marie Nivet would probably have been included, that is, baptisms from 1734 to 1744 and marriages from 1734 to 1758.

in 1791 name Marie Nivet as his widow and heir. The couple had no children or close relatives, and apparently lived contentedly together. Marie assisted her husband in his business, for his letters occasionally mention her performing various transactions in his absence.

We know relatively little of the details of their daily life. The large number of books listed in the inventory of Fitzpatrick's property after his death and the occasional mention he makes in his letters of volumes purchased or loaned imply that he was a man who enjoyed reading. His library contained the works of several major literary figures of his day, as well as works on a variety of other subjects. He also enjoyed gambling, an indulgence which got him into some difficulty with the officers stationed at Manchac in the late 1770s, and seems to have appreciated a bottle of fine wine. His home was comfortably furnished, as the inventory indicates, and much of the furniture and houseware was imported from England. At the time of Fitzpatrick's death he owned eleven slaves, including two who worked as house servants. Despite the uncertainties of frontier life, it must have been a fairly comfortable existence.

This busy, peaceful life was permanently disrupted by the American Revolution. At first, the unrest in the northern colonies went virtually unnoticed in West Florida, marked as it was only by a gradually increasing influx of loyalist refugees fleeing the growing dissent in their home colonies. In West Florida, there was little revolutionary fervor. Isolated from the other British colonies and surrounded by powerful Indian tribes, the colony was also cut off from the conflicts over foreign trade, local rights, land distribution, and other factors which inspired the rebellion. In West Florida, the energies of the colonists were largely consumed by the problems of frontier existence, and the influence of the loyalist refugees, many of whom were wealthy, well-educated, and came to assume important positions in the colony, only strengthened these non-revolutionary tendencies.[70]

In 1774, the Continental Congress addressed a letter seeking support to the speaker of the colonial assembly at Pensacola, who merely referred it to the royal governor.[71] The colony failed to send delegates to either the first or second Continental Congress, being almost totally engrossed in local problems. But despite its lack of sympathy for the revolutionary cause, West Florida could not escape involvement in the war. Following instructions from Lord Dartmouth, Governor Chester issued a proclamation establishing the colony as a sanctuary for loyalist refugees, and by April, 1776, the immigrants were coming in large numbers.[72] By

70/Starr, "Tories, Dons, and Rebels," 92–93.

71/Robert R. Rea, "British West Florida: Stepchild of Diplomacy," *Eighteenth-Century Florida and Its Borderlands*, ed. Samuel Proctor (Gainesville, Fla., 1975), 69.

72/Starr, "Tories, Dons, and Rebels," 88–89, 91.

Introduction

early 1776, also, the colony began to receive reports of an impending attack by the rebels, warnings which, with one exception, did not materialize but which created a state of apprehension that continued throughout the war. The fact that the British government did not at once provide additional troops for the defense of the province or send funds to pay for repairs to fortifications only increased the general sense of insecurity.

At this same time, relations between British West Florida and Spanish Louisiana were worsening. The normal tensions between the two neighboring colonies were exacerbated by continuing friction between the mother countries. Encouraged by national policy and by friendship with New Orleans merchant Oliver Pollock, who was an ardent supporter of the American cause, Louisiana governor Unzaga began to provide covert support for the rebels. In the summer of 1776, two American officers from Fort Pitt, Captain George Gibson and Lieutenant William Linn, arrived in New Orleans after journeying down the Mississippi in a *batteau* with about twenty hands, all disguised as traders. They sought powder, drugs, and other supplies, and through Pollock's intercession Governor Unzaga was persuaded to accede to their request. On September 22, 1776, Lieutenant Linn, with forty-three men, set out up the river with about nine thousand pounds of powder. Linn and his men wintered at the Arkansas Post and finally reached Wheeling, Virginia, in May, 1777. Meanwhile, Captain Gibson was briefly imprisoned to quiet the suspicions of the British consul in New Orleans, and in October sailed for Philadelphia aboard a vessel purchased by Pollock flying a Spanish flag, and laden with over sixteen thousand pounds of powder and other supplies.[73]

Unzaga's successor, Bernardo de Gálvez, displayed partiality toward the Americans from the moment of his arrival in Louisiana. Following royal orders, Gálvez permitted the sale to American agents of powder, drugs, guns, and other military supplies from government warehouses. To avoid arousing English suspicion, the supplies were sold through intermediaries as surplus or deteriorated goods. By the end of Gálvez's first year as governor, about $70,000 worth of such goods had been sent up the river.[74]

Besides the hospitality and material aid which Gálvez gave to the Americans, he also undertook direct assaults on the British position in Louisiana's commerce. On the night of April 17, 1777, he seized eleven English boats engaged in contraband trade on the river and followed this action with a proclamation on April 18 ordering all British subjects to leave Louisiana within a fortnight. The proclamation was not seriously enforced, since Fitzpatrick continued to correspond with English merchants in New

---

73/James Alton James, *Oliver Pollock: The Life and Times of an Unknown Patriot* (New York, 1937), 61–70; John W. Caughey, *Bernardo de Gálvez in Louisiana, 1776–1783* (Berkeley, 1934), 86–87; PRO, CO 5/593, p. 107, 5/594, pp. 170–71; Starr, "Tories, Dons, and Rebels," 91, 112–16.

The Arkansas Post, or Fort Carlos III, as the Spanish called it, was located on the north bank of the Arkansas River near its confluence with the Mississippi. The importance of this location, which controlled the entrance to the Arkansas River basin and provided an approach to Spanish New Mexico, was recognized by the earliest French explorers of the area, and a settlement was first established there by Henri de Tonti in 1686. After the Spanish assumed control of Louisiana, they constructed a new fort beside the Mississippi for the convenience and regulation of river traffic. The post also functioned as a trading center for the neighboring Indian tribes and supported a small population of white traders, hunters, and farmers. Stanley Faye, "The Arkansas Post of Louisiana: French Domination," *Louisiana Historical Quarterly*, XVI (1943), 633–721; Faye, "The Arkansas Post of Louisiana: Spanish Dominion," *ibid.*, XVII (1944), 629–716.

74/Caughey, *Bernardo de Gálvez*, 91–92.

Orleans and visited there himself after the spring of 1777, and smuggling continued. However, by a series of proclamations in the same year, Louisiana was given commercial privileges, such as freedom of commerce with Yucatán and Cuba and virtually free commerce with France and the French colonies, that soon destroyed British contraband trade with the Spanish colony.[75]

While the security of John Fitzpatrick and his neighbors at Manchac was seriously damaged by these commercial proclamations, it was completely shattered by the arrival of the long-threatened American invasion of West Florida in February of 1778. The excursion of James Willing, brother of a wealthy Philadelphia merchant and a failed Natchez planter and merchant (and one of Fitzpatrick's former correspondents), was the only military venture the Americans made into West Florida. After proposals for larger expeditions down the Mississippi were rejected, the American Commerce Committee instructed Willing in the autumn of 1777 to go to Fort Pitt and there equip, arm, and supply a boat and twenty-four men. He was further directed to deliver dispatches to Governor Gálvez and Oliver Pollock in New Orleans, to convoy supplies back up the river, and to "capture whatever British property he might meet with in the said rivers."[76]

Willing left Fort Pitt on an armed boat in January, 1778, with a force of about thirty volunteers, which increased to over a hundred as they moved down the Ohio and Mississippi. By early February the party reached the Arkansas River and plundered the small English trading settlement at Concord. They landed at Walnut Hills on February 18, where they captured four Indian agents and informed a local resident that they were an advance force for a larger expedition which would follow in May. The next evening, February 19, Willing's force landed at Natchez, captured all the magistrates of the district, and seized their property. Part of the force raided the home of Alexander McIntosh, a prominent planter with strong British sympathies and a longtime associate of Fitzpatrick's, where they killed some livestock and stole several slaves. Another group went to the plantation of former British army officer Anthony Hutchins, an outspoken Tory and local magistrate, and took him prisoner. Articles of capitulation were forced on the local inhabitants, providing for their strict neutrality.[77]

Apparently relatively few depredations were committed by Willing's troops around Natchez, except for the plundering of the Hutchins and McIntosh plantations and some minor thievery. Between Natchez and Manchac, however, the behavior of the rebels changed drastically. They pillaged, burned plantations,

75/*Ibid.*, 71, 76.
76/Memorial of James Willing, October 29, 1781, quoted in Starr, "Tories, Dons, and Rebels," 149.
77/*Ibid.*, 151–55.

killed livestock, stole slaves, and forced the residents to flee. Early in the morning of February 23 they attacked Manchac, seized a British ship anchored there, and made prisoners of the inhabitants on their parole. They then proceeded to lay waste to most of the settlements between Pointe Coupée, Manchac, and the Amite River, destroying whatever they could not carry away. The devastation was enormous; as one settler observed, "They have cleared all the English side of the river of its inhabitants, and nothing to be seen but destruction and desolation."[78] Many British settlers fled into Spanish territory seeking sanctuary, carrying with them their slaves and movable possessions. John Fitzpatrick with many of his neighbors took refuge in the Spanish fort across the bayou from Manchac, where they were given protection and shelter. Willing's troop, meanwhile, left a small force in Manchac and proceeded to New Orleans. At Oliver Pollock's urging, Governor Gálvez gave them shelter. Much of the raiders' plunder was sold at public auction, and weapons and other supplies were purchased. They continued to make sporadic raids throughout the summer against British ships on the river and British settlers in the region.

The main body of Willing's party remained in New Orleans until late summer. Finally, at the end of August, Robert George, a nephew of George Rogers Clark, assumed command of the company and proceeded north. Willing sailed from New Orleans in November, but his ship was captured by the British and he was held prisoner in New York until exchanged for a British officer in 1781.[79]

In response to news of Willing's expedition, British officials in Pensacola immediately began to take measures to protect the colony. A ship was sent to the Mississippi, and reinforcements were detached to the armed sloop *West Florida* on Lake Pontchartrain to prevent any penetration by the rebels through the lakes. Another group of twenty men, commanded by Captain Richard Pearis, was sent through Lakes Pontchartrain and Maurepas to the Amite-Comite area to protect the inhabitants and assist those who wished to leave. They were also directed to attack the rebels at Manchac if they were still there.

On March 14, a small detachment of fifteen British soldiers, accompanied by Adam Chrystie, a local planter, arrived at Manchac just before daylight. In a brief surprise attack—the only land clash between British and American forces to take place in Louisiana—the British killed and wounded five Americans and took thirteen prisoners, while the remainder of the rebels fled across the bayou into Spanish territory. On hearing that the Americans were returning, the British withdrew from Manchac with

78/*Ibid.*, 157.

79/For a detailed discussion of the Willing expedition and its consequences, see John Walton Caughey, "Willing's Expedition Down the Mississippi, 1778," *Louisiana Historical Quarterly*, XV (1932), 5–36; Robert V. Haynes, *The Natchez District and the American Revolution* (Jackson, Miss., 1976), 56–100; Caughey, *Bernardo de Gálvez*, 102–34; Starr, "Tories, Dons, and Rebels," 145–210; Robert V. Haynes, "James Willing and the Planters of Natchez: The American Revolution Comes to the Southwest," *Journal of Mississippi History*, XXXVII (1975), 1–40; Matthew Phelps, *Memoirs and Adventures of Captain Matthew Phelps, Particularly in two voyages from Connecticut to the River Mississippi, 1774–1780* (Bennington, Vt., 1802), 112–13.

their prisoners, as they considered their force too small to hold the position. The Americans offered the fort to the Spanish commander at San Gabriel, then apparently abandoned it.[80]

Meanwhile, the council in Pensacola was considering additional measures for the defense of the colony. On April 27, it unanimously recommended the establishment of a military post at Manchac, with Lieutenant Colonel Alexander Dickson as commandant.[81] About sixty-five British regulars were ordered there, and Colonel John McGillivray, who was in charge of the colonial militia, was ordered to detach about one hundred men from Natchez to Manchac. Another company of colonial militia under Captain William McIntosh was also ordered to Manchac. This establishment was contingent upon the return of the Manchac residents from Spanish territory where they had fled after Willing's raid, for the West Florida Council unanimously resolved that "Should the inhabitants of the Manchac district neglect to embrace the protection now offered to them but rather choose to continue under Spanish protection, the said post at Manchac after its having been established two months [will be] withdrawn and the troops be sent to take post at the Natchez for the protection and security of the loyal inhabitants in that district."[82]

When the British government sent military reinforcements to West Florida in 1779, to operate under the command of Brigadier General John Campbell, more attention was given to Manchac. Lord George Germain considered that "the command of the navigation of the Mississippi, and of the communications from thence to the Indian nations in the southern district, is essential to the security of His Majesty's possessions in West Florida, and to the protection of the king's faithful subjects, and their property, and also of great importance to the trade of this country."[83] The most proper place for a post that could further the accomplishment of these objectives was at Manchac, on or near the site of Fort Bute. Campbell was ordered to send the necessary troops, engineers, and equipment to construct a permanent fortification there for a garrison of three hundred men.[84] Two galleys were also ordered to Manchac to protect British navigation on the Mississippi,[85] and there was apparently some discussion of attempting to clear the bayou again, for a plan by Thomas Hutchins dating from this time has been preserved.[86] By the end of the year, plans were being made for General Campbell to proceed from Pensacola up the Mississippi River with a sizable force of men to build forts at Manchac and Natchez.[87]

The disorderly troops and other difficulties which Fitzpatrick described in his letters were a reflection of very serious problems which Campbell and his men encountered at Manchac. In the

80/Ellis, "American Activity in Louisiana and West Florida during the Revolutionary War," 10; Starr, "Tories, Dons, and Rebels," 181–85.
81/Wilbur H. Siebert, "The Loyalists in West Florida and the Natchez District," *Mississippi Valley Historical Review*, II (1916), 471.
82/Quoted in Starr, "Tories, Dons, and Rebels," 199.
83/*Ibid.*, 232–33.
84/Milord George Germain to British Commander, July 1, 1778, Archivo General de Indias, Papeles Procedentes de Cuba (AGI, PPC), Leg. 1232 (photographic copy in Department of Archives and Manuscripts, Louisiana State University, catalogued as Gálveztown Papers).
85/Siebert, "The Loyalists in West Florida," 472.
86/PRO, CO 5/595, p. 318.
87/John Stuart to Alexander McGillivray, December 19, 1779, Henry Wilson Papers, Department of Archives and Manuscripts, Louisiana State University.

first place, the site itself was far from ideal—the whole area was flooded during the spring, the bayou was dry during part of the year, and the point of land upon which the fort was to stand seemed in danger of being swept away by the river. Moreover, Campbell found himself without money or credit for contingent expenses (such as the use of Fitzpatrick's houses and supplies), without adequate transportation, without men skilled in construction, without tools or materials for building, and without even adequate provisions. The frustration which Fitzpatrick experienced in trying to obtain payment for property taken by the troops was more than matched by that of General Campbell, who considered his situation "the most disagreeable, the most irksome, the most distressing of all situations to a soldier and a man of spirit."[88]

Spain declared war against Britain on June 21, 1779, although General Campbell did not receive word of the commencement of hostilities until September 9. By that time, Governor Gálvez had already begun to move against West Florida. Painfully aware that New Orleans was virtually defenseless, Gálvez regarded British defense efforts at Natchez and Manchac as intended "as much for the attack as for the defense" and viewed the arrival of British reinforcements as a threat to Louisiana.[89] His suspicions were further aroused by reports from Spanish commandants at Manchac and Pointe Coupée that the British were planning an attack on Louisiana, either to take New Orleans or to attack Spanish settlements farther up the river.[90] In early 1779, when the British were preparing to send troops from Pensacola to the Mississippi River, Gálvez believed that the real motive for the troop movement was that the British intended a surprise attack on Louisiana in the event of a rupture with Spain, or else they expected the arrival of a large number of colonists and were using the threat of further American attacks as a pretext for expansion into Spanish territory.[91]

It is not surprising, then, that Gálvez was eager to combat the British menace when, in the summer of 1779, he was informed that Spain had declared war on Britain and was ordered to drive the British out of West Florida. He was convinced that the best way to defend Louisiana was by a swift surprise attack on the British posts along the Mississippi and began to make secret preparations. On August 27, his small force of 667 men left New Orleans, marching up the river toward Manchac, their first objective. By collecting local militia companies along the German and Acadian coasts and enlisting local men, Gálvez raised his force to 1,427 men, although about a third of them were disabled by sickness and other causes by the time they reached Manchac on September 6.[92]

88/Starr, "Tories, Dons, and Rebels," 234–35, 238.
89/Gálvez to Don José de Gálvez, June 9, 1777, Survey of Federal Archives, *Confidential Despatches of Don Bernardo de Gálvez to his Uncle Don José de Gálvez* (Baton Rouge, 1938), 25–26.
90/Juan de la Villebeuvre to Gálvez, July 6, 1778, Don Carlos de Grand-Pré to Gálvez, July 8, 1778, *ibid.*, 31–33.
91/Gálvez to Don José de Gálvez, February 25, 1779, July 3, 1779, *ibid.*, 57–58, 119–20.
92/Caughey, *Bernardo de Gálvez*, 151–54.

In the meantime, the British commandant at Manchac, Lieutenant Colonel Alexander Dickson, had decided that the post could not be defended against an expected American attack and had withdrawn the main body of his men to Baton Rouge, where a redoubt was hastily constructed on the plantation of Stephen Watts and Dr. Samuel Flowers. The few men left at Manchac were unable to defend it when Gálvez made his assault early on the morning of September 7. Although one British soldier was killed and eighteen others taken prisoner, the action was apparently very minor and quickly finished.[93] Fitzpatrick, who by this time had returned to Manchac from the shelter of the Spanish fort, made no mention of the Spanish attack in his letters or of any damage to his property. Since many of the inhabitants of Manchac had already left the settlement for more secure homes elsewhere in West Florida or in Spanish territory, Gálvez must have occupied a nearly deserted post halfheartedly defended by a tiny contingent of soldiers.

After a few days rest at Manchac, Gálvez set out for Baton Rouge, where the British had by this time constructed a substantial fort. On the morning of September 20, the Spanish cannon opened fire and inflicted so much damage that by mid-afternoon the British were compelled to surrender. Gálvez insisted that Fort Panmure at Natchez be included in the act of surrender, to which Lieutenant Colonel Dickson agreed. A detachment of fifty Spanish soldiers under Captain Juan de la Villebeuvre was sent north to Natchez with a letter from Dickson instructing the British commander there to surrender the fort. Other British posts on Thompson's Creek and the Amite River were seized by Carlos Grand Pré, commandant at Pointe Coupée. Gálvez then returned to New Orleans, leaving Grand Pré in command of the entire district with small garrisons of regular troops at the various captured forts.[94]

Even before setting out against Manchac and Baton Rouge, Gálvez had begun to plan the conquest of Mobile and Pensacola. Preparations were carried on through the last months of 1779, and on January 11, 1780, the expeditionary force, consisting of 754 men and twelve ships, embarked at New Orleans. On February 12 the fleet entered Mobile Bay, and on the morning of March 14, after a brief attack, the Spanish took possession of Fort Charlotte. Preparations for the conquest of Pensacola were undertaken immediately. However, the attack was long delayed, partly because the Spanish government at Havana was hesitant to commit the necessary troops and ships to the campaign and then, when preparations were finally made, they were destroyed by a hurricane which struck the fleet soon after its departure from Havana in October, 1780. An assault was finally begun on May 1, 1781.

93/*Ibid.*, 155.
94/*Ibid.*, 156–59.

After a shot from one of the Spanish howitzers destroyed the British powder magazine, killing at least eighty-five men, and further heavy Spanish fire weakened remaining defenses, General Campbell ran up a white flag in the afternoon of May 8. Formal surrender of the fort took place on May 10, an act which included the surrender of the entire province of West Florida to Spain.[95]

Meanwhile, the settlers at Manchac were accommodating themselves to Spanish rule. Fitzpatrick had fled to the Spanish fort across the bayou after Willing's raid in February, 1778, and remained there through the summer, living with his wife in a tiny hut. During the summer, British troops arrived at Manchac and occupied Fitzpatrick's buildings, so he had no place to return to. The destruction of his property by the troops, coupled with the refusal of the officers to pay for the damage and for the provisions with which Fitzpatrick had supplied them, thoroughly disgusted him.

By September of 1778 Fitzpatrick was expressing his intention of becoming a Spanish subject. At that time, this transaction involved a simple oath of loyalty to the Spanish crown, which he must have taken in the next few months. By July of 1779, he was enlisted as a soldier in the Second Company of Militia at Gálveztown,[96] and it is possible that he participated in the capture of Baton Rouge, since the Gálveztown militia companies were among those involved.

Fitzpatrick had other connections with Gálveztown. In December, 1778, he offered to build some houses at the new settlement; on December 31 Gálvez accepted Fitzpatrick's offer and assigned him to build four houses, "thirty-two feet long, sixteen wide . . . with galleries along one side." However, on the following January 11, Fitzpatrick left for Pensacola to petition the provincial government to pay him for the property used and damaged by the troops at Manchac, and the houses were never built.[97]

The change of government in West Florida seems to have had relatively little impact on Fitzpatrick's ideology. His great concern during these years was to recoup his losses and to collect outstanding debts. Like many of his neighbors, he considered leaving the province and moving back to English-speaking society. In 1781, he mentioned that he planned to move to Charleston, but he was unable to settle his affairs and so never left.

The last ten years of Fitzpatrick's life reflected in many ways the changes which Spanish control brought to West Florida. After giving the required oath of loyalty to the Spanish king, the British inhabitants were treated leniently and considerately by the Spanish authorities. Trade with Louisiana was, of course,

---

95/*Ibid.*, 172–85.
96/Seguna Compañia de Milicias de la Villa de Gálvez, June 27, 1779, AGI, PPC, Leg. 2351.
97/Gálvez to Fitzpatrick, December 31, 1778, Collell to Gálvez, January 15, 1779, *ibid.*

open to them, and New Orleans was available as a trading port. The Spanish commandant at Fort Bute held authority to settle all civil disputes, which solved one of the great problems which the Manchac settlers had faced during the years of British rule, the absence of local judicial authority.

There were other changes as well. The clandestine trade upon which the settlement had previously depended was ended. The Spanish did not prevent the British merchants who remained at Manchac from continuing to trade, but the conditions of commerce had been greatly altered. Goods had to be obtained through legal channels and sold according to Spanish commercial laws. Although some contraband trade continued because the Spanish were still unable to supply the colony adequately, this trade was mostly in the hands of Americans, and the goods came down the Mississippi, not through the Gulf Coast ports. By 1785 so many flatboats were coming down the river each year that Louisiana could not absorb all the produce they brought.[98] Local merchants were unable to compete with the prices or variety of this merchandise.

Moreover, the economy of the area was changing rapidly. The great floods of furs which had annually swept down the river were now in Spanish or American hands and were destined for merchants in New Orleans. Consequently, the trade route between Manchac and Pensacola lost most of its significance. At the same time, the population of the area was growing. In 1785, Manchac had 77 people, Gálveztown 242, Baton Rouge 270, and the country south of the bayou 673. By 1788 Manchac had 284 people, Gálveztown 268, Baton Rouge 682, and the St. Gabriel area 944.[99] Local farms found a ready market in New Orleans for surplus foodstuffs and provided staples for the overseas trade. Indigo remained the most important export crop during most of the Spanish period, and prices were high throughout the 1780s. Although the dye was very expensive to produce, requiring specialized machinery and considerable labor, the increasing availability of slaves made large-scale production possible for more people. Tobacco was also more widely grown than before. In 1776 Louisiana was granted a monopoly on tobacco production for the Mexican market, and after delays caused by the war a genuine tobacco boom developed in the 1780s, spreading north beyond Natchez. Although the bulk of the crop came from Natchitoches and Natchez, tobacco was grown throughout the region.[100]

Fitzpatrick's activities paralleled these economic changes. Trade occupied a decreasing amount of his attention. He no longer supplied fur traders or expeditions into the Illinois country, and the goods he ordered from his suppliers in Pensacola and

98/Bruce Tyler, "The Mississippi River Trade, 1784–1788," *Louisiana History*, XII (1971), 262–63.

99/Martin, *The History of Louisiana*, 239–40, 251.

100/Clark, *New Orleans, 1718–1812*, 186–91.

New Orleans consisted mainly of items which he expected would find a quick local sale. Increasingly, he turned his energies toward developing his plantation and growing cash crops. Chafing under the idleness imposed by the collapse of trade, he occupied himself in 1780 with repairs to his fences and with cultivating his household garden. Then, to keep his slaves occupied, he repaired the levee in front of his plantation and then worked on the road between Manchac and "the forks." By 1790 he was growing indigo and had produced a crop of tobacco which he hoped to sell to the royal monopoly in New Orleans.

Fitzpatrick also assumed a position of respect within the Manchac community. The records of the Spanish commandant at Manchac mention his name frequently as a witness in various legal transactions in the community, serving as a "witness of assistance, in absence of a notary."[101] Still attempting to settle his debts, he sold three slaves, a woman with her two infant sons, in 1789.[102]

On January 20, 1787, Fitzpatrick and his wife made their will before Lieutenant Francisco Rivas, commandant at Fort Bute. Having no children or other descendants, each named the other as sole heir to all their property.[103] On March 21, 1791, the local priest, Father Bernardo de Limpach of San Gabriel Parish, recorded the death of "felixpatria irlandés," who died too suddenly to receive the last sacraments.[104] The death had actually occurred late in the afternoon of the previous day, March 20, for Lieutenant Rivas was summoned about seven that evening by one of Fitzpatrick's slaves, who reported that her master had just died in his house next to the fort.

In accordance with the standard practice of the time, Rivas proceeded to make a detailed inventory of Fitzpatrick's property to facilitate the settlement of the estate.[105] There were many debts still unsettled, and the widow Marie found that she had inherited a maze of financial complexities. A few months after Fitzpatrick's death she sold part of the plantation, consisting of a house and land one arpent wide by forty arpents deep, for 1,500 pesos in order to try to settle her debts. In June of 1793, she applied to the New Orleans Cabildo for permission to sell more of her husband's property in order to pay debts.[106]

Marie Nivet died in 1797 or early in 1798 with her husband's estate still unsettled. Francis Poussett, a prosperous Baton Rouge planter and former acquaintance of Fitzpatrick's, was appointed to settle all the affairs of the Fitzpatrick family. Two auctions of the property were held to raise money to pay off all debts.[107]

In the end there was nothing left except the letterbooks, which eventually ended up in the hands of the Hicky family of Baton

---

101/Survey of Federal Archives, *Spanish West Florida Records*, I, 68, 70, 71, 140, 141, 143.

102/Slave sale, July 14, 1787, *ibid.*, I, 83–85; Receipt, April 18, 1789, for 600 pesos, Elizabeth Becker Gianelloni, "Louisiana's Spanish West Florida Records," *Louisiana Genealogical Register*, XVII (1970), 3.

103/Joint will of John Fitzpatrick and his wife Marie Nivet, *Spanish West Florida Records*, I, 158–65. Also recorded in Acts of Pedro Pedesclaux, Vol. 13, p. 410, New Orleans Notarial Archives.

104/Registres mortuaires de blancs, 1785 á 1856, St. Gabriel Church Records, Diocesan Archives, Catholic Life Center, Baton Rouge.

105/See Appendix, p. 425.

106/*Spanish West Florida Records*, I, 203–205, 929; Petition, June 20, 1793, Spanish Records, Archive and Manuscript Collections, Louisiana State Museum.

107/Poussett to Thomas Durnford, February 21, 1798, Fitzpatrick Letterbooks.

Rouge. The estate was sold, the debts settled, and the village of Manchac swept away by the river. But the letterbooks are legacy enough, for in them we see the development of a region, the history of a frontier, the spirit of a pioneer. John Fitzpatrick endured. He still endures.

Part One
1768–1769

To JOHN FITZPATRICK, *New Orleans*

Pensacola, June 13, 1768

I receivd. your favour of the 19th last with an Account Current of the Sundrys Concerns Betwen us; and as I find some Errors in it; I send you inclosd. Mine; in Order; you will peruis it; & which youl see Ballance in my favour of $297.2¾ Which hope you will Endeavour remitt me said Sum by the first oppertunity Being in Much want of it, for to remitt home; and by the Sd. my Account you'll Observe I did Credit you for the Martin Skins which I have sent you; Back some Time ago; as also for the $10—in Your Order on Henry Smith, sent you Back by Mr. Haigh When Harrison comes back At your place hope you will git from him what you Knows & you'll oblige Mr. Stephenson in regard of Corn; the price you tell me is very high for this Markett, & I can buy here by the Single Barrell at 18 Bills, and Accordingly it will not Answer; I Confirm you what I had the plasure to Write you; by my last hopeing you would Oblige of Acquainting Me How affairs goes on at your place; and What Appeerence have have Regarding the present (Discentions)....

[*signed*] Jac. R

To JAMES AMOSS, *Pensacola*[1]

New Orleans, June 30, 1768

Since you left orleans I have not been able to sell any More than 4 Whips & 1 heat [hat] As there is no money to be seen [at] Pressent; Although, if I had Had the 6 saddles I should have sold Them with all that belongs to them at your price. if you should thin[k] Proper to send me that number by the first Oppertunity, as so[on] As sold shall Remitt you the Amount, or to Mr. Barrow. if you think of Sending them it must be by first Oppertunity Or not att, all....

1/ Two badly torn letters at the front of the first volume have been omitted. James Amoss was a Pensacola merchant and represented Pensacola on the West Florida Provincial Council.

To JOHN STEPHENSON, Pensacola[2]

New Orleans, June 30, 1768

Your kind Letter of 31 Ullto. I have now Before me, and no[te] the Contents. it Came to hand this Morning, and am much perp[lexed] that you have not Receivd. the 4 Casses of wine that I Bough[t] of Monsr. La Coste for you; I have shipd. on board the schoon[er] Polley[3] one thousand Boards on my proper Account and they [are] Consind to your self; if you would be so good as to sell them [to] the Best Advantage as I was obliged to Take them in p[ayment ?] from a french man that owed me the money; that is to say 6 Hundred ten foot at 2 sols p[er] foot—12 foot at 2 sols p[er] foot, t[hat] is $216—and the Remaining part have shipd. on your A[ccount] and Risque with sundry small things as p[er] Invoice, w[ith an] Accot. of Sales & the money, for what I sold of the thing[s] Sent me p[er] Captn. [*blank*] I have sold all your printed lin[ens ?] With [*page torn*]

Captn. More[4] Arrivd. hear on the 16th and Settled the 23d Instant For the havana to bring the money so that we are all in great Hopes; that I shall be able soon to git in all that is Due; I hope Are [ere] this that you have Receivd. the Second of the same tenor & Date, the first on Messrs. McGillivarey & Struthers[5] for $881.8½ r[eales] Mr. McGillivary is hear at present But I cant git any thing from Benvenur & Co.[6] to give him—as they have not as yeat Recivd. Any Skins[.] I toald them that if I could not git th[e] skins, so [as to] Let Mr. McGillivary have them; that I could not take [any] thing in payment Excepting Cash or Sterling Bills [they] Have promised me the Latter at the Arrivel of the Con-[voy ?] I have got out an Execution against LeRoux & Co. [and will] Git it Executed by Mason,[7] so that I am as farr, fro[m] Money as when you left Orleans.

I am for ever obliged to your Kind offer in keeping a Coers[pondence] With me, if in Case that it is for any thing that lays in [my] Power that Regard Your Interest; you will always find m[e] Disposed to Serve you; if you can find any sale for the prod[ucts] of this Place, Such as Boards[,] Chingles [shingles] Tobaco;

{38 *Merchant of Manchac*

2/Pensacola merchant, attorney, and member of the provincial council. A map in Howard, *The British Development of West Florida*, facing p. 42, shows Stephenson as the grantee of a town lot on the north side of the central plaza.

3/A ship named *The Polie* is listed in the New Orleans Superior Council Records as the property of David Ross and Company, New Orleans. See Laura L. Porteous, ed., "Index to Spanish Judicial Records of Louisiana," *Louisiana Historical Quarterly*, VIII (1925), 731.

4/Captain William Moore of New York, master of the ship *St. Peter*, was the New Orleans agent of a New York firm which contracted to supply flour to the Louisiana colonial government. A creditor of the Spanish government of Louisiana to the amount of 24,000 pesos, Moore waited more than six months to receive payment for a shipment of flour; then, in early 1768, requested permission from Governor Ulloa to sail to Havana to pick up Spanish specie needed for Louisiana's commerce. After a delay of several months, Ulloa finally consented, and Moore sailed some time in June, 1768. See Laura Porteous, "Index to Spanish Judicial Records," *Louisiana Historical Quarterly*, VI (1923), 162; Ulloa to Bucareli, February 20, June 22, 1768, in Kinnaird (ed.), *Spain in the Mississippi Valley*, Pt. 1, pp. 42–43, 50–52; Clark, *New Orleans, 1718–1812*, 165. Apparently Fitzpatrick was in error about the date of Moore's departure, because Ulloa's letter of June 22 indicates that he had already sailed.

5/The Mobile-based mercantile firm of John McGillivray and William Struthers controlled much of the Indian trade in West Florida. The company maintained a branch in Pensacola, where other partners resided, and had traders scattered throughout the province. The company and its partners played a prominent role in the political and economic life of the province.

6/Possibly the New Orleans mercantile firm of J. Bienvenu and Jean Brunet.

7/Joseph Maison, bailiff or *huissier* of the New Orleans Superior Council until his resignation in January, 1769. See Petition, January 24, 1769, New Orleans Superior Council Records, Archives and Manuscript Collections, Louisiana State Museum. On June 3, 1768, Fitzpatrick, holding power of attorney for a Mr. Hazelton, petitioned the Superior Council to permit him to recover 32 piastres owed to Hazelton by the Sieurs LeRoux and Jouannis. See Document D–68–122, *ibid*.

I should always Make quick Sales, or [either] in Skins and money when it offers[.] I am in hopes that things will soone, Change for the Better And I will be able to make quicker Returns then has been Already Done—If in Case any of your friends has a Negro Man that they will sell; at a reasonable price, there is a spanish Gentleman that will Take him payable when the money comes in But the price must [not] Exceed $250: or $260: —and [he must be] a fellow that does Not love liquer. Having nothing worth your Hearing; only that the persons in [*blank*] has put me off from time to time waiting for an Answer to your Letter. . . .

To JOHN STEPHENSON, *Pensacola*

New Orleans [August 1768]

Yours of 22d Ulto. I receivd. on the 8th Instant by favour of Mr. [*illegible*] Acquainting me that you had recivd. the 4 Casses of wine; [I am] sorry to hear that the wine was Sower [sour] when it came to [you] as they Ware very good when they left this [place]; I am glad to [hear that you] Have not paid the Duty as it would have been a great Loss to [*illegible*] And as for the Boards I neaver saw them my self but Trusted Capt. Preston to Receive them for me; as Mr. McGillivray was [in] Town; the man that came to Town to lave [leave] the Bills of Leading [lading] Toald me he neaver saw Better to other[?] Boards then they ware[.] Flower [flour] is now 7 $ per ba[rrell] of 180 lb. french weight and [*illegible*] will soon be [twi]ce, as the [New] Yourkers are not as ye[t] Expected in this [area for] s[ome] Time; and [there is] no flower in Town to spe[ak of.] Boards Seems [to] keep up the price of 2 sols per foot & Chingles [sell] at 35 and 4[0 sols per] thousand; we have hear a ship from provance [Provence, France] w[ith] Wine, but her Comming in has not lowerd the price of wine for Provanc wine is $20 per hhd. [and] soap 15 Dollers per lb. Monsr. Monsa[nto][8] Has not as Yet paid the Bill of Exchange in full[.] all that I Recivd. was only $100 an [on] Acct. which I will send you; per Monsr. [*illegible*]. As I am not well Acquainted with the Bearer, I dont chuse to Trust the money with him—the Spannards have not as yet Begun to pay out the money; but it is Expected in 3 or 4 Days Time[.] Deer Skins in the hair are at 45 sols & 50 per lb. and the Leath[er] 37½ Sols to 40 per lb. Messrs. Benvenrs & Brunet[9] would have given Me some Deer Skins with a bill on [New] York for £48: that [is] $120 but I have not as yet taken them; by Reason that the skins Take A great Deal of Care in this time of the year and the Bill was [not] A Sterling Bill According to there promise to you when here; [or] to me since your

1768–1769

8/Isaac Rodrigues Monsanto (1729–78), a Dutch-born Sephardic Jew, came to New Orleans about 1757 or 1758 and soon became a prosperous merchant carrying on business with firms in Europe, the West Indies, New York, the Gulf Coast, Louisiana, Arkansas, and Illinois. His home, store, and warehouse were located on Chartres Street, New Orleans. In 1769, Monsanto was expelled from New Orleans by Governor O'Reilly, as were Fitzpatrick and numerous other foreign merchants. After a stay in Pensacola, Monsanto set up a warehouse at Manchac in partnership with his younger brothers Manuel and Benjamin. This business apparently did fairly well, but Isaac was never able to recoup the great losses he had suffered by leaving New Orleans. Between 1770 and his death in 1778, he traveled widely in Louisiana, and at the time of his death he was running a small store and warehouse in Pointe Coupée and apparently planting indigo on land belonging to François Allain. For a fuller account of Monsanto's career, see Bertram Wallace Korn, *The Early Jews of New Orleans* (Waltham, Mass., 1969), 9–40; and Monsanto to Oliver Pollock, February 10, 1775, in Oliver Pollock Papers, Library of Congress (xerox copy in Department of Archives and Manuscripts, Louisiana State University). It is apparent from Fitzpatrick's letters that Monsanto's financial troubles began before his expulsion from New Orleans when he, like most other merchants in the colony, was unable to collect or pay debts or to carry on business because of the colony's lack of acceptable currency.

9/The mercantile firm of

Departure—if soap is sold at [*illegible*] per lb. I shall Send you 500 lb. per first Occation; or any Other thing that [*page torn*] proper To Demand; you Mentioned in last that if I could m[ake] Sale of any of your printed [*illegible*] to let you k[now by the first] Oppertunity But [*rest of page illegible*]

... with 1 p[iece] Green and 5 pss. your Common—hank[erchiefs] Win[e ?] them are the Things that will Sell, with one thousand Shott or Balls; if Balls from 28 to 30 per Lb.—Monsr. Boisdo[ré][10] [has spoken] with me one sundry Time to see if I would Join him to [ope]n the Trade on the side of Lake ponchartreen, he Tells [me that] if I can gitt Liberty for him and me; that he will Make this Winter $1200—Clear money and if I Dont think Proper to Join him that he will give $250: for the permitt for him self; therefore Sir if you can upten [obtain] me that Liberty You shall have the half of what I git for said Licence. The small Bundle was Deliverd to her Self. . . .

To JOHN RITSON, *Pensacola*[11]

New Orleans, August 19, 1768

You have here inclosed two Orders the one on Majr. Hutc[hi]son for $43 for Sundrys fournishd. Lieut. Fraizer,[12] and the Other for $100 on Mr. William Bar[ber ?] Corrospandant of Messrs. GoDly & Raincok[13] of your place—the Spanish Work men[14] are not as Yett paid, but when they are, I shall [*illegible*] And send you the Remainder with your Account Current; pl[e]ase to let me hear wheater or no that Mr. Stephenson has sold [the] Boards and wheather or no that you Recivd. the neat prosseed [net proceed] of Them—As with out that I cant Settle your Account[.] please Let the Majr. see Mr. fruezeis [*sic*] Letter to me, and that wi[ll] Serve in stead of a Letter of Advoice [invoice]—as I have not Time [as a] Mans a waiting. . . .

J. Bienvenu and Jean Brunet had been active in New Orleans since at least 1766, when they were included among signers of a petition to the Superior Council. See Alcée Fortier, *A History of Louisiana* (2nd. ed.; Baton Rouge, 1972), I, 161. In December, 1769, Jean Brunet was included among the merchants exiled by Governor O'Reilly for suspected participation in the rebellion against Spanish rule and for illegal trade with other Spanish colonies. See Archivo General de Indias, Santo Domingo, Leg. 80, no. 1–7.

10/Possibly Louis Boisdoré, a New Orleans merchant with whom Fitzpatrick had later business dealings. The shores of Lake Pontchartrain were a center for tar, pitch, and lumber production during the colonial era.

11/John Ritson was a Pensacola merchant and business associate of John Stephenson. See Fitzpatrick's letter, May 5, 1769. His name is included in a list of "transient traders" taxed by the West Florida government, and a land grant of 600 acres near Fort Adams (Natchez) was recorded in his name on July 30, 1772. See "Tax on Transient Traders," January 30, 1769, PRO, CO 5/577, pp. 70–71; Gordon M. Wells (comp.), "British Land Grants—William Wilton Map, 1774," *Journal of Mississippi History*, XXVIII (1966), 155.

12/Probably Lieutenant Alexander Fraser, a British army engineer charged with clearing operations along the Iberville River in early 1768. Fraser and his crew worked on the project into the summer and succeeded in sailing their schooner from the Iberville into the Mississippi River during high water on July 28, 1768. See Brown, "The Iberville Canal Project," 491–516. According to the citation included on a sketch map of the Iberville River, drawn by Lieutenant Fraser in 1768, he was a member of the 9th Regiment. See PRO, CO 5/587, p. 335.

13/The Pensacola mercantile firm of William Godley and George Raincock prospered during the British rule of West Florida, and both partners were active in the affairs of the colony, for their names appear frequently in the colonial records. George Raincock served as a member of the West Florida Provincial Council.

14/On March 12, 1767, a schooner arrived in New Orleans from Havana bringing workmen and materials to build or repair fortifications in the newly-acquired Spanish colony. Twelve of these workmen were sent back to Havana with Captain Moore's ship in June, 1768, having been discharged as unsatisfactory. The others remained in the colony and worked on various government construction projects. See Ulloa to Bucareli, March 20, 1767, June 22, 1768, in Kinnaird (ed.), *Spain in the Mississippi Valley*, Pt. 1, pp. 24, 50–52.

To JOHN STEPHENSON, *Pensacola*

New Orleans, August 19, 1768

I have Shipd. on Board Monsr. Covons Peteauger[15] a 11 Casses of Soap with a Case of mighty good wine that I Bought at Monsr. La Costes; I hope that you will Receive it in a bett[er] Condition then the last—with one hundred and three Dollers—$100 is them that I Recivd. from Mr. Monsanto—Being all I have got fr[om] him as Yett & the $3 are for some fills [files] I sold; the Spannards Have Begain to pay out the money to the Merchants; but on[ly] pays the ½; work men are not as yet paid; as soon as they are I Will see what I can do with them; Monsr. Valliseous[16] the Spanish Capt. Leavs this on the 22d Instant for the Havana, and is to be hear In 3 months aGain with $100000—but God knows wheather or no it is True; while he was hear he Bot. [bought] all Mr. Bradleys Goods; Mr. Ross[17] I Believe will be obliged to Take his goods Back again, as there is no Sail for them; fine Goods do not sell hear at present, By Reason that Cash is so scarce; if you should want any fowles; Tobaco Indian Corn Boards Chingles or peas let me know, some Time Before hand that I may Git them Ready— if you think proper to send me the Things I mentioned to you in my list; you may Depend on quick Sales as they are in Demand at Present....

To ROBERT ROSS, *Pensacola*[18]

New Orleans, September 20, 1768

You have hear Inclosed the Second Bill on Mr. Aikman for $52.2¾ with one on your self in my favour for $78 Drew By Captn. WarCarton [*sic*]; for Sundries furnished him hear, as also the Invoice of Sundries Shipd. on Board the Schooner your Account; the Schooner Master and mens Accounts, amounting in all to with My Commission there on $740.6¼—if I coud have Barterred any of the Dry Goods for any of the things that you Demand in my Letter the Schooner would have Been Loaded in

---

1768–1769

15/Variant spelling of *piragua*, in this context referring to a type of open, flat-bottomed schooner-rigged vessel much used in the West Indies and some of the continental colonies.

16/Don Lucas Villaescusa was a Spanish ship captain responsible for specie shipments between Havana and Louisiana. In early August, 1768, Governor Ulloa requested that Cuban governor Bucareli send additional money to the colony by way of Villaescusa, because an allotment of 100,000 pesos which arrived the previous month was not sufficient to pay the obligations of the colonial exchequer. See Ulloa to Bucareli, August 10, 1768, in Kinnaird (ed.), *Spain in the Mississippi Valley*, Pt. 1, pp. 62–63. For a detailed discussion of problems of currency and specie supply encountered by the Spanish in Louisiana, see Holmes, "Some Economic Problems of Spanish Governors of Louisiana," 521–43.

17/Probably David Ross, a prominent New Orleans merchant and owner of the schooner *Polly* (see this volume p. 38, *n.* 3). His business affairs were widely extended, as his name appears frequently in the British West Florida records as an active resident of Pensacola, and in 1776 his name is included on a list of jury members. He also held substantial grants of land along the Mississippi River, acquired in 1771 and 1772, including a plantation between Manchac and Baton Rouge and houses in Baton Rouge. Ross was also owner of one of the "floating warehouses" confiscated by the Spanish governor Bernardo de Gálvez in April, 1777, in an attempt to end British contraband trade along the Mississippi River. See Wells (comp.), "British Land Grants," 158; "List of Grantees of Town Lots in Pensacola," in Howard, *British Development of West Florida*, 42 and facing; Caughey, *Bernardo de Gálvez in Louisiana*, 76; "Louisiana's Spanish West Florida Records," *Louisiana Genealogical Register*, XIX (1972), 144.

18/Merchant of New Orleans and Pensacola, and brother and business partner of David Ross. He resided in New Orleans by permission of the governor. He also speculated in land. Besides a town lot in Pensacola, Robert Ross held a land grant of 1000 acres on the Mississippi River below Natchez, granted July, 1772, and another of 200 acres on Thompson's Creek. He was a native of Scotland. See Howard, *British Development of West Florida*, 42 and facing; Wells (comp.), "British Land Grants," 153, 157; PRO, CO 5/595, p. 349.

full, But no you have nothing But what I paid the C[a]sh for. if I could have Detained her Some Days Longer I should have sent you 2000 Carrots[19] pint Coupie [Pointe Coupée] Tobaco that I Expect in Town every Day from that place; if you think of Sending the Schooner hear again Let it be as soon as possible With the following Goods Viz: 20 ps. stript Holland 50 ps. Comn. Check at 9½ d: 10 d per Ell, 50 Pss. Osnaburghs, 2 ps. blue English Bred [broad] Cloth—100 or 130 with a Blue or Black Strip and 3 doz: black Silk Handkerchief—all on Your own proper Account & Risque[.] the Dry Goods off but slow, but hope that things will soon Turn to more Advantage; on the Arrival of the Spanish Soldiers that are Expected in hear soon, I might have sold some goods for Indego if I would take it at 4/10 sols per lb. But would not pass the Limmited price you left; if you have any more Coffee Send it per the Return of the Schooner as soon as possible for in some Time hence it will not be in Demand on Account of the Ships that are Expected in from the Cape[20]; as the[y] Will Bring a Large quantity with them. . . .

To JOHN STEPHENSON, *Pensacola*

New Orleans, September 28, 1768

I have made Inquirey about the price of the Mules that you mentiond. in your Letter and have been with Monsr. Aubry[21] to see if they could Be Exported out of the province. he toald me that he would see the Spanish Governor on that; But as for him self he would give Me all the Liberty that lay in his power—and that he would if possible, ingage the Spanish Governor to give his Consent there on, Monsr. armon is the man that will furnish the mules But not at under $28 or 140/ per head although if I had the Cash in hand I am Shure to have them for $25 the one with the Other. such a quantity as you Demand Cant be had hear at present, and to git them will be obliged to go [to] the Nacitosh where the greatest part of what is here Comes from; thence, this affair Requires near 4 months Time and you Then Could not have Delivd. You 60 mules that is to say in the Month of January Ensuing and the Other 60 in the Month of May[.] I offered them Bills on London

---

19/During the latter part of the French regime in Louisiana and most of the Spanish, tobacco was an important product of both Pointe Coupée and Natchitoches, although the latter was considered far superior. After being cured and stemmed, the tobacco leaves were rolled together lengthwise somewhat in the fashion of a huge cigar, about four inches thick at its largest diameter and tapering toward each end. This bundle, called a *caret* by the French and a "carrot" by the British, was then covered with a cloth and tied with rope until dry, at which time it weighed about ten pounds. The cloth was then removed and the "carrot" was tied with twine, ready for shipment or sale. For a description of colonial Louisiana tobacco culture, see Bernard Romans, *A Concise Natural History of East and West Florida* (New York, 1775; Reprint edition, New Orleans, 1961), 102–103; Syndor, *A Gentleman of the Old Natchez Region*, 10–11.

20/Cap François (modern Cap Haitien) on the northern coast of the French colony of St. Domingue, was an important distribution point in the commerce of the colonial Caribbean. Customarily, merchant ships coming from France unloaded their cargoes there, where they were repacked and carried by local traders to New Orleans and other points. A Spanish decree of May 6, 1766, permitted French ships to bring wine and flour (and apparently some other commodities) into Louisiana from Martinique and St. Domingue, provided they carried return cargoes of colonial products. See Clark, *New Orleans, 1718–1812*, 42–43.

21/Sieur Charles Philippe Aubry, professional officer of the French army, became director and commandant of troops and thus ranking officer and acting governor of Louisiana after the death of Governor d'Abbadie in February, 1765. After the arrival of Spanish governor Ulloa, Aubry remained in command of the French soldiers in the colony and acted as executor of the governor's policies. After Ulloa's departure in the fall of 1768, Aubry again assumed the role of acting governor until the arrival of General O'Reilly in 1769. In January, 1770, Aubry sailed for France and was lost when his ship was wrecked at the mouth of the Garonne River. See Moore, *Revolt in Louisiana, passim*.

[for] the Amount; but 1 half money And the Other in Bills will git them at $25, and as for the Deer Skins, there is plenty in Town at 3/r per lb. this money[.] it is true they Ware at 35 $ per lb. but at present, they cant be got for that price[.] if you think to purchass any Quantity; let me hear as soone As possible for in all Appearence they will Augment are [ere] long As there is sundry Vessells hear at present that will be going Home for old France[.] Monsr. Venne has near 4000 lb. that he Will Dispose off—Monsr. Poupet[22] has a large quantity, with Many others in Town, which I am Shure to git; you; Bills may Be Exchanged for Cash with the Messrs. Durads[23] and another French Gentleman hear that has offers in London. . . .

To McGILLIVRAY AND STRUTHERS, *Mobile*

New Orleans, April 13, 1769

I have before me your Esteemd. favour of the 5th Instant inclosing invoice and bill lading for sundrys by Monsr. Dominique Amounting to $187.9¼ which is passed to your Cridett, as soon as I receive your Acct. shall rectify any Errors that may appear therein[.] I have likwise receivd all the Articels sent for Mr. McIntosh which Shall forward him per first Conveyance, I shall pay Monsieur Dominique the freight hear for your Government, I shall likewise honour any Draught of Mr. McIntosh for peltry in (Consequence of your orders) if in my power[.] I deliverd your Letter to Mr. Monsanto and intimated him that he must Not think of baffling me any longer about the payment & that if Continud. Pleading his Accostmed Exccuses I would present a petition to the Council to Request they would see me Redressed by giving me up the Neoxus[24] Untill an Entire Satisfaction was made for what he ows to all this he promised Faithfully to Endeavour to pay me as soon as in his power Which I shall Strictly remind him off. I am afraid your Suspicions about Carass[25] are so well Grounded, for I have Taken all means to reduce Them to a Settlemt. but all to no purpose suing I think will answer no End, however should you think it advisable I shall follow your Directions[.] if William Smith, who you Mention, should Come to this quarter you may Depend on my Exerting my self all in my power in your Behalf—on Receipt of your order on Mr. Durring I aplied to him he toald it was not then in his power but would as soon as He was able he is at present a soldier only which does not screen Him from paying it as on Application to the Governor he will always Oblige him to it[.] I shall forward all your letters when ever any opper-

22/Possibly Pierre Poupet, a New Orleans merchant who was one of the leaders of the rebellion against the Spanish government in 1768. See David K. Bjork, "Alexander O'Reilly and the Spanish Occupation of Louisiana," in Lawrence Kinnaird (ed.), *New Spain and the Anglo-American West: Historical Contributions presented to Herbert Eugene Bolton* (Los Angeles, 1932), 165–82; Moore, *Revolt in Louisiana*, 166.

23/The Duralde brothers, natives of Geneva, dealt in diamonds, watches, laces, and other luxury goods. In December, 1769, they were exiled from Louisiana because of their suspected participation in the rebellion and because of illegal trade which they had been carrying on with Mexico. See Korn, *The Early Jews of New Orleans*, 31.

24/Probably the name of a boat owned by Monsanto.

25/Pierre Caresse was a wealthy New Orleans merchant and one of the leaders of the rebellion of 1768. After the arrival of Governor O'Reilly, Caresse was arrested, tried, and executed by firing squad. See Moore, *Revolt in Louisiana*, 199–208.

tuy. Offers. on Receipt of Mr. Le Goutries Letter Immediately forwarded it his son was in town some Time Ago. I realy do not know anything About their Trade, if they owe you anything, please send me their Acct. With a power for me to act for you; I have obtaind a final Judgment Against Madame Phillipeaux[26] but I cannot git it Executed[.] I have Receivd. to the amount $28½ in Spanish Bills and shall right [write] her for the Remainder[.] I shall be Obliged to Repack some of the flour that was Damaged which Mr. McIntosh can inform you after which I hope to be able to Dispose of most part of it, I send you by this Conveyance 3 Casses sweet oil, 10 [?] flasks in Eeach case; there is no Good Wine here at present or should have sent you the quantity You wrote for; there is Vessels Expected Daily with a large Cargo[.] When she shows[?] shall buy up the quantity you wrote for— And send it by the first oppertunity for your place; I have made all Enquiry About Alexander Cerving intimating my having a letter for him from Europ[e] thinking it the most Essential Way of finding him as Mentioning the real Circumstance might allarm him, he is not at present hear, I have met some That knows him and they tell me he is up the Mississippi[.] should he come to this place; you may Acquaint Messrs. McIntosh & Co: that I shall not [fail to act] the needfull—I have paid Monsr. Andre Heaut Brother in Law to St. Pe[27] $87:3 for Amount Sundrys Mr. McGillivary had 20th May 1768 as will Appear by the Inclosd Coppy of this Acct. which was Mr. McGillivarys orders to Me when hear last and not being in Cash to pay that Account I paid him Him [sic] part in Bear Skins and part in some of the Inferiour sort of Deer Skins Which would not suit your Markett. the former I sold at 5 r Each and the Letter [latter] at 40 sols per pound, I applyed to Mr. St. Pe for an Account of Sales of some Goods he Recivd. from Mr. Terry[28] on Account of Mr. McGillivary which He said coud not give untill you could send him the perticulars that Mr. McGillivery left with Terry—I have nothing more at Present to add but remain most Respectfully . . .

To PETER SWANSON, *Mobile*[29]

New Orleans, April 16, 1769

I delivered your letter to Captn. Solomon who informed Me that he has obtained Judgment against Dixey but has not not [sic] As Yet recivd. a farthing neither Can We learn where he is[.] Solomon Offerd to give up all the papers on paying him the Expencess he was At which was $7 which I did not chuse to do, untill

---

26/Madame Philippeaux, a resident of New Orleans, owed Fitzpatrick 36 piastres for flour she had purchased from him. Originally she gave as payment two bills due her by Crock and McIntosh, merchants of Mobile. Fitzpatrick was unable to collect them and petitioned the New Orleans Superior Council. On October 12, 1768, the council ordered Madame Philippeaux to pay what she owed. Apparently she did not comply, because a month later, on November 20, Fitzpatrick, acting as McGillivray's proxy, again petitioned the Superior Council for assistance in getting payment from Madame Philippeaux. See Doc. D–68–207, New Orleans Superior Council Records, Archives and Manuscript Collections, Louisiana State Museum.

27/Pierre St. Pé, New Orleans merchant who was exiled in December, 1769, for suspected participation in the rebellion and illegal trade with Mexico. See Bjork, "Alexander O'Reilly and the Spanish Occupation of Louisiana," 165–82.

28/Jeremiah Terry, a prominent Indian trader and member of the West Florida Council, was also active in the New Orleans trade. His name appears in various documents of the New Orleans Superior Council and in West Florida documents as a resident of Pensacola.

29/Mobile merchant. Along with the McGillivray company, his firm controlled most of the Indian trade in West Florida. See Claiborne, *Mississippi, As a Province, Territory and State*, 112.

I heard further from you as probably it may be a matter that Did not regard your Interest, I omited in Mr. McGillivarys Letter to mention the Amount of the Oil which is $13 I could not gitt less as it is a Scarse Article here at present, you have Inclosed an Order on Mr. Daniel Ward for $10 which if Excepted please to Carry to my Creditt[.] you have Like wise a note of hand the Widow Aransure[?] for $10 to be paid on her first Arrival at your place, if you have any Turlingtons Balsam please to send me a Doz: Bottles, and 6 or a doz: felt Hats[.] I have Been Repacking the flour these three Days past and foud [found] Several Barrels Quite Rotten. I would be Much Obliged to you to Caul on Mr. Ward and ask him if he will Except of one Lewis Boisdors draft on him for about $206 for Which he will Take Goods; and if I should not have all the Articles he may want I intend to write to you for them for which I will Draw in Mr. McGillivarys favour and any Over plus in my favour of the Goods I send for please to Carry to Captn. McMins Credit; We are still in suspence about the French And Spanish Revolutions[.][30] the Spanish Frigate Sails to Morrow. this is all the News I can afford you at Present And Remain . . .

To DANIEL WARD, *Mobile*[31]

New Orleans, April 17, 1769

on Receipt of your favours of 20th Ulto. I immediately took the needfull Steps to procure your Negro Wench and Child for which I applyed to the Governor &c: but to avoid much Expencess (after Taking all necessary Measuers to attach her Judiciously I thought it visable to Demand her Amicably of Mr. Farriseon who on seeing I was ready to Carry the Affair into due Execution of Law, he directly Deliverd her and her Child to me, and brought Them Both to me, at my house. And Kept a Close watch on them least she Should Abscond Being married to a black Silver Smith and not wanting to quit him at this place;

You have [the] negro Wenches Bill of sale left me by Mr. Barrow also Damig ues [damages?] for her and Child you are to pay him for their passage $7 he would Not take less. I am glad my Assiduity has proved to Successfull &c. I Supplyed her with provisions and a Letter to pay some Triffle She Owed here[.] my Charge thereof together with my own Trouble is 10 Dollers for which I have this Date Drawn of you in favour of Messrs. McGillivary & Struthers which hope you will Honour[.] I have nothing more at present to add & Remain . . . P.S. one Louis Boisdore has Applied to me several times for a Credit for which he prom-

30/Fitzpatrick is referring to the New Orleans uprising of October 29, 1768, when a group of French merchants and planters led a rebellion against unpopular Spanish authority, and to the subsequent popular movement to evict the Spanish from the colony. After the revolt, the people remained quiet, although there were repeated demands for the withdrawal of the Spanish packet *El Volante*, along with all the Spanish officials and soldiers in the colony. The packet, carrying Governor Ulloa, left New Orleans on April 20, 1769, but other Spanish officials remained behind, partly to uphold Spanish authority and partly because they were unable to pay debts owed by the Crown and had been ordered not to leave the colony until all such debts were paid. The situation remained unsettled until the arrival of Governor O'Reilly and a large convoy of Spanish troops on August 17, 1769. See Loyola to Bucareli, April 20, 1769, and O'Reilly to Muniain, August 31, 1769, in Kinnaird (ed.), *Spain in the Mississippi Valley*, Pt. 1, pp. 84, 90–91. For further information about the rebellion, its causes and consequences, see Moore, *Revolt in Louisiana*; Bjork, "Alexander O'Reilly and the Spanish Occupation of Louisiana," 165–82; and Richard Ira Matthews, "The New Orleans Revolution of 1768: A Reappraisal," *Louisiana Studies*, IV (1965), 124–67.

31/Daniel Ward operated as a merchant in Mobile and New Orleans during the 1760s, when his name appeared on various documents of the Superior Council. By 1769 he had

ised me Draughts on you[.] I would be much Obliged to you to informe me if you Will Except [accept] them, and to what Amount. I am as before ...

To JOHN STEPHENSON, *Pensacola*

New Orleans, April 22, 1769

I hope are [ere] this comes to hand you have recivd. the things I sent you By Savon, and Should this not overtake you at pensacola hope it will find you safe arrivd in England, which Shall be always glad to hear; the Spanaish Frigate Saild for the havana 3 days ago We are Still in Suspence About the Result of the Rupture between the French & Spanards but is the General oppion of the people here that it will fall to the Spanards if so Cash will Circulate in this place, and the Articels you was kind Enough to promise to send me will Answer extream Well, I omited to Mention Blankets in the Memorandum, which if you think proper to send please to let them be good Blankets proper for making Blankett Coats with Either black or Blue Strips only[.] I am afraid Mr. Monsanto Will Shortly be pushed very hard for money he owes at Mobile to Messrs. McGillivary & Struthers for Negros Bought of them a long time Ago[.] I have nothing more at present worth your notice but should this Reach you at pensacola refer you to Mr. McNamara who no[w] goes there[.] I am with due Esteem ... P.S. Youl please to send me the Universal History well bound with proper Cutts and Maps tho they should Cost 6d or a Shilling More a Vollume.[32] ...

To VALENS STEPHEN COMYN, *Pensacola*[33]

New Orleans, April 22, 1769

this Serves to aquaint you that Mr. Olivie and his Wife are Gone from hear to the Opisite side of the lake, he became a Bankrupt. I recivd. to the Amount of your Debt in Bonds on Sundry persons a part of which I Believe will be paid in Time And there are some all ready paid for which the people produced his Receipts in full to them, as when they paid him he said he had Lost their Bonds, this I Knew nothing of while he was hear But Should he Return I Shall use my best Endeavours to reduce him to payment[.] if you have any Such thing as a Mahogony framed looking Glass about 18 Inches by 14: I should be much Obliged to you to send it Me by the first Oppertuinity, there is nothing here at present Occurs worth your Notice; I refer you to Mr. McNamara who Now goes to your place & am ...

---

moved to Mobile, and in 1772 was elected to serve as one of the representatives of Mobile in the West Florida General Assembly. He also speculated in land, for he is recorded as the recipient of a tract of 1500 acres below St. Catherine's Creek near Natchez, granted August 3, 1768, and of a town lot in Pensacola. See Wells (comp.), "British Land Grants," 154; Howard, *British Development of West Florida*, 42 and facing; "Written Evidence of Notice No. 982," Ellis-Farar Papers, Department of Archives and Manuscripts, Louisiana State University; Contract, August 21, 1769, Acts of Joseph Fernandez, New Orleans Notarial Archives.

32/The inventory of Fitzpatrick's property made after his death lists "a Universal History of only one volume ... estimated at fifteen pesos." See Survey of Federal Archives in Louisiana, *Archives of the Spanish Government of West Florida* (18 vols.; Baton Rouge, 1937), II, 459.

33/Valens Stephen Comyn was a Pensacola merchant.

To JOHN RITSON, *Pensacola*

New Orleans, April 22, 1769

I hope Savin is arrived are this, and that you have recivd. the Things I sent by him. I lay under great Concern about what I owe you[.] I Assure you the Spannards I sold your Goods to are Still hear, if Spanish Bonds payable on Arrival of the Treasury would Answer your End I will send them to you on Acquainting me therewith, I would be Sorry that Mr. Stephenson or you should think me Remiss in any thing For your Interest which I have as much to heart as my own[.] if Before this Arrives Mr. Stephenson should have Sailed for England Youl Please to Forward the Inclosed by first Oppertunity for England[.] there is nothing more at present occurs from ...

To McGILLIVRAY AND STRUTHERS, *Mobile*

New Orleans, April 22, 1769

I this morning recivd. a letter from Mr. Lafarac Intimating he had Recivd. a Letter from me Concerning a Debt he owed the House[.] this I immagine Could be no Other than the Letter you Inclosed me for him, in his Letter to me he Seems a little surprized You was not paid Long are now by Parung his Brother in law at your Place as he left Effects in his hands for that porpose and Insists on your Looking to Parung for payment. for which you have a letter from him to Parong Inclosed and Likewise a Small list of Sundry Articles which I Belive may be the Debt. .... P.S. Mr. Bradley[34] who Arrivd. Yesterday from Natches informs me that Mr. McGillivary is Expected there from the Chickesaw Nation....

To DANIEL HICKY, *Pensacola*[35]

New Orleans, April 22, 1769

the french man who promised me the Bill for 100 D. now seems to Equivocate he has offered Spanish Bills but I Refused them as there is no Certainty of the Time [of] payment, he promised me Draft on Daniel Ward of Moblie [Mobile] which I have wrote Mr. Ward about to Know if he would Except [accept] if so I Shall Draw on him in your favour[.] the hole [whole] of your Stone ware are Still on hand[.] Mr. LaCount told me he Wrote you by his own Vessell and ordered the man who Comman[d]ed

---

34/Merchant John Bradley was granted 1000 acres in the Natchez district in 1767 and together with Henry Fairchild operated the only trading post in that area before 1770. After the British withdrew troops from Fort Panmure in 1768, Bradley remained behind, occupied the fort, and made plans to form a settlement there with the help of his slaves. Early in 1770, Bradley and the few other inhabitants of the Natchez settlement were forced to flee when Indians entered and plundered the fort. See Ulloa to Grimaldi, October 6, 1768, in Kinnaird (ed.), *Spain in the Mississippi Valley*, Pt. 1, p. 71; Faye, "The Arkansas Post of Louisiana," 632–33; John Bradley to Elias Durnford, February 1, 1770, in PRO, CO 5/577, pp. 233–40.

35/Daniel Hicky, born in County Clare, Ireland, in 1740, was at this time an "Indian Commissary" or licensed trader operating out of Pensacola. He was granted 500 acres of land on the east side of the Mississippi River, about six miles below Pointe Coupée, on November 29, 1768, but did not occupy it until later. In 1780 he served on the grand jury of Manchac. His son, Philip Hicky, born in 1778, developed the plantation and became a prominent figure in the early history of the Baton Rouge area. Daniel Hicky died in 1808. See Hicky Family Genealogy, Morgan Family Papers, Department of Archives and Manuscripts, Louisiana State University; Land grant, November 29, 1768, Daniel and Philip Hicky Papers, Department of Archives and Manuscripts, Louisiana State

her the Ps. 28 for the Strouds—if not I think you would do well to oblige Him to it there, LeCount[36] has got Command of the Spanish Sloop which Sailed 3 days a go for the Havana[.] there is nothing new hear at Present and Remain . . .

To DANIEL HICKY, *Pensacola*

New Orleans, May 3, 1769

since writing you the 22 Ulto. I have recvd. your favour of the 14th same of Mr. Bastison and note the Contents, I could be of Little or no Service to him in Disposing of his Iron work; further then Speaking to severals it is an Article at present not in Demand[.] I have furnished Mr. Batison with Sundry Articels amounting to 81.¼ Dollers as you will see by your Accot. Current here Inclosed . . Ballance in your favour D. 43:8 Exclusive of outstanding Debts which Am sorry I have not been able to gitt in as yet to make you a good Remittance[.] as to what you Mention with Respect to Smith I certainly Told him I would send (him) you [sic] a bill but Mentioned nothing more how Might he Know but it may be one I sent you to Receive for me, I send You by this Conveyance, a Box of Soap, I would have sent you the wine You wrote for had you not Limitted me to the low price you Did, I would When it was to be had—I have not as yet heard from Mr. Ward concerng. the Bill I mentioned in my last; all the Earthen Ware is Still on hand Owing to the Dulness of Trade hear at present for which I Refer You to Mr. Batison[.] I have Nothing more at present to add Remain . . . P.S. You will please to observe I have Charged you no Commission which is to be 7½ pCt. [percent] which if Deducted the Ballance would be in my favour; I conclude Storage in Said Commissions as you know I cannot Consider the out Standing Debts Value, untill Recvd. tho I Believe the people are good. . . .

To JOHN FALCONER, *Pensacola*[37]

New Orleans, May 4, 1769

I have been this morning at the vandue[38] to see if I could Dispose of the Cheese most part of with [which] is Rotten and Stinks which Mr. Batison Mr. Wilton & Hood who are Going to pensacola & have seen it Can Inform you[.] the Vandue Master Said he would not keep it in the House And that it would not Fet[c]h Nothing so reather than Keep it untill I am Obliged to throw it away, I will Send it about the Town with a Negro to Sell to the

---

University; Elias Durnford to Montfort Browne, January 13, 1770, in PRO, CO 5/577, p. 260; Address of the Grand Jury of Manchac, November 15, 1780, PRO, CO 5/580, pp. 309–11.

36/The Spanish sloop *La Alegre Cazadora* sailed from New Orleans on April 20, 1769, under the escort of the packet *El Volante*, for the purpose of bringing money from Havana to pay Spanish troops and officials in Louisiana. The sloop was commanded by a Monsieur Le Conte. See Loyola to Bucareli, April 20, 1769, in Kinnaird (ed.), *Spain in the Mississippi Valley*, Pt. 1, p. 85.

37/John Falconer was a merchant and freeholder of Pensacola.

38/I.e., *vendue*, a public auction.

Best Advantage, I Expected to have heard from You are now, in answer to a Letter I wrote you some time ago. I am Sorry to Acquaint you that Trade is very Dull here at present. I shall Continue remitting [to] Mr. McGillivery as usial as it lies more in My way[.] there is Nothing more at present Occurs worth your Notice & am . . .

To GODLEY AND RAINCOCK, *Pensacola*

New Orleans, May 4, 1769

I am Desired by Mr. Barrow[39] to write you any thing That may occur relating to his affairs left in my Care in Consiquence of which, have now to Acquaint you that the peltry he Expects from Maxant[40] by the summer Convoy I Shall Endeavour to Change for Deer Skins in the Hair, and Shall give Maxant Credit for the same At the Cash price they Shall be Vallued at by 3 or 4 of the principal Merchants hear who Deal in that Article agreeble to his Request and Shall punctually observe his order in keeping the Skins in good Order.—Mr. Cavalier hear for the Ballance he says Mr. Barrow owes for his Board upon which I presented him Mr. Barrows Account Settled with him, which he acknowledged to be very fact[?], but Added at the same Time there was a Ballance of Ds. 30 Still remaining Due. and which he requested I would pay, which I refused and toald him As the matter was of such a Nature he must wait Mr. Barrows Return to Settle it, upon which he Threatned to seize upon Mr. Barrow['s] Effects which I Defied him to and Since I have not heard further About it, I have Settled with Mr. page for his note of Ds. 280 but was first under the Ne-

39/William Barrow is identified in several documents in the New Orleans Superior Council Records as an English merchant resident in New Orleans. He operated out of Pensacola and apparently maintained a residence there, for his name is included on a list of Pensacola merchants in 1766, and Fitzpatrick addressed a letter to him there in 1770 (August 26). Together with Robert Barrow, probably a brother, he was granted 2000 acres near Second Creek, below Natchez, on December 10, 1768. William Barrow left America in the early 1770s and eventually made his way to Liverpool, where he was living in 1777 (see p. 227). See PRO, CO 5/574, pp. 978–79; Wells (comp.), "British Land Grants," 160.

40/Gilbert Antoine de St. Maxent (1724–94) was born in Longy, France, and came to Louisiana in the 1740s. He purchased a building on Conti Street and entered the commercial life of New Orleans as a supply merchant for fur traders. By 1763 he was the leading merchant of New Orleans and a prominent military figure in the colony. As a reward for his service in the war with Britain, Governor Kerlérec granted St. Maxent the exclusive right of trade with the Indians of the Missouri River as far north as Lake St. Peter. St. Maxent then became a business partner of Pierre Laclède Liguest, who, in 1764, established the trading post that was to become St. Louis. By 1766, St. Maxent, Laclède and Company controlled virtually all the fur trade from the Illinois. The monopoly was cancelled in 1767, and the partnership dissolved in 1769.

After the change of regime in 1766, St. Maxent showed public support for the Spanish and became a close friend of Governor Ulloa. Governor O'Reilly named St. Maxent commissioner of Indian affairs for the entire colony in 1769 and ordered that all goods distributed to Indians anywhere in Louisiana had to be purchased and delivered through the firm of St. Maxent and Ranson, which had been formed for the purpose of carrying out this commission. In this position St. Maxent dominated the fur trade as before and became one of the wealthiest men in the colony. St. Maxent's children also enjoyed positions of prominence in Louisiana. One daughter married Governor Unzaga, another married a wealthy planter named d'Estrehan then, after his death, Governor Gálvez. His oldest son, Antonio de St. Maxent, served with distinction in the Spanish colonial army, was named commander at the former British Fort Bute in 1780 and commander at Gálveztown in 1781. The complexity of St. Maxent's financial affairs is revealed by the legal battles over his estate which occurred after his death. See James Julian Coleman, Jr., *Gilbert Antoine de St. Maxent: The Spanish Frenchman of New Orleans* (New Orleans, 1968); and Documents Concerning the Estate and Succession of Don Gilberto Antonio de St. Maxent, 5 vols., Louisiana Division, New Orleans Public Library.

cessity of Bringing him Before the Councill,[41] I was obliged to Take a Spanish Bill for payment.

I am Sorry Mr. Barrows Letter of the 4th Ulto. Desiring I would Git Security from page for the Ballance of the protested [debt] came too Late as page had sailed some time before in the Spanish Frigate for the Havana; I Sent you by the Convayance a peice of Cambrick which was the first I could gitt here it cost me 8½ D. Which should it Suit you please to pay the Amount to Baptist & if it Should not suit you please to return it Back by him[.] I would not Desire you to pay Such a Triffle, but I assure you I have Not as yet been able to git in any part of Mr. Barrows out Staning Debts, I could not git any Glass of the Demetions Mr. Barrow Wrote me to send you as their was none at Mr. Cavalier, Who is the only man that has any at present, less than 12 Inchs By 10 Except some of 7 Inches by 5. which I apprehend would Not Suit you; and he would not give the former Under 3 reals this Money the pane, and Mr. Barrow limitted me to 2 Rs. the pane[.] if you have any of your white Ground Cotton left please to send Me 6 double ps. such as Mr. Barrow brought here of No. 11 & 12 for which I will reumburs you in Corn Rice Deer Skins or Indego in the Ensuing Crop if Agreable to you; I have nothing more At present to add & Remain . . .

To JOHN RITSON, *Pensacola*

New Orleans, May 4, 1769

Agreeable to Mr. Stephenson's Letter I send you by this Conveyance a Box Marked JR Containing 37 ps. Printed Cottons perticulars, as per the Annexd Invoice, I have been Often with Bein Venu & Comy. upon Mr. Stephensons Bussiness they can give me Nothing unless I would take 150 Ds. in Tobaco A part in Liquers in quart Bottles at 6 rs. [per bottle] and some soap which I Declined doing untill I receive your Orders on that head—I would be glad to know if you Receivd. the things sent by Savon And if he lost any thing when Cast away[.] I have nothing more to add at present But Remain . . . P.S. please to forward Mr. Stephensons Letter per first Convayce. . . .

To VALENS STEPHEN COMYN, *Pensacola*

New Orleans, May 5, 1769

Since writing you the 22d Ulto. have not had the pleasure of Hearing from you, the present servs to inform you that 15 or 20 ps. of

41/On March 22, 1769, Fitzpatrick, acting as proxy for William Barrow, petitioned Intendant Foucault for an order to prevent Joseph Page from leaving the city until he paid off a note for 200 piastres which he had promised to pay Barrow when he received money owed him by the Spanish. On April 5, Foucault granted an order for a summons against Page. The hearing was held on April 8, and Page was ordered to pay Fitzpatrick the disputed sum in Spanish notes. See New Orleans Superior Council Records, Archives and Manuscript Collections, Louisiana State Museum.

Strouds would Anser very well hear at present, for your Government As you Desired me to acquaint you so if this meets your approbation you May send me; 10 ps. blue with a small Stripe & 5 ps. red to be of a good Quallity—I shall use my Best Endeavours to dispose of them for Your Account, for their are a good many Boats Expected here Shortly from the Nactosh [Natchitoches], they may in all probility want some Negroes all this I advise you offf in Conveyance of your Verble orders to me when You was hear[.] I have nothing more at present to add & Remain ... P.S. if you have not as yet sent the Looking Glass I wrote for please to send it by Baptist. ...

To JOHN STEPHENSON, *Pensacola*

New Orleans, May 5, 1769

I have now to Answer your favours of the 15th March & 5 April[.] I this day (Agreeable to your Orders) Shipped the Cottons directed to Mr. Riston [*sic*] at pensacola, I have Acquainted Mr. Monsant that you Could not procure the Articels he mentioned[.] Monsr. Deturts is in the Country at present on his Return to Town you may Depend on my Acting the Needfull with respect to the power of Attorney against Roberts, I Shall punctually observe your Orders in sending some Wine to Mr. Ritson, I was Yesterday at Bein Venus and they Could give nothing Unless I would take 150 Ds. in Tobacco a part in Liquer in quart Bottles at 6 rs. Each, and some Soap which I refused untill I had Either your or Mr. Ristons orders who I have this day wrote to on that Subject; I am Infinetely obliged to you, for your kind promise of Establishing my Creditt which favour I shall always Endeavour to Merrit and use All assiduety to give Content as well in Remittance as Otherwise; Affairs here are in the Same Situation as when you left it, we daily Expect to here the remot[?]; there is nothing more at present worth Your Notice and Remain most Respectfully ...

To GODLEY AND RAINCOCK, *Pensacola*

New Orleans, May 5, 1769

Since Sealing my Letter of the 3 Instant I Had the Disagreeable News of hearing (by Individuals) that all Mr. Barrows papers sent by Serpee;[42] are lost as the Boat was Blown up by some powder they had on Board; I Expect Mr. Serpee Will Write me about it as I can then furnish him with Coppies of the Hole Taken by the Notary publick. I am Sorry to Conclude With Such a Message of ill News & am ...

42/Jean Baptiste Sarpy, born in Funel, Gascony, France, was a prominent merchant in both New Orleans and St. Louis. After the death in 1778 of Pierre Laclède, founder of St. Louis, Sarpy was appointed coexecutor of the Laclède estate. He died in New Orleans in 1798. See Coleman, *Gilbert Antoine de St. Maxent*, 94; Louis Houck (ed.), *The Spanish Regime in Missouri* (2 vols., Chicago, 1909), I, 200 n.

To JOHN RITSON, *Pensacola*

New Orleans, May 17, 1769

I have Before me your Esteemd favour of the 4th & 12 May And note the Contents, Inclosed you have an Abstract of your Accot. Currt. Ballance in your favour $260.7¾ which should have been able to have Remitted you long are now if the Spanish Bills had been paid which We are Daily in Expectation of: I have Bartered your Martin Skins for Blankets, which when Sold Shall pass to your Credit. As this goes by a Conveyance to Mobile, I Cannot send the Turbits Or Corn you mention, the former I Shall git made and Send them per First Oppertunity; when Harrison Comes here you may Depend On my Acting the Needfull; the Corn I Can gitt but As you Mentioned a Low price, thought proper to Acquaint you that it Will be 1½ Dollar for the Corn and Barrel here is Shipped in this place, and if Obliged to send it to the Bayoux[43] will Stand you in $1–6. Exclusive of freight. for your Government there fore would not send it without your approbation[.] the man that Roberts bought the White Lead of is in the Country, so when he Comes to Town Shall Ask him for one[.] there is Nothing more at present occurs Worth your Notice & Remain . . .

To PETER SWANSON, *Mobile*

New Orleans, May 19, 1769

I have now before me your Esteem'd favour [of the] 6 instant And am much obliged to you for the Trouble you have Taken in Wai[t]ing on Mr. Ward; on the Receipt of yours I waited on Mr. Boiedore, who shewed me Mr. Wards Letter to him on that Subject by Which it appears it was for a protested Bill which Mr. Ward has Since recovered from the Drawer on said Boisdores Account, who is no way inclind to Take any other payment but Cash[.] he leavs this Tomorrow Morning and as he has not recivd. an Answer to his last Letter did not write by this oppertunity[.] he has left Mr. Durrant his father in law his attorney who intends Drawing on him per first oppertunity after this in my favour for What Boisdore Owes me as well on my own Account as that of your Sales, it is true I have had a great Deal of Trouble with Madame Phillipeaux And all I Could git of her was $28½ in Spanish Bills and I believ the law Charges will Neaver be recovered from her; for she fulfill[s] the old proverb sue a Begger & youl Cetch a Louse; I would have Sent you the Cherit [claret] if there was any Good to be had they ask $40 per hhd. for an Inferiour Sort and that ready Cash, we are Daily Expecting a Cargo here when able to send it you the quantity you mention[.] An Op-

---

43/Bayou St. John, New Orleans' "back door" into Lake Pontchartrain, was the head of a convenient route through the lake and the Rigolets to the British trading towns in West Florida. A road was maintained between the town and the bayou to allow carts and horses to carry goods back and forth.

pertunity offered some time ago to send the Cheese to pensacola to Mr. Falconer but all the Gentlemen that saw it said it was not Worth the freight there fore Declined Sending it, I have nothing More at present to add & remain ... P.S. my Compliments to Mr. McIntosh & let him know I would have wrote him But the man is Waiting—Please to forward the inclosed Letters.

To McGILLIVRAY AND STRUTHERS, Mobile

New Orleans, May 19, 1769

I recivd. your favour of the 6th may and obser[v]e there was A Bottle of oil wanting in the 3 Casses, I sent them to you first as receivd. So Cannot Account for it; the Day I recivd. the Cranks I immedeately Sent thim to the smiths, where they are Repaird the following day and Shipt on Board this morning; the smiths Charge is $13 the Cartage from and to the Bayoux $1½ which I have placed to your Debit the Smith, Inshurs their Goodniss and Strenth with Respect to his work[.] I hope Mr. Lizzard will find them as Such, a Sett of New ones would Cost him upwards of $60—the 12 Bottles Turlington you sent Came All safe and have passed the Amount to your Creditt, I am sorry that I have to Inform you that Mr. Monsanto s[t]ill puts me off in the Usall Manner, tho the last time I was with him he promised to pay me the latter end of next Month I was very Ingenious with him & Toald him if he did not, Comply with his promise, that I would present A petition to the Councill to gitt the Negroes into my possession Untill full Satisfaction was made, I have waited so long on blass & Carass that I almost Dispair of ever Bringing it to a Conclusion, they have Reapeatedly toald me to T[ak]e what Measuers I pleased, I Cannot furnish you with the Sundry Articels I sold for Mr. McGillivry in 1767—as I only had a rough skeath [sketch] of it in my pocket Book; which I lost at pensacola in July 1767, when Mr. McGillivary Was here in March 1767 I give him an Account Sales of the Hole. I think nothing of the Trouble I have Taken about the flour, all I wish for is to be able to make Sales of it, which will soon be able to do, as their is not Much in Town at present, I have nothing More to add at Present & Remain ...

To GODLEY AND RAINCOCK, Pensacola

New Orleans, May 19, 1769

Since writing you the 5 Instant have not rece [*page torn*] of yours the present serves Chiefly to inform you I this Day saw a le[tter] from Mr. Saint Pee, to one of his friends in town in which he Desired [his] Friend to acquaint me that he had Saved his Trunk, where Mr. Barr[ow's] papers ware; other wise; would have Taken out Copies at the Notery publicks[.] if you think it Convenient to send me the Cottons please to Advise me; I could have sold them —Several Times if here for the Articels I quoted in my Last; I have nothing more at present to add And Remain . . .

To JOHN FALCONER, *Pensacola*

New Orleans, May 25, 1769

I have now Before me yours of the 29th Ulto. and note the Contents I inclos'd you have Invoice of the Goods upon hand belonging to Cap[tain] McMain; and at foot an Accout. of the Uble Linus [*sic*] sent you by this Conveyance in a Small Box Marked IF which I wish Safe to hand.

With respect to the Spanish Bills, I never took but one on his Acc[ount] Which I was Obliged to do when the Spanards; ware ordered from hear; Which will be paid on Arrival of the Spanish Preanier [*sic*]; Expected here in a Next month; When ever I am in Cash for Captn. McMins Sails I embrace the first oppertunity of Remitting it to Messrs. McGillivary & Struthe[rs] The out Standing Amount to about Ds. 250 for which hope to Receive D[eer] Skins in all next month, which I shall remitt Messrs. McGillivary & Struthers Being an Article that will suit them; as well as Cash W[ill] I hope to be able to remit, them Gentlemen the hole of what I have sold [or] May sell Before Captn. McMins Arrival; what I have sold heathere[to is] at about 50 per Cent on the prime Cost. as to the Condition of the Che[ese] I refer you to my last of the 4 Instant; you may Depend I shall use my Best Endeavours to Dispose of it to the best Advantage; I have sold about 115 lb. [at] 15 sols which is Equal to 1½ royals your money[.] I wis[h] it was all sold at the same which it would have been if not prevent[ed] By Several Arrivels from the northward which Glutted the mar[ket] With that Commodity[.] I am of Opinion that the Goods on hand are Very Suitable here the Slowness of which is Occasioned thro scarsity of money; I have nothing more at present to add & am . . . P.S. the Quantity of Cheese specified in the Invoice is what should be on hand According to the weight Deliverd me but Since Mouldering & Grown Rotten will fall Short of that Weight.

To JOHN McGILLIVRAY, *Mobile*

New Orleans, June 10, 1769

You have here inclosed a Letter from one Mr. Durant a French Gentleman of this place Father in law and attorney to Mr. Lewis boisdore Who is at present up the river[.] he Beged, the favour of Me to request that you would act the Need full; there in which I pray you will do if not incovenant to you; how ever on reading the Inclosed you will be Better able to Judge; if agreeable to you; or not to Act in Conformity[.] I am most Respectfully . . .

To McGILLIVRAY AND STRUTHERS, *Mobile*

New Orleans, June 10, 1769

You have Inclosed Mr. Dussins draft of this date My favour on Messrs. Daniel Ward & Comy. for Ds. 164:6½ this money Which please to present to them and if Excepted. please to pass the Same to my Creditt. this Bill is for the Amount of Bosdores Acct. With me he has left said Dussant his Attorney should he not Chuse to Except it youl; please to gitt it Duly protested, and remitt it me back[.] I have not heard any thing from Mr. McIntosh for some Time; I here he is to be hear Shortly. I have all the Goods you sent for him here Still. I have paid to the Amount of $40 for him since I wrote you Last I have at Last Recovered Mr. Swansons Money in Spanish Bill from Madame Phillipeaux with Charges which when paid I Shall remitt him; I have nothing more to Acquaint you with But that money is Scarser than ever. I hope Times will soon Alter [for] the Better; & am . . . P.S. Skins begin to Come here pritty plenty and I Belive Could be Bought for Cash at 32 to 33 sols per pound[.] I have been Informd from some people that Came down the river that Monsant will have Skins Down very Shortly which may probabily be them he Intends for you.

To McGILLIVRAY AND STRUTHERS, *Mobile*

New Orleans, June 26, 1769

Since writing you this 10th Instant I receivd. your Favours of the 6th and 10th same and note the Contents, I then Remited you a first Bill of Mr. Dussins my favour on Messrs. Daniel Ward & Comy. for $164:6½ with which please to send the needfull; I now inclose you a Second of the same to serve in Case of Need[.] you will receive by this Conveyance 3 Hogsheads Rum and One

Hogshead Taffia[44] Amounting to 70½ Ds. as per Invoice for Which I was obliged to Borrow the money payable at a month In which time I hope you will be able to reumburs[.] the Rum Was Usial here, and has a very Stroung [flavor?], therefore make no Doubt But it will please, there is but one or Two that has Gott Clarritt [claret] Here and would have spared 2 Hhds. on paying them Down 90 Ds. Which was really out of my power; as you see by the above As I have not Been able to gitt in any Money, there is some Vessells in the river therefore if you Could send me money for the Quantity you Should want I would sent it you by the first Safe Oppertunity. I have the Amount of about 100 Ds. of my own In Skins which I intend to Send you; with them of McIntoshs— had it been posible for Domenigoue to send you with them (you, for he says his Boat is Two Small, and Battison was not Going Your way. Coffe[e] is at Present at 20 Sols, which I thought Two Dear or would have sent you 50 lb. I have not Sent Mr. McIntoshs things as I Expect him hear in a few days[.] the Skins I mentioned in my last of Monsanter are not yet Arrived being what at present Occurs from . . .

To JOHN BRADLEY, *Natchez*

New Orleans, July 12, 1769

I recivd. your favour of the 4th Instant per Mr. Hayton who was Speechless a Day Before the Boat Arrivd. I Had him Brought to the House; and Immediately sent for a Doctor who administred every Reamedy he could think of for his Recovery but all to no purpose; he Expired Yesterday at 12 Oclock, and had him Intered the same night as he was in Such a Condition that he would not keep any Longer[.] his Geniral Charges Doctors Fees &c aMount to 18 Ds. tho I have not Asked the Doctor his Charge but I Belive it will not be More, and if any thing Less Shall Credit you with the Difference

I inclosed you here an Inventory of all his things in presence of the Witness'es there unto Subscribed[.] I have sent you all his papers sealed up in A Pillow Case as you will See by the Inclosed receipt of Thomas,s[.] you have Like wise Inclosed Messr. Hayton & Williamss Account Sales Agreeable to that Given Mr. Williams when here, an abstract of Mr. Haytons Account Current as I always Charged him with any thing they which he Said he would Settle with you; there fore would be glad to know how how [*sic*] I am to be reimbursed; I am Sorry I Cannot Send you the Taffia for here it Cannot be gott without ready Money which I have not at present, tho I have Been with sevaral people Who

44/A rum-like distilled liquor obtained from low-grade molasses and refuse brown sugar.

owe me Money this long Time and all put me off; I have About Ds. 10 in the House which I must pay for Mr. Haytons Charges if I should hear of any News worth your Notice. I shall Acquaint you by all oppertunities[.] I am with respect . . . P.S. Mr. Maghear desiers his best Respects to you; Monsant has had No Vessell as yet and god knows When he will;

To JAMES SUTTON, *Pensacola*[45]

New Orleans, July 17, 1769

I recvd. yours of the 5th Instant with the peice of Cotton you sent Me; I have not as yet been able to Dispose of any of your things nor doI see any prospect of Selling them to any Advantage. I spoke to the Vandue Master about them, and he assurs me they would not all Togeather fetch $40. so reather mairr [*sic*] any Consarve about the sale of them I wish you would Impower Smith or parker to bring them duty or Take them out of my hands and pay me the freight for it Is Disagreeable To have such unsaable [unsalable], Articels on hand Especially Recommened by a freind. I shall Expect your answer and am . . .

To GODLEY AND RAINCOCK, *Pensacola*

New Orleans, July 17, 1769

I recivd. yours of 7th Instant with the peice of Cotton you sent you sent [*sic*] me by Mr. parker I am Sorry you shoud think un-mercantile to return the others where as your Quoting the price You sold some at to the Spannards is no General Rule And I thought it necessary to Specify what I could Afford to give [in] Advance as I never was Charged more than 50 p Cent upon Any Dry Goods I ever had Either from Pensacola or Mobile and you Charged Almost 100 pCt. According to Mr. Barrows Invoice of Goods of the same kind in the sails of which I assissted in part my self And the Best of Them No. 12 was only Charged 5 ps. per yard which Is $15 Ds. per ps. I am surprised Donaldson should plead Ignorace of the peice Githing wett and Likewise of the Contents of the Box when he was present at the Time I packed thim And give him a Strict Charge about them[.] if that Accident of the Ink fauling on the peice I kept [had not happened] I would have Likewise Returnd. it as it was Spotted with oil Occassioned by your Sending them in a Case that had oil Bottles in it; Mr. Maxan[?] Arrivd. hear Yesterday from the Illinois and Informs me that the french Boats Will Soon be down with skins in Such

45/Pensacola merchant. His name is included on a list of grantees of town lots in Pensacola. See Howard, *British Development of West Florida*, 42.

Case you may Depend on my Acting the Needfull with Respect to Mr. Barrows affairs[.] the man Incharged with his affairs and papers has not wrote me a Word about it As yet but I Expect Letters in the Boats Cumming Down. . . .

To McGILLIVRAY AND STRUTHERS, *Mobile*

New Orleans, July 17, 1769

I have Before [me] your Esteemd favour of the 4 Instant With which recivd. the 71½ Ds. sent by Dommick; which Came very Seasonable. I note the Draft on Ward for $164.6½ is Excepted which Is well[.] I could not prevail on Dominick to take less than 4 Ds. per hhd. for these Small Boats Generally Ask more than a large Vessell On Account their Small freights. I have not as yet Spoke to any the Inhabitants here who Deal in peltry as there is no great Quantity as yet Come down—when make no Dout but I Shall be able to gitt Skins at the Credit you Mention. as Soon as I recivd. yours I immediately waited On Mr. Monsanto & Toald him it was absolutely necessary to come to some Conculusion & that your patience was quite Exhausted Upon which he came on; the following Terms that is to say. there Is a parcel of Peltry now Shipping for pensacola & the french man Mr. Chouteaux who has the Care of Delivering them to Sundry Creditors will on Your producing Monsants note of hand for Ds. 401:4 Take it up paying you the vallue in Skins at the rate of 37 Sols per lb. to say the drest Leather and if in the Hair at 42 Sols per skin that being the Tenor of his note of hand here inclosed for that purpose, if the Skins had been Delivered here the Wt. would have been 1085 but if paid in pensacola the Difference of 8½ pCent must be added to the above Wt. which Makes 1177 and it will be necessary to loose No time on Sending the note on Receipt of This Should you be frustrated in this send me back the Note Immediately; but I am in hopes you Will not as he Tels me; he has Taken all Necessary Steps for its meetg. Due Honour there on the above Terms[.] the young le Gentry has been in Town some Time till with in these few Days to who I Spoke about Your affairs as Mr. Swanson wrote me before on the same affair he toald me as to his part he new nothing about it, therefore Immagin it must be his father if so you will please to send me his Acct. Currt. And if obligation of his to Enable me to use proper Deligence there in Not with Standing he lives on the opposite side of the lake and is Become a british Subject.

You have here inclosd. Mr. Alexr. McIntoshs[46] first of Ex-

46/Alexander McIntosh began his career in West Florida as a captain of the provincial troops and as an Indian interpreter. In 1769 he was apparently operating as an Indian trader. In 1770 he was granted 500 acres near Fort Natchez; another 500 acres near Petit Gulf were granted to him in 1772 and 500 acres opposite Point Coupée in 1771 and 1773. Apparently he settled on the Point Coupée plantation for a time, for his name appears in 1772 as a witness to the wedding of a Pointe Coupée couple. During the late 1770s he moved to Natchez and was there when the Spanish captured the settlement in 1779, for his name is included among the inhabitants of Natchez who signed a letter commending the British commander there. During all this time he continued his trading activities, often in partnership with Fitzpatrick. See Howard, *British Development of West Florida*, 27; Wells (comp.), "British Land Grants," 152, 153, 155; Winston De Ville (ed.), *Colonial Louisiana Marriage Contracts*, Vol. III: *Post of Point Coupée, 1736–1803* (Baton Rouge, 1962), 20; Kenneth Scott (ed.), "Britain Loses Natchez, 1779: An Unpublished Letter," *Journal of Mississippi History*, XXVI (1964), 46.

change of you my honour for Ds. 187.4 which please to pass to my Creditt. you have likwise inclosd Mr. Henry Leflowr[47] (kings Indian Interpretor at Fort Natchez) Drauft on Mr. Charles Steward[48] (Deputy Intendant of Indian affairs) your favour for Ds. 254 as per said Leflowrs Letter of Advise to said Mr. Stewart. I woul assteem it A favour of you to Endeavour to Recover it for Said Leflowr And remitt it me observing to Deduct Ds. 41.4 which he owes me Which if Receivd. you will please to pass to my Credit. you will receive By this Conveyance Mr. McIntoshs Skins made as follows

		Skins	
2 packs Contg. each 30 Skins in the hair	. .	60	
1 ditto Small		7	
14 packs Drest Leather Containing	.	420 Wt.	995
IF one pack on my Acct. 22 Skins in the hair at 45 Sols Livs.		48.10	
5 packs Drest Leather Contg. 142 Skins wt. 280 at 35	.	490.	
		538.10	Ds. 107.5½

		Ds.
1 Hhd. province Wine		25.
1 Hhd. Wine De Ville		35.
Chartge [cartage] package and Cordage	.	7.2
		67.2
		174.7½

For all which you have here inclosed Mr. Swansons receipt you are to pay Savon Ds. 4 per hhd. the Wine and Ds. 8 for the Skins you will please to pass the Amount of the Wine & Skins Cartage to my Credit being Ds. 174.7½ As per anext abstract. Mr. Alexr. Solomons lent me in 1764 after Coming from being a prisoner from the Indians Ds. 10 which I neaver Recollected till the present. therefore woud be much obliged to you to pay Him that sum in Cash. for my Account. if there Should be any ¾ or yard Wide Checks Among the Goods you Expect would be much obliged to you to send me 20 ps. for which I shall/Send/say/Reumburs you as I sell them Which I cannot do immediately as I want to remburs you for your & Capt. McMins Sales as soon as I can recover the outStanding Debts[.] if you have got any of your Best English beavour Hatts please to send me Two 7⅓ Inches Diameter in the mould and 3¾ Inches in the Depth or as Near that as posible, as they are for a french Capt. Beloning to Marticco[?] there is no news here worth your Notice and refer you for the little there is to D. McIntoshs Letter. would be obliged to you to give me part of any With you; or from Carolinas where I wish you an agreeable passage And am Most respectfully . . . P.S. since writing the above I gott Mr. Monsants note regersterd for fear of any Accident which Cost Me a Doller.

1768–1769

47/ Henry Lefleur served as British Indian interpreter in the Natchez area in the late 1760s and was official interpreter for Lieutenant John Thomas, deputy superintendent for the Small Tribes at Manchac in the early 1770s. In 1772 Lefleur was granted 500 acres near Fort Natchez and eventually settled there, for his name appears on a list of inhabitants of Natchez in 1779, after the Spanish occupation of that territory. See Memorial of Henry Lefleur, April 10, 1771, PRO CO 5/578, p. 201; Wells (comp.), "British Land Grants," 153; Scott (ed.), "Britain Loses Natchez," 45–46.

48/ A cousin of British Superintendent of Indians John Stuart, Charles Stuart served in the Seven Years' War with the 78th Regiment, was commissioned as lieutenant in 1760, and left the service in 1763 to go to South Carolina. In November, 1764, he was sent by John Stuart to West Florida to assist General Campbell in making peace with the Small Tribes. He was appointed commissary to the Small Tribes, and was promoted to deputy superintendent in January, 1766. He continued in this position until the end of his life. When the Spanish captured Mobile in 1780, Charles Stuart was imprisoned and died shortly after his release. See Alden, *John Stuart and the Southern Colonial Frontier*, 212 n.

To VALENS STEPHEN COMYN, *Pensacola*

New Orleans, July 18, 1769

Since your Negroes came I could have sold them several Times for Indego or a Short Credit both which I refused Knowing How Circumstances are at this Crittical Time—

There is a french man going to your place with a per cell of peltry to whom I have made a proposal about the Strouds that Is Ds. 24. per ps. and you to receive the peltry at your place at 37 Sols per H. [hide?] if agreeable to you to take the peltry on them terms I shall on sight of your Receipt for the quantity you may take let him have the Strouds. and in Case you agree with him you Will please to send me the same quantity as before Assorted for Boats that are Expected Down if not shall want no more Untill those Are Disposed off for not with standing what I here write you I shall Embrace you; the first oppertunity of Selling them in the Interval.

if you have any ¾ or ⅞ Cotton Linen Checks by that vessell Lately arrivd. and that 50 pCent upon the prime Cost would Suit you please to send me 6 pss. of the handsomest patterns if you have Any large files say flatt [?] half round three Square, and Small round & that from 50 to [?] 65 pCent would suit you please send to the Amount of £6 prime Cost. for which I shall reumburs you in 3 or 4 months in peltry or Cash or Sooner if sold, any Checks narrow[er] than whate quoted will not answer if wider so much the Better

You may Depend if the Negroes are sold for Cash I shall Remitt you Immediately and if for peltry Shall Take Care to have it kept in Good order untill I receive your orders How to act there With; there is nothing more at present occurs worth your notice And remain most respectfully . . . P.S. Mr. Hayton Arrivd. hear last Week from the Natchez. when he come AShore he was Speechless Expired Next Day.

To JOHN RITSON, *Pensacola*

New Orleans, July 18, 1769

I have Before me your Esteemd. favour of the 6th Instant By which I observe you have Given me Credit for Mr. Haghs note of Ds. 43 which is well. I am sorry I could not git the Medecins You wrote for As none of the Doctors here would sell any as they Import none but what they use in their own pratice, and their is not one Druggist or Apothecary Shop here therefore return your order.

You will receive by this Conveyance a Hogshead of the Best wine Could be gott in Town as it was for your own Use. it cost me $35 wch. please pass to my Credit. it is Marked JR at the Bung. you have Capn. Smiths Receipt inclosd for the Same. you will likewise Credit me for the Cartage in Town & to the Bayoux D. 1. when you Write Mr. Stephenson please to present my Compts. and if any thing New at pensacola you will be kind Enough to give me part[.] if the British King[49] Should bring any newspapers I should be much Obliged to you; to procure me the presiual of a few or if any from the Norward. I am very Sincerely . . . P.S. Mr. Cowthers at your place owes Ds. 6 you will oblige me in Waiting on him for the Same; if not in his power Dont Distress him.

To JOHN RITSON, *Pensacola*

New Orleans, July 20, 1769

Since Writing you the 18th Instant have now to Acquaint you that Mr. Viviat[50] a french Gentleman that is now in Goal here on Account of a law Suit now Depending Concerning of percell of peltry Which are Consigned to you; with his InstruCtions how to act there in Which begg you will Adher to; in the Strictest manner—Mr. Hardy has wrote to you [*sic*] on the same Occasion as it is a matter Must be Decided At your place. Mr. Viviat says this peltry was not his own and Was Given him at the Illinois by one Mr. Blaan and one Bosserau to sell for their Account. but as I cannot give you a perticular Discription of the real Neature of the Affair you must Consult Mr. Viviats Letter, to you in french where no Doubt the whole Is properly Illustred, in all appearance there are some french Gentlemen that have a Demand against the owners of the Peltry; Which they are to pay in Bills of Exchange when the Convoy came Down; now those people here want to seize on this peltry tho they, Never made any Legal Demand for payment of the propritors Who will no Doubt. be making a provision for the Compliance of their promise

If the Suit should be Given in favour of the proprietors You will please to send me the Articles Specified in the inclosd Memorandum as I am to send them to the Illinois[.] you will please to have the Skins beat and Taken care of, Especially the raccoon Skins as it will be necessary to beat them Twice a Week, you will Observe that the raccoon Skins Cannot be Given at the very lowest Under 15 Sols or 1½ bitts your Money per Skin which you must recor. in Good Sterling Bills or for the Articels Mentioned in the [*blank*] And some part must be in Cash to send here; Should

49/Apparently the name of a ship.

50/Sieur Louis Viviat, wealthy French merchant and land speculator of Kaskaskia, Illinois, with interests in New Orleans. He was the Illinois representative of the Wabash Land Company, and was involved in the illegal but highly profitable importation of goods from the Spanish side of the Mississippi River into British Illinois, which brought him into conflict with British traders. He died in 1777. See Max Savelle, *George Morgan, Colony Builder* (New York, 1932), 47, 65; Clarence Walworth Alvord, *The Illinois Country, 1673–1818* (Springfield, 1920), 320, 327; Clarence Walworth Alvord and Clarence E. Carter (eds.), *Cahokia Records, 1778–1790*, in *Collections of the Illinois State Historical Library*, Vol. II (Springfield, 1907), xxx.

you not be able to dispose of the rackoon Skins at the price Quoted you will please to have them Taken Care off. and hold them at Mr. Viviats Disposial Or Ship them as he shall Direct[.] I would Esteem it a favour of you to prevail on Mr. Hardy to push the Matter forward; as soon as posible. . . .

To JOHN RITSON, *Pensacola*

New Orleans, July 20, 1769

this Serves to Strengthen my former request of praying you to adhere Strictly to Mr. Viviats instructions relative to the peltry &c there in Mentioned[.] Mr. Monsanto Assuers me that Viviat has wrote you to pay a Note of his to Mr. McGillivray for Ds. 401.4 in peltry; if so You will please to act the Needfull; this Supposing that Viviat gains the Suit. . . .

To McGILLIVRAY AND STRUTHERS, *Mobile*

New Orleans, July 20, 1769

This serves to inform you that the Gentleman I Mentioned that was to go with the peltry can not go, as he is much indisposd. And the Skins are now Consigned to Mr. Ritson who will pay you the Note in Case he gains the law Suit about them of St. pee. and if St. Pee Gains it I Suppose he woud have no Objection to Settle his own affairs With you; you have here Inclosed 2 Letters from Mr. Monsanto, if you are not paid you will please To return the noat; to receiver of Monsanto. . . .

To VALENS STEPHEN COMYN, *Pensacola*

New Orleans, August 1, 1769

I have now before [me] your favour of the 15th Ulto. Mr. Gradinego[51] & note the contents. I have Given him all the Assistance in my power in looking out for the Portugeze (who have Absconded themselvs And all to no purpose. we Waited on the Governor who gave an order to Search for them; telling us at the same Time he could not at present Act with such Strictness as he otherwise would on Accot. of Arivel of the Spannards Commanded by his Excellency Lieut. General Oreyly[52]—

The Strouds and Negroes are Still on hand which Mr. Gradenigo; can in form you but am in hopes they will be Shortly In

---

51/ John Gradenigo, Pensacola merchant with interests in the province of West Florida. He owned a town lot in Pensacola and a plantation of 550 acres on the Mississippi River opposite Pointe Coupée, granted in 1772. He apparently settled there, for his name appears as a witness to a Pointe Coupée marriage in 1772. See PRO, CO 5/574, 978–79; Howard, *British Development of West Florida*, 42; Wells (comp.), "British Land Grants," 158; De Ville (ed.), *Colonial Louisiana Marriage Contracts*, III, 20.

52/ Alexander O'Reilly was born in County Meath, Ireland, in 1722 and was among many Irish soldiers of fortune who emigrated to the Continent in the eighteenth century. He enlisted in the Spanish army in Italy, and his abilities were quickly recognized. After the end of the Seven Years' War, O'Reilly was appointed inspector general of the Spanish army, with orders to restore its efficiency and discipline; his performance in this position made him the most respected figure in the Spanish military establishment. Intelligent, energetic, self-confident, and ambitious, he was a logical choice to lead the expedition to regain control of Louisiana. O'Reilly returned to Spain in 1770 and died there in 1794, after a distinguished military career. See Moore, *Revolt in Louisiana*, 190–93.

Demand. I could have sold the Negroes a few Days ago for Indego or Bills on New Yourk but declined it not having your orders to do so.

Had your Letter arrivd. five days sooner I could Have sent you the articles you wrote for but it is now Imposible . . the Governor having Given Strict orders to the Contrary under a Sevire Penalty as the Spanish Army Consists of 4800 Men and it is reportd. there is More; Expected; I waited on Capn. Prant, who with some Difulcity Condesended to Take Dublin for James upon Giving him 3 doz: Good Madeira, Boot which hope you will approve of, and Send it first Safe Oppertunity, inclosed you have Capn. Prants Bill of Sale for him

As to how affairs will be regulated here it is not as yet Known, but shall soon bee able to advise you, as Shall if their should be any Demands for the Negroes you Mention. . . .

To ARTHUR STROTHERS, Pensacola[53]

New Orleans, August 1, 1769

on recipt of yours of the 15 Inst. I waited on Mr. Voye, and Informed him of the Quantity of pimento you Intended to send him for which he promised me Cash on its Arrival; he likewise will Take any quantity you may send after provided it can be Hear by the latter End of September next; as he then leavs this for Old France; and I know of noBody here would by it Except himself

Wine has rise to Ds. 40 per hhd.—occasioned by the Arrivel of 4800 Spanish Troops; so if it suits at that price; shall send you the Amount of your Piemiento in that Article or cash as you shall Advise; the price of produce is not broke here as yet, so cannot Inform you; I cannot give you any Encouragement; about sending Any Goods, Neither can I inform you the price goods will bear; Untill the Spaniards Git up the River and Settle themselves, here. . . . P.S. Good Britannies would fetch Ds. 272 per ps. for your Government

To JOHN RITSON, Pensacola

New Orleans, August 1, 1769

I recvd. yours per Mr. Gradinego and have now to acquaint You that I send you by this Conveyance the six pounds hair powdr. their is no good ponsatum to be had at present. the french Governor Will not allow any Stock or produce to be Shipped from here at Present as their are 4800: Spanish troops Arrivd.—and

53/Pensacola merchant and member of the provincial council. One of his pursuits was the supply of military stores to the army. See Arthur Strothers to Nathaniel Green, Commissary of Stores and Provisions, July 12, 1770, British Museum, Add. Mss. 21729, Haldimand Papers (microfilm in Department of Archives and Manuscripts, Louisiana State University); Howard, *British Development of West Florida*, 42.

now in the river destined for this place which Gives me hopes that I Shall soon be able to remitt you the Amount of your Accot. I Delivd. Mr. Durad your Letter. I have nothing more to add . . .

To PHILLIPS COMYN, *Pensacola*[54]

New Orleans, August 1, 1769

By recommendation of Mr. Gradenigo I take the Liberty to Tender you my Service hear and to Cultivate a Correspondence that may here After be Mutually advantageous to us; I hitherto had a Connection with your Brother and other Gentlemen of your place.

There are 4800 Spanairds arrivd. in the Ballice [Balize] it is Generally Beliveed they will make new regulations in point of Commerce which if so Shall in course advise you thereof for yr. Government. and am on all Occasions of your Commands . . .

To THOMAS HARDY, *Pensacola*[55]

New Orleans, August 1, 1769

I receivd. your favours of the 29th Ulto. and note the Contents[.] As to Monsr. Viviats affair in Question I am quite a Stranger to it Only what I heard say in Common reports. which is of No Signification in pint of Law, where in Authentick proofs are Required to Authori[ze] a final Decision[.] my Connection with him was but Triffling at the Illinois the year I made my Escape from the Indians and in Compassion to the Distressed Estate I then Laboured Under shewed me Some Small kindness in Attention there to. on hearing of his being In Custody here I paid him a Vissit but toald him nothing More[56] Meterial then his having a Suit Depending about his Confinement; In some Time after; when the Governor. and Council of your place Gave orders to have the Skins sent to pensacola; with proper recourse to the Concerned to make there Begal [legal] demands; where upon Monsr. Viviat sent for me requesting to recomend him to my friend Mr. Riston to address the Skins too; and you as his Attorney; in Consequence of which he Sent me the Letters for you and Mr. Ritson Requesting to forward them whose Contents I Ignor Except [*i.e.*, except] the Translation of a Bill of parcels Inclosed to Mr. Ritson[.] this is all I know of their Disputes.

Said Mr. Viviat Made his Escape out of Geoal 6 or 7 Days before your Letter Arrivd. to what place he retired is Unknown. . . .

54/Pensacola merchant and member of the provincial council. In 1772 he was granted 1900 acres on the Comite River, and he owned another plantation on the Mississippi River, opposite Pointe Coupée, where he resided. See Wells (comp.), "British Land Grants," 159; "A Plan of the Lakes Ponchartrain, and Maurepas, and the River Ibberville, and also of the River Mississippi from its Mouth to the River Yazou. A Distance of 450 Miles," by Thomas Hutchins, January 24, 1779, PRO, CO 5/595, p. 341A (hereafter cited as Hutchins map, 1779).

55/Pensacola merchant, attorney, and clerk of the West Florida Assembly. Besides two town lots in Pensacola, he held two land grants on the Mississippi River below Natchez, one consisting of 500 acres granted in 1769 and the other, also 500 acres, granted in 1772. See Howard, *British Development of West Florida*, 42; Wells (comp.), "British Land Grants," 154, 155; Cecil Johnson, *British West Florida, 1763–1783*, (New Haven, 1943), 86.

56/I.e., ". . . but he told me nothing more." In the spring of 1769, Viviat, his boat, and cargo were seized by Spanish authorities near Manchac, apparently because he was suspected of trying to smuggle furs into British West Florida. In an extraordinary session, the Superior Council in New Orleans annulled the seizure and ordered the matter turned over to Governor Browne in Pensacola for a decision on the disposition of the boat and its cargo. See Henry P. Dart (ed.), "Cabildo Archives," *Louisiana Historical Quarterly*, III (1920), 96–98.

To JOHN RITSON, *Pensacola*

New Orleans, August 2, 1769

I wrote you Yesterday to Which refer; I have to Acquat. You that one Mr. Lagoutre who you have formerly seen at Pensacola; will Shortly be Going your way to receive money there Due him from the Government and as he is indebted to me about Ds. 46.2 as will appear by the inclosed Accot. I beg the favour of you to use your Endeavours to recover it for me; as he will Certainly have it in his power to pay it and Should he make any Objection you will please to Stop him their and if you receive it pass the Amount to my Creditt. . . .

To McGILLIVRAY AND STRUTHERS, *Mobile*

New Orleans, August 4, 1769

This serves to Acquaint you that there Are 4800. Spanish Troops in the river Destined for this place and it is Immagined their will be no Trade permited here but that of Old Spain however that wants Conformation; on General Oryleys Arrival as he—Commands we Shall know on what Terms, which I Shall in Course advise you of, they have brought Dollers 500,000. with part of which it is Expected they will pay of all the Spanish Bills. so as soon as the people have any money Among them I shall I Shall [*sic*] Use my Endeavours to gitt in All the outStanding Debts. I shall Likewise use my Endeavours to git paid of Blass & Carass and as I am Apprehensive Monsanto's note will not be paid on Accot. of some things that has passed Since I Sent Said note you will in such Case please to Send it me back with an Account of the Charge Attending it

You have here Inclosed Mr. Leflowrs second Bill of ExChange to serve in Case of Need for Ps. 254. and Mr. Alexr. McIntosh's Second order for $187.4. Should be much obliged to You; to let me know if the Wine and Skins got safe and if Leflowrs Draft was Excepted, if so youl; please to Carry the Whole to my Credit; and I shall Settle it with Leflowr here; if the Vessel you Expected; is Arrivd. I would Esteem it a favour of You to send me the 20 ps. of Check I wrote for some Time ago as they would be Immediate Cash at present & if there should be any Other Articels that you think would Suit the Spaniards you May Send them Either on your own or on my own Account. if the Latter beg you will be as reasonable as posible, in Case you Should send them; you'll please to give the Capt. that may bring them a Strict Charge; to Contrive to send me your Letters before He Enters the port; that I may Take the Necessary steps to prevent Any Seizure by the Spaniards Should they be inclined that way Which as Yet is not known. and it will be some Time before they Git up; as their are 22 Ships 20 of which are Frigates .. and the General will have all to come up together. . . . P.S. I have this day wrote Mr. Alexander McIntosh acquainting him of the Arrival of the Spanairds & to send Nothing down Before Matters Ware Regulated here When should Advise him—

To JOHN RITSON, *Pensacola*

New Orleans, August 11, 1769

I have now Before me your favour of the 29th Ulto. And Observe you have receivd. 81 packs peltry and 19 skins now Under an Atteachment act, Mr. Viviat Escaped out of Goal About 6 or 7 days ago, therefore Can Give you no [a]dvice concerning that affair, my notice for having them Addressed to you; was With a View, of your Giting some thing by them; for my Acquaintance with Mr. Viviat was at the Illinois after I Escap[ed] from the Indians with whom I had been Prisoner, who seeing my Dessolate Condition gave me some small Assistance in Attention There to; on hearing he was here in Custody I paid him a Vissit But he Toald me Nothing Material Except that of his having A law Suit Depending about his Confinement & Requested of Me to recommend him to you to whom the Skins was to be Addressed, and to Mr. Hardy as his Attorney in Consequence of Which he sent me the letters for yu. & Mr. Hardy requesting I would forward them whose Contents I Ignor, Except the Translation of the Bill parcels I Endorsed you[.] as to the price of Skins I Cannot Quote none Concerning that affair as it is not a matter Relates me; & he being absent; as allready Mentioned; there are no Green Umbrellas here at present; if their Should be any by the Next Conveyance, Shall send you one and the Black lace; the Note I had of Barnards I Returnd it to the owner. . . .

To GODLEY AND RAINCOCK, *Pensacola*

New Orleans, August 11, 1769

I recivd. your favour of 26th July and note the Contents; there are only two Battoes as yet come down one of Which Belongs to Mr. Morgan;[57] and the Other to French men that Came down in it, by Neither of which have recd. any News from Mr. Sarpée

---

57/George Morgan (1743–1810), Philadelphia merchant and partner in the firm of Baynton, Wharton and Morgan, was from 1766 until 1771 supervisor of the firm's extensive trade with the Illinois country. During the Revolutionary War, he became an Indian agent for the new United States government on the western frontier, later worked on problems of supply for the American armies on the frontier. For a full account of his life and career, see Savelle, *George Morgan, Colony Builder.*

which prompted me to wait on Mr. Maxant who is replaced in all his former Employments with the Spaniards and Assurd Me; he is Daily Expecting Letters from Mr. Sarpée Concerning what He has done in Mr. Barrows Affair up there; adding that if he did not receive the whole above he would Settle it him Self with me; As it is supposed he will be paid all that the Spaniards owe Him—

I Waited on Mr. Morgan with your Compliments for which He returned you thanks; and Desired me to inform you that he leavs this in A Couple of Days bound for Philadelphia which prevents him the plasure of Seeing you; for the present; I am sorry I had not Time to wrote you by Mr. Gradenigo to Acquaint you of the Arrivall of 4800: Spanish Troops Now in the river; and Expected up in Town in a Couple of Days, they are Under the Command of General Oryley....

To VALENS STEPHEN COMYN, *Pensacola*

New Orleans, August 11, 1769

I wrote you the 1st Instant per Mr. Gradenigo to which Refer. I have now to Answer; your favour of the 29th Ulto. Inclosing Bill of parcels for some files Amounting to Ds. 14½ This money Which is to your Credit.

Since Mr. Gradenigo's Departure I was offered Ds. 120: A Head for the Negroes to be paid in Drest Leather at 40 Sols which I would not Except of; I offered them for Dollers 130 and would have Taken the Drest Leather; at 35 Sols which the person Refused; the Negroes are in very Good Order and I think worth what I asked[.] the Strouds are Still on hand but hope the Spanairds will soon rid me of Them; for the Troops, perticulary the Blue Strouds, & perhaps the red if Not I am in hopes to be able to sell them, when the Boats Come Down for Here there is infinity a better Chance to Sell them than with you And if all fails they will be here at your Disposial, it is Certain I Omitted Giving you the name of the french man that Should have Gone With the Skins but he was Taken so Ill that he Could not Proceed so they ware sent to Mr. Ritson....

Since Writting your Letter of the 11th Instant I receivd. from Mr. Smith a parcell Rasps which in your Bill parcels you Term files. I Shall Neaver be able to Dispose of them; here, for I had a Great many of the same on hand[.] I think it was a little Remiss (in you) as you took the Trouble of Sending any thing; not to adhear more Strictly to my letter of the 18th Ulto. where in the quality Was Spacified[.] however reather than return them I have Credited your for the amount—New Orleans 15th Augt. 1769.

To PHILLIPS COMYN, *Pensacola*

New Orleans, August 13, 1769

Since Writting you the 1st Instant I had an Opperunty. of Speaking to some of the Spanish Officers in Conversation I asked them if they thought English Manufactures Would be prohibited here to which they Assurd me they Could not Tell, as it was a Matter that lay intirely at the Generals Brest, but said they ware well Convinced that Beer. Porter. Cyder, hams Bacon & Chees, will be Gladly receivd. and meet A very quick Sale. for your Goverment a Small trunk of Cottons printed and one of prusianas would sell Well, and Believe there Would Be a Demand for your Best pinch back Buckels & 3 or 4 Gold Watches, should you be inclined to send any of the above Mentioned Articles would be Glad to serve you in the sail in which You may Depend I shall Regard your Interest the Same as my own . . . P.S. a few peices of your Linen Not Callendered would Sell very well And Some Dimothy—

To ARTHUR STROTHERS, *Pensacola*

New Orleans, August 13, 1769

Since writing you the 1st Inst. have not recd. any of yours. this serves Chiefly to Acquaint you that I spoke to some Spanish Officers lately concerning what Goods they thought would be in Demand Most here; and their oppinions was that 2 ps. blue Broad cloth from 15 to 18 Slg. per yard 1 ps. Scorlet from 17 to 20 per yd. would meet Quick Sale. Likewise a Small Trunk prusianas some Blue & White Handkerchfs. Such as I had Before No. 11 & 12 and a Doz. Good Hats. which should you Chuse to send this way would be Glad to serve you in the Sale of them, In which you may Depend; I shall Study your Interest Equal to that of my own Interist . . . P.S. you may probably know of many Other things that may suit the Spaniards Which I leave to your own Disposial

To McGILLIVRAY AND STRUTHERS, *Mobile*

New Orleans, August 26, 1769

I have now before me your favours of the 25th & 28th Ulto. and note the Contents. that of 25th is Copy of that wrote by Savon which I have not yet Receivd. I observe you have Given me Credit for Ds. 174:7½ but you make no Mention of Alexr. McIntoshs &

Coys. Draft for Ds. 187:4[.] I have spoke to Mr. St Pei concerning the 20 ps. Cotton you Mention and he Toald me that when Mr. Terry, was Evacuating his Store, he left 6 or 7 pieces with him, which he Believd. to be your property tho he recvd. them from Mr. Terry and when I asked him if he would Account with me for them he Gave me No positve Answer tho I Shall see if I can oblige him to it in a few Days. your opinion of the Badness of the flour is well Grounded for it is realy in Shocking Order not with standing the pains used in Shifting it and taking out the Best of it to make it saleable, and had I not Been befriended in a barril I sold a man here, it would been all thrown in the Mississippi for the man Complaind to the High Sheriff of the Badness of it[.] on reecipt of Mr. LaGouttres, account I Got it Translated And inclosed in a Letter in Transacting that unless he Used some Expedition in Selling it; you would be under the Disagreeable Necessity of pushing the Matter—& Should he Come here you may Depend on my Exertion in the Recovery of it; you will please refer to my letter of the 13th April by Which you will see I paid Monsr. andree Neaut (Brother in law to St. pee Ds. 87.3. with 187¾ lb. deer Leather at 40 Sols which Makes Ds. 74:7 and 20 bear Skins at 5 rs. Makes Ds. 12:4 which is Equal to the Sum of Ds. 87.3. the 14 packs Drest Leather sent you Containid 420 Skins And Weighed by the Skillards [?] here which I reivd. them by 995 which with 187¾ Makes 1182¾, and what Mr. McIntosh brought down in all Was 1191 lb. so that the Difference of the Whole is only 8¼ which Impute They lost in Beating them so often to keep the worms out, and please to Let me know if Savon left the 6 Bear Skins I Gave him, to Cover the Leather; since the 18th Int. being the Day General Oreyly took possesn of this place; in his Catholick Majestys Name the face of affairs Has been Mightily Changed[.] on the 20 he gave orders to Take up the head Men that Revolted against the Spannairds which it is thought Will be Delt With according to their Deserts; but for the poorer Sort the General promised to be their protector as farr as Consistd. With Law and Equity, it is Supposed the English will be Allowed no further Trade; here; but such as are here will be allowd. A Sufficent Time to Collect in their Debts; and Settle their affairs tho his Excellency has not Communicated his Opinions in publick As yet Concerning that affair; Among the Number of them is Mr. Carrass

Your Crank that you sent to be mended I had it Immediately Done; and would have sent it by Dominick but poor Man was Seized very Ill, and Capn. Hays promised to Call for it When his Cart was Going to the Bayoux & Never Came near me; Had I not relyed on his promise I would have Sent it Down my self Which I was about Doing when I was informd. he was Gone from the head of the Bayoux.

I am sorry Mr. McGillivray is Gone as I promised My self the pleasure of Seeing him, as Soon as they Give out the Spanish Money, as I had something to Communicate to him that if Backd in; Would prove to our Mutual advantage; with out any Danger of Confiscation from the Spaniards, which I Shall Write you more at Large about in my next as I shall of all regulations here Enterim....

To VALENS STEPHEN COMYN, *Pensacola*

New Orleans, September 1, 1769

On Receipt of yours of the 18th Instant (say Ulto.) per Mr. Gradenigo I Deliverd that Gentleman the Sundry Bons I recvd. on Account of Olive, and the Spanish Bills Remaining of yours in my Hands for which he Gave me a Receipt Copy of which you may have Transmitted you if you require it, I cannot but thank you for your Kind Usage to me in Ordering me to Deliver the Negroes & Strouds to Mr. Jones which Shall be Done on Either his or Mr. Gradenigos Requiring it observing that they must first pay me the Account of Your Accot. Ds. 66:1 to prevent further After Claps Mr. Jones Will no Dout Transmitt you Copy of the Account Arises for I would Not be your Slave nor no mans for nothing, as I was in a manner Last Winter, having nothing furthur to say upon the Matter I Remain ... P.S. you think I shall be obliged to leave this place; I think should this be Brought in question I should have the prifference of Staying to Mr. Jones; this I do not intimate with any View of Craving any furthur favour from you but I am Certain I had as Good an Oppertunity to sell your Goods as Jones And always as rady to make good Remittences

To GODLEY AND RAINCOCK, *Pensacola*

New Orleans, September 1, 1769

I have now before me yours of the 19th Ulto. and note the Contents; that you mention to have wrote 26th Same Neaver Came to hand—Mr. Maxant has not yet recvd. his money from the Spanish Treasury Neather has any of the Inhabitants; as they are Excessive busy Regulating the Affairs of this place which whin done its Generally Supposed every Body will git paid in Such Case you may be Assurd I Shall urge Maxant to Come to a Settlement. I am inclind to think he will Not be very ready to do before he hears from the Illinois Concerning the Obligatory papers he gave Mr. Barrow, however this I Shall be Better Assurd off as Soon as I learn that he has Got paid from the Spanairds When Shall wait on him on that affair. . . .

To JOHN RITSON, *Pensacola*

New Orleans, September 1, 1769

This serves to Acquaint you that the Spanish money Is not yet paid out; as they are Excessive Bussy in Regulating the Affairs of this place but you may Depend the first I Receive from them Shall be remitted you—for it is Immagined they will soon Pay all off. . . .

To McGILLIVRAY AND STRUTHERS, *Mobile*

New Orleans, September 2, 1769

Since Writing you the 26th Ulto. have now to Inform you that after a Strict Serch by the Justisses in Town for all Bad flour to seize it and Throw it into the Mississippi I through A stratagum Saved yours and happily met with a Chap for all that Was Good of it; for which I Took peltry and as the flowr was Excessive Bad; Such that if met with by the Justice could not Expect mercy from his hands; I was obliged to give Something More for the peltry than Other wise Should have done; indeed if flowr was not so Excessive Scarce as it is at present I am of opinion I should neaver have Been Able to Dispose of it; their are about 18 or 19 Casks on hand quite rotten Which I would not Venture to sell to any Christian at this Critical time, Should the Bearer Donsinick be Coming this way you will please to Deliver him the 20 ps. Check my Account Recommanding to him Caution in Sending me your Letters. first as Mentioned in my Letter of the 4 Ulto. to which refer; the Spaniards have not as yet Commenced to Make any payments therefore; Cannot as yet recover any of the out Standing Debts; but it is Generally Immagined they will Shortly pay Every Body; when Shall be able to make you a remittance Equivelent to the Sales; what Skins I may have you Need not Expect them untill Some Time hence—

I have sent you the Crank by this Conveyance and had Capn. Hays the least Complieance he would have Taken it along with him; as he promisd. Me; by Next oppertunity Shall furnish you yours & Capn. McMins Account Sales wch I cannot do at present. being in Such a hurry; I would be much Obliged to you; to let me Know if Le flowrs Bills ware Excepted and if you have passed A: McIntoshs & Comy. for Draft $187.4 to my Credit As you make no Mention of it in your last Letters of the 25th & 28th July Last. As to Blass & Carass Monsanto and Others that Owe Money I am in Great hopes of Gitting paid now sooner [?] than Ever as General O Reyley is inflexable in these Cases; to whom I Shall Apply for Redress should they Equivicate much longer tho a person Must be under the Necessity of Shewing a Little Lenity untill the Money of the Trausery Circulates Among them—Things are in a very Critical State here at present as the General Will not Allow any forneigers to Vend their Merchant Dize here in Future; they are allowd to Dispose of what they had in Store before his Arrivel; of which they ware all Obliged to give in an; Inventory to him[.] In mine I included the 20 ps. Chex and some other Goods; the Same as if in Store, for your Government. . . . P.S. the sum I Recvd. from Madame Phillipeaux Was $34 in Spanish Papers.

Mr. Swanson
Sir

The wig you wrote for in July last is now Making and will Be According to the Dementions you gave and Shall be sent per next Oppertunity. . . . P.S. I am Quite out of Strouds at present. therefore if you Chuse you may Send me 10 or 15 ps. of Blue Strouds & 4 or 5 Bales Blankets with blue And black Stripes as the Season is advancing in Which Cloth will be in Demand

To HENRY LEFLEUR, *Natchez*

New Orleans, September 7, 1769

This serves to acquaint you that your Draft on Charles Stewar[t] Esqr. for $254 is Returnd to me Protested, Said protest Spacifying th[at] Mr. Stuart Reason for Refusing payment; was that he paid you you[r] Sallery for the Time you Acted as Commissary; the Expence attend[ing] it is Ds. 3 which with the Amount of your Accot. Ds. 40:1½ Makes Ds. 43: 1½, Which would be much obliged to you remit me, as I intend to [leave] this place Shortly; if you Can procure Mr. McIntoshs Draft my Favour on Messrs. McGillivray & Struthers it will Suit me the Same as Cash; I Shall Expect to here from you as Soon as posible. . . .

To ALEXANDER McINTOSH, *Natchez*

New Orleans, September 7, 1769

This serves to Acquaint you that I have wrote to Mr. Le Flowr by this Conveyance; and as he informed me when here; that You owed him a Certain Sum; I have wrote him to ask you for a Dra[ft] My favour on Messrs. McGillivray & Struthers for Ds. 43.1½ the Amount of his Accout. with me which I wrote him I Esteemd th[e] Same as Cash; Should this be a fiction (which I have no reason to Suspect) you will please to procure me payment of the afore Mentioned Sum; which favour I Shall Acknowledge; as I inten[d] Leaving this place; Shortly as all English Subjects who are no[t] Married or have no fixed Settlements here are Ordered Away by h[is] Excellency General O Relley; I would not Advise you to send any Thing Down before you here furthur from me, or Mr. McGillivray[.] I have Nothing More to add . . . P.S. You will please to observe that No English Subject is allowed to land Any thing here; for your Government

To ROBERT BARROW, *Natchez*[58]

New Orleans, September 7, 1769

This serves to acquaint you that all English Subje[cts] Here who have no Settlements are Ordered away by his Excellency Gen. Oreyly for which beg the favour of you of you [*sic*] to use some means of Setling my Accot. for Ds. 66.1¼[.] I was in hopes of having the pleasure of Seeing you here are now but According to the present Situation of Affairs Cannot by any Means; recommend to you to bring any thing Down Unless you Could Immediately Dispose of it in the River as the General has Given Orders to Impale all Englis[h] Subject to land any Goods for your Government; you will please to write me [?] per first oppertunity. . . .

To BAYNTON, WHARTON & MORGAN, *Illinois*[59]

New Orleans, September 11, 1769

This serves to inform you that your Mr. Morgan Left me orders to Dispose of a Batteau of his here and to Remitt you the proceeds in Six Barrels pitch and the Ballance in Taffia; I ha[ve] Not as yet been able to Dispose of her, but I Sent you by Mr. St. p [Pé] 10 Barrs. Pitch Before Mr. Morgan's Departure from here, which I hope You will have Recevd. are this; Reaches You; as per his

58/Apparently a brother of New Orleans merchant William Barrow. See this volume, p. 49 n 39.

59/Philadelphia mercantile firm in which George Morgan (see this volume, p. 66 n 57) was a partner.

own Advice to you, You may Depend that as soon as I Despose of the Batteau I shall Remit you in Cash Deducting my Commission and the Amout. of the 10 Barrels pitch Remited you as above Specified, as no products Can be Shipped for your side of the River which the present Situation of Affairs Will not permit me to give you a Detail of; it is Immagined that all the English Subjects here will Shortly be obliged to leave it which is Reasonable to Expect being Universally known the Spanish Government will not allow any Foreigners in their America Settlmt. therefore we Must Submit to their Accustomed Rules of Government Altho such as has any outstanding Debts rely on his Excellency's Clemency for Time to recover them; the result of wch God only knows; I purpose Going to Settle at Iberville where would be Glad of your Commands in Any thing I can Serve you in; Either from your place or philedelphia As it is Supposed there will be a great Intercourse of Bussiness Carrd. On there for we are Daily Expecting 2000 Troops at Pensacola when Arrived we Expect that Iberville and the Fort of the Natchez will Be Re Established. . . . P.S. should I not be able to Dispose of your Batteau before my Departure which Expect Will be in a Month from pensacola I shall Leave her in Trusty persons hands; to remit Me the money to Iberville or give it me on passing this river to go their; which if posible Will remit you; if not to your home in Philedelphia—

To JOHN FALCONER, *Pensacola*

New Orleans, September 11, 1769

This Serves to inform you that I intend Sending you by Mr. Marshals Schooner now here; a Small parcel peltry which please be so kind as to receive, and remit it to Messrs. McGillivray & Struthers by first Conveyance from your place to Mobile, as none offers from here to that part at present. . . . P.S. as there is money now in the Collony; I am [in] hopes to be able to recover some Spanish Bills I have and Finish Capn. McMins Sales as farr as is already Sold—

To JAMES AMOSS, *Pensacola*

New Orleans, September 11, 1769

This serves to inform you that I was something surprized to Learn that Mr. Barrow never reumbursed you the $16.4 ballance of your Account as I settled with him in account here; for the performance there of; however; as I have Still an Account open with Sd. Gen-

tleman And shall have to Remitt Godley & Raincock on his and
their Accot. per first oppertunity & Since you Defered Asking
them Gentlemen all This Time you may Expect I Shall Remitt it
your self by the same Conveyance. . . .

To PHILLIPS COMYN, *Pensacola*

New Orleans, September 11, 1769

I am Glad to learn you have Ingaged with a Gentleman Hear to
do your Busseness; and Wish you Success. . . .

To ARTHUR STROTHERS, *Pensacola*

New Orleans, September 11, 1769

I am much ob[liged] to you for your kind offers to serve Me in
which I am sorry I cannot act at present; as the Situation of the
Affairs frustrate the Whole; which you must be kind Enough to
Excuse My Giving any further Detail off. . . .

To JOHN RITSON, *Pensacola*

New Orleans, September 20, 1769

This serves to inform You that I am making all Dispatch for
Mobille and your place, as I am Ordered away by the General—
And not able to receive in Neither your nor my own outstanding
De[bts] Which oblige me to leave them; to the Care of Gentle-
man here notwithstanding I have Remitted you by Mr. Fanning
the Bearer here of Ds. 100 in Cash Which I wish Safe to hand. . . .

To JOHN BRADLEY, *Natchez*

New Orleans, September 21, 1769

I would have wrote you long are now; but had the Disagreeab[le]
News of hearing you had Departed this Life which I am over-
Joyed to Learn it is but a fiction, I am at present prepairing to
leave this place it Being the Generals orders I have Disposed of
all your Oyle and send You the Ballance of your Acct. $11.6¾
which is reducced to that Sum By my Chargeing you with $25 the
Ballance of Haytons & Williams Account with me; Immagining
it will be more in your way to Settle their Accot. than mine as Mr.
Williams will be Shortly at your place[.] however should this not

be agreeable I shall Settle it any other respect You may Chuse on the River which hope will be in about five weeks as I Purpose Going to live at Manchac where would be glad to serve you in any thing in my power; and as I am informed you have some Housses in Manchac would be much Obliged to you to let me have one for which I Shall pay you with thanks—

Should you Come down here before I Return from Mobille you will receive from Madame Lain[60] (who lives Still at my old House) all Mr. Haytons things agreeable to the Invoice Except one White Hatt which I took for my own; use; for which Shall pay any Demand You may Chuse to make....

To ALEXANDER McINTOSH AND COMPANY, *Natchez*

New Orleans, September 21, 1769

This serves to inform you that I intend Leaving this place To Morrow being Ordered away by his Excellency General Oreyley; I have Likewise to inform you that Was an Order of yours for Ds. 10:4 presentd to me for pay ment this Morning; which I Did not pay neither could you Expect me to pay; for youl please to observe I had no Advices as yet from Messrs. McGillivray & Struthers of their Excepting your last Draft tho I receivd. Several Letters from them Since you Drew and not the least Mention of them Made....

To ARTHUR STROTHERS, *Pensacola*

Mobile, November 7, 1769

Your favour of the 3d Septemr. last I have Answered per Capt. Smith[.] Am now to Acquaint you that of Mr. Silvester Fannings Untimely Death he was Drowned the 1st Int. opposite Mr. Dunfords plantation in this Bay in which Misfortune I am afraid you will be a Sufferer; as the Three watches which I suppose to be yours, that Remained unsold ware all Damaged by the Salt Water in his Trunk of Cloths the Amount of the Other four Watches that was Sold he had in Cash; Togeather with what he had of his own And one hundred Dollers of Mine; all in afore said Trunk; which the Master and Crew of the Vessell Alledges they found aShore Without a Bottom; and Nothing appeard of what it Contained but About Nine Dollers had in Different places on the Shore or Strand Which seems very Strange and Suspicious as being the most Valuable And as there was no Loggs nor rocks

---

60/Madame Marie Jeanne Blain, née Nivet, at this time apparently Fitzpatrick's housekeeper, later joined him at Manchac as his reputed mistress and later wife. See Introduction to this volume.

towards the Shore to cause its; Being Broak More than the other Two Trunks; which mett no Such Accident; Containing Nothing but his Body Cloths; and the Afore Said three Watches—the very Inst. I heard of the Disaster Being in Two Days after it hapned I with two more persons; went in order to procure what I could of my own and friends property; But found Nothing only the afore said watches and Cloths which I Brought here to Git washed and Dryed

Am now to Advise you of my Determination to Settle at Manchac or Iberville up the River Mississippi which I hope will Answer my Expectations in the Sails of Sundry Goods Suitable to the french and Spanairds at point Coupei &c as no Credit can be Given them; and in all Likelyhood Goods henceforward will be very Scarce in Orleans; they will always find Means to pay for What they want; in Deer Skins Indego Cotton Tobaco rice & Cash therefore if you Should think proper; to send me a trunk of Cottons And handkfs; to say blue & white Linen Handkrfs No. 11 & 12 from 14/6 to 15/6 per Doz: some Dimme Cottons Copper plait Gold Couller no. 9, at 2/8 per yard of the Latter as many as you Can Conveniently Spare. Also some of any Other Good Coullours well Assorted including a few ps. of 28 yds. Each white Grounds and all to be Dimmi Cotton; Excepting the Handkfs. for all Which Ill reumburs you next September or Sooner if posible in any of the produce of the Country Such as Indego; Rice Indian Corn Tobaco Deer skins or Cash allowing You 50 pCents on the prime Cost as Coted [quoted] in Your former Invoices; Should this meet your approbation you;l please to Ship them to my Address here in Mobille per the first favorable oppertunity of a good Vessell; but in Case you should not Admit this proposal you'll please to Advise me there of per first Occation for my Government; as I prepos parting from hence as Soon as possible with Sundry MerchantDize....

To MONSIEUR LAFITTE, *New Orleans*[61]

Mobile, November 23, 1769

As I Expect some Goods from Philedelphia per Capt. More from Mr. Morgan which I Suppose will be addressd. to my self; as in all Likelihood I shant be at your place till the 20th of the Ensuing Month; this to beg the favour of you; that if the Afore said Goods Should Come to your place; that you would be Kind Enough to let great Care be Taken of them untill my Arrival; for which I will reumburs you for whatever Expencess You ware at on the Accot. of the Afore Said Goods—

61/Probably Jean Lafitte, a New Orleans merchant whose name appears frequently in Superior Council documents of this period.

We have nothing here worth Acquainting you; but that We Dayly Expects a Vessel from England which we hope will bring Something New....

To BARTHOLEMEW MACNAMARA, *New Orleans*[62]

Mobile, November 23, 1769

I had the pleasure of Writing you sometime ago but in Such a precipatated Manner; that in Case it Should Come to hand which I Expt. wot. I dont think youl be able to Make any Sense of it; occasioned by the unhappy Death of Mr. Fanning; who was Cast away on all Saints Day last; by which I am a Considerable Sufferrer.

I Should have Been in the river long ago had it not ban Occasioned by Capt. McMins long stay, which is n[o]t yet Arrivd. But is Expected in every Moment. I Shall Carry a Small Cargo— of about 3 m. [thousand] Ds. and was I to think I would find Sale for a larger Cargo—I Should have Taken More; as I had offers to Take what Quantity I wanted; but knowing the Circumstances of that place At present I thought proper; to Try the above quantity first

When Mr. Morgan went to philedelphia he promd. To Send me 3 pss. Broad Cloth. and Some Checks; which in Case Capt. Moor Should have Arrivd. I Beg you to take the Goods from him and Pay him freight for the Same Should they not be in Mr. Lefittes Hands. . . . P.S. I Should take it a perticular favour to give my Complts. Capt. Cransburg and Newgion; also madame your Spouse and All other inquiring friends.

To JOHN BRADLEY, *Natchez*

Mobile, December 1, 1769

I have Recivd. A Letter from Orleans where in I was informd of your side being laid open and Nothing can give me More pleasure than Hearing of your Recovery; this serves to inform you; that I Shortley shall have the pleasure of seeing you Either in N. Orleans or in the River On my Voyage to the Ebrille. I some Time hence have wrote to you Concerning a house there; as I am well Convinced you can supply me; if so please to leave Directions with Madame Blain; where I formerly Lived; with respect to it: As to your Accot. Currt. with me; which if in your favour; if you'll allow Haytons & William'ss the Ballance I shall pay you

[62]/Bartholemew MacNamara, British or Irish native resident in New Orleans. He acted as agent for Baynton, Wharton and Morgan in New Orleans, and apparently performed the same service for other British mercantile firms. He also acted as a translator for the Spanish government. See Savelle, *George Morgan, Colony Builder*, 38 *n*; and Kinnaird (ed.), *Spain in the Mississippi Valley*, Pt. 1, pp. 137–38.

to Mr. Laffitte or Mr. Macnemara on your leaving my Accot. with Either; with an order to receive the same[.] I long are now Expected to see you; but the Delay of Mr. McMins Arrivel was the Only hindrence; and as this place cant afford me an Assortment Suitable for that place; untill his return from England am Still Obliged to wait that oppertunity; which I hope for and Expect Every Day; if you have any of the Dimie Cottons that I formerly had of you & the former price to suit you; please to leave one Trunk At Lafittes or McNamara's let them be of the white Ground for Which I Shall pay you as soon as Convenient; if aGreeable to you; there is nothing new to inform you of But a report of Mr. Dunfords[63] Being Made Lt. Governor in place of Governor Brown; and Assurity of a Redgment to come to pensacola Immediately....

To MONSIEUR LAFITTE, *New Orleans*

Mobile, December 3, 1769

I had the pleasure of Writing to you on 27th Ulto. Acquaintg You that if Capt. Moor is Arrivd. at your place; and if Mr. Morgan has Sent me the Broad Cloth and Checks; that he promised to send me When he left Orleans; I Should be much Obliged to you if you would Be so Good; as to pay Capt. Moor his freight; and if posible to keep them at your house Just untill my Arrivel whch I hope will be soon And when I Shall Have the pleasure of Seeing yourself; Shall reumburs You for what cost you have Been at on my Account....

To WILLIAM MARSHALL[64]

Mobile, December 6, 1769

This serves to acquaint you that I shall Stand in need of such a Vessell as your Schooner to go with me to Manchacke; And as I am not as yet provided with one; Should be much obliged to you to let me know your lowest price for that Voyage per the first oppertunity for this place; after Capt. McMins Arrival in the province. as till then I Cant leave this place[.] Messrs. McGillivary & Struthers will be fourth Coming to you for the payment if I Cant pay if my self in Cash at Orleans; which I Expect to Receive some money as we are Going up the River Mississippi; if this is aGreeable to you; you will let me hear By the first Occation; so that if we Dont aGree about the price of the freight that I may provide my self with aNother....

63/Elias Durnford, engineer and surveyor-general of the province of West Florida, was appointed lieutenant governor in 1769 and in 1770 served for a short time as acting governor. He was a member of the first provincial council in 1764, and was in command of Mobile at the time of its surrender to the Spanish in 1780. See Alden, *John Stuart and the Southern Colonial Frontier*, 317; Howard, *British Development of West Florida*, 26; Johnson, *British West Florida*, 71–72.

64/Pensacola merchant and shipowner.

Merchant of Manchac

To JOHN RITSON, *Pensacola*

Mobile, December 12, 1769

You have hear Inclosed an order in your favour on Monsr. Vincent; a french man and Watch Maker lately Arrivd. at your place from N: orleans for $20 that sum being the Ballance of his Accot. with me—Which should be Much Obliged to you to recover for me; if he Cant Produce you Monsr. Macnamaras Receipt for that Sum; if you Recover it Place it to the Credit of my Accot. But dont let him leave the Province Untill paid you; or produce the above Receipt. I have Wrote him on that same Head my Self; Should be much obliged to You if you would send me Monsr. Dela Goutreas Accot. as there Is no Acct. of his Comming this way and on my Return to Orleans I may be able to Recover it; if posible. . . .

Part Two
1770–1775

To JOHN RITSON, *Pensacola*

Manchac, February 15, 1770

I had the pleasure of Writting you from N: Orleans—Acquainting you that I had money; to send you and Mr. Stephenson Which I promise you I would be Glad to find a proper oppertunity to send it; as I am at present, in a place Distitute of Inhabitants (and As one may Say among the Savages) had the Bearer Been in a Good boat or one that I could risque Sending the Money in you Should; have had it Sent per this Occation; But his Cannoa I would not Risque my old fouse[?] in; I hear that Capt. Blomart[1] is to Come up to this place; if he Dus; Shall Remitt it you; by him or per Mr. Gerome when he comes hear; I hope that you have Recivd. Monsr. Vancents old watch and that he Has paid you the $20. if he has you will please to Advise me there of if you have time to write; should there be any Letters for me from Mr. Stephenson please to send them per the first oppertunity; I shall Louse [lose] per Orleans Near 750 Dollers if after Generl. OReyleys Departure I dont gitt leave to recover my outstanding Debts that Are Still Due; me in that Town—I having nothing more to add for the present; only that I am in hopes of Doing something for my self In this place; More than ever I had an Oppertunity of Doing in Orleans—if you have anything New in your place; or any Newspapers Please to let me hear. . . . P.S. my Compliments to any that may Ask About me; tell Them that I am in Good health And would have wrote; but the oppertunity was Waiting for the present.

To McGILLIVRAY AND STRUTHERS, *Mobile*

Manchac, February 15, 1770

I had the pleasure of Writing you; from New Orleans Acquainting; you how the Spanish Iresh man Served me; on my Arrivel

1/ John or Jean Blommart, born in Geneva, Switzerland, served as a captain in the British army during the Seven Years' War and retired on a lifetime pension of half-pay. In the early 1760s he became one of the chief merchants in Pensacola. In January, 1769, he was granted 1000 acres on the Mississippi River at Bayou Sara, and was living there by 1770. At about the same time he was granted 1000 acres near Natchez, and in 1775 he transferred his family and his business as an Indian trader to Natchez. There he developed his mercantile business and a small but profitable distillery. In 1776 he became a justice of the peace. Blommart was active in the trade of the Arkansas area. By early 1777 he held at British Ozark (later called Concord), on the east side of the Mississippi, the principal stock of merchandise for trade with the Osage Indians in Arkansas. He became associated with Spanish commandant De Villiers in a scheme to supply goods for De Villiers' trade with the Osage, an arrangement approved by Governor Gálvez. In practice, the partnership provided that Blommart's money supported De Villiers' falling credit, allowed Blommart's hired British hunters from Natchez and Concord to join the French *voyageurs* and specially licensed Americans hunting along the White River and the Arkansas, and granted Blommart a

Merchant of Manchac

Spanish passport which freed his cargoes from paying import duties in New Orleans. The partnership was dissolved in 1779.

After James Willing's raid on the British Mississippi settlements, Blommart was appointed captain of British militia and quartermaster in Natchez. When the settlement was occupied by the Spanish in 1779, he became a leader of local British royalists and, in 1781, led the volunteers who besieged and captured the Spanish garrison in Natchez. When the fort was reoccupied by the Spanish, Blommart surrendered and his property was confiscated. He was imprisoned in New Orleans for a time, but was released by Governor Miró in April, 1783. Shortly afterward he went to Jamaica. See Robert V. Haynes, *The Natchez District and the American Revolution* (Jackson, Miss., 1976), 12, 19, 135; Wells (comp.), "British Land Grants," 155; and Faye, "The Arkansas Post" *passim*.

2/On January 21, 1770, a band of eighteen Choctaw Indians entered the ruined and defenseless fort at Natchez, then inhabited by a few British settlers, and plundered the store of merchant John Bradley. Bradley, with a group of friends, pursued the Indians and attacked them, killing two. They then fled down the river to New Orleans, warning other traders that the Choctaws were about to go to war. The Choctaw chiefs, however, expressed a desire for peace, and eventually most of Bradley's goods were returned to him. See John Bradley to Elias Durnford, February 1, 1770, Account of

in that place; he put me in prison and Kept me there 36 Hours; and when he let me out would not allow; Me time Anough to git my things out of the Town; but have got some things Up to this place; and s[h]all git the Remainder when he leavs the Country— Mr. Macnamara got in only the Spanish money; and about 150 Dollers of the outstanding Debts; for which he Charged Me 5 pCent for Recovering them the money that I owed the house Capt. McMin & Mr. Swanson is all ready; had I but the pleasure of finding a proper Occasion to send it you; I should be quite Easy to what I am at present on Account of the Affairs that Has passed at the Natchez; with Mr. Bradley and the Indians there; all the Inhabitance that ware there are at present here or At point Coupée;[2] Mr. MacIntosh and his wife is on a plantation Near to the point Coupée; what he will do I Cant Tell you; as he he [*sic*] has not wrote me; Since he has been there; Mr. Bradley Seems Mighty Jeoulous about my Being here; we have heard that Monsr. Dunford came out Leut. Governor of the province; I have some reason to think he has wrote him Concerning the House that I am in at present; Should you hear any thing of this please to Advise me per the first oppertunity; as Also if there is any Troops Coming this way; if there should and for this place; I then should be much obliged to you if you would Send me some things proper for them; such as 2 Hhds. Norward Rum; Sugar tea & Coffee; with any other small Article you may think proper to serve them with; as there will be no Body here to Supply them; but my self as Mr. Bradley setts of for England, on his Return from the Illinois; Where he is gone with a large Batteau and 25 Negroes to see if he can Dispose of them; as we shall not be able to git any thing More out of the Island of Orleans—if the Schooner has not left your place Before this comes to hand please to charge Monsr. Gerome; when in the Mississippi not to offer to stop on Any Accot. at the Town of Orleans; but to proceed up the River Without loss of Time; as I am in hopes of Making Good Sales; as there is No Goods here at present—I have sent to the point Coupée for 200 Carrots Nacotosh Tobaco to send in the schooner; if you have Any files please send me 10 Doz: of Different sorts; As all them I left in Town ware sold while I was at your place—having nothing More to Add for the present only I am in hopes of Doing something More for my self then I did in the Town. . . . P.S. if Capt. McMine has Brought me the Gunn he promised me from London please to send it me; and if you will be so good; as to pay him for it I Shall Send you the Cash; as soon as I know the price —if Mr. fraruh Is S[t]ill with you please to give him my kind Compliments—

To JEAN BAPTISTE SARPY, *Illinois*

Manchac, March 5, 1770

This serves to acquaint you; that I am something Surprized; that since your Departure from; New Orleans; that I Neaver had the pleasure of hearing from you; Concerning Monsr. Barrows, effects, that you have under your care; to recover at your Place; I think they are something worth Writing about; as you are Not in want of Occasions; for Orleans or this place should be much Obliged to you; if you would write me per the first Conveyance; as I Am Charge'd with the Recovering and finishing, all Mr. Barrows; effairs in this province; Should be Glad to hear what Measurs you have taken for the Recovering that Gentlemans Interest; and if there is nothing to be Done with them that owes the money; please to Remit me the Papers that are in your hands, as soon as posible; so that I may know How to Act with Regard to Monsr. Maxant; in that affair; and as I am not able to bring him to any Settlement Just till I know the Result of what you have Done; your Compliance in Wrighting per first Oppertunity will Oblige . . .

To JOHN RITSON, *Pensacola*

Manchac, May 11, 1770

Your kind Letter of the 24th January and the 9 feby. I have now Before me; and note the Contents and aGreeable to your orders Have sent you per Mr. Gradingo on Mr. John Stephensons and your Account and Risque the following Sums Viz.

His honor. Elias Dunfords note for	$118.7r	$276.7r
Leut. Wm. Featherstons Ditto for	158.	
in Gold { 11 Doubble Louns [doubloons] at $16	176.	
5 half Joes³ . . at 8½ . . .	42.5r	223.3
a light pistole	3.6¼	
In Silver	1.1¾	
as per Recipt inclosd.		$500.

of which there is for Mr. Stephenson $340 and for you $160— you will Please to give me Credit on Mr. Stephensons Books for $357½ As I was obliged to pay 5 pCent for Drawing the Spanish Money & so have Charged Mr. Stephenson's Accot. with me $17½ Commissn. for the payment of Leut. Fetherson's note you'l please to present it to Capt. Innis (if Leut. Featherston is not with you) who has the money in his hands a Long time (as Mr. Bradley

---

Mr. Fergy, in PRO, CO 5/577, pp. 233–44; and Alden, *John Stuart and the Southern Colonial Frontier*, 316.

3/The "half-Joe" was half a "Johannes," the name by which the Portuguese gold *peça* of João V was known in the British American colonies. A full Johannes was worth 6400 *reis*, and the more common Half-Joe about £3 (Pennsylvania currency) or $9.6 (Spanish milled dollars). See Savelle, *George Morgan, Colony Builder*, 33 n.

toald me) for the paymt. of Said Notes; I Gave him the Cash for them; thinking them saffer to send; as I have Taken coppies of them Before Witnesse's—out of the money that was owing me at orlean,s to say $1994½ I have Not been Able to Recover no more than $904½ as yet; Although I have Employed a Gentleman to Trans act for me there; to whom I am Obliged to Give 5 pCent Commissn. and have bein twice in Orleans my Self to see if it was posible to finish my small affairs But all to no Accot. as I cant appear in Town my self without the Governors permission which I am in hopes of Abtaining as my friend wrote me last week; so I live in Expatation to go Down And Finish all I have to do in that province Shortly; if so you May Depend that I shall Remit the Ballance of your Acct. by the first oppertunity that shall offer for your place—I have Receivd. this Morning the Trunk of printed Linens; all in Good order; & Shall do all that lies in my power for Mr. Stephensons Interest & more over you shall be Reumbursed Either in Skins Indego Or money; by next October or November at the furthest—Monsr. Vensant Behaved to me like a Great raskel in Serving me as he Did for I promise you as God is my Saviour; I had no Other in my keeping[.] if you Should Recive any News from Mr. Stephenson, please to let me here how he does & if he is already with you; please to present him my kind Respects; & Tell him I Shall Wright him by Capt. Gerome as I Shall your Self; having nothing more to add for the present only beg You to write me; per first appertunity; if any of the produce of this Place is in Demand with you; Your Compliance will Oblige . . .

To McGILLIVRAY AND STRUTHERS, *Mobile*

Manchac, May 31, 1770

I have now Before [me] your favours 9th Feby. 13 & 15th Mar[c]h And the 12th Ulto. with Invoice and Bill Landing of Sundry MerhtDize pd. the Schooner fortunes Rivenge; which have Recivd. and Noted in Confirmity; Amounting toGeather with the Articles to my Debit in Your Accot. dated the 14th March last; (Execlusive of the Ballance of former Accot. Setled) $3320.5/4 Which Ile Remit you in Octor. or Novemr. Next & Sooner if possible; as well the Amount of Two hhds. Rum $214.2rs yr. letter Omitted in yr. Accot. your are Sensible the Sales of Strouds Blankets &c is over untill the Autumn occationed By their Not comming timely to hand; which If [*illegible*] not Remedy—agreeable to your orders I now Remit you per Captain Gerome; all the skins and Cash I possibly cou'd as per inclosed Receipt & the

Abstract accot. thereof; as to the money I Recivd. From the Spanish Treausury; the Detention of the Schooner obliged me to Employ the Major part in Goods at orleans; the proffits there on will I hope Reumburs the heavy Expencess my precipitated Departure from Orleans has Caused; Occasioned by Genel. Oreyleys ill Natured proceedings; also in Building my self a house as none here was Habitable Except them Occupied before my Arrival by Monsantos Brother & Mr. Bradley, the latter Endeavourd to prevent my taking of the house I live in, which have been Under the Necessity of Repairing untill my own is finished; had not been the order I had from Governor Brown to Dwell in any I found with in the fort; his Motives for such proceedings is quite Apparent covetousness predominating too much—of the list of Debts I Shewed you left in Macnamaras hands there are yet outstanding about $650 which hope will be Recoverd towards the fall;—the french Merchts. Who lately Saild from Orleans for old France were hitherto purchasing all the Skins they met; with; which left me no Chance to come at any Except at the same price then Current; which would neaver Answer Your Markett; the few I now send you have bought of an English Man; chosen by Mr. Campbell & to his approbation; hope toward the faul [fall] to procure a good many my own Accot. & if any over plus shall recomd. them to you as you require—no corn to be had at point Coupee nor down the River, which Mr. Favory of pearl River & others lately here with Cash have Experienced[.] Monsanto's Bror. Disappointed me in the Nachit. [Nachitoches] Tobaco which I bespoak having as I am well informed sold it to Mr. Bradley[.] I used Other Deligence but could not Succeed; as the Commedant of Nachitosh Obliges the Buyers to carry him back proper Certificates of Delivering it in Orleans; there is no rice to be had at your limets as General Oreyley's Taxation is $4½ per Barrel weighing about 170 lb. besides no Emty cask to be had with out sending to orleans; which woud like wise Attend with too much Cost—Mr. French's friend Mr. OConner Was lately promoted is now 500 leagues Distant from his late Govnmt. At the Adaies.[4] however the former wrote to some of his Acquaintance's there Advising the Comedities they can meet with here for Cash or Merc[han]table Skins which hope will have Dissired effect; the need full Preacaution of not Trusting them; nor any [?] other; any way Doubtfull of true Compliance Ile Strictly observe—as [I] Ignor what lands are Taken up ajecent to this; you must in such case apply to the Secretarys office in pensacola for proper Inteligence there of—Beaton Rox [Baton Rouge] about six leagues Distant from hence; is held by all Judges to be very fine land and from thence to this fort—your Uisal imports are the Goods Generally

4/ The Spanish mission and presidio of San Miguel de los Adaes was established in 1717 as the easternmost outpost of the Spanish establishment in Texas. An important frontier outpost originally intended to bar French expansion out of Natchitoches, a few miles away, Los Adaes became a major center of Spanish Indian administration after the cession of Louisiana to Spain in 1763. Hugo O'Conor served there as ad interim governor from 1767 until 1770, when he returned to Mexico. In 1772 he was appointed *inspector comandante* of the Interior Provinces of New Spain. See Herbert Eugene Bolton (ed.), *Athanase de Mézières and the Louisiana-Texas Frontier, 1768–1780* (2 vols.; Cleveland, 1914), I, 127 n.

Demanded here of English Goods or Commodites if you'l order the contents of the with in Memorandum to be shiped with the Rest of your Cargo Ile; take them at the Accustamary Advance, as well any other Necessary Assortmt. I might then want; observing that you'l be pleased to suspend the Order Mr. French gave Mr. Swanson relatives to the 8 ps. Hair and Wirsted Shagg as the sails there of to the Spanairds at the adies is Now frustrated by the departure of Mr. Oconor for whom they ware Intened

Please to send me per first safe Conveyance Badon & Roshon's Notes of hands in Order to Deliver them to the hoalder of my obligation for the payment thereof Conditionally on their Being duly paid—pursuant to your Instructions I wrote to Mr. A. McIntosh; who immediately brought Down all the skins he had & Shipt them on Board the Schooner Capt. Gerome; and goes by the same Occasion himself, I understand by his conversation that nothing wou'd do him Greater pleasure than to have all his Affairs Setled to your intire Satisfaction[.] the Negro he already sent by Mr. Cambell.

On rexammining your afore Mentioned Accot. dited the 14th March last I find you Charge me $148.8rs Ballance of an Accot. Settled 21st Novembr. last; by which you'l see (as per Coppy there of now before me; its only $116.2½r Amount of your Inclosed bill parcels sent you for your Govert. Which as not to my Debit in the Afore Said Acct. Ile likewise make you Good the Error to my prejiduce being $16.4r which if you'l make appear to the Contrary (as I at present Ignor any other charge) I conform there to; I am Greatly obliged to you for your kind Offer in Supplying me hence Forward; with any Goods I might want & may Rest satisfied all my Connections in that as hitherto will Meet Reciprocal complyance, being the Commercial Expediancy to Support mutual Interest friendship and free the Supplyers from Apprehensions in case of Accidents; which Ile Always Endeavour to provide against, as well for your sakes & other friends As my own; You have here with Capt. Gerome's rect. for 181 Good Deer Skins in the hair Wt. 386 lb. whose Amount youl be pleased to Credit my Accot. with; On the Best terms of price; I only Recvd. them two days ago—am promised By some White people 6 or 800 skins more in a month hince and then Deliver their Amount in MerchanDize; Immagining your house would Not Chuse to be Troubled with a Trifling Commission I Addressed per this Occasion 400 Carrots of Choice point Coupee Tobaco & 2 hhds. french Clarrit, to Mr. Swanson with orders to pay you the neat proceeds Crediting me there With; if it suits you to Take the Tobaco at 3 bits your money the Carrot I am Satisifed there at; as well the wine if you want it at the price quoted to Mr. Swanson;

please to send me (if it suits you) per Mr. A. McIntosh 150 lb. Gun powder Dubble F 200 Wt. Ball 3 doz Check Shirts, 1 doz felt hats & 4 pss BengAl Stripes 2 Red & 2 Blue; Being the Merct.-Dize Dailey Demandd. here; their Amount I,le duly remit you equal to the formers before Capt. McMin Sails; after his Return in the fall from England Shall Esteem you Advise me per first oppertunity for my Governmt. if you will take Merhantable indego in part payment and the most You'l give; Also if admited to an Entry with you; & if any Duty Attends there on with all perticulars on that head; please to carry the Ballance my favr. in Acct. Current (which herewith goes) to my Credit in New N/A being $108....

To PETER SWANSON, Mobile

Manchac, May 31, 1770

I Recivd. Your kind favour 13th March last, Where by observe Your Assiduity in the choice of the Goods; & in procuring from Others the part your house had not; which if Occasion permits will mett A Reciprocal Return; Interim Sincere thanks— Inclosed you have Mr. A. McIntosh's Rect. for $61 out of which youl please to pay Doctor Chastom $28½ I recvd. his Acct. in Orleans his order was for $30: from which I have Deducted 5 per Commissn. same as Macnamara charged me for Recovering the Spanish bills &c which I find is the Customary practice in Orleans—the Remainder of Said Recipt. being $32½ is your property Recovered of Madame Phillips by Mr. Macnamara with his Commisn. at 5 pCent. please to tell Doctor Cheston that his Black is At Mr. Subi,s; but had not in my power to use any Deligence about Him—Being purswaded of your Integrety towards my welfair; I take the liberty to Address you 400 Carrots Choice point Coupée Tobaco no way inferior in quality to that of the Nacatosh & 2 hhds. french Clarit. the latter; cost $25 Each Exclusive of freight &c Which youl please to sell to my Best Advantage & pay the Neat proceeds to Messrs. McGillivray & Struthers Deducting your Commissn. & any other Charges Attending there on; but if your house Should Require the Tobaco may let them have it 3 Bits your money the Carrot As well the wine at $40 Ea: if not youl Act the need full in the sales there of to others— Mr. French prays his Compliments to you ... P.S. for your Governt. in the Sale of the Tobaco, the planters of Nacatoche nor pint Coupee Will rase [raise] none this year Except for their own Use for want of Encouragmt. in orl[eans] [last line illegible]

To McGILLIVRAY AND STRUTHERS, Mobile

Manchac, June 4, 1770

Referr you to my last 31st May per Capt. Gerome who parted hence 1 Instant & hope will be safe arrivd. at your port are this reaches; at foot you have Abstract of what I shiped on Board his Schooner agreeable to your orders and for your Acct. & Risque as well for Capt. McMain and my own, also that which Mr. A McIntosh shipt for his & Co. Acct. who Goes by the same Conveyance[.] I Since got a Small percel of Skins in the hair; & am in hopes in about a Month hence to have about 600 more; not having to Add I Remain . . .

Your Acct. Viz
  53 Skins in the hair . . . . at 5rs. Eeach
  59 Ditto do . . . . at 45 Sols E.
  94 Ditto hand Dresd 218 lb. . . . . 37½ Sols p
  Cash $260.8¼ rs. of which $101.8¾rs Acct. of Capt. McMain
  from which Deduct My own Accot. . . . . Comissn. 5 pCent paid

  181 Skins in the hair ⎫
  400 Carrots Tobaco ⎬   Macnamara
  2 hhds. french Clarit ⎭

    Accot. of Mr. A McIntosh's Viz
    35 packs Skins in the hair & Seperated

To McGILLIVRAY AND STRUTHERS, Mobile

Manchac, July 23, 1770

Referr you to both mine 31 May & 4 June last the Former per Capt. Gerome; who hope is longe are now Arrivd. at your place with Desired Sucess, the Contents of the latter (via Dolphin Island) intimating what I Shiped you Capt. McMains Accot. & my own; as well the Skins of Mr. Alr. McIntosh's & Comy. I have now 7 hundred Skins in the hair & about one hundd. Drest, which am purswaded will meet your Approbation; in all next month I hope to Recive as Many more; I have Also 200 Choice Carrots of Nacatoche Tobaco; Towards the fall I Expect 2 thousand Skins in the hair from a french man (of whom I had some of the fore-Mentioned) and take their Amount in Merchandize; he Yearly Carrys to Orleans about 4 thousand Skins—the Sales of Goods as yet are very slow perticularry the Wollens Untill the faul— as all the powder & Ball I had are almost Disposed off, I Stand in Great Need of the quantity I wrote to you for in my former; as above Which you'l please to send me per Mr. A. McIntosh or Any Other Conveyance by the lake or New Orleans; if to the Latter to be Delivered to Monsr. Ranson[5] at his plantation about ¾ League

---

5/Louis Ranson or Rançon was a prominent New Orleans merchant and planter who amassed a considerable fortune by the end of the French period and during the 1760s frequently loaned money. In 1770 he became attorney general of Spanish Louisiana and was partner of Gilbert Antoine de St. Maxent in the state monopoly of Indian goods. See Clark, *New Orleans, 1718–1812*, 105, 196.

below the Town, on the left hand side going up the River, Always prefering Sending them by Mr. McIntosh in Case his Detention should not be Verry long—Ile greatly esteem; You'l be pleased to write to yr. friend in pensacola; on Rect. here of to petition in my Name for a lot of the land on which my house is built a small Distance from the fort; being as I am Informed to be made a Town Ship off;[6] Mr. French prays his Compliments to you Mr. Swanson and all other friends . . . P.S. this instant I opened a Barl. of powder which the Buyer would not Take except at less then the first cost being mostly in dust and hard lumps Which condittion it must have been in when Shiped as it Recd. no Damage on Board nor here all the Rest of the Barrls. turned out very Good & have now Only one left; I Just Recivd. One hundred Skins more in the hair; please to let me know as Soon as posible the most youl Give for good Merchantable Indego; and if admitted to any Entry at your Custom House with particularities Relative to its Imports & Exports for my Govermt. . . .

To GODLEY AND RAINCOCK, *Pensacola*

Manchac, August 6, 1770

I Recivd. your favour of the 28th June last & another from Mr. Barrow to whom you'l please to forward the Inclosed left open for your presuial having Noted there is every Circumstance Relative to his affairs With Maxant & my self for his and your Governmt. —As to Mr. Frenchs Bill in your possn. for £15 am Assurd; as he wou'd Recivd no paymt. there of Untill I had an Acct. of Its Being honour'd; tho he neaver Doubted the contrary As the person on Whom the Bill was drawn transacts and receivs the Major part of the formers possessions in Ireland being £120 in Ireland per Annum and hitherto Duly paid his Draft and Orders, by Letters which Mr. French Shewed me; I find he is ill used; which the Other will in course Repent. I Will Next Novemr. go to Mobile & your place and then pay you the Amout. of Said Bill; with the Charges Attending there on; same Time Shall Settle Mr. Barrows Acct. with you; as he Requiers; observing that part of his Outstanding debts are not yet recovered; Neither can I go to Orleans till I have the Governors permissn. which my friends are Soliciting for And hope soon to obtain it in Order to Settle my Affairs there. . . .

6/No petition in Fitzpatrick's name has been found among the records of the West Florida government and apparently none was ever submitted. On February 17, 1772, the council granted Fitzpatrick's request that he be permitted to remain in his home on the reserved land at Manchac until it was needed for the use of the government, and that he have liberty to remove his effects from this land when he was ordered to leave. See Minutes of Council, February 12, 1772, PRO, CO 5/589, pp. 356–57; Minutes of Council, March 4, 1775, PRO, CO 5/634, Pt. 1, pp. 236–37. Fitzpatrick eventually acquired legal title to his plantation under a grant signed by Louisiana Governor Estevan Miró on February 14, 1786. See Act of Congress, February 9, 1833, No. 802, "An Act for the Relief of Josiah Barker," *Acts of Congress Pertaining to Louisiana*, 358, Louisiana State Land Office.

In 1771 the British colonial government considered the establishment of a town just above Fort Bute and plans for such a town were drawn up. Petitions for town lots were presented to the provincial council in April, 1772, but action on them was postponed. The following November lots were granted to twelve men. In August, 1776, the council directed that the town, to be called Harwich, be marked out and lots sold. Between 1777 and 1779, 58 lots were sold, many of them to colonial officials. The town itself was never built. See Cecil Johnson, "Expansion in West Florida, 1770–1779," *Mississippi Valley Historical*

To WILLIAM BARROW, *Pensacola*

Merchant of Manchac

Manchac, August 26, 1770

Your favour of the 25th August last came to hand the 4th Inst. & note the Contents—as to your Affairs with Maxant have according to promise Used my utmost endeavours to reduce him to a favoble. Conclusion there of but to no Purpose; he woud terminate Nothing untill he first recivd. proper advice of the bits Or notes he gave you payable at the Illinois; ware complyed with or not; I wrote to your Attorney Mr. Sarphy; from whom I Recivd. a letter dated in September Last which Only came to hand last may Being five months in the post office in orleans Caused by my Absence from thence[.] he sent me a bill for 2550 livers [livres] on Mr. Dubray [?] in Orleans which was protested for non acceptance & now in the hands of Monsr. Ranson who is a Gentleman I can confide in to procure payment there of when the Drawer comes to Town and he is Daily Expected[.] Sarphy mentions in his letter that the want of Due compliance to said Bills obliges him to sue for the Same & hopes to succeed there in; that if he recovers the hole or any part there of will Remit it by the Convoy which is Expected in all Next Month & that he will Use his Utmost Endeavours to bring them to a favoble. Conclusion; I wrote him by Mr. Bradley to which I have [?] No Answer as yet; all the Spanish Bills which Maxant had to the Amout of $15000 As am informed were Stopped by Generl. Oriley to pay a mercht. in Spain to whom the former was owing said sum which has been a Mighty prejeduce to the Rest of his Creditors who now bears the same fate as you Do; but in case his Affairs With you should terminate as you quarl [?] shall observe your Instructions there in[.] When Genl. Oriley ordered me from Orleans I petitioned him to Redress the Deplorable State of your affairs; with Maxant; he answered that he had Three Years Time for the paymt. of his Debts & till then nothing could be Done, the out Standing Debts due to my self and Other friends; he in like manner obliged me to leave them to my friend Mr. McNamara & after wards quit the place Which I was obliged to do; the major part of said Debts are not yet recovered; Except the spanish Bills which ware all Duly paid; therefore am Sorry you Did not Admit of them offered to you by Maxant; in payment of your Demand on him—As to my being Instrumental to this affair; you know I had no further connextions in it only to interpit for you, he then Appear'd to you, as well as to me; & all the Rest of his Creditors to be a man of Good Credit; transacting all the Spanish Bussiness, with Sundry other negiotiations, & the Cash from the Havana then daily Expected to pay all the Spanish Engagements which Doubtless annimated

---

Review, XX (1934), 487, 493; Council minutes, November 2, 1772, PRO, CO 5/589, pp. 46–49; Peter Chester to Hillsborough, September 20, 1771, PRO, CO 5/588, pp. 499–512; "Plan of the proposed New Town also the proposed Cut from the Mississippi to the Iberville," [1772], British Museum, PS 8/15276.

you to let him have the goods; otherwise you was Master to keep them; you likewise know that all the Goods, I sold your Acct. have Recovered & paid you the Cash before; you left Orleans—As the Skins that I Assisted in prizing out for you; they were all Merchantable for the french Market which I immagined wou'd Answer Equally at the English; being the Same qualities whch the British Merchts. in Cannada Shiped during my Recidence their, it may be Supposed the Buyers find fault when there is none; in Order to Come at them the Cheaper; Being over Stocked with them; and no Recourse of any Other Market, Mr. Carrass was Executed[7] he remained insolvent for upwards of Ten thousand Dollers so that his note you left me for $22 will near [never] be paid, Your order on Legotry I fear will Meet the Same fate he is owing me $56 & cant Git it—as to the Articels which Remained in my hands part of the Shott is yet insir, & some out Standing Debts; which hope to recover this fall; as I am to go to Pensacola Next Novemr. Shall Settle your Accot. to intire Satisfaction with Messrs. Godley & Raincock whose Directions Ill Observe Relative to your Affairs as you Require; as I cant appear in Orleans, with out the Generals permission my friend are Soliciting with him there on; which hope soon to Obtain in Order to Settle my Affairs on the Best Terms I possible can; you may be Assurd that I have your well fare as Strongly Attacked as my own—& do Sincerely wish You all Desired Felicities in your future Undertakings . . . P.S. I was Obliged to sue Mr. Page when he was Going the Havana, he paid Me in Spanish Bills, which I Gave Messrs. Godley & Raincock—

To McGILLIVRAY AND STRUTHERS, *Mobile*

Manchac, August 30, 1770

I Recivd. your favour of the 4th July per Mr. McIntosh; as likewise 200 Ct. of Balls & 150 lb. powder, Amounting as per Invoice to $82.4½rs which have passed to your Credit; tho the latter is not of the quality I Required and so bad in its kind (without Receiving the least dammage in the Carage) all in hard Lumps; that after it was Dryed and Drifted Deminshed ¼ part; which Mr. McIntosh knows;—I note your having Receivd. the Cash and skins per Capt. Gerome; & Carried to my Credit; am Sorry the Drest Skins Did not mett Your Approbation; the loss I Sustain by them is Evident; but it shall serve future Goverment; to confide in none to chuse any but my Self;—am Glad you Make Appear the Error quoated in my former which did not then Recolect;

7/Pierre Caresse was executed by a Spanish firing squad on October 25, 1769, for his participation in the New Orleans revolt of 1768.

Being in the Article of the Sheep; which Mr. Swanson toald me would be left to Mr. McGillivray; however; as its no meterial affair Between friends am Conformable to your Settlement there of;—my endeavours will not be wanting to Collect as soon as posible the Remainder of yours & Capt. McMains outstanding debts[.] Mr. Delile left Mr. McIntosh in Cat Island as well tuo of his men the former Asserting to be Sick; the Vessell Remained there 14 Days as well by Contrary Winds as the want of hands, which, with the want of provissions Except a few Biskets; obliged Mr. McIntosh to hire tuo men & proceed up the lake to Transyraho; & there Necessiated to employ eight Indians Giving Each of them one Stroud Blanket & each a Shirt; to row him up to the landing place; Ten miles from this Distant; from thence had to Carry all his Goods on Peoples Backs by Land to here; the worst of all the Carage was the hhd. of Rum; to provide Caggs to Start it into; which attended with great fetigue & Expences I assisted him as much As possible other wise woud not Succeed as well as he Did; he intends to sue Delile for all cost and Damages; his AGreemt. being not properly Complyed with; I have 1000 Choice Skins in the hair, most red; on an Naverage about 3 lb. Reather under as you Required, am Daily Expecting 1000 more and hope in the fall to Succeed better; the few Drest Skins I have are very Good as already Intimated in my former; its well you countermanded the hair Shaggs—Mr. French prays his Compliments to you . . .

To PETER SWANSON, *Mobile*

Manchac, August 30, 1770

I recivd. your Esteem'd favour of the 4 July and note the contents, Being well Assur'd that you will embrace all favorable Oppertunities in the Sales of the Clrarit & Tobaco; perticularly the former; which whilst on hand the Accustomry care to be Taken for the preservation of it; your being no Stranger to the Method there of I need not Recommed to you; am fully Satisfied of your Integrity in any thing Commited to your Care; I observe your having paid Doctr. Cheston his $28½ as Likewise Capt. Gerome $6 the Remainder of his freight; which have Carried to your Credit,—I used all deligence when in Orleans to Dispose of your Wigg; but cou'd not Succeed; which Occasioned my Sending it to the Illinois by Thomas the Cooper who went with Mr. Bradley; but met the Same Disappointmt. having brought it Back; however am yet in hopes Mr. Monsanto on his Return from Orleans may buy it;—if you find an Appearance of Corn to answer at your Market, please to advise me in course thereof; and if you will take any Interest in 200 Barrs. Shelled; which I can have deliverd me here at 10 bits this Currency say 12½ bitts your money; if a Greater quantity wou'd suit Can have it, for your Government the freight to Your place I belive can be had at ½ Doller per Barl. . . I flatter my Self the Tobaco will in Corse very favble. sell as the planters as the planters [*sic*] at point Coupee [*illegible*] year only for their own private use . . . [*rest of line illegible*]

To GODLEY AND RAINCOCK, *Pensacola*

Manchac, August 30, 1770

I Refer you to the above being a Copy of last forwarded by Mr. Jones, With another for Mr. Barrow—Am now to Acquaint you that all the Illinois Boats are come Down except one Expected; in the fall; I Recivd. no Answer to the Letter I wrote Mr. Sarphy by Mr. Bradley Relative to Mr. Barrows affair Which I Greatly Strange at; as Mr. Williams toald me that he is active and Deligent in any thing committed to his Care; with the CaraCter of an honest Man; & belive will Use his Endeavours to Reduce the people, (whoes notes he has) to payment, if not Insolvent; one of which whose obligation is for 14000-Livers [livres] is become a bank Rupt, I wish the Same fate may not befall the Others as no Recourse can be had of Maxant for three Years Commincing last Jany. Except he Volentary condesends to a Settlemt. thereof; which I,ll Earnestly Solicit; when to Obtain permissn. to go to Orleans—Mr. Dubray the Drawer of the Bill in Mr. Ranson's hands for Livers 2500—as Mentioned in my letter to Mr. Barrow, is not yet come from the Illinois but is Expected in the fall Which Bill Mr Williams believs will be Duly paid—and Agreeable to Mr. Bradleys promise to me (who now goes to your place,) you'l please to Call on him for the Amount of the Bill of £15; in your possn. togeather With the Charges makeing an Estimate of the whole Exa. at 4/8 per Doller Which he will pay on Demand Giving him a Recpt. to have Recvd. the same—My Acct. which I,ll in Confirmity carry to his Creditt being due to me; you'l Likewise please to send me Sd. bill with your Recipt. there on by a safe Conveyance in Order to Deliver it to Mr. French. . . .

To GEORGE MORGAN, *Illinois*

Manchac, September 12, 1770

I have now befor me your favour of the 27th July Inclosing a Rcipt. for a Barge oars & Rudder; which I'll Endeavour to dispose off; as soon as possible to your best Advantage & in Course Advise you; thereof[.] I have Mr. Bradleys Certificate of his having Deliverd me but five Oars, the Deficiency of the Other five he thinks him self no way Answerable for, that Your men lost out of his Battau a Greater Number; as to your Other Barge I Offered to sell her to Genel. Oriley & others before I left orleans soon after your departure from thence but could not Succeed, which obliged me as having no Other Recourse to give her in Charge to Monsr. Maxant who promised me would Act the Needfull in this Sale of her; but on my Return from Mobille to this Place gave me the Disagreeable Acct. of her being lost night Occasioned by the Rapidity of the River; he believs She Sunk as cou'd git no Intelligence of her Drifting down the River; which Accidence gave me more Uneasiness than if She had been my own; tho not in my power to prevent;—as yet there is no Encouragemt. for your sending any flowr, nor Mault liquor to these parts; The most of all the British Inhabitants are very poor; Glad when able to attain to the Common Necessarys of Life; the french will Always prefer Taffia which they can have much cheaper from the Havana than yours can be afforeded at; New Orleans and Several of the plantations are at present well Stored with Good Merchale. flowr lately from New York, sold on Board $6 and 7 per Barrl. of 180 or 200 Each; if yours turns out Equal in quality to the Best in pensiloa. You may in such case send me on your own Acct. 6 or a Doz: Barrels per first Oppertunity for Tryal, which if Should Take place; both in quality, price, & well packed may After Wards serve for a Continual encouragemt. to large parcels quoating the lowest price; you can afford it at in Orleans with the Weight of Each Barrel—Tea Coffee Sugar, linens and Sperrits [spirits] none to be had here therefore cant send the Barrl. of Sugar & Tea you now Require; as I cannot Go to Orleans; without the Governors permissn. which my freinds are Daily Soliciting for in Order to enable me to go there and Settle my Affairs of out Standing Debts &c. . . .

To McGILLIVRAY AND STRUTHERS, *Mobile*

Manchac, October 30, 1770

I Receivd. both your favours of the 1 Ulto. & 8 Instant and Observe their Contents[.] Capt. Gerome is down the River, belive he will not be able to proceed His Voyage; thither Untill Deceemr. Next; AGreeable to your Arders I will Send by him all the Skins hitherto Recivd. being about 1800 in the hair and 100 Dressed.

I hope before he Sails to have a Good many more to Ship on him in a word Shall Endeavour; as much as in my power to give Content in my Engagements and Connextions with you as well for your sakes as my own, I will be as Carefull As posible in the Choice of Skins; Shall take no Scraped ones; as to the weight of the Skins in the hair; am Obliged to take them as they can be met with in Weight when Merchantable; the Sales of Goods will I hope henceforward will Commince to some Advantage and Continue till february next, in Decemr. and Jany. Will be in greater Quantities coming to markett in these parts then at present does; —I observe you Expect per Capt. McMain a large & well Assorted Cargo—God send him Safe, by being so well Assorted will Doubtless favour the Sales thereof—As to the Crackers they Shall have no Credit from me—Nor any Other but such as Can Depend upon—

Am Obliged to you for your Care in procuring me a licence which have not recvd. it must have Remained with you out of a Mistake, therefore shall Esteem you'l Send it me per first safe Conveyance as I yet Ignor; the place and Limits there in Expressed to trade with Indians as Mentioned in the Act of Assembly for the Regulation of Indians Affairs, copy of which I Sent to Mr. A. McIntosh Pursuant to your Desire thereof—Mr. McIntosh Mr. Miller and Mr. Falkener arrivd. here 30th Instant; am sorry the place would not permt. My Using them with the Civilities I wou'd Willingly confer on them, but hope they admitt the Good will for the Deed; as well for your recommendation as My own desire thereof—the former will Inform you how affairs Stands Effected here more or less—Mr. French prays his Compliments to you ...

To PETER SWANSON, *Mobile*

Manchac, October 31, 1770

I Receivd. Your favour of the 3 Ulto. & 12 Instant and note their Contents[.] I observe that the Wines & Tobaco are yet Unsold, the former you,l Please to dispose of Soon as possible at first cost including freight being p 28 Ds. Each hhd. which they Stand mo [now?] in—also the Tobaco you need not be in haste to Sell it; Except can git 3 bits or upwards the Carrit, as none Will go from Orleans hence forward thither; being all that was & is Merhable. Bought up for the kings Use; who Sent a Vessell from La VaraCrux [Vera Cruz, Mexico] with $15000: to purchass the Same and Gives 5 Sols more the carrot for point Coupée than it sold for before the Arrival of Said Ship & Nacatoche tobaco 11 Sols per

Ct. so that in a few mo[n]ths hence it will be very Scarce or none to be had in the province for Exportation; which will in Coarse Cause it to Rise Considerably as well with you as in Orleans &c—

I note the Disappointment of not obtaining the Grant for the lott on which My House is Built, to proceed from the person you mentioned with whom Shall have as little Connection as posible for this and Sundry Other Motives Needless to incert; However hold in Oppinion with you that the Governor &c will Consider me in a More Equitable light, as it is with in the Limmits of the Town Ship in Case of any; I flatter myself with yours and freinds Interest there in my favour in case of Need—Am Rejoiced to here yr. finger is on the mending [?] Hand; Mr. French prays his kind Complimts. to you and Mr. McIntosh ...

To GODLEY AND RAINCOCK, *Pensacola*

Manchac, December 27, 1770

I Recivd. Both your favours the latter of the 15 Octobr. and note the Contents being, Glad you Recvd. payment for Mr. Frenche's Bill Amounting with Interest &c £20.9.6. also Mr. Barrows affairs Relative to Maxant am sorry My Endeavours when last in Orleans in soliciting the laters complyance proved to no purpose; Still Alledging had no Answer as yet from the Illinois about the Notes he gave Mr. Barrow if paid or not; and they ware not; that its out of his power to comply therewith; to commince a suit with him woud be of no Signification as he Obtained from the General three years for the paymt. of his Debts—the Bill of 2500 livers drawn by Mr. Dubray is yet unpaid in Mr. Barrows hands in Orleans as mentioned in my last to you 30th Augt. last, but as said Drawer is soon Expected to Twon [town] hope to reduce him to payment thereof—I'll send you per Capt. Gerome the Sales of the Two Remnants of Cloth left in my hands per Mr. Barrow, also the part sold of the Shott togeather with what triffle of Cash I recovered his Acct. thereof, when last in Orleans—please to be Assurd I Acted in his Affairs as much as on me Depended & Remain on all Occasions of your Commands ...

To PETER SWANSON, *Mobile*

Manchac, January 21, 1771

I am duly favourd with yours of the 15th Ulto. and Note the contents[.] I observe your having sold part of the Tobaco at 3rs per

Carrot which is well, and Doubt not of your Integrity & Assiduity in Disposing of the Rest (say Remainder to best Advantage as well the wine—it gives me Singular pleasure to here of Mr. McGillivrays safe Arrival & hope Capt. McMain is in like manner are now Arrivd. in Your port; As to Capt Gerome he has not yet finished the Repairs of his Vessell which gives me Great Uneasiness fearing should not arrive Timely for Capt. McMain to Take in the Skins, which I have Ready packed this month past; had any Other Oppertunity offered should not have waited for him; by some Accots. I lately recivd. from point Coupee I dont Expect him Before the last of this month; Neather is it certain if then; Mr. French Prays his kind Compliments to you . . .

P.S. Inclosed you have Mr. David Williams Acct. & pray youl Recover the Balle. apperg. Due me; there on Being $26.¾ Agreeable to his order to me Creditting my Acct. with Messrs. McGillivray & Struthers for the same; you likewise have Henry Smiths of tanchipaho [Tangipahoa] Acct. Currt. that you may be pleased in case he may go to your place with skins to secure or Attach them for the Ballance due to me there on; being Ds. 242.4rs but in case he should Deliver them Volentary not to put him to any Expence, when he came here last with Mr. McIntosh he faithfully promised me he woud return here in a month with Skins to discharge Sd. sum; or part there of, but as yet did not appear—

To McGILLIVRAY AND STRUTHERS, *Mobile*

Manchac, January 21, 1771

I Recivd. your favour of the 12 Ulto. and note the contents; and Obliged to you for the Licence; that of Mr. McIntosh have forwarded as well the paragraph in your Letter to me Relative to him; As to Capt. Gerome to Whom have forwarded your letter; I fear he will not be ready to [leave] Cupee Before the last of this month; which Greatly afflicts me Dreading the Disappointment; of his not arriving timely for Capt. McMain to take in the skins— Which I have Ready packed this month past; being 2600: in the hair & 120 Dressed; I am Daily Expecting 3 or 400 hundred more Skins; which if come to hand before Capt. Gerome parts Shall in like manner send by him; had Any Other oppertunity offered should not have waited on him; the most of the Hunters & Indians are yet on their hunt & by late Accts. will not be down before the latter end of Next month or begining of March Which will cause a Staguation in the Sails of the Goods I have on hand—I observe you intend to have A Vessel of your own property for this Trade which Shall be Glad off in order to prevent here after the Delay and Disappointment now likely to Accrew, I'll acquaint Mr. Ranson what you Mention about his Order in case Should determine there on as you propose; Inclosed you have a memorandm. of Goods which youl please to send me, as Soon as possible freighting the Vessell on the best terms you can; with orders to the Capt. that on his Arrl. in the Mississippi at the first plantations to advise me there of under cover to Mr. Ranson in New Orleans by an Express to be paid by Sd. Ranson who Will have my Orders Relative there to; that I may on Rect. of the Captains letter Carry my Large Barge to unload him at once Down the River; proceeding Always to proceed his Voyage up the River untill I meet him which will Save him a long detention, trouble; & cost of not coming here; Same time I will have all the Skins I recive from the Departure of Capt. Gerome Ready packed to Carry down to be Shipped on him, which I hope will be Sufficint to Discharge the Ballance due to you of my Acct. Last year—

I have 7 Barrs. Good Havanna Sugar Clayd,[8] tolarable white about 20 lb. Which if to suit you at 12 $ per lb. Including fraight I'll send it by said Vessell; as well 100 Barrels Shelled Corn if You Require it Advising me there of per first oppertunity by the Lake or Mississippi. . . .

P.S. Since writting the fore going I Receivd. 450 Skins in the hair which I Will send by Capt. Gerome who is not yet come from point coupée but Dailey Expected by his last Accot. the whole Number of Skins which will go by him are about 3200: Including the Dressed—

To McGILLIVRAY AND STRUTHERS, Mobile

Manchac, February 8, 1771

The foregoing is a Coppy of my last I wrote you per Mr. Murray to which Referr since am favoured with yours of the 24th Ulto. per Mr. Williams and Note the Contents Seeing that Capt. Gerome did not come here from point coupe Agreeable to his last mesage to me; I dispatched a boat 5 Days ago (which is Not yet Returned) desiring him to come as soon as possible; am Vastly sorry for the Disappointmt. Likely to aCrew in not Arriving timely for Captain McMain to Take in the Skins; but you are Sensible its not my fault as Having no Other Conveyance to lay hold off;—I observe what you say about the Clarott which if not Turnd Vinegar you'l please to send me by the Vessel that Brings the Goods;

8/ A nearly white sugar refined by a process employing clay.

as I can Sell it here; for the Wine in Orleans is now $40 and 45 the hhd—but in Case it shou'd be pricked you'l be kind Enough to Dispose of it the best manner you can, as Vinegar or Other wise—Inclosed you have a letter from a french Gentleman at point Coupee for Doctor Grant Relative to a Negro wench in the latters possession which if he'll buy and be Accountable to you or paying you $400 Giving him a recpt. for the Same which Receipt he'll be pleased to send Said French man and I will Satisfy him as aGreed on already betwen us—I delivere'd Mr. French the leter You inclosed for which thanks you; & Desires his kind Compliments to you Mr. Swanson &c. . . .

To JOHN RITSON, *Pensacola*

Manchac, February 9, 1771

You have here inclosed, Mr. John Bradleys funt [first] of Exchange my favour; on Messrs. Walker & Dawson, Merchants in London; for Ninety five pounds ten Shillings & five pence Sterlg. payable at Sixty days Sight; he has not Given me the letter of Advice; But promised that he wou'd Deliver it to you at your place; I have not time at present to send an Acct. of Sales not having Time as the Bearer can inform You; but shall send it per Gerome; your sales Does not Amount to that Sum; we shall Settle that matter aNother Time. . . .

To GODLEY AND RAINCOCK, *Pensacola*

Manchac, February, 1771

Inclosed you have Mr. Barrows Accot. Current & Sales of the Goods left by him in my hands, Exclusive of 100 lb. Shott Yet unsold, with Capt. Geromes Receipt for the Ballance of Said Acct. being $128.4½rs In hard Dollers—I did not yet Recover Monsr. LaBlons Outstanding Debt as per his Note in my possn. for Ds. 41.6rs which as having past it already to Mr. Barrows Credt. in former Account I now Debit him there with as well $16 paid Capt. Danelson by orders Mr. Amois who wrote me Receivd. of Mr. Barrow but $27.5½ for his Sales Amounting to $43.5½ which I likewise posted to Mr. Barrows Credt. in said former Acct.—as yet have Receivd. no Accot. from the Illinois Relative to the latters affairs with Maxant, the Bill of £2500 mentioned in my formers is yet unpaid in Monsr. Ransons hands in Orleans waiting untill the Drawer Comes to Town; who is Expected by the funt Boats from thence. . . .

To ELIAS DURNFORD, *Pensacola*

Manchac, February, 1771

Inclosed you have Mr. Bentleys[9] Receipt for $180 which he Ordered me to Remitt you; he left me a letter to be forwared you per first Safe Conveyance which have Accordingly complyed with to the care of Mr. Commeneo New Orleans—if in any thing I can be servicable to you here may freely Command . . .

To McGILLIVRAY AND STRUTHERS, *Mobile*

Manchac, February, 1771

The foregoing is a Coppy of my last to you per Capt. Lum—to which Referr; Inclosed you have Capt. Gerome's Receipt for [blank] Packs Skins in the hair containing [blank] Weight and 3 packs Drest Quantity [blank] Skins [blank] Wt. [blank] lb. the Ballance of your Acct. last Year I will Remit you per the Return of the Vessel; that Brings the goods As per my former orders there to, & flatter my self you will Act in the Same frindley Manner as you do with the Indian Traders in Allowing Me the Same price as you do them, having Sundry Articels had of you Which will be a long time on hand before I can Dispose of them, and would Now be Glad to Take the price they Stand me in Being the following Goods Viz: Nankeen White Shirts proper, Brass Kettles & Wine Beeds Looking Glasses; ribbans; Mohair Silk Cambricks . . Ons. thread—Hoes & Saddles; the best of the Goods I have on hands will soon meet Speedy Sales; When the white hunters & Indians &c Comes in who are Expected in this or the Next Month—I am Dailey Expecting 1400 Skins in the Hair already paid for in very secure hands Exclusive of what Smith of Tenchipo ows me who will soon Come to Discharge the same AGreeable to his Letter to me a few Days ago on that head; You'l be pleased to Specify in the Agreement; or Charter partley with the Cap[t]ain Who brings the Goods According to my Orders there to; that is to Carry back [?] to you the Skins which I will Ship on him freight free, which will save him the Cost & Trouble of Taking in Ballist for his Return; I formerly Advised you that Mr. John Campbell[10] would

---

9/Thomas Bentley came to West Florida from London and established a store at Manchac about 1765 or shortly thereafter. In the 1770s he moved to Kaskaskia and there managed a successful mercantile business. He probably died in Virginia in 1783. See Alvord, *The Illinois Country*, 321; Houck (ed.), *The Spanish Regime in Missouri*, I, 179; Alvord and Carter (eds.), *Cahokia Records, 1778–1790*, cix.

10/John Campbell, New Orleans merchant, was a native of Scotland, born about 1747. He was the owner of one of the "floating warehouses" seized by Gálvez on the Mississippi River at New Orleans in April, 1777, in an effort to end illicit commerce on the river, and also of the *Neptune*, seized by James Willing in 1778. In 1780 he was a resident of Manchac and served on its grand jury. See Caughey, *Bernardo de Gálvez in Louisiana*, 76, 119; Testimony of the Spanish process, 1778, PRO, CO 5/595, p. 334; Address of the Grand Jury of Manchac, November 15, 1780, PRO, CO 5/580, pp. 309–11.

pay me $4.6r this Currency which you will be kind Enough to procure; if not alrearddy Complyed with—I pray you not to Send me the Two hhds. Rum Mentioned in my Bill per Order Capt. Lum being a Coppy of that sent By Mr. Murray; for Upon Exammination I have yet of the last Had of you goG [?] all, which as the Consumtion how [now] is not much, will Be as Much as I Shall find Vent for this Year, perticularry as Mr. Bently has a Good Deal hear & can Always under Sell me—Mr. Monsanto has Likewise some so that it will not aneswer My purpost to Engage in any more at present. . . .

To JOHN RITSON, *Pensacola*

Manchac, February 22, 1771

You have here Inclosed John Bradleys Second of Exchange my favour on Messrs. Walker & Dawson Merchants in London for Ninety five pounds ten Shillings & five pence Sterling Exchange at 4/8 per Doller; is Ds. 409.3¼r this money payable at 60 Days Sight—the Amount of your Sales my Commissn. Being Dated is $413.6r so that there is S[t]ill Remaining due the Sales; $5.2¾ Which Mr. Gerome, will Give you in Cash as per his Receipt Altho I send you the Amount of Sales there is Still Outstanding $94.¼r; and What I have Receivd. is in Indian Corn; at 1 do. per Barrel; Sheled, and in Havana Sugr. at 10 Dollers per Hundred[.] Monsr. LaBlanc was to have paid in Good Indego—But as his Crop faild him Which Obliged me to take the fore Mentioned Corn—as I did the Sugar from Senior Don Barnard; please to let me know, whether these things Sell so as to pay the freight at your place; for Mr. Gerome Demands 1 Ds. per Barrel for Corn; & 2 Dollers per Hundred for the Sugar; if they will Bear to pay that freight Advise me by the first Oppertunity; and I will Send 200: Barrs. & 2000 lb. of Good Havana Suger—I hope are this comes to Hand you have Recivd. my last of the 9th Instant a Coppy of which you have Hear Inclosed with an Account of Sales; to this day; there is Still 35 pss. which I Shall Dispose of [to] the Best Advantage; as soon as Occasion offers—I am in great hopes that the Sterling bill will suit you Much Better than the Corn or the Sugar; and Mr. Bradley are this has Given you the letter of Advice, I am fully Assur'd that it will meet due honour; or if I had Not thought so Should not have Taken it; please to let me hear (if you have Any Nuse of Mr. Stephenson; and how he does, and when you Expect him Out aGain) I really thought to have Sent you the Ballance of your Acct. had I not been Disappointed; by

Sundry persons, but if the Corn or Sugar Will suit you they are at your Disposial when you think proper to send Me word; and they Shall be Shipped in Your Acct. per first Occasion; no More at present . . . (The Above not sent)

To JOHN RITSON, *Pensacola*

Manchac, March 6, 1771

you have here inclosed Mr. Bradleys Second of Exchange my favour on Messrs. Walker & Dawson; Merchants in London; for Ninety five Pounds Ten Shillings & five pince, Sterling Exchange at 4/8 per Doller; is $409.3¼r this money payable at Sixty days Sight the Amount of your sales is $413.6r Neat proceeds; So that there is Still Due the Sales $5.2¾ which S[h]all send you per Mr. Gerome; with a quantity of Indian Corn; if you will be pleased to dispose of it to the best advantage for my Acct.; and Credit my Account with the Neat prosseeds; there is Still Remains due your Sales $94.4r the Indego that I was to have for the Goods I did not Git; but was obliged to Take Corn; I shall wrote you more fully per Gerome whom I have Expected here this 40 Days. . . .

P.S. I hope are this comes to hand that you have Recivd. My last of the 9th Ulto. by Mr. Lum; a Copy of which you have inclosed with An Accot. of Sales to this Day, there is Still 36 ps. on hand which I Shall Dispose of to the best advantage, when Occasion offers, I make no Doubt but that Mr. Bradley are this has Given You the letter of Advice and that you have sent the funt to Mr. Stephenson [?] for Axceptation—I am fully Assurd it will meet his honour

To JOHN RITSON, *Pensacola*

Manchac, March 17, 1771

Since my last of the 6th Instant Monsr. Gerome, arrivd. here from the pount Coupee; and brought me 182½ Barlls. Indian Corn; which I promised to send you on my Acct. & Risque but he would not Take it as his Schooner Was so deep loaded; so that I was Deprived of the pleasure of Sending it to you, as I promised, as it wont dow to keep it long on hands, shall see if I can Sell it at Orleans; and send you the money per the first Conveyance, you have here Inclosed Mr. John Bradleys third of Exchange to serve in case of Need, as Likewise Capt. Geromes Receipt for the Ballance of your Sales to this day; if you Think that I Empose you may demand of Mr. Gerome who will Certify what I Say to be True; if you have any Nuse from Mr. Stephenson please to let me know how he does. . . .

To JOHN RITSON, *Pensacola*

New Orleans, April 20, 1771

You have here Inclosed Mr. Gradingo Receipt for $337.2r In Indego & Cash; of which their is $137.2r for the Ballance of your Acct. and the Other $200 are on Acct. of Mr. John Stephenson as Also 6 ps. printed linen that remains Unsold; as for what you mention in Your Letter of the 22 Jany. last Concerning Mr. Bradleys, paying Me $57.3½r I know Nothing of Any Such thing; all that I can say of the Matter is that Mr. Stephenson; left me an Order for $28.3½r for Which I Accounted with him for in my Acct. of the 28 Jany. 1769; if you can prove to me by the Coppy of your letter that ever you sent an Order on Mr. Bradley; I am Willen to pay you; but Neaver no such Order came to hand; as I can prove by your letters—so that I Cant be accountable to you for any thing I neaver got; nor Receivd.; their is still Some out Standing debts on Accot. of your last sales—for which I cant be Accountable for before I Receive them they are persons that are in Expectations; of paying me in a Short time; as they Expect Skins or Tobaco from the Nactosch Every day—As Soon as I Receive them Shall Remit them to you; as I have Not my papers here cant send You your Accot. Sales by this Occason; but Shall Send them per the first Conveyance, after my Arrival at Manchac —Having Nothing more to add for the present . . . P.S. Sent you 7 Dollers for 1 pss printed Linen No. 8.

To JOHN RITSON, *Pensacola*

Manchac, May 9, 1771

I had the pleasure of Writing you on the 20th Ulto. from New Orleans by Mr. Grandingo Inclosing you his Receipt for 6 ps. P. Linnens & 7 Dollers in Cash; for 1 ps. Linnen No. 8 sold as I was putting them up to remit to you, as Also aNother for a percel of Indego, Amountg to ps. 337.2r of which there is for you $137.2r and the other $200 for Mr. John Stephensons Accot. Which I hope are this is safely Come to hand—

You have here Inclosed Mr. Stephensons Account Current and

Account of Sales; by with [*i.e.*, which] you will see that their is still due the Sales $243.3r Which Shall Remit you as Soon as it is Receivd. but cant Advance money Before) I acquainted you on the 19th of Septr. 1769 per Monsr. Cavon; that I had Setled Mr. Stephenson's Affair with Messrs. Benvenu & Comy. on the 17th of Said Month; but did not Git cash in payment; but was Obliged to take Spanish bills in payment; for $340. and Sundry Other bills for $172.1½r Which latter Amount Mr. Ranson payed me for Indego as Mr. Gradingo Can Inform you) Should be Glad that you would let me hear when you sent Me an order for Your Acct. on Mr. Bradley to recover money for you; for My part I am Un Acquainted with any such a thing; all the Orders I ever Had Either from you or Mr. Stephenson was one of $28.3½r that the latter left me and for which I Accounted for in my Accot. Given in Once 28th Jany. 1769

Mr. Harrison[11] whome Mr. Bradley has left here with care of his Bussiness and Books; can prove what I say to be the Truth; dont be Uneasy on Account of your outstanding Debts; as they lay in the hands of Honnest men; and as Soon as they are Recovered Shall remit you them by the first oppertunity—had your letter of 22 Jany. last come to hand sooner Should have sent you all the linnens that Remaind Unsold 20th Feby. last According to Account Sales sent you per Mr. Gerome; but it came to hand only On the 12 Ulto. per Mr. Blanchard—I hope you will favour me with a letter by the first oppertunity for New Orleans or this place, as I neaver have heard from you since I sent you Mr. Bradleys Bill of Exchange; and Wheather or no he gave you the letter of Advice as he promised me hear—Your Complyance in Wrighting by the first Occation will Greatly Oblige . . .

To EDWARD MESS

Manchac, June 6, 1771

I have taken the liberty of Drawing on you; for the Amount of your Accot. Being $33.7r (this money) for Sundrys Furnished Samuel Lewis According to your Order, to me from the Natchez; relative thereunto; I should not have Troubled you for so Small a Triffle had it not; been for the great want of cash that is hear at present—

Shall your men Stand in Need of any More provision, shall supply them on Demand; if you have any thing as are With you Relative to the Ware; Should be much Obliged to you if you will favour me with a few lines; You will Greatly Oblige . . .

11/George Harrison, Manchac merchant, signed a petition to the West Florida Council in March, 1772, protesting the behavior of Lieutenant John Thomas (see Introduction, p. 18). Harrison was killed in a fight with Thomas later that year. See PRO, CO 5/579, pp. 55–60, 241–45.

To McGILLIVRAY AND STRUTHERS, Mobile

Manchac, July 11, 1771

I have now before me your Esteemd favours of the 7 March the 17th 24th of April and the 18th May and Note well their Contents; as for the Letter per Monsr. Favour; it neaver came to hand[.] I have Spoke to Matthews about paying the $50 that you Mention in Your letter, he offerd me Cattle for the Same; and toald me at the Same Time that he had Nothing Elce for the present; but, that in the faul he would pay to me part if not the Hole; and as there is Nothing Elce to lay hold off; has given him till then to pay it;

I observe what you Mention in Yours of the 17th April concerning the difference in the Weight of my Skins per Mr. Gerome to be 212 lb. on the whole altho the Number of Skins Exceeded what was Mentioned in the Invoice 22 Skins—for which I cant Account for Altho I belive it, to be owing to my Stillards—I am Greatly Obliged to you for the price you ware pleased to Allow me for the Skins At that Season of the year; and Shall always Acknowledge it as such; but at the sam[e] Time you will please to Observe that if you had not ordered me by your advices At Sundry Times to send them by Gerome; that you would not have lost the Oppertunity of Sending them to England; I would not have lost in the price of them $201; but as Your Orders; ware Such thought it the most Advisable to follow them—I Shall take the Greatest Care with Regard to the large Bucks that lays in my power; and Shall not take but as few as I can; with Out they are with Other Skins; in Such Casses Shall be Obliged to take them As they come; but as for Disposing of them at any Other Market then at Your place or pensacola is a thing I Cant Comply with—

I Receivd. in Good Order (Excepting Some Blankets) the Sundrys Sent me per the Sloop Dolphin; but am sorry to find that the Blankets are not so good As they ware last Year; Altho the price is Still the Same; I have Credited Your Acct. Current with the Amount of the Invoice per the Dolphin and the Goods bought of Mr. Struthers Being in all $3818.9¼r Your Money—for the Reumbursment of which I shall Use all proper Measuers that lays in my power that the Remittance Shall be made in proper time

I Remited You by the Sloop Dolphin; 490 Deer Skins in the hair Weight 1249 lb. and 439 Drest hides; Wt. 942 lb. which I hope are now Are Safe Arrived—I would be much Obliged to you if you wou'd Send me by the first Oppertunity my last years Acct. Including in the Same Time; the things Bush had on my Accot. at the Common Advice. . . .

P.S. I paid Mr. Struthers my part of the freight and $40. on Acct. of the Housse's Sales—and possible shall remitt the Remainder of Yours and Capn. McMains Out Standing Debts this faul—

To McGILLIVRAY AND STRUTHERS, *Mobile*

Manchac, July 25, 1771

Since Writing You my last of the 11th Instant a Coppy of Which you have Anexed) I have had Occasion to Open the 8/4 Bed Blanks. And found One of them quite Damaged & Unsaiable; which I promise You Neaver hapned Since in my possession; I Omited Mentioning in My last, that Mr. Artr. Struthurs was please to promise me that the 50 pCt. on the Old Trunks that my Goods Came in Should be Taken off; When any Occasion; for this place or New Orleans Offers; You will please to send me my last years Acct.; and let me hear how my last Skins Turnd out. . . .

P.S. I have Got since I came from New Orleans 640 Good Skins in the Hair—and Dailey Expecting More—

To HENRY LEFLEUR, *Natchez*

Manchac, July 29, 1771

You have here Inclosed Your Accot. Current Amounting in all to $168.6½r; of Which there is a ballance that Remains Due me of $62.5¾—Which I hope you will Endeavour to pay sooner than you have Dun in former Dealings; I am sorry that I Cant Comply with your Demand; of Goods as you are Senciable you Wrote for a large Amount, had You Come your Self; you might had Something More; But with out having proper Security I cant let so much Goods Go;—as for the partnership that I spoak to you about it cant take place as I have a Great Oppertunity of Selling here for Cash in hand—but at the same time if you think proper to come your Self; I will let you have Two Hundred Dollers worth of Goods At a time; and When you have payed for them; you may have as many more; So to trade on your own Acct. and Risque— you may Depend; it will be the Best way both for Your Intersest and my own; As I promise You; You shall Always have goods from me; As Cheap as I can possible let them go; and then You will have no Acct. to render to no one but your self; as for your Skins I have paid you as much as I could afford; Seeing that they ware Drest with oil And I must git them all done over aGain—

Your Illinois leather I have paid You the price it sells for in town; where they Git french Weight, which is 8½ lb. in hundred More than ours; I have sent Madm. Leflour 6 Coffee Cups 2 lb. Coffee for her Butter; and at the same time humbly thanks her. you Will please to let me hear from you; by the first Oppertunity; and let Me know if you will Except of my proposals. . . .

P.S. I will Sell your Elk skins for your Acct. As I take none of them—

To BAYNTON, WHARTON AND COMPANY, *Illinois*

Manchac, August 7, 1771

I have Shipped on board Monsr. Moranic'es Bataux Sundrys as per Invoice here Inclosed Amounting to $99.5¾r on your Account And Risque; as per order from your Mr. George Morgan—Should have Consignd them to Engenear Hutchins;[12] but heard Since Mr. Morgan left this that Sd. Hutchins has left the Illinois; I have Sold 24 Barrels of your flower at $3½ per Cent [hundredweight] that being the most I could Git; by Reason of the large quantity Lately Come down from your place; I am sorey to Acquaint you that it was Not in my power to Comply with your Instructions in Regard of sending up Your Barge; with the Loading You Required; Cash being so mighty Scarse Hear at present & the Remittance that I am Obliged to make this fall to mobile put it out of my power for the present; as Soon as Your sales are finished; Shall Remitt the Ballance with the Account of Sales there of; in the mean time Should be Glad to hear from you; and let me know wheather you will have the Ballance Sent you in Cash or Merchandize;—Should You have any thing that Requiers my Assistance in this part of the Country Should be always Glad to serve you. . . .

To McGILLIVRAY AND STRUTHERS, *Mobile*

Manchac, August 14, 1771

The fore Going is a Coppy of mine of the 25th Ulto. Since which I have been favoured with yours of the 3d & 26th Ulto. Inclosing my Account Current which I have now before me; and note the Contents; I find on Examination that their is some Errors or Amissions in my Credit; a Note of part of them You have here inclosed; and the others Shall Advise you of as Soon as I have

{109
1770–1775

12/Thomas Hutchins was born in Monmouth County, New Jersey, in 1730 and entered the British army in 1756. He spent several years as an officer of the first British garrison in the Ohio Valley, where he worked as a quartermaster and engineer, and was employed in exploring and charting that area, the country around Lake Michigan, and the Illinois country. He came to West Florida first in 1766, when he explored and charted the Gulf Coast and the Mississippi River, and returned in 1772, when he was assigned as an engineer at the fort in Pensacola. During this time Hutchins produced numerous maps of the West Florida area and detailed reports on the Spanish defenses in Louisiana. He also acquired considerable holdings of land in West Florida, including 2000 acres near Natchez, near the holdings of his brother Anthony, 2000 acres on Bayou Sara, 2000 acres on the Comite River, and 600 acres on the Homochitto River. He left America for London in 1776 to arrange for the publication of his geographic studies, which occurred in 1778, and returned in 1781, when he was appointed "Geographer of the United States." He continued his exploration, charting and writing until his death in 1789. Thomas Hutchins never married, but he left a will acknowledging three illegitimate children, one of whom, Margaret Hutchins, was living at Manchac in 1774. Hutchins' study of West Florida, *An Historical Narrative and Topographical Description of Louisiana, and West-Florida*, first published in Philadelphia in 1784, is one of the most important contemporary

Examined the Low Account (if any) I Observe that you have Credited my Acct. with the 50 pCt. that was Charged me on the Trunks; for which I am much Obliged to you for; I Shall Always be Glad to Come to a Settlemt. as you propose once a Year; as by that Means Shall Always know how I am; and think, it far the best way both for your Interest & mine; I find You have made No Difference in my last years Skins & this Years—But as that is a matter of no Consequnce and all to the Same as if in Different Accots.—John Francis is not here at present, it will be the Spring are he Comes Down; and then Make no doubt of his paying the Amount of his Accot.; As I have Reason to believe I Shall have his Skins & Shall Stop it in my hands; as likewise the Amount of Mr. McIntosh And Co. Accot. which I beg You will be pleased to Accquaint them of My intention on that head....

P.S. I Still keep in gitting some Skins—

To McGILLIVRAY AND STRUTHERS, Mobile

Manchac, September 22, 1771

—the above is a Coppy of mine of the 14th Ulto.; Since Which I have receivd. Yours of the 14th and the Original of yours 3d July Inclosing; John Francis Acct. Which when he is here Shall Act the Needfull if in my power;—Since Writing my last there is nothing New Occurd; only that the Sale of my Welling Goods is Mighty Slow; But hope they will soon be in Damand; as hear is the Winter Comming In; I have now about 12 or 1300 Skins Mestly all Red; and am in hopes are long to have a larger Quantity; Which propose Carr[y]ing with all That I Shall be able to git betwen this and the latter End of Deccemr. Insuing to Monsr. Ranson's plantation; Below the Town of New Orleans; to be ready to send by the first Oppertunity that may Offer for Your place; or to be Delivered to your order if your Slo[o]p Comes into the Mississippi; so as yt. you may not meet with such a Disappointment as that of last year in not sending home the Skins—having Nothing more to add for the present...

P.S. if you approve of my Carring My Skins to Monsr. Ranson's planta[tion] Please to Acquaint me in Your Next—

To PETER SWANSON, Mobile

Manchac, September 22, 1771

I had the pleasure of Wrighting you the 14th Ulto. to which Refer; since there is tuo french Gentlemen, that wrote me Concern-

---

descriptions of British colonial Florida. See Hutchins, *An Historical Narrative*, Introduction by Joseph G. Tregle; Anna Margaret Quattrocchi, "Thomas Hutchins, 1730–1789" (Ph.D. dissertation, University of Pittsburgh, 1944).

ing Some runaway Slaves that they have About your place the one; is Monsr. Trenonay; that lives at point Coupie; he has 2 Negro man Has Run away from his plantation some time aGo; which he has been Informed keeps about Mr. John Murrays plantation with his Negros Or at least they has been Seen there Some Time ago; he says he dont Value What Expencess there may Arrise for having them taken and well Secure'd; with Irons &c, and that they may be sent by the first opperturny, to the Adress of Monsr. Bonrepaux in New Orleans; who has orders from the Said Monsr. Trenonay to pay on Demand all the Expencess that may Arrise for the taking the said Two Negroes; their provisions Irons passage &c; to New Orleans—the Other is one Monsr. Daniel fagot that has been a french Officer here to fore; and is now at the Illinois; a Gentleman that Used me with the Greatest politeness when the Indians Gave me up at the Iillinois in 1764; I have neaver had it in my power to Return them since; but by this Occation and your Interest (if it is possible to git him his Molato man that run away from the Illinois about 21 months aGo) And is now in the Chicasaw Nation; with some of the Traders; if they have Been at any Expence in Giting him from the Indians (as is Generally the Case) he is very Willing to Reumburs and pay all Charges that may Attend (if it is possible to git him from the Nation) You will please to send him by the first Conveyance to the Address of Monsr. Pierre freenier Obiere Regidor & all Paid) at new Orleans; who has Orders from his Master the Said Monsr. Daniel fagot; to pay all the Expencess it may Cost in sending him there) And to prove that the Molato is his property you have here Inclosed; a Curtificate to that purpose Discribing his name and marks &c—

Now Sir; if you Can be of any Service to Either of these Gentlemen in halping them to Recover there property; with out putting your self to too much trouble; You will Greatly Oblige Sir . . .

To McGILLIVRAY AND STRUTHERS, *Mobile*

Manchac, October 9, 1771

I had the pleasure of Writing you the 22d Ulto. Since Which I have been favoured with yours of the 7th last March; Inclosing Sundry Accounts aGaint one Conner & Mathews; the former is not hear Nor hant Been these some Months past; he keeps with the Indians about the Grand Gulph above the fort Natchez; so as there is no such thing As my seeing him; and if I did I am Affraid it would be to no purpose As he hant where with to git him self a Shirt; as for the latter he is hard At work a Making pickets & Staves to carry to Orleans to see to pay off this faul; if possible; as his Crop of Corn has failed him by Reason of the Bad Weather & high Winds; that has been in this part this year;

I Acquaintd. you in my last of having 12 or 13 hundred Skins But as I have Augmented the Number; the present is to let you know that I have in House at present 2228 Good Skins of which there is About five Hundred that I have had Dressed; and am in Great hopes of Soon Adding Some hundreds more to them that are already paid for; and in Good hands—I have neaver had the pleasure of Receiving an Answer to any of my Letters since I Recivd. the last goods; there fore Should be Much Obliged to you if you will favour me with a few lines....

To McGILLIVRAY AND STRUTHERS, *Mobile*

Manchac, November 9, 1771

Since Writing you my last of the 9th Ulto. I am favoured. With yours of the 28th Septr. which came to hand the 3d Instant and Note the Contents; well; Inclosing Accts. AGaints Monsr. Perring & Henry Leflour[.] I am Sorry that the former has Imposed so much on Mr. Walch; for he is a Mighty great roge and has been been [*sic*] Guilty of a Roberry at the Illinois; he and his Companions; have robbed a man in that Country of Near $3000 Worth of Skins; and Six Indian Slaves; and I make no manner of Doubt But his Excellency Goverr. Chester;[13] has been are now made Acquainted With there Being at the English Natchez; With the Skins and furrs; for it is above 2 Mon. Since I saw the English & Spanish Commanders of the Illinois orders for taking them up; if found on Either Side of the River for said Roberry; but as Leflour is Bound for the paymt. As well as Permigs have Wrote him about Sending it Down; he is [not] as Yeat Returnd to the Natchez, as I have been Informed By the Arrival of Capt. Thomas, that Came thence 2 Days ago; I am Truly obliged to you; for your kind Offer of Sending of sending [*sic*] me a New Supply of Goods (if in Want of them) but as I have of the last Cargo; Cargo [*sic*] more than I Can Dispose of; this some Time to Come; and as I would Not Chuse to demand Any thing More; till all old Accots. are paid off; I expect to send you by the first Conveyance after the 26th & 18 Next moth. 3000 Good Skins or more; of them I have now in the House; 2516 of Which I have; Upwards of 600 Drest Skins; and am Dailey in Expectation of 4 or 5 Hundred Skins that are Already payed for;—in stead of my Being paid the $4 that Wm. Bush; owe the House; on Settlemt. he Owed me; $24 and as he had No Other way of paying than by Going a hunting; I fitted him Out; so that at present his Accot. with me is; $77.4r, all Which I am Well Assurd will be paid When he Comes Down; I have heard from him not long ago; and he had then 170 Deer Skins and Some Beaver, he wont be Down; Untill the Spring; as he proposses hunting After Oyl;—as it is a thing almost Emposible for Me to leave this my self, till all the hunters are Come down—I Cant think of Going to your place till next may or June; and then Am termed for Your place—and hope to Carry with me where with Either in Cash or Skins to pay off my Account; the Ballance of; to your Satisfaction; and as you are at present Acquainted with the Goods that Is proper for this place; hope that you will keep me a proper Assortmt, With Cotton Cards that You have Already Receivd.; and in the mean Time Should be verry much Obliged to you; if you would Settle with Capt. McMain; for the Remainder part of his Sales, at the same Time Observing to Expect Monsr. Veniens the Watch Maker Debt of $24 Ds. as he has left this Country and is gone to new York I Wrote to Mr. John Riston of Pansacola to recover it for me; but Said Venien, did not pay it as Riston has Informd. me by his letter So that it is left I dont think that I ought to bear it—I have had the feavour this 24 Days past But thanks be to god I am Gitting the Better of it; having Nothing more to add . . .

P.S. When Your Blankets Comes in if they are not of a Better Quality than the last; I had reather you woud not keep any of them for me; for that them that I have at present wont bring me; hardley 25 pCt. more than What they Cost me;—

To McGILLIVRAY AND STRUTHERS, *Mobile*

Manchac, November 20, 1771

I had the pleasure of Writeing you the 9th Inst. per Via New Orleans; and a Coppy of which you have here inclosd. to Which refer;) Since which I have been favoured With yours of the 26th Ulto. and a Coppy of that of the 28th Septemr Last; and Note well the Contents Notifing that the Sundry Omissions; Mentioned of mine of the 14th August; had been Rectified; As for Mr. Williams asure [?] as He is not Going Back to Pansacolo this some Time to come but is a Coming up the River to this place, Shall Settle it with him—Either By Gitting the Money or an Order; for it on Mr. John Miller;—Leflour; is not as Yet returnd. to the Natchez; as I have heard; by a boat that came from; thence this

Morning But as Soon as I have Intelligence of his Arriva[l] S[h]all Write You; (as I have Already done) to bring down the paymt. of his Note and Acct. I have receivd. a few Skins Since my last aBout 4 or 500 that Expected are not Come in—We have Nothing Strange here only That the Indians are Coming in & Receiving there presents having Nothing to add . . .

P.S. I omited to Mention in my last to Mr. William Struthers about the Birds Caulled popes; there is none of them at this Season of the year; But in the Spring I will send him a Doz: of them—

To PETER SWANSON, *Mobile*

Manchac, November 20, 1771

I am favoured with Yours of the 26th Ulto. and note Well the Contents I am sorry to find by Yours that the 2 Hdds. of Wine are quite lost and that they have Given you so much trouble; But as the wine has lost Its Quality I am in hopes it will make good Vineger; Which is Mighty Saleable in this parts so Shall Bring it up with me when I go Down—to your place;—as for the Sales of the Tobaco it is no meterial point when the Sales are Clousd as the Amount will Still remain in the hands of the Gentlemen; of the house) Being Always Intended for that Use—In the mean Time am very much obliged to you for your kind offer of service; and if ever I have it in my power Shall most Greatfully Acknowledge them in the Entrame if there is any thing Where in [I can] Be of any Service to you in this parts should be Glad of an oppertuny. to prove how much I am . . .

To McGILLIVRAY AND STRUTHERS, *Mobile*

Manchac, [December] 11, 1771

The fore Going is a Coppy of mine of the 20th Ulto. Since when then I had not the pleasure of receiving any of yours informed You of the 9th Ulto. of having at, that time 2516 Good skins but at present I have the plasure of Acquainting you that I have 3206 now in the House Which I am apacking up with all Expedition with A determination to Leave this place with them Sd. Skins by the 28th of the present or the 3d Or 4th of the Ensuing month; at the farthest and am in hopes are I leave This to add to the above 4 or 500 or may bee 1000 Which are already paid for) I shall do all that lies in my power that You may not Meet with the like Disappointmt. in sending home the Skins as You Did last

Year; Which was a Determt. to Your Interest and mine thinking it the most Advisable; I send You here Inclosed A memorandum of the things I Shall want next Spring after all old Accots. Is Settled, there fore would be much obliged to you to Reserve for me;—Where as it is Out of my power to go Down; Untill Spring upon Acct. of Out Standing Debts among Hunters and Others; as I Shall Stand in Need of some Trifling things make out an Assortment against the Spring or the Arivel of the hunters; would be much Obliged to you; to send me by the first Oppertunity Directed to the Care of Mr. Ranson in New Orleans 2 ps. blue Strouds 100 lb. Good Gun powder; in 25 bags 12 felt Hats No. 9 and 10 and 20 Blue Stript Duffils if they are any thing larger than them I had last; for with them it is Imposible to make a Blankett Coat for a man; You have here Inclosed Mr. William's order $26: Which When Receivd. please to place to my Credit. . . .

To McGILLIVRAY AND STRUTHERS, Mobile

New Orleans, March 8, 1772

I Arrivd. here Yesterday; had 9 Days passage; no Accot. of Cap. Gerome; its probable he may be at the Balize Wind bound; if so Mr. Miller who parted him the 4th Cunt. will Doubtless advise y there of Also that his Capt. would not take the skins for freight only for pensacola, which Ranson would not adher to my Orders to him being for your part where by to Satisfie your selves; of their Qualitys before Shipped for London; am Extreamly sorry for the Disappointmt. no reamedy but Patience; they will be sent per the first conveyance; Capt. Gerome or any Other offering there are 7 or 8 packs which Mr. Ranson receivd. in my Absence Could have had a Greater Quantity; but prevented by Capn. Thomas's Unjustifiable proceedings since my Departure which youl partly see by a Coppy of a paragraph from Mr. Kelleys Letters Inclosed in Mr. Frenche's Leter to me per Mr. Miller for your peresual—[14]

Mr. Thomas Seems to pay you no more attention then to me; having DeClaired to Mr. Kelley that if in Case you Espoused my Cause would by Two lines make your house Trimble which Accumulates his Absurdity And Depraved Enimity to me perticularly as he Ignors not my Connictions with You; therefore flatter my Self your Assistance & Assiduity Will not be Wanting in Conjunction with me to procure proper redres Before John Stewart Esqr.[15] parts the province; Uneasy to know how my Affairs Stands Effected at Manchac am Determined to sale of the 11th

{115
1770–1775

14/For a discussion of the Lieutenant Thomas affair, see Introduction to this volume, pp. 16–18.

15/John Stuart was born in Inverness, Scotland, in 1718 of a reputable burgher family. After early training in business, he entered the Royal Navy in 1740 and saw active service during the War of Jenkins' Ear. In 1748 Stuart went to South Carolina as a partner in a mercantile firm, which soon failed. He held a number of local offices and in 1756 began a career as a frontier military officer. His superior abilities in Indian diplomacy led to his appointment as Superintendent of Indian Affairs for the Southern Department in 1762. Because the management of Indian affairs affected so many aspects of colonial life, this office was one of the most important in the imperial hierarchy. When the American Revolution began, Stuart remained loyal to Britain. In 1775 he fled Charleston to Florida where he continued the management of Indian affairs from St. Augustine and, after 1776, from Pensacola. He died there in March, 1779. For a full account of Stuart's life and career, see Alden, *John Stuart and the Southern Colonial Frontier*.

Instant from whence shall write you more at large for further Govermt. relative to the present matter in question—and shall Leve the Necessary Dispossisions with freinds here to forward me [?] the Goods on Capt. Geromes Arrival; who You know had Nothing to Detain his voyage to this river; agreeable to Agreement wind & Weather permitting; Mr. French prays his Compliments to you ...

To PHILIP LIVINGSTON, JUNIOR, *Pensacola*[16]

New Orleans, March 9, 1772

I have Used proper Deligence to come at the Aritcels [articles] of your Memorandum; but sorry to tell you none to be had at present Except the 3 Barrels best St. marys Wine—Which have bought to be sent You per first Safe Conveyance; no good Clarrit to be had Untill Monsr. Ransons Vessell Arrives from the Cape; which is Daily Expected; than Shall procure one of the best [hogs]heads; on Board being my perticular friend who will forward it Cearfully to you; togeather; with a Case of Olives Capes oil & an cloves; and in Case of my Departure from hence Before the Arivel of Sd. Vessell; also the Buffollow Blankets & painted Deer Skin; if any should here After Come As probable may from Nacatoche; there Amount will Settle with you at Meeting for—When to Arive at Manchac I will in Corse Advise you of Mr. Thomas's proceedings during my Absence; for your province or Governmt. in Acting the Needfull Judiciously my favour if Accations Requirs Engageing some Time Mr. Morrices Assistance Jointly with You; if Necessary; Interim, do pray your Cerumspaction & Viligence, in Any thing Elce; Unknown to me at present, Which he might Write to the Governor; &c to my prejudice; as he Declard to severals would Use his Utmost Endeavours to oversell me by any means, possible in his power. ...

P.S. One of the Barrs. of Wine is for Mr. McCoullough; my Intire Confidence is reposed in you to Extricate me from the Depraved Attempt of Thomas for Your Governmt. to be Vigilent there in—

To PETER SWANSON, *Mobile*

New Orleans, March 11, 1772

On my Arrival here have presented your Order on Monsr. Burgar; could by no perswations reduce him to payment Untill his noat

16/Philip Livingston, Jr., related to the Livingston family of New York, came to West Florida in 1771 as Governor Chester's secretary and was given the title of "deputy provincial secretary." Under Chester's patronage he became an important personage in the province, was appointed a member of the council and receiver general, and held several other offices. Livingston also acquired large tracts of land and by 1778 may have held as much as one hundred thousand acres. See Johnson, "Expansion in West Florida," 489; Johnson, *British West Florida*, 130.

Appeared; that when it does his Immediate Compliance there to will not be Wanting; the Same Day arrd. from point Coupie one [?] Butler by Whom Mrs. McIntosh Sent Said Note; which I demanded of him (as your property) in Vertue of the fore mentioned Order; Which I likewise Shewd. him in presence of Mr. Lafite; all to no purpose; absolutely refusing Delivering it to me; in Consequence of which I obtain Mons. Burgars promise not to pay him; nor any Other person untill I proceeded for his Government Mr. McIntosh's determination there on; which shall Solicet after my Arivel at Manchac—this day I set off; my Acting in this manr. I hope will meet your Approbation; as I hold it the Most ready Meathod your being reumbursed there of—

Mr. Thomas Deputized Mr. McIntosh his Constable which Commision he Admited of to Search my house for Wine and Rum; by what protext I know not but his Attempt was frustrated by my people in not Delivering him the Keys of the Store —Mr. French prays his Compliments to You; and am With due Esteem . . .

To JEAN BAPTISTE SARPY, St. Louis

Manchac, March 26, 1772

In Answer to yours of the 17th Novemr. 1771 that Came safely to hand; and note well its Contents; I am in hopes (on Mr. Barrows Acct.) that you will not fail in fulfilling the promise that You gave me in Your Letter; sending Down what skins you have Got in the month next July; or sooner if possible; and if there is Nothing to be had (which I cant beleive) You will send me all the Bills & Accounts; that you have belonging to Mr. Barrow; that I may have it in my power to oblige Maxant to Come to a Settlemt—

You have here Inclosed Monsr. Dubriuel['s] Bill on his Brother for £2750 Which I nor Monsr. Ranson could neaver make pay; he alledging that he had no founds [funds] of his Brothers in his hands; and more that he Would not Advance a farthing on his Accot.; Monsr. Peeraut; offered Me a percel of Spanish & french; Bills or Bons to the Amount off £1900 But I would not Except [accept] thim; Knowing them to be Nothing More than Immagenery Coyn; therefore have Declined having any thing to do with them —on Mr. Barrows; Accot. for I promise You that Mr. Barrow, has been Laying a long time out of his Money; and if I Take the Bills he Might lay a Great deal Longer; this being the Needfull for the present. . . .

{118
Merchant of Manchac

To CHARLES STUART, *Mobile*

Manchac, May 5, 1772

By Orders of the Honourable John Stuart Esqr. I receivd. from Mr. John Thomas; the Goods Mentioned in the Inclosed list signed by the latter; to be held at your Disposial; which I will Observe when to have your Orders there to; you have also Inclosed the Inter Peter Laflours receipt for necessaries which he requested me to give him for his Voyage to the Aleanzas or Cappas[17] to facelatate said Voyage—I was Obliged to wait on the Commanding Monsr. DuCaudraux[18] at Spanish Manchac for a passport for Leflour which he Granted on his Gitting a Coppy of the letter Wrote by Said John S[t]uart Esqr. to Said Leflour; Translated into French; Other wise would not Grant it with out having the Governor of New Orleans Orders for so doing which would Delay his proceeding timely[.] I Suppose before this comes to hand you will here of Mr. Thoma's killing Mr. Harrison in the House built by Mr. Bradley Betwen the hour of 8 or 9 o clock at Night on the 22d of last Month; the Indego Machine which I promised to send Mr. John Stuart Esqr. was Defective which the maker Toald off; & Desired to let him have it in order to Compleat it in a propr. Manner, for the Intended purpose and as soon as finished I'll send it you per the first Ensuing Conveyance. . . .

To JOHN MILLER, *Pensacola*[19]

Manchac, May 5, 1772

I receivd. your Esteemed favour of the 5th Ulto. and note its Contents, am informd. Capt. Gerome Arived in the river 6 days ago. I'll Sett off for Orleans the 7th Instant as to the Average aCrewing cant Advise you there of Untill the Goods are Examined; the Skins I will send by Antonios Schooner; if She Can take them all in no Oppertunity hither to; offered; You will Doubtless hear from Mr. Jones who parted this some Time past of Harrison's Unhappy end killed by Mr. Thoma's; the nues papers you sent him neer Came to my hands, the place at that time Being all in Confusion; which I hope will be hince forward Remeded—Please to tell Mr. William Swanson that I got his suord repair which Cost $3 and shall send it per Antonios Schooner to be Delivered to his Brother; am Much Obliged to you for your good Wishes & Desire of Contributing towards; my wellfare; & may be Assured of my Inclinations Equally Reciprocall to you. . . .

17/The Quapaw Indians of the Arkansas nation were a Siouan tribe living along the Arkansas River.

18/Captain Charles Descoudreaux was appointed commandant at the Spanish fort San Gabriel de Manchack in 1771, where he served for two years. Perhaps French-born, he had previously commanded the garrison at the Balize. See Faye, "The Arkansas Post," 630.

19/Pensacola merchant, partner in the London firm of Swanson and Miller, and member of the West Florida Provincial Council.

To McGILLIVRAY AND STRUTHERS, Mobile

New Orleans, May 13, 1772

The above is a Coppy of Last to you to which referr; Since I am favoured with both yours 20th March & 7 Ulto. whose Contents I Note; the want of an Oppertunity of Shipping the Skins hitherto gives Me Vast Concern; as well for your sakes as my own; tho no fault of mine As I had not in my power to remidy it; but had you sent your sloop at the Time Mentioned in Your former; the Skins in all likely hood Would arive timely winds & Weather permitting) for the Chester; to take them in being as I toald you; they ware at Mr. Ransons plantation Since the 14th of last Jany. Waiting for an Occasion to be Shipped but as I Apprehend you will find it two late to Ship them on Capt. Vaughn who is now ready to sail; youl in Such case allow me the price which you think Most acquittable; AGreeable to your Usial Goodness CreDiting me there With the Quantity as per Bill Lading herewith being 92 Packs in the hair And Dressed Containing 4548 Skins Which is 589 less then the Number Mentioned in my last; as Accasioned by the Afore Sd. Disappointmt. of the persons who promised faithfully to bring them long are now; and paid for these 6 Months past my only Consolation for the same is that they are Sure people—Inclosed You have the Coppies Against Leflour and his Accot. which I Setled With Thomas if any Error Appears please to advise me there of; you,l see by the fore going the manner of his paymt. Which was all I could then Obtain; or Elce let him proceed prisoner to; Panacola [Pensacola]; You may be Assurd I Acted With the same Integrity to your Interest as if it had been my Own; Since the Settlemt. of the Above; I receivd. from Mr. Thomas $63.6r in part paymt. his fore Mentioned Note which Would have sent you Now but that Mr. Thomas promised he would Endear. to pay me the Ballance on my return to manchac; you have herein; like Wise goes Henry Smyths order for $173; on Mr. Daniel Ward with a Letter of Advice, there of which if Accepted & paid youl place to my Credt. But if Should not meet Compliance send it me per the first Conveyance that I may procure pay ment Otherwise;—

Capt. Gerome arrived here the 4th Instant; and my self from Manchac the 19th the Average is not so much as I apprehinded; but on a Naverage; Will be I believe about 8 or 10 pCent; the Chiefest part of all the Good ware Wett; and After wards Dryed; which will lessen there Value in the sale there of; and remain the longer on hands; the same must bear with Patience; as it would have been ours if all ware lost; the powder & some other Trifling

Articels receivd. no Damage one Cask of the rum Entirely lost; I cant be quite Certain of the Damage; Untill all are Examined on Arrivel at Manchac; which will be in presence of Capt. Gerome; as he goes up With me; the Schooner in Which said goods Came in Would not Take Above 50 packs being very small; besides hur upper parts and Deck is so lakey could by no means Venture the Skins in her; as they would be all Wett & Damaged; the first Rain &c; Which is always to be Apprehended may offer before to Arive at your part; there fore meeting with no Other oppertunity and the hott weather Comeing apace; Also the Danger of the Worms; I Determined to send them by Capt. Vaughn Consigned to Messrs. John Miller & Comy. who am perswaded will Take the Necessary care in Gitting them Beat on Arivel; and Advise you there of to be held at your Disposial AGreeable to my Orders $147 which I likewise remitt them as per the Inclosed recpt. to be sent you by a sure hand; Seventy Dollers of Said money is the freight of the Said Goods per Capt. Gerome; the remaining part 77 Dols. the Cash receivd. of Mr. Thomas Accot. of Leflour; as per Abstract; here with the Tobaco mentiond in Said Abstract I will send by Antoneys; the Oyl is not yet sold the town Is Glutted when sold Shall remit you the Amount—an Edict is to be published hear in a few Days prohibiting the Wearing of any Callicoes; Stampt linens Muslins &c; Under Sevear pennelltys; to any of the Spanish Inhabitants thay [that] may hence forward buy any from foreigners parts for their own Use or Other Wise.[20]...

To JOHN MILLER AND COMPANY, Pensacola

New Orleans, May 13, 1772

I referr you to my last of the 5th Instant; the Vessell that Brought my Goods Could not Take in above 50 packs of Skins being two Small besides hur upper Works & Deck quite leakey; that I would by no Means Venture to Ship the Skins on her as they Could not aVoid Gitting wett & Damaged by the rain &c; Which may be well Expected before to Arive at her Distined Port; there fore Metting no Other Oppertunity, and the hot weather Approaching Also; the Dangers of the worms, I am Determined to sind them by Capt. John Vaughn Consigned to you as per receipt here With in being 92 Packs Containing 45 Hundred & 48 Skins Indian Dressed and in the hair which you will be pleased to freight and hold them at Messrs. McGillivary & Struthers Disposial giving them Timely Notice there of; as you will als[o] be pleased Immediately After their Arivel; to open all thei packs and them Well

[20]/One of the measures taken by the government of Carlos III to reform Spanish colonial commerce, this edict struck particularly hard at the English cotton industry. See Clark, *New Orleans, 1718–1812*, 171.

beat as Customery for fear of the Worms which this hott Weather will OcCation; and any Expencess you are at I will make it good to your Order;—the average On the Goods is not as much as I Expected tho I cant be quite Certain how Much untill they are Exammined on my Arivel at Manchac in presence of Capt. Gerome he goes up with me; in Case I can have any recourse against him & poles Russon. . . .

N.B. Capt. Vaughn will Also Deliver You $147 Which youl be pleased to Remit Messrs. McGillivary & Struthers by some sure hand—

To EVAN AND JAMES JONES AND COMPANY, *Pensacola*[21]

New Orleans, May 13, 1772

I Receivd. from Mr. Macnamara forty Seven Barrs. of flour some of Which not well nriditroud [?] Caused by the Badness of the casks; which I will Endeavour to Dispose off to the best advantage your Accot. and When Vended; Shall in Corse advise you there off—As to what your James Jones Spoak to me off relative to the Goods you have from New York; I Cannot give the least Encouragemt. to you,r Sending any at present; as an Edict Is to be published in a few days hence prohibting all kinds of Cottons to be Imported nor wore by the Spanards on no protext Whatsoever; under severe penaltys to any Transgresser—

Please to let me know by the first oppertunity if I am or not to Buy the Cattle You spoak to me off Your Acct. and if Capt. Canty Is to take take [*sic*] them; in Case, of their Being Bought. . . .

To McGILLIVRAY AND STRUTHERS, *Mobile*

Manchac, June 5, 1772

I Referr, you to my last, Capt. Vaughn under cover to Messrs. John Miller & Co. and a Dublicate by Antonies Skooner on my Arivel here the 20th Ulto. have Exammined the goods per Capt. Gerome the average Is not nigh so much as I ExpeCted; the knives & the rest of hard Ware suffered most; the remainder of the Merchadize but Trifling; a ps. Raven Duck & 1 doz: Chick Shirts are Wanting; Capt. Gerome says that nothing was lost in the wrack; but a few Body Cloths; of his own; that an Exact In-

1770–1775

21/The Evan and James Jones Company of New Orleans was one of several British firms which opened up the first commerce between New Orleans and the Atlantic coast colonies of Great Britain, importing flour and other provisions, British manufactured goods, and slaves and purchasing furs and local agricultural products. Evan Jones was born in New England about 1739 and came to New Orleans from Mobile in 1765. He remained there for the rest of his life, eventually becoming a Spanish subject, pursuing an active commercial career, serving as a militia officer, and later serving as acting vice-consul of the United States, as a member of the New Orleans City Council, and as a bank director. In 1781 Evan married Marie Verret. His brother James directed the company's affairs in Pensacola, served as a member of the West Florida Provincial Council, and maintained a plantation on the Amite River. See Clark, *New Orleans, 1718–1812,* 164–65, 255, 336, 351; Johnson, "Expansion in West Florida," 489; "Memorial of the Inhabitants of Pensacola," PRO, CO 5/577, p. 39; Report of Peter Chester, 1778, PRO, CO 5/580, p. 107; Sidney A. Marchand, Sr., *An Attempt to Re-Assemble the Old Settlers in Family Groups* (Baton Rouge, 1965), 52–53; Jack D. L. Holmes, *Honor and Fidelity: The Louisiana Infantry Regiment and the Louisiana Militia Companies, 1766–1821* (Louisiana Collection Series of Books and Documents on Colonial Louisiana, No. 1.; Birmingham, Ala., 1965), 193; Sale document, November 28, 1765, Acts of Jean B. Garic, No. 1, Sec. 34, New Orleans Notarial

ventory was taken at the Opening of Each bail Casks & Trunks by him Monsr. Mason; & Sergant Scott; then Commanding at rose Island;[22] that the latter Remains with said Inventory Signed the Coppy which aGrees with your Invoice; Except the Afore Mentiond Raven Duck & Shirts which may be your Mistake in packing ore; if shoud Be so; please to Credit in Conformity; but in Case of its not being your Error Monsr. Peter Ruschon[23] must be Answerable for them; to which Purpose Capt. Gerome now Writes him; also his Inclosed draft on Sd. Ruschon my favour for $48 being the amount of one Cask of Rum; the price Sold at here; Which Rum was Expended on the Soilders &c—Who Assisted in Saving the Goods when the Vessell was Stranded; his Compliance there to Youl please to Solicit in the most Judicious maner; in Case of his Making any Objections & if Recovered to Credit me there with[.] Leutn. Governor Dunford is Surveying up the River; on his return to this; I will Send you his bill; which he promised for all my Disbursments on him;—Being 70 or 80 £ Sterling— Mr. Thomas parted last week for Pensacola per Via the lake, in Custody of Oriley the Constable Deputized by Mr. Bentley; he Offered me some Old Iron Works and Other trumperys in part payment of his Note; which I would not admit of, as Useless to you and no prospect of Reducing them to Cash here; therefore I here with send you a Coppy of Sd. Note properly Attested that you may procure paymt. as falls Due; the Originall I hold Untill to meet a safe Oppertunity of Remitting it—You Doubtless are no[w] have heard of the Edict Published in New Orleans; prohibiting the Importation; or Wearing any kind of Cotton Manufactries, by the Spanish Inhabitants who are the only people that Consumes Most of them; for your Government in Susspendg [?] Your Orders for any those parts Except the Indian Callicoes for the Savages,

I hope you,l are this Reaches Receive the Skins I sent per Captain Vaughn; to the Care of Messrs. John Miller & Co. Abstract of which; With the price you make me good; Shall be Glad You advise me off per first Oppertunity for my Government to regulate aGreeable there to—our Accots. on that head. . . .

P.S. Instead of the Copy of the afore Mentioned note the Original goes

Archives; Archivo General de Simancas, Sección de Guerra Moderna, Legajo 7291, Cuaderno 2. Regimento de Milicias Provinciales Disciplinadas de Alemanes. Floridas, p. 10.

22/Santa Rosa Island, opposite the harbor at Pensacola Bay.

23/Pierre Rochon, French merchant at Mobile. His company competed with British agents for army contracts and was employed by the British army to repair Fort Charlotte. See Howard, *British Development of West Florida*, 15; several letters from Rochon in Haldimand Papers; List of transient traders, January 30, 1769, PRO, CO 5/577, pp. 70–71.

To PETER SWANSON, *Mobile*

Manchac, June 5, 1772

I referr you to both my formers; the last of the 11th Ulto. Relative to your order my favour on Mr. Burgar which you have Inclosd.

Mesrs. McIntosh went lately to Orleans she promised would recover the money her self; and remit it you; She Arrivd. here Yesterday but did Not Tell me how She Acted there in; at hur Departure from hence to Town Deman[d]ed Sd. Order; Alledging that the Want of Which might Prevent Burgar; of not paying; I answered that her Motive of requiring it was of no Signification; as the Note was payable to order; which would Be Complied with to the Bearer; there off. . . .

To JOHN MILLER AND COMPANY, *Pensacola*

Manchac, June 5, 1772

I referr you to my last 13th Ulto. am now to crave Your favour; to Day Mr. James Serving Toyner $16 my Accot. on his Giving You Mr. Messers Accot. of $33.7rs With Samuel Lewis's Recipt. for the same; and as You have one of Sd. Messers Negroes in Your Service You will Greatly Oblige me; to stop Said sum of $33.7r in your hands But if not agreeable or in your power to serve me; there in to Acquaint me there of per first Occasion; as well about the Skins Delivered you by Capt. Vaughn to be held at Messrs. McGillivarys Disposial, & your Expencess Attending them my Accot. which Togeather with the Above $16 to Irving I Will remit to your Order with Infinite thanks. . . .

To McGILLIVRAY AND STRUTHERS, *Mobile*

Manchac, June 26, 1772

The fore going is a Copy of last to you per Mr. Ross to Which Referr; Inclosed You have Elias Dunford Esqr. Note for $122.7r. With which please to Credit my Accot. when recovered and Debit me 51 Ds. which I receivd. your Accot. from Ireal [*sic*] Mathews; for whom his being a poor man Mr. Dunford paid $26 of Sd. sum; and that he would Complimise matters With you relative to the Interest there on; which Demanded AGreeable to Your Instructions; but Inter Nose[24] as his Abilities is weak by all Accots. I was Glad to come at the principal I wanted Mr. Dunford to Include; in his said Note the Ballance of his Accot. paid me in Cash; which he Did not Chuse to be Burdoned with as he said I Suppose; to avoid the Wresk of Carrying it; that Mr. Wilton would

24/Probably Fitzpatrick's version of *entre nous*, French idiom meaning "just between ourselves."

soon be hear; and his Draft on him would meet Due hounor, for the remainder of my Disbursments on the latter which I believe ods of $200 the same shall remit per the first Ensuing safe Conveyance. . . .

To JOHN STEPHENSON, *Pensacola*

Manchac, June 28, 1772

I had the pleasure of Writing you per Mr. David Ross to which refer; Since which their is nothing new; hapned here; on Setling my Books; I find that I have Commited error Against my self in Setling with Mr. Riston; And paid him $82.9¼ more than was a Comming to him; I have wrote him On that head and have sent the Coppy of his Accot. for his Government there in; You have here Inclosed; an order on him for the Balla[n]ce; that he Ows me; and when you Receive it; you will place it to my (Accot.) say Credit with you. . . .

To JOHN RITSON, *Pensacola*

Manchac, June 28, 1772

On Stating & Setling my Books; I find that I have Committed an Error, in the payment; that I have made you; at Sundry Times; to my Disadvantage $82.9¼r More that I have paid You than was Comming due to you; as you will see by the Coppy of your Accot. sent me the 13th June 1769 Where in it appears that at that Time; I remained Owing you $297.2¾ Since which; I have sent You Mr. Haighs Note for $43; that you Acknowledge the receipt of the Same; in Your Letter 6th July the same Year; as Also a hhd. Wine 36 Dollers sent you per Henry Smith; & 4 Ds. paid the same Smith For the freight of the Said Wine; your Accot. for all those Articles You have never Given me Credit for; as You will see more fully per the Accot. here inclosed;—I hope you will find it Just; and as You know all Accots. are Signed With Errors Excepted; that you will pay the Ballance to Mr. Stephenson; in whos favour I have Drawn on You; at Sixty days after Sight. . . .

To EVAN AND JAMES JONES, *Pensacola*

Manchac, July 19, 1772

I receivd. your favour of the 17th Ulto. Advising the recipt. of mine 13th May Without being Signed; which Amission Was

Owing to my being in such a Great hurry; at the Time Unloading my Goods &c; its Contens I now Confirm of having Receivd. from Mr. Macnamara; forty Seven Barrels of flour of Which have sold 8 Barrs. some at 8½ $ and Others at 9 Dollers, part Yet out Standing but in sure hands; ready to pay When Demanded for your Govermt. and Disposial; You may Depend I will Use my Utmost Endeavours to Vend the remainder; to the best Advantage to prove, but am affraid the Sale there of will be verry Slow, perticularly as the flower is very Old, not of the Best, and a large Quantity of new flower trouly Expected from New Orleans belonging to Mr. Pollock[25] & one Mr. Willing[26] lately from Philadelphia now here With a large Boat of dry Goods all averaged; and Some flour; which will Always be preferd to yours; if not averaged; as to the Merchabl you Mention; I realy hold it not Advisable your sending any; for the place is over Stocked and no buyers worth Noticing—Capt. Canty has been here last Month; but Determined Nothing relative to the Cattle preposed by You to him; he bought some at point Couppie payable in six months; this all I know of the Matter....

To THOMAS HUTCHINS, *Pensacola*

Manchac, July 19, 1772

I receivd. Your favour of the 12th Ulto. also Messrs. Bayton Wharton & Morgan whose sales here with goes for your Governmt.; the neat proceeds being 383 Dollers 1½rs of Which I have already agreeable to their former Orders remited $133.7rs; the outstanding debts hope to recover in a Month or Six Weeks and perhaps Sooner; at least the Major part shall Remitt you per the first Ensuing safe Conveyance, being as Desirous as they are; to have it in my power to Ballance Accots. to there Satisfaction I have a part at Present of Sd. Out Standing Debts in my hands but Want some Sure Oppertunity of remitting it; by; as no bills is to be had On your place; must go in specia....

To THOMAS HUTCHINS, *Pensacola*

Manchac, August 10, 1772

The above is a Coppy of my last to you; to which refer; Inclose'd You have; Messrs. Bayton Wharton & Morgans Accot. Currt.

1770–1775

25/Oliver Pollock was born in Ireland in 1737 and came to Philadelphia in 1760. He began his career as an independent trader centered in Havana, moved to New Orleans in 1768, and developed an extensive mercantile business with ties in Illinois, the West Indies, Europe, and the British seaboard colonies. Governor O'Reilly granted Pollock complete freedom of trade in Louisiana, and he soon became one of the leading merchants and landholders in the colony. He operated a plantation near Baton Rouge and bought and sold other land along the river between Manchac and Natchez. Sympathetic to the revolutionary cause, Pollock provided assistance for the Americans in New Orleans and in 1777 was appointed "commercial agent of the United States," in charge of all American financial affairs in New Orleans until the end of the war. He provided substantial material assistance to American revolutionary activities in the Mississippi Valley and helped influence Governor Gálvez' anti-British policies. After the war Pollock was appointed U.S. agent in Havana but his service was handicapped by his need to settle personal debts and large claims against the United States. He returned to New Orleans in 1789, then moved to Pennsylvania in 1791. After the death of his wife in 1814, he lived with a daughter in Pinckneyville, Mississippi, where he died in 1823. For a full account of Pollock's life and career, see James, *Oliver Pollock*.

26/Member of a prominent Philadelphia mercantile family, a younger brother of Thomas Willing, and partner in the firm of Willing and Morris

also Mr. Wm. Wiltons[27] Bill at 40 Days after Date on Leut. Governor Dunford Esqr. for $153 Which is all I have in Cash; togeather with what I Already remitted AGreeable to their former Orders to Mr. Morgans Absent in the Illinois as per receipt there of in my possession; the Remainder of the outstanding debts there Accot. is $86.6¼; which when Recoverd shall remitt you; at last of said Accot. Currt. you have a list of Sd. out Standing Debts, which I will Endeavour as soon as possible to Recover. . . .

To McGILLIVRAY AND STRUTHERS, Mobile

Manchac, August 10, 1772

I receivd. Your Esteem'd favour of the 30th June With a Coppy of yours of the 23d of the same Month; the Original of Which Neaver Came to hand nor the Accot. Curt. there in Mentioned; there fore Shall be Glad Youd Send my Accot. there of per first opperty. for my Governmt.; also to know the Amot. of the Skins; some of Which You say has been hurt by the Worms (to say the raw) and some by wate[r] in the Voyage; from New Orleans to pensacola; the latter Greatly Surprises me as Mr. Miller; lately Wrote me; that he receivd. them In Good Order; from on Board Capt. Vaughn; so that the Damage of the Water must be from pensacola to your place; when to receive yr. Afore Sd. Accot. Curt. Shall Examine it; & if without Error of Either, Side; Shall note the same aGreeable to your Desire; am Obliged to you for the price You Allow me for the skins; which shall let no person know as You Require; least it should Come to the Ears of Your Traders; I observe Mr. Ward would not Except Mr. Smiths Draft On him; the latter was here at the Time I receivd. Your afore said letter And toald me as he Goes Immediately to Mobile, would Endeavour to Settle there if so or not; Youl please to advise there of per first Ensuing Conveyance; to prove paymt. Other wise in Case of his Non Complyance to this; as the Mistake of the pss of Raven Duck & 1 doz Check Shirts Was not Committed by you; Shall be much Obliged to you; to procure if possible there Amount; from Mr. Peter Russon; Your Care there in flatter my Self there with; as there is no Recorse to be had from Capt. Gerome; Annext you have a Coppy of my last to you; per Leut. Governor Dunford to which referr. . . .

---

and Company, James Willing came to West Florida in the early 1770s. In 1772 he was keeping a store at Manchac, selling Indian goods brought from Pennsylvania; at this time he formed a brief partnership with Oliver Pollock to supply flour to West Florida. He was granted a town lot in Manchac in 1772, as well as 1250 acres north of Baton Rouge. He later moved to Natchez, where he established a store. Unfamiliar with agriculture and unsuccessful in business, James Willing was accused by his associates of dissipating his fortune. In 1777 he abandoned his unpaid debts in royalist Natchez and returned to Philadelphia, where he was soon commissioned to lead a military expedition down the Mississippi. See Starr, "Tories, Dons, and Rebels," 147–48; James, *Oliver Pollock*, 117–20; Haynes, *The Natchez District and the American Revolution*, 56–57; Willing to Haldimand, January 3, July 6, and November 11, 1772, in Haldimand Papers; Caughey, "Willing's Expedition Down the Mississippi, 1778," 5–6; Council minutes, November 2, 1772, PRO, CO 5/589, pp. 46–49; Eron Rowland (ed.), *Life, Letters and Papers of William Dunbar of Elgin, Morayshire, Scotland, and Natchez, Mississippi* (Jackson, Miss., 1930), 60–62.

27/Surveyor and engineer under Governor Peter Chester.

To JOHN STEPHENSON, *Pensacola*

Manchac, August 28, 1772

Your Esteemed favour of the 28th Ulto. I have now Before me; and note well the Contents; I am sorry that I had not heard of your Sloops being in the River; to have sent your Canno that has been here this Six Weaks; Should have sent her per the Way of the Lakes long are now; had their been any Water,—in the Bayaux; but it has been Dry this three Months past. Yours of the 27th of last May onely Came to hand; per Mrs. Urquhart; the 20th of the present which I answered the same Day per Via of New Orleans; was Realy Sorry that it did not Come to hand in Due Time so as that I might have had the quantity of Ash oars you Wanted for Your Sloop; I have in my last of the 20th past Assigned you My reasons for not having them Got at present; but will refer it Till the Beginning of Novemr. if aGreeable to you; of not please to let me have Your Answer per the first Oppertunity; and Shall then have them Got; and Sent to Monsr. Ransons plantation below Orleans, as Mentioned here before;—You Desire me in Yours to Give You an Accot. of the spot where the new Town[28] is to be built; Above this place; all that I can say on that head is that it is Situated in the Bottom of a large Bite where the Missisippi after Comming down through a large Reach of Near 5 Miles; Strikes the Banks of the New Town with Great force; and at the lower End of the Town it is subject to flowing in When the river is low and that thier have many heavy Ruins; But as to the overflowing of the Ground in the front it happens only when the river is at a Great hight; but that may be asly [easily] Stopt by good Ditches or leavies as their is in Orleans; as to the Ground that lays behind it; it is low Sipruss [cypress] swamp & some Cane brakes for many miles back—with many Small lakes Occasioned by the overflowing of the Mississippi; when at its hight; and in the most part of Which there is Water the hole Year Round; this body of Water Comes about 10 or 12 Miles Above the place where they propose building the Town where the River takes a large Turn; & where the Ground is Mighty Low—on this side— This Sir is the Best Account I am able to Give You on that Subject; Yet for all these Ill Convenincies you might Git you a lot in the Town; Where You would not be Troubled with the Overflowing of the Waters; Nor the faulling in of the Banks; and for Many Reasons Should Recommend to you; if Possible to Git one of the Uper End Lots; being by farr the Most Convenient; in the first place it is handier to any Trade that may be Carried on up the river—And Secondly its being more Under Cover of the land from the N.W. and N.E. Winds that blow here; with Great force;

28/See map in this volume, following p. 162.

the Greatest part of the Winter; Now Dear Sir; should be Much Obliged to you; to keep the Infurmation to Your Self; as may be the Leut. Governor would not like that I should say so Much; about a place that he has Chose for the Building of the Town; having Nothing more to add at present Only to Desire you to Acquaint me in Your next if Mr. Riston has payed the $82.9½r as per my Order on him of the 28th June last for an Error Committed in his Account Currt. a Coppy of which I Sent him and Youl Oblige . . .

To PETER SWANSON, Mobile

Manchac, August 29, 1772

I Wrote You the 10th of the present to which referr Since Which Your Esteemed favour; of the 23d of last June Came to hand; I observe well Its Contents; as to the money Mr. McIntosh Was to have paid me Your Accot. have heard Nothing more of it since My last to you on that head—tho I am Apt to think that he has Remitted the whole; or some part there of by Leut. Governor Dunford though am not Certain; all that I Can say, is that I heard his honour Say that a man up the river had Committed Money to his Care; without Nameing any One; as for the Trouble I have had about it; it is Nothing at all; am Only sorry for Your Sake that I had Not Got it in Due Time; to have sent it to you; if any thing Elce I Can at any time be of any Service to you; in these parts you may freely Command; and Shall Except them; if in my power with all Attention possible;—I am Much Obliged to you for your kind offers & Shall Always be Glad to have it in my power to repay you with Many thanks; I had a letter from pensacola; the Other Day; in which their is Mentioned of the New Govermt. taking place; and that its Brown[29] that Will be Governor; I hope he will Act with more prudence then here to fore when Leut. Governor of Your province; perhaps That Experiance will Teach him Better he is to Act when in possession of this New Employment—I am sorry to Acquaint you that Trade is mighty Dull with us Yet; there Neaver was so many Merchts. And so many Goods on the river at one Time as there is now, for my part I am trying to Git in all Out Standing Debts as fast as possible, with A determination of Crediting no More; Except men that always paid Me at the Time Appointed; having no more at present and remain . . .

P.S. Should be much obliged to you; to Close the Sales of the Tobaco as soon as you Can Conveniently

---

29/Montfort Browne arrived in Pensacola in 1766 as lieutenant governor of the province. He was a veteran of the French and Indian War and held large grants of land in the province. He assumed the administration of the colony after Governor Johnstone's recall in 1767, remaining in control until the arrival of Governor Eliot in April, 1769. Browne's administration was marked by disputes and accusations of wrongdoing. After Eliot's suicide on May 2, Browne resumed control until he was recalled in August, 1769, and replaced as lieutenant governor by Elias Durnford. Browne departed for England early in 1770. Peter Chester was governor at the time this letter was written and remained in that office until 1781. See Johnson, *British West Florida*, 61–73.

To McGILLIVRAY AND STRUTHERS, Mobile

Manchac, September 3, 1772

—the fore Going is a Coppy of my last to you of the 10th Ulto. Since which Your Esteemed favour; of the 23d Came to hand; With my Accot. Curt. which after Examination find to be Right; Excpt in the first place you paid Capt. Macmain $24 to much being the Amount of Monsrs. Vincens the Watch Makers Accot. that in my Absence from New Orleans by orders of Oriley; he went to Pensacola And from thence to New Yourk; so that Mr. Riston to who I sent his Accot. To Pensacola; at my Return from Your place to New Orleans to recover the paymt. for me; sent me the Accot. Back the said Vincens Having been gone before the Accot. got to Pensacola, there fore it would be Very hard to oblige me to pay money I neaver Receivd. but shall leave that to your Consideration Wheather I ought to pay it or not—and as for the Others I have Marked them in [blank] of an Acct. for your Governmt.—Trade has been very Dull Since the Arivel of the last Goods here Inclosed; Yet hope to send You by the 20th Novemr. 2000; Good Skins a part of which I have now in the House and a 1000 more I Expect in every Day; from the advice I receivd. 6 Days ago and for which I have sent my Boat this Morning—

Goods are sold here very low by one Mr. Willing from philedelpha that brought here a large quantity and sels out at 45 pCent from the Sterling Cost which puts it out of my power to Dispose of So many; as I should have done; had he not Came here; Yet I am of opinion that he will repent it are long; this all for the Needfull . . .

To GODLEY AND RAINCOCK, Pensacola

Manchac, September 5, 1772

Your favour of the 26th Ulto I have now before Me and note its Contents I am sorry not to have it in my power to Acquaint you of the Arrival of the promised peltreys or flour; from Monsr. Sarpee; at the Illinois; but as Yet their is nothing Come to Hand I Receivd. a letter from Mr. Patrick Morgan;[30] of the 19th last month Where in he Mentions that Mr. Sarpée will soon make some remittances but to what Amot. he Cannot Tell; as soon as any Comes to hand Shall inform You per the first Conveyance—

I am sorry that I Cant Give you any Encouragemt. to send any of the Goods You Mention this way; for, there is large quantities of them Now in Orleans; point Coupee and at sundry Other

30/Patrick Morgan was the owner of one of the "floating warehouses" operated by British merchants in the Mississippi River near New Orleans. His vessel was among those seized by Gálvez in 1777.

placess on the River; so that they are sold much Cheapper here than they Could Be Expected from Your place; or You would Care to give them. . . .

To JOHN STEPHENSON, *Pensacola*

Manchac, September 16, 1772

The fore going is a Coppy of my last to You of the 28th Ulto. since which there is nothing new Accourd in this place; only that all the Witnesses are Cauled down to pensacola to give Evedence AGainst Thomas; the Bearer is one and a Young man who lives with Me who will if You please Acquaint you with the whole affair as it passed; and was on the Spot almost all the Time; Should be much Obliged to you; if by his return you will favour me With an Accot. How things turns out; and Wheather he [*i.e.* Thomas] is Cleare'd—

And if he is to return to this place a gain; for if so it will be Imposible to live here; I must leave it; or if I dont Shall be always in Disputes with him; Your Compliance will Greatly oblige . . .

To PETER SWANSON, *Mobile*

Manchac, September 16, 1772

I wrote you the 29th Ulto. per via of New Orleans to which Referr; since which I have been Informd. that one Abner Bush that is some thing in debt to me; as You will see; per his Accot. and Note of hand Hear Inclosed; Lives with one Mr. Buckels; that Trades for the House; if so; Should be much Obliged to you; if he Comes down that you will Recover the Amount for me; as in all Appeareance it will be a long Time Before he Comes this way again; You will please to Observe that the $7¼r that Remaind due to me Besides the Amount of his Note; was an Error Committed by me when I Setled with him; & his Company for the Amo[unt] of the results; having Crouded his Accot. $152.7¾ Insteed of $145.7½rs. I hope he will be Nothing aGainst paying it as I Believe him to be an honest You[n]g man; Your Compliance will Greatly Oblige . . .

To JESSE LUM, *Natchez*[31]

Manchac, October 12, 1772

Your Esteemed favour of the 22d of August I have now Before Me; and note well the Contents; I am really sorry that I have not

---

31/The Lum family was among the early inhabitants of the Natchez district. In November, 1776, Jesse Lum was granted 300 acres at Villa Gayosa, as was his wife Hannah; a son, William, was granted 350 acres. When James Willing left Natchez in 1777, he sold the effects of his mercantile business to the Lum brothers. See Norman E. Gillis, *Early Inhabitants of the Natchez District* (Baton Rouge, 1963), 9–10; Edith Wyatt Moore, *Natchez Under-the-Hill* (Natchez, 1958), 18.

in my power to Acquaint you that; I had heard Some thing of your Negro;—But I Promise You that I have made all the Enquiry possible; Both here at Orleans the point Coupée; and have sent Advertms. to Sundry parts on the Mississippi; where I thought He might have Got too; with out Ever being able to here any thing Certain as Yet; But if here after I should hear anything you may Depend on my Dowing the Needfull in that Affair....

To DANIEL McINTOSH, *Pensacola*

Manchac, October 12, 1772

Your Esteemed favour of the 1st Ulto. I have now before me and note well the Contents; and I am Much Obliged to you for your Kindness and realy thank You; for the Trouble you had on my Account; If any such thing Should, lay in my way; Where in I may Serve you; and there in shall always be Glad to Receive Your Commands It gives me a Great Deal of pleasure to find that it Comes so Seasonable to the poor Womans hand; for my part I Promise you thats so much Loss to me; for the man I Sent the things by; at first has give me but a flemish Accot. of them Saying that he was drove back by Distress of Weather & he had Near lost his life; and that all he had was Intirely Lost; and as there is no such thing as to prove to the Contrary I must Put up with the loss—We have no News worth Relating Excepting that Trade is Mighty Dull with us; the Cargo of Goods that I had from yr. Place are Still Mostly on hand; and am Determined to keep them With out Either Good Skins or Cash in hand; for Trusting will no Longer do;—if you here any thing of the New Settlemt. that is Propossed to be made, at this place; Should be much obliged to you if you would give me Advice there of; per the first Conveyance....

To PETER SWANSON, *Mobile*

Manchac, October 12, 1772

I Wrote the 16th Ulto. to you; which referr; since which your Esteemed favour of the 9th of Last month Came to hand; per Mr. Stuart, And I Observe well its Contents; I am realy sorry that I have it not in my Power to Aquaint you Something Concerning Mr. Lums Negro; But I promise You; I have not spared any pains; and have made all the Enqury Both at New Orleans and at point Coupée; Since I Came from your Place; and have sent Advertisements to the Natchez; offering a Reward of $30 to any one that Should bring Sd. Negro, or only Acquaint me Where; he Resorted; but as Yet to no purpose; here after if I can hear Any thing You may Depend on my Doing the Need full in the Affair— in my last to you; I sent you Inclose'd Abner Bushes Accot. Currt. and his Note of hand & if he should Come down I hope you will Endeavour to Git him to Settle that small affair. . . .

To EVAN AND JAMES JONES, *Pensacola*

Manchac, October 16, 1772

Your Esteemed favour of the 2d Ulto. I have now Before me; And Note well the Contents; I realy am Sorry; to Acquaint you; that saels of Your flour has been mighty Slow; not being able to sell but 2 Barrs. Since my last to you of the 19th July; But at present hope are long to be Able to Dispose of the remaining partly; at the price you have Coated; in Your last to me; I have Acquainted Sundry people at Point Coupée that they shall have it $7 and they sent me word that when they go Down with their Indego they will Take 18 Barrels at that price—if so Shall be able to Close the sales; and remitt you the Amount per the First Conveyance that shall Offer after they are Close'd; Either in skins Indego or Cash; this Being the Needfull at present . . .

P.S. Capt. Canty is something in my Debt; should be Glad to hear if you would Except his order for $35.

To CHARLES STUART, *New Orleans*

Manchac, October 16, 1772

This mornning I Remembered that I omited to give You the Receipt for the 2 Doz: Garlix Shirts; goes here Inclose'd & at the same Time Acquaint you that 1 of the pss. Strouds that I had of You has been Cut; it is Marked 22 Yards there is only 16 Yards remains so that their 6 aWanting; I promise You that the piece was Cut when it Came hear; as I neaver touched any of Your Strouds to give the Indians; Mabee Sir you Can Remember; Wheather you gave any Blankets away for it is as I inform you; at the rate that I bought the Strouds is £5.5 Sterling or $22½; the peice; so that the Six Yards Amount to $6.1½r the same Rate Allowing 22 Yds. the peice as they all run; which you Will please to Endorse on the Back of the Note;—After your Departure I found in Your room a handkf. with some Cloths in it; which I Send you per this Conveyance; and that will Still find you at Orleans Having no More at present to add, only that I wish you a Good Voige . . .

To McGILLIVRAY AND STRUTHERS, Mobile

Manchac, October 17, 1772

I had the pleasure of Writing the 16th Ulto. which I Hope are now have Come to hand; since Which Your Esteeme'd favour of the 31st Augt. came to hand per Mr. Smith; By which I observe Mr. Rushon did not Except Mr. Geromes order for the Amount of the sundry things that was lost; at St. Rosses Island; Which things are Only Charged at the price they cost me; the rum Excepted which I have Charged him at the Curt. price; that it sold for here; at the Time of his Arrivel; the money receivd. from Isreal Mathews was for the Amount of his Accot. with the House Being $35 & the Other is for the Estate of the Deecd. Joseph Crow $16) to which Estate I believe Mr. Swanson to be Executor, if so he will know what to do with $16.

Trade Continues Mighty dull; but hope are long it will be Much Better as the Season for the Wolling Goods are Dailey coming on—You Cant Immagine Gentlemen the quantity of Goods brought up this way; every day some new one maks his appearence and Sooner than they will Carry them Back; they sell at Most the prime Cost; for my part I cant help thinking that some of them will Give a flemish Account if they Continue Selling as they had Begun; I have now in the house; 1400 Good Skins and soon Shall be able; to Augment the Number; as the season; for the Hunting daily Comming on; this Being all from . . .

To MONSIEUR LAFITTE, JUNIOR, New Orleans[32]

Manchac, October 20, 1772

Your Esteemed favour of the 9th Ulto. with my Accot. Curt. Came duly to hand & I note well Its Contents; and after due Examination find it to be quite Right & have Credited your Accot. with me for the same; Now Dear Sir; this is to beg Your Assistance in a small affair Between Jaique Taniscion; and me, the Subject where of will take up the remaining part of this letter; and for your Governmt. in the afair have sent you here Inclosed; all the Accots. and Letters from Monsr. Duvall Who Wrote all Monsr. Tanisions Letters, himself Not Being Capable;—The affair is this; I Being in Orleans in the Mo[n]th of June 1771 Mr. Tanision proposed to let me have all the Skins that he should Receive From the Indians, that ware at 48 sols per Skins in Consequence of which I Took all the red Skins that he got the last

[32] Son of New Orleans merchant Jean Lafitte.

Merchant of Manchac

summer; at the price aGreed On; for the Hole Years Skins always in Expectation of having the Winter Skins; as he had promised; When he proposed the affair to me at first; He sent me at Sundry Times 1728½ Skins the amount of which was $829.5½r Which sum I paid him in full as Youl see by his Accot. Currt. No. 1 and the same Time Commited an Error AGainst my Self $7.7¼ that I over paid him; Which sum I have Charged his Accot. No. 2 with As You will see there in Coated; Now Dear Sir; you will please to observe that the Amount of his Accot. No. 2 was for Sundrys Goods I Gave to Mr. Tanision the 1st July & 25th Augt. to sell for our Amounts to the Amot. of $319 on the Conditions that follows; that he should have the Indian Goods that he took the 1st July at the price they cost me; at, Mobille; Without allowing any thing for the freight as per McGillivary & Strs. Invoice thereof; and furthur that I run the Risque of any thing that migh[t] Happen them; Till they ware Landed at point Coupée; and if any part of them Remained Unsold they ware to be returnd to me at the price Coated in the Invoice; the Amot. of What Goods that ware sold Mr. Tanision Was to pay me for in Deer Skins at 48 sols per Skin as soon as the Indians came in from their Winters hunts to whom he had gave my Goods too on Creditt; and the profitt arising on the Sales if any; he to have the one half part & I the Other half; now Sir; he sold all the Indian Goods at least to the Amount of $159.1½ & the Others he returnd to Mr. Duvall the 11th Octobr. 1771 to the Amount of Ds. 159.6½r as You will see More plainner By the Accot. of Goods returned No. 3 Which some [sum] I passed to the Credit of his Accot. No. 2 Always in hopes that the Goods that ware sold Would be paid me last spring According to Our aGreement the Skins at 48 sols; but Instead of paying me the Hole Amount of the things he sold he only Gave one hundred and then he made Me pay 3 lb. Skin which was 20 pCt. more than our AGreemt. he neaver; has Given me an Accot. of Sales; and has had my Goods Almost 16 months in his hands; and Seeing that I Could not bring him to Give me a proper Accot. of the Sails; have placed the Amount of the Goods Sold to his Debit, in his Accot. Curt. No. 2 and have Charged him 25 pCt. on What they cost me; Which Advance I beleve no man Can Demand less and Wait 16 Months for the paymt. as I have done you will see that their is a Ballance due me of $299 as per his Accot. Curt. No. 2 Which Sum I have Demanded of him the 24th Ulto. when at the pt. Coupée; his Answer was that he owed me Nothing that in the presence of Monsr. Duvall; Monsr. Crousée & Monsr. Perisch all good Honnest Men of the point Coupée Saying that he neaver took Monsr. Duvilliers Obligation; on his Accot. Although Mr. Duvalls Letter will prove that he Expected it; for his Accot.; and further it Can be proved that Monsr. Duvelleer has paid him $250: on Acot. of Said Obligation; which Sums are Indorsed there on as may bee Seen by his producing the said Obligation & that it is payable to the Bearer—at Present it only remains to Acquaint You that since I made the demand the 24 Ulto. & that he refused to Pay; as before Mentioned I receivd. a letter With a Note of hand there in for $180 On Accot. of the Ballance of his Acct. No. 2 Which was $299 so that there Still remains due me $119; to finish all Accots. with Mr. Tanision & me which last sum; he promised to pay as soon as he goes to Town which will be in a few Days; if it is According to the Accot. in his Wifes keeping; which Accounts are Eronious; these that I send you here Inclosed being the Right one's; as you will see your self as yo. are well Acquainted with the Meathod that Bussiness is done;—and that all Accots. are Signed (Errors Excepted) should be much Obligd. to you; if he will Settle Accot. that you will Draw the remaining Balle. and Place it to the Credit of my Accot. with you; to Conclude I Shall Be Glad to have all things Settled in the Easiest manner possible; And Shall be quite willing sooner than have any more Disputes about any thing that; (in my Opinion) is so plain; to leave it to any two Gentlemen Either french or Spanairds that knows any thing About Mercantile Affairs; & What Ever they shall think the most Equitable between man & man I shall agree to; and for my part if it should Come to that Extreemety (should beg the favour of you to be one of the Two Your Self) if Your Bussiness will permitt there of) and What Ever you shall think the most Advisable to do in the Affair will Always be agreeable to me & Shall Always Always [sic] Acknowledge the favour with Greatest Return of thanks; Possible, as I Cant leave My House at present. . . .

To McGILLIVRAY AND STRUTHERS, *Mobile*

Manchac, October 31, 1772

You have here Inclosed a Coppy of my last to you; of the 17th Instant by Mr. Steuart via of New Orleans; Since which your Esteemed favour of the same Date Came to hand; which I have now Before me; and note well the Contents; I Observe Your having Mentiond. to Capt. McMain the Affair of the $24 of Monsr. Vincen the Wat[c]h Maker not having been recovered; and that the Capt. Said I had posetively Agreed to pay it; its certainly an Error in his Memory; for all that I Ever said to him on that head While at your place was that Mr. Swanson; would Settle with

Merchant of Manchac

him; that had been receivd. on Acct. of [*illegible*] Sales, Neaver Immagind that he would have Demanded the $24 Untill they had Been remited if he that ows them should return to his place; though at the Capts. return he Will not allow it; I must only repay it with thanks to you; But at the same Time I took the Captain to be too Honnest a man to require me to pay it as it was not owing to any Neglect, of mine—that it was lost in the Accot. Curt. Mentioned in mi[ne] of the 3d Septemr.—was not omitted But went by the way of Orleans Which hope are now is Come to hand; as Also that of the 10th of Augt. You Mention in Yours that you Expect; Capt. McMain in the Next Month; and that I should Acquaint you by the first Convey Ance what things I might want for the Ensuing Year; in Answer to Which I am Sorry to Acquaint You; that I am not so farr Advancd In the Sale of my last Cargo; as to be in Want of Another this some Time to Come; with out Trade Alters or Times Grows Better than It has been sum Time past with me in the first place as I have t[he] Major part of them on hand though am in hopes of Being able to Dispose of them Mostley this Winter; & may bee sooner if there Is no Europien Ships in the river; this two months to come—Secondly knowing the Balla[n]ce that still remains due to the Hous and the small profits that can be had by the sales at present; Occasind By the Great quantity of Good that are Dailey; Comming this way And the small Demand there is for it, at Present; the Town of Orlean Having such large quantitys in it all which prevents my Daring To Attempt to send for any thing more Till I See the house paid of[f] And how things are like to Turn out with us in these parts; which Reasons Gentlemen I hope will meet with your Approbation—in As much as I would not Chuse to Take more on my self than I could be Answerable for Yearly; as I have been here to fore; But you may Depend that as soon as there is any prospect of Times Growing Better; that I Shall loos no Time in Acquainting you both for Your Interest & my own; of the things that shall be Wanting; both for [*?*]; As to Your Brigs Comming to the Mississippi; and her Being able to make a Saving Voyage; Will be owing Intirely to the Time she Comes in; if there is any Other before her it will Lower the price of Your Goods; But that is not all You must Consider at present their is no Such thing as Landing any thing with out its Costing You Dear; and at the same Time your Running the Risque of having Your things Seized Upon; While on Board the french will tell you if they ware on Shore they would take Such & Such things and When aShore; they will want them at their price; Saying among them Selves (they have been at the Expence of Gitting them ashore And Must sell at our price; or be Obliged to be at further Expence to git them on Board aGain; all this I Mention to you is no more than the fashin; the french at Orleans; have got into Since the Spannairds Keeps such look out; as they have this some time Past; the Consequence of which I think my self Obliged to Acquaint You off; and leave to your Superior Judgmt. to act as yr. long Experienced amongst the french of the province & your own Interst will Direct; Having Nothing More To add . . .

To PETER SWANSON, *Mobile*

Manchac, October 31, 1772

Your Esteemed favour of the 17th Instant Duly Came to Hand; and I Observe well its Contents; by which I find that the Letter I wrote to you the 29th Augt. per Via of New Orleans n[eve]r Came to hand but hope are now it has[.] I am Greatly Obliged to you for your Attention in regard to Abner Bushe's affair & Mine & am in Expectation yt. you will be Able to receive it & recover it for me; if or not I return you my most Humble thanks for your Trouble Not having it in my power to repay it any Other way for the present And at the same time to beg Your Assistance in aNother; which I was Obliged to Take the Other day in part from H. Smith knowing that all I can Git from him is so much that one gits out of the fire he gave Mr. Kraps; Note of hand payable to the Bearer, for $30.2r which if any Occasion offers and that you Can Inform; him that you have his note; I am well Assurd; that he will pay Soonner than smith—Trade Continues Mighty dull with me; But hope are long it will Be more favorable than it has been this some Time past; as You Will see; more plainner by my letter to the House on that head; having Nothing more to add for the present only to Assure you that I am . . .

To CHARLES STUART, *Mobile*

Manchac, November 9, 1772

I Receivd. the honour of yours of the 29th Ulto. from New Orleans the 7th Instant, and note well the Contents—I Observ What you Mention Relative to the Strouds that was Wanting is mig[hty] Well and Will Answer the same End; I am sorry that you lost your little Sow; but as the loss is not Unreaparable you need not be Uneasy, for Madame Blain promisses to send You aNother of the same Breed by the first Conveyance that shall go for Your place; by the way of the Bayaux;—I am Much Obliged to you for your offers of service and [*edge of page cut*] which I return You my most Harty thanks &c; if there is any thing in these parts where I can be of any Service to you; Shall always be gl[ad] to receive Your Commands; In the mean time should be much Obliged to you; if you will be so good as to Informe me by the first opperty. that may Offer for this place or per Via of New Orleans if you have Any thing Heard Relative to the Government; having Given orders to have my house Pulled Down; if so or not should always be much Obliged to you to favour me with a few lines; there is nothing new With us Since Your Departure from this Excepting that old Mobelian Chief Went to the Spanish Commander at Point Coupée to recover presents with the Bullix Indians and that Mons. Duvillie toald him he had no presents for him; as being a English Indian; we have a report here of Mr. Thomas's Returning to this Place; aGain with more power; than Ever; if so I promise You that he will have the place to him self for my part I am Determind Neaver to remain in the place where such a Turbelent man as he is Shall Reside; having Nothing more to Add ...

To JOHN STEPHENSON, *Pensacola*

Manchac, December 14, 1772

Both your Esteemed favours of the 24 & 26 of last Octor. duly Came to hand; & I observe well their Contents; Especially that of the 26th where in you Mention the peacans and the Tongs Which shall Procure for You; if possible; and having on Receiving Yours Wrote to a Gentleman; at the point Coupée to procure the Nutts; if they was to Be had in them parts; as for the Tongues & beef you want for yourself And the General; will purchass from the first Hunting Boat that shall Come here in their way to Orleans; though it is not aften; they do at present nor heant since Thomas's Transactions last Winter; Trade is migh[t]y Dull with us; no Boat Being permitted to come AShore; till She has had Permission of the Commanding officer at the Post on the Other side of the Bayaux; we have a report here of Thomas's returning here AGain; if so I Promise you that he shall have the place to himself for me; as I am Determd. Not to run the Risque of having my self Butchered; and as no one Can live nigh him without Runing that I had reather leave the place and loss all the Improvements that I have made; here which have Cost Me above a Thousand Dollers; as all the Gentlemen of your place that ha[ve] Been here can inform you; then to remain in a place where such a man Shall reside; as soon as I have been able to git your Nutts tongues &

Beef You may Depend on having them sent you; per the first conveyance[.] we have Nothing New worth Acquainting you off as the Bearer Mr. Jas. Jones Can Inform You. . . .

To McGILLIVRAY AND STRUTHERS, *Mobile*

Manchac, January 6, 1773

Your Esteemed favour of the 18th last Novemr. Came to hand the 4th Instant per Via of Orleans; it having by mear Chance fell into the hands [of] Mr. Poussett;[33] who was so Obligeing as to send it me; under the Cover of one from himself; acquainting me of Mr. Touns; having Landed Mr. McIntosh's Goods at the Bayux of St. Johns near to Orleans; instad of Bringing them to the river of Amett or to this place; Where the Goods woud have been in Safety; Till Mr. McIntosh Could have Come for them; when the Waters would have permitted him to pass in the Bayaux of this place; on Receipt of the Letters I sent a man off with Mr. McIntosh's and sent him the Bill of lading for his Governmt. so that I Expect him down in a few Days; to go to Orleans; to see about Monsr. Touns and his Goods; I am afraid from What Mr. Poussett Mentions in his letter that Mr. McIntosh will not git Purmission to have his Goods Transported a Cross the Island of Orleans;[34] to have them Shipped for his place; by the way of the river; but make no Doubt but he Will git leave; to have his Boat Brought aCross the Bayaux; to have them Brought to this place by the way of the lakes as the Navigation will be opped [opened] As the Mississippi; risses mighty fast; in observing the Contents of your kind Letter; I cant help Taiking perticular Notice of Your Generos Offers; of Still Contunuing to Supply me with more Goods (tho them that I had Already are Not paid for;) for which Gentlemen; I return you most hearty thanks; the many conceiving proofs that I have had of your; Genirosity towards me And on so Many Occasions since my Comming to this province; Leaves no reason [?] to doubt of your Generosity & Good Intentions to serve me Still; if I have not Sent you a Memorandum for Goods; It is intirely owing to the small prospect that their is here at present for the sales of them after they ware Come; Occasiond. By the large Assortmt. lately Imported by Captn. Wagh; and an New EnGland Man; and the low price that the latter sels at; putts it Quite out of my power to send for any thing more; till I have sold them that are on hand; as I have still in the House; for $2000; Besides to the Amount of $900 that I have sent to the

33/Francis Poussett was one of the earliest residents of Baton Rouge, where he held 10,000 acres on the river directly south of the town. He previously resided in Pensacola and was elected speaker of the General Assembly in 1766. The date of his move to the Mississippi River is unknown, but he was granted a town lot in Manchac in 1772, and it is certain that he was well established there by 1776, since some of his slaves were involved in a conspiracy in the summer of that year. Poussett apparently maintained a residence or store at Manchac, since he is recorded as being resident there in 1777. A census of 1782 lists his occupation as planter and records that he owned 14 slaves. After Fitzpatrick's death in 1790 and that of his widow in 1797, Poussett was appointed one of the executors of the Fitzpatrick estate. Fitzpatrick's letterbooks contain a number of Poussett's letters relative to his duties as executor. See Council Minutes, November 2, 1772, PRO, CO 5/589, pp. 46–49; Rowland (ed.), "Diary of William Dunbar" in *Life, Letters and Papers of William Dunbar,* 27; Baton Rouge Census Document, Department of Archives and Manuscripts, Louisiana State University.

34/The "Island of Orleans" was not a true island but rather a section of land, bounded on one side by the Mississippi River and on the others by the Gulf of Mexico, Lakes Pontchartrain and Maurepas, and the Amite and Iberville rivers, upon which New Orleans is located. It was the only territory on the east side of the Mississippi to be included in Louisiana after the territorial cessions of

Merchant of Manchac

Natchez some Time aGo; and as I Should be Glad to have them that are here Disposed off are I send for any thing further; More over Gentlemen; when I think on the large Ballance that Still remains due to the house The small Trade that is carried on hear; al which prevents my Dearing to Engroce any further on Your Goodness, Till you are paid; oir till there is a Greater prospect of being able to do something more then there is to be done here at present; for Your Interest as well as for my own; as I should Be Extreamly happy to have all my former Dealings Settled and to pay the Ballance of my Accot. to the House;—before I Enter into any new Engagements; and which is and always shall be my Constant Study till fully Effected (though in the mean time if I find any Change in the Trade of this place; and that it should be for the Better; you may Depand that I shall loss no Time in Acquainting you of the goods that will Answer here; I hope You will not Blame me for Exposing to you the Reasons that prevents my Not sending for any thing more as yeat; for Really Gentlemen in so Doing I have had Your Interest; as much at heart as my own—for had I where with to pay for them on their Arrivell; I should not hisatate A moment; about sending; but as I have not dare not Venture any further Out of my Depth; then where I am as you know; that I have Nothing more than what I have been able to make these fours Years passed; & that by yr. Generous Assistance, and that it self not mine untill you are paid; I have Now in the House; about 4 Thousand Weight of Leather in the Hair (and According to Sundry Obligations in my hands for Goods sold may Expect before the End of this Month 4 or 5 thousand Wt. more; (but in what manner I shall Send them You;) Excepting some Vessell comes to Orleans; so that I may Send them that way; Cant say having no Boat of own; that could go to your Place with such a load; I have Desired Monsr. Lafite Mercht. at Orleans to Purchass from me the Martin Skins that Mr. Struthers Mentioned in his letter of the 25th of last June; as no Boats stop here when aGowing down But as there is none Come Down this Year; with there skins as Ussial; he has not been able to Git them; for me But should any Arrive before I send my Skins I'll be shore to git them; and send them by the same Conveyance[.] there is three English hunters Expected in Dailey with a fine parcell; of Beaver; and as they are in my Debt; hope to have their; Beaver if so shall send it all to you; having Nothing more to add . . .

P.S. shall be happy in having the Pleasure of seeing Mr. McGillivray at this place when he shall think proper to honour my house with his Company

---

1763. Since its possession allowed Spain to control both sides of the river near its mouth, the unrestricted access to the river promised to England (and later the United States) was totally dependent on the good will of the Spanish masters of New Orleans.

To FRANCIS POUSSETT

Manchac, February 2, 1773

Your Esteemed favour of the 15 Ulto. Came to hand the 1st Instant per Mr. Urquehart which surpissed me a little to find that you have Not been paid by Mr. Pollock long are now; as I Delivered the Amount of the ps. of Blankets to Mr. Willing on receipt of your letter in Deecemr. last As at that Time there was no safe Oppertunity; offered to send it you—Should be much Obliged to you; if you will speak to Mr. Pollock; about it as I make no doubt but he will pay it you on Demand; for I am Well Assurd that Mr. Willing wrote him on that head a longe time ago; I spoke to Mr. Manuel Monsanto;[35] Relative to the Indego or Cash; you Mention; he Writes you him self per this Conveyance to which refer you;—I am much Obliged to you for your kind Affers of Service; in return if there is any thing Up this way in which I can be of any Service or Use to you; shall Always be Glad to Receive Your Commands. . . .

To JAMES WILLING, *Natchez*

Manchac, February 3, 1773

According to your request of the first Instant I send you; per this Occasion; 400 lb. Gun powder 4 Gross Bead lace all the other things that you mention went with Mr. Dusole; which I hope are now is Safe Come to hand; You have here Inclosed an Accot. of the Hhd. of Taffee; that was drue off hear Containg 54 Gallons of which I have taken for my Accot. 13¼ Gallons; should be Glad you will let me hear per Your next how much I am to Charge myself per Gallon; Mr. Pollock has not Paid Mr. Poussett the $27 as the latter acquaints me in his Letter; no matter I Shall Send him the money this day; louis has Got the hams that was here; and them that was at Mr. Fargusons with the Beacon. . . .

P.S. my Compliments to Mr. Fields;

To McGILLIVRAY AND STRUTHERS, *Mobile*

Manchac, February 11, 1773

I had the pleasure of Writting you the 6th Ulto. per Mr. Romans, which I hope are now is Safely come to hand; and to which referr

[35] A younger brother of Isaac Monsanto, Manuel was born about 1734. He left New Orleans in 1769, when the family was exiled, and became a business partner with his brothers in a store at Manchac, dealing in dry goods, cattle, slaves, and local commodities. He also maintained a home or plantation in Pointe Coupée. With his brother Jacob, Manuel moved in the early 1780s to New Orleans, where the two established themselves in business on Toulouse Street. He died there about 1796. See Korn, *The Early Jews of New Orleans*, 10–67.

Merchant of Manchac

You; Concerning the Trade of this place; since which there is nothing New worth your Notice; only that I have been informe'd by Sundrys that Mr. McIntosh is about selling his Skins to Messrs. Pollock & Willing for Cash and with which he propposes, to pay of[f] his Account with the house But wheather so or not I cant realy say but I believe he has wrote you him Self on that head; By his boat; for my part all that have to say in regard to Skins; is that all I have and all that I shall be able to git here After; you May Depend on them the same as in your Store; (if some Unseen Accident does not happen to them on their passage from hence to your place)—I am Expecting with great Deal of Expectations; the Arivell of some Traders With their Skins that has been daily Expected down this some time Past; but are not as Yet arrivd. or I should have Gone from here to Orleans With my Skins; but shall loos no time after their Arrival; to go down; With them so as they may be sent you; per the first Conveyance from that Place; Mr. Bently since he finds that he has no Goods Come out in Capt. Waugh by whom he Expected a large Cargo, as he Often toald me; before the latters Arivel; has throud out many hints; as if he should be Glad to have A Supply of Goods from your house—he has often spoak to me something in that way; but I as Often toald him I could not Tell how it might take With you—I have nothing to say aGainst Mr. Bentley; knowing of what Consequence it is to say any thing aGainst a man; with out having Convincing proofs; of what one may Advance; but this I Can say it is a hard Matter to Git any thing out of his hands for he has owed me $350 Since the first of last may with out my being able to bring him to a Settlemt. he still Keeps putting me of from one Time to another; and further I have reason to Believe that he has some large Engagements already in this province, Without saying what he may have at home; I only Mention these things to You for Your Governement; and hope Gentlemen; that you will Excuse the Liberty I have taken in so doing; for I promise you it is out of no Motive of Malice; but for Your Interests sake; in such you will Act as you think Proper; Should he want any Goods from You; the Bearer Mr. Lum has Meet with a Great Disappointment; Mr. Willing not keeping his promise of Supplying him with Goods; as he will be able to Acquaint you more fully him self; You have here Inclosed a Small Account aGainst him for $8.4½r Which he promised to pay to the house for my Acct. we have Been in Expectation of Seeing Mr. McGillivary long are now here; but As Yet have heard Nothing of his being on the way; this Being the Needfull . . .

To CHARLES STUART, *Mobile*

Manchac, March 10, 1773

This serves to Acknowledge the receipt of your Esteemd favour of the 28th Ulto. which is now before me and shall Observe well Its Contents; But that you ware pleased to write me per Mr. Salt Kill neaver Came to hand—I make no doubt but the few Inhabitants that lives on the Est side of Mississippi; on their hearing of Mr. Thomas's having nothg. More to do; or say in the Indian affairs; this way, will be Extreamly Glad for had he remained here any longer; its Certain no man would have been Able to reside on this plantation; (for a proof of what I advance let anyone Only remember What hapned at Mr. John Bloomants; last Spring; who Was on the brink of Loosing his life; and all the mens lives that was at the Plantation with him;—for only Offering; to stop the Indians from robing his house; one of Mr. Bloomants hands was Stabbed through the thigh And aNother Slightly Woanded; When the Afair came to be inquired into the Indians had for Answer; that Mr. Thomas; had toald them to take provisions Where they could find them; this an affair; that almost every Inhabitant On the river Can aVouch for; if Demanded I can further say that had he Continued much longer in this Department that we should have been Obliged to abandon the place to him self; and his party—there being no Such a Thing as living where he had (or pretended to have the Command in Chief) for the small time that he was here (By his Exampels) the Indians have Conceivd. Such strange Notions a mong them as I promis You Sir; will require a long time to ware off; the Indians presents that Was left in my Possession I have shipped for your place by the Occasion of Capt. Brown; who goes with Mr. Miller and Whos receipt for the Same and an Accot. of the Goods You have here Incolosed which added to the things Given to Leflour; as per Receipt a Gun and Blankett to Govorr. Dunford And what things you had your self when here) will Compleat the Amount of the Accot. of Goods receivd. of Mr. Thomas the 5th of last may—I am really sorry to be obliged to send them Back should have Excepted your Offer with pleasure of Changing them; and have Given You an order on Messrs. McGillivary Struthers & Comy. for as many of Each Epeau;—but Trade has Been so Dull with me this long time past; that if it dus not Change this sumer; I have more Goods on hand then I shall be able to dispose of this year to Come; the Gentlemen of the House Can Acquaint you that I have Ordered Nothing more this Year; the Country being quite over dun with all sorts of Indian Goods

Merchant of Manchac

As to what you Mention; Relative to the great Confusion; among the Indians on the Mississippi (as the great man says) Occationed by your Jorney to this parts; is so strang a thing to us that live on the river; that I Believe not one Inhabitant; since Your Departure from hence Can Complain of the least I'll Usage; from the Indians; all the Indians that have come to My house; have always seemed Mighty well pleased with the Talk you gave out when here;—they have often demanded of me when you ware to Return aGain I have always toald them that I could not Tell—[36]

As for the Certificate that you request to Justify your Behavior; while With the sundry tribes of Indians when here; I cant send you per this Conveyance But shall send it you in a short time hence; as I am aGoing to the Point Coupée in 5 Days hence; will take it with me and have it signed By all the principal people up that way; as I make no doubt but every Inhabitant will Sign it; as there is not one that I have heard off that has reason to Complain of the Indians since Your Departure this being the Needfull . . .

To PETER SWANSON, *Mobile*

Manchac, March 10, 1773

Your much Esteemed favour of the 27th Ulto. is now Before me; and I note well its Contents; But the letter you Mention that Mr. McGillivary wrote me from Pensacola is not as Yet come to hand —the first Account Certain that I had; of the Alterations in the House I had from Mr. Miller; I am heartily Glad to hear that you are in the House; it is such AGreeable peice of News to me; to here of your well fair; that I realy wish all Your Affairs, and all your Undertakings may be Crouned with the Greatest Suckcess, [?] for if success; is any way Owing to Personal Merritt—I am well Assurd that Your Portion will not be the Smallest—

I am Much Obliged to you; for your favorable, Opinion you have of me; Which Opinion I Shall always Endeavour to uphold —in Your Esteem; As for the Continuance of my small Custom you may Rest Assurd Tho I am afraid that it will not be so Considerable as I could wish,—for Your Interest as well as my own; for the Times and the Trade that is Now Carried on in these Parts at Present must meet with a Considerable Change; which for the present we Can only hope for; Occasioned by the Many failures that have Hapned at Home; I have Been very misfortunate this last Year both in the sales of my Goods; and in recovering my Out standing debts—But hope I shall be able to do more in both

36/To counteract the confusion created by Lieutenant John Thomas among the Indians along the Mississippi and the general distrust which he aroused in the minds of the neighboring Spanish, Charles Stuart was ordered to visit the Mississippi area in late 1772 to smooth over the whole situation. Stuart went to New Orleans, where he met with Governor Unzaga, and also held a conference with the Small Tribes. See Alden, *John Stuart and the Southern Colonial Frontier*, 333.

ways this Year;—I belive I shall take some small things from Mr. Millers Cargo; when Arrivd. here; to Assort the goods I have s[t]ill On hand it being the Same; as if they came from the House; Both Your Housses being but one at present; if I should want any sml. thing to keep up my Assortment; and that Mr. Miller should not have them; I shall desire the Gentlemen; of the House; to send them me which I hope they will not refuse; Although I have not been; so Successfull as I could Wish for in my Remittance as Yet this Year—I say Nothing to you Relative to skins and Skins affairs in these parts; as Mr. Miller will Be able to Acquaint you more fully Your self; I am very Well Satisfied with Abner Bushes Behaviour; and Could Wish I could say so Much for his Brother William that owes me $76.6r; Which has been Due me Since may 71—and which McIntosh Assumed the payment off when at Your place last year; in presence of Mr. McGillivary Struthers & your self One Evining as we all sat in the Roum; You may Remember something of it; and of my Speaking to yourself; on the Subject in the Coumpting House; Since his return he refuses to pay any part; though when he Assumed the paymt, he had Where with in his hands—as to the Tobaco that still remains unsold should be much Obliged to you; if you will do With it what you think the most Advisable; for all that you will do in the Affair will Always be aGreeable to me—I most sincerely wish You happiness in all Yoar Under Takings. . . .

P.S. I had the pleasure of Writting You the 31st last octobr. in which was Inclosed Mr. Kraps note of hand payable to the Bearer for $ [blank] which letter yo do Not Acknowledge the receipt of; if it is not Come to hand are now; please to Acquaint me in Your Next, that I may send You a Coppy of the letter & Note—

To McGILLIVRAY, STRUTHERS AND COMPANY, Mobile

Manchac, March 12, 1773

This serves to Acknowledge the receipt of your Esteemd Favour of the 27th Ulto. Relative to the Goods; Mr. Stuart had here Mr. Miller has taken some part of them; and I have taken one hundred of Gunn Powder; 426 lb. Bullits; 7 Trading Guns & 200 Gun flints; for which I have Given in an Order in favour of Mr. Stuart; on the house; I have Delivered to Mr. Miller 1271 Skins in the hair & 140 Drest Skins; (it being all I had in the House; which was no ways Answerable to the Quantity; I Expected long are this) for as yet I have not recvd. any thing worth Mentioning from the People up the river—But hope are long to have the pleasure of Acquainting; You of having you more than I have Delivd. to Mr. Miller; if they Should Arive in Time; shall send them by the Schooner that comes With Mr. McIntosh's Goods; I Shall say Nothing; to you Concerning the Trade of this Place; as Mr. Miller Can Inform you how things Stands in the Quarters; having Nothing further to add for the present; Only to assure You Gentlemen that I am most Respectfully . . .

To CHARLES STUART, *Mobile*

Manchac, March 13, 1773

Since writting you the 10th Instant which goes here Inclosed Mr. Miller has Taken some Part of the goods that was here; that is to say 2 Doz Garlix Shirts 1 ps. Strouds 5 lb. Vermillion 16 Blankets & 150 lb. balls Which he will Deliver to you or Your Order, at Mobille; I have Taken 100 lb. Gunn powder, 426 lb. Balls 7 Trading Guns and two hundred Gun flints for which I have Inclosed You an Order on the Gentlemen of the House;—the Remaining part of them Shall be Obliged to keep hear; as Capt. Brown mentioned in my former is not sure of Gowing to Mobille; as Mr. Miller; Proposses Shipping the Skins at Orleans for England, if I can Dispose of the remaining party; Shall send you an Order; to receive to their Amount But if I cant shall send them you; per the first Conveyance;—

If you should leave the Province before my Note becomes due should be much Obliged to You; to leave it in no Other hands than that of the Gentlemen of the House; the Storage of the Goods from the 5th May to the 5 March is 11 Months at $2 per Month is $22; which you will please to allow me, or Indorse it on my Note; Your Compliance will Greatly oblige . . .

To MILLER, SWANSON AND COMPANY, *Pensacola*

Manchac, May 8, 1773

You have here Inclosed for your Government; Your Accot. of Sales of the goods that Came in Carpenters Sloop—which you Will find (I hope) agreeable to your Invoice and Instructions that I recivd. from Your John Miller; while hear and by his letters from Orleans—(This only Excepted) Two small Errors; which you may see by Comparing the Invoice with your sales; the first in the Pomeranis Linens No. 8 Being Marked in the Invoice 213 Ells instead Of 183½ ells that is 5 pss each Containing 30½ Ells & aNother 31 Ells Which makes the 183½—second Error is in the Box No. 77 ought by Invoice to contain 267 Cautaux —Knives—I only found 243 as you will Observe per the Accot. of Sales; which I suppose must been Owing to some Error Commited in the Number of ps; and in Counting the Knives—You have also hear Inclosed James Kelleys draft my favour on Elias Dunford Esqr. for one hundred & Ninety five Dollers & ¾ payable Sixty days after sight; which have Indorsed to your House—have at the same Time Sent you an Account sales of an Old Negro Wench that I sold for Mr. Dunford for $150 the Charges and Commission to be Deducted the Neat proceeds as per Sales $138.4 which if he Excepts the Bill; you will please to allow him; in Account of said bill; As I am very Desirous to have Kelleys Bills Excepted before Freemans and Wiltons comes to hand; which will be for near $400 which shall have On their Return from the Natchez; I have further to Acquaint you that Mr. Caudaux the Spanish Commanding officer of the Spanish Manchac;[37] is a Going to the point Coupée to be Commanding Officer their; he has been with me this Morning and Toald me that if you thoug[h]t Proper to send here two Bales of Strouds; one Bale of your 2½ point Blankts. at 10/ per pair one of Your Common at 8/ per pair; 6 hundred Weight of good Gunn Powder; 12 hundred of Bauls; 1 Case of Guns; some three quarter Checks he would Take them and pay for the same in the month of Novemr. Ensug.; Or Deecemr. Either in Cash or Skins; he will take them at the price of Your place; and pay their freight; I should not have taken the liberty of Writing to you on any Such Subject if I thougt. that their was the least Risque for your Interest; I can only add that since he has been hear I have had the Greatest Proof of his Punctuallity in all his Ingagemts. that he Contracted from time to time; shall leave it to your selves to Act there in; as You shall thing [think] the most Advisable for Your Interest—If their is any thing further this way in Which I Can be of any Service to your house; shall always be Glad to Receive Your Commands. . . .

P.S. Mr. Lum in Taking out the Goods toald me; that Mr. Mc-Gillivary had Given him his word; that he should have his Goods at 60 pCent Advance So have Charged no more; as you will see per his Bill; hear Inclosed till I hear from You; have Taken his note for the Amount payable in Nine Months—N.B. there is a letter of Advice with the Bill—

37/Captain Charles Descoudreaux, Spanish commandant at Manchac.

To PETER SWANSON, *Mobile*

Manchac, May 8, 1773

You have here Inclosed Sundry Letters that Came With Mr. Lum; Two of Which Came to the Adress of Mr. John McGillivary I have Opened; By reason of Mr. Lum's Telling me that he was well Assurd that their was Mention made in them to Supply him with some Cash, Although he toald me so; I should not have Taken the liberty had it not been for the Distress he was in; Occasioned by the Oxen that and the Cart that Mr. Mac Intosh Brought with him from the Point Coupée to draw their Goods from the forks to this Place; Neaver Could be maid to draw; altho I sent an Got an Accadien[38] to Drive them;—so that they have been Obliged to Git horsses at 30 And forty Dollers per head; as also a New Cart; or Else they should have been Obliged to have Waited till the river was up; to have them Brought by the Bayaux; Which in all Appearence will not be this Year—

All these reasons Induced Me to Open Said Letters—and further—for fear that their should be any thing wanting . . that I could Comply for the Interest of Both your Housses; Altho I found; Nothing said On that head; I Supplyed him with $30 With out he Could have Neaver Got his Goods to this place; I further lent Lum 125 lb. Gun powder; as you had more hear; Which please Send me by the first and same Conveyance; that my Other Goods Comes by; I also Oppened a Letter of Allexr. McIntosh's Esqr. that Mr. Lum Toald me he had Orders for so doing; in Case Mr. McIntosh was Gone from Daniel McIntoshs, because it Contained a Note of Mr. John Bloomarts for $17½ which Note I have; and Wrote to Mr. Bloomart concerning the Payment; I have Mentioned something to Your house Concerning one Monsr. Des Coudieux; for the perticuculars [*sic*] I referr you to the letter for Pensacola; in which Letter I Omitted to Mention; to Mr. Miller; But should be Glad you would Incase that Mr. Durnford should not Except the Bill to have it protested Infourm; and if possible to take out a Writ against the drawer for the Amount & Charges with out the loss of time; for without Some Such Meathod of Prooceeding I may wait a long time for my paymt. Should Mr. McGillivivary be still at your place; to present him with my Most humble Respects; should have wrote him; but look on it that he Is gone; are This; having nothing futthur to add I remain most Respectfully . . .

P.[S.] S[h]ould the Bearer Mr. Jacqueaux; want any thing in the Store; on his Accot. please Supply him; and Charge the same to my Acot.

38/The Acadians were French-descended Roman Catholic refugees from British Nova Scotia who began arriving in Louisiana in 1756. Many settled along the Mississippi River in Ascension and St. James parishes as far north as Manchac, an area which soon became known as the "Acadian Coast." Many of these settlers engaged in various types of farming.

To EVAN AND JAMES JONES AND COMPANY, *Pensacola*

Manchac, May 8, 1773

Your much Esteemed favour of the 2 Ulto. per Mr. Dutton Duly Came to hand; it is now before me; and I note well its Contents; I am Obliged to you for your Good Intentions; and sorry to find that it did Not meet with the Desired Effects but since their Can be Nothing Done that way; s[h]all only be Obliged to put up with the loss; which I promise You is a little two Much for me to losse in these hard Times; I wrote You per Via of the lakes last Feby. By a french man Named BonArm that went from this place with Intententions [sic] of Going to pensacola—I am sory to hear; it did not come to hand; But as things has happned; It is not so much loss; I am Glad you have not sent your Rum this way the New England Man has Supplyed all them that would want rum at 4/ per Gallon hear; Your flour would Meet with Good sale in Orleans at present there Being none in the place to be had for love Or money; Mr. Par'rs letter I deliverd to himself; as also his Barrl. of pork; the small things that came per Mr. Dutton he Receivd. them himself at forks of the Amitte; their is one of the Negroes Dead on the plantation; I belive it to be Mr. Parrs the Other Being Dailey Runing Away Occasioned as all people on the Amiett says by his Starving them; (if so or not Cant purtent to say) Bush has Complied with some part; of his Engagements; such as Making a Cabbin and fencing a Garden .. therefore have given him some part of his Goods; but shall not Deliver the remaining part Untill I hear from You; as his wife will not go to live at the plantation; as I have finished your sales; send you an Accot. there of; as Also an Accot. of Sundrys furnished to Mr. Perr; for the Use of your plantation as per Receipt; a Coppy which you have at the Bottom of the Accot. & lastley you have a General Accot. By which you will see that their is a Ballance due me of $140.4½ Occasioned by the Unhappy Affair that hapned; to Mr. Jacob Monsanto; the french man at the pt. coupée that was to Deliver the Cattle; on his agreemt. saying that as Mr. Monsanto; was a Spanish prisoner; there was no such thing as recovg. the paymt. it is Certain that the poor Monsanto has lost by the Affair of Near to $1500; and is a prisoner; in Orleans; and God only knows when he Will Git Clear; from their hands—this being the Needfull; from ...

P.S. the Umbrilla was lost at sea.

To McGILLIVRAY AND STRUTHERS, Mobile

Manchac, May 8, 1773

By this Occasion I send You 551 Skins in the hair & 9 Ds. it being all that I have receivd. since I deliv[er]ed the Others to Mr. John Miller; for Your Accot. their weight I Cant purted to Mention Occationed by not having proper Weights & Scales; which should be glad if Could procure for me a sett; As for my Note that was in Mr. Stuarts hands that you was so Obliging to take up you may Depend on my Sending You Bills on Mr. Dunford for near the Amount as soon as Mr. Wilton & freeman; Return for the Nachez Which I may Expect Before it becomes Due; I inclose you an Coppy of a Inventory that I sent you by Your; Mr. John McGillivary with some small Additions should be Glad if you Shiped the former; to send me the latter by this Conveyance[.] the Clearing the road to the forks & Carting Messrs. McIntosh's & Lums Goods to this place has been Atte[n]ded with such Expencess that you Neaver Could Immagine; Till you see their Accots. there off; Occasioned by the Disappointmt. they Mett with from the Cart and Oxan; that Mr. McIntosh Bought for the Accot. of the House; they Could neaver be maid to draw; for which reason I did Not think it advisable to give a receipt as Mr. McGillivary Desired me to dow; for them; he has Disposed of the Oxen for what they cost and have been Obliged to Git horsses at 25 & 30 Dollers per Head which for the future will be much Better; the Sheep that Mr. McIntosh Brought Down to be sent to the house; it was Imposible to send them by the Occasions the Sloop being Obliged to heive Down; Being so leakey that shee Could not Take nothing in—the Schooner so small that the few things fils up her hold; there fore shall keep them hear; till some good Oppertunity shall offer to send them[.] having nothing more to add; only to Aquaint you; that there is a Greater prospect of Doing something this year; than the last; as there does Not as Yet appear to be so many Strangers on the river with Goods; as there Was the last; this Being the Needfull from . . .

To PETER SWANSON, Mobile

Manchac, May 10, 1773

Your much Esteemed favour of the 27th Ulto. I have Just time to Acknowledge; the receipt of; But not to Answer; as the man that is to Carry the present is aGoing where he will; Meet With Monsr. Jacqueaux Before he git to your place; I have sent you the Coppy of Mr. Hugo Krebs Note the Original having sent you last Octobr. if you have Charged Mr. McIntosh's Accot. with the 150 lb. Gun powder; please to Charge it to me; as he has Returned it to me this day; Please to Excuse hast[e] and Belive me to be Most Sincerely Dear Sir; Yours to Command . . .

To McGILLIVRAY AND STRUTHERS, *Mobile*

Manchac, June 30, 1773

Yours favours of the 18th & 31st Ulto. are now before me & Carefully Observe the Contents[.] the Goods per Jacquo safely Arrivd. and in good Order; I am Much Obliged to you for Your; trouble in sending for the Skcales & Weights the Accot. you sent me of the goods had from Mr. Stuart is verry Just; but you will Please Credit me for Twenty tuo Dollers for my Store Accot. as also Six Dollers & 1 bill for 6 Yards of Stroud that was aWanting in a peice that he sold me for a Whole one; Both which he has Acknowledged to be Just and that he would Credit Me with; and for the powder sent Mr. Lum I cant pertend to take Mr. Stewarts In lieu of it; as it is partley Dammaged Lum took 50 of the Best of it and woud have taken the Whole had it not been so very Bad; so you may Charge Lum With the 50 lb. and for the 125 lb. Sent him I shall Settle with him as Easy as posible; as for what servises I might Rendered to him; they shall be Continued if in my power upon the Account of your House; as for Drest Skins I have none at present; and What I have in the hair; will not answer to send them this Season of the Year; I am Extreamly sorry to find your Accot. of the sales of Skins in England to be so very Bad; if them if them [*sic*] on the Mississippi should Not Answer You; it would be an Easy Matter for me to Exchange them for cash As there is a Great Many looking after them this way; and for my perswadg. Hunters and Other people to keep Skins free from pelt; and from Killing out of Season; I might as Well pertend to preach them into a More Regular and reformed way of life; though I shall Endeavour all that lies in my power Towards procuring Skins such as I hope; there shall be no Occation for any Objections; in my last to you; I was then in hopes of Sending you before now Some Bills of Mr. Willtons & Mr. Freemans on Mr. Dunford but as they are only ten leauges above this I Expect them Dailey I shall send them by an Oppertunity which will go from this in 8 or 10 Days by the way of the Bayoux[.] this Being the Needfull I remain . . .

P.S. if you should send me Goods or any thing Addressd. to

my Care; you will so Agree for the Freight; as I was Obliged to pay three Dollers for the freight of Leflours Box Before Mr. Bently would Deliver it.

To PETER SWANSON, *Mobile*

Manchac, June 30, 1773

Your kind favours of the 27th April and 31st Ulto. I recivd. And Note the Contents, I shall do my Endeavours to send you your Quantity of Tobaco, I have none my self at present, but shall write my friends in Orleans to ship as Much if they have it, on reasonable Terms the same you shall be Acquainted with as Soon as possible, and for Bears oil its very Scarce the season Being past; & Brings here a Greatter price than with you; as for Leflours oil I receivd. from him 53½ Gallons at 4/r per Gallon; and was sold for the same at Orleans the Amount of the hole Being $26.6 last year that Article was in Abundence there and very Cheap; the sales of which I only receivd. las[t] Winter from the man Who Sold it; relative to the Curried & Tand Leather I have wrote to Messrs. McNamara & Conway to Ship the quantity Mr. McGillivery spoke to them for; & to let me know the Amount there of, as I am Ignorant of the quty. Spoak for; or upon what terms; Although fully perswaded these Gentlemen will Not Charge more than to their Customers, and that I would Settle with them for it, having Accounts with one of the partners; I have had no Oppertunity of Sending up Blanchards letter; but Shall per first Conveyance; all that I am afraid of it Will be some Time before you Can git Your money; he ows me much about the same Sum these twelve Months & have not been Able as Yet to git the least payment; When I have the pleasure of seeing him I shall do all in my power for your Interest, I have sent the remainder of Mr. Stewarts Goods per the Schooner & Accot. of Which & receipt you have hear Inclosed[.] Beging leave to Conclude . . .

P.S. some time aGo Mr. Bentley made Application to Me for the horsses to Carry things for the use of his plantation to the forks; which I refused; as not having the Housses Answer to Whom they Belonged; as they ware left with me by Messrs. McIntosh & lum; it is very Certain that Mr. McGillivary When hear toald me that the Oxen or horsses kept hear was only for the Use of The House; & people that was Concerned With it when they had Either Skins or Goods to Cart to or from the forks; if you think proper he should have them for the Use of his plantation; I beg you will give him an order to take them into his Care; as they are, as they are [sic] of no Service to me; I been at the Expence, I Been Attended with Expence, by making a New fence to keep them from Going, to the Spanish fort—and a man to look after them—

To McGILLIVRAY AND STRUTHERS, *Mobile*

Manchac, July 4, 1773

Since my Writting you of the 30th of June last Captain Sassier Engaged him Self to go to point Coupée for some prisoners, which he is to Carry to pensacola; in Consquence of Which he says; he Cannot possibly Stop at Orleans to take in any thing therefore must Embrace the first oppertuy. from the river, or by way of the Bayaux; of Sending the Tobaco & Leather and Upon the Same Reason he Cannot take in any of the Sheep or any thing Elce—Being Incumberd with the prisoners & people to Gard them and the Schooner Being so Small; if Mr. Stuart is with you please Acquaint him of the Imposibility of Sending him his things at present, But shall per first Oppertunity if not Disposed off, Being the Needfull; at present . . .

To MILLER, SWANSON AND COMPANY, *Mobile*

Manchac, July 4, 1773

I Wrote you the 8th May last which referr; you Inclosg. You a Coppy of Accounts Sales of the goods that Came by Capt. Carpenter; Which I hope was found AGreeable to your Invoice & Instructions as also first Copy of James Kelleys Draut on Mr. Dunford for $195.3¾r which was I hope duly Honoured[.] I am now to acquaint you that the freight of the Goods per Capt. Carpenter; I was Obliged to draw on Mr. Morgan for being $87— Mr. Carpenter Neaver Spoake to me; Concerning it untill the Evening before his Vessell; was to sail for the Cape; and having not so much Cash in the House laid me under the Necessity of Drawing which I would not Have Done had I done had I got from him the least timely Notice[.] if any Servises Occurs to you where in I may be Usefull; Up this River yo. may at all times Freely Command . . .

To EVAN AND JAMES JONES AND COMPANY, Pensacola

Manchac, July 7, 1773

Your kind favour of the 23d may last Is now before me, and in Answer there to; Should be glad in Your Next, to find the Sundry Accounts Inclosed in my last to you; was Examined to your satisfaction; the first Accot. of Sales of the flour; have Examined & find that I have made an Error in the Addition by making it $177.6r Instead of $167.6r Which is $10 in my favour & Comissions being Deducted from the $10 remains $9.2r this money; I Am much Obliged to you for the Trouble You have Taken in Hamiltons affair and that you Still will Employ your Interest towards recovering that Dubious Debt; as to the Accounts given You last, relative to Your Amitte affair, was No more than what I heard from Sundrys whom I thing Might be Depended Upon; having my self Neaver been on the Spott; I have Assisted Mr. Parr, with my advice and Every thing Else in my power when required[.] I am Informed by Bushes Neighbours that he has got a pritty fieald of Corn, But as I Can Say Nothing of the Improvements he has made; Mr. Parr who goes for your place Will fully inform you; his wife still remains in this place but when she Intends Joining her husband on the plantation I cannot say but the first time he Comes to this place I am fully Determed to know when he Intends removing his family left here; which I Shall let you Know; in my Next; I have forwarded Mr. Frenonays letter it was now Needless to mention the persons Name as I had taken up the Cattle & am to pay for them in the Month of August a part of which is already paid; when You see Mr. Parr; he will give You the french Mans reason for not delivering the Cattle According to aGreement with Mr. Monsanto; in Sending the Umbrilla Delivered to Mr. Dutton on Accot. of Madame Blain was lost when last in Orleans, I took one from Mr. Saviray price $6 which if you Did not think proper to Accot. with him for; I promised him payment; it is verry true a few Days aGo Mr. Dutton sent me one; but it must be far Inferiour to that Designd. Madam Blain; & so returned it; there fore you will Charge Mr. Dutton with the One he lost; I should have kept the one he sent me, but it was so very small; that Little or no use Could be made of it—as for Mr. McIntoshs land adjoining the Reserved of this I Can say Nothing about having Never been in the back parts of it; but shall let you know in my Next fully Concerning it, as I will employ Some person or Indian who shall fully inform me of the Situation of the same[.] having Nothing further to add . . . [postscript illegible]

To JOHN MILLER, *Pensacola*

Manchac, July 7, 1773

Your kind favour of the 24th May last I receivd. only Two Days ago, & am Glad to hear that Mr. Durnford Accepted my order on Mr. Wilton & am very sory to find the Skins not Shipped home this Season should be Attended with so much Expence[.] I heard from Mr. Swanson to the same purport about them; I heartily wish Messrs. McGillivary & Struthers a hapy a Safe Speedy return to this province, & to have the pleasure of Seeing you at Manch[ac] I referr to mine of the 8th May & Jacquo; & of the 4 Instant per Capt. Woods a Gentleman from the Norward; & am much obliged to you for kind Endeavours for Securing my Enterest from that Damn'd Villian Hamilton you'l Eease [?] . . .

P.S. Sir. Inclosed have sent you for pensacola a Copy of a letter which Mr. Bentley sent me last night; upon what reasons or motives my Weak Judgmt. has not been able to penetrate into the Grounds of which seems to arise from a paquet with Mr. Mansanto sent me Yesterday which packet was from your Self; Immediately on receipt of it; sent him his letter; which was inclosed upon Which some time After wars he sent to know from whence the letter Came; I returned for Answer I was Surprized that he Should then Enquire after he Had Opened the letter; he After wards sent to know by what Oppertunity it Came; I then a second time Desired the Messenger to let me alone—as I was Conscious of not having Detained his letter; if my Brief Answer Did not suit Mr. Bently it was altogeather owing to him self as he gave Orders to Mr. Maison when he went aboard Capt. Saucier not to receive any Letters that was for me, or to have any hand in forwarding them; this the Capt. When here Inform[ed] Me of; and the Truth of Which will be assertained by him to you (if required) As he is now at your place You'l please to Communicate the same of the Inclosed to your Mr. Swanson & I remain with respect &c. . . .

To JAMES JONES, *Pensacola*

Manchac, July 7, 1773

Inclosed You have a Coppy of a letter which Mr. Bentley was pleased to Write me last night upon what Motives I Cannot pretend to say; I should be Much Obliged to you; that you would Communicate the Inclosed to Mr. Morrisson and Giving him on my Account his Customery fee; Desiring him to give his Opinion in Writing (to be sent me by first Oppertunity) if their be sufficient Grounds for Entring a petition [?] aGainst Mr. Bently[.] you may Depend I Shall spare no Cost in Vindicating my Character so farr as my Abilities Will admitt of; for to live under Such a Scandolous one as he Intimates in the Inclosed; Should have Taken my own revenge; had he not been effectivily Screened By the Tittle of Esquire; which in one Sence is quite Arbitrary on thise River Having no Superiors present to answer to for their abuse of power, which has Been the Case of late in some of them; Neglecting their Duty towards some prisoners taken up for Murder & Roberry & now sent to your place[.] you may if You think proper take the Advice of Mr. Levingston Along with that of Mr. Morrissons whose Opinions with your own you'll please to forward per first conveyance, You'l Excuse the trouble I Give you in this Disagreeable Affair & Believe I am at all Times . . .

To JEAN LAFITTE, *New Orleans*

Manchac, July 20, 1773

I Receivd. Your Eesteemed favour of the 14th Instant is now Before me the Contents of which I duly Observe I am Much Obliged to you for your Complisance in Complying with your Order for the Tobaco; since Capt. Sauceir refused taking the said Tobaco; Should be Glad you would send it By some Oppertunity of Going Directly for Mobille for Messrs. McGillivary & Struthers; and the freight of the same I Shall pay here; and if no Vessell offers of Going soon there; I desire you will be so kind as to send it up to this place; I have frequent oppertunities of Sending it by the way of the Bayoux from this; I Beg if you have any Sugar about $7.4 or $80 per Ct. Should be obliged to you to keep or send me Two or three Barrels and one Hogs head province Wine; Inclosed You have Two Notes of Messrs. Polock & Willing at Sixty Days Sight Amounting to $331.6r which you'l please to git Excepted; please after Acceptance to Acquaint Monsr. Ranson and When due to be kind Enough to take up my Note; in his hands & the Balla[n]ce Youl please to keep in your own hands; untill I have the Pleasure of Seeing You in the fall; or perhaps Sooner; and the Remainder I shall settle With you then; Your Goodness I hope will Excuse the Trouble I am Continually Giving you. . . .

To JOHN STEPHENSON, *Pensacola*

Manchac, August 1, 1773

Your Esteemed favour of 7th Ulto. is now Before me the Contens. of Which shall Duly Observe as for the three letters you ware pleased to write me while at Orleans I neaver recivd. But that in which there was a nother for Patrick Morgan; in which you neavour Mentioned to me wheather or Not you would have me Git the Oars; as I proposed to you; in mine of the 28th Augt. in 72. as for the Canoe I had made here [her] Agreeable to your Dementions with a Sett of Oars which Cost $12. She lay hear about Six Weeks with out Being Able to sell her; for want of a proper, Conveyance the Water at that Time Being so low; that shee would not pass per the Bayoux; of this place or would have sent her by the lakes, she was Stole from me; But by Whom I was neaver Able to find out; the tongues Nutts & Beef that you required me to purchase for You, I did all in my power to procure the Two first Could not be had althoug[h] I sent to point Coupee Grand Gulph & the Natchez for them, the Beef I Did Git & have it properly Smoaked & ready & ready [*sic*] to send you; which Should have Done by Mr. Kelly [?] last Spring; but he toald me he could not [*illegible*] of Taking the Beef with him to your place and should have Embraced the Oppertunity of Mr. Bruce had it been possible of Transportg. it by Land to the River Amittie, which would be attended with more Expenc than the Value of the Meet; & When the hot weather come on it got full of Worms, that I was Obliged to Sell it, or should have lost it all; but hope to be More Successfull this Ensuing Winter as Intending to pass some part of it up the river When I Shall be able to git you Beef Tongues Nutts &c. if you should want any of them[.] I have sent you the Rushes & have requested Mr. Swanson to forward them for you per first Oppertunity—as the Nature of my Demand on Mr. Riston is only requiring him to pay you on my Acct. $82.9¾ that I over paid him; which Error happned by not having my Accts. With me at Orleans the 20th April 71 when I sent (I sent) [*sic*] him a percell of Indego; per Mr. Granigo; to the Amount of $137.2½ instead of $54.2¾ Which was the Ballance due him; as soon as I was Assured of the Error, I Acquainted him there with; & sent him at same Time a Coppy of his Acct. Current hoping he would not be Backward in repaying the overplus to you; I say Nothing Concerning the $100; that sent him by poor Mr. Fanning the 20th Septr. 69, that was lost, but have repayed in Consideration of his laying out of his funds so long, Altho you will see by his of the 13th June 69 Where in he Desires I should make him remittance per the first Conveyance Which letter and Acct. you have here in; Inclosed for your Government in the Affair, there fore I hope there will be no Dificulty in the way to Hinder him from Complying with my first request; Should there be any thing this way in Which I Can be of any Service to you; should be always G[l]ad to receive Your Commands and Beleive I am at all times with Sincerity . . .

To EVAN AND JAMES JONES, *Pensacola*

Manchac, August 1, 1773

Your favour with that of Mr. Van Tyul of the 24th Apl. I receivd. the 14th Ulto. inclosing a list of Sundry goods sent to my Care for Mr. Jaques Rapalje[39] which when they Come to hand I shall take Immaginable Care off, But am not a Little Surprized that I have never heard anything more about them or which way they was to come; however Shall Make Inquiry about them; have Wrote to Mr. Rapalje Advising him there of, What Ever Servisses lie in my power to render Mr. Rapalje Shall not upon my Account be Wanting Being the Needfull . . .

To McGILLIVRAY, STRUTHERS AND COMPANY, *Mobile*

Manchac, August 16, 1773

I had the pleasure of Writing you the 4th Ulto. to which refers Since have not Been favoured with any of yours; this serves to Acquaint you that you that [*sic*] I have got the leather & Tobaco you Mentioned in your last which Should have been sent long are now, if their had Been any Conveyance to Your Place to Orleans from Whence I came the Other day, & Desired Mr. Lafate & Conway to send you the leather & Tobaco as soon as possible; which they Promised they would, here in You have Inclosed sundry Bills &c.—Viz.

Quien John Freeman on Elias Dunford Esqr. for	348.3/4
John McGillivarys Accepttance for	28.3/4
John Fitzpatrick on James Bruice Esqr. for . .	51.5/8
	$429.1/8

Which when paid You'll please place to my Cr. I shall Want some small Things a list you have here inclosed, to make an Assortment for the Ensuing winter as I shall be obliged to pass some of it up the river on Account of Recovering my Outstanding debts there

---

39/Jacques Rapalje, son of Garrett Rapalje, a New York land speculator, came to West Florida in the early 1770s to look over the province on behalf of his father and his business associates. In April, 1773, Rapalje and his associates were promised a reservation of 25,000 acres in return for promises to settle a certain number of families on the land. Jacques also purchased land near Baton Rouge, where he settled. See Council minutes, April 19, 1773, PRO, CO 5/630.

Being so many on the river; looking out for Skins that if I dont take that meathod I shall Be in the same Labirinth I was in last Year; Occasioned by the persons Not Being punctual to their Agreemt. as one Could Wish; they meeting with many Merchants Before they Come this lenth; this Being the Needfull; I remain with respect . . .

To PETER SWANSON, *Mobile*

Manchac, August 16, 1773

I Omited in my letter to the House to mention that the Messrs. Wards had now in my house, Sundry Goods left with me by Mr. John Gradinigo to be sent them per first Conveyance since which their has None offered for Your place; Among Which there is 15 pss German Ozns. [osnaburgs] Some of Which I may want haveing none on hand[.] should be much Obliged to you; to speak to the Gentlemen & Desire to know What I shall do with their Goods & at same Time if it would Suit the House; that I should Take any part of the Oznabrigs; I Beg you would Settle the same with them; or return them the quantity; if Agreeable to you let me Know per first oppertunity and Youl Oblige . . .

To DANIEL AND BENJAMIN WARD, *Mobile*

Manchac, September 13, 1773

Inclosed You have a receipt for Sundrys left in my Care by Mr. John Gradinigo to be sent you by first Oppertunity of which this is the first that has offered from this place; I have kept for myself One of the Saddels & Bridles & have Given Mr. Swanson order to repay the Same to you of as Good a Quality[.] You'll Please pay the said Gentlm. 5 Dollers & a half Being for porterage & Storage on said Goods being the Needfull . . .

To McGILLIVRAY, STRUTHERS AND COMPANY, *Mobile*

Manchac, September 13, 1773

Your Esteemed favour of the 28th July is now Before me and Hopes are now you have mine of the 16th Ulto. to which refers You[.] I am now to advise You of having Shipped from Orleans on Your Accot. 100 Carrots Tobaco on Board Monsr. Baptist for your place it is Charged ½ Doller a Carrot As for the leather it is ready & your Brother will Take Charge of it in Town & let you know the price for Both which Articles You'll please Credit my Accot. By this oppertunity have sent what Goods was in my hands of Mr. Stuarts addressed to your Jno. Miller; with an Account of their Being disposed off; I Shall have a house Built ready to receive any skins that may for the Account of the house Come down; the river. I am much Obliged to you for your advice concerning having any Connections with Mr. Blackwell; which you may Depend on I shall Observe, the Sundry Articles Mentioned in my last You'll please forward per first oppertunity if not Sent Before this reaches you Being the Needfull I Conclude . . .

To MILLER, SWANSON & COMPANY, Pensacola

Manchac, September 14, 1773

Your favour of the 23 July by Mr. Swanson I recivd. and Observe the Contents[.] inclosed you have an receipt & an Accot. of Mr. Stuarts goods which You'll please take Charge of[.] your Acot. you sent Me finds it very right only you have Omitted Charging me with the Coffee had of Mr. Hodge which you will see by the Inclosed, I intend selling out to morrow or next day for point Coupée on purpose to Acquaint Decod [illegible][40] What has pased; the result of which Shall make you Acquainted with per first Conveyance, What goods Mr. Swanson has not Disposed of; I shall take Charge of and Dispose on Your Accot. what I can of them[.] I have Taken a few things on my own Accot. for any perticulers Referrs you to Mr. Swanson As for Gradinegoes Notes I shall take with me and Settle the same with him if possible I can[.] Being the Needfull I Beg leave to Assure You . . .

To LUKE COLLINS, Natchez[41]

Manchac, October 7, 1773

Your favour per Blakely of the 24th Ulto. I Receivd. and Also 45 Skins 5 of which was light & Damaged & therefore Cant Ascertain the price of Them Untill you Come this way[.] the Other 40 Weighed 75½ lb. at 25 Sols per lb. Or 2 rs Which Makes 18 Dollers & 7rs I paid Your Order to Blakely being £13 Pensilvany Money Which Makes in Dollers 34.5rs which have paid to Your Debite & Given you Creditt for the 40 Skins[.] when you come Down if You Should have Occasion for Rum Taffia, Wines or sugar I can Easily Supply You upon such Terms as Shall be of

---

40/ I.e., Descoudreaux.

41/ Luke Collins came from Virginia and saw military service during the French and Indian War. He arrived in the Natchez district with his family in 1773 and in 1776 received a grant of 600 acres on Fairchild's Creek north of the town of Natchez. He moved to Louisiana about 1780 and settled near Opelousas, where he was granted 640 arpents of land by Governor Miró in March, 1784. By 1789 Collins was well established in the Opelousas area and still titled himself "Major in the service of the provincial troops of Great Britain." He died in 1801. See William S. Coker, "Luke Collins Senior and Family: An Overview," *Louisiana History*, XIV (1973), 137–55; Luke Collins Documents, Department of Archives and Manuscripts, Louisiana State University; Winston De Ville, *Opelousas: The History of a French and Spanish Military Post in America, 1716–1803* (Cottonport, La., 1973), 37.

Advantage to your self[.] as for Your Barge you Mention I have not any Occasion for, having one Built on purpose for my own Use about a month ago[.] Should be glad to have the pleasure of seeing You here & you may Depend what Bussiness we may do to Geather shall be to your proffitt & Satisfaction, Being the Needfull I conclude wishing you happy Sucess in Your Affairs . . .

To JESSE LUM, *Natchez*

Manchac, October 7, 1773

Yours of the 12th August duly came to hand have it now before Me and Observe well its Contents[.] as for the Powder in Question I have recvd. it from Messrs. Miller Swanson & Co. With whom you will Account with for it; But not in the price you Coat in Yours; But Leave that Matter to Your self; to settle; I have sent you per Monsr. Jacquax your Account Curt. With your Notes which should be much Obliged to you to pay to him; as he is a person that you may Depend Upon; as for the Authors of the reports Spread hear; Concerning Your Turning away the french Boat with the Flour; was a Gentleman Named Capt. Wood and the five young men that Was with him Named Boumen; which Report was Still further Confirmd. By all Mr. Swazeys people; and Still went further; & said that was the Occasion that made them leave the Settlemt. of their lands near the Natchez they not Being able to git provisions, Except they would Buy your flour at $5 Dollers per hundred; and that the french Boat would have let them Have it; for $3 the Hundred; if so or not Cant say—they toald every one here that had a Mind to hear it; that hooper had Been Seen at your house Since his Brother was Taken; and that he had been seen aSetling Accou[n]ts With you; Mr. Rapalji when here the Other Day said that he had heard the same; story from sundry Inhabitance of your place when there And lastly Spencer toald here that the day he went to the Natchez to have Mr. Willings Horses Marked that you toald him to Take Care of himself for that hooper had Been at your house while he had Been Over at Weds'es[.] if I take the Liberty of Writting you as funt on that Subject, it was Only on Account that I should Be sorry that any man; should have Such a thing aledged AGainst him, and Especily one that has Connects. With the Gentlemen You have; I have now Quoated all the Authors As You required, therefore you may Act as you shall think the most advisable; in the Affair—having Nothing further to add only should be Much Obliged to you to Remitt me; the Ballance of Your Accot. as I am In Want of Money and Oblige . . .

{162
Merchant of Manchac

To THOMAS JAMES, *Grand Gulf*[42]

Manchac, October 20, 1773

Your much Esteemed favour per Nelley I receivd. and have Sent the things by her agreeable to the Invoice inclosed[.] I am very sorry that I could not send you it Being Scarce on the river and none to be had in Town & what I have sent is out of some that was apart for the Family use & Charged you no more than the first Cost at Orleans, I Wish it had been in my power to have sent you the Striped Duffills But them I have sent I am in hopes they will Answer Your porpose Quite as well and if not, I will take them aGain when I Shall have the plasure of Seeing you up the River; in about two Months; what things you may Want I Begg You may let me know of; as I shall bring them up with me[.] Having Nothing new to Acquaint off I am ...

P.S. the Bearer Skins Weighed 72½ lb. Neat & the Gross of the whole 75 lb. which shall be sold on your Accot. & the proceeds passed to your Creditt as they would by means suit the English Markett;

To DAVID HODGE, ESQUIRE, *Pensacola*[43]

Manchac, October 22, 1773

Your much Esteemed favour of the 25 Ulto. duly came to hand per Williams Burns & am very sorry that their is no possibility of sending You the Corn yo. Want (not that it is wanting on the river) Occasioned by the hand Carage over to the forks which would be Attended with more Expence then the first price, but should Any oppertunity offer for your place from this river and should still be in want of the Articels you mention only let me hear and you may be assurd if possible Shall send it You; What Grain they raised on the river Amitte will be scarce Sufficint to Subsist them Selves having Nothing further to add ...

To GODLEY AND RAINCOCK, *Pensacola*

Manchac, October 22, 1773

I have this moment Receivd. a Letter From Monsr. Sarpée of the Illinois relative to Mr. Barrows affairs in which he promises to send Me Down the next spring all the Bills he has not been able to recover Payment off, as also the Amount of them for which he has receivd. paymt.—he Resquest me that I should have his Receipt that he gave to Mr. Barrow Ready for to Deliver him up

---

42/English trader, resident at Grand Gulf. For his role in the dispute between Fitzpatrick and Nelly Price, another trader, see this volume, 348–49.

43/Pensacola merchant and member of the provincial council.

or to the person that he s[h]all send down the things by; & as I have not got it but suppose Mr. Barrow on his leaving the province left it with you; Should be much Obliged to you to send it me per first Conveyance, for should he Come or send with out it; they will deliver; up Nothing. Being the Needfull . . .

To MILLER, SWANSON AND COMPANY, *Pensacola*

Manchac, October 22, 1773

Your much Esteem'd favour was handed me last night by Capt. Burns, in which You Mention the Bad State of Mr. O Kelleys affairs for which I am Sorry to here; but it is no Other wise than what I long Expected; for my own part I think myself happy in Comming off so well; let his Circumstances be as they will; I shall not be a loosser above 9 or 10 Dollers; in my last to you per Mr. Swanson I Acquainted you of Setting out Next day for P. Coupie to see Mons. DesCoudraux to which place I have been But to my Great surprize found him quite Changed from What I Expected; he toa[l]d me he was sorry that the Goods had been detained so long; he Being Obliged before they Arrivd. here; to send to Orleans where with to supply his Traders, & at same Time toald me would Take part of them; to which I Should Neaver have Consented; had there been any Meathod left to Oblige him But knowing there was not thought it the most Advisable for your Interest to let him have what he would Take; & that upon Conditions of paying in the month of March Next; an Account of Which you have here in Inclosed[.] I have sold some part of them to Emanuel Monsanto & since I have been the Cause of your sending them hear; be assurd I Shall do every thing in my Power to dispose of them; more to your Advantage then if Descaudraux had Got them; the house at Mobile Acquaints me they will send hear for the [s]kins Next Month. You well know that is not the Time, for my part I shall set of about the last of that month to go up the river where I Propose passing 8 or 10 Weeks to recover my Debts; so that it will be in February Before there will Be any Quantity here; there is nothing New here since my last worth Notice & what there is Shall referr you to Mr. William Swanson to whom I have Wrote having Nothing more to add but Wishing you health and prosperity . . .

P.S. Should have sent Mr. Hodge the Corn the land Carage and Other Charges would have been more then the first Cost—Since Lum; has been at the Natchez I neaver Receivd. a letter for you; But what he is aDoing I don't Know & God knows—

To PETER SWANSON, *Mobile*

Manchac, October 22, 1773

Your much Esteemed favour of the 30th Ulto. duly came to hand & is now Before me; & Shall Observe the Contents Instead of Making Use of any of the Oznabrigs with out Your Answer; having shipped them per Capt. Sauciers Schooner for them & am heartily glad to have had Nothing to do or say to 60 pCent Gentlemen; altho I am quite out of that Articel the Other day Mr. Monsanto came to me with his Invoice from Miller Swanson & Co. Requesting me to put the prices & the name of the Goods in french & there in found to my great Surprize that he was only Charged 6½d Sterling for his German Oznabrigs & that mine is Chargd. 9d per Ell first Cost which makes a Difference in the Cost; 2 peices I had Left from the house Amounting to $12.5/7 if by Mistake should be Glad you would Acquaint me in the Next; Other wise must suppose that the house at Pensacola; has its goods so much the Cheaper; so as to be Able to sell so much the lower; as both Monsantoes and mine ware of the same quality; having Nothing new to Acquaint You . . .

To McGILLIVRAY, STRUTHERS AND COMPANY, *Mobile*

Manchac, October 22, 1773

The coppy of yours of the 6th last August & yours of 30th Ulto. Came to hand with Mr. Guilory as also the Sundry Goods in good order, & found all right; having Credited the house for their Amount as also what things Mr. Guillory had Being in all $68.3½ this money[.] Your Orriginal of the 6th of August & the Case of Guns has not yet come to hand, tho I dailey Expect to here some thing of them from Mr. Ranson; to whoes care they ware sent; I observe by your last that propose sending here next month for the skins that the Sundry Housses may have at that Time, for my part I shall have No Large Quantity to send you then; Neither do I believe that any of the Others can; have many; it Being not the season of the Year; that we can Expect great things; it Being Just the Time When the Trade Comminces with Us; but whatever I may have Shall send them You; I Mentioned in my last that I proposed passing some part of the Winter up the River, the reason for Which I mentioned you at the same time; so that it will be February Before I have any quantity of Skins here worth your sending for; & you may be Assurd that will be near the Time; that the Other Housses will be ready to send your way[.] I should have been happy had it been in my power to have Acted Other wise, but there is so many here abouts looking out for Skins that it is Imposible to act in any Other Manner; I have not Credited your Acct. with the Guns & locks as you have Sent me; Mentioned their Price Neither in the Coppy; or yours 30th Septemr. But Shall on your Acquainting me with the prices; I hope long before now the Draugfts on Durnford and Mr. Bruice are honoured if not I Expect you will Do the Needfull; & by all means to have Freemans Settled Before he leaves the Province; the Bearer here of Being Waiting I conclude . . .

P.S. I had a letter from Mr. Conway in Town where in he Acquaints me that Mr. [*illegible*] had not taken the leather with him altho it was ready for Delivery what may be the Reason of its not Going I Cannot say—

To PETER SWANSON, *Mobile*

Manchac, November 18, 1773

Inclosed You have a Note of hand of one Nathaniel Wests who Lives above this[.] I beg you will be so kind as to git out a Writ against him For the same & send it me along with a Deputation leaving the Name of the Person Blank who is to serve it; dont Miss the first Occasion of forwarding It, as he is Dailey Making way with his Effects; he is the first person That I ever Served so; but if I dont take this meathod; I am afraid I Shall be Too late[.] Mr. McIntosh Arrivd. here safe two Days ago; as his things is not Yet come up from the forks have not had the pleasure of Receiving yours But as I intend for Town in a few Days shall then Answer them being the Needfull . . .

Coppy of Nathaniel Wests note of hand

Manchac 16th Augt. 1773

Two Months after Date I promise to pay John Fizpatrick or Order the Sum of Sixty four Dollers and six royals for value Receivd. of him as Witness My hand

Witness   his
Tho. Gregory   Nathanel R. West
                                             Mark

Pay the Contents to Mr. Peter Swanson or Order for Value in Acct.

[*signed*] John Fitzpatrick

To PATRICK MURPHY

Manchac, December 26, 1773

Mr. Blanchard pased pased [sic] here Some Days ago & spoke to him Concerning the Two Notes he toald me he had no Money with him but he Would leave it for me at the Commanding Officers at Point Couppée, if so As I leave this to morrow for my Voyage to the Grand Gulph I shall be able to Send it you from their per the first Conveyance; I have Spoak to an Accadien Woman about the Butter; which she is making for you; when she is to Bring here & the woman of the house will send it you; by the first Oppertuy. that may Offer for your place; I should be Glad to find a Good Occasion to Send you the Barrel of Rum; but cant find any that I may Depend on[.] Monsr. Vailure a Gentleman that has been in the same place with Hamilton aTrading last summer Toald me this morning that Hamilton is a Cumming down with seventeen hundred Deer Skins with which he is a Going to your place; I am in hopes You will be able to git Something from him And if you find him any way Inclined to pay that if you Can git only $400 in hand give him up the Note Your Attention in the affair will much Oblige Dear Sir . . .

To MILLER AND SWANSON, *Pensacola*

Manchac, December 26, 1773

This serves to Acknowledge the receipt of your last Letter Which should have Answered are now, but as I proposed Writing to you, before I sett of for the Grand Gulph; which Voyage shall Commince to morrow & Shall Carry With me to the Amount of; $2700, the sales of Which and What is already due me in them parts; will I hope at my return Enable Me; to make you a suitable return to your Expectations, I have taken some Part of Your Goods with me; some part is Sold; & a proper Account of Which Either of your; Gentlemen that comes to this place will find in my Books[.] Mr. Isaac Monsanto came here the Other day & had some Cotton Checks for Sale & as I was in Much want of to Carry with me And as he (Carried) sold them very Cheap I Bought to the Amount off $102, and drew on your house for the payment; as I immagined you Would have no Cash to disburse in the Affair; I hope you will not think hard of my Drawing on you; for if I thought you should have the money to pay; I should not have drawn on You—Mr. Kelley has not as Yet been here when he has run the land; shall pay him at your Mr. Millers Request and send You the Certificate and Account, per first Conveyance[.] Mr. Alexr. McIntosh of point Coupée Goes up with me to the Gulph; having Nothing more to add . . .

To McGILLIVRAY, STRUTHERS AND COMPANY, *Mobile*

Manchac, December 26, 1773

I had the pleasure of Writing you the 24th Ulto. per Vie New Orleans to which referrs; since which I neaver; Been favourd with Any Yours; the present is to Acquaint you; that I sett of Tomorrow for the Grad Gulph & Carry with me for $2700—the sale of which and the money already due me; in them parts; will I hope Enable me to Make you a suitable remittance this Ensuing Feby. at the latter End of Said Month or the Begining of March; I Expect to be here my Self or to send down the Skins; so that you need not meet with a Disappointment in Sending them home as has been the Case these Years past; there Neaver was so many Vessels in the river with Goods as there is at present; since the french lelft the province;—I am of Oppinion that some of them will make but a flemish sales they way they are Selling their Goods; for my part I cant think of Sending you any further Orders for any more Goods; Untill I come Down; the River; at which Time I am in hopes of Being Able to go to Your, Place my self, & shall then be a Better Judge how Trade will stand[.] having Nothing more to add only Wishing You the Compliments of the Insuing Year . . .

P.S. I have heard this Morning that Mr. Lum; has given a power of Attorney to Deliver up the Horsses to Mr. Bentley Because I lent one of the horsses that Lum Purchased to Capt. Carpenter to git in his Corn as they ware doing Nothing here Which horse is lost; Capt. Carpenter is very ready to pay for him; or Reinstate him, which ever I think proper; if the Horse is not found; as I always thought the horses Belonged to the House; & your Mr. Millers last request to me was to render all servisses laid in my power to Capt. Carpenter Being one of his Perticular friends in Pensacola; as the Sheep that Mr. McIntosh left here; for your Mr. McGillivy. Cant Conveniently be sent you, if you have a Mind to let me have them at the Price they are Charged to you; Ill take them for my Account—

To JOHN STEPHENSON, *Pensacola*

Manchac, December 26, 1773

Your much Esteemed favour by Mr. Carr & a french Gentleman duly came to hand the contents of which I duly Observe[.] Should Be Extreamly happy, if their is any thing in my Power to oblige you or Your friends that come this way; as for the latter he Deliverd me your Letter in Orleans; & the former Remains at my house; I leave this To Morrow for the Grand Gulph; About 120 Leagues from this place; I hope at my return to send you the Buffillow Tongues & Paucon Nutts that You wrote to me last year about, be assurd there shall be nothing wanting to procure them for money or Goods, if they are to be had in the parts where I am a Going to; I hope are this you have been able to Bring Mr. Ritson to a Settlement and that he has paid You; the Ballance that is so Justly due so long if their be any thing this way where in I can be of any service to you or your friends you may freely Command ...

To McGILLIVRAY, STRUTHERS AND COMPANY, *Mobile*

Grand Gulf, March 22, 1774

Your much Esteemed favour of the 2d Ulto. ha[ve] Now Before me, the Contents of which Duly Observe;—

I am Realy sorry that it was not in my power, to have Sent you my skins in Time to have Shipped them By Capt. McMain, but his Going off But his Going of [*sic*] at the Time you Mention; it was quite out off my Power; to have sent them; But hope that they will not meet with any Disappointmt. (as to being in Time) By Captn. Waugh; as Mr. McIntosh of point Coupée left this the 18th Ulto; with all the skins we Could Git togeather at that Time so that I am well Assurd; that all the skins he Took with him (what of his own at his house & them of mine at manchac; are Delivered to your Mr. McIntosh are this at my Place; or at Orleans Since Mr. McIntosh left me hear; I have Got since Tallow oil Beaver; Otters & Deer Skins; the former we porpose Disposing of for Cash at Orleans; and the latter; and the latter [*sic*] to Carry to your place; with as many More as wee shall be able to git; togeather; Before I go down[.] I Expect to leave this about the 20th of Ensuing Month (if the hunters Comes in that are Daily Expected with their skins; and After my arril. At Manchac shall loos no Time; But shall proceed for your place Then hope to have it in my power to have all things settled to your Satisfaction (or at least as farr as lies in my power) tho there has been Many a fleemish Account up this way this Year) having Nothing Further to add for the present only to Assure you that I am with much Esteem ...

To ALEXANDER McINTOSH, *Pointe Coupée*

Manchac, June 4, 1774

the present is to Acquaint you that by the Bearer I have sent You $400 in Gold there Being no Silver to be had in Town; as Also sundries the Amount of $159.4, Expended for your Account, as per Accot. here Inclosed for your Government; with Acct. of sales[.] I am realy sorry to have made You wait so long but I promise you it was not for want of Taiking all the pains possible to Dispose of all the Goods; which I was on the point of Bringing up aGain Not Being able to gitt a Doller per lb. and at Last was I Obliged to Take 4½ sols that Being $5 p Ct. weight [*i.e.*, per hundredweight] More then the Beaver sels for in Town at Present as all the ships are Sailed for England & for my part I am realy Glad that it is off our hands, the more so Instead of our Loossing any thing by the Weight; being obliged to sell it french Weight we Gained 117 lb. that is 43 lb. that was light and Dammaged & 74 lb. Good the Otter skins I left at Monsr. With's on Accot. of Mr. Ransons Request; the Cased Otters at 10/r Each; the split ones at 7/r Each; The raccoon skins at 10/sols Each Could I have returnd to Town; I should have got the money; but realy could not; therefore thought it as well to leave them; as to bring them up aGain knowing that the money is always ready for us; I have paid Robertson the amot. of his and Carters Accot. that is $505: as per his receipt. I gave him 261 Dollers in Cash on Accot. of paying prices Wages but Since You have paid price he will give you the 160 Dollers as he Dus not want the money to Carry with him; should be Glad how soon Wee could come to a Settlement for our Gulph Affairs; as I shall want to Go to Mobille as soon as possible; I shall go work next monday and Shall neaver quit them untill they are finished; which I am in hopes I can do in 15 Days; should be much Obliged to you to send me an Account of the Beef; and the Charges you have Been at; on our Accot. Shall Write you more fully in a few Days. ...

To MONSIEUR [*Blank*]

Manchac, June 18, 1774

I take the liberty of Inclosing you three Notes of hand,—Payable to the Bearer for the Amount; off $278.6 for the recovery of Which will pay you any Commission you shall think reasonable—As for that of Monsr. Vallieree; I request that if he does not pay you On Demand; that you; will put it in the hands of Senr. Don Henry; as I promise you he has used me most Cruelly; and as for the Messrs. Morants if they wont pay Please to Act with them as with the Other—I am realy sory to have to Trouble you on any such Occation my Necessity has no Law; there fore Rely on Your; goodness; and you ware So Obligeing to offer me Your kind Assistance; and if Ever in my power to Oblige you in any thing this way you may Depend that I shall Always Be . . .

P.S. Monsr. Vallieres Note was payable to the; Bearer, But through a Mistake I had Indorsed it; which Indorsemt. I have Cut out; & Inclosed the same; it Being of no Consequence but for your Satisfaction have Inclosed it to you—

To JOHN McGILLIVRAY, *Mobile*

Manchac, June 23, 1774

Your Much Esteemd favour of the 31st Ulto. is now Before me; the Contents of which Shall duly Observ—I am much Obliged to you for your Good intentions for my well fare; in regard to what you ware pleased to Mention, in Yours; Relative to your Stopping the man that run from this Place; Such are the Behaviour of many in this lawlis Parts; when Occasion Offers; for them to make there Escape; But for my part I lost Nothing by him for Madame Blain took such Care that she maid him pay what he was Indue me some Time Before he left this place; I am realy Sory to here that any part of your Bussiness should Take; any Disadvantages Turn; so that you Cant Supply me on the same Terms; as to here to fore; sooner then pay the 60 pCent; I had reather Take them at your Place & pay the freight, as I am well Assurd they will Neaver Cost me 10 pCent freight; as to the skins I should be sorry we should loos any Thing by them; sooner then that should be the Case; I will Dispose of all the light Skins at Orleans; for Cash; at a Good Advance & them that Weigh Sell to the New Englanders; as they are Always Demanding after Skins when in the river and Will give three royals your Money per lb. I am for ever much Obliged to you & the Gentlemen of your House for the many Repeated Servisses that I have so ofteen Receivd. from you & them; Be asSurd that I shall Neaver Request; any thing that may be Deter mental to your & there Interest; I have to Acquaint you that your sheep and mine Are reduced to a Small Number; at present; out of 72 large & small there Is not above [*blank*] left; Occasioned By the Overflowing of the Mississippi—And them that is left is 2 Miles from this in the High Lands; for the Perticulars of the river Overflowing; and the Dammages that I recivd. I referr you to Mr. Miller; who was Witness to the Whole; I have Nothing more to add only to Acquaint you that I have Taken part of the Cargo; TB Amounting at 50 pCt. to $3403.¾ But Cant say it was Properly Assorted; for this part of the Country; this Being all for the Present . . .

To JOHN MILLER, *Pensacola*

Manchac, July 1, 1774

Your much Esteemed favour of 21st Ulto. is now before me The Contents of Which I duly observe; I am Really Sorry to hear of your Continuing in the same Condition; but hope are this comes to hand; you Will be able to undertake your Voyage; for your place; with safty[.] Mr. Mr. [*sic*] Swanson Arrivd. hear about three hoars after you left this; but As Yet there is Nothing Come from the Schooner; I am affraid the Unlading her will be attended with much Expence; as there is Neither Water or Land Carage; Practable for the Present; I have paid the 2 Hands $5 Each and have Charged your Accot. with the same; I shall forever be Much Obliged if you will not for gitt me; about the promise You were pleased to give me Concerning Gitting a Licence for James Banks; for which I will be his Sequerity for Keeping a Publick House at this place[.] Your Compliance will Ever Oblige . . .

To JOHN STEPHENSON, *Pensacola*

Manchac, July 10, 1774

I have sent you by the schooner Swan per Via of Mobile; a Small Cask; Containing 15 Dryed Bufflow Tongues and as small Bagg of Nutts; Being all that I could procure the last year And Winter when up the river; the former; the Hunters would not Unstow their Boats to let me have them without Taking all their Beef & the latter the season was passed Before my Arrival; at the Grand Gulph the few that I now send you are some that I got from Thomas James; that was so obliging as to let me have them altho they ware promised to another—I am realy Really sorry that I had not Been more Successfull in Gitting Ten Times the Quantity, if I had you may Be Assurd should have sent them You; But hope in some Other Occation to be More Successfull; which you may Depend will always Give the Greatest Pleasure; to have it in my Power—having Nothing further to add only Wishing you and Madam Stephenson hea[l]th and happiness on all Occasions . . .

To JOHN MILLER, *Pensacola*

Mobile, August 4, 1774

Your much Esteem'd of the 29 Ulto. duly Came to hand the Contents of which Shall Observe; I am sorry to find that your Prognostication on Lums Acctions seems to be so much verifyed in his late proceedings at my Place; I am well Assur'd; of what you mention; and the Disadvantage that you & your Gentlemen Labour Under; therefore for your Interest must Endeavour to make the Best of it; though at the same Time know it will be verry Determental to him and me; in the sales of our Goods as you are well Acquainted with the place your self must Leave it to your Better Judgmt. I am for Ever Obliged to you for the Copy of Minutes of Councill as they will Be of much service to me; I return you my hearty thanks for the Trouble that I gave you in Looking out for a hatt; But since there is none to be had I am Always Obliged to you; as if it had been sent;

Should be Glad that per the first Conveyance that you send me the Licence for Banks—Seeing that you; ware not able to git the Box of Tools for Monsr. Dusall; have got him 2 Hear; so that he may have his Choise But as for the Glass that Mr. Swanson took with him none of them will Suit; there fore if you find a Good one; and sent it him I am well Assurd he will be much Obliged to you for it;—I am realy sorry that I Have not in my Power to give you sum Insite Relative to Rumseys note for my part Ignor any thing Concerning it; though at the same Time they Might came to the House with my Letters; I am well Assurd that I neaver Sent it; therefore I cant say Nothing in the Affair may bee on some Other Occation I may be more happy; if so Shall Always be Glad to Receive Your Commands; Till which I am with much respect ...

To PETER SWANSON, *Mobile*

Manchac, August 18, 1774

I have the pleasure of Acquainting you of Our salf, Arrivell here, the 16th Instant about 9 Oclok at night; after a very Disagreeable passage; of Eleven days; though Thanks to almighty in good health; though I had Not the Pleasure of finding your Brother; in the same state of health as when I left this; he has Been; Ill with the feavour; but is now Gitting the Better of it; so that I am in hopes are long will recover his former Liveliness; I return You Your; Box with many thanks; shall send to Town to have your Buckel & hat band; sent me by the first Conveyance; so that I am in hopes I shall have them to send you by the first Conveyance; or By Mr. McGillivary When he returns; from the Natchez; I have Taken—the Liberty to send to your Address; a Book Intitled the Greek Rudiments; it being Quite Usless to me; which you will please to present to Doctor Gordan; With my Complaints to him & his good Lady; I make no doubt but it may Be Exceptable to him—I say Nothing about; I say Bussiness but Referr; you to Mr. McGillivivarys Letter Consisting of how matters Stands hear; this Being the Needfull; for the present...

P.S. My Compliments if you Please to Doctr. Grant & his Lady

To ALEXANDER McINTOSH, *Pointe Coupée*

Manchac, August 22, 1774

By this conveyance I have Sent you the Books; for your Examminatn. You will find that their is some Accots. that are not Closed; which hope you will Be able to Close Especily that of the Beef; as you are Better Acquainted with it; as to the quantity; that Mrs. McIntosh; took for your own Use; I now Nothing off; it, all that I have Been made Acquainted with is that she sold for $14 Dollers in Cash; and 70 Carriots of Tobaco; which Allow to be worth 10 sols Each; there was 40; Tongues at first 16 of which you sent me; and I have Chargd. My Accot. with them; the first Cost; as I Expect you will do with them you Kept for your own Use; all which you Omitted giving Creditt for in Your Acct. of 6th June; furthur You Omitted giving Creditt for the Amount of the Beaver And Otters; of ours; and some of my Own; that you Carried with you to Town With the deer Skins and sold there for Cash, I furthur Observe in said Acct. that You have Charged the Comy. with $611.5½ that you paid to sundrys With out ever Mentioning or Crediting for the money that Robertson Returnd you to help to pay Prices Wages; that you had Assumed; with out Your Knowing that I had paid off their Accot. in full as per Receipt. Be assurd; that their is nothing would give me a Greater Pleasure; then to have our Small Affairs finnished in the most Amicable Manner Possible; for it Would give me the greatest Uneasiness Imaginable to think we should be Obliged to carry things; any further; then to Judgment of friends and the Gentlemen that you propose your self—to whose Superior Knowledge shall LEave it with Pleasure; I furthur think it a Little hard that I shoud be Obliged to pay half of Steels Time that is two Months; as You Deliverd our Skins 30th March as per Miller & McIntoshs Receipt for them and the Remainder of which time he was in your private Imploy—You will please to Observe the Accot. of Bills

Merchant of Manchac

Receivable; that sundrys are made Dr. to them that is for Sixty Dollers; of which 43.7½ was Due to the Comy. Accot. from Major Collins & the Other 16.½ Due me upon my privat Accot. as you are Well Acquainted with your self—I have Assumed all the outstanding Debts that I had Contracted in Your Absence; so that I hope there will be no Dificulty on that Accot.—and have Taken in all the Goods Unsold & Remaining On hand; at the price Coated in Our Invoice Amounting to $ [blank] as per Inventory taken here; a Copy of which have sent you for your Government[.] Now Sir, I hope that you will have Nothing further to say; in regard of keeping the Books; and Breaking through any part of our Agreemt. and I Should be Glad how soon; them affairs ware brought to an End; I have Creditd Your Accot. with every thing that you Either paid or Supplyed Excepting 95 lb. Salt, and as for that I dont think you have a right to Charge, as I had Above a hundred Weight at first that I neaver Mentioned in the Invoice therfore if You Credit your Accot. with the same; must Insist on your Creditting my Acct. with mine Also; Lastly I am in hopes that you will not forgett that I recivd. in Rum Gunpowder & Balls from Wm. Gilchrist for $76; which ware Added to the Cargo; though their was no Mention made of them in Our Invoice; it Being the day after our aGreemt. was Signed; which I have Charged to the Voyage As the Other goods; for the skins that we have on hand; I am of Oppinion that it will be most Advantages; to let the Gentlemen of the house have them all At once as there is some that Cost 25 some 22½ and Others 20 Sols per lb. and let them Creditt our Accounts with Each mans part; for I am Determined to have no Concerns in having them Dresed; as there will be a loss in them; if Dressd. As You have been at home all the Latter part of this year; I am in hopes You will Come down with Mr. McGillivary when he returns from the Natchez so that all may be settled in his presence to our Satisfaction As I realy look upon it that I have already lost Time anough in the affair[.] This Being the Need full . . .

To RICHARD WINSTON, *Kaskaskia, Illinois*[44]

Manchac, October 7, 1774

I have had the pleasure of your Mr. Kennedy's Compy. here this four or five Days in Which Time; we have Transacted Some small Affairs togeather; which I am in hopes will not be the Last as he Acquaints me that you Propose sending this way Yearly A Large quantity of Provision for Sale if so; I Offer you my service in that way & Shall only Charge 5 pCent for Storage & Commis-

44/Richard Winston came to Illinois from Virginia in 1766. In partnership with Patrick Kennedy, his firm became the Kaskaskia agent for the Baynton, Wharton and Morgan Company of Philadelphia. Many of Winston's associates suspected him of dishonesty, and his partner Kennedy accused him of having sold the cargo of a *batteau* in New Orleans. Winston also speculated in land and by the late 1770s was one of the most prominent men in Illinois. He gave considerable sums to aid the American cause and was made commandant at Kaskaskia in 1779. He died in 1784. See Savelle, *George Morgan, Colony Builder*, 73; *American State Papers, Public Lands*, II, 207; Alvord and Carter (eds.), *Cahokia Records, 1778–1790*, Introduction.

sion; And if I am Obliged to purchass any thing that you may stand in Need of for Cash Before your sales are Made; shall Charge 2½ pCt. there on Should this be AGreeable to you; You may freely Command ...

To JOHN WAUGH, *Pensacola*[45]

Manchac, October 26, 1774

Your much Esteemed favour of the 20th Ulto. Came To hand; but no Raisins Mr. Johnson toald me you had Commanded him to Deliver them to OKeffe as per his Certificate Relative there unto; Since that Yours of the 26th Ulto. come to hand Acquainting me that You had Sent me four Doz: Plates per Mr. Lafountt; which When I Demanded he said you had Neaver Putt them on Board his Boat; as therefore since You have Not sent me the above Articles Request that you do not; As I Expect to be in Town as soon as I have finnished Sending the Skins that I have on hand Away as the Schooner is now Waiting for them at the Amitt; this Being the Needfull ...

To JOHN STEPHENSON, *Pensacola*

Manchac, October 26, 1774

your much Esteemed favour of 7th Instant Is now be four me; the Contents of which Shall duly abserve, Be assured that if Mr. Gradenigo Sends me the Effects of the Desistd that I Shall take Proper Care that they Shalle be Sent you per the furst Convance, after they Come to hand; I have taken the Liberty to Send to your Care Sum Europing & armaricans Letters; that came to me Under Cover from Gentlemen at the Illinois; therefore should be Glad thay ware sent off per the first conveyance; this Being the Needfull ...

To CAPTAIN FITZMORICE O'CONNOR

Manchac, October 30, 1774

According to the Promise I Made you when at your place; To Inquire at New Orleans for a Water fountain with a Wash hand Basion; But there was none at that Time; But since I left Orleans There is Many Vessels Arrivd. from the Cape and Other Places; so that As I am aGoing to Town in a Short time; if any be there

---

45/John Waugh was an English merchant who owned several ships operating on the Mississippi River near New Orleans and who made frequent voyages to Pensacola and England. In 1772 he was granted a town lot in Manchac. He owned one of the "floating warehouses" seized by Gálvez in 1777. See PRO, CO 5/594, pp. 169–70; Caughey, *Bernardo de Gálvez*, 76.

then shall Bring you one; and send it per the return of the Schooner; Wishing you A Better state of Hea[l]th then You have Injoyed since I left you . . .

To McGILLIVRAY, STRUTHERS AND COMPANY, *Mobile*

Manchac, October 30, 1774

This will be handed you by your Mr. McGillivary, to whom Refer you for the Nuse of this place, I have only to Acquaint you that I have sent you a State of my Accounts, both; with McGillivray & Struthers & McGillivray Struthers & Co. which hope you will find Right; if not you will Please to note me the Defaults in Your Next; I have Given Mr. McGillivray Mr. Alexander McIntoshe's draft On you; my favour for $435.7¾ Your money which I request to pass to my Creditt with McGillivary & Struthers as also the Amount (this my half of the Skins that is Marked F & Mc of Which you will only Receive per this Conveyance 23 packs; as the Schooner could not Carry any more; therefore must wait Till she comes Again to remitt you the Others; Which is about 4500 lb. of Good skins; I have some Skins of my own which shall ship per the Next conveyance for the Comy. Accts. and hope are the Schooner Returns to add More to them; As this is about the Time that they are aComming down; with Skins; In the Companys Accot. I have not aded to it the sundrys that I have Supplyed the Schooner Swan with; But have Given them to Mr. William Swanson; Who will send them you; Having Nothing more to add . . .

To PETER SWANSON, *Mobile*

Manchac, October 30, 1774

Your Letter of the 20th Augt. came to hand the Commencement of the Present; on the Receipt of which I wrote Monsr. Ranson; to send you the wine, and that I would pay for it; if he has Dun it; or no Cant say; as I have neaver had any Answer—Yours of the 11th Ulto. is also befour me; have Observd. your Orders in having all the Skins beat and Properly Packed; that is all them that was hear; But them of mine and McIntosh's; it was Impossible to pack them any other way then what they are the Skins Curing [?] So very hard; But the others that you will Recave per next Convance will be much Better maid up; as we shall Be better provided for it; I have Sent you per Finlay Mc McGillivray [*sic*] a pr Cotten Gloves & your hat Band & Button &c which Cost me $3.⅞[.] I also [paid] a Gold Smith 2:2/4 for a Small Plain Gold Buckel; which I have not as yeat Recevd. But Daily Expect it from town when it Comes to hand Shall Embrass the furst Convance to Send it you. . . .

P.S. for god Sake Send back the Lashings of the packs for we Shall be much put to it to find any thing hear hear [*sic*] to make any Excepting we take Dipin [?] Lin[e]s—

To MR. MACNAMARA, *New Orleans*[46]

Manchac, November 4, 1774

Mr. McGillivray that Left this the 1 Instent; Requsted me to acquaint you of his not Being able to write you or would have dun it himself But the Inclosed order on Senr. Don Hendry for a note that I Left with him will prove the partenership that Subsisted between them; (that is Blank & Carrass . . .

P.S. my Respects if you Please to Mad. Macnamara & your Cousin [?]

To MILLER, SWANSON AND COMPANY, *Mobile*

Manchac, November 17, 1774

Your much Esteemed favour of the 2 Instant, is now befour me; the Contents of which Shall Duly Obsarve; if Gentlemen; I have Neglated Writing you this Sum time pass,d it was intirly Owing to my being well assured; that Mr. Swanson Capt you Dully advised of all that passed; hear and as I thought that a repetation of the Same things would be quit usless; the more Sow as I had nuthing of moment to acquaint you with my Self; I have Exemined your account and found it Right; therfore have noted the Same with me according to your Requst; Have Charged Miller Swanson & Co to Swanson Miller & Co for the things I had from Mr. William Swanson; we Have nuthing hear worth acquainting you off only that we had the honour, the of the Governur & his Compy. During five Days; he Left this the 12 In. for the Natchez; I am verry Glad to hear that Mr. McIntosh is Gating the Better of his Elment; Mons. Lafite's vessell is arived from york with 1500 Barrel of flour; now acct. as yeat of Mr. Pollock. . . .

P.S. if you have any fourther accounts from the norward please favour us with Sum part of the news; you will please to put Mr. Bruin [?] in Mind to pas his Acct. with the Interst

---

46/Possibly Bartholemew MacNamara, with whom Fitzpatrick had earlier dealings. See this volume, p. 78.

{178
Merchant of Manchac

To JOHN WAUGH, *New Orleans*

Manchac, December 6, 1774

As I am much in whant of Sum Small articls from your Place; and Cant Leave home for the Prasent; on account that I Expect hear daily to pay off there accounts Sum Peopel from Point Couppée; Should Be much obliged to you if you Can Send them Me Viz—
1 or 2 Barrel of Coffee
4 Boxes of Soap
& 2 hhds of Provence wine; for which will Rem[b]ource you; ether In Cash Skins or Indigo; By the Last of the Insuing month or the Commencemt of the other; if Convent for you you will Send them by the Bearer; and In so dowing you will oblige . . .

To PETER SWANSON, *Mobile*

Manchac, December 24, 1774

Your much Esteemed favour of 21st Ulto. Came To hand the 15 Instant; the Contents of which have duly obsarved, I am verry Glad the Cotton Gloves Came to hand so verry (a pru paux)[47] as the[y] did—your Brother that Leaves this By the furst Convence for New Orleans; to See Monseur Conand; that is Come Down from the Illinois; with Skins—Will Send you; your Buckele; from thence if any Occation Shall offer; as the Smith has amitted Sending it me—all though I paid him for it are I Left town—

Your Schooner has not Been Detained Hear on[e] moment on account of the Skins; they beening all packed are She Cam; But the Road Beeing so very Bade has occationed her Terring [tarrying] so Long—

I am verry Sinciable of what you Say on account of the Skins; and the Grat Disadvantage it is to you; in not having them in due time; But I Promise You there has Been nuthing whanting on my part

Your Brother Sent Mr. McIntosh's Letters per the furst Occation that offered; But as yeat have had no account from him; this Beeing the need full; wishing You the Compliments of the Insuing Season . . .

To McGILLIVRAY, STRUTHERS AND COMPANY, *Mobile*

Manchac, December 24, 1774

Your much Esteem'd favour of 21st Ulto. Is now be four me; the Contents of which Shall Duly Obsarve—I am Relley Glad to hear

---

47/*I.e.*, à propos.

that the account I Sent you is Right, and as for the mistack (or the things you did not Credit my acct. with) Shall Explain; in a proper manner in the Note hear Inclosed; &c, have allrady Charged Miller Swanson & Co with there part of the Expences; for the Skins they had hear, which was only 669 lb. of Drassd Leather; that Mr. Miller had from Thomas James, all the others belonged to yr. House,

Should have Been glad that the Skins that whint In the Schooner had not Been mixed But Since they have & there is no halp for it; have Sent you the wight of Mr. McIntoshs & mine; that is what whint in the Schooner be four and now—So that I am in hopes yll be able to Come at the troue Knolege of each man part; as for the Skins marked F & Mc & Mr. McIntosh's own Skins, you had them as the[y] Came hear; But for what I had maid up hear, I had them dun as I always dow;—I am verry Senciable; of what you Say in Regard of the Skins Beeing Sent home in due time & of the advantage accouring there on; But it is a near [?] Imposible to have any quantity; till the hunters and Traders Comes Down with them; and that wont be till About the 15th of Feby. Insuing; what fur I have Recved for any account; have Sent them you markd F the amount of which you will place to my Credt with you and the Others [illegible] In my Last per Mr. McGilly.

In the Small account of the Charges of the Schooner that Came with mr. Bentleys Goods & mine; is Erronios as there is nuthing Charged to Miller Swanson & Co for the fraight of 7 hundred of Gun powder; and Since Ever one is Charged according to his Amount; they ought all to be put on the Same futting; that is the Sterting Cost; and then it will Stend as per account of it hear Inclosed; So that there will be to my Cradt. $4.3:¾

I obsarve By the account you Sent me of the Cargo TB that I was formally over Charged $8:4¼ which have placed to your Debte; as allsow $4.7¼ on account of Mr. Stuart which is yr money $13.4¼ and have noted the Same in my books, have Placed to your Cradite $25.7r for my part of the fright of Mr. Baptists Schooner; the Balls that Came in the Schooner to Remplace, them of Lum's I have taken for my own acct. as I neaver Sent them any; which you will Please to Debte me with; I amitted Sending you in my Last Mr. McIntosh's Draft my favour for $435.7:¾ your money; but Inclose It now; with a Draft on Mr. Charles Stuart for $65.1:¼ at 30 days, Sight when Recevd you will place to my Cradt. with you; we have nuthing new hear Excepting that the Franch Gentleman that Commaded at the Spanish manchac is Changed & a Spanerd put in his Place;[48] which I am afraid will be nuthing to our advantage, hear—wishing you the Complements of the Insuing Season ...

48/Charles Descoudreaux was replaced as commandant at Fort San Gabriel de Manchack by Sublieutenant Thomas de Acosta, who held the post until 1777.

To ISAAC JOHNSON, Natchez[49]

Manchac, December 27, 1774

Your much Esteemd favour of 20th Instant is Now befour me; the Contents of which have duly obsarved—

As to what you Say; Consar[n]ing Ellinor Prices not having Been able to as yeat to Discharge the Small Cradite I gave her with you; Viz: for I quarter Cask of Taffia Twenty five pounds of Gun powder & fifty wight of Lead or Balls; is Sumthing Surprizing to me; the more Sow as I wrote to her Sume time ago to know if She had paid it; her answer (or at Least Mr. James by her Request) was that She had Setteld that herself with you and that I had no Reason to be uneasy on that head; and that it was no longer an effer of mine—Now Seeing that She has not Complyed; nether with or Promise or the Letter (although it is a Long time Since she had the goods) must Request that you give her nuthing further as I will not bee accountable for any thing She has had; the quarter Cask of Teaffia the Gun powder & Balls; as above menchend; Excepted at the Same time Should be forever obliged to you if you will Indevor to Recover, there amount from hir as you are at hand; for if she Obliges me to add that to her fourmer account; which was on Settelment the 29th of Last march in Pracenes of Mr. James $880.6r & Since that have Paid an order She Drew on me for $12 So that the Ballance at Present is $892:6r, without Interest; I promise you She may Expact no further Linilly [?] from me—

I Should be glad if you would only for one moment Take it under your Considration; think of the amount she all[r]audy owes me; In whos hands it is in; and the Prajudse it is for me to be So Long Capt out of So Large a Sume; the Small Praspact there is of Geting it out of her hands; when you have Considered all this Sarcamstances; am will assured; ware you in my Place; you would go no further; and Parhaps not So farr as I have dun; for all this had She Been; Possessed of the Least Since of Gratitude towards me Since I Left the Goulph, ether By writing or Remitting me; Sum part of my Just Demand I should have Been the furst to have halped her again—But in Steed of thinking anything about me; or the Large amount She is indue me per her Bond; she has Retaliated with Ingratitude for all my pasted Indulgences; there for must Be verry plain with you; Since you have acted; with so much freandship to wards me, In tilling you that I am of Oppinen the Longer She is Let alone the more they (that have Been so unhapy) as to advance her any thing; will Louse by her at Last; though at the Same time if Mr. Johnson, Relley is of Oppine; By Letting her a Lone till next Spring she will be then able to pay

49/Natchez trader, planter, and justice of the peace.

off her Dabts; Be assured that I Shall due nuthing that Shall be any ways Determentil to his Interest; But at the Same time Cant help thinking that all her Promises will prouve a [*illegible*]; at Last; I once more Repeatte my fourmer Request; that you Let her have nuthing with out it is on her own acct. as I will not be answerable for any thing But as Before menchened; It only Remains to acquaint you with the news we have hear at Prasent; By the Last advice from North america is that the Genl. [?] Congress that was heald; at Phileda. is Broak up; and the Results of which is that they will not Importe any thing from the mother Countrey after the furst of this month; & that all Exportations Shall be Stopped after the furst of Next may; or at Least till Such time that the Parlement Recoalls; all the acts that have Passed in the Houses; aginst america; & Particularly the Canada act[50]—No account as yeat of Pollock & willing; David Williams & Docr. flowers; are arived with 80 prime Slaves half for Sale & the other for there Plantation; this Beeing the need full; with wishing you the Compliments of the Insuing Season . . .

To STEPHEN HAYWARD, *Concord, Mississippi*[51]

Manchac, January 28, 1775

Your of the 9 Instant is now be four me; the Contents of which have duly observed; I am Relley Sorry to [say] that; I had it not in my Power to have Compleated your order; But as Mr. Dannella is a going up to your place with Sundrey Goods; Betwen what you will Reseve from him and In your Boat, will be near to Compleat your Order; (the Blanketing only Excepted) and for them theres is nown in the River for Sale; for my own part I have not 10 in the world; Till more goods Comes in; which Cant Expect this Sum time to Come; you have hear Inclosed an Invoice of the Sundries Sent you; amounting to $1106.5¼r as alsow an account of the wight & numr of your Deer & Beaver Skins; the Latter I have not Pack on my own acct. But such another parcel of I have not seen this Sume time (I mean so fowl) be assured that if you take them so that you will Louse by them—as no one will take them from you with out triming them as I have dun; I have Been as Particuler as Posible On account of Charles Howard's Skins; as you will See per the account; and them fur you had from James Countiton Lost 21 lb. in Bashuff [?] &c—I have pased them all to your Cradite with me; the Deer Skin at 2/r per lb; which is Relly more then any one on the River gives; nor Should I have given it; had it not Been that I Expect that the Gentlemen from

1770–1775

50/The first Continental Congress met in Philadelphia on September 5, 1774, and adjourned on October 26. Its most significant action was an intercolonial agreement known as "The Association," by which a policy of stringent nonimportation was adopted, no British goods were to be consumed, and no colonial goods were to be exported to Britain. The "Canada Act" to which Fitzpatrick refers is the Quebec Act of June, 1774, which provided for the continuity of French civil law, governmental institutions, and Roman Catholic religion in that formerly French province, and extended the boundaries of the province to include all lands between the Ohio and Mississippi rivers and the southern edge of the Hudson Bay basin. Many of the English colonists were bitterly opposed to the act, denouncing its recognition of the Roman Catholic establishment, its abandonment of representative government in Quebec, and particularly the new boundaries, which seemed to close the trans-Alleghany west to exploitation by the old colonies. See Savelle, *A History of Colonial America*, 536–37, 544–47.

51/Stephen Hayward, a Natchez trader and hunter, was one of several British hunters who operated on the Arkansas River. In 1778 he was arrested, along with two others, for violating Spanish trade laws and sent to a New Orleans jail. In June of the same year he was sent to Havana for trial. Lacking sufficient evidence, the Spanish authorities were never able to carry out the trial, and the men were released. In 1788 Hayward returned to Natchez, coming from Virginia, and

Mobille allow me the Same again; if not shall Louse By them, your Bond that you gave Mr. Alexander McIntosh of pt. Couppée for $495.2¼r I have taken up and have passed my word to Mr. Dutton; to see your order paid of ninty Dollars, and the Interest acc[r]uing there on So that it will be up wards of one hundred Dollars; in all I therefor must Expact that you will make me Suttable Remitance; in Consquance to inable me to pay them off—

If you find your Interst in taken oil Tallow from your hunters Will take them from you; the former at 6/r per Gallon; & the Later at 9 Sols per lb. franch wight; or if Or if [*sic*] at the time you Come or Send Down, will take them from you at the Orleans, Price; what ever Skin you Can Send me; Send if Posible by 12th of April; for after that Time; Shall be obliged to Keep them on hand all Summer which will be a great Loss to us Both; in the first place as I will not give the Same Price; when you write me again Rember to Signe your Letters & orders you Self; as Mr. Armstrong's Signing, will not Due; having Nuthing further to add only to wish you hea[l]th & Suckess . . .

To JOHN MILLER, *New Orleans*

Manchac, February 2, 1775

Your much Esteemed favour of the 22 Ulto. Is now befour me; the Contents of which have & Shall duly Obsarve; as to Sending an order for goods is a thing that I Cant think of Till Such times as I have Sold off what I have Still on hand; and Setteled with your house's for them alrady Taken; the more so as there is Nuthing to be had by them at Present; on account of the havey advance; the Low pr[i]ce that there is for Skins; and the number of Traders; from all parts; that are hear & hear abouts; which Surcomstances Provents me from Daring to Lay in [?] any further; till I see how things are Lick to tourn out; & as to Mr. McIntosh's Intentions on this head Cant purtend to Say But I amgine that they the Same with mine—But more of that from himself when he Recves your favour—

I Dont Imagin in the Least that your Coming to Manchac will be any ways Determantil to me; be assured that it will give me the gratess Pleasure; to have So good a Freand and Nabour; so near at hand as Mr. Miller has always Been to me; and as for Trade [?] it is usless to think any thing further about it; hear the futer; I have Sume Skins in the house and Expact more Daily; as this is the Season for them, which Shall hold at your Disposel; I have

---

established residence there, serving the Spanish as an Indian interpreter. See Faye, "The Arkansas Post," 653–54.

Spoak to Mr. nicholson Concar[n]ing the house; so that on your arivill you will find an apartement Redy for your Receptance; having nuthing more to add . . .

To WILLIAM WILTON, *Pensacola*

Manchac, February 2, 1775

Your Esteemed favour of 13th of Last Decmr. Is now befour me, the Contents of which have duly Obsarve'd; I am Relley Sorry that I Cant take the artils you menchen for my own account; as I make no Doubt but you Could Let them go on a Reasonable advance from the Starting Cost; But Since that is not the Case; if you will Send me the foll[ow]ing articls for your account Viz the Indin Gun's; 500 lb. of Gun powder; one thousand wight of Balls assorted; and hand & Cross Cutt Saws; with fills [files] for them; youll please to put your price on them or the advance you Demand that they Should [be] Sold at hear and If I Selle any of them Be assured that your money Shall alway Be Ready at your Command. . . .

To JOHN STEPHENSON, *Pensacola*

Manchac, February 2, 1775

Your Ever Esteemed favour of 16th of Last Demr. Is now befour me; and have noted well its Contents; I am Relly Sorry to find that Mr. Riston; has not ere now Complyed with my Just Request; which if he Dus not to your Satisfaction Ere Long; he may rest assured that I shall be abliged to mak him; which will be much agenst my Inclination; I am S[t]ill more Sorry to hear that he has Lost your good will on Lousing of which he has Lost that of his Best Freand In this Provance—Be assured that if any good opperty. Should offer for the Sale of the Land; that I Shall not Let it Slip; Shall always Keep you advised; of what poposilles may Be maid me on that head; though as yeat has not Been non; as the Gentlemen that Comes hear at Prasent are not So much Mississippi Sick as others have been Her to four; As to the Books you menchen Should not Chuse to part with them; as I Sent home for them for my own Use; though if a good Oppertunity offered; to Send them you; they are at your Searvess for Perusal—

If any thing Else Should accer for your Searvss In these parts you will Please to Rember that I am Still, D Sir, yours . . .

Merchant of Manchac

To DANIEL McGILLIVRAY, *Pensacola*[52]

Manchac, March 6, 1775

As Mr. Miller nor Mr. Swanson is nether of them Hear at Prasent; I have taken the Liberty; to Inclose you a Bill for $200 at 30 Days Sight; as also a note of Mr. James Kelley's for $52.2½r at 40 Days after Date which when Reecoverd; you will pleas to place to my Cradt. with Miller Swanson & Co—this being the need full I am with Respect . . .

P.S. as Mr. Kelley is agoing to Pensacola to Sittel his affairs with Mr. wilton; he will have it in his Power to take up his note; there fore Please Dont Let him Leave your Place Till he has Setteled it with you—

Copy of Kelley's Note—

Manchac 6th March 1775

Forty Days after Date I promise to pay to John Fitzpatrick or his order Fifty Tow Dollars Tow & one half Rayel; Beeing, for the Ballance of all accounts to this Day; as witness my hand—

(Signed) James Kelley

$52.2½r

The above a true Copy
Tho. Gregory

To CAPTAIN COLLIN GRAHAM, *16th Regiment, Pensacola*

Manchac, March 6, 1775

Since your Departer; from hance I have not Been favour with any of yours; I am Relley [sorry] To hear; that your Regt. has Receved order to hold itself in Radness; to go on so Disagrable an Expedition; as agants the Bostonins[53] (But when the Roff Comes one must away; as the old Saying is) may this find you In the Same good health you injoyed; whill with us on the Mississippi; & may the gods Protack you; when you Shall Be Exposed to Danger; & Bring you Safe Back hear again; that I may have the honour of Trating you to a Bottel of the Best; that our Place Can aford, these are the Sincr wishes of, D Sir, yours . . .

To JOHN MILLER, *New Orleans*

Manchac, March 26, 1775

By the oppertunity of Mr. James I did myself the pleasure of writing you; inclosing my order [?] Beeing then in a hurry I

52/ A partner of the Pensacola branch of the McGillivray company. The firm employed numerous family members.

53/ Although the Revolutionary War had not yet begun, the situation in the Boston area at the beginning of 1775 was one of open hostility to Britain, and British military forces already in the New England colonies were being reinforced as additional coercive measures were adopted to bring the colonies to submission.

omitted Some Small articls which you have herin; which Should be much obliged to you to add to the fourmer; if you Send it home; on the Condition you offered me; that is a 40 pCent to Be delivered in the Mississippi, at or about New Orleans, which will be Equal to me a Littel above or below; as there will be always Vessells enaugh where they Can be put on Board; for I Cannot think of having them by the way of the Bayaux for the Charges on them that way would Exeed more there [?] Then half of the fright from Europ; I flatter myself as the Books & Silver watch are for my own use; that you will Lay aside the advance; and Require only the fright & Charges[.] as for the watch you will be kind enough to minchin to your Corrospondent to get one that is warranted, I Should not have Sent for one; but that which is in your Trunks I can have $30 when I please—

You'll also obsarve to your Correspondent To Let the Sundries articls in my order to be rather under than Exceed the menchend prices; & those that has non menched to be upon as good Tirms as posible; If the advance & Plaice place [sic] of Delivring do not meet with your approbation In that Case you ll only Send for the Books & watch; upon the Usual advance; being the needfull . . .

To STEPHEN HAYWARD, Concord, Mississippi

Manchac, April 8, 1775

I had the pleasire of writing you Sundries Letters Since your Barge Left this; But as yeat have not Been favoured with any from you; which I Suppose has Being owing to a proper Occation; which is Relly offen the Case on this River; the Prasent; will be Deliverd to you by Mr. James To whome; have given a Coppy of your account; Current with me, which Should be much obliged to you if you Could Settel with him at his Place; as it will be Seaving you much Trouble In Coming hear—the morsow; as I am Relly in whant; of wherwith to make Remittence, not having wherwith; has Pravented me from Daring to go any further; till Such times; as them that are Indue me; payes me off; Be assured that if you Comply with your Obligation; that you Shall not be in whant of a good Supply of Goods again; I have Got for you 5 Doz of fine Beaver Traps which Shall not Dispose off but to your Self; this Being the needfull . . .

P.S. Should have Sent your Bonds per Mr. James But was not Certen when you ware to be at his Place; or whether you Should Call ther or now—if you pay him off; Shall Send them you per the first Convance; after I Recve your orders for so dowing—

Merchant of Manchac

To GARRET RAPALJE, *Baton Rouge*[54]

Manchac, April 12, 1775

The Bearer of the Present is a Person from the Illinoise, that has Brought me Down a Quantity of Flour Pork and Beef from Messr. Winston & Kennedy of that Country for Sale[.] they Demand, a Quantity of Liquours In Return and as You Told me You had Norward Rum for Sale and You that would be Glad if it Lay in my Power You would Sell of it therefore Lay hold of this Occasion, and Inclose You a List of Some Other things that they want; which if You Can get them have You may Depend, that As Soon as I have Disposed of their Effects which are [*illegible*] Don and I will See You Payed; if not Sold in Time Enough for you to Remit by Schooner Mr. Kennedy will be here himself in all the Ensuing Month, and will Bring Down Some Good Bills which will Suit You & which I Promise You Shall have in Payment if I have not his Effects in time. . . .

P.S. my Best Respects to Mr. Jaques if You Please

N.B. if the Bearer Mr. Louis Charleville Should want any things Be Assured he is very Good/ if the Bearer Should want Cash

To WINSTON AND KENNEDY, *Illinois*

Manchac, May 10, 1775

Your Esteemd. favour of the 27th of Last march Duly Came to hand; the Contents of which I have obsarved

I am Relley Sorry it was not in my power to have Complet'd your order; But it was not posible; for the Prasent; having Recev'ed no goods this year; or had I Been in Cash to have Purchd. them Should have Dun it; But I rally was not; owing to the many Disapointments I meet with this Last winter

You have hear Inclosed a Bill of Lading for Sundries Shipd. for your acot. & Risque By Mons. Charleville amounting to $851.5r as alsow an acct. Current Ballance due me $1127; I have Chargd. you 5 pCent on what Cash I advanced for you; your flour is Still on hand; occationed by the Larg quantity of Norward flour that is in the provance; But Should any Occation offer for the Sale; be assured I Shall Dow the needfull; this Beeing; all for the present . . .

54/New York land speculator who acquired extensive holdings along the Mississippi River above Natchez as well as a plantation near Baton Rouge. The Baton Rouge census of 1782 lists Garrett Rapalje as a planter and owner of 17 slaves. Sometime during the 1780s he moved to the Big Black River near Grand Gulf, leaving his Baton Rouge property in the care of his sons Jacques and Garrett, Junior. See Johnson, "Expansion in West Florida," 488; Baton Rouge Census Document, and George Rapalje Notebook, both in Department of Archives and Manuscripts, Louisiana State University.

To WILLIAM WILTON, *Pensacola*

Manchac, May 14, 1775

Your favour of 23d of March and the 10th Ultimo are now before me with an Invoice of Sundries You Sent me to Dispose of for Your Account Amounting to £66.8-6 Sterling But the Invoice is Erronious for in it You Mention 500 lb. of Gun Powder and there is only 15 Kegs of 25 lb. Each which is 375 lb. So that there is wanting 125 lb. at 95 s. per Ct. is £5.18-3 to be Deducted from the Invoice So that it only Remains £60.10-3[.] You Say the Price You Mention in the Invoice is the Sterling Cost if So you have Been Impased upon 10/ in Every hundred wt. for it Cast no more than 85/ I have not as Yet seen Your Guns But if they are Common Trading Guns, they Ought only to be Charged 10/6; But more of that when I have Seen them[.] Be Assured I Shall Dispase of them to Advantage when Occasion offers[.] I shall be happy, if there is any thing this way in which I Can be of any Further Service to You, and if I find that these Goods turns to Good Advantage when they are Sold Shall Send You Another Order, Tho in the mean-time I Should be much Obliged to You to Keep me Advised of the Differrent Goods You may Receive from time to Time as I may Stand in Need of them for my own Account[.] This being the Needfull ...

To STEPHEN HAYWARD, *Concord, Mississippi*

Manchac, May 15, 1775

Your Letter per Mr. Donneldson of the 25 of last March I received the Perusal of which was much Alarming to me not for my Sake alone, But on Account of the Gentlemen whase Effects that I had Simplicity Enough to Intrust You with to Enable You to Corry You on Your Trade Never Expecting Such a Return of Ingratitude from a man whom I had Obliged in the Manner I had You—

It Really apears that I am much Your Enemy for in the first Place my taking up Bond of $495.2½ from Mr. McIntosh Secondly to have Passed my word to Mr. Dutton for $90 & its Intre[st] [*illegible*] Thirdly by my Sending You to the Amount of $250.6½ [?] at a Time when You were in Due me $2012.2[.]

By Your Bond in all is	$3703.1½
And of which I received Only	619.1½
So that ye Balance Due me	3084.—

All this without Interest all which Instances Shews how much I was Your Enemy, which of the two I must Leave the world to Judge—my own I am much Afraid will will [*sic*] Apear But Two Convincing in the Sequel; If one may Judge from Your Last Proceedings, Your Letter was much Surprising to me, But Your Draft of the 24th March for $1200 in favour of Mr. Babtist Boisis (and not to his order) without so much as Writing to me or Sending me the Cargo to Enable me to Pay Said Demand, You might well have Inagined would meet with no Receptance from me, Let me tell You Sir, That the Plain Honest Dealer will Always meet with Esteem from his Creditors, But when he has Taken off the Mask, and from The Honest man Becom[e] A Sharper, Then when to Late we find out whome we have Been So Misfortunate as to Place our Confedence In; This Sir, I am afraid from Your former Actions is the Case therefore there is Nothing Left for You at Present to Retrieve Your former Caracter, than by Your Showing the world Your Intentions never was to Defraud any man of his Property which for Your own Sake I hope may realy be the Case[.] I have nothing more to Add only to Aquaint You that I Bought the remainin[g] [*illegible*] Amounting to $663.6¾ of which I Paid Mons. Poussett $600, and have Drawn on You for the Balance beeing $63.6¾ which I have Indorced to Your Bond to me . . .

To WILLIAM WILTON, *Pensacola*

Manchac, June 7, 1775

I had the pleasure of writing you 14th Ulto. by Mr. James Elliott, to which Refer, since which all your things are arrived here, and on Examination find that your Invoice is not Right, in the first place you mention fourty nine Guns, & there are but fourty Seven[.] Secondly there is but 377 D. of Balls and say there ought to be 432 D. therefore finding that the things did not agree with the Invoice, I sent for Mr. Swanson and Mr. Munsanto & had every thing Examined, in their presence, an account of what was found you have here inclosed for your Gouvernement Since their Arrival I have been able to dispose of some of them, to the Amt. of Ds. 284.5r at 30 pCt. advance[,] that being all I could get for them, payle. in October I nowing there's a number of them that I shall never be able to Dispose of Vizt. the Axes the Bullet mould, and Malles though if any Accassion Offers Shall not let it Slip— Having nothing more to Add . . .

To PETER SWANSON, *Mobile*

Manchac, June 7, 1775

Your much Esteemd favour of the 11th of Last April I Duly Received, The Contents of which shall Observe, I'm realy sorry for the Death of poor Mr. McIntosh, which I heard of long ear' your Letter came to hand; & the more so to hear the Manner & where he ended his days, which when I heard of I Expected, of Course would Cause Some Alteration in the Terms of your Houses—

I'm much Obliged to you & all your Gentlemen for your kind offers of Serving me, which from the long Experience & the many convincing proof; I have had on all Occassions laves no room to think otherwise, I farther return you my hearty thanks for your own Good Oppinion of me, & be assured that I shall always endeavour to uphold the same with you—

I Delivered to Mr. Miller all the Skins I had at the time the Vessel was here of which I make no Doubt you have been made acquainted with from himself ear' now. I have about 400 Good Skins in the House, but had reather beat them all Summer then give them at 20 Sols per lb. having cost myself 35 therefore Can never think of Letting them go under that Sum—

I have recd. Sundry Letters from Mr. McIntosh, Requesting me to send him an Account of the Amount of Our Skins, that went in the Schooner last fall But as I never received any could not Send it him. I shall be forever Obliged to you if you will send me the Amount of them; as also of my own, for without which I am not able to settle my Books, which should any thing happen to me may be a Loss to you & your Gentlemen therefore Request that you Send me the Amt. of them by the first Convenient Conveyance as also please to Let me hear if you ever found Mr. Krapps Note for Ds. 30.7½ for if you have not found it ear' now I must Louse its amount, which will be something hard on me[.] In my Letter to your House I have Requested a few Small Articles that I'm much in want of if Convenient Send them it will be rendering me a great Service[.] Having nothing farther to Add . . .

To JOHN McGILLIVRAY, *Mobile*

[Manchac], June 7, 1775

Since your Departure from this I Did myself the Honour of writing you Sundry Letters, an answer to any of them I Never as yet Received which makes me Imagine they never came to hand; some time ago Mr. Miller acquainted me that you Requested the Money, you were so good as to lett me have last fall; at the time he Demanded it I had it not in the House, therefore will pay you

Interest for it till paid[.] In part I enclose you a Small Draft on Mr Chs Stewart for ps. 104.1½ payble. at 30 Days Sight which when Received you will please Indorce on my Note for the Cash Borrowed[.] be assurd the Remainder I will pay to Mr. Miller ear' long with Interest, I have nothing new to acquaint you with, all things stand much in the same manner as when you were here as for Trade Mr Miller wil no Doubt Acquaint you with it's progress, therefore have nothing farther to Add . . .

NB Please Send my note to Mr. John Miller with the Indorcement for 104.1½, & also for 50 Dolls pd. Mr. Miller ommitted in the Body of the Letter.

To McGILLIVRAY, STROTHERS AND COMPANY, *Mobile*

[Manchac], June 8, 1775

It's now upwards of five Months since I have been favoured with any of yours—Your long Silence I aledge has been owing to your Continuall hurry of Bussiness, or to the neglect of forwarding your Letters[.] Therefore the present is to Request that you favour me with an Account of the Sk[ins] that went in your Schooner Last October Both of them Belonging to me and Mr. McIntosh & my own; withou[t] which I Cannot Settle my Books[.] I'm Really Sorry that it was not in my power to have done more than what I did in the Remittance way this Last Spring But Really Gentleman it was not owing to any Neglect in me, But to many Dissapointments that I met with of which your Mr Miller is well Acquainted with But hope that wont be the Case this Year—

I should be much Obliged to you if any Accassion offer, to this place to send me the Small Articles that you will find a Note of Inclosed as I'm much in want of them (that is if convenient) you will please to Observe in the Account I sent you last fall by your Mr McGilliwray I only Charged for Mr Elliots Note 330 Dolr. & it was for 333.5rs so that you'l be so good as to Credit my Account for 3 5/10 Ds. Having nothing more to Add . . .

follows the Order

2 ps. German Oznabrigs	4 ps. Blk Ribbon
4 ps. Dowlass at 20/ or 21/6	4 ps. flowrd Do.
6 ps. ¾ linen Check	2 doz. fishing Lines
4 D Garlox thread	3 ps. Irish Linen 12 at 14d
4 D Black Do.	1 doz Good penknives

If it was Convenient should be Obliged to you to Dble the Above Order

To JAMES WILLING, *Natchez*

Manchac, June 16, 1775

According to your request of the 14th Inst. I have sent you your Bottle & Spoons, But the Copy of Mr Blommarts Receipts, for the things delivered him, that Belonged to the Estate of John Finney I [c]an't send you, as you are not the Administrator thereon without you will Assume to me, the payment of what the Estate is due me, the More so as I have wrote to Pensacola to Put in a Cavett against Mr. Pollocks taking letters of Administration as he lives in Orleans Don't look on it as right he should have them, Neither do I imagine any one on the River has any thing to do with the Effects till such time as Letters of Administration are Obtained for that purpose which I am well Assured are not as yet, therefore must know who I am to look to for my payment Ear' any Copys Or Originals get out of my hands—I have nothing else to add only to Assure you that on any thing Else I can be of Service to you, you may freely Command . . .

P.S. Since writing the above I have received a Letter from Mr. Bloommart wherein he expresses himself in a warm Manner at the Information I gave you in New Orleans Concerning your Affairs which I had from some people who came down from that Quarter[.] I'm sorry I did it as I find it is made so bad an use of. But beleive me it Shall be a warning to me if I was to see them parish Should give my self but little trouble about other peoples Affairs for the future

To JOHN STEPHENSON, *Pensacola*

Manchac, July 23, 1775

Your much Esteemd favour of the 23d Ulto By Governer Brown is now befour me the Contents of which I have duly obsarved; I am relly Sorry to hear of your Ilness; but hope it will not be of a Long duration; as at your Place you Injoye the Binifits of the fine Sea Brizes; that we are deprived of on the Mississippi;—I am Glad to hear that you are to Come this way; this Insuing winter; but Shall Be much more So when I Shall have it in my pouer to to [*sic*] Bid you wilcome to Manchac; I am Extreemly hapy that you did not Come with the govr. on account of your health; as this has Been a verry Sickly Season this way. The winter will be much more agrable; and much Better; as then you will be able to Travill with more Ese; and be Better able to See the face of the Contry— According to your Request; I have Sent Mr. Bowker his Letter;

by assafe Convance; Should he the Papers Be assured I Shall deliver them to the Governer—

I furthr obsarve what you say Consaring the New Town; that is to be Bilt at the Cliffets. In answer to it I only Can for the prasent; Till I have the pleasor your Self Say; that all Plains of this Kind will when well dun by a masterly hand Look well on paper; to Parsons that is not acquainted; with the Place and its Sutuation; Both of which I am So well Convenced of that I have Discisted from making any Demands for a Lott; having Nuthing fourthr for the prasint . . .

P.S. Please Let me hear in your Nixt if you have Sent for my Box to England—

To WINSTON AND KENNEDY, *Illinois*

Manchac, August 9, 1775

Both your much Esteemd favour's of the 20th of June & the 21st Ulto; are now befour me; the Contents of which, I have duly obsarved; as to your fourmer Should have answered by Mr. Bentley; but as your Mr. Kennedy has Retourned with him from New Orleans; and is on his way upp having Been Disapointed in geting a passege to the northward; he will be able to Infourm you fully—Relative to the prices your Cuntry Pradice takes for hear as alsow the Discount that is allowd in Nigotiating, your Commands. Bills. they are now at 3:04 & 5 pCent Discount; the Discradit they are now in Partly if not wholy; owing to the Distorbance in North america—

By yours of 21st Ulto I obsarve with Pleasure that Monsr. Louis Charleville was arived (a Bon part) the goods in good order; and the account of there amount right, I am in hopes that things will Tourn out more faverable with you; then you Seem to; Expect; I mean in the Sale way; (or at Least so as to Inable you [to] Realize your own) with Some advance thereon; as is Evry honest man's Right To Endemify him for the many Risqus his Property rins a going up and Down this Rivir—Be assured D Sir that the goods I Bought for you at orleans; with Cost ware Lay'd in at the Common p[r]ice then Current; there and as for the goods I Supplyd you with from hear; war not Charg'd you above 15 pCent more then what the[y] Cost me at Mobille; which will not Leave when fright Insurance & Cartage &c is paid not above 10 pCent Cleer; I am Sorry that it was not in my power (at that time) to Dow more for you & your worthy friend Mr. Kennedy, the Occation of which I menched. to you in my Letter of the 10th of Last may—

I Expect this fall a Small Cargo from England by one of the furst Vessills; that arives in the River from that Contry; to the amount of Eight or Nine hundred pounds Sterling if you Should whant any part there of in (the Dry Goods way) you'll Send me your order per the furst Convance; that I may be able to Keep you a proper assortement—as to Remittince; the pr[i]ce of Deer Skins Beavr furs &c I Refare you to Mr. Kennedy; as he has had an oppertunity; Both hear and at New Orleans; of making him self accauntd with the Common Prices at Both Places; and will be a bethr abl[e] To Judge; whether it will not be more advantage for you to Dispose of your Skins above for good Bills; then to bough them down; having Nuthing further to add only to assare you; that it will allways give me please to hear from you; by evry Convance; as for News We have nuthing New (only much the Same as what you menchind. Should any thing new accer and any occation for your Place; Shall Keep you advised thereof; this being the needfull ...

P.S. my Best Rispects to Mr. Kennedy—

To MONSIEUR RENAUX, *Illinois*

Manchac, August 9, 1775

Your favour from Pt. Coupée of 8th July per Mr. Maison I have Recvd and Note its Contents; as to what you Say Consar[n]ing your demanding me if I would Store your goods for you till the other Bataux's Came up; I told you I would; and at the Same time maid Bold to Demand; your Reason for So doing; you gave me for answer; as you hand maid your Bargin with Mr. Bentley; at New orleans; for the fright of 8 hhds. on your furnishing him with 3 good hands and your Self; making up the forth; you had a Right to Compleat your fright wher you Could find it; and as you ware not able to dow it in Town; the goods that you had bought of me; would about Compleat it; you further Said that Mr. Bentley Demanded a note for $15 Surplus; that you would not Consent [t]o; which was the Reason for Landing your goods; your talking of Leaving the Boat I my Self [*illegible*] on your Talking of Landing your effects. I herd Sundries of the hands Say that if you and your 3 men Left the Bataux they would go no further; this Sir is all I Know or all I heard of the affer you menchd. in your; and is all that I Can Say on the Subjet. ...

194
Merchant of Manchac

To CHARLES STUART, *Mobile*

Manchac, August 10, 1775

Your much [esteemed] favour of the 10th Ulto. is now Be four me, the Contents of which have Obsarved; you acqut. me that Mr. Nicholsons Draft my favour meetg. with due honour; for which I am Much obliged to you; it is very True the Swamps have Cost you Some Cash; But be assured it will Retourn with good Interest (that is Sum hundreds advance provided there is But a few years Tranquillit with our nabour's)

As for the Hibernia Chife and his 15,000 Cuntry men aComing to the Mississippi we have hard Nuthing fourder about them; I have Seen Governer Brown; he did me the honr. to Remain four Days with me hear; whilt his Things was a geting over from the amitt, in which time I had an Oppertunity of Seeing the plan of the Proposed New Town all I Can Say for the p[r]asent; is as it is will Dun by A mastely hand; it Looks will on paper; But as for his Dowing any thing for the provance; I Belive will be owing (Like all his prudesars) as farr as he find it Comabrats with his Intrust; But on the wholl I Cant halp wishing there neaver had Been worse Enemys to the Provance; then he; we have had the Indian Chife with us that you minchen; I Rember to have Seen him when a boy about 10 years ago; I Belive him to be a good Red man—& at Present it will not be no hard mater for him to brng the Remaing part of his Nation; to the arkansas; as they have meet with a grat Defit the 10th of Last June, having Lost upwards of 70 men women & Childers; By there Enemys from towards Michillimackina; the affer Lasted from the 4th till 7th this I have in a Letter, from Richard Winston of that Contry,

It is verry Just what you obsarve; that with 18 punchns. of Northward Rum; we may Expact grat things the morso as the man that has got them; is Intiteled to give out grat Taiks; But more of this hear; after—

You Request that I will Infourme you; what Prospects the Inhabitans have this way; I Can Say with much Certinty there Could not Be grator; for the Short time the English has Been at work; there Planta[t]ions; are will Stored with Corn &c; and as to the Indigo maiking we must put Mr. Clark at the head; its Said he will make 3000 Wight this year; the Messrs. Jones 14 or 1500 Wight—& Mr. Dun [?]5 or 600[.] this Sir is near the Generall oppinon Both on the amitte & Mississippi; all Say they Shall have fine Crops; I am Relly Sorry to hear Such Dismell news Both from your quarter; and from the Illionis; all much to the Same End; as you are about to Leave the province (as I have Been Infourmd) Should there be any thing this way in which I Can be of any Searvess; to you in your Abstence; you may freely Command...

P.S. my Compliments; if you Please to Mrs. Hatfild & Littel Johnney—

To PETER SWANSON, *Mobile*

Manchac, August 12, 1775

This Searves to acknowladge the Recept of your favour of the 11 Ulto; as alsow the Letter from the house; with an Invoice of Sundrys per The Schooner Swan, amounting to $94.9¼ your money all in good order; which have placed to the Cradite of Messrs. John McGillivray & Co.—I am well assured of the Necessity that there is in having your fourmer affers Brought to a Close (wish to god it was in my power to Dow my part of it this moment) it is all most Imposible to Represent to you in its True Light the many Disadvantages I Laber under here; In Collacting in Outstanding Debts; mer[e]ly for what of Some Methoud of obliging them; without Being oblige to Pensacola; or your place; the whant of Such halp has Been a grat apstruction in my Remittance from time to time; you may Rest assured D Sir I Shall Exart myself this fall and winter in making all the Remittence posible, though I must tell you that I Dont think I Shall have many Skins; as I am Determind Never to Receve another; if there is any thing Else to be got for the Debt; as I find there is nuthing but a Continal Loss on them for me; in them that Messrs. McGillivray & Struth[ers] has Last Jany. I Louse upwards of 5 pCt this and many Shuch Losses will purvent me from having having [*sic*] any thing further to dow With them whill they are at 25 & 40 Ct. per lb; as I Cant See my Self Buy them at that Prce.

Should have wrote to your house by this Convance; But as Mr. Miller has not a moment to himself Since he Retourd from pant Coupée; we have not Come to a Settelment; till Such times as that is Dun Shall defare it—

I have Spoak to Mr. Miller Consaring your having Lost Mr. Kribs Note to Pensacola; he Sames to Rember Sumthing about it so that I am in hopes I Shall not Louse its amount; having nuthing further to acquaint you with...

To DAVID HODGE, *Pensacola*

Manchac, August 14, 1775

Your favour of the 12 Ulto. is now befour me[.] Mr. Elsworth is not as yeat arived; when he dus Shall Pay him the Ballace of your acct. 22Ds. 7r. we have nuthing new with us only there is a grat Demand for Corn [?] Goods; and nown to be had; this Beeing the needfull . . .

To LAURENT ERMANTINGER, *Montreal*[55]

[Manchac], August 24, 1775

This is the fourth Letter I have don myself the pleasure of writing you; Since the Time of my satteling hear; which I am afraid have all miscarried, which I flater myself will not be the Case with this; as Mr. Rapalje, the Carrier and an Inhibitan of New York; has Given me his word of honour that he would forward it by the fir[s]t Oppertunitty after his arrivell, in all the formers, I requested you would Send me my note for the Watch and my account of the Sundries you supplyed me with in the Winter of 1765 after my return from Captivity, as I am realy sorry you Should have Laid out of your money so long. I Say the Note (if not all ready paid you) for in my settelmen with my partiner Francis Lavaring at the Illionis in November 1765, I Left wherwith in his hands to pay it, and which he promised he would forward that Winter; or the Next Spring by some one of the Bay Traders that he should have; an occation of Seeing; as he was to winter up the Mississippi that winter, but if he has Diseved me in the affair, as he had on on [sic] many other Occations; I will pay the Note with the amount of the account; when was presented, as thanks to the Almighty have it in my power; and am allways willing[.] if you have no Correspondent in these; parts; Let me only Know if or to whom you'll have it remitted to in London, and it Shall be dun By Messrs McGillivary Struthers & Co Merchants at Mobill & Pensacola. having nothing further to add . . .

Sent by Garret Rapalje

To DAVID ROSS, *New Orleans*

Manchac, December 1, 1775

This Searvess to acquaint you, that I have now In the house 650 lb. of fine Copper Indigo; and as I Can Dispose of it hear at one Dollar per lb. English wight; and get Cash or good Bills on hand or from a Gentleman; that has property anouf in the provance; But would not accept it till I herd from you; The presant is to Request; that you Let me hear per the furst Convance; whater the Indigo will answer you Bether than the Cash or Bills, if it dus you may have it On the Conditions abov menchd; your Emitty answer Will much Oblige . . .

---

[55]/Montreal merchant with whom Fitzpatrick was associated in trade in the early 1760s. See Introduction to this volume, p. 4.

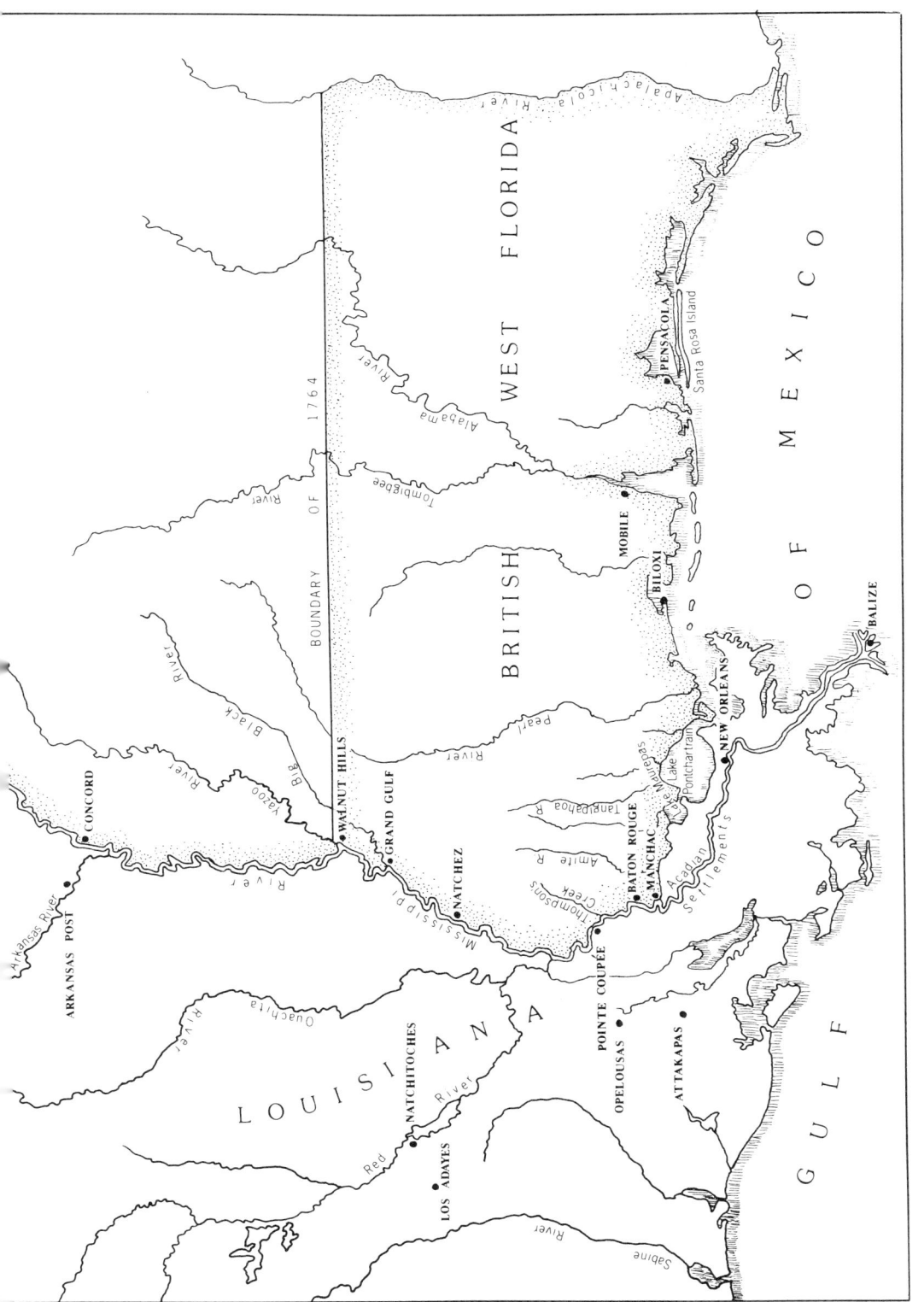

Louisiana and British West Florida, 1776.

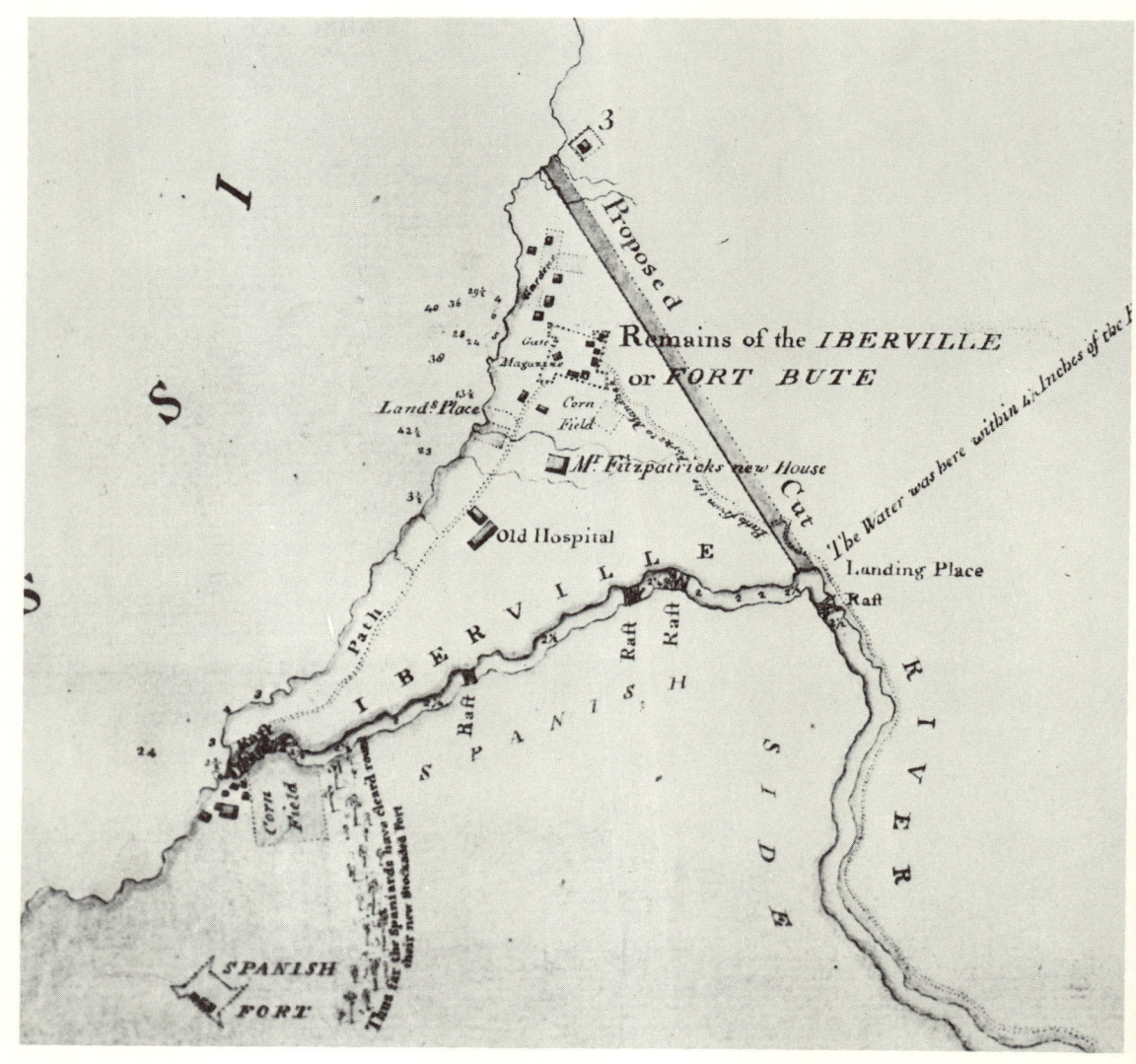

The settlement of Manchac, 1772. From "Plan of the proposed New Town also the proposed Cut from the Mississippi to the Iberville." British Museum.

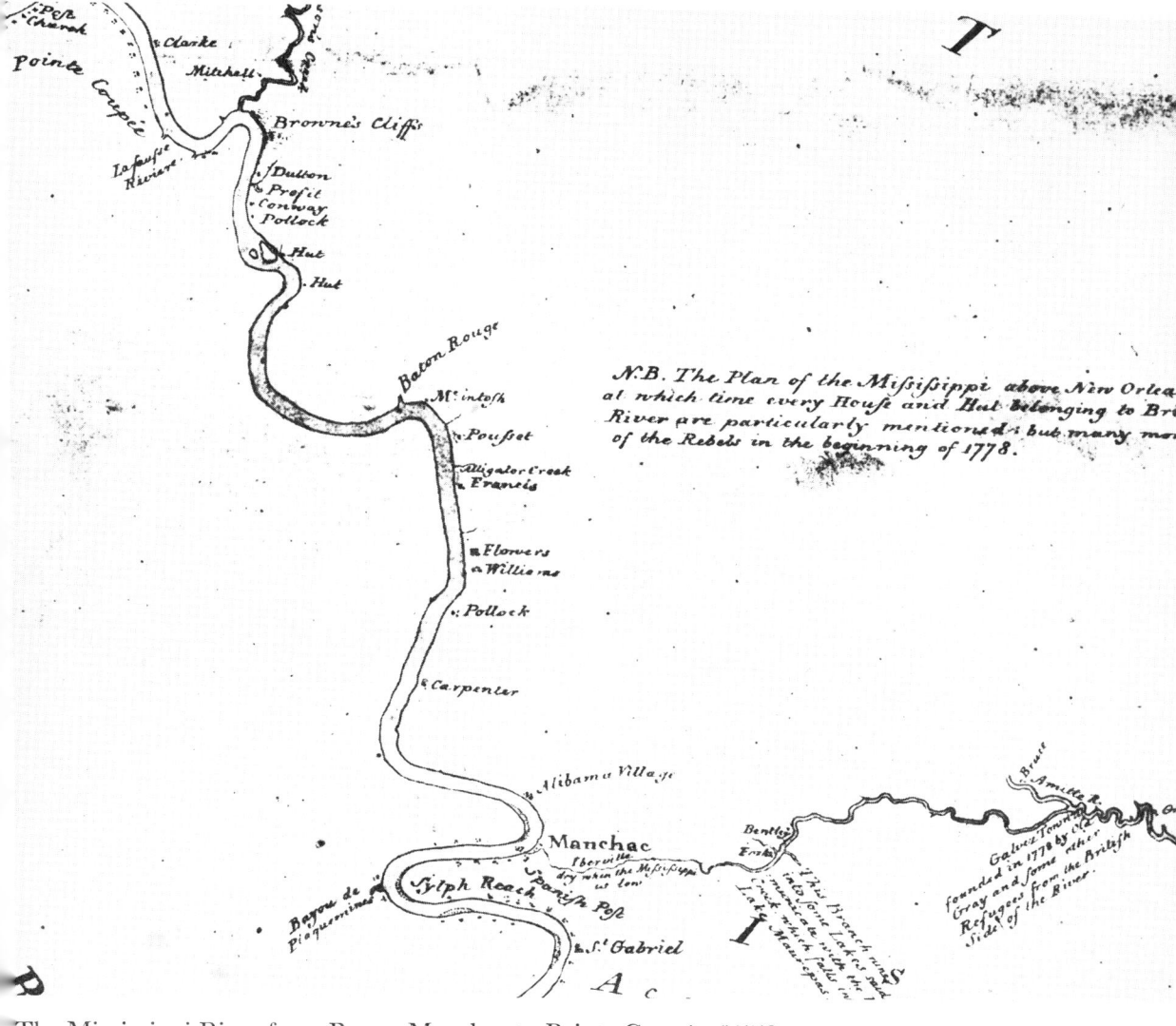

The Mississippi River from Bayou Manchac to Pointe Coupée, 1778, showing settlements and plantations. From George Gauld, "A Plan of the Coast of Part of West Florida and Louisiana including the River Mississippi from its entrances as high as the River Yazous." British Admiralty, photostatic copy in Map Library, Louisiana State University School of Geoscience.

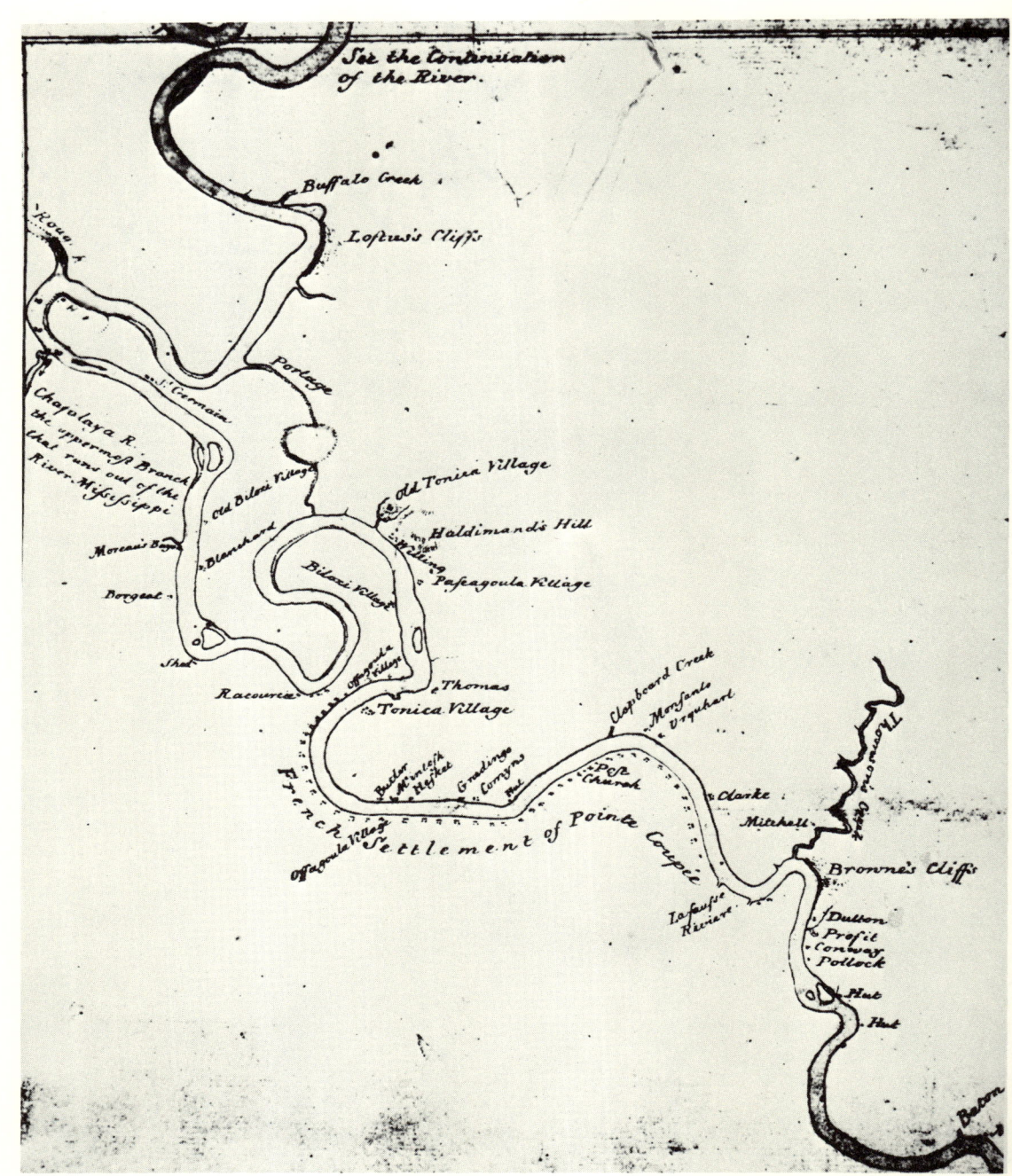

The Mississippi River from Thompson's Creek to Buffalo Creek, 1778, showing settlements and plantations. From Gauld, "A Plan of the Coast of Part of West Florida and Louisiana."

To OLIVER POLLOCK, *New Orleans*

Manchac, December 1, 1775

As I make no doubt but your Vessell from the Cape will be arved are this; the prasint is to Request you will Keep for me the folling articlls. Vizt. 8 hhds. of Good wine [*page torn*] Barrells of Caffee; 10 Basckits of Liquers and [*illegible*] Doz Suains of fill de pupillong[56] (if any Comes) for Which I shall pay you in hand $150 or 200; and for the Remainder Request till the month of April; Insuing—Should thes Conditions meet with your aprobation you'll Please to advice me per the furst Convance; that I amy [*sic*] whold myself In Raddiness to Send for them on the furst advce this Being the needfull . . .

56/A type of thread.

Part Three
1776–1778

To HOOPOCK AND STAMPLEY, *Concord, Mississippi*[1]

Manchac, May 9, 1776

By the Occation of Monsr. Bayer fils; you will Receive Two hundred Wight of Gunpowder; and 224 lb. of Balls; Beeing all that is as yeat Come to hand; the Gun Locks are not Come; or Should have Sent them alsow; But you may Rest assured; they Shall be Sent you By the furst Occation after they Comes to hand—

I have paid him your account; $8 for the fright of things; which I think verry Reasonable; inded. I have Sent your Spun [spoon ?]; But the Suger I have Capt as he Could not Carry it with Saftey; therefor will Cradt. your acct. with its amount—

I will be much obliged to you to Let me hear from you By every Convance; that may offer for this place; that I may Know how things Gose with you—and above all things; must Recommend to your Particuler notic to Be ware of Giving too Large Cradits for its much Better to get But a Small advance on your things; and Be Sure of your Payements; then to run any Risques; But for this point Shall Leave to your Own Knowladge that you [have] of of [*sic*] the Peopel wher you are—

For god's Sake above all things Take good Care of your powder as that is the main Chance; and there is nown to be had hear for Love or money; nor will there Bee any Till affers are Setteled &c

Having nuthing further to add only to wish you health and Suckcess in your undertakings & Belive me to be with Regards...

Messrs. Hooppock & Stamply
    Bot. of John Fitzpatrick
2 hundred Gun powder . . . . at $64 per Ct. $128
244 lb. of Balls . . . . . . at 12/4r per Ct.   28
                                                            156
Paid Monsr. Bayer fils for the frght of Do.   8
Placed to your Debte with me . . . . $164.—

[1] Indian traders and hunters, operating out of British Ozarks or Concord into the Arkansas River area.

(The following is the editor's translation from the original French.)

To MONSIEUR LOUIS VIVIAT, *Kaskaskia, Illinois*

Manchac, May 11, 1776

Sieur Louis Charleville has no doubt told you that I have on hand your bill of exchange, drawn on Messrs. Levy and Franks, contractors at Philadelphia, to the order of Mr. Louis Charleville at 30 days sight, for 120 pounds New York money, dated 17 March 1775, which the Sieur Charleville gave to Mr. Garret Rapalje in payment [of a debt], for whom I am commissioner. As it was protested for lack of acceptance and payment, when I had the honor of seeing Sieur Charleville, I told him of these things and he promised me to acquit it in town, that you would also except him from changes and exchanges and would have taken only the interest and expenses. As he has not carried out his promise, I cannot for the sake of Mr. Rapalje now excuse myself from requesting from you, Monsieur, the change and replacement and the interest accrued by the default of attention that Sieur Charleville has brought to this, for which reason I advise you to see to this matter, whether I may draw on you for the full sum or whether you will send here the necessary funds.

I am very sorry that in my first letter to you I have the disagreeable task of telling you prejudicial news, which perhaps may prove to be only a misunderstanding of your correspondent or an error of two letters of exchange drawn for the same sum, which they fear may be a duplication of the same bill. However, if I can be of some use to you in this part of the country you may call on me . . .

To HOOPOCK AND STAMPLEY, *Concord, Mississippi*

Manchac, May 31, 1776

Your Esteemed favours of the 25th Ulto and 15th Instant are now Both befour me; the Contents of which Shall duly Obsarv, In your furst you Acquaint me of your having Been Imposed upon By a negro of Mr. Cumyn's & that you ware oblig'd to Draw on me for 30 Dollars &c the Draft Came to hand, But I have not payed it as yeat as Mr. Cumyns is full as will able to Lay out of it Sum time Longer; or I am to pay it; though I have promised to pay it this fall—

In your Last you acquant me of your Safe arivell at Concord

for which I am Relly Glad to hear; But on the other hand am sorry to hear of your meeting with the Loss of part of your win[e]s; as Imagin they are verry Salable with you; at prasent. therefor Lay a havir [heavy ?] Strain on the Remaing part to mak up for what has Been Lost; I Did my Self the pleasur of writing you By Monsr. Boyer fils; the 9th Instent; and by his occation Sent you 200 Wight of Gun powder and 224 lb Balls all which I hope you have Recevd in good order are this—But my Gun Lock nor guns are not yeat Come from Mobill or Should have Sent the Locks—all the Draft you Drew on me in Behalf of you[r] men, have paid and Debted your acct. with there amount; Should you Receive any quantity of Skins in this Season; without you are verry Carfill of them; you will Suffer by them; though if you think Proper to Send them me I will Recieve them; at the price that any one will give for them at the time of there arivill, (if Cleen) if you Should think proper to Remitte my any thing to Dispos of for your acct. or to my Self; Be assured will due the Same for your Interest as if you war Personaly Present—

We have Receved nuthing new from the norwards yeat[.] if any things Com to hand Shall advis you of the Same....

To HOOPOCK AND STAMPLEY, *Concord, Mississippi*

Manchac, July 2, 1776

I had the pleasar of writing you 31st of Last May By Monsr. Ginge, to which Refair; Since that your Letter of the 14th of apl. that you Left with Mr. Blomard Came to hand; the Notes in it for $111.6 is vary Good therefor have Plased the Same to your Cradt. with me—

Since my Last we have hard nuthing new worth Retaling But we are Daily In Expatation of Receving Tralle [trail ?] news; when any Comes to hand; that is True or that Can Be Relley'd on be assured that I Shall advice you of the Same By the furst Convance; for your Governement in your effers—

You will please to Rember; what I have menchd. to you in all my Letters; which is Beware of Contracting Bad Debts, for Small profits; and quick Retorns will in a Short Time Inable you to Come on a Considerable trad to the your place; I have Still further to advice you to take grat Care of your powder; as there is nown to be had hear for Love or money under a Dollar in 10 Rayels per lb[.] this with my most hea[r]ty wishes for your hea[l]th & Suckcess is the needfull from Dr Boiys Yours...

Merchant of Manchac

To WINSTON AND KENNEDY, *Illinois*

Manchac, July 2, 1776

I have valued my Self on you this day; in favour of Monsr. Darchute; for Two hundred Dollars; which hope will meet with Due honour; when presented; Beeing for Skins Bought of him; your Complince will much oblige . . .

To JOHN STEPHENSON, *Pensacola*

Manchac, July 2, 1776

Since my Last to you; in which I maid menchen; of Captn. Lords having Left the Illionis; nown of yr. favours have Come to hand; By a Bautaux from the Illionis the other Day; we hear that Fort Dutroit, is taken by the amicans; and that Captn. Lord & his men ware on there way Back to there old port the Illionis; as all this is feunch News it whant further Convirmation;—[2]

In one of your fourmer Letters you Desired me me [sic] to pay Mr. Elliott; his account for Some Surveys he had to Dow for you; which I Promised I would; and on that account Supply'd him with Sundres provisions to the amount of $53.2 But when he had Dun the your work he would not allow me the $53.2; But Insisted on my paying him his account in Cash allthough in due me $465.0½ as you will see by his Draft on Mr. Durnford my favour for Said Sum—When I found that he acted in So unrasanable a maner I Refused paying; any thing further; and hope that my So Dowing will not meet with your Displeasur, for had it Been any other wise Should; have paid it the moment the Demand was maid; I have taken the the [sic] Liberty to Inclose you Said Draft; which if you Will be so obliging as to have it accept for me youll Gratly oblige me in so doing; Should not have Given you the Trouble, But as I am in Some hopes part of the money; that he will Receve from the Surveyer General will be through your hands (that is if Govr. Brown & Captn. Babbage, have Remittd you wherwith to Clear out there Lands; Should this be the Case you will Oblige me By paying Mr. Wilton $230.6; and the Remander Keep in your hands till I have the pleaser of hear from you; a number of Negroes in the Settilmen of Banton Rough; had Laid a Skime to put there masters to Death; But happly Decovered are it was put into Execution; and three of the Brighands has Been put to Death &c for the particulers of which Refare you to Mr. Wilton;[3] having nuthing more to add . . .

2/Despite several attempts, the Americans never succeeded in capturing Detroit. Fitzpatrick's source was mistaken.

3/In June, 1776, a conspiracy was discovered among a number of slaves in the Baton Rouge area. Apparently their headquarters was on the plantation of William Dunbar. Slaves owned by David Ross were the informers, and when the plot was discovered, one of Dunbar's slaves threw himself into the river and drowned. Three of Dunbar's slaves were arrested, along with one belonging to Francis Poussett, one belonging to Garrett Rapalje, and one belonging to the plantation of Stephen Watts and Samuel Flowers, along with several others. They were tried on June 30, and two of Dunbar's slaves were sentenced to be hung the next day, as was one of Watts's and Flowers's. See Rowland (ed.), "Diary of William Dunbar," in *Life, Letters and Papers of William Dunbar,* 27.

To JOHN STEPHENSON, *Pensacola*

Manchac, August 4, 1776

I had the pleasure of writing you the 2d Ulto By Mr. Wilton; Incloising you James Elliotts Draft; on Mr. Durnford for $475.0½ which hope you have Recieved are this; Should Mr. Durnford make any Deficualtey in accepting it; in that Case you will much oblige me to Keep it in your hands; Till Mr. miller's arivell with you; whom is to Set off in a few days, to whom Shall give an order; to take out a Write against Said Elliott for that Sume; the Ill usage I received from him; about my Due Desarves no further Linity from me—

Should neaver have taken Such Bills Drue on Such Conditions, had it not Been that I whanted to have a proper Voucher to Shue that he was in due me that Sume; he having alrady Denied the Dabte; we have nuthing New hear; worth your notice and it only Remains for me to Assure you that I am with Respect . . .

To CHARLES BLANCHARD[4]

Manchac, August 11, 1776

Your much Esteemd favour of the 6th Instant from your Plantation; Came to hand this moring and I retourn you my most harty thanks; for the trouble you gave youself ABout my affers with George Kaiser; further I am much obligd to Mrs. Thomas; for her good Intentions to Sear[ve] me; in Said affers As I am will pursweded She will fulfill her promise; and if ever In my power will Retourn the Compliment—But when I Came to that part of your Letter in which you make menchen; of Morice's having Denied; his partnership in traid with Le Crox; it surprized me a goodele (as I allways Looked on him as a verry honest man till then) But to prove to you that they are Relley in due me the amount of there Note (Now in your hands) for $133.3 and $9.2½ more then is menche'd in Said Note; as you will find hearafter menchend; furthere to prouve there Copartenership; I have Sent you there Joint Letter of the 12th Septemr. 75 Requesting me to Let them have goods and Lastly of the Compys account Currant; amounting Last Novemr. to $269.2; and part of which I have Receiv'd at Sundries time, as per my Recipts 126 Dr. 4½r which with the Note for $133.3r ought to have Ballanc'd there account; But as I had Nether my Books; nor there Proper account Current with me; at Point Couppée; the whant of which Occa-

4/Charles Blanchard owned one of the English ships that traded along the Mississippi, as well as a plantation on the Mississippi River above Bayou Sara. He resided in Manchac in 1772, when he signed a petition protesting the actions of Lieutenant John Thomas. See Caughey, *Bernardo de Gálvez*, 49; Hutchins map, 1779, PRO, CO 5/595, p. 341a; Petition of the residents of Manchac, March 9, 1772, PRO, CO 5/579, pp. 55–60.

tioned my Committing; the Error of the $9.2½ at the Time of taken the note for the $133.3r So that there account ought to have Stood as this—Vizt—

Dr. Messrs. Morices & Le Crox In acct. Current with Jno. Fitzpatrick Cr.
1775 Novemr 7
To the amount of yr. acct. Current $269.2r—By Sundries as per acct.
                                                   Curent . . Ds. 126.
To . . . . 000.00—By your Jo[i]nt Note
                                                     for . . . 133.
To . . . . 000.00—By Error on Settlement
                                                                9.2
                         Ds.269.2r   Ds.269.2r

This Sir I have Stated there account afrasch; that you may See with more Ease how the Error happened; and Should they offer to Refuse To Settel for Said Error; or make any further Dificalty about there account (that has Been So Long due) In that Case you will oblige me; to Embrass the furst Safe Oppertunity; to Send me all the papers; that I m[a]y Sand for a write; By the furst Convance for Pensacola; which will oblige them to pay my Just Demands; for I am Determined Now that I have found out the Error Committed; on Settelment to have it as it is my right; as much as the amount of there Note

I further make Bold to Trouble you with a Small account aganst Monsiur Olivier; for $21.2¾ which is the amount of his Priv[ate ?] acct. and for fear of his Den[y]ing this as he Did his Connactions with Le Cro[x] I have Inclosed his order on me for the Same; of the 10th June 1775 and have passed the Same to you or your order, therefor Request you will Indever to Recover its amount with there Compys. account, and Should he not Comply with your Demands; Retourn it with the other papers; and Shall have Same Distination; and as for John Bowle's account for $34 I positivly Refuse paying; that part in which he says that I assum to pay for Dail Carter (say $20) and to which that Villion; has atested; Befour Corll. Hatchison; and for that purgry, I am Determined to have have [sic] Crossed; if ever I find him in a place whir there is Law or Justis to Be had; the $14.5 for the oil is Just, and you may allow them that Some; On Settlement (if they think proper to Settel without going to further Extreems) as they may be assurred; if they oblige me to it; that I will put them to all the Expences; that the Law will allow of, But not one Singel Sols More will I allow in Bowles acct. the Said $14.5—

Having nuthing further to add only to assure you that I am with much Esteem . . .

P.S. Dont forget that the Interest goes on on [sic] the Note till the day of payt.

To JOHN STEPHENSON, *Pensacola*

Manchac, September 18, 1776

Your much Esteemd favour of 2d Instant is now before me; the Contents of which have obsarved; I am Relly Sorry to hear; of your Disapointement in Regard; of the Spott of Land that you So much whanted; But in now Respacts, am Surprized at Elliot's Behavour in the affer, for my own part; have not Experenced more Ingratitued from any man, Since in the Province (of them that I have Suarved in the manner I did him) then from Said Mr. Elliott, as for his paying me anything Since he gave me the Draft on Mr. Durnford; Not one Sole; the $53.2 was inCludid in Said Draft, therefor if you Can Sequare me that Sum; it will allways Be reducing the Debt, I am Verry glad to hear; you are in Expactation of Receiving Some money are Long; on account of Govenr. Brown, if so you will then have it in your power to Keep sumthing more; on account of the Bill; But in the Intrime, Shall be much oblig'd to you; to have the Bill Protested with out Loss of time; that he may not have it in his Power to take advantage of its not Being Protested; for I am will assurd. he will not Let any Occation Slip to keep me out of my money; as you will See more fully By his Letter, hear Inclosed; for your Parruselle—

After your having the Bill protested; Shall be much oblig'd to you to advice with Mr. Harrison or Bey [?] on that head of the Cost of which will Repay with Thanks, and if Ether of them Gentlemen; aprove of my aisining him for the amount of Said Bills; Please Let it Be Dun as Soon as Posible; as you may Rest assured; that he Looks on my Linity as No obligation in Whating So Long as I have dun on him; I would not Chuse to Be to [*i.e.,* the] Villint in the affer; or to Dow any thing; without your advice; therefor Dear Sir; Leave it all to you; if I am write and you aprove of the Same; Let the Write Be Sent per the furst Convance; he [k]now[s] what to Charge me as you See by his Letter; of having assumed to pay the Survaying of Govranour Brown's Lands, I Dont Denie; But what the Govr. Spoak to me on that head are he Left this; But I Told him I had ma[n]y Debts to Discharge of my own Contricting which I told him ought to be dun are I offered to pay for others; on which he told me he did not Expact I Should advance one farthing; be four he would get you to write me to autherize me to Draw on you his account, for the amount of Elliotts Demand (on these Conditions and now others) I promised as Sone as your Letter Came to hand; to assure me that I might Dow; to See him paid; it would have Been will for me; as he was in due me at that time upwards of $300—Seeing no Letter from; you on that Subjet I wrote you in august 1775 Requesting you would Let me know; in you[r] nixt; if the Governer had Setteld that Point with you are he Left the Provance, But your Sillance on that part of my Letter; gave me to underStand; I had nuthing to Expect on that head, on Recept of your Letter I acquanted Mr. Elliott he gave me for answer he was Sorry on my account; But was no ways afraid of the money; are Mr. Thomas Hutchins Letter to him to Dow the work was anouf; and if the Governer Did not pay him; he would See him paid payd [*sic*], this is all I Know of there affers; and now he Seemes to Insist on my beeing accountable; for the Same; which I neaver will; beeing [*illegible*]

I have Taken the Liberty of Sending you, a Panted Boufflow Skins; which Beg; you will Except of; as you will find it verry usefull in the Winter, in a Chese [*i.e.*, chaise] &c—we have a grat dell of flying new's But nuthing to be Depunded on as it is for the most part franch news; having Nuthing to add . . .

N.B. Sent this Letter by John O Brient; that whent in Burnes Schooner

To STEPHEN HAYWARD, *Concord, Mississippi*

Manchac, September 24, 1776

I have Did my Self the pleasure of writ[ing] you Sendries Letters within these Twlve months passd, But as yeat have not Been favourd with an answer to any of them; which makes me Imagine; they have miscaried and neaver Came to hand[.] The Prasent is to acquaint you; that I have no further Demands on you for the Bond you gave Mr. McIntosh for $495.1¼; as I have Retourned; it owing to what you; menchin in your Letter of 21th March 1775; that Mr. Harrod Refused; to pay you the amount of the Sundries Notes you Took up from Mr. McIntosh; for which you gav in Said Bond; But on[e] in particuller; of $180; which you Say harrod paid Mr. McIntosh himself; therefor to End all Disputs, thought it most advisiable to Retourn it; as not Beeing acquant'd With the originill Transactions; in your Letter Last Coated; you Tell me; that it was not in your power; to make me any remittance for that Season, Beeing oblig'd to Let mr. Donnallon; have all the Skins you had then on hand; on account of his Supplying you with goods (though you are will assured at the Same time) as you had my Goods in your hands; that I had Supply'd you with a much Larger amount; then Mr. Donnallon; had Dun; and on much more Reasonable Conditions; therefor might have Expactd. a part with him; Since which I am Glad to hear you have paid off a number of Debts you Contracted Since you have had my Effects in your hands Vizt. to Mr. Blommert Mr. Maison & Many others indeed all your Cradrs. have got Sum thing But me; Be assurd. Such proceedings has given me much unesaness this Sum time passd.

I have now waited Till the time you Limitted to pay me Expired; therefor hope you will Comply with your promise as far as Lays in your Power; and to make the affer the more Esey for you have Delivered all your Letter, orders men's Recpts account Current & Bond; to Mr. William Williams; with whome you will please to Settel; for there amount, So that if any Error has Been Committ'd that it may be rightifed; to Both our Satifaction by Mr. Williams; whom has my power of attorney for So Downg—

I therefor Beg that you will act the Needfull In Letting me have all you Can this year; to toward Clering your account; for Should you Detain my payment any any [*sic*] Longer it will be of a grat Detirment to me; and no advantage to your Self; Be assured if you Comply with my Just Demands as I am in hopes you will, if in your power; and if so if Ever in my power; Shall with Pleaser halp you again; I relly would for your own Saik advice you to Come; Down and Self your affers with Messrs. Pollock Willing & Blommart and as I am well assd. evry honest man that Sees your accounts (that Mr. Topham maid out for you) will Say you have Been put on[.] This Beeing the needfull ...

P.S. in your account Current you will only find Charg'd $40 paid Mr. Dutton; your account; the Ballance of the 90 Dollers which is 50 ds. you are in due him; if you Can Send it him you will much oblige me, as the man has Been Laying out of his money this Long time—

To JOHN STEPHENSON, *Pensacola*

Manchac, October 2, 1776

I had the Pleasure of Writing to you the 10 ulto. (by John OBrient) which hope you have recd are this; and to which refer, since which have thought it adviseable to Petition for some Lands not as yet having one foot in the Province, tho' in it since the year 1764[.] I have now 8 Negroes, self, & Wife, therefore think I am entitled to some & leave it to you to mention the Quantity I may reasonably expect; for my Family Rights without saying anything of my 3½ years service as a Volunteer with Robert Rodgers in the last french wars in America, Certificates of which service I had, but Lost them with many other Papers when taken prisoner in August 1763 by the Indians, I have not been able to send you per this Occasion a Certificate of my Head Rights, having no Justice here at present but shall embrace the first Conveyance after this. I have Indo[r]sed you a Blank sheet with my Name to it, which you will be so Obligeing as to have filled up with my Petition, being unacquainted myself with the tenor of Petitioning for Lands, therefore must intrude so much on your wonted goodness to me, as to get it done by a proper person; the Cost of which Mr. Alex. McIntosh will reimburse you, he will further acquaint you where there is some vacant Land near the Natchez, which would be Glad to Locate if I can get the Warrant for them, We have nothing new with us worth mentioning excepting that the American Barge that went to New Orleans some time agoe; has repassed here in her way to fort Pitt, the other Day; it is said she has 15000 some hundreds of Gun Powder on Board; she never called here going up or down[5]—having nothing further to add . . .

P.S. Please don't Petition for less than 1000 Acres—

To JOHN FALCONER, *Pensacola*

Manchac, October 2, 1776

I have taken the Liberty to Inclose you, Mr. Henry Smiths Note to me for dol.143.3½r payable 2 Months after date; this Money has been due to me since your first Voyage on the Mississippi; without my ever been able to recover it, which has induced me to Indorse it to Messrs. Miller McIntosh & Co. therefore as he is often at your place shall be forever Obliged to you, if you will endeavour to recover it or get Security for the same ere he leaves the place. should never have troubled you on such disagreeable subjects, but as we are deprived of all manner of redress at this place must have recourse to some Gentleman at yours, to see ourselves Righted. therefore your Obliging me in this affair shall be most Gratefully acknowledged . . .

To WILLIAM STROTHER, *New Orleans*

Manchac, October 2, 1776

Both your last favours duly came to hand the last of the 21 Ulto. by Mr. Campbell; with the Bottle of Mockaba I recd. last Night & for which I return you my most hearty thanks, about an hour after your Letter arrived here Mr. Dutton in his way for your place, to whom I deliv'd the Letter you wrote him; as you will now see him yourself shall say nothing further on the score of

---

5/See Introduction to this volume, p. 24.

your accts. together, but it stands me in hand to acquaint you, with an expression that he made use of here, relative to you & me which was, when I asked him how he could use you in the manner he had done; in getting you to assume the Amt. of his acct. to me, and to send him other goods on your own Acot. in expectation of being reimbursed by Mr. Chrystes draft on Pensacola for $56; but when it came to hand, it was only payable to himself; which Mr. Chrysty has done on purpose to serve his friend Mr. Amise, to whom he was in due more money than that, he told me it was no such thing, & that it was a made up matter between us, to deprive him of his Right. I then told him I was very sorry you was not here your self, to prove the falseness of the Acusation, but promised him I should acquaint you therewith the first conveyance[.]

I have got with a very good hand at present, that will suit me very well, therefore shall have no further Occasion for OBrient to doe any thing for me for the future; OBrient came & made out the Ballance sheet that you had Commenced, which took him about 4 Days, when done he made a demand of 10 Dolls. saying that you had promised that to his Wife, I told him I could not take upon myself to pay him more than 4 rs. per Day till I heard from you. therefore if you made him any promise of that kind let me hear in your next as I shall not pay any thing till I hear from you again, I am much Obliged to you for getting me the Casks of Claret on the Conditions you did; I have sent per Mr. Manuel Monsanto [blank] lb. Beaver when sold please to pay yourself for the Wine & Soap, (the latter of which is not yet come to hand) & keep the remainder in your hands till further orders from me, for Gods sake send me the wine per the first conveyance as I have not one drop in the House, I am well assured that you will doe for the Best, therefore leave it to your self to dispose of the Beaver as you shall think proper. I am much Obliged to Messrs. Morgan & Mather their good Intention, but as their terms is too hard for me, therefore shall follow your advice & defer all engagements of that kind till the Arrival of the Vessalls from England, & then if on no better conditions, what they mention shall only have to send for them to the House at Mobille; where I am sure of any assortment I may want & Nine Months Credit for the Amt. should your Vessell arrive according to your [e]xpectation, be assured you shall have the Refusal of Supplying me with what few things I shall want, when she comes in[.] I leave this in 10 days hence for p Coupie where I am going to recover what Money is due to me there; & from the sundry Letters I have lately recd. am in hopes of Meeting with good success. shall be much Obliged to you to write to me per first Conveyance after the arrival of the first Vessell from England, I can't but thank you for the trouble you gave yourself on Waiting on Mr. Pollock about settling the affair of dols.75 for Poor Hickey for which he returns you his most Hearty thanks. having nothing further to add . . .

To WILLIAM STROTHER, New Orleans

Manchac, October 10, 1776

I had the pleasure of writing to you the 2nd Inst. per Mr. Campbell; to which refer; since which Captn. Holly arrived here and delivd. me the Box of soap Wt. as it is marked 54 lb. Gross 8 Tare 46 Neat, but you don't mention in yours the price, I have sent you per Mr. James a small Bundle of Beaver; Wt. 80 lb. English; which if Messrs. Morgan & Meather will take at one Dollar per lb. Please let them have it my acct. further you will find here Inclos'd my Draft on Mr. Clarke for 37.3 your favr. being for the ballance of his acct. with me; which he promised to pay on demand to me or my order; with which you will remember yourself; and if any thing left keep it in your hands, if Morgan & Meather dont chuse the Beaver at the price mentioned, Please Dispose of it to the best advantage for me & pay them the Neat proceeds. we have nothing new this way excepting poor Elliott lost his Wife after 4 Days Illness this being all . . .

P.S. my Wife presents her Compliments to you—

To THOMAS O'KEEFE, New Orleans

Manchac, October 17, 1776

The Bearer, Mr. Hooppock; is a very worthy young Man, and to whom I have advanced at sundry times to a large Amt., he has some affairs to present to the Governor, relative to an affair that has happened him a few days ago; at the Arkamanas;[6] where he called in to get some provisions for sick people he had in his Boat; he was permitted to call in by the Commander Monsr. Viller,[7] and then seized on him, and took 11 hundred Deer skins 280 lb. Beaver with a Number of Otters; and then let him goe with his Boat. he will acquaint you fully himself; therefore if you can advice him how to goe to work in a proper manner to Recover his Skins, shall be forever Obliged to you, I rely much on your good Office in this affair, and be you assur'd I shall look on it the same as done myself and shall never be forgot by . . .

6/*I.e.*, Arkansas Post.

7/Captain Balthazar de Villiers, commandant of the Arkansas Post, was among the French military officers who accepted the Spanish invitation to continue military service in the colony. He served as commandant of Natchitoches until 1769, then of Point Coupée until 1776, when he was transferred to Arkansas Post. See Faye, "The Arkansas Post," 629–30.

To WILLIAM STROTHER, *New Orleans*

Manchac, October 17, 1776

Your esteemed favr. of the 26 ulto. per Monsr. Nicholet is now before me, the Contents of which have duly Observed, I am realy sorry you could not procure [?] an oppertunity of sending me the Hhd. of wine, as I am in great want of it—therefore request you will lay hold of the first conveyance. the present will be handed you by Mr. Hoppock, who is gone to your place on some Business that [he] has with the Governor, the relation of which shall refer you to himself for if you can be of any service to him, in advising him what he should doe to recover his Effects, shall be much Obliged to you. it may be that he will want about 20 Dollars in Cash, if you can supply him with that sum you will much Oblige me, if you have not disposed of the Beaver or got the $37.3 from Mr. Clark 'ere this comes to hand Please to let him have the forementioned sum, & be assured I will remit it you per first Conveyance after receiving notice of the same from you[.] your Compliance will forever Oblige . . .

if the Bearer should want a few Articles let him have 'em which Charge to my acct.

To OLIVER POLLOCK, *New Orleans*

Manchac, October 17, 1776

Your favr. of the 5th Inst. is now before me, the Contents of which have duly observed. I am sorry to acquaint you, that White Oak Staves are not to be had hereabouts under $30 Dollars per thousand; to be taken from the Landing where they are got, between here & Pt. Coupie, as that is the Price they bear at your place, it would not answer to give it here & loose all the Expence that must attend Rafting 'em to Orleans. Mr. Thoms. Pollock spoke to me in his way up about the Negroes; I told him it was Impossible for me to take them, as I have not Provisions for the few I have myself; but if I could doe anything with them at Pt. Coupie, to which place I am going in a few days on Business, shall doe it with pleasure; you request me to supply Mr. Henderson with three or four Hundred Dolls. Cash, is a thing quite [out] of my Power at present, as that article is very scarce with us—

I have already supply'd him from Time to Time, with sundry Goods for him and his Men to the Amt. of $290 and for which I am to have a Draft on you; should he stand in need of anything further in my way, he shall have it with pleasure[.] further have supply'd your Plantation with sundries to Amt. of $50 which I expect you'll discount on settlement; for the Remainder of my old acot. & my Note for $600 payable in Feby. Insuing shall hold ready to discharge when said Note is due, this being the needfull ...

To FRANCIS POUSSETT, *Baton Rouge*

Manchac, November 21, 1776

By the Occasion of Mr. Bonhomme you will receive the remainder of your Blanketts & Ruggs excepting the following which was sold since my Departure. Viz.

1 Rugg	. . . .	£0.8.0		
2	. . 12/4 Blanketts	. . . .	2.18.	
1	. . 11/4 . . Do	. . .	0.18.	
1	. . 10/4 . . Do	. . .	0.12.9	
		£4.16.9		brt. forw.
brought forward	. . . . . .	£4.16.9		
advance at 40 pCent	. . . . .	1.18.8¼		
		6.15.5¼		
Commission & Storage at 7½ pCent		.10.1¼		
		£6.5.4		
Exchange at 4/8d Ct per $			is $26.7r	

the whole amount I have not yet recd. but will in a few Days, therefore at the latter end of the ensuing week you may draw upon me for the Amt. I am apprehensive you have committed an Error in putting up the Blanketts as I found but thirty four when they were opened to keep 'em from the Worms &ca, I am confident that there was no more sold than the four mentioned at the other side[.] I have said nothing to Mr. Munsanto about the salt, as I have purchased some from him since my arrival at tuo Dollars per Barrell, as he will not sell it under that price[.] this being the needfull ...

To RICHARD CARPENTER[8]

Manchac, November 21, 1776

By the bearer Mr. Francis you will receive fifty Dollars which should have left at your House as I was coming down, but Night coming on & having the appearance of bad weather prevented me from the pleasure of seeing you and family. the remainder of my acct. with you, you may depend on having it Paid in the run of the ensuing Month. this being the Needfull ...

8/Richard Carpenter was granted a town lot in Manchac in 1772, and he resided on a plantation a few miles north of Manchac. See Council minutes, November 2, 1772, PRO, CO 5/589, pp. 46–49; Hutchins map, 1779.

To CAPTAIN CORNELIUS VAN HORN

Manchac, November 23, 1776

The inclosed is a Letter from Mr. Philip Francis to you, [rel]ative to two Negroe Men, that you have at his plantation for sale, a french Gentleman of Point Coupie by name Mr. Bohomme, offered to take them, if you will let them goe, for two hundred and forty Dollars each payable in Indigo next Novr. should his proposition meet with your approbation, and that you want security for the same I will myself in his stead and be forthcoming to you or your order for said sum when due, your answer to this by the first conveyance will much Oblige . . .

To WILLIAM STROTHER, *New Orleans*

Manchac, November 23, 1776

All your esteemed favours came safe to hand, the first of the 18th the 2 of the 22nd the [third] of the 23rd ultmo. and the last of the 6 Inst. have noted the Contents, In the first you acknowledge the receipt of the beaver & Mr. Clarkes order, I also recd. the Cask of wine that you mention in good order, but you don't say any thing about the Price—I have Credited your acct. for it and the soap

In your second you mention you having had an Explanation with Mr. Chrystee about the order on Mr. Amoss you say nothing further, if the Explanation you had put you in a way of getting your 50 Dollars that you advanced for Mr. Dutton or no but more of that when I shall have the pleasure of seeing yourself—

As you agreed to pay Mr. O Brien the 10 Dollars on the conditions you mention which he never complied with, when I came home I sent for him & shewed him your Letter (he having got the one you sent to him before I got down) that he might be noway Ignorant of your Intention on that head; he told me that he thought it was well worth the Money, on which I paid him 10 Dollars and took his receipt for it—

I have had but poor success at Pt. Coupie this year as yet, but am in hopes of receiving much more than what I brought Down 'ere long, as my small affairs would not permit me to remain any longer from home And as it is in very good Men's hands am no way afraid, but they will fulfill their Promises when due, but that same will prevent my being able to go Down so soon as I expected. by this Conveyance you will receive the Remmt. of your Coatee that I got from Allman—

You say in same Letter that you can't sell the Beaver but for 80 sols, which is less than what it cost me therefore request you will keep it till a better price is offered—provided that you are not in immediate want of the Money you advanced for me, in that case sell it for what it will fetch sooner than you should lay out of your due.—

I am well assured of your good intintions for my Interest therefore return you my hearty thanks, and shall be extremely happay if ever in my River to return the Compliment—I am in hopes are this you have recd. the Amt. of my order on Mr. Clarke, Mr. Miller will pay you the twenty Dollars you was so kind to advance Mr. Hooppock my acct. which added to the 10 Dollars Paid O Brien your acct. will reimburse you—If Mr. Dutton says that he had not the 10 Gallons of Rum (which was put in tuo keggs instead of one) its a falshood in him or else his Man destroyed it ere he got home, as I was neither Drunk nor out of my sences when it was Delive'd, therefore am ready if called upon to attest the Truth of the same—I am sorry that I cant send Mr. Laville the ps. of Corderoy that he wants on his Conditions, but if he will have it & pay you the Amt. it shall be sent to him per 1st Conveyance after your answer comes to hand—I am no ways pleased with Mr. Conans behavour to me about the spoons &ca, after a Man breaks his promise, when has it in his power to comply, I have nothing further to say to him.—

I have sent to Mrs. Blanchard time after time for your Gloves but have not been able to get one Pair, and as I know you are in want of them at present as the cold weather is coming, shall purchase the first that comes here for sale, provided they dont exceed the price you Limitted & forward 'em per first Conveyance—

Yours of the 23rd Ultmo. as it contains nothing particular therefore refer you to what is already said in Answer to the 2nd—

Lastly yours of the 6 Inst. per Mr. Profit it informs me of the arrival of the Vessells from London which am glad to hear of and realy wish that your one may arrive (Bon Port) I say nothing to you about the Goods I may want for the present; as your Vessell is not come in, should she arrive 'ere this comes to hand, you are well acquainted with the things I shall want, as you have an account of them already[.] having nothing further to add for the present...

To DAVID ROSS, *New Orleans*

Manchac, November 25, 1776

According to your directions when at Pt. Coupie I applyed to the sundry persons that was in due you, for payment, but was not so happy, as I could have wished, for your or my own Demands, as

I got nothing for you only, from Mr. Gradingo, who paid me the amount of his Note & your acct. against him being 226 Dollars, and that in Indigo which on my Arrival I put in Mr. Miller's Store, I should have been paid all that Mons. Duval is in due you if I had orders to receive it and give him a Discharge, which was a thing I did not chuse to do, for fear of accidents, your payment is ready for you, and he requests you will send for it as soon as possible, as he is not going down himsf. or to send his Indico this fall.—

By your Letter from your Plantation of the 26 Ultmo. You desired me to inquire after an Overseer for you, which I did, and have got a very good one (tho not a Married Man as you wanted) he is one of the best Indico Makers in the Province his Conditions are $240, from Decemr. 20th, till such times the Crop is housed, if his conditions & price suits you, Please to let me hear per first conveyance, that I may advise him of the same, as I have promised to do, & yo'll Oblige ...

P.S. the Inclosed Letter I imagine came from your Plantation—

To FRANCIS MILLER[9]

Manchac, November 25, 1776

I have this Morning taken up your Note of hand for £24 New york Currency from Mr. John Van Allen, which note was Payable in October 74, further I have paid him the Interest thereon, being £4.4 said Currency which makes in all £28.4 or Ds.70.4rs as I did it to Oblige you am in hopes you'll approve of the same & as soon as convenient for you to Draw, Reimburse me with a bill on Pensacola this being the needfull ...

To RICHARD CARR

Manchac, December 5, 1776

The bearer of the present Mr. Terince McMahon, has lately come from the West Indies, with an Intent of setling in the Province, provided he can be be [sic] able to obtain Lands, & as he is a Stranger will stand in need of some assistance to obtain them, I have recommended him to you as a person worthy your acquaintance, if you can be of any service to him in that affair shall esteem the same as done to myself this being the needfull ...

my Wife & Madam Maison presents their Comps. to you—

9/Possibly Captain Francis Miller, an army engineer in the command of Lieutenant Colonel Alexander Dickson. He later participated in the construction of defenses at Manchac and Baton Rouge. See Haynes, *The Natchez District and the American Revolution*, 117–18.

Merchant of Manchac

To JOHN STEPHENSON, *Pensacola*

Manchac, December 5, 1776

Your much Esteemed favr. of the 28th October is now before me the Contents of which have duly Observed, and should have Answer'd long 'ere now had any Opportuy. offered for your part—I am much Obliged to you for your kind attention to my small affair with Mr. Elliott shall Esteem my self happy if ever in my Power to return, according to your request have sent you his acct. properly attested, to serve in case of need, he is now going to Pensacola himself, and if you have not been able to settle the affair agreeable to your expectations he will be at hand where he can be served with a writ; without putting him to so great expence as it would be if it came here. am in hopes this will not be the case, but should it be, please do not let him leave your Place without having the writ served, as it may be I shall never have so good an opportunity again—I am in hopes that you & the Gentlemen of your Place that their fears are Expell'd in regard to the three Rebel Ships of 18 Guns each that was sent out to prevent McMinns [?] and the other Vessels for the Mississippi arrival, as there is six of them safely arrived now in the River, make no doubt but McMinn and the Store Ships is safely arrived 'ere this as it is supposed they have enaugh to do at home if the defeat of their Troops on Long Island is true

I am sorry to acquaint you that there never was such a scarcity of Provisions on the Mississippi these fifty years past as this year Corn is sold at 1½ Doll. per Bushell Pease at 3 Ps. & so on, and at that Price not to be had when wanted[.] as for Illinois flour there has not one Barrell come down this fall yet, but we are in Dayly Expectation of some, but God knows what Price they will make us pay for it, as there is none in those Parts to be had for Love or Money, but should any come and that it is on reasonable terms, you may depend I will purchase all there is to be had for your acct. and when I have got the Main point will be answerable Vessels will not be wanting to convey it to your place—

As to The Mr. Gibson[10] you mention he did not return with the Boat up the River as was supposed, but went to the Norward from New Orleans in a Large Sloop with Captn. Bethell Oord [?] & one Sign. Don Basille a Spainard that lives at Orleans, it is said the Boat that went up the River had on board 13,500 lb. Gun Powder but as she never Stopted here in her way up or Down, I realy can't say what Quantity she had but this is the Common report, as for the Sloop it is reported she had on board 30 wine Hhds full of Powder which was Intended for the Americans if they could arrive (a Bon Port) which was Loaded at the Levee

10/See Introduction to this volume, p. 24. Gibson left New Orleans bound for Philadelphia accompanied by Captain George Ord, an American whose vessel had been seized by a British sloop and who had been protected by Oliver Pollock during his stay in New Orleans. See James, *Oliver Pollock*, 70.

before the Town of Orleans[.] this Sir is all the News of these parts that can be depended on in regard to the American Boat & Sloop—If any thing else should occur be assured I shall advice you of the same by all Opportys.—In your Note 30th sd. Month you acknowledge the receipt of mine per Mr. McIntosh, that you proposed to apply the first Council Day for my Land, all I can say is that I leave that Intirely to yourself, to act as you shall think proper, & can only for the present return you my most hearty thanks, for the many services you are always rendering me having nothing further to add only to assure you that I am with the greatest Respects . . .

P.S. I have ½ barrl. Puccaun Nuts to send you but could not do it this Oppory. but shall imbrace the first that may Offer by the Lakes[.] since writing the above the Bearer Mr. McMahon is so kind to take a small keg of Puccaun Nuts for you, the remainder shall forwd. as soon as Possible—

To JOHN McGILLIVRAY, *Mobile*

Manchac, December 6, 1776

Your much esteemed favr. of the 19 ultmo. per Mr. McIntosh is now before me the Contents of which have duly observed, I am sorry that the acct. you mention (has been omitted) as it was not in the Letter, or should have sent you my Bond for its Amt. per this Conveyance—

Be assured Dr. Sir there is no one on Earth that is more sinsibel of the favours confered on him, than I am, penetrated with sensibility for them received from your hands time after time, am realy sorry to acquaint you that I thought to have paid your acct. off last spring, in this manner having paid Miller Swanson & Co., Miller McIntosh & Co. all their old demands against me, there remained in Mr. Miller's hands 2242 $ of an overplus which I intended for you, and never knew any thing to the Contrary till the time I came to settle with him for the goods that came from England, which was payable as per my agreement in the Month of Feby. insuing he then told me that he was determined to keep that sum in his hands, on acct. of sd. Goods, and for which would allow me the Common Interest for sd. sum therefore it was to no purpose for me to say any thing further on that subject, as he was determined on it, as for the Interest you may have charged on my Acot. I am well perswaded, it is nothing like what might have been charged, therefore this & the many other Benefits, I have experienced from you so often, for which I return you my most hearty thanks, for the present, and you may rest assured, that this winter, or early in the spring time enaugh for Shipping, I will exert myself to the utmost, to pay of your acot. I have paid your Gentlemen here abt. 2400 $ in Skins Indico and other Effects, although there is none of my People as yet come down with any thing this fall, am well assured that I shall recover to a considerable Amt. this winter, as there is due to me from three Men alone 8758 Ps. their comg. down this winter is most certain (if not prevented by Death) without saying about the many Debts I have outstanding in this District, Point Coupie, Nachitoshex, Natchez and other parts of the Country, which I am in great hopes to receive this Winter, (or the greatest part of them) it will be very hard with me, if I can't make out to pay your, and every Demand any other Man may have against me e'er the Month of April Insuing.—its most Certain wee Labour under many Difficulties, more than any other part of the province, as every other district, is providd. with a Court of Common Pleas but this, by which the plantiff may recover to the Amt. of 10£—here if you make a demand of your right, they only Laugh at you, all tell you must goe to Pensacola to get your Money for they have none.

This Sir, and many other such affairs, that have happened to me, for want of Authority to see myself righted, has been in a great measure the reason, that you & Mr. Strothers was not Paid before this time (not that I am by a means fond of Law or suits) at the same time it is necessary for some such thing to be established here, if you can service in getting such a thing done, I entreat for to have it & request you will use your endeavours to have such a thing Establis'd in this Place—you accuse me of having forgot you so much by not writing to you so often as I might have done, the Former part of said accusation, I promise you I never was guilty of, as to the Latter part much acknowledge to have been much so, not thro' any neglect in me, but as Messrs. Miller & Swanson were both here, who I suppose kept you properly advised of the affairs in this parts. I thought anything further I might have said, would have been Superfluous—for the future be assured I shall not neglect any Opportunity that may Offer.

For the present it is not in my power to make you a further Satisfaction, or else should have been done with the greatest cheerfulness Imaginable: but hope e'er long that will not be the case, as I am in Dayly expectation of recovering a considerable sum from the Illinois, this is the time the Boats from that country is expected down—Mr. Miller had no Tobacco himself[.] I let Mr. Swanson have 100 Carrts. of Pt. Coupie, which will be answerable for the Goodness of. as for Nashitosh there is none here, excepting the little Mr. Swanson got from Mess. Monsanto's and has sent per this conveyance. I have sent you a Doz. Carrotts which Mr. McIntosh told me you wanted for your own use & per the first conveyance after this will send you the 100 you wanted [?] this with my most humble respects to you & Mr. Strothers to whom shall be much Obliged to remember me is the Needfull . . .

To REUBEN HARRISON, *Natchez*[11]

Manchac, December 8, 1776

It is now near tuo Months since your Note has been Payable, and as I am much in want of its Amt. shall be much Obliged to you to remit me per the first Conveyance, either Deer skins, Cash, or Corn, to discharge the same this being the needfull . . .

To JOHN PRIEST, *Pensacola* [?][12]

Manchac, December 10, 1776

The bearer Mr. John Simes, acquainted me that you are in want of a Store, to Store a number of Goods that you have till such time as you can procure a proper Opportunity, to Convey them to the Natchez[.] if that is the Case, the present is to inform you, that I will supply you with a good Store &ca, and if there is any thing further, in which I can be of any service to you, in these parts, shall be glad, in being made acquainted with the same from yourself, this being the needfull . . .

To DAVID ROSS, *New Orleans*

Manchac, December 10, 1776

I had the pleasure of writing you the 25th ultmo. per Mr. Miller which hope you have recd. ere this, yours of the 23 last, Month per Mons. Lamatte with tuo Cross Cut saws, came to hand this Morning, and yours for your plantation and the Saws sent of half an hour afterwards by Captain Barry therefore am well assured they will be deliver'd this afternoon, at their Destination. As to what I was able to recover for you at Pt. Coupie, have mentioned in my former, therefore say nothing further on that head, there has no Letters come here, but one which was from Mr. Gordon, & that I sent you per a frenchman, that came from the Natchez in Messrs. Morgan & Mathers Batteaux, if any others come for you, be assured I shall forward them by the first safe conveyance, this being the needfull . . .

11th. since my writing the above the Inclosed Letter came to

11/A settler at Natchez who joined James Willing's force in 1779. In 1778, Harrison was granted 300 acres near Natchez. See Starr, "Tories, Dons, and Rebels," 194.

12/John Priest left Jamaica with his family, slaves, and an overseer in October, 1776, because of scarcity of provisions caused by the war in the northern colonies. In April, 1777, he petitioned the West Florida Council for a grant of 900 acres on the east side of Thompson's Creek. His slaves were said to be among some involved in an insurrection in Jamaica, and when he tried to sell them in Louisiana the Spanish government prohibited the inhabitants from buying them. Priest then took his slaves up the river to British territory and sold them there, many at Manchac. On receiving his petition for land, the council recommended that it be denied and that the attorney general "be compelled to remove this dangerous Banditt from the Colony." See PRO, CO 5/594, p. 12.

hand by the Gentleman you desired me to pay the Money to that I might have recd. your acct. at Pt. Coupie. I told him for Cash there was none but if he would receive the Indico I was ready to deliver it to him[.] he told me that it was not money, and that and nothing else that he wanted, on which I offered him all the Money, I had in the house which was 80 Dolls. (having giving 30 Dolls. already to Mr. Paussett for a Draft on you, he has not yet excepted it, if he does shall acquaint you per the first Conveyance, I am realy sorry that I had not more Money by me or should have Paid him his Demand, which was 200 Dolls. for you acct. having nothing further to add, only to assure you that I hourly expect down about 400 lb. of fine Indico from Pt. Coupie which I promise you; is Destined to Discharge my Notes in your hands. . . .

P.S. if you have any Common Romalls at 9/ or 10/6d per ps. any Jimmy Dimmy handkfs. at 21/ or thereabouts please to send me 4 ps. each per first Conveyance.

To ISAAC JOHNSON, *Natchez*

Manchac, December 11, 1776

You have Inclosed a Copy of y/a Currt. by which you will see there is a ballce. due me of Dr.67.5R out of which, there is the amt. of the oil you delivered me to the 10 April 1775, in your way to Orleans, an acct. of which I gave you in on your way up. but have omitted Crediting your acct. for its amt. in my Books, therefore as you have the acct. of its amt. yourself will please to deduct the same, and remit me the Real Ballance per the first Conveyance, or deliver it to, Mr. McPherson for the same my acct. your Compliance will much Oblige . . .

To DAVID ROSS, *New Orleans*

Manchac, December 12, 1776

Since my writing to you the 11th Inst. Your favr. of the 28 ulto. came to hand, in which you acknowledge the receipt of mine per Mr. Miller, in my former I acquainted you of Mr. Shaus having been with me for money & my having Offered him all I had then in the House, since which he has been here again, & I have paid him on your acct. 70 Dollars, and gave him orders for more as [?] your settlement, what success he may have, shall inform you per next Opportunity as he is to send me word,—I shall acquaint the french Man per first Conveyance that shall offer for Pt. Coupie, that he may not be disappointed—I am much Obliged to you for your kind offer, but as I am in no way in want of any goods for the present, only the few ps. of hanf. that I mentiond in my former, can say nothing further, till such time, I see what Money I may receive this winter[.] Should any thing offer be assured I shall advise you of the same. . . .

To JOHN CAMPBELL, *New Orleans*

Manchac, December 12, 1776

The Bearer of the present Captain Wm. Thomson will pay you on my acct. 129 Dollors an order for which you have here Inclosed, which is not the whole Amt. but as you have committed an Error in the Bill of Parcells you sent me, for you have charged me with the Barrell of sugar N 2 Wt. 30 lb. Gross tare 22 that you sold Mr. James Jones because it came from the Brig in my Boat its amt. is drs. 22.7 this with drs. 10.7¾ that there is a differance between your Invoice & what the things weighed here, but all these are trifles, and shall be settld to your satisfaction, on our first meeting. . . .

Manchac 12 Decr. 1776

Sir

 Please to pay to Mr. John Campbell or his order the sum of one hundred & twenty Nine Dollars being for value delivered you and Place the same to acct. of Sir . . . . . your humble Servt.

J: F

To Captn. Wm. Thomson
 Mississippi

To DAVID ROSS, *New Orleans*

Manchac, December 18, 1776

Your favr. of the 9 Inst. & a small sheeded parcell came to hand yesterday, this day have sent yours for Mr. Gordon & the parcell by a Boat of Messrs. Munsanto's that [was] going to Point Coupie.—Mr. Miller informs me you have some provisions to Dispose of, as I am much in want of some at present, you will Please to send me one Barrell of Pork per first Opportunity which charge to acct. of . . .

To THOMAS TOPHAM[13]

Manchac, December 19, 1776

I have inclosed you two Notes one of Monsr. La Chance from the Illinois for Ps.100, the other Monsr. Conans for twenty six Dolls. the former is the Patroon of Monsr. Dubrays Beautteux who will pay you on demand and Monsr. Dubray will pay you that of Monsr. Conans. they both stopped here and requested I would send them per first Conveyance, this being the first good one have embraced it—when you have recd. the Money, Please to Indorse it on my Note with you & advise me per first Conveyance when you are Paid. when Mr. Profit comes shall indeavor to settle the remainder; as I am hourly in expectation of Monsr. Colletts arrival with 290 lb. fine Indico, according to his Letter of the 4th Inst. with that and Mr. Profits acct. & a Little Cash, will discharge my Note, having nothing furtr. to add . . .

To ANTHONY HUTCHINS, *Natchez*

Manchac, December 29, 1776

Yours of the 22 Inst. came to hand yesterday the Contents of which have duly Observed, you will Please to draw on me at one Month after sight for the Expences on Locating & Surveying the Land Granted to Mr. Gerrard Raphelji, which shall be duly honoured, if at any time I can render you any service here, shall think myself happy. . . .

To DAVID ROSS, *New Orleans*

Manchac, December 29, 1776

Your favr. of the 14 Inst. is now before me, with the with the [*sic*] Bill of Parcells for the handkerfs. Amt. Ps.38.4 have placed the same to your Cradit. I am sorry that the Indico that I expect from Pt. Coupie is not Come to hand yet, or should have sent it per this Conveyance, I have about 50 Packs 5500 lb. of fine Illinois Scraped Skins, fit for the french Markett, if you know of any one that will Purchase them, please to let me hear per first Opportunity & if you have an Occasion for them yourself, you may have them, they cant be sold under 40 sols per lb. french Wt. having nothing further to add, wishing you the Compliments of the season . . .

the Inclosed came to hand this Morng.—

13/Thomas Topham originally came from England. He was granted a town lot in Manchac in 1772 and resided there for a time as business partner of George Proffit. He later managed a successful mercantile business in Natchez and married a sister of Isaac Monsanto. See Korn, *The Early Jews of New Orleans*, 47; Council minutes, November 2, 1772, PRO, CO 5/589, pp. 46–49.

To JOHN STEPHENSON, *Pensacola*

Manchac, January 14, 1777

I was favoured with your kind Letter of the 14 last Novembr. the 3 Inst. the Contents of which have duly Observed—

I am sorry to hear that your Endeavours to get me the Land met with so many obstructions, further am much Obliged to his Excellency for his good Intentions to serve me, but same time can't help thinking that I have as good a right to my head rights as another, in the first Place I have been in the Province since the year Sixty four, secondly for my past services in the last War in America, thirdly having made a Demand of my head Rights in the year 71 & had tuo Tracts surveyed for me, but before Mr. Wilton acquainted me that he made said Surveys for me, they were Granted away, the one to Mr. David Ross & the other to David Hodge Esqr. these Sr. are all the Claims I ever made heretofore, and if they are not valuable with the Governor & Councill you will much Oblige me, in never making any further Application for Land for me, as I have done without it till now shall be full as well able to do without it hereafter, but same time return you my most hearty thanks for your Good Intentions to serve me—

Mr. Miller acquainted me that he believed you are Attorney to Messrs. Godley & Raincock as them Gent. was to Messrs. William & Robert Barrow, the Letters left in my hands, with some papers & a Power to settle an Acct. with Mons. Jean Baptist Surpy of the Illinois, whom Mr. William Barrow before he left N: Orleans, had authorized to recover the Amt. of sundry Bills, Bonds & Notes of hand, that he had recd. as security from Mons: Maxant, for the Money due him from that Gentleman, with orders to remit me the Amt. that I might be able to settle Mr. Barrows acct. with Mons: Maxant; since Mons: Surpy went to the Illinois (which was in Feby. 69) he has never remitted me one Sol, till the other Day, an acct. of what he has sent, you have here inclosed for your Governt. in the Affair, for when Messrs. Godley & Raincock left the Province, they never wrote how I was to act, when I recd. anything from Mons: Surpy, therefore as I really don't know what to do with the Skins as they will not suit the English Markett, being all Scraped Skins, and if shipped home on Mr. Barrows acct. there will be a Loss of at least 50 pCent Exclusive of freight, Insurance & all other Charges, this I acquaint you with, that you may favour me per first conveyance with your Answer, or send an order to Mr. Wm. Strother to receive them, to dispose of them to the french at N Orleans for Cash, so that the Amt. may be sent per first Opportunity to Poor Mr. Barrow, as it has been a Long time due & may be of service to him, if you send an order to Mr. Strothers to receive the skins, Please to advise him to pay me 50 Ps. that I paid for the freight 'em from the Illinois to this Place, with the Storage & Porterage will be 7½ Ps. Please to loose no time in favouring me with your Answer, for if they be kept on hands all summer a great Loss will attend them. having nothing further to add, only to wish you & Mrs. Stephenson Compts. of the Season . . .

To WILLIAM STROTHER, *New Orleans*

Manchac, January 16, 1777

Your favours of the 13th, 14th & 30th ulto. are all before me, the Contents of which have observed, should have answered them ere this, but really had it not in my Power, when Opportunity Offered for your Place, therefore hope you'll excuse me on that head. In yours of the 13th you Say you can't get more for the Beaver than what you mentioned in your former as they Imagine it to be killed by English Hunters; but I promise you it is not, for I had it from Mr. Lafavour a french Hunter, therefore since you have not been able to dispose of it till now for the Price & that you are not in want of its Amt. to discharge my small Acct. with you, you will please to keep it till I come down myself, as I shall have a large Quantity in the run of next Month, & then will be able to dispose of it all together, & may be to better advantage, than to sell it under Price, as it cost me 7r per Lb. last May

I am glad to find Mr. Clark was on the Point of Paying you, the Amt. of my order yr. favr. hope you have recd. it ere this.—the Amt. of the soap & Wine sent [?] y/a have Passed to your Credit with me.—I am Pleased to hear you app[r]ov[e] of my Behavior with O Brien y/a & wish the Money he got may be of service to him But am apt to think he is still the same Man.—it is very true my success at Point Coupie was not according to my expectations, therefore must say as every one has been Obliged to say this fall, if bad Luck now, Better another time—Mr. Miller told me he had the Receipt for the 20 $—

Be you assured there was no Mistake in the Rum for Mr. Dutton and when I shall see Nash shall inform myself of the Size of the keggs, for our General Satisfaction—as there is no great demand for the Goods that Mr. Sulzer left with me, and as you have orders to settle that Acct. have thought proper to send you them that remain unsold, as you will have a much better Opportunity of Disposing of them than I have here, Inclosd. is an acct. of the No. Amt. £164.18s.10d the Acct. Sales shall furnish you with when I go down myself.—as for the spoons I want shall let you know when I have the Pleasure of seeing you, and if you can get them for me shall be much Obliged to you.—I am sorry to acquaint you that since your Letter came to hand I have not been able to get you the Gloves though have offered a Dollr. per pr.

In yours of the 14th you acknowledge the rect. of mine of the 11th in which you mention there was no flour at the Price I had heard & none but what you had yourself for sale, I am much Obliged to you for the Barrell you sent me per Maison, as nothing ever came to hand more timely—its amount is to your Credit with me, till such time as I have the Pleasure of seeing yourself which will be ere Long, when all the small Payments you have made for me shall be discharged with thanks.—

In your last Letter of the 30th you mention having recd. mine of the 23rd, a few Days before, and as there was no Vessells in from France, you could not give me any incouragement about the Illinois skins, till some arrived from thence, further you advise me not to bring down the Skins, till there is a prospect for sale, the last part of your advice was what I allways proposed to my self, knowing full how you are Lumbered, on Board your Vessells, with your own Effects; without being Troubled with Others—I am much Obliged to you for the abatement you have thought proper [?] to mention you will make on your flouer for me, therefore request you will keep me tuo Barrells let the Price be what it will till I go down myself, which you may depend will be in the run of the Insuing Month—

I have taken the Liberty to Inclose you sundry french Bills Amoutg. to £2558.6s.6d that Monsr. Sarpy of the Illinois sent me, in part payment for acct. William Barrow of Liverpool, but as the Bills are of no acct. to Wm. Barrow or any one else at this time being long since out of Date, with both french & Spainards; therefore can't think of taking them for that Gentleman's acct. as the B[ills] Notes & Bonds delivered Mr. Sarpy in feby. 69 was only on Conditions as security for the sum of $5440 due by Mr. Maxent to said Barrow, and it is to be further understood, that Mr. Barrow was to be at no Expence, on acct. of Transportg. what might be recovd. on acct. of said Bills to New Orleans from the Illinois, Monsr: Maxents agreement is such, that only the Nt. proceeds should go to his Credit, this he Obliged himself to do at a Notary Publicks Office, Now Sr. as these Bills was taken in Part of a Debt due Mons: Maxent by Monsr. Dubreuil St. Crox, and that Mr. D. St. Crox Paid them to Mr. Surpy, when quite out of date I look on it that Mr. Maxant has it still in his Power, to Oblige Mon: Dubruil St. Crox to Reimburse him said sum; therefore the present is to request you will Oblige me so far as to Deliver them, to Mr. Maxent and get his rect. for the same, the more so as Mons. Dubruel St. Crox is now in Orleans, so that they may settle it as they Please, for I would have nothing to say to them for acct. Mr. Barrow, as you will see per the Copy My rect. here Inclosed. I am sorry to be Obliged to Intrude so far on your good Nature, but the Offer is such that I realy could not help it, being well convinced that you will not take it amiss on such an Occasion as the present. this being the Needfull . . .

P.S. my best Complts. to your Brother—Inclosed him Mr. Barrows Letter to J: F

Sent by Isaac Johnson

To OLIVER POLLOCK, *New Orleans*

Manchac, January 23, 1777

Your favour of 6th Instent is now before me; the Contents of which have obsarved; I am Much obliged to Mr. Proffit for having menchened to you that I had a number of Illinois Scrapd. Skins on ha[n]d; But as they have Been Remitted to me in payement at the rate of 40 Sols per lb., Cant think as yeat to Let them go for Lase; then what they Cost me, I Shall be Down with them myself in the rune of the Insuing month and if nuthing more Can be had for them then 35 Sols; you Shall have the refusll

I am much oblig'd to you for your Kind offer; & Should with pleasure have Daitle [dealt ?] with you; But have found an Occation of Supplying myself hear; on Such Reasonable terms that I Could not Defur Suppling myself Pruttey plantifully for the Sale of the Insuing year; with out; it is much more Larger then I ever found it at Manchac; this with my Best Respects to you & Mrs. Pollock is the needfull . . .

To JOSEPH PINHORN, *New Orleans*[14]

Manchac, January 23, 1777

Your much esteemed favr. of the 13th Inst. with your draft on Messrs. Miller McIntosh & Co. came to hand this afternoon, the Contents of the former have noted, and the Latter presented which was accepted on sight, as for the little Ballance that may be due me, please to pay it to Messrs. David Ross & Co. as I owe them Gentlemen some Money, by so doing you will much Oblige me, it is realy the case with me; that since your Departure from this I never had the pleasure of hearing from [you] once, till yours of the 13th of the present came to hand, if you have wrote me

---

14/Joseph Pinhorn was a clerk for Robert Ross in New Orleans. He later moved to Pensacola where, in 1779, he was employed as a clerk by John Miller. See Petition, August 4, 1779, PRO, CO 5/580, pp. 147–71.

sundry Letters, be assured I never recd. but the present and another which I answered on recg. it, as for your Tea, I say nothing about it, till such time it comes to hand and if before my Departure for town, which is fixed upon for the middle of the Insuing Month, shall settle that point with yourself, when I have the pleasure of seeing you. Madam Maison joins my Wife in their best Compliments to you, this with my most hearty wishes for your welfare is all . . .

To DAVID ROSS, *New Orleans*

Manchac, January 23, 1777

Your favr. of 8th Inst. is now before me, the Contents of which have duly Observed. I am sorry my Letter came to hand to late for the Pork but there is no help for it at present.

I further Observe you have passed to my Credit Ps.95.5 that I paid Mr. Shaw your acct. but can't help thinking Mr. Poussett did not use me well to draw on you if he had no authority for so doing, therefore shall request he will pay me the Money on his return, as I only did it, thinking it was to Oblige you

I Return you my most hearty thanks, for the Trouble you gave yourself in informing me of the Price of Illinois skins, but as them that I [h]ave was remitt'd me at 40 sols per lb. cant think of letting 'em go under that [pr]ice till the last Extremity, therefore shall keep 'em here, till I hear of some Arrivals from france, You may depend that the salt you are in due Mr. Marshall shall be sent him per first Conveyance, as for the Oil I have none at present but you may rest assured it shall be sent him the first I receive, and am Dayly in Expectation of receiving some from the Arkansaws. having nothing further to add . . .

P.S. you have here Inclosed an order on Mr. Joseph Pinhorne for Ps.30.5½ and Ps.10 that I paid the other day to your overseer by Mrs. Sally's orders, which please to pass to my Credit with you—

To WILLIAM WILTON, *Pensacola*

Manchac, January 23, 1777

Your esteemed favr. of the 27 Ulto. by Captn. Offurd is now before me, the Contents of which have duly Observed.—I am glad to hear of your Brigs safe Arrival and the quick sale you have made of her Cargo, which is more than any of the English Vessells, now in the River have been able to do, this year partly owing

Merchant of Manchac

that the French have a free Trade now with Orleans, which will be of no service to the English hereafter, as they certainly undersell us, and their Goods are better calculated for this Province they will always have the proferance.[15]—According to your request I Inclose you your acct. Currt. & Sales, which am in hopes you will find right, and by which you will see, there is a Ballce. due you of $43.¼ having charged your acct. with Mr. Hodge's Acceptance your favr. for 63$ now here Inclosed—further my Draft at three Days sight on Mr. Adam Chryste for $43.¼ being the Ballance, and which you may depend will be duly honoured, on his Arrival at your Place, he being already advised of the same, —I should with a great deal of pleasure have paid you in Skins, had you authorized anyone to receive them here your Acct. but for me to send them to your place, to pay the Land Carriage, freight, & run the Risque of the Sea, would not suit me, therefore have thought the Method I have taken to be the most adviseable for your Interest.—In the Acct. Sales delivered you 1 July last I am apt to think I Committed an Error against myself of $5.2 but as I have not a Copy of said Acct. refer to yourself, which you will be able to see, by comparing them with this now furnished, but should the Sales furnished you when here be right; then I shall be in due you $5.2 more than appears in your acct. Currt. and which Mr. Chryste will pay you with the Draft, what Goods of yours that still remain unsold, shall send to you on order by the first Vessell that comes to the Amit (after there is water in the Bayeaux) Should have sent them now per Offurd, but Land Carrige is so high, that it will not answer,—I am much Obliged to you for your kind Offer of supplying me with Goods but as the french Trade is now open with Orleans, English Goods will not suit, as the others comes much cheaper. this with my hearty wishes for your health during the Voyage & safe return is the needfull...

To PHILLIPS COMYN

Manchac, January 24, 1777

Your favr. of the 22nd Inst. from Mr. Williams Plantation is now before me, the Contents of which have duly Observed the Letter for William Morris shall be forwarded by first Occasion, and if he sends the Indico seed here, be assured proper care shall be taken of it till you or Mr. Booker advises further about it, comes to hand—

On reexamination I found everything right as per acct. thereof, excepting one ps. of the printed Cotton N 25 price 29/s which

---

15/In 1776 an agreement between France and Spain granted limited trading privileges to the French West Indies for commerce with specific Spanish colonial ports, including New Orleans. Governor Gálvez was extremely liberal in interpreting these provisions, even permitting direct imports from France, and French merchants were allowed to import slaves from the West Indies to pay for Louisiana products. In 1778, the agreement was extended to allow colonial produce to be exported to any port in France or Spain which enjoyed the privilege of trade with the Spanish colonies. Between 1776 and 1778, as a result of this agreement and the disruptions caused by the war, the British were replaced by the French as the dominant element in the economy of New Orleans and the carrying trade of the colony. See Clark, *New Orleans, 1718–1812,* 222–23.

suppose in the hurry through a mistake has been put up in the JF [?] Trunks, if so or not, you will be able on your examining 'em at your Place to know, as there was but 2 p of that No. in Trunk N 1—

The Bearer of the present Jacque Timmée will receive the half of the Goods you have at your Place, and for which this will serve you as my receipt for the same, I have wrote to Mr. Tounoir for his large Pityauger, and as Mr. Manuel Munsanto has my Tarpoling [tarpaulin] at your Place, have requested him to deliver them, but should Jacque Miss him in the Night and not get them shall be much Obliged to you to lend him one of yours which shall be sent up with Mr. Tounoirs Boat, as it would be dangerous to come without covering this time year, I have a Large Quantity of Rum myself on hand West India & Jamaica for the present, but should any Occasion offer to purchase more than what I can supply them with be assured shall not fail in acquaing. that you have that Article for sale, Maderia wine comes to high for frenchmen and as all the English Troops have left the Illinois, it will not suit them, having nothing further to add . . .

To ADAM CHRYSTIE, *Manchac*[16]

Manchac, February 3, 1777

I have valued myself on you in favr. Mr. William Wilton for Ps.43.5¼ mill'd Money—which being the Ballance due him as appears by my Books at present, though by an Error committed in his favour when he was here, it appears Ps.5 more, therefore I have requested that he will examine the sales and if he find them right to Demand the five Dollars from you which shall be much Obliged to you to pay my acct. taking his receipt for the same having nothing further to add only to State that I wish you a pleasant Voyage . . .

P.S. Please to send my Book ere you go to Pensacola—

To DONALD McPHERSON, *Natchez*[17]

Manchac, February 3, 1777

Since your Departure from hence I have not been favoured with any of yours, which I suppose has been owing to your great hurry of Business, since your return to your Department. I shall be much Obliged to you if you will favour me with a Line per first Conveyance to let me know what you have been able to do for me —further to request you will acquaint Mr. Philip Allston, that I

16/A resident of Manchac in 1777, Chrystie also owned a house in Pensacola and a plantation on the Amite River, and served as both speaker of the house and member of the West Florida Provincial Council, representing two districts, Mobile and Manchac. See Starr, "Tories, Dons, and Rebels," 183; Haynes, *The Natchez District and the American Revolution*, 104.

17/Natchez merchant and planter.

offered his Notes to Mr. Miller in Payment, but he would not accept them, therefore as I am likely to be pushed for Money ere Long myself—I shall be under the Disagreeable necessity of Pushing others, but should be sorry it should commence with Mr. Allston having nothing further to add only to assure you that I am with Esteem Dear Mack yours . . .

Sent by Mr. Lyman

To PHILLIPS COMYN

Manchac, February 4, 1777

Your favr. of the 28 Ulto. whith an Invoice of Goods sent per Jacquex is now before me the Contents of which have duly Observed—

In my former I requested that you would examine your goods—the half of them that went from here, to see if the ps. Printed Cotton N 25 was not among them through a mistake it being the only thing found deficient in that Parcell in yours you say nothing in Answer, to said request, which I imagine has been owing to your hurry of Business—I am sorry the 300 lb. Gun Powder I expected is reduced to one, as without it I know not what I shall do, on examining the Goods you delivered Jacquex, I find there is sundry things wanting to compleat your Invoice an acct. of which you have here annexed for your Government, which you will Please to Rectify—I also found sundry Goods partly Damaged, so much as to make them unsaleable, therefore have put them by themselves till I have the pleasure of seeing yourself (as I allways understood when I agreed to take half your goods here, and at your Store they were to be Merchantable and Good) therefore shall say nothing further on that head, being well assured that you will admit of my reasons when you see the Effects

As for my Note or Bond I am no way against giving you any security you shall request (though as yet all the Dealings I have had with McGillivray & Co. I never gave a Bond) but that is no reason for you, having nothing further to add . . .

Should be much Obliged to you if an Opportunity Offers to send me the Powder

the following Articles Deficient

1 blue bordered handkf . . . at 23	0.1.11
1 Cottn. waistcoat shape backs but no front	0.3.—
¼ Bunch white Barleycorn Beads	0.0.9
1 Pair oiled Ramskin Breeches	0.13.—

1 doz: broad Hatchetts N 2		0.13.6
1 doz: 10 Inch Stock Locks		0.14.6
½ doz: blue & yellow handkfs . . . 20		0.10.—
2 butchers knives		0.0.5

no staples came with any of the Stock Locks

The undermd. Goods Damaged

the Scarlet Cloth stained & worm Eaten
a Number of ps. of Brittanias stained with water being wet I suppose on Ship Board
the Blue & some of the red bordered handkfs. do. . . . do. . . .
1 ps. Teapay soiled & Dirty
2 pr. Ram skin Breeches not sound

To MR. EASON, *Natchez*[18]

Manchac, February 6, 1777

As you was so obliging, as to Offer me your service & that you are now on your way for the settlemt. of Concord, the present is to request that if Messrs. John & Thoms. Cummings, should offer you any Payments on my acct. you Will please to receive them for me, also from Geo. Williams & Zebulon Mathews a Note of each mans acct. you have here annexd.

In case of your receiving any thing from the aforesaid Persons, you will Please to Observe they are to be at all the expence & risque of sd. things till such time as they are delivered here, this being the place of Payment, for whatever they deliver you, you'll give them a receipt in my Name, which shall be valuable the same as from myself on acct. of their Note or Bond—wishing you a good Voyage &c—

John & Thoms. Cummings acct. as Inclosed them		208.7¼
Zebulon Mathews . . . . . Do		125.6
George Williams . . . . . Do		11.1½
		Ps.345.6¾

To HOOPOCK AND STAMPLEY, *Concord, Mississippi*

Manchac, February 6, 1777

Your Letters of the 24th Decr. that of the first Jany. with the Skins & one of the 13th same, are all now before me, the Contents have duly Observed.—In your fi[r]st you requested to pay of your

18/Probably William Eason, originally from Pennsylvania. He served in the Indian Department in Illinois but left in 1775, when the American Revolution began, accompanied by loyal Kaskaskia and Peory Indians. He was granted 500 acres about 25 miles from Natchez near Homochitto Creek. See Council minutes, August 28, 1777, PRO, CO 5/594, pp. 88–89.

hands which I did, in yr. 2nd you desired me to pay Mr. Charleville 12 Dollars, which I done & charged as you desired, that is to your acct. 7 Ps. & to shoots 5 Ps. lastly I paid your order in favour of a French Man 12 Ps. & Paid Mr. Comyn your acct. Ps.37.4 should have wrote you ere this, but was afraid my Letters should meet with the same fate they did last year, I have sent you none of the things you requested Mr. Boles to send by the first conveyance, as I imagine the season for Trade will be over, ere you could receive them, I have a Compleat Cargo ready for you come when you will, therfore for your own Interest, Loose no time in sending down your skins, for if they come to hand after the Vessells sails for England, you are well convinced their Price will fall, excuse haste and believe me to be with Esteem Dear Boys yours ...

I have no Oil, therefore depend on you for my Provision of that Article, all the Tallow you can get bring Down.

Sent by Mr. Eason

To PHILIP LIVINGSTON, JUNIOR, *Pensacola*

Manchac, February 7, 1777

Having been informed that Mr. Pollock of N: Orleans had out Letters of Administration on the Estate of the Deceased John Finney late a Trader at the grand Gulph on the Mississippi, and as said Estate is in due me, as I had the honour of acquainting you, when you was here last, since which I have not been able to get a satisfactory acct. from Mr. Pollock on that head, therefore have recourse to you, to request you will favour me with a Line, and let me know if Mr. Pollock has made a return of said Estate to your Office or no, your compliance in Obliging me so far shall be gratefully acknowledged by ...

To OLIVER POLLOCK, *New Orleans*

Manchac, February 13, 1777

Agreeable to your order of the 2nd last March, I paid Thoms. Taylor 38 Ps. and took his Note payable to you or your order for said sum, which I now inclose you, to receive its amt. as he is going down & has wherewith to discharge it and any other further Demands you may have against him with honour, on his Arrival here I demanded the payment, which he told me he did not think proper to pay till he saw yourself, as you were in due him, as the order you gave him for the Powder had not its Intended Effect, therefore have passed its Amt. to your Debit with me, I shall be down at your place some time this Month, or the beginning of the Ensuing when all our small affairs shall be settled to your satisfaction[.] having nothing further to add . . .

P.S. the Effects that Mr. Russell left here for you shall be sent per first safe Conveyance—

To JOHN WAUGH, *New Orleans*

Manchac, February 13, 1777

I have this Morning recd. an Express from Mr. Hooppock informing me that his partner Henry Stamply had been taken Prisoner by the spainards of the Arkansaws, & sent to your place in Irones, he passed by here yesterday, but did not stay long enough for me to see him, although I made all the haste Imaginable, as the poor fillow may be in want of some small necessary's in the Clothing way (if delayed long in Prison) shall be forever obliged to you if you will supply him to the Amt. of Ps.20 or thereabout in any thing he may want, which you may depend I will reimburse you with all other demands you have against me, on my arrival at your Place, which will be some time this Month or the Commencement of the ensuing without fail, further if you can be of any service to him in helping to extricate him from Prison (as he has not been guilty of any crime than that of being found with Two kegs of Rum, agoing to the Indian Village to get Corn that they wanted for their subsistance) it will be most gratefully acknowledged By . . .

To DAVID ROSS, *New Orleans*

Manchac, February 13, 1777

By this conveyance I have sent you the Inclosed Letter that I recd. from your Plantation last Night by your Carpenter, which will no doubt inform you, that one of Charles Clarkes Negroes that was at your place has run away, there was a Letter for his Master, which shall forward this Morning—& am Realy sorry that it was not in my Power to have complyed with the Tenor of my Obligation in your hands ere this, but you may rest assured I shall be with you in the run of this Month, or the Commencement of the ensuing without fail, and will have it in my power to reimburse you the Principal & Interest that may remain due—I have this

Morning recd. an Express from the Arkansaws from Michael Hooppock, acquainting me of his partners having been Taken by the spainards of that Part, going with tuo Kegs of Rum to the Indian Village, to get corn that they wanted for their provisions and that they had sent him to Orleans in Irons, if you will be so complisant (as you are now in Town) to go to the prison & see if the poor fellow is in want of any Clothing, if so please to supply him my acot. to the Amt. of Ps.20 of any thing he may want, and if you or your Brother can be of any service in helping to extricate him from Prison (as I am greatly Interested in his preservation) it shall be most gratefully acknowledged by . . .

To MICHAEL HOOPOCK, *Concord, Mississippi*

Manchac, February 14, 1777

Your favour of 7th Instant per MacCartey is now be for me; the Contents of which have observed, I was Sorry to hear of Poor Stamply's unhappy fait; he passed hear the day Be four your Letter Came to hand, I sent over to the Spanish for (as I Could not go my Self for that instant; having a number of franch men in the house at that time) as Soon as I hard of his arivell there; to Know if he whantd any thing; but he was gon; they did not allow him to Remain there ten minits when I found that to be the Case I wrote Sundries Letters to English Gentlemen in Orleans; to Supply him with any thing he Might whant; and further Request'd them to use there Interest to Extricat him out of Prisen; and which am in hopes they will Be able to Effect with Ese; as the New Governer[19] (Latley arved at Orleans) allows the English Liberty to trad or hunt up any of the Rivers on the Spanish Sid they Please; further—all the English merchants that Capt there Stores on board the Vessells have now there Shops in Town; So that I am in Grat hopes he will be with me are your arivill—

I am Sorry that it was not in my power to Comply with your order in favour of Mr. Jaccob MacCartey, having been oblig'd to Pay Mr. Mcmahan; a few days Before the amount of the Rum you took up (when Last hear) as he was a Leving the provance; and Could not be put off any Longer; this and the orders you have Drue on me from time to time has Draind me of all the Littel Cash I receive daily; for this sume time passd, the morsow as Mr. Miller is verry prassing for his payments; which ought to have Been have Been [*sic*] paid Some time ago; and for which am paying Interest daily; there for Shall be for ever oblig'd to you to make all the heast possible with yr. Skins; the arivalle of which; will Inable

19/Bernardo de Gálvez was born in Málaga, Spain, in 1746. He was a nephew of José de Gálvez, minister of the Indies, and son of Matías de Gálvez, who became viceroy of New Spain. His military career began early and he saw many years of distinguished service in Europe and New Spain before arriving in Louisiana as governor in 1777. He left the colony in 1781, after the fall of Pensacola, and was made viceroy of New Spain in 1785. He died in Mexico in 1786. For a full account of Gálvez's career in Louisiana, see Caughey, *Bernardo de Gálvez*.

me to Discharge my affers with that Gentleman; and put me in a Condition of Supplng you farther; if you Should whant it, as I have a fine assortement of Goods now in the house; not that alown; But if your Skins Came to hand after the Vessells have Saild for England, they will fall in there Price Besides the trouble and Expances that will atend Keeping them on hand all Summer—I have supplyd Mr. MacCarty with Sundries; an account of which you have hear Inclosed for your governement; when Setteling with him; having nuthing further to add for the Prasent; having wrote you fully the 6th Instant per Mr. Eson . . .

P.S. I shall take proper Care of your Corn [?]—

Sent by Jacob MacCarty

To JOHN STEPHENSON, *Pensacola*

Manchac, February 14, 1777

Your obliging Letter of the 7 Ulto; Came to hand Sum days ago, the Contents of which have obsarved; and am for ever obligd to you for having Termenited the affer of Elliotts in the manner you did, it Beeing By fare the Best for me, and according to your order have Drue on you in favour of Messrs. Miller McIntosh & Co. at thirty Days Sight, for the amount; we have nuthing new with us; Excepting; that I have Been will Infourmed; that the Boat that whent up with the powder; has Left the fort of the arkansaws—and is gon in Company with three smaller for fort Pitt—She was meet By one Thomas Tayler; near the Iron mines; that is about 100 mills Below the mouth of the Ohio; 16 Days ago; and as they ware in what of hands; they took one of his; he further Says they told him they Expectedd to Be Reinforcedd By 500 men; about the mouth of the Ouabachi; that is about 60 mills up the Ohio; & that Said Reinfor[ce]ment was to Come from fort Pitt; this I have from Said Tayler himself how is now hear with me, having nuthing further to add . . .

To DAVID ROSS, *New Orleans*

Manchac, February 21, 1777

I have only time to acquaint you that by the Occasion of the Schooner Mississipi Captn. Fouls I have sent you the Indico that I recd. your acct. last fall at Point Coupie, a rect. for the same you have Inclosed, if nothing extraordinary happens shall be with you some time next week. . . .

To DONALD McPHERSON, *Natchez*

Manchac, March 2, 1777

I have taken the Liberty to Inclose you an acct. against Charles Thomson properly attested ballance due to me $37.1[.] shall be much Obliged to you, if you will acquaint him of the same, letting him know it is my request if he does not discharge said Acct. of hand; that you will be obliged to put the Law in force, & if he does not comply with my request, beg that you doe not spare him the first Court that you have, as he deserves no further Linity from me, you[r] compliance will much Oblige Dr. Mack yours ...

P.S. please to let me hear from you per first Opportunity, any Expences you are at for my small affairs in your hands, shall be paid on Demand to you or yr. order

Sent by Henry Stuart

To PHILLIPS COMYN

Manchac, March 18, 1777

Your much esteemed favr. of the 8th Inst. came to hand last Night with the ps. printed Callico N 25 cost 29/s with advance is 9 Ps. though it is much damagd. have added its Amt. to the tuo former accts. given in which is in all Drs.5158.7r to your Credit with me, and hope when wee come to examine the same will find right, if any Error has occurred, all shall be righted at our first meeting, as for the damaged Goods that I have put by, am well assured we shall settle ourselves to mutual satisfaction without callg. a third Person, as for the hatchetts N 2 there was certainly charged 2½ doz in yr. Invoice [per] Jacquex, but only 1½ doz: found when examined here, I am much Obliged to you for Delivering the powder to Mr. Tounoir, as he had my order for the same, the back of the Cotton waistcoat shape is here, & shall send or deliver it to yourself, if you are coming down if you stop at this place, Mr. Boles will rectify any Errors that may have been committed as I shall be at Orleans, any thing that he shall do will be the same as if done by myself[.] this being the needfull ...

To THOMAS O'KEEFE, *New Orleans*

Manchac, March 19, 1777

I have shipped on board Mr. Winstons Batteau 43 Packs scraped skins, the property of a Gentleman now in England, which are marked & Numbered as per Invoice here Inclosed for your Government; shall be much obliged to you if you can dispose of the same for Cash at the Markett price, as I shall want to remit the Amt. per first conveyance to his attorney, if not you will please to put them on board some English Vessell if possible till I am with you, which will be in a few days hence, further there is four Bundles of Beaver skins weight unknown & 2 bundles of Deer skins in the hair, which you will dispose of in like manner to the best advantage, the amount of the Beaver skins in the hair you will give to Messrs. Morgan & Mather taking their rect. for the same my acct.—further have to request you will present for acceptance the following orders to Mr. Olivr. Pollock Viz

Alexander Hendersons . . . . . for Ps.262.0¾
Phillip Lyons first 38.6¾
Do. . . . second . . . . 9.— —Ps.309.7½

you will Please to observe that there is a small Pack of Beaver 21 skins on which is marked Samuel Shoots that you will weigh by it self and keep an acct. of the same as it belongs to said shoots & he is not here—any Expences you may be at on acct. of the skins shall be reimbursed you on our meeting[.] having nothing further to add . . .

P.S. further you have Mr. Raujote Note for D.145.6r which if you [illegible] before I go down pay to the Messrs. Ross—

To DONALD McPHERSON, *Natchez*

Manchac, March 19, 1777

Your esteemed favrs. of the 15th 26 & 27th ulto. are now before me, the Contents of which have duly obser[v]ed—

In that of the 26th I found a Note of Dan: Bush's for $40 and an order your favr. on David Williams for Ps.18.4 which keep till I have an occasion of seeing him and if accepted shall be applyed to your Credit with me, if not shall remit it to you per first conveyance, as for the Note that Mrs. Truly sent I will have nothing to do with it, for I think the Drawer has not wherewith to discharge it when due, therefore Inclose it to you again that you may receive its amt. I am pleased you have reduced the sum, as now you have brought it within the Verge of your Court, therefore must request you to have no further Linity for the old woman, but Push her at the first Court, without she complys at your first demand, I am Glad you acted in the manner you did with Thornhill, as the Money for my Goods is the only assumption that will suit me at present, therefore do your utmost, I am obliged to you for the Pains you took with the others and hope they will comply with their Promises, realy your Countrymen are very long winded, I also return you my hearty thanks for the advise you gave your friend Allston as I found it has had some effect on him, I have seen Mr. Johnson and settled with him but no money yet, this is often the case on the Mississippi, having nothing further to add . . .

P.S. I wrote to you the 12 Inst. per Henry Stewart Esqr. Inclosing you an attested acct. of Charles Thomson which please do the needfull with—

I am sorry to hear that you & Mr. McIntosh has had such a Difference would be glad you could settle that affair yourselves without the trouble or expence of going to Law

To MESSRS. MORGAN AND MATHER, *New Orleans*[20]

Manchac, March 22, 1777

You will find here Inclosed Mr. Donaho's order your favr. on Mr. Oliver Pollock for Ps.200 which when you receive Place to my Credit with you, I am realy sorry that I have not been able to go down ere this, but it will not be many days before I shall have the pleasure of seeing you, as I have defered my departure from here, till the last of this month, if then the Boats that I have been hourly expecting these 20 days past is not arrived here, shall leave this place without fail & be assured that on my arrival with you, all our little affairs shall be settled to your satisfaction[.] I delivered Mr. OKeefe four small Packs of Beaver which when sold desired him to pay you its amt. & am well assured he will, having nothing further to add . . .

P.S. Please to forward the inclosed—

To THOMAS O'KEEFE, *New Orleans*

Manchac, March 22, 1777

I have Inclosed to you a Letter for Mr. John Campbell with a draft on him for Ps.150 at ten days sight which please to get accepted & keep till I have the pleasure of seeing yourself; should any unforeseen accident prevent my being with you when the Bill should be come payable, you will please to draw the Money your Compliance in this affair, will add to the many Obligations already conferr'd . . .

20/The New Orleans mercantile firm of George Morgan and James Mather, established in 1776, continued until 1783. Mather was also associated with Arthur Strother of Mobile in a concession from the Spanish government to supply Indian goods to Louisiana. See Arthur P. Whitaker, "Alexander McGillivray, 1789–1793," *North Carolina Historical Review*, V (1928), 187.

To JOHN STEPHENSON, *Pensacola*

Manchac, March 28, 1777

Since my writing you the 14th ult. your much Esteemed favr. of the 7th of the same Month came to hand, the Contents of which have duly Observed—I am much obliged to you for your attention to my small affairs & since you are so good as to give yourself further Trouble about the Land, I have nothing further to say only what I have already mentioned to you in my Letter of the 14th last Jany. excepting that the tuo tracts that was surveyed for me in 71 only contained 850 Acres and my Petition was for 1000, which if you can procure for me with the governor & Council shall be glad to have in tuo tracts of 500 each, as for pointing out the spot it is almost impossible; as all the Lands near here are already granted therefore must take on the vacant Lands near to the Natchez—I have sent all Mr. Barrows skins to Orleans, to have them sold for Cash, the Nett pro[ce]eds of the same shall be delivered Mr. Wm. Strother as per your request—I am glad to hear that his Majestys Troops was in so fair a way of bringing the Americans to a proper sense of their duty, & hope ere this that all is finished—from what I can learn from below the french & spainards seem inclined to a Rupture, (the following is a Piece of news I have from a french Gentleman that was here the other day on his way to the Illinois) that he saw a Letter dated at Dunkirk 4 Jany. 1777 from a Colonel Commanding a Reigment there, to his Nephew in Orleans in which he acquaints him that there is 38.000 Men employed in rebuilding the walls in sd. Place, that the English Engineer had protested against their proceedings, yet the work was continued which gave many reason to Imagine that there will be something to do this Summer between England & France, but hope this will turn out nothing but french News.— There is a young man Living with me who has been obliged to Leave Philadelphia on acct. of the present Troubles—which has been of great hurt to him, as he was in a very good way there. when he arrived in this province (which was in May last in the Schooner Sally Capt: Collart) he waited on his Excellency who promised him Lands, but as he then did not know whereabouts he should settle would not take it up, I inclose you his affidavit, you will please, to get his Petition drawn he requests to have what Land may be granted him near the Natchez. I beg your assistance in procuring him the same, whatever Expences there may be attending his warrant, you will please to charge to my acct.— which shall be paid per the first Conveyance after recg. yours if you favour him in this affair it shall be acknowledged with the many confered...

P.S. since my writing the above I have seen one Lewis from the Natchez who informs me there is no vacant about there without going a great way back, therefore would be glad to have the Locations on the first vacant Lands I can find—

To DONALD McPHERSON, *Natchez*

Manchac, April 10, 1777

I recd. your order on Phil. Alston for Ps.10 but as he did not pay it think proper to return it, as you are on the spot you will have an opportunity to receive the amt. it being accepted payable on demand—

yours of the 7th Inst. came to hand yesterday in which you acknowledge the rect. of tuo from Mr. Fitzpatrick who is now at Orleans, when he arrive here you may expect to hear from him. . . .
for J: F/ G. B–

To FRANCIS POUSSETT, *Baton Rouge*

Manchac, April 19, 1777

The order you gave me on Mr. Henderson was accepted by him, which he paid me with a Draft on Oliver Pollock, but as I could get no money from that Gentleman, was obliged to take it out in the way, therefore as I shall be in Cash in a few days you will please to draw on me at 10 days sight for the Ballance which shall be duly honoured, this being the needfull . . .

To JOHN CAMPBELL, *New Orleans*

Manchac, April 22, 1777

This Morning Mr. Edwd. Peyton drew on you my favr. for drs. 63.5½ being for the ballce. of his acct. with me. should it not be convenient for you to pay the Cash, as I have sent my Boat for Tobacco & provisions it will be all the same if you can get the Tobacco from any that are in due you at the Markett price. if any your Vessells comes down from Jamaica and brings Sugar or Coffee, please to keep for me of the former 1000 Wt. & of the latter 500 Wt. the manner of payment that I p[r]opose is the one half in hand & the other at the Crop, should that mode of payment be agreeable & the Articles comes, you'll Oblige me to let me have an acct. as soon as Possible that I may send for the same. . . .

To JOHN WAUGH, *New Orleans*

Manchac, April 22, 1777

The inclosed letter came from Mr. Chrystee with one for me, the Negro that brought 'em, did not take proper care to keep them apart, so that in separating them, the seal on yours was broke in the manner you'll find it though not opened[.] I am sorry it should have happened but realy it was done inadvertenly—There is a Gentleman living at my House named Doctor West, to whom I was speaking about the Books, you have still on hand for Sale. he requested me to write to you, for to send him by the return of the Boat, Rollins Antient History & them tuo Vols. that are on Physick which was among your books and as you are to be this way in a short time yourself he will see you paid for the same, should you have any Tobacco for sale, Please to let my young man have 200 Carrotts of Nachitosh, and for which I will acct. with you for with the Things I had already amt. as per Bill to Ps.75.4½ this being the needfull...

P.S. the bearer has orders to receive some Money in Town, if he gets it he will pay you for the Tobacco, or part of it—

To THOMAS O'KEEFE, *New Orleans*

Manchac, April 22, 1777

P.S. since Writing the Inclosed, Mr. Shakespear came here, and requested me to Inclose you Captain Phillip Lyons Draft on Oliver Pollock for Ps.113.5 which he requests you'll receive for him & deliver to Jacquex the Money he further desires me, to acquaint you that he is willing to allow you any Commisn. you may charge him for receiving the above, therefore deliver to Jacquax the nett proceeds & you'll Oblige...

To MESSRS. MORGAN AND MATHER, *New Orleans*

Manchac, April 22, 1777

According to my promise I have sent you all the receipts for your Powder & Balls, and hope you'll find them right accor[d]ing to yr. orders, excepting that of Mr. French's for 50 lb. Gun Powder, which he told me would admit of no dispute, as he had dealings with you & for which he obliges himself to you or your order for its amt. I deliverd to Mons. Dartugo for Mr. Le Blond 275 lb. of yr. Powder which I thought was all, but on making out the acct. find there is 50 lb. of yours here yet which shall be delivered to

Merchant of Manchac

21/In April, 1777, the British armed sloop *West Florida* under the command of Lieutenant George Burdon seized a small Spanish schooner and two canoes on Lake Pontchartrain for engaging in contraband trade. Less than twenty-four hours later, on the night of April 17, Louisiana governor Gálvez used this action as a pretext for seizing eleven British boats and "floating warehouses" on the Mississippi and the next day ordering all British subjects to leave Louisiana within a fortnight. Gálvez hoped in this way to end British smuggling on the Mississippi. The boats and their cargoes were valued at about $70,000 and belonged to John Waugh, John Campbell, Patrick Morgan, David Ross and Company, Thomas Collar, and two other merchants named Norton and Calvert. The British in West Florida were alarmed and outraged by Gálvez's action. In early August, John Stephenson, Pensacola merchant and attorney, and Lieutenant Colonel Alexander Dickson arrived in New Orleans to investigate the situation but soon returned to Pensacola without having changed Gálvez's attitude toward the British smugglers. While relations between the British and Spanish were henceforth gravely strained, it does not appear that the expulsion of British subjects from Louisiana was seriously enforced, because many British merchants in New Orleans continued their business activities there. See Caughey, *Bernardo de Gálvez*, 71–77; Starr, "Tories, Dons, and Rebels," 121–26.

your order, as for the deficiency on the Balls be assured it never happened here, as I was particular in every draught I weighed, they was brought here in very bad order, being spilt in the boat & the heads out of the Casks,—Inclosed you have my acct. Current with you which if you find right please Note the same in yr. next for our general satisfaction—I shall have some bills ere Long on Pensacola which shall send to Mr. Stephenson to receive their Amt. if it would suit you to receive the Money that way, please to let me know, & on my receiving advise of the same, shall Draw on him your favr. for the same—I have sent down some Deer skins that Mr. Barbour sent here before he came down & when he passed could not take them in, therefore if he is not with you, please to receive them for him & give my young Man a rect. for the same Mr. Barbours acct. he also sent here 100 Bushells shelled Corn, which he said was for your Negroes, which I have stored—Mr. David Williams sent here yesterday to know if sd. Corn was here, same time acquaints me he is to be here to Morrow for it, which I suppose is by authority from you. having nothing further to add...

P.S. my best respects to Mrs. Morgan, have sent her a small bag Puce [pecan] [nu]ts agreeable to my promise,—since writing the above I recd. an acct. from your place, that the English have taken some spanish Prizes & the spainards made reprisals of several English Vessels in and about Orleans (but it's not true) don't think it prudent to send the skins till I can doe it with safety—

To JOHN STEPHENSON, *Pensacola*

Manchac, April 23, 1777

Last Night between Nine & ten O Clock a friend of mine on the other side the water, sent me word, that the Spainards of N Orleans had seized on all the English Vessells; at or about that place, that all the English Merchants there had orders to quit the place in 15 days—as for the Vessells being taken and the English Gentlemen ordered out of town is true, what the reason is for so doing can't say without we have a War with spain, if so I make no doubt you have better information yourself than what I can give you, therefore have thought proper to advise you of the present, when any thing further occurs and an opportunity offers shall acquaint you of the same....

P.S. the acct. of Vessells taken. Morgan & Mathers Brig with 25 Negroes. Mr. Waughs Brig & Sloop with all his goods on board. Pickles Brig with his goods & several others names unknown to the amt. of 13—[21]

To ALEXANDER McINTOSH, *Natchez*

Manchac, April 28, 1777

Your favour of the 18 Inst. is now before me, the Contents of which have observed, I am sorry to hear that your Negro got away from you when so near home. the other has been taken up and deliver'd to Mr. Poussett, for all he was well Bolted made out to git away from him—should either of 'em come this way, be assured I will have 'em secured, and advise you of the same per first conveyance—On my Arrival at Orleans, I endeavoured to get the Quantity of wine for myself and that you Spoke to me about, the wine might have been got but not without the Money, which obliged me only to bring up but 3 Casks 1 for you and 2 for my self. the Wine is good and only cost Ps.22 which I assure you is very reasonable[.] if any good opportunity shall offer shall sent it to you. if not keep it till you come or send for it—when in Town I made a demand of your acct. Curt. from the Messrs. Ross' but they was so hurried that I could get nothing but a rect. for the bill you gave me, which I have thought proper to keep to deliver to yourself for fear of any thing happening to the Letter—I saw your acct. in their Books, you are still in due them some small Matter, the just sum can't say. I then asked Mr. Ross if he had done any thing for you about the Land affair he told me not, on which I went to the Office and had all the Registers overhauled, but all to no Effect. nothing further could be found than Deplantes Bill of sale to Gerome, which if I recollect right you have already, if not can get it for you when you please, Monsieur Garrish[22] requested I would call again, which I did, he then told me that no such paper was in his Office, and it was useless for me to look any further about it, as the Book in which it was registered was not in the place, but was sent to France in the year 1749 therefore it's useless for you to look any further about it—for which I am realy sorry & be assured I did all that lay in my power; for had you been there yourself you could not have done more,— as for the small accts. you left with me I have not been able yet to recover 1 sol, therefore hold them at your disposal—out of the Money I recd. from Mr. Campbell I layed out Ps.22 for the Wine the other Ps.28 shall be paid to your order on demand—I make no doubt but you have been informed ere this comes to hand of what has happened at Orleans & that all the English Vessells in & about that place have been taken by the Spainards, the Captains, Mates & me[n] are all in prison, Messrs. Morgan & Mather lost a Vessell with 22 Negroes on Board, Mr. Waugh 2 Vessells Loaded with goods, another that had sailed for England, that had not got out of the River was taken, in which Mr. William[s] of

22/Jean B. Garic acted as a notary in New Orleans from 1739 until 1779. See Acts of Jean B. Garic, New Orleans Notarial Archives.

your place had shipped on his acct. his Beaver, as he could not get a price for it that he wanted, what is become of him I can't yet learn, as there has not been any late arrivals from Town, this I am certain of that all the English Merchts. are ordered out of Town & had but 15 days allowed 'em to prepa[re] for their departure, what all this means God only knows, but am much afraid we are on the Eve of a war with Spain—if any thing further occurs worth acquainting you with shall embrace all occasions of letting you hear from me. . . .

To DONALD McPHERSON, *Natchez*

Manchac, April 28, 1777

Both your favrs. of the 7 & 11 Inst. is now before me the Contents of which have duly Observed. your last Inclosed me Mr. Bushs acceptance for 10 dollars, payable in Money or deer skins. the former he said he had not. the Latter he would have given me if I had taken them at 2r per Lb. which I would not do, as all the Vessells had sailed, since which he has sold them for 20 sols per Lb, I therefore return you the order to doe the needfull with, also John Hostlers order on David Williams for 18 [*illegible*] as Mr. Williams will not pay one farthing of it, the Drawer has deceived him. therfore return it that you may have it in your power to receive the amt. if Thomson com[es] your way pray do the needfull —I am very sensible of the Trouble you have given yourself about my affairs at your place, therefore expect to pay you for any thing you do for me, the same as another & request you charge me as you do everyone else, Draw on [me] for any Expence you are at on my affairs, which shall be honoured on Demand, besides returning you my hearty thanks for your Complaisance—

I make no Doubt but you have heard ere this comes to hand, of what has happened at Orleans, and that all the English Vessells at and about that place have been taken by the spainards. the Captains, Mates, & Men are all in Prison[.] Morgan & Mather lost a Vessell with 22 Negroes on Board, Mr. Waugh [*page torn*] Vessells Loaded with goods, another that had sailed for England, that had not got out of the River, was also taken, in which Mr. Williams of your Place, had Shipped on his acct. his Beaver, as he could not get the price for it that he wanted, what is become of him I can't learn yet, as there has not been any late arrivals from town, this I am certain of that all the English Merchts. are ordered out of Town & have but 15 days allowed them to prepare for their departure, what all this means God only knows, but I am much afraid we are on the Eve of a War with Spain—in yours of the 11th you mention of Mr. Gibson drawing an or[der] on me for Ps.30—I have no Money of Mr. Gibsons in my hands, but if Mr. Alex. McIntosh draws on me his favr. for that amot. shall be duly honored, if anything further occurs here worth acquainting you with, shall embrace all occasions of letting you hear from me. . . .

To PATRICK KENNEDY, *Illinois*

Manchac, May 1, 1777

On your Mr. Winstons arrival here I was in great expectation that you would have made some remittance for the Money so long due, but to my great surpise found there was nothing, which Answer give me leave to assure you was very alarming to me, the more as I realy expected you would have exerted yourself according to your promises made from time to time on that head—Another alarming circumstance, was to find that I have not been favoured with a Letter from you this long time—(it may be you had no paper) if I thought so would have sent you some long ere this, by which I might have been in some measure armed against what has turned out to be the case, that is, no payment,—Mr. Winston has given me your joint Bond for the Ballance which is Ps.898.7 payable in December Insuing—Now Sir it only remains to request that you'll exert yourself in such a manner that I may be paid said sum as agreed upon, I will leave it to yourself not wanting a better Judge in this affair, as you was the person that contracted the greatest part of it, how hard it is for me to be used in this manner, by Men that I sacrificed my Interest to Oblige, & am sorry to say has treated me in a manner I never expected, this being the needfull on so disagreeable a subject . . .

P.S. if Convenient to you Please to write to me & let me know what I am to expect—

To MICHAEL HOOPOCK, *Natchez*

Manchac, May 1, 1777

Since the unhappy accident happened & you have been at the Natchez, you have not favoured me with a Line, to acquaint me with any part of your Misfortunes, which circumstance is rather surpising to me. I realy expected to have heard from you ere this, if you have not been able to make the Remittance you might have wished for, that ought to be no hindrance to your writing me from time to time—I shall be happy in seeing you here ere you return to the settlement of Concord. that wee may have all accts. properly settled, which always gives satisfaction to both Parties—I have done all in my power to help Mr. Stampley by applying to a Number of the first Inhabitants in Town but all to no Effect, when I saw that I could do nothing, I helpe'd him to Money & Cloths which will enable him to bear his confinement something Better till Mr. Devilles Letters come to hand which must come ere he can be released[.] having nothing further to add . . .

To JOHN WAUGH, *New Orleans*

Manchac, May 3, 1777

The order you gave me on Alexr. Bell have presented to him for my Note which he would not deliver, alledging for reason that you was in due him 5.000 Dollars that you had given him a Number of Notes to recover, but could get no money for them, as mine is paid should be glad to have my Note, request you will take it up & send it to me per first Opportunity. . . .

To FRANCIS MURPHY, *New Orleans*

Manchac, May 5, 1777

On receipt of yours of the 26 ulto. Inclosing Mr. [*illegible*] Mr. Smiths acct. I apply'd to him for the Ballance $27.5 he gave me for answer, that he had no Money, but would give me his Note payable one Month after date, which I would not accept, as he is setting of for the Natchez this Morning, and as I am well assured that he would not comply with his Obligation in due time, the more so ere that time is expired he will have imbibed the Maxims of the Natchez—which is never to think about the Debts they contract untill they are forced to it—as you have wherewith in your hands would recommend you to avail yourself of it, as I am apt to think you may wait a long time for Payment—By this Opportunity have sent you two Notes of Charles Blancards, as there is no likelyhood of getting anything from him—we have nothing strange here, all hands enjoys a good state of health. having nothing further to add . . .

P.S. if there is any thing this way in which I can serve you, favour me with your commands. N.B. Smith says beside the wine he left a Barrell of Coffe wth. you request you'll send me a small keg of good white wine vinagar, for which I will immediately remit you the amt.—

To THOMAS O'KEEFE, *New Orleans*

Manchac, May 6, 1777

Your much esteemed favour of the 26 ulto. is no[w] before me the Contents of which have duly observed—I return you my most hearty thanks till you are further paid for the Trouble I give you from time to time about my small affairs in Town, which hope you'll excuse, as you are well convinced that I have no one in town, on whom I can rely but yourself when you receive the money for Mr. Shakespear & self please to hold it in your hands and acquaint me per first conveyance of the same—I am happy to hear wee may still go to town as usual and hope the squall that has been in your parts some days ago will soon blow over but can't help being heartily sorry for Mr. Waughs Misfortune—I now inclose you Mr. Edward Peytons Draft on John Campbell for 63.5½ which get accepted, if not have Indorsed it that you may recover its amt. from Mr. Peyton, and if you get the Money and want to make use of it till next fall, as I shall not want it till then[.] having nothing to add . . .

P.S. If Mr. Campbell does not accept the Bill, Mr. Peyton has affairs with Mr. Pollock, who may pay it, but at any rate don't let Peyton go till he has settled it, for it may happen that he never returns

To OLIVER POLLOCK, *New Orleans*

Manchac, May 6, 1777

I had the pleasure of writing you the 22nd ulto. which hope you have recd. ere this by which occasion should have sent you the sheathing Nails, but was prevented by the News wee recd. from your place, the Eve of my sending the Boat down to Town—therefore if the Nails comes to late for the sloop, shall be sorry for your disappointment—there is 153 lb. of them I charge you the same price they cost me, which is one Ryall per Lb. their Amount & the acct. here Inclosed against Captn. Lyons please to pass to my Credit with you—If you are not over hurried shall much obliged to you for the Copy of my acct. Currt. by which I may see if any [err]ors has occured which should be glad to have Rectified for our general satisfaction[.] Mr. Peyton that was making staves at your place is gone down with an Intent of going home with Captn. Bell he is in due my $63.5½ for which he has given me a Draft on Mr. Campbell[.] should it not meet with Acceptance from that Gentleman, if you have any affairs to settle with him & you can Keep that sum in your hands for me, you'll much oblige me, I have sent the Bill to Mr. Okeeffee who will inform you whether or no it has met with acceptance, which if it has not, & that you have it in your power to act the needfull, it will be gratefully acknowledged by . . .

P.S. my best respects to Mrs. Pollock—

To DAVID ROSS AND COMPANY, *New Orleans*

Manchac, May 21, 1777

I had the pleasure of writing you the 22nd Ulto. which hope you have recd. ere this, if so or not have not been favd. with an answer which I imagine is owing to your great hurry of Business this some time past—

By this opportunity have sent you your acct. Currt. in which you will find I have placed to your Credit the Ballance due to Messrs. Robt. & Geo: Ross which I suppose will be all the same, I have charged to your Debit $66.5/2 being the amt. of Mr. David Ross Private acct. with me, so that there remains a ballance due you of $330.5/2 which I believe the Beaver will about ballance, should there be any thing wanting to Ballance the acct. please to Note it in your next and by the first conveyance shall remit it to you, therefore request you will send me my tuo Notes, & if convenient for you send me by the same conveyance the following Articles payable next fall which charge as reasonable as you can afford—

    20 lb. de fill du Rain   20 doz: de fill de papillon   1 Gro:
    White Tape   2 doz: sheets Pins   2 ps. Blue Pollenese
    1 ps. red do.   1 doz: bright drawing knives abt. 12/
having nothing further to add . . .

P.S. as my young Man Jacquex goes with the Bateau if you have any things to send this way on freight, please to give 'em to him—

To MESSRS. MORGAN AND MATHER, *New Orleans*

Manchac, May 21, 1777

I wrote you the 22 Ult. per Mr. Jean inclosing you all the receipts for your Powder & Balls & my acct. Currt. which hope you have recd. ere this but am not Certain as I have not been favd. with your answer—The Bearer will deliver you for my acct. $80 and if he receives some money that is due me in Town will give you as much more, be assured I shall by every Occasion remit you what Little I can get in Cash till such time the Bill you took from Mr. Profit is discharged, which I am sorry I have not been able to do ere this, owing to the many disappointments in payment that has occurd this spring. I have sent you the remainder of the Corn & Skins sent here by Mr. Barbour for you, Mr. David Williams had for the use of himself & your place 35 Bushells Mr. Daniel Hickey 6 for which he has accd. with Mr. Barbour for, so that there remains (or aught to doe) according to Natchez measure 59 if so or not can't say, but it was all of it, for the freight of the Corn and skins I expect you will allow the Common price, having charged Mr. Barbour with the Storage, Porterage & taken care of his Skins &c having nothing further to add...

P.S. if you should have any freight to send this way Please to give it to my Man & he will take care of it

To OLIVER POLLOCK, *New Orleans*

Manchac, May 21, 1777

I had the pleasure of writing you the 6th Inst. which with Nails hope you have recd. ere this. In which I requested you would favour me with a Copy my acct. Currt. and if not already sent beg you will forward it to me per this Conveyance—I am in want of 200 [car]rots Tobacco Nachitoshes (having been disappointed by a Gentleman of that Country that was [to] have sent me a Large Quantity) therefore as I saw you had a Quantity of it by you when I was in town, if you will let me have that Number at the Currt. price I will pay you for [it] in the Month of August Insuing—I hope you have kept in your hands the amt. of Captn. Lyons small acot. for sundries furnished him here, & passed the same to my Credit [wi]th you. There has been no arrivals from Pensacola this sometime past, therefore have nothing new with us from that Quarter—should you have any freight for your place shall be much obliged to you for it, it shall be delivered at your plantation the next day after [its] arrival here, as I am obliged to send the Boat to Pt. Coupie on her return—having nothing further to add...

To MR. JENNINGS, *Baton Rouge*[23]

Manchac, May 21, 1777

I have taken a Hhd of your Mallases that was at Mr. Millers, Contents unknown not having Gauged it, I only took the wantage

---

23/Probably John Jennings, listed in the Baton Rouge census of 1782. No profession is given for Jennings, but he owned a house and was perhaps employed by James Smith, a planter. Baton Rouge Census Document, Department of Archives and Manuscripts, Louisiana State University.

which was 3½ Inches for its amt. shall acct. with you for on our first meeting—

The present is to inform you that my Boat will have but a few Trifles to bring up for my self, if you should have any freight shall be obliged to you for the same, it shall be delivered here or at any Plantation you point out at Richmond settlement,[24] if you have none yourself, if any Gentleman of your acquaintace should have any, Please to recomend 'em to my young Man. should your Vessell that you expected in be arrived and you have any sugar, please to send me 4 Barrells at the Current price. the amount will settle with you on your arrival here, having nothing further to add . . .

To DAVID ROSS AND COMPANY, New Orleans

Manchac, June 7, 1777

Your favr. of the 28 ulto. with my acct. Currt. and the Goods sent me came to hand in good order the amt. of the Goods being Ds. 97.7r. is to your Credit with me, in my acct. Currt. you have charged me Ps.2.4 for a Trunk that I got in March 76. sd. Trunk I took for D.2.4r. that your Mr. George assumed to pay me for one of your hands named Isaac Newton in June 1774, therefore expect you will Credit my acct. for the same—If any of your Vessells comes in from the Cape and brings sugar please to keep for me three or four Barrells and advise me of the same per first opportunity. this being the needfull . . .

To THOMAS O'KEEFE, New Orleans

Manchac, June 7, 1777

Your much esteemed favr. of the 28 ulto. with Mr. Willings Draft & Smiths Note are now before me, the Contents of which shall duly Observe—

I am realy sorry Mr. Peyton should have given you so much Trouble about paying his Obligation which now proves to me how necessary it was to have Endorsed it to you without which I am well assured I should have lost it, therefore return you my most hearty thanks for this favr. with the many others,—Mr. Shakespear is much obliged to you and is pleased to hear you have got his Bill accepted by Mr. Pollock—I shall take the first Op-

24/The British name for Baton Rouge was New Richmond.

portunity of sending Mr. Willings draft to Mr. McPherson at the Natchez to get it pay'd or Accepted, but as for Smith's Note I realy do not know what to do with it, as he is now at the Natchez, & sold the Boat on his arrival here for 18 Ps. to Mr. Shakespear. therefore if the Effects that our friend Mr. Murphy has in his hands is not sufficient to pay you both, I am much afraid you ll be a looser for in my Opinion he has acted his part in such a manner here & at your place that he will not be in a hurry a Coming from the Natchez but should he come down or I hear [he] has wherewith there be assured I shall act the needfull, in any thing that shall regard your Interest—I have Spoke again to the Taylor, he has promised me your Cloths the Insuing week, when finished shall send 'em per first Conveyance till which I am . . .

P.S. I have been informed you are coming to pass a Month with us this Summer if agreeable there is Room & a Bottle of Generaus stuff at your service—

To WILLIAM WALKER, *New Orleans*

Manchac, June 12, 1777

On your return to this place you will please to bring for me 2000 lb. good sugar in Barrells & 500 lb. Coffee in do. for which I will pay you the Current price it sells for in this River, or if agreeable will take [it] at the price you purchase it at in the West Indies, paying Insurance, freight Commission all all [*sic*] Charges, wishing you an agreeable Voyage & safe return . . .

To DAVID WILLIAMS, *Baton Rouge*[25]

Manchac, June 14, 1777

This Morning Mr. Blancard presented your order on me for D: 91.2r which I have accepted on Condition of your giving me a draft for its amt. on Miller McIntosh & Co. or your Note bearing Interest, as this is not an affair of the present year, but is Money due this long time you will also please to settle the Ballance due by you to Smith & Castles and you'll Oblige . . .

P.S. the six Dollars charged Mr. Blancard in your sales for 1 doz: Cotton Cords he never would settle with me, as he told me at the time he recd. 'em that it was by your Verbal order & that they was to be disposed of for your acct. I know nothing further about it—

25/Listed in the Baton Rouge census of 1782 as a planter. He owned 26 slaves, the largest number held by any person named in the census, and included in his household William Williams, apparently a brother. See Baton Rouge Census Document, Department of Archives and Manuscripts, Louisiana State University.

To MESSRS. SMITH AND CASTLES

Manchac, June 16, 1777

Your favr. of the 12 Ultimo is now before me the Contents of which have duly observed[.] should have answered long ere this, but Mr. Miller would never Consent to take the skins at any more than 20 sols per Lb. till this Morning and then on Condition of having the Ears & hoofs cut of, which I consented to that the affair might be finished

Inclosed is your acct. Current (ballance yet due me 29.2½ I have Endorsed the remainder on your other Note for D:131.6r, Inclosed is your Note for 21.2—this being the needfull . . .

To MONSIEUR RICARD, *Pointe Coupée*

Manchac, June 16, 1777

I have received the honor of yours, dated the 16th of this May with the works of Montesquieu in good condition, but I am very sorry to tell you that it is impossible for me to send you the works of Jean Jacques Rousseau at present, since I lent them some time ago to Mr. Stephenson of Pensacola, but he should return them to me as soon as he has finished reading them, so I hope to receive them shortly, and as soon as they arrive you may be certain that I shall send them to you by the first occasion.

Following the permission which you gave me, I send you here inclosed two bills with the account current of Jean Baptiste Mai-Caunce [sic], hunter on the Red River, who should arrive at Pointe Coupée at any moment. The bills are not for merchandise sold to him, but for money which I paid for him in 1774 at Grand Gulf, so I hope that he will not be against paying me the interest. If, Monsieur, you can get me the amount of the sum of the bills, you will render me a great service, as it is impossible for me to leave here at present, and if I miss this occation to be paid, he might return to the woods or I might not see him soon. As for the expenses (if there are any) I shall reimburse you with much pleasure. Awaiting the pleasure of your response, I am . . .

To MESSRS. MORGAN AND MATHER, *New Orleans*

Manchac, July 3, 1777

Per the opportunity of Mr. Geo: Mather I have sent you $100 which request you'll endorse on Profit & Tophams Note[.]

The remaining ballance of said Notes being $106.5½ shall remit you ere long. the 50 lb Powder was delivered agreeable to your request—if convenient for you would be much Obliged to you to send Me per Mr. Bacon one Barrell French Flour provided it does not exceed 16$—Mr. Maison is safely arrived at this place from Aux Post, with a pretty parcell of skins which I suppose he will bring to your place, ere long. having nothing further to add...

To DAVID ROSS AND COMPANY, *New Orleans*

Manchac, July 3, 1777

Your Esteemed favr. of the 15th Ulto. duly came to hand Covering one for Mons: Dussall which was delivered him[.] he has not paid the order yet but says he will ere long—I shall depend on your promise in Regard to the sugars when they come in. if convenient please to send me 1 Barrell french flour per first Opportunity as I am really in want which will Oblige...

To MESSRS. MORGAN AND MATHER, *New Orleans*

Manchac, July 7, 1777

I had the pleasure of writing you the 3 Inst. per Mr. Geo: Mather, by whom I sent $100[.] he also got a p. Ginghams amt. $9 which please to Credit my acct. for—Inclosed is Mr. Henry Stewarts Draft my favr. on you for $50 which place to my Credit—Please to send per first opportunity the Barrell of flour I wrote for if it does not exceed the price Limited....

To DONALD McPHERSON, *Natchez*

Manchac, July 8, 1777

Your Esteemed favours of the 13 May & 29 June are now before me the Contents have duly observed—I recd. from Danl. Lewis your acct. 32 Deer skins in the hair Wt. 56 lb. at 20 sols $11.5½ & 4 do. scraped 84 [pounds] at 25 sols .. 2$ .. is 13.5½ which is applyed to your Credit; I am realy sorry to hear you had no Court not on my own acct. alone [?] but for the Good of the Country in General, as I am well convinced without one at your place business must go on in a very lame Manner, I paid Daniel Lewis 1$

for the freight of the skins which is to your Debit—I recd. from Mr. Alexander McIntosh d.10.4r the 20 March which is placed to your Credit. The Linen & Paper you wrote for shall send per Mr. Bacon as Mr. Stewart has not proper covering in his Boat. I have sent to Pensacola for a few Blank Writs, which when I receive shall send you some—

If Mrs. Truly[26] does not settle her Note directly request you will serve her with a writ as soon as you get one which I am in daily expectation of, I am very Glad to hear you & Mr. McIntosh have settled your affairs amicably—I must request again them small affairs of mine in your hands, that you'll settle as soon as Possible give them no Quarters next Court—I never heard a word from Mr. Gibson about the $30 you mention, no news worth notice except by a Letter I recd. from a Gentleman in Orleans who informs me that sundry Letters are arrived at Orleans from the Cape & Port au Prince giving an acct. that the Kings Troops are at last in Possession of Philadelphia, having nothing further to add . . .

To MICHAEL HOOPOCK, *Natchez*

Manchac, July 8, 1777

I did my self the Pleasure of writing you the 1st may last, which I am well assured you recd. in due time for all which you never have been complaisant enough to answer it, and I may say with a great deal of Propriety you have have [*sic*] not answered one of my Letters properly since last November. what your reasons are for so doing I am an Intire stranger to, but can't help saying you have not used me with that Civility that might have been Expected. was your silence owing to your not having made a Proper remittance that both of us expected you are then blameable, for it is well known to every one that you have met with with [*sic*] a number of Misfortunes, which be assured that no one has a more sensible feeling of than I have, and wish that it was in my Power to have prevented them. I can't help being Plain with you & inform you Ingenuously of what I have been told by a Number of Persons, that is that I did not get the Number of skins you recd. last winter, the smaller Part came to me, but the larger Part was sold at N: Orleans—the Authors of the above information was tuo french me[n] that went up with you last fall, one named St. John that assissted Kennedy in the sale of them last april in N Orleans, was it that the sale of said Skins turned out more to your advantage there than what it would have been to have Paid 'em to

26/Mrs. Sarah Truly, a widow, came to the Natchez district in 1773 from Virginia as a loyalist refugee, along with six of her children and three brothers. She moved to a site north of Natchez and was beset with considerable financial difficulties for the rest of her life. She died in 1792. See Madel Jacobs Morgan, "Sarah Truly, A Mississippi Tory," *Journal of Mississippi History*, XXXVIII (1975), 87–95.

me, be assured that I am glad for your sake, as it will always give me pleasure to hear of your every thing to the best advantage. Mr. Bloomart, Mr. Bacon & Mr. Eason have all informed me that they [saw] Kennedy on his way up to Concord where he was going to take Possession of his Effects having informed these Gentlemen that he had Purchased the remaining Effects of Hooppock & Stampley which if true is a very alarming Circumstance to me as I am much afraid that you will have such another flemish acct. rendered you in for your Effects as Mr. Morgan had heretofore. you can't say that you was Ignorant of his Character, as I cautioned you of it last Spring before he left this with you. in my former I requested you would come down here, that we might settle your affairs ere you went up—But now request in a Particular Manner that you loose no time (provided your Arm will admit of it) but proceed directly to Concord & bring your affairs as soon as Possible to a Close, for give me leave to assure you that nothing is Equal to a person being on the Spot himself. I recd. a Letter of the 6th of last Month from Henry Stamply by which he informed me he had got the Better of the small Pox, & was sent to Prison again[.] he seemed to be under great Concern that they were going to send him to the Mines (if so or not God only Knows as I have heard nothing about him since) I have nothing further to add only to request you will do your utmost that I may be paid the ballance of your acct. this Insuing Winter this being the needfull...

P.S. Please to favour me with a Letter ere your departure for Concord—

To MESSRS. WILLIAMS AND FERGUSON

Manchac, July 8, 1777

When your Mr. Williams was last here he gave me your joint Note for $180 Payable 10 days after date as it has been due since the 21 of last May & that Mr. Williams promised to remit the Money immediately after his arrival[.] The present is to request that you'll send it to me per first Conveyance as I realy am in want of it, secondly that you will remitt me the amount of the four Petticoates if sold if not send them per first safe Conveyance as I want to Close them Sales—

I should be much obliged to you to inform me what progress you have been able to make with Mr. Harrisons Note having Nothing further to add...

To ALEXANDER McINTOSH, *Natchez*

Manchac, July 8, 1777

Your Esteemed favr. of the 12th May duly came to hand which I would have answered in course but as you informed in yours of coming here the latter end of May prevented me of writing sooner as I expected to see you dayly also of sending the Wine knowing the difficulty of sending it this season of the year—I assure you I took great care to fill it up &c. notwithstanding by some accident or other which I can't acct. for the Cask Bursted and about six doz: of the wine was lost[.] I then took it to my own acct. as it would be spoiled had it been deferred one Day longer, I expect some wine up from Town Dayly if it comes before your arrival shall keep a Cask for you if not will pay you the Money. as yet have not been able to recover any of the Notes or accts. you left me, though have made Several applications. we have nothing new here except several Letters which are arrived from the Cape & Port au Prince to Orleans giving an acct. that Philadelphia is at last in Possession of his Majestys troops having nothing further to add...

My wifes Compts. to you & Mrs. McIntosh. remember me to Mr. Foley

To PHILIP LIVINGSTON, JUNIOR, *Pensacola*

Manchac, July 16, 1777

Your much Esteemed favour of the 25 last March I duly recd. and should have answered long ere this but waiting for the bearer of the present Mr. Eason who is the most proper person to administrate to the Estate of the Deceased John Finney as he will make appear by his papers. I should much rather it was him than myself having already a number of affairs of my own on hands & as he is to be accountable to me for my proportion of what he shall be able to recover from them that has the Effects—

I have delivered him Mr. Bloomarts receipt for the Effects & Notes found in said Finney House by Mr. Thomas James & self as per Inventory taken by us. If Sir you can serve him as he is a very honest Man you'll greatly oblige me, should his Money run short, and be any thing behind hand in your way if he gives you a draft on me for 25 or 30 $ it shall be paid to your Brother on Demand. any assistance you can render him in his Little affairs at your place shall be most gratefully acknowledged as if done my self by...

P.S. the Bearer is a Stranger at your place & may want security in the Course of his business getting out Letters of administration if I can be admitted as being here will be bail for him with pleasure—

To PHILIP ALSTON, *Natchez*

Manchac, July 24, 1777

Your letter of the 18 Inst. is now before me the Contents of which I have duly observed—I am sorry to acquaint you that you have put it out of my power to comply with any further orders from you, till such time as you have dischargd them so long due. I am further sorry to acquaint you that Mr. Miller is not here now but is gone this some time past to Pensacola, what are his intentions towards entering a sute against you can't say. all that I can say with safety is that I am well assured he is much in want of his money, as the Gentlemen of the House of Miller McIntosh & Co. are to settle all their affairs this Insuing Winter that belonged to sd. House and I am further assured that they are determin'd to recover in all their outstanding Debts without loss of time—If this advise can be of any service to you I am glad I gave it if not all things remains as before—having nothing further to acquaint you with only to assure you that I shall expect the payment of the Note due me in all the Month of November Insuing, if not be assured I can't wait Longer though at same time should be sorry you would force me to such Extremes—which I must certainly do if you don't comply with my just demands—I shall add nothing further as I am well assured you do not Love to be troubled with long Letter on such a disagreeable Subject, therefore shall conclude with once more putting you in mind that I shall expect my payment at the time I mentioned, if not be not surprised at finding that I have kept my promise as before mentiond. . . .

To DAVID ROSS AND COMPANY, *New Orleans*

Manchac, August 14, 1777

Your favour of the 3 Inst. with the Black Jacks safely [came] to hand their Amt. to your Credit D.22.3r and 1 Ps. for the freight—I have some Beaver by me which I propose bringing down in Novr. Insuing but not litt them except you will agree to pay me 1 Ps. per Lb. as it is of a good Quality, and I will not part with it under that, wee have nothing new with us excepting an acct. of the Death of Philip Comyn Esqr. which happened some time last week having nothing further to add . . .

To MESSRS. MORGAN AND MATHER, *New Orleans*

Manchac, August 14, 1777

I make no doubt ere this comes to hand but Mons. Maison has been with you & hope he will settle all things to your satisfaction if not shall esteem it a particular favour that you will insist on his settling with you for the Amt. of the Goods you was so obliging as to Credit him with on acct. my Letter his favour last year—we have nothing new from Pensacola (per Capt. Offurd) excepting that there was a number of Vessells expected in Dayly from England & Ireland. no acct. of your Powder yet, when it comes shall act the needfull. yesterday we had an acct. that Philip Comyn Esqr. departed this Life last Week, this being the needfull . . .

Sent by Captain Davis

(The following is the editor's translation from the original French.)

To JEAN DATCHURUT, *Ste. Geneviève, Illinois*[27]

Manchac, August 19, 1777

I received the honor of yours by Monsieur Duprée the 14th of last month, with the 5 packs of deer skins marked FP which you had the goodness to pull out of the fire for me. I say out of the fire because these men still owe me more than 900 piastres, and I much fear that I shall never receive one more sol from them. However, Winston was here. If he has sent something down, I don't know anything about it, because he has said nothing to me of it, nor have I received anything from him, except their bond payable next December. Mr. Winston says that he will charge Mr. Kennedy with all the mismanagement of their affairs in this country, but it is he alone who is really the reason that I have not been paid this long time past. I have made you here an itemized list of Winston's affairs with me. I don't mean to trouble you, but as you have already done something in this matter for me, for which I am very obliged to you, I beg you to take the trouble before you come down to find out everything possible in this respect,

---

27/A Juan Dachorat is listed among individuals harvesting flour in Ste. Geneviève in 1774. The Monsieur Duprée mentioned in this letter is probably Louis Duprée, formerly a resident of Kaskaskia. He is recorded as a carrier of furs from Illinois to New Orleans in 1774, and in 1770 he carried freight to New Orleans for Datchurut. See Houck (ed.), *The Spanish Regime in Missouri*, I, 93, 95.

in what situation their affairs are, and if I can count on something from this dastardly or [*illegible*] man. Monsieur Duprée, who was charged with the payment of your little affairs, has settled with me in peltry, that is to say, in two packs of deer skins weighing together 247 pounds at 35 sols per pound, makes the sum of £432.5s. Deducting the balance of your account of £308, there remains £124.5s, which I paid him in cash. But the next day, on opening the packs that I took on Monsieur Duprée's assurance, I found 61½ pounds were damaged, and in this case I took back that much money from Monsieur Duprée in New Orleans, returning to him the [damaged] skins mentioned above, as I have no doubt he will mention to you in his letter. I hope to have the pleasure of seeing you next December as you advise me . . .

(The following is the editor's translation from the original French.)

To JEAN BAPTISTE SARPY, *St. Louis, Illinois*

Manchac, August 25, 1777

Your letter of the 23rd of last November I have received with the pelts in due time, all in good order, according to the invoice which you sent me, showing a balance of £9,800, that is to say, the price of your shares [?], but for the £2,558.6.6 which you sent me in letters of exchange and bonds, I cannot accept it as a payment for the account of Mr. Barrow without keeping my rights and claims [?] on what it may bring, since this paper was in disrepute a long time ago, and I am very certain that Mr. Barrow never had to accept such payment when he entrusted his papers to you. In one of your letters written the 17th of November 1771 you tell me to send you Monsieur Dubrieul's letters of exchange, which would be paid to you at once. This I did by the first opportunity that presented itself. Then you told me that Monsieur Rasadeau [?], who had been absent for a very long time, was then to return, and not being able to pay you in pelts, he was going to pay you in flour to the value of 16 or 18,000 pounds. If, according to your letter, you received it on time, with the £2,500 in goods which he paid you and which you promised to send me the following July, I never received it before last December. Then you told me there was not much to be expected from Monsieur Robinet, as he was insolvent. However, you hoped to receive about £3,000 in effects from him. If you have received all the objects which you mentioned, they would have been a very nice remittance, and I would have forwarded these funds to Mr. Barrow, who then had great need of them and was even detained in a prison in London partly because of this miserable affair. Allow me to say to you that it is now nearly eight years that you have had these papers in your hands and the bonds and notes which Monsieur Maxant guaranteed in New Orleans, by which he promised that if any of these papers should not be paid he would be responsible to Mr. Barrow or his order, and to me, who am charged with his power of attorney. Since I did not have the papers in my hands, you were the means for me to receive anything from Mr. Maxant. I beg you, consider for a moment the wrong that this does to both Mr. Maxant and Mr. Barrow, since Mr. Maxant is obliged to pay the interest until payment is completed and Mr. Barrow must wait so long for his money. When you have considered all these circumstances, you must see that both parties have suffered badly by waiting so long. I beg you to send me the papers that remain to be paid, with whatever you can or will collect, so that I can terminate this matter with Mr. Maxant, who seems very much disposed to do it every time I speak with him on this subject.

I have no news from New England to tell you, as we are in a state of almost complete ignorance here about what has happened this summer. Having nothing further to tell you . . .

To JOHN PRIEST, *Thompson's Creek*

Manchac, August 29, 1777

This Day Mr. Berwick presented me your order his favour for [*illegible*] out of which I gave him Drs. 40 in Cash & discounted Drs.31 with him being his acct. with me/ for the Ballce. your order being forty six Doll: 1r I gave him my Note payable in October[.] I would have given him the Cash, but ever since I came from Orleans have been very unwell which has confined me entirely to the House & of course rendered me scarse of Cash as I was not able to go about my affairs[.]

I understand Nicholas Vaughan is Building a House for you & Capt: Hindson, he owes me sixty one Dollars I have sent to Pensacola for a few blank writs one of which I intend serving him with if he does not comply very soon with my just demand, if not assumed by you or Captn: Hindson as I will not be put of with his Promises any longer, if you do not come this way as soon as you expect, shall take it as a favour if you will write me per first opportunity & let me know if you will assume the same for him or not—I spoke to you when last here about White & Scarse concerning the Negroes, as you did not speak to them when here I request in a Particular manner you will write to them for I am apprehensive of some unfair dealings will occur ere the time of Payment comes which makes me very uneasy & have been this some time past, having nothing further to add till I have the pleasure of seeing yourself which Mr. Berwick informs me will be soon I remain & my best respects to Mr. Hindson—

To JOSEPH PINHORN, *Pensacola*

Manchac, September 6, 1777

Your esteemed favour of the 16 ulto. with your order on Mr. Ben: Ward came to hand in due time the Contents of which have observed—and should have answered ere this, but hoped to have sent you the Ps.30 with the answer[.] I have presented the order for Payment from time to time since it came to hand till this Morning when he told me I might send it Back and he should write you himself on that head therefore return you the order, I am sorry that I could not doe otherways. it may be I shall be more successfull in some other of your affairs, if you think proper to Employ me, I will with pleasure use my endeavours to recover any thing you may have due you this way[.] as for your Tea my own being allmost out I will take it at your price 5 rs per Lb and for which you may expect the payment in all the Month of october if this is agreeable please to Note it in your next if not I will dispose of it at Vendue to the highest bidder. having nothing further to add...

To JOHN MILLER, *Pensacola*

Manchac, September 19, 1777

Since your departure from hence there has nothing new occurred in this place excepting that Trade has been very dull with us, as is usual every summer to be[.] there is a very great prospect of a fine Crop at Pt. Coupie their Indico turns out wonderfull well so that I am in very great hopes they will be able this fall to make good payments, there has hardly ever been known such a sickly summer as this has been both here and down the River poor Mons: Dussall has paid the great Debt due to Nature therefore the Spanish fort is at present without a Commander but there is one Dayly expected and it is supposed it will be Mons: Ville-Beef.[28] but if so or not it is not positively known[.] I am much obliged to you for having acted the needfull in the affair of Mrs. Cantys by which I am now in some hopes of being paid some time or other, I hope you have not forgot me about the affair of

28/Captain Juan (or Jean) de la Villebeuvre was named commandant at Manchac in October, 1777, replacing the deceased Luis Dessalles. A professional military man, de la Villebeuvre was born in the French province of Brittany about 1737 and came to Louisiana about 1764. One of the first French officers to transfer to the Spanish army in Louisiana, he served at the new Spanish fort San Luis which was constructed opposite British Natchez in 1767. In 1777 de la Villebeuvre was named commandant of Fort San Gabriel de Manchack and also of the small Spanish settlement across the Iberville River from British Manchac. In the spring of 1779 he left Manchac to join Gálvez's preparations to occupy the British posts along the Mississippi River and, after the surrender of Baton Rouge, was sent with a force of fifty men to occupy Natchez. He remained there as commandant until forced to capitulate to British loyalist rebels in May, 1781. De la Villebeuvre later served with distinction at various posts in Louisiana, Mississippi, and Alabama, and died in Mobile in 1797. For a detailed description of his career, see Jack D. L. Holmes, "Juan de la Villebeuvre: Spain's Commandant of Natchez During the American Revolution," *Journal of Mississippi History*, XXXVII (1975), 97–129; see also Archivo General de Siminas, Sección de Guerra Moderna, Legajo 7291, Cuaderno I. Regimento de Infanterio fixo de la Luysiana, December, 1787, p. 16.

Mr. Kraps &c—I have been well informed that Henry Smith is on the point of going over to the Island of Orleans, there to become a settler, for which reason I have thought it adviseable to Inclose you his Note for drs.143.3½ as he has Land & Cattle to discharge the same if pushed should be much Obliged to you if any occasion should offer up this way that you would have him served with a writ, I am sorry to be obliged to go to such extremes but can't help it the greatest part of said sum has been due me since June 1770—I have further to request that you will remember me when you are coming up this way yourself & bring if possible 10 or 12 blank writs by which I shall be able to bring my good Gentry to reason—having nothing further to acquaint you with excepting that my wife & I have been very ill with a fever & Deafness the Latter of which I have not got clear of yet but hope ere Long to get the better of it. . . .

P.S. if any of your Gentlemen is with you please to present them with my best respects if you will send me a Barrell of Irish Pork per first conveyance I shall be much Obligd. to you

To DONALD McPHERSON, *Natchez*

Manchac, October 4, 1777

Yours of the 18 ulto: per Mr. Newman is now before me the Contents of which have observed[.] the Money & Bill you sent per him have applyed to the Credit of the sundry persons as per acct. here Inclosed for your satisfaction, I further have sent you a Copy of the accts. & Notes that I delivered you as per receipt— I am sorry that you omitted charging the Interest on Thornhill & Truly's Notes as they realy deserved it from me but now it is all over & I promise you it will be some time ere they will owe me so much again—On recept of yours I sent over to Mr. Swanson for your Note but he acquainted me as per his Note here Inclosed that Mr. Miller had it with him at Pensacola or should have sent it as you desire. I am forever obliged to you for your kindness as you will not accept of any payment for what you have done for me at your place I must only for the present acknowledge the Kindness till such time I have it in my power to make it appear more plainly to yourself—this being the needfull . . .

P.S. when I was at Pt. Coupie last fall I sold some Cattle to Timothy Hotchkiss for 30 drs & took his Note payable for the same last December now as he did not pay the Note in Time, I sent it to you or some other person (who I can't say) to recover for [me] if you should see it please to inform me whose hands it [is] in & you Oblige me—

Sundries	Dr.
To Sarah Truly Note & acct.	62.7
To Ephraim Thornhills Note	37.0½
To Saml: Lewis acct.	9.3
To Vousdons . . . do	5.4
To ballce. due Mr. McPherson & Carrd. to his Credit with me	.5
	dollrs. 115.3½

Sundries	Cr.
By Alexr: McIntosh assumption	30.
By Wm: Hinsons draft on Watts & flowers	37.
By Cash from McPherson per Tho. Newman	48.3½
	dollrs. 115.3½

To THOMAS WALTERS, *Pensacola*

Manchac, October 4, 1777

Your favr. 20th Augt. (for Mr. Wilton) is now before me the Contents of which have duly observed and according to your advice have passed to his Credit the drs.5.2rs so that the Ballance you mention of drs.51.6¾ (your money) is very right and as I have not been able to dispose of any part of the Goods remaining in you hands as per acct. sent as they are quite unsaleable with us, I have value'd my self on you as Mr. Wiltons attorney for said ballance in favour Messrs. Miller McIntosh & Co. & for my draft on Mr. Chrystee for drs.43.1¼ in favr. Mr. Wilton, as there is no other way of disposing of the articles on hand but by that of Vendue therefore shall embrass the first & when sold shall remit you the Amt. with the Sales. . . .

To JOHN MILLER, *Pensacola*

Manchac, October 6, 1777

Since my writing per Mr. McCormick the 19th ultmo. your favour of the 18 August came to hand the Contents of which have duly Observed—Mr. Francis Miller on the rect. of your Letter to him came up hear to acquaint me that his Draft my favr. for Ps.104.3½ had not met with that honor he expected from Mr. Durnford who is in due him upwards of Ps.1800 he further added he is going to Pensacola with Mr. Elliott, that I might rest as-

Merchant of Manchac

sure'd he would settle it with you ere he left the place—according to your request have sent you the Copy of your receipt of my small accts. I troubled you to recover for me—I have Drew on Mr. Thoms. Walters attorney to Wm. Wilton your favour for Ps. 51.6¾ your money being a ballance due me as per his Letter of advice of the 30 Last Augt. which when you recover place to my Credit—further an order for my Draft of the 23 last Jany. on Mr. Chrystee in favr. Mr. Wilton for dr.43.1¼ which Mr. Walters acquaints me is not paid nor has he any right to pay it having already overpaid Mr. Wilton the Ps.51.6¾ which I have drew for the order you will please to destroy or send it me as you shall think proper[.] there is a report here that Mr. Geo: Morgan of Philadelphia is arrived at the Illinois with a Large Number of Batteaux from Fort Pitt apart of which they expect at the Natchez ere Long but all this wants further confirmation[.] I am well assured that the Spainards have no accts. of any such arrivals in that Country this I have from Mons. De Villbeef the Commander of the fort—By a Letter of the 15th last month [from the] alkansaws Informs me that the Ozages Indians that made a Peace with Monsr. Deville last Spring did it with no other intent than to get ammunition which when they had supplyd themselves with they fell on all the French Hunters they could find in the River Alkansaws there is 60 of them missing many of them have been found in the Woods with their Heads & Legs cut of this is all wee have with us worth acquaintg you with having nothing further to add . . .

Manchac 6 Octor. 1777

for Drs. 51.6¾
Sir

At Sight please to pay John Miller Esqr. or his order fifty one Dollars six Ryalls & three quarters being for so much overpaid my account by Adam Chrystee & please the same to my Debit with Wm. Wilton—
To Mr. Thoms: Walters   J.F.
Mercht. Pensacola

Manchac 6 Octor. 1777

Sir

Please to deliver to John Miller Esqr. or his order my Draft of the 23 last January on Adam Chrystes in favr. Wm. Wilton for Ps.43.1¼ and his receipt it will be your discharge from Sr. your very humb: Servt.
To Mr. Thom: Walters   J.F.
Mercht. Pensacola

To OLIVER POLLOCK, *New Orleans*

Manchac, October 6, 1777

Your favr. of the 26 last August came to hand a few days agoe the Contents of which have observed—The Money you requested me to pay to Mr. Jennings your acct. shall be complyed with when ever he thinks proper to call for it—I should be extremely Obliged to you for a Copy of my acct. Currt. settled with you last April as I am realy in want of it & without can't settle your acct. in my Books which shall be always glad to have done for our mutual satisfaction as wee are all Mortall. having nothing further to add . . .

To OLIVER POLLOCK, *New Orleans*

Manchac, October 7, 1777

Both your favrs. of the 25th & 26 ultmo. came to hand since my writing the Inclosed of the 6 Inst.—the Letter in which you request me to take an acct. of the deceased Wm. Davis Effects and to send it you I can only give you for answer in the affair that there has been an acct. taken of 'em already and Letters of administration have been sent for some time agoe which are dayly expected on the arrival of which all his Effects will be appraised and Sold at Publick Sale[.] you say his Estate or Effects owes you largely in that case send your acct. against them that you may partake with the other Creditors or that it may be ballanced by Large accts. that are in his Books against you & Mr. Alexr: Henderson for work done by Orange Grove having nothing further to say on the subject . . .

To DONALD McPHERSON, *Natchez*

Manchac, October 11, 1777

Since my writing you the 4th Inst. Rodgers Ross has been here of whom I demanded payment of the within Note which has been due me these three years, & since I can't Obtain it by fair means, must have recourse to the Law to Oblige him, therefore request on your receipt of the present you will enter a suit against him for the amount, at the time he consented to give me his Note, I gave him a Certificate as he said he had paid Nelly Price that sum already that if he could produce any authentick proof of the same such as a receipt &ca, that was prior to the Note in that case it's amount should stand for the Note if not to remain in full force

&c[.] now as he has not produced any such thing to me these three years, I am apt to think he never had any, or he would not have neglected it so long as he has done, therefore Dr. Mack don't let him leave the Landing if Possible without having him served with a Writ or Summons as you shall think proper to secure the same[.] wee have nothing new with us, except Daily Confirmations of Philadelphia being in Possession of the Kings troops this being the needfull . . .

Grand Gulf 27 March 1776
Six Months after date I promise to pay to John Fitzpatrick or order the sum of thirty Nine Dollars four Ryalls being for Value recd. of Elinor Price as Witness my hand
                                    Roger Ross
Present at signing James Gauy,
                                    Endorsed Jno. Fitzpatrick
a true Copy from the Original
                                    Witness Geo: Boles

To JOHN MILLER, *Pensacola*

Manchac, October 13, 1777
Since my writing you the 6 Inst. per this Conveyance there is nothing new with us, nor have we heard any thing further of the Americans being at the Illinois therefore have nothing to say upon that Subject—William Davis the Blacksmith Died since your departure from hence, and as he did not appoint any person to administer to what little he had left and the Effects are in due to sundry persons here, none of which chuse to administer as the sums due them are so triffling, James Banks Excepted as there is due him Ps.48 as per his proved acct. he desired me to write to you on that head, further requesting you would take out Letters of Administration in his Name by which means he may be impowerd to act for the good of himself & Creditors[.] whatever Expences there may be on the Letters he promises he will pay you on your arrival here with Interest on the money you you [*sic*] may advance on said Occasion, as security will be required. I will freely give mine as the Effects are all Lodged in my Store, say his Tools Iron & Steel &c. and as the Estate is in due me about 23 dolls. should it be that Letters will not be granted to Banks on sd. Effects which I would much rather they should than to myself, in that case please to get out in my Name[.] he has wrote himself more full on the subject[.] having nothing further to add . . .

To JOHN KENNEDY, *Natchez*

Manchac, October 16, 1777

Your favour of the 15th last Month is now before me, the Contents of which have duly observed—I am glad to hear of your recovery from your late Ailment and hope that the good state of health you now enjoy may long continue

The breaking out of the ozages Indians with the Hunters on the River Alkansaus is realy alarming (or ought to bee) to every person that have any concerns in your parts but since you do not mention that they have meddled with the English Hunters, am In hopes things will not be so bad with you as if otherwise[29]—I am much afraid for Mr. Hayward as you say he is gone up the alkansaw River, for to get the English hunters skins, for you may depend that the Commander, from the disappointment he has met with in his Trade will leave no stone unturned to get all he can into his hands, to endeavour to make up for his losses which I imagine must be considerable after what has happened, & as there is no dependance to be put in the Indians that you say are with him whom I look upon as capable of betraying their best friend for a Kegg of Rum, which I most heartily wish will not be the case with Mr. Hayward—it realy gives me pleasure to hear you are in a good way of doing something for yourself & hope, for your own sake, that you will make a good use of the opportunity. I am much obliged to you for the Kind offer of your assistance in my behalf with Mr. Hayward about the payment of his Bond but as the conditions are of such a Nature as I can't in Justice to myself accept, have not sent you the said Bond, for in the first place the Bond is payable in Money, & not in skins at any fixed price, secondly the price of Skins at your place where there is 150 pCt. advance on the goods sold here is no regulation for the Marketts in these parts, thirdly as I delived my Goods here, therefore may expect the paymt. at the same place. Lastly as I have been well Informed that Mr. Hayward proposes coming down himself this Insuing Winter, if so had much rather settle with himself, than any other Man, Though I have not accepted of your kind offer for the reasons above mentioned I still return you my most hearty thanks & if ever in my power will return the Compliment—I am realy [sorry] to hear that you have been so unfortunate in recovering the outstanding Debts of Messrs: Hooppock & Stampley am in hopes things will go better ere Spring, you say you have collected about 500 Dolls. worth of Skins and that you propose keeping them till Spring (if you do not meet with a good Occasion to send them[.] I would advise you to send them per the Illinois Batteaux if Possible, but you & Mr. Hooppock who I hope is with

29/During the summer of 1777 a band of Osage Indians robbed four white hunters on the bank of the Arkansas River. They were pursued by Caddos friendly to the Spanish, and five of their number were killed. Two who escaped set out for their village to raise their tribe and make a war of retribution against the white hunters on the Arkansas River. On their way homeward they encountered three white hunters and killed them. Captain de Villiers, commandant of Arkansas Post, had been working to develop a profitable personal trade with the Osage, and this episode forced him to abandon it. Faye, "The Arkansas Post," 651-52.

you ere this will be better able to Judge yourselves though at same time must intreat you will loose no opportunity as I am much in want of them, or money having large demands to discharge this winter—I have nothing new to acquaint you with excepting that the Kings Troops have taken Philadelphia and that it is generally Imagined that the affairs of America if not already settled will be ere long to all our satisfaction this being the needfull . . .

P.S. Please let me hear from you per all occasions my Wife desires to be remember to you & Mr. Hayward—

To STEPHEN HAYWARD, Natchez

Manchac, October 16, 1777

I did myself the pleasure of writing you a Number of Letters from time to time these tuo years past, the last of which was per Mr. William Williams of the 24th Sepr. 1776, but as yet have never been favoured with any Answer from which long silence I imagine they must have miscarried which I hope will not be the Case with this. In a Letter that I recd: from Mr John Kennedy he acquaints me that you told him that if I would send up your Bond & acct: you would pay them this winter if I would take Deer Skins at six ryalls per Skin & Beaver at a Dollar per lb them being the Common prices at your place of such skins & Peltrys— But for Sundry reasons which I have mentioned to him & which I am well assured he will shew you, has prevented my complying with such hard Conditions. be assured that I want nothing but my own & I am as well assured that you are to honest a Man to require any thing further of me than what is right—for my own part I don't want to have the handling of another Skin while I am in business, neither do I want to take any advantage of you or any other Man. Send your Skins or bring them yourself, dispose of them to whom you shall think most proper for your advantage[.] all I want is that you discharge your Bond & acct. Currt. & that wee could settle it together which I am well assured will be much more satisfactory to ourselves than any one can for us—

Since my writing my last I have been obliged by Law to pay the remaining 50 dollars due Mr. Dutton with Interest &c—for the amount of your draft on O: Pollock, therefore hope you will as you now have it in your power to discharge the ballance due me this winter, having nothing having nothing [sic] further to add, only to request if nothing further you will favour me with an answer to the present, and let me Know from yourself what I may expect. this being the needfull . . .

To MICHAEL HOOPOCK, *Concord*

Manchac, October 21, 1777

Your favr. of the 20 last Month from the Natchez I duly recd. by old Mr. Stamply and according to your request supplyed him with some Money your acct.—I have also received from Mr. Kennedy acquainting me that he has got in about 500 dollars worth Skins for you since he has been up—God send that he may continue in the like way, till all your Outstanding Debts are got in—you will lay hold of the first Conveyance of sending me what Skins you may get from time to time, which will enable me to discharge some part of the large sums I have to pay this Winter—wee have nothing new with us excepting that they say Philadelphia is taken by the Kings Troops & Captain John Waugh departed this life the 7 Inst: Please let me hear from you per all Conveyances & you'll Oblige . . .

To WILLIAM WEIR, *Pensacola*[30]

Manchac, October 29, 1777

The present is to request you will send me as soon as possible 3 or 400 lb Gun Powder also the flour for Commandant & Self the Tea & Pepper I recd. in good order, the last of which Articles wanted 5 lb of the Wt. the Seal that was on the Bag was not broke, therefore you'll please to Credit my acct. for the 5 lb. deficient. . . .

for J: F ———— G: B

To OLIVER POLLOCK, *New Orleans*

Manchac, November 17, 1777

Your favours of the 24 ulto. & 5 Inst. I found here on my return from Pt: Coupiée the Contents of which have duly observed—yours of the 24 Octor. you mention having Inclosed a Copy of my acct: settled last April as also the new acct—neither of which came in the Letter, which I imagine has been omitted through the hurry of Business—if you have Credited my acct. with Ps.100 you have committed an Error as I only paid Mr. Jennings P.75 as you requested per your Letter of the 26 Aug[.] as for me pretending to settle Davis's acct. or to send you a state of them, I realy cannot for the present, as it is not me that wrote for Letters of administration, for I am a Creditor like yourself but you may rest assured that when I have a little time more than I have at

30/William Weir came to West Florida from North Carolina in September, 1775, to escape the rebellion. He eventually settled near Baton Rouge and served on the grand jury at Manchac in 1780. See Address of the Grand Jury of Manchac, November 15, 1780, PRO, CO 5/580, pp. 309–11; PRO, CO 5/594, pp. 111–12.

present I will get the accts. Drawn out & send you as you request[.] in yours of the 5 Inst: you desire me to pay Doctor West Ps.27 which I have settled & placed to your Debit with me, further you will Credit my acct. Ps.113.5r for your Acceptance in favour Stephen Shakespear of the 14 May payable in 3 Mo: which I have settled with him, that is I have assumed it to him payable in the month of Feby. (as till then my Note in your hands is not due) should I hear any person Inquiring about a place be assured I shall let them know that Guinea Estate is for Sale, but as for the present there is nothing stirring in that way. there is now a Schooner from Pensacola now in the River but nothing new from that quarter[.] having nothing further to add only to request you'll not fail in sending me my acct. without which I am realy at a Loss about some small articles in our accts—your Compliance will Oblige . . .

P.S. I am obliged to you for striving to procure me a Saddle, a french one would not answer me therefore have wrote to Pensacola for an English one—

To THOMAS O'KEEFE, *New Orleans*

Manchac, November 17, 1777

Your much Esteemed favour of the 14 ulto. with Philip Lyons on Oliver Pollock I found here on my return from Pt Coupie the Contents of which have duly obsd.

I am much Obliged to you for your kind concern for our welfare and be assured [I] return you our most hearty thanks. For Gods Sake don't Imagine that your silence was ever looked upon in such a Light as that of your being in Possession of Drs. 113.5r should stop you from letting me hear from you, Especially as it did not belong to either of us; if I wrote to you about your silence, be assured it was because I was always happy in hearing from you & how you was. further I heard that you got the place of Interpreter which if so would have often prevented you from having time to acquaint your acquaintance how you do, for whin a Man is in that post, he is not always his own Master, we have a Schooner now in the Amit from Pensacola, but no news from thence if you have any at your place that can be depended on please let me have it in your next. You say you will be shortly up the Country if so remember I shall lay an Embargo on you & shall expect you will favour us with your Comy. for 10 or 20 Days at least if your affairs will permit of it. having nothing further to add, only to assure you that I & wife are with much Esteem Dr. Tom . . .

To MESSRS. WILLIAMS AND FERGUSON

Manchac, November 26, 1777

I have done myself the pleasure of writing you sundry Letters since your Mr. Williams departure from hence all which I am well assured you have recd. in due time, but as yet have not been favoured with an answer from you[.] therefore the present is to request you will endeavour to send me the amount of your sundry Notes, which have been due this some time, please to let me know if you have recd. the Amount Mr. Harrisons Note, & if you have sold the four quilded Petticoats you had from me last Decr. if not sold please to return 'em per first Conveyance as they belong to Mr. Priest your Compliance will Oblige . . .

To STEPHEN HAYWARD, *Natchez*

Manchac, December 31, 1777

Having duly authorized & Empowered Mr. Wm: Eason (who will deliver you this) to receive any Payments for me up the River I Should be much obliged to you if you will be so good as to make me some Remittances by him when he returns & his receipt for same shall be a sufficient discharge from . . .

P.S. Any Payments made to him on my Accot: shall be immediately endorsed on your Bond as soon as I shall receive Advice from him of the same.

To MICHAEL HOOPOCK, *Natchez*

Manchac, December 31, 1777

Since my last I have been credibly informed that what Skins You had got together as per Mr. Kennedy's Letter of 16th last September amounting to upwards of 500 Dollars which he promises to forward to me per first Conveyance have been given to Mr. Poulteney which report I would not willingly give Credit to after the promises You have made me since your Departure from hence—

In another Letter from Mr. Kennedy dated 15th Ulto. he acquaints me that I need not expect any remittances from you this year as all your Hunters have been robbed and that You was gone up the river which if so is really surprizing to me to think that any Person in whom I have ever repose'd so strong a Confidence as I have in you should treat me in such a manner—Therefore weigh within your own Breast how I have ever strove my utmost to serve you and your People and You cannot but on this Consideration join with me in allowing I have not been so well treated as I deserve—

This which goes by Mr. Eason (who is a Gentleman I have duly authorized & empowered to Act as my Attorney as in my Lieu) will serve to acquaint you that any Payments made to him on my accot: will be sufficiently discharged by you on his rect: for same and either on his return here or Advice received from him, such Paymts. shall be immediately endorsed on your Bond. —I have nothing further to add at present but with wishing you the Complimts. of the Season . . .

To ALEXANDER McINTOSH, *Natchez*

Manchac, December 31, 1777

Mrs. McIntosh favr. of the 29 ulto. I have duly recd. the Contents of which have observed, sametime recd. a Pot of Butter & Cheeses which you was so obliging as to send me, all in good order. therefore return you my most hearty thanks for the present till you are further P[aid ?]— I am sorry that I have it not in my Power to send you a Large assortment of Garden seeds, as I have been unlucky in that way this year my self—I am sorry to find Mr. Hooppock has used me in the manner he has done after all my Linity to him on so many occasions but I don't blame Hooppock so much as I do that Villan Kennedy—

I am much obliged to you for your kind offer in serving me when you go up the River should have embraced it with pleasure, if I had not already settled that Point with Mr. Wm. Eason whom I have Impower'd as my Attorney—

I am further Obliged to you for your kind Enquiry of my health[.] I promise you that neither I nor my wife have enjoyd any at present. she has been under a disagreeable complaint of the swelling of the Liver this some time past & I am Deaf with my right Ear, since last August & to compleat my misfortune, I have lately been poisoned in the Legs, which is very uneasy to me at present & is attended with a great inflamation in the parts affected —I have sent you 10 lb. Coffee that John Watkins told me you was in want of. further have Paid Mr. Wm. Weir your acct. Ps.28.6 as per your request. we have nothing new from the Norward that can be relyed upon; therefore say nothing on that head[.] it only remains with me for the pr[esent] to wish you the Compts. of the Season & believe me to be with much Esteem . . .

P.S. my Wife joins me in her best respects to you & Mrs. McIntosh

N.B. the drs.11.5 which you Paid to Mr. Priest on acct Mr. Foleys Note he has got Credit for the same, and as Mr. Priest is on the Point of leaving the province should be much obliged to Mr. Foley for the ballance per first safe Conveyance—

To THOMAS BOOKER, *Pointe Coupée*

Manchac, January 2, 1778

Your esteemed favr. of the 27 ulto. I recd per Mr. Monsanto & am sorry to acquaint you, that I have not at present so much Money in the House, having given what I had to Mr. Bradley for the Inclosed Bill for £100 on his Brother at 30 days sight, which you will please to acknowledge the rect. of in your next. I have only sent you the first shall send you the 2nd & 3rd with the Letter of advise per Mr. Gooding & if I receive so much Cash ere he arrives shall send you the Ps.200 if not rest assurd. I shall remit you per the first good Conveyance that shall offer this with my wishing you the Compts. of the Season is the needfull . . .

3rd Jany. 1778

Dear Sir

Since my writing you the Inclosed of the 2nd Inst. I have found those 3 European Letters at Mr. Hickeys the postage of which I paid being Ps.1.7 have debited the E[st]ate with the same be assured that I shall not omit your order for Cash which I shall send you per the first Conveyance after I receive so much. . . .

To JOHN PRIEST, *Thompson's Creek*

Manchac, January 7, 1778

Inclosed you have all your of Sales & Acct. Currt. by which it appears there is a Ballance due you of Ps.563.64—exclusive of Ps.190 outstanding on acct. your Sales as per acct. thereof all which I am in hopes you'll find right if not all mistakes shall be rectified at our first meeting[.] out of the above Ballance Doctor West will pay you my acct. Ps.236 and the remainder shall endeavour to make out ere your departure having nothing further to add . . .

P.S. my Complts. to Captn. Hindson—

To THOMAS DICAS, *Manchac*[31]

Manchac, January 9, 1778

Since my writing you the Other Day; I have Recved from Mr. Oliver Pollick; your note of the 24 of Novemr. Last payable on Demand for Ps.153; which he Requst me to Receve & Pay to Mr. Lintot, his account, as he is indue that Gentleman; money and would be Glad it was pay'd; I Request your answer per the furst Convence; that I may advice Mr. Pollock the Results of the Same....

To ROBERT ROSS, *New Orleans*

Manchac, January 10, 1778

Your favr. of the 19 ulto. I duly recd. with Sundry Goods most of which I have forwarded as you directed, as Jamaica Rum is scarse here please to send me 2 hhds Taffia per first opportunity, please to secure them for me as soon as you can, as I hear it is now at 25 Dolls. per hhd. & Store them for my acct. till an opportunity offers, as the Illinois Batteaux will be comeing down—

Inclosed is Frans. Poussetts draft on you for 20 Dolls. which please to apply to my Credit....

P.S. please to inform me in your next if you accept the Inclosed draft

To OLIVER POLLOCK, *New Orleans*

Manchac, January 10, 1778

Your esteem'd favr. of the 30th ulto. with my acct. Currt. is now before me and after due examination only find the ballce. due you to be Ps.294.7¼ which is owing to the Articles you have omittd. giving me Credit for. therefore refer you to my acct. herewith Inclosed the Ballce. remaining due to you am ready to discharge at any time in Scrap'd Deer Skins or Beaver, at the Currt. price of your place the freight of which I will pay & Insure them to your place, as for Money or Indico I have them not, or can I get them from sundries that are in due me. for which reason am sorry to acquaint you that it was not in my power to pay Mr. Lintott as he would not accept of skins. therefore wrote to Mr. Dicas & have sent your Letter to Mr. Williams. what the Result will be shall acquaint you per first Conveyance. This with my best respects to you & Mrs. Pollock with the Complts. of the season is the Needfull ...

31/Thomas Dicas resided in the Manchac district and served on the grand jury of Manchac in 1780. See PRO, CO 5/580, pp. 309–11.

To JOHN MILLER, *Pensacola*

Manchac, January 14, 1778

I am favd. with your three Letters the first by Mr. Trist of the 11 Octor. the 2nd of the 22nd Do. & the last of the 15 Novr. by Mr. Wm. Weir, the Contents of which have duly observed—And according to your request have assisted Mr. Triest every thing in my power his effects are still in my store—I am much Obliged to you for your kind concern for me & be assured I shall follow your advise in every Point—as to Bonds in Judgement he shall never have any from me—I have seen Mr. Booker since poor Mr. Comyn's death & spoke to him on the subject & of my verbal agreement with the deceased. as to the modes of payment he told me that the deceasd had often mentioned & I might be assured he should never do anything in the affair that should be contrary to the deceased Intentions—I have made him some paymts. my acct. as I have also done to Mr. Swanson for further particulars of which refer you to his Letter per this conveyance[.] exclusive of 20 Packs of Skins in the Hair now in your Store not yet weighed of I have not fixed any price of the skins in the hair [de]livered Mr. Swanson as yet[,] as I have seen an order for to Purchase skins in the Hair at 30 sols per Lb. from your place to be taken here the payment to be made in good Bills at 30 days on London or Cash. I am well assured if other Gentlemen give such prices you'll not be against allowing me the same, as it is to be supposed that Skins are in a greater demand now in England than they have been heretofore—In yours of the 27 Octor. you mention that Mr. Francis Millers Draft my favour on Mr. Durnford for Ps. 103.3½ was still unpaid for which I am realy sorry, but hope it will be honoured ere Mr. Miller leaves your place

Mr. Bay in a Letter of his of the 20 Novr. has forwared me a Writ against Henry Smith which I have not been able as yet to get served, as he is in Orleans but is Dayly expected over when I shall put it into execution if Possible

I shall be much obliged to you if you Write to the Widow Crepps on the affair I am well assured she will not be against paying it. As good Luck would have it I have got Mr. Valears Notes for what is due to you & my self otherways you may rest assured we should have had a flemish acct. for Desalls effects will not pay six shillings in the Pound. Valears Notes shall send to Mr. Duforrest [by] the first good conveyance, having already wrote to him on that subject & he has promised to do the needfull when they come to hand—

In yours of the 15 Novr. you say Mr. Miller promised he would take up his draft which I hope he has done as also Mr. Walters

Merchant of Manchac

acceptance my draft your favour therefore debit you with the same but you say nothing about the Drs.5.1r of Mr. Bruce's

I have wrote to Mr. Bay per this conveyance riquesting if Possible to send a few Blank writs to Mr. Watts and beg that you'll assist my endeavour in perswading him to it, as it will never answer if I am obliged to send for 'em to your place—God be praised the americans have got a flogging. I am in hopes that some of their friends on this River will be obliged to look out for some other method of paying their debts than what they have long expected (that is of an Army coming down the River) I have spoke to Mr. Livingston about the Effects of the deceased Davis & he told me I might act in the manner you advised me which I have done—I have now to acquaint you that James Banks deceased the 11 Inst. at Thompsons Creek where he went to recover Money on the news of which have taken Posession of his Effects (as he is indue me upwards of 400 Drs. per his Bond & Note) an Inventory of which shall transmit you per the next conveyance—as also the amt. of my acct. therefore request you will apply for Letters of administration on receipt of this for me, being the principal Creditor & am well assured there will be enough to pay all his Debts if properly managed[.] having nothing further to add only to wish you the Complimts. of the season . . .

P.S. my wife desires her best respects & is much obliged to you for your kind Enquiry—

N.B. Dr. Sir do not fail to apply for Letters of administration before any body else should apply as Mr. Livingston is now up the Country shall speak to him upon that subject & see what he can do for me here. the Expences attending the Letters of administration shall pay Mr. Swanson in Cash on recipt of the same this with the many other favours I shall always retain a gratefull sence of as it would be a great detriment to my Business to leave home at present or if any body else should obtain sd. Letters of administration

To ELIHU HALL BAY, *Pensacola*[32]

Manchac, January 14, 1778

I recd. your favr. 20th last Novr. Inclosed from Philip Livingston Esqr. the 17 ulto., since which no occasion has offered for your place till the present—I am much obliged to you & Mr. Miller for the trouble you have given yourselves in the affair of Mrs. Canty & her son & as the commensment of the Estate Accts. was with me in the year 71 & has gone through a Number of Blotters without which I could not settle a Number of accts. still Outstanding,

---

32/Elihu Hall Bay came to Pensacola from Charleston and served as a deputy provincial secretary under Governor Chester during the Revolutionary War. He held plantations under British grants near Natchez and at Walnut Hills. After the war he returned to Carolina. See Claiborne, *Mississippi*, 103–104; Johnson, *British West Florida*, 99.

have attested to it as also to that Mrs. Canty & that of her son should this not prove effective the affair must remain till some time next spring, at which time I can absent myself from Home— As all the Clerks that was with me at the time of the delivery of the Goods are Dead—But for the present it is impossible for me to go—as this is the season in which the French from the upper Country make their remittance & this the time I have all mine to make—

I have done the needfull in regard to proving Henry Smiths Debt before Mr. Watts but as yet cannott get it served, as he is still in the Island of Orleans but is Daily expected back to his place which when I am assured of shall loose no time in having him served with the writ & when done shall transmit it you—I return you my most hearty thanks for your kind offer of serving me in your way, & accept of it with pleasure—though if you could fix it so with Mr. Watts that he could have a number of Blank Writs it would be much more advantageous to me than by sending for them to your place, for it often happens that a Man that is indue me money & whom I can't Oblige to pay will remain here only one or tuo days therefore for want of proper means to stop him, I may be kept out of the Money a number of years Longer— which if they was in his hands I could get them as they might be wanted—which is not the case from your place—If Sir you could in any manner facilliate this you would greatly oblige me—and if there should be any deficiency in your sending the Blank writs & your filling them up yourself I will with thanks reimburse you the differance on demand—As I am quite unacquainted with the amount of the sundry fees attending a writ when properly served should be much obliged to you for a Note of them that I might at any time settle with the person on whom it was served having nothing further to add . . .

(The following is the editor's translation from the original French.)

To MONSIEUR TOURNOIR, *Pointe Coupée*

Manchac, January 20, 1778

I hoped to have the pleasure of seeing you several days ago, but as you did not come down I fear that you have fallen ill again. Here enclosed you will find two notes of Monsieur Lafitte Junior with his account current, by which you see that he still owes me Drs.482.6, and as I expect that he should arrive soon I am sending you the present, requesting you to receive the balance from him whether in deerskins, tobacco or other things that he may have to remit to you. If I have taken this course, it is because I fear that when he comes down here, the commandant will not allow him to unload anything here, and if they are with you they will be in a safe place.

All the expenses which will attend this affair you will be paid with much gratitude and many thanks.

If in case you have among your mules two that are broken and suitable for indigo-making, please let me know by the first opportunity, as I have need of a couple like this for a special friend, and at the same time tell me the price of the mules, as it is I who will guarantee you the payment, since my friend has no money to pay you at present.

I have nothing further at present to tell you, only to ask you to give my respects to Madame your wife and also to our friend Monsieur Dubour...

Copy of the account sent in the letter of Monsieur Tournoir:

Monsieur Cadet Lafitte . . . Owes to John Fitzpatrick
1776
April 12. For the balance of your note payable next November   334.5
1777
August 10. For the balance of your note payable in December   221.1
          For the money paid to the doctor for you (after
          your note was made) . . . .   4.—
                                        225.1
                                    Ps.559.6

Credit
1776
November 7. By 3 mules received on account at Ps.32 each   96.—
                                    463.6

Debit
          For 12 months interest on the remainder of your
          first note at 8 percent . . . .   19.—
                                        Ps.482.6

Without errors and omissions
Done at Manchac the 20th of January 1778

(The following is the editor's translation from the original French.)

To MONSIEUR LAFITTE JUNIOR,
New Orleans

                                Manchac, January 21, 1778

I write you the present to inform you of the reason that I have sent your account current and two notes to Monsieur Tournoir.

It is, Sir, so that I shall not be obstructed from receiving the payment which you will bring me here, because perhaps the commandant at Manchac will not permit you to land it here, but by placing it in the hands of Monsieur Tournoir I shall be very content knowing that when it is in his care it will be safe, and I can send for it when he advises me that it is with him. So I ask you not to take it badly that I have done this. If in case you do not find it convenient to place it in Monsieur Tournoir's hands and you would rather bring it to me here, you must come here at night, warning me in advance. Otherwise you will do me more service by placing it in the hands of Monsieur Tournoir as I have told you.

Having nothing further at present to tell you . . .

To RICHARD BRADLEY, *Natchez*

Manchac, January 23, 1778

According to your request have debited your acct. for the following sums vizt.—for the Ballance of Mayo Grays acct. as per acct. Current with a receipt here Inclosed Ps.54.2½ & Ps.13.5 for acct. of Wm. Scott with a receipt Amt. Ps.67.7½, the remainder of your Indico seed is not yet come, though the Commander promised it should have been here ere now, so that I may hourly expect it[.] be assured you shall not be disappointed, for should it not come in 10 or 12 days I will send my own People for it to the Pilleasaws[33] where it is to be had having nothing further to add . . .

To MESSRS. MORGAN AND MATHER, *New Orleans*

Manchac, January 26, 1778

I am favoured with both yours of the 9th & 15th Inst: the first per Mr. Allen without the Effects which I have since recd per Mr. Williams. the Letters have been forwarded to their address. that of the 15th per Mr. Gooding Inclosing an acct. & Note of Messrs. Ml. & Jab. Monsanto for Ps.94.7½ which I this day made a demand of they told me they had no money, but if I would take Indico they would pay it directly[.] In informed them my orders was to take nothing but Cash & shewed them your directions to me on that head, therefore wait your answer for my Government—I am sorry to find Mr. Maison so backward in discharging the sum due you[.] I have wrote to him per this conveyance on that subject therefore expect he will comply without further delay

33/*I.e.*, Opelousas.

if not poor Fitz: must make it good—though I am in hopes that will not be the case—the Bearer will pay you my acct. 90 or 100 Dollars, which if he does please give him a receipt for the same—I shall be with you soon am only waiting for Charlevilles arrival who is hourly expected here from the accts. I have had & then all my affairs with you shall be discharged to your satisfaction. . . .

(The following is the editor's translation from the original French.)

To MONSIEUR MAISON, *New Orleans*

Manchac, January 27, 1778

By a letter that I have just received from Messrs. Morgan and Mather, dated the 15th instant, they tell me that you have done nothing with regard to the payment for which I stood security for you. Be assured that their letter showed me much about the promises that you made me when here to send me my letter of credit as soon as you had time to go to town. However, it seems that nothing has been done there and that I shall be obliged to pay this sum, according to the terms of their letter. You told me that Monsieur Villeboeuf would pay me sixty and some piastres for the debt that was owed to you by the late Monsieur Des Salles, but the news has come and Monsieur de la Villeboeuf can pay nothing unless they show some notes or bonds, and he has sent all his [Des Salle's] effects to the government, where you ought to be paid the money that you are owed. Now the time has come when I have some payments to make, and if I am obliged as I know the laws will oblige me to pay Messrs. Morgan and Mather, I shall be very embarrassed for not having politely obliged others [to pay me]. Do me the pleasure, I beg you, to settle with these men, and if you can send me the balance that you received for Lillywhite you will oblige me, but preferably pay Morgan and Mather, so that I shall hear no more about this affair. . . .

(The following is the editor's translation from the original French.)

To MONSIEUR VALLIÈRE, *New Orleans*

Manchac, January 28, 1778

Much time has passed since all your notes were due, without your having informed me when you intend to pay me. Since you have apparently forgotten me, I take the liberty of sending you your account current, by which there appears to be a balance due of

207 pesos, that is, 197 pesos for your two notes, and the other ten pesos for the 25 pounds of powder that my wife [*illegible*] you on the 29th of December 1773, for which you gave neither a receipt nor a bond. I am really convinced that since the time you [*illegible*] me, if you had really wished you could have found the means to pay me before now, but my absense from New Orleans made you believe that I had no need for my money. Allow me to say that this is not the treatment that I expected to receive from you when I gave you my goods. I did it honorably as I expected to be paid, but unfortunately (for me) I have found everything otherwise since the time you made me do it. I ask you to observe that when the late Monsieur Des Salles remitted to you your note for 233.6 pesos payable to the bearer and you paid him 50.6 pesos on account, there remained a balance of 183 pesos on your first note, and instead of endorsing the sum that you paid him on account he completely cancelled my note by remitting it to you without my consent, and for the remainder of the note, which was 183 pesos, he took your note payable to him alone and not to the order of the bearer. If I entrusted my first note to him, be assured that it was not with the intention of having it cancelled. But no matter. I hope that what is owed to me will be paid just as if it was on the first note. It appears that the note for 183 pesos mentioned above is endorsed on the back to the effect that you paid 36 pesos, so there remains a balance on this note of 147 pesos, this being adjusted with the 10 pesos for the powder and the 50 for your other note makes a balance of 207 pesos, according to the account enclosed herewith.

I am sending your notes with a copy of your account to Monsieur Du Forest for him to ask you to pay it, which I beg you to do without forcing me to get assistance from His Excellency Don Gálvez to force you to pay me a debt so legitimately and so long due, and I hope by the justice of my cause and the manner in which it was contracted to obtain from His Excellency as much justice as if I were a subject of His Catholic Majesty. If I am forced to take this course it is because I see no other way to be paid. So, Sir, for goodness sake spare me from being forced to pursue you, seeing that I shall be forced to do this if you do not pay me. Having nothing further to say . . .

To THOMAS BOOKER, *Pointe Coupée*

Manchac, January 29, 1778

The Inclosed 8 Letters Directed for Mr. Comyn I got at Mr. Hickeys & Paid drs.3.4r postage for the same. I am in dayly expectation of receiving some Money from the appalosaws, having had advise of the same, when I am in Cash you may rest assured I shall send what you wrote for per first safe conveyance....

P.S. in order to make the Bearer more punctual in delivering the Letter have given him 1 Carrott of Tobacco for performing the same—

To THOMAS BOOKER, *Pointe Coupée*

Manchac, February 9, 1778

I had the pleasure of writing you the 29 ulto. & Inclosed you a number of European Letters that I got at Mr. Hickeys which hope you have recd: ere this.—I now Inclose you Mr. Nichs: Trist first of Exchange for £100 Sg. or Ps.428.4½ (he having sent the Letters of advice by the Pacquit) which please to apply to my Credit.—I am realy Glad to hear that you have been so happy as to get on the Scent of the Robbers & hope that you will be soon be able to bring the offenders to Justice—Be assured that I shall do all that is in my power for to make you from time to time all the remittance possible but as yet no Boats are come down that are indue me. this being the needfull . . .

To MESSRS. MORGAN AND MATHER, *New Orleans*

Manchac, February 9, 1778

Since my last of the 26 Ulto. I have been favoured with yours in which you request me to send you six or seven hundred [pounds ?] sheet Lead, I am sorry it did not come to hand some time sooner having disposed of it some days before yours came to hand—I am in hopes Mons: Cadet Lafite has 90 or 100 Ps. as he promised me he would which if so place to my Credit—I send you here Inclosed Mons: Frans. Vigo's receipt for a Note he has of mine to recover & pay it to you the amount say Ps.146.5 which I am well assured you will receive if not oblige me So far as to make him deliver you up the Note with his Indorsment on it then put it into the hands of some of the Gentlemen of the Justice to [o]blige the Drawer to pay it ere he leaves toun as it has been due this 3 years this being the needfull . . .

To MESSRS. MORGAN AND MATHER, *New Orleans*

Manchac, February 11, 1778

I had the pleasure of writing you the 9 Inst. in which I inclosed you Frans. Vigo's rect. &c. to which refer—Since which Messrs. Manl. & Jab. Monsanto offered me the Inclosed Draft in payment of their acct: & Note which I accepted as you have further affairs with the drawer, am in hopes it will meet with your approbation. the more so as ready Money is realy scarse with us at this place— Charlevilles Batteau is not yet Arrived, nothing further for the present . . .

To DONALD McPHERSON, *Natchez*

Manchac, February 12, 1778

Your esteemed favour of the 29 Ulto. per Mons. Richard I duly recd: the Contents of which have observed[.] I paid your order have debited your acct: with the same—I am glad to hear that Hodskiss Note is still in being for God sake don't defer putting him to all the Expence that your Court will admit of as he has used me like an old sharper[.] I have Inclosed to you Richd: Bacons Note for Ps.26.2r fourteen dollars of which I went security for & which I was obliged to pay last October therefore request you will not take any thing in payment but Cash or Deer skins if the Latter make him pay the freight to this place, charge Interest from last October—I am in hopes you have ere this finished the small affairs of mine that remained in your hands, if so remit them per the first Opportunity as this is the time to make remittance therefore should be glad of them to help all I can get,— Jacquaux acquainted Mons: Tounoir of Pt: Coupiée that there is a Man at your place acoming down with a raft of Boards say 10,000 feet that he wants to Exchange them for Cattle Mons: Tounoir has requested me to write to you to inform yourself who the person is if you find him out let him know Mr. Tounoir will take his boards & pay him for them in Cattle at the current price, provided this Man stops 4 or 5 Miles above his House, and comes & acquaints him the Boards are there that he may get hands to help doun with the raft for if it goes by he will have nothing to do with it, as the getting them up will be attended with great Expence you will much Oblige me by Inquiring after the Man & let him know Tounoirs intentions, be assured it will be as much service as if done to myself. . . .

Merchant of Manchac

To PATRICK MORGAN, *New Orleans*

Manchac, February 18, 1778

Your favours of the 3rd & 10 Inst. have duly recd: the Contents of which have observed—I shall supply your man with anything he may want from time to time to the amount of what you have Limited him to have—yours of the 10th Inclosed a Letter for Mr. Francis Poussett which I sent him Express he is now here on his way for your place—Messrs. Jones sent here some time agoe a pot of Butter for you which I sent you per Mons: Pickear of the Illionois hope you have recd. ere this[.] I have had occassion for some provisions which I got from Mr. Charlo Charleville to the amt. of drs.39.5 I will be much obliged to you if you will acct. with him in your Settlemt. as I realy have not money in the House, having paid all away this Morning (nor can I get any from our Gentlemen planters that are in due me hereabout) I am in hopes you have ere this recd. the Money from Mons: Lafite & Vigos, if so please to acquaint me in your next[.] Mr. Danl. Lewis leaves this in 3 days with his raft he will pay you my acct. Ps.300 this is what I always promise you[.] The 14th Inst. I send you per Mr. Campbell 152 lb. sheet Lead at 2 sols per lb. amt. 300 Ps. to your Debit. this being the needfull . . .

(The following is the editor's translation from the original French.)

To JEAN JOSEPH DUFORREST, *New Orleans*

Manchac, February 28, 1778

Although I have not had the honor of corresponding with you, I have known you for a long time, so I am so bold as to take the liberty of sending you the papers herewith enclosed relative to the manner I have been treated for so long in some business that I have with Monsieur Vallière. First, you will find a letter for him which I have left open so you can read it. When you have done that, please seal it and send it to him. Then there is a copy of his account current, by which you will see that he owes me a balance of 207 pesos. There are also his two notes, one for 147 pesos and the other for 50 pesos, making a total of 197 pesos. The other 10 pesos are for gunpowder, according to the account current mentioned above.

I have no doubt that you will be surprised to see a note made by Monsieur Des Salles for 183 pesos. This is endorsed on the back for 36 pesos, so there remain 147 pesos on this note as mentioned above. But here, Sir, is the way this affair happened. Monsieur Des Salles, commandant of the post at Spanish Manchac, came to my place with Monsieur Vallière to get some merchandise on credit. I told Monsieur Des Salles that I did not know Monsieur Vallière, that is, I had never had any business with him, and as for the merchandise, I did not have enough for a trip I was about to make to Grand Gulf. He replied that it was all the same whether I sold them here or up there, and that by giving some merchandise to supply Monsieur Vallière in his trade to the Attakapas I would render him a great service, because if he was obliged to send to New Orleans for them the season for trade would be passed before the merchandise arrived and his opportunity would be lost. Seeing the insistence of the one and the need of the other, I agreed and gave Monsieur Vallière merchandise amounting to 233 pesos and 6 escudos, for the balance of which he gave me his note payable to the bearer the following April (that is, 1774), but as I had not returned from my trip to Grand Gulf at the time Monsieur Vallière left for the Indian Nation, I was not paid on time. I arrived in New Orleans the following May, but unfortunately his house had burned. That was not the time for me to demand my money, and although it was not to my liking I agreed to give him more time to pay me. After eight months I sent my notes to Monsieur Surere to collect the balance, which he was never able to do despite the legitimate demands that he made. When I went down and found that Monsieur Surere could get nothing, I then had recourse to the late Monsieur Des Salles (who by then had returned to his post), telling him that he was the cause of the debt contracted with Monsieur Vallière and that he gave me his word of honor that I would be paid in the time stipulated by the bond. He replied that this was true and that if I would give him an order to get my note from Monsieur Surere he would see me paid before much longer. I gave him the order, and he received my notes according to his letter, dated the 9th of February, 1775, herewith enclosed, and I expected to receive my money shortly. I received nothing from him until his death in 1776. When I asked him if he had received any payment, he told me he had not. Then I told him to return my notes and that I would see the Governor on this matter, but much was my surprise when I found that the note herewith enclosed was not the same that he had received from Monsieur Surere. He had collected one part of the first note and then took a note for the rest payable to himself alone and not to the order of the bearer. When he gave me the said note he told me, "There, I have nothing else to give you." I was obliged to take it, and for the money that he had received on the first note and the

Merchant of Manchac

36 pesos endorsed on the second he gave me the letter herewith enclosed dated the 6th of February 1776, addressed to Monsieur Donicant Darby, who was then in charge of all his livestock at Manchac, so that I could sell them to reimburse myself with the money. I received the livestock and sold them and took the surplus into account for him a long time ago. Here, Sir, is the subject of my complaint, and if you can help me in this affair I shall pay you whatever expenses you may have along with your commissions, with much gratitude, and if ever I can be useful to you in this place, I beg you to let me know and be assured that I would do everything I could to reciprocate. Awaiting the pleasure of your reply...

P.S. If Monsieur Vallière is disposed to settle this matter with you amicably, give him a general receipt for me. If not, keep the papers until I have the pleasure of seeing you.

Summary of the account mentioned in the two letters preceeding:

Monsieur Vallière owes John Fitzpatrick

1773
December 26 For various goods given to you according to your bond, dated this day, payable to the bearer next April 233.6

29 For 25 pounds of gunpowder given you by my wife for which you gave neither receipt nor bond, telling my wife that you would pay her with your note at 40 sols per pound . . . 10.—
                                                                 243.6

Credit

1775
April 29 By what you paid to the late Monsieur Des Salles on account of the note of December 26, 1773, for 233.6 pesos 50.6
                                                                 193.—

Debit

1776
February 4 For the balance of your note, dated this day, payable next March . . . . . . 50.—
                                                                 243.—

Credit

By what was paid the 29th of April 1775 to Monsieur Des Salles, according to the endorsement on the back of your note for 183 pesos . . . . 36.—

                                    Balance remaining . . . Ps.207.—

January 28, 1778

To WILLIAM WEIR, *Pensacola*

Spanish Manchac, April 10, 1778

Your favor of the 27th Ulto. I duly received and note the Contents, Inclosed is your Accot. Currt. ballance due you 776 Dolls. which is not payable this sometime—

I have a large quantity of Tobacco by me at present cant get a safe opportunity to send it to Pensacola, if any offers, shall send it to your Care to sell for my Accot: Mr. Boles desired me to pay you Ps.14.5 but first requests you will send him Jackson's Bookkeeping that you got from Mr. French, as he would not lose it on any account whatever, therefore requests you'll send it him per first Opportunity, & when he receives it will pay the Money to You on your Order—The Barr Lead that you Left at my house I have brought over with my own Goods, shall be deliver'd to your Order on demand, or if I want it will take it to my own Accot: & Credit yours with it—The two pieces of Muslin remaining in your hands request you'll dispose of to the best Advantage and credit my Accot: for the Amot:—You need not be uneasy about the Balance due you as I hope things will be settled on this River soon & I shall have it in my Power to pay you & every other Person I am indebyed to—This being the needful . . .

To McGILLIVRAY, STRUTHERS & COMPANY, *Mobile*

Spanish Manchac, April 10, 1778

Your Esteemed favor of 26 Jany. I duly received & note the Contents[.] Two days before it came to hand a small Party of Americans arrived at English Manchac which has interim broke up all the English Settlements on this River, for want of a small Assistance in due time[34]—I shall be a considerable Loser by it as Several have joined them that are in my Debt for large Amount however I am determined to call my Creditors together as soon as possible, if there is not a Sufficiency saved to pay them will give up my Negroes & everything else I have as I wrote last month to Mr. Miller on the Subject; when Mr. Miller was here I gave him a Draft on Pensacola to discharge my Debt with John McGillivray & Co. therefore think I am not in debt to him & Co.

I have delivered Skins Indigo & other Effects at sundry times to Mr. William Swanson for accot. of McGillivray & Strothers and Miller Swanson & Co;, each half as Accot. of which I suppose he has sent you e'er this. I can't exactly say the Amount but its upwards of 2500 Dollars—the whole I was in expectation of dis-

34/See Introduction to this volume, p. 26.

charging before this time as there were a great quantity of Skins coming to me which the Americans have got and God only knows if ever I shall receive a ryal of it—this being the needful ...

To ROBERT ROSS, *New Orleans*

Spanish Manchac, April 30, 1778

Your esteemed favour of the 26 Inst. I duly recd. this Morning & according to yours & Mr. H: S. request have not detained Mr. Bloomart a moment have supplyed him for his own & the Mens use with sundry Provisions &c. to the amount of $103.5¾ as per acct.—without which he could not proceed therefore hope it will meet with Mr. H. S. approbation—Having nothing further to add only to request if anything further of the same nature should offer that you will recommend them to yours ...

P.S. Please to acquaint the Gentleman that is Purser of the Hound for want of a Boat I can't send him doun the Tobacco I promised him—

To ROBERT ROSS, *New Orleans*

Spanish Manchac, May 2, 1778

I had the pleasure of writing to you the 30th Ulto. relative to Sundries supplied Mr. Blommart &c: and on the 1st Instt. per Doctor Cap de Vielle who goes down with Francis Lassley who was one of Stuart's Rangers that came here with Mr: Christe and was wounded in the Affair that happened at this place the 15 of last March.[35] Messrs. Christe & Paris requested I would take proper Care of him which I have done as far as lies in my Power[.] They told me that all Expences should be paid on demand at Pensacola. Now as I look upon it that the Doctor's bill is rather Extravagant have valued my self on you to have his Bill examined by the Gentlemen of the faculty in town; and whatever is right request You will see him paid[.] Mr. Christe told me either to draw on John Stuart Esqr. or himself for the money and that it should be honored on Sight; if it is not inconvenient to discharge his Accompt, you will oblige me to see to have it properly examined and to let me know how much I shall have to pay as I shall be obliged to pay him on his return from Town if you do not settle the Affair. ...

35/*Ibid.*, p. 26.

P.S. The NB in my other Letter to you by Cap de Vielle for the Ps.32 is for necessaries furnished by him which I request you also to pay him apart.³⁶

(The following is the editor's translation from the original French.)

To MONSIEUR ROUJAUT

Manchac, May 9, 1778

It is now two years and some months since you have had my goods, which I very honorably gave you, believing that I would be paid in the time specified by your note. However, you have come down since your note was due and gone up again without having had the kindness to let me know either by letter or other means when you intend to pay me. That is why I take this opportunity to ask you to send me the balance of your note with the interest that has accrued since it was due.

I shall wait until the middle of next month to receive your response or the payment, and if I have not received either one or the other in that time, do not be surprised if I take another means to obtain my payment. For goodness sake, Monsieur, spare me such a step which I promise you will be very disagreeable to me, but not being able to do otherwise in my present situation I shall be obliged to do it. Having nothing further to add . . .

To THOMAS O'KEEFE, *New Orleans*

Spanish Manchac, May 13, 1778

I have Inclosed to your care sundry papers, and if you are not too hurried with your own affairs shall be much obliged to you if you will transfer the following small ones Vizt.—Mr. Pollocks acct. Currt. & his acceptance by which you ll will find there is 4 Ps. 0¾ Ballance due me by that Gentleman, please to deliver him up his acceptance & receive my Note now in his hands with the Ballance; pass receipts with him in my Name & remit in [my] Note per first conveyance. In the next place I send you the Widow Lewis Bill of Sale for a Negro Man named York now in the common Prison of Orleans having run away but some time ago he was taken up in the accadian Country as I suppose, and [brought] to Town[.] you'll Oblige me much by paying the expences that will attend on said Negro Imprisonment should it happen that you are not in Cash to pay the Charges in that case you'll apply to Mr. Bay if yet at Orleans who will supply you with wherewith to redeem the

36/On May 10, 1778, Robert Ross sent the following reply to Fitzpatrick's letter: "I am favored with your Sundry Letters of the 30th April 1st and 2nd May, and observe that the Expences Attending Mr. Blommarts Voyage to the Natchez Amount to a Very Considerable Sum. I make no doubt of your Account being paid by Mr. Stuart but he must needs think Odd that Mr. Blommart Should take upon him to Expend twice the Sum he was limited to—Francis Lessly is lodged in Our Hands, and You may Assure Mr. Christie that he Shall be treated with the greatest Care and Attention[.] The Governor has directed two Surgeons to Examine Cap. De Ville's Account and from $190 they have reduced it to $76, which I have accordingly paid and taken his Receipt." Blommart had gone to New Orleans in order to recover property stolen by Willing's raiders and was returning to Natchez to help organize British defenses there. He availed himself of Fitzpatrick's services on his return trip, for on April 6, 1778, he reported to Ross that he was going to Manchac and would "get dispatched either by Land or water by the means of Fitzpatrick." See Ross to Fitzpatrick, May 10, 1778, J. Blommart to Ross, April 6, 1778, PRO, CO 5/595, pp. 283–84, 293–94.

Negro, but should Mr. Bay have left Toun ere this comes to hand, then apply to Mr. Jab. Henderson for what will pay the Expences which Money I will remit him when I Know how much per the first opportunity. when this is done before you take him out of Prison go to Mr. Dojeans who will supply you with a proper pair of Irons which I request you'll have well secured, send him to me per the first conveyance giving the person you deliver him to a strict charge not to take the Irons of on any acct. till I receive him[.] whatever you agree for his passage shall be paid on his arrival here, I should not be so very particular if It was not that I know him to be a very great Villan & would have nothing to do with him if I could have been paid any other way, but is him or nothing. Lastly I have sent to your address 8 Ells fine Linen for Madam Guidraz, which with her Letter request you'll send her. you'll charge me what you think proper for your trouble in these affairs which shall allways be acknowledged by yours . . .

P.S. Please to acquaint Mrs. Martin at Mr. Murphys that the Letter she gave me for Mr. Mills have sent to him who is now at the appalausas but have got no Ansr.

To OLIVER POLLOCK, *New Orleans*

Spanish Manchac, May 13, 1778

My short stay at Orleans when last there & your hurry of business prevented me from taking up my Note in your hands for the ballce. of the Negroes therefore as I cannot for the present leave home have sent you your Acct. Currt. (which I am in hopes you'll find right ballance due me Drs.4.0¾) and your acceptance my favour to Mr. O Keeffe to deliver you therefore request you will deliver him up said Note & pay him the ballance & his rect. shall be the same as from Dr. Sir yours . . .

To THOMAS BOOKER, *Pointe Coupée*

Spanish Manchac, May [*blank*], 1778

Since your departure from hence I have done all in my power to find out the Cambrick but all to no Effect as at the time we packed up the Goods had not time to take an Inventory, therefore can't say whether [we put] it in a case trunk or Barrell & as I have no place to put my Goods into (they are still in the fort) untill I have time to build another Cabbin which I am in hopes will be in a few days hence then shall embrace the first conveyance of sending it to you. Inclosed is your Acct. the other I sent it per Mr.

Comyn which am in hopes you'll find right[.] as yet nothing new from the Eastward, things still remain as when you left us. Mr. Bay is gone to Town for his Negroes to make a Crop in the Accadian Country[.] this with my respects to Mr. Comyn is all at present . . .

P.S. Thomas Wescoatt has been here since you left this I spoke to him about going back to the Plantation but he says it would be attended with Danger as there is nobody on the English side of the Amit [*remainder of line illegible*]

To THOMAS BOOKER, *Pointe Coupée*

Spanish Manchac, May 15, 1778

Your order per Michael Routher for twelve Dollars came to hand this Morning which have paid & placed as advised we have nothing new with us though in Dayly expectation of Men from Pensacola—In my former per a French Batteau I requested you would let me know if Mr. Wescoatts Draft my favour would meet your acceptance for Ps.149 but as I have not been favoured with your Answer have deferred making any demand of it till I hear from you—you'll Oblige me to acquaint Mr. Comyn that I expect Doctor West here soon, therefore request he will send doun his Gun per first opportunity[.] this with my best Respects to you & Mr. Comyn is the needfull . . .

To ADAM CHRYSTIE, *Pensacola*

Manchac, June 8, 1778

Since your departure from hence till now I have not had an opportunity of writing to you nor of furnishing you with an acct. of sundries supplied Francis Lesley according to your & Mr. Pariss request[.] the Doctors demand against him was paid by Messrs. David Ross & Co. according to my request & for which I suppose they have valued themselves on you ere this for the amount if not you may expect it soon[.] I have supplied him with sundries as per acct. Inclosed Amt. Drs.29.4Rs I also send you your small acct. with me say 28.3½ amt. in all Drs.57.7½Rs which request you will pay to Mr. John Miller or his order my acct. having advised him of the same per this Conveyance[.] if you have finished with my Books shall be obliged to you to forward them to me per Mr. Smyths return. . . .

To JOHN MILLER, *Pensacola*

Manchac, June 9, 1778

Since my writing you the 14th last March per Mr. Chryste I have not been favoured with any of yours though there has been frequent Occasions from your place to Orleans[.] your long silence makes me Imagine that you are offen[ded] with me if any thing of that is the case please let me know in your next the Bearer of the present Mr. Henry Smith has given me his promise that he will discharge his Note now in your hands on his arrival at your place with all cost and Interest thereon—Mr. David Williams offered me a draft on you for Drs.428.4Rs which I did not accept till I hear from yourself if agreeable to you shall forward the same per first opportunity with a Draft of Henry Stuarts Esqr. for 250 Dollars which I shall have from him on his arrival here which is Dayly expected[.] I have taken the Liberty of enclosing to your care sundry Notes & [bonds ?] amt. Drs. 349.5Rs as per acct. here inclosed, which if you receive place to my Credit[.] Mr. Smith will deliver you an old Watch that belongs to Charles Clarke—it having been found among the Effects of the deceased James Banks by whom I should be a considerable sufferer as the Dammd Woman that he had with him on Willings arrival at Manchac went & swore that the Major part of the deceased Effects was her property on which I was obliged to deliver them up or should have been in Danger of Loosing all my own for the Particulars of which refer you to Mr. Swanson—your Negro James, Mr. Bentleys Collins and Mr. Swansons Negroes are still with mine[.] I have not sent them over the Water, having no place for them or my own, myself and wife remain in a small Cabin scarse Habitable at another time. the Gentlemen officers have taken possession of my house the Soldiers have occupied all the out Houses. Mr. Dutton, Lieut. Wilson, & Lieut. Graham have taken up the large store with their Effects all this without my knowing if I am to be paid for the same—if Mr. Swanson is not coming this way for some time request you'll let me know what I shall do with the Negroes at present they are doing nothing but running their respective owners to Expences—in all probality we shall have a good trade here this Summer and as I want a few articles for an assortment as per Inclosed acct. for which you may depend to be remitted in due time your sending them per first safe Oppty. will greatly oblige yours . . .

P.S. the widow Cantey died about a Month agoe shall be much obliged to you to send me an acct. of the Cost of the writs &c for her & Geo: Cantey—

2 Punchs. Jamaica rum put into Porter Casks   6 ps. scotch osnaburghs   16 ps. Irish Linen from 13 to 16½d per yard   16 ps. ¾ Check   1 Gro: Common Knives & forks   1 Gro: Pewter spoons   1 Piece fine blue Camblett with trimmings for the same   4 doz: black Handkfs. from 38/ to 44/   6 Pieces black Ribban   6 ps. sorted Ribban   6 ps. blue strouds   6 Nests Tin Kettles,   2 doz: fine white plain thread Hose   2 doz: ribbed Do.   4 doz: Mens shoes   2 doz: womens Callimanco shoes   10 pieces red strip Ginghams   10 ps. blue do.   1 box Common pipes   20 lb. Hyson Tea   1 lb Cinnamon   1 lb Nutmegs   1 Cut Single loaf Sugar   2 Pieces broun holland   1000 fish hooks Sorted   6 doz: Common hemp Lines   1 doz: deep sea Lines   2 doz: Hambourgh Lines   500 best black oil flints—

as Mr. Smyth will be coming here directly he will take a Trunk full of Goods for me which please put the Tea, Ribbans Handkfs. & other small articles into it as I am in want of them—

To THOMAS O'KEEFE, *New Orleans*

Spanish Manchac, June 18, 1778

Your esteemed favour of 23rd ulto. is now before me the Contents of which have observed & according to what you was pleased to mention had reason to have expected my Negro ere this his not arriving I suppose is owing that you had not a good opportunity[.] should that be the case and that you have [not] sent him ere this comes to hand request you'll embrace the first safe opportunity to send him up that I may have him here to send to Pt. Coupie with others that I am going to send to that settlement to dispose of payable at the Crop—this with my best respects to Mr. Murphy when you see him is the needfull . . .

   P.S. please to get my Note from Mr. Pollock & send it per first safe oppy. seal & deliver the Inclosed

To MICHAEL HOOPOCK, *New Orleans*

Spanish Manchac, June 18, 1778

Since my departure from New Orleans I have not been favoured with a Line from you relative to our affairs I am happy to hear you have been able to recover some part of your effects that was taken by Captn. Willing that is that you have recd. payment for them[.] if so requst you'll please to remember that it is now a long time since your Bonds & other obligations have become due.

the losses I have sustained since this unhappy contest & the many demands that is dayly coming against me obliged me to have recourse to them that are in due me, to see if they can help me with some part of the respective sums, Now Sir if you can't pay the whole please let me know what part you'll be able to discharge that I may send your obligations to my friend Mr. O Keeffe to have what you can pay Indorsed thereon your answer per the first opportunity will much oblige ...

To THOMAS BOOKER, *Pointe Coupée*

Manchac, June 19, 1778

Your esteemd favour I duly recd. should have answered it by the same conveyance but realy had not time. I am realy sorry to hear of your ill state of health & your Malady continues so obstinate that you have not found means to remove it. I am of opinion that if you could spare time & your business would permit that a voyage to Pensacola where you would enjoy the Benefit of the sea Breese would be of great assistance towards your recovery for without health what is life to us? You request an explanation of the small differances that is in my acct. in the first place the 2 dolls. to Joseph the Portague I paid him by Mr. Comyn's Virtuel order[.] the abatement on the Goods was also by himself on his way to Orleans in the presence of Messrs. Miller Swanson & Boles as he took of the advance on 24 ps. Brittanias 2 Pair ram skin Breeches 1 ps. Teapay 7 doz & 2 printed Linen Handkfs. these being water damaged he Let me have them at the prime cost therefore I debited his acct. for the same Amt. D.37.2¼ as for the Salt when at your house you requested I would leave word with Mr. Collison to let you have three Barrells I not only left him word but left him a written order to let you have the same which order he delivered to Mr. Weir and I paid him for it—now Sir as you have not recd. the Quantity I charged please send me an acct. of what you have recd. & I will oblige Mr. Collison to refund the differance and Credit the acct. for the same[.] I am sorry Mr. Boles Book is not found since it is lost Mr. Gooding must pay pay [*sic*] for it. Mr. Wescoats recd. your Letter and answers it by this opportunity his acct. with me is Doll. 148.2½ which I would chuse if convenient to be passed to my Credit than any other way but an order on Mr. Morgan is as good as the Bank for me—be assured that I am realy sorry for your Losses the more so as there is no prospect to retrieve them if things continue in the situation they are at present[.] this with my sincere wishes for your health is the needfull ...

To DAVID ROSS, *New Orleans*

Spanish Manchac, June 27, 1778

As I am much in want of some small articles to make out an assortment, as per annexed acct. if you can supply me with them shall be much obliged to you if you should not have all of them yourself shall be obliged to you to procure 'em for me and for the amount of which will pay you on your order at the Crop. please to deliver them to the bearer Jacquax and take his receipt for the same. my best respects to your Brother George . . .

2 Reams writing Paper   1 Hhd: Taffia   10 Kegs Brandy
2 Boxes or Barrells of Sugar   1 or 2 Barrells Coffee
4 Boxes Soap   10 Pieces blue & red Ginghams
2 Pieces Osnaburghs—

not sent

To MESSRS. MORGAN AND MATHER, *New Orleans*

Spanish Manchac, June 27, 1778

You will receive from the Bearer Mons. Jacquax 176 Deer skins in the hair Wt. 598 lb. which cost me 20 sols per lb. hope you will allow me the same as your Mr. Morgan told me when I was last in Town he would allways take them from me at 2 ryalls per lb. now as they will cost something for having them wormed willingly allow the difference—The paper you was pleased to send me I recd. & am much obliged to you for it—Please to send me per Bearer tuo Blank Books three Quire Each & one Ream paper for which he will pay you, let me Know the price of the Ream paper you sent me that I may Credit your acct. for the same. . . .

not sent untill 8 July

To THOMAS O'KEEFE, *New Orleans*

Spanish Manchac, June 27, 1778

I had the pleasure of writing to you the 18 Inst. to which refer, if you have not found means ere this comes to hand to have sent me my Negro, the present is to request you'll deliver him to Mr. Jacquax with my Note (if you have withdrawn it from Mr. Pollock) if not request you will before Jacquax Leaves Town as I should be glad to have it as it is paid[.] Jacquax will be in want of a little of your assistance in the purchase of some small articles that I stand in need of your assisting him with your advice will add to the many favours I have recd. from you[.] my Wife desires her best Respects . . .

this not sent

To THOMAS O'KEEFE, *New Orleans*

Spanish Manchac, June 29, 1778

Your esteemed favour of the 15 Inst. with the Negro & Bill of Sale I recd. from Mr. Strother the 27 Inst. and return you my most hearty thanks for your trouble in the same & I observe what you say about Mr. Strothers paying me 41 dolls. your acct.—which he promises he will do if he receives the amt. of the Note at Pt. Coupie

I further observe that you have sent me a sketch of your acct. but as it does not agree with my Books have sent you a Copy of your acct. for your Government by which you will see there is due me Dolls.69.5½ and if you recd. the 12 dolls. of Captn. Lyons & 9 drs. of Doctor Wests it will be Ps.90.5½ these tuo last sums I allways thought that Mr. Pollock had assumed as you never mentioned any thing to the contrary in any of your former Letters therefore had charged them to that Gentlemans acct. should this be the case Mr. Henderson is right in saying that I am still indue Mr. Pollock for instead of having the ballance drs.4.0¾ being due me there is due Mr. Pollock Ps.16.7¼ this provided he does not charge Interest on my Note since my furnishing him with my acct. should he charge Interest thereon I expect he will allow me the same—Doctor West says he knows nothing of Mons: Duforrest or the Ps.20 you mention, therefore will not have anything to do in the affair, for my own part I know nothing of it but should it be that it was any Money Paid on my acct. & I may have omitted the transaction please to explain yourself more fully in your next & be assured it shall be allowed you[.] my wife desires her Compliments to you . . .

To DAVID ROSS, *New Orleans*

Spanish Manchac, June 29, 1778

As I am much in want of some small articles to make out an assortment, as per annexed acct. if you can supply me with them shall be much obliged to you, if you should not have them all yourself shall be obliged to you to procure them for me, & inform me of the same per first opportunity & that I may send my Boat for them & Cash to pay for the same[.] my respects to your Brother George . . .

3 Reams writing paper   1 Hhd: Taffia   10 Keggs Brandy
2 Boxes or Barrells sugar   1 or 2 Barrells Coffee
4 Boxes Soap   6 Pieces blue stripe Ginghams   6 Pieces red Do.   2 Pieces Osnaburghs—

To JEAN JOSEPH DUFORREST, *New Orleans*

Spanish Manchac, June 29, 1778

Mr. Wm. Strother acquainted me that you was on the point of settling my small affairs with Mons: Vallier & that the only obstacle was that he could not pay it till the Insuing Crop—in that case if you will oblige me so far as to deliver him up the acct. and his tuo Notes, take his Note for them payable to the bearer in the Months of October or Novr. Insuing with Lawfull Interest and in so doing you will Oblige him who is with regard . . .

P.S. the account of your charges for Transacting said affairs let me Know & I will remit it you per the next conveyance. please to forward the Inclosed to Mr. O'Keefe & you ll oblige yours . . .

To THOMAS O'KEEFE, *New Orleans*

Spanish Manchac, July 5, 1778

I had the pleasure of writing to you the 29 ulto. to which refer—I have sent Mr. Jacquax to Toun to buy a few articles I am want of your informing him where to get the goods on the best terms will be acknowledged with the many favours conferred on [me] . . .

P.S. Please to forward the Inclosed—I believe Jacquax will get an order from Mr. Alexr. Henderson of the Homa Village on Oliver Pollock for d.68.0½R if he does he will give it to you which please to present to Mr. Oliver Pollock for payment[.] get my Note from him & pay him the ballance I owe him the remainder please to give to Jacquax—

To MESSRS. MORGAN AND MATHER, *New Orleans*

Spanish Manchac, July 22, 1778

Your esteemed favour of the 13 Inst. I duly recd. and am much obliged to you for your Kind offer relative to Mr. Haywards affairs in consequence of which I have inclosed to you his Bond, Note Receipts & Acct. Currt. by which it appears there is a ballance due me of Ps.3057.7¼ whatever you do in this affair will be agreeable to me as I am well convinced you will do what is in your power for my Interest—If Jacquex should call on you for the undermentiond goods please to let him have them, & for their Amt. shall send you the Cash as soon as I know how much it is—Inclosed is Thomas Bowkers draft on you favr. Thomas Wescoatt for 160 Drs. which please to apply to my Credit. . . .

2 Boxes Sugar   4 Boxes Soap   2 Hhds Taffia   2 ps. french or Engh. Cottonade   1 Barrell Coffee—

To JEAN JOSEPH DUFORREST, *New Orleans*

Manchac, August 3, 1778

Your esteemed favour of the 16 ulto. by Mons: Rose came to hand the 27th & according to your request have supplyd him with Sundries to amt. of ps.183.1—I am much obliged to you for the trouble you have given yourself with Mr. Valier & if you have not been able to get his Note or Bon for the Amount payable at the Crop—request you will give yourself no further Trouble but put all the Papers into a Lawyers hands of your own chusing that he may push the affair to the greatest Length as I am determined to put him to all the expence possible, since he has used me in such a manner & endeavours to put me of still longer after my having waited so long for my Money—

I have nothing further to add only to request of you if you have any thing this way in which I can serve you that you will favour me with your commands . . .

To ARTHUR STROTHER AND COMPANY, *Pensacola*

Manchac, August 3, 1778

The Inclosed Letters was left with me by your Mr. Wm. Strother on his way to N: Orleans he requested that I would remit you by the first opportunity the ballance of my acct. with you, but as it is dangerous to send Money have exchanged it for Captn. Wm. McIntosh Draft my favour at thirty days sight for Ps.497.3¾ on Humphry Grant Esqr. which request you will have accepted & advise me of the same per first Conveyance. . . .

To WILLIAM STROTHER, *New Orleans*

Manchac, August 3, 1778

According to your request I have forwarded your letters by the Express that left this for Pensacola & with it sent your Brother Captn. Wm. McIntosh first of Exchange my favour on Humphry Grant Esqr. for Ps.497.3¾ being the Ballance my acct. with you & Co. and for fear of any miscarriage have Inclosed you Second same tenor & date. your Book shall be forwarded by the first good conveyance. . . .

To HENRY STUART, *Pensacola* [?]

Manchac, August 3, 1778

Since your departure from N: Orleans I have not been favr. with a line from you allthough this is my third Letter I have thought it adviseable to forward your acct. with me by which you will see there is a Ballance due me of Ps.105.4 for which have valued my self on you in favour John Miller Esqr. if there is any thing this way in which I can be of any service to you request you'll favour me with your commands. . . .

To DAVID ROSS, *New Orleans*

Manchac, August 7, 1778

As you was so obliging as to offer to send for a few things that I want the undermentiond is a list of them   Vizt.—
2 puncheons Jamaica Rum put in Porter Casks   6 ps. Scotch Osnaburghs—30 ps. Irish Linen from 13d to 18 per yard   1 Gro: Common Knives & forks   1 Gro: Pewter Spoons   4 dozen Black silk Handf. from 38 to 44/   10 Pieces Black Ribban   5 ps. sorted Do.   4 ps. blue Strouds   6 doz: pair Mens shoes mostly Strong   2 doz: pair womens Callimanco Do.   10 ps. red Stripe Ginghams   10 Pieces blue Do.—25 lb. Hyson Tea   2 Pieces Broun holland   500 best black oyle flints   1 doz: Saddles Compleat—3 Reams good writing Paper   4 Pieces Cotton-

ade[.] if no good opportunity offers by the Lakes, please send them up the Mississippi & if you think requisite get 'em Insured & I will pay for the same...

To WILLIAM WEIR, *Pensacola*

Manchac, August 12, 1778

By this conveyance I thought to have sent you Bills to the amt. of three or four Hundred dollars for supplies furnished but when I applyed for them the officers told me they could not draw till the latter end of this Month[.] therefore you may rest assured that when I get them shall remit them to you per the first conveyance[.] in the Interim have Inclosed to you my draft on Richard Bradley for 66.5½ which you may depend will meet with due honour having advised him of the same per this conveyance, which when you have recd. please to Credit my acct. for the same. I hope ere this that you have disposed of the tuo Muslin Patterns of mine that you had on hands

The appearance of things is such at present that I have given over all thought of Trade[.] therefore am endeavouring to settle all my affairs as soon as possible in these parts being allmost assured there will be troublesome times this way ere long, for which should be happy if all the Gentlemen that I have had connections with was paid—I have paid the House of McGillivray & Struthers & out of the many thousand Dollars due from time to time to the House of Messrs. McGillivray Struthers & Co. it is reduced to 1300 dollars I have paid Mess: A: Strother & Co. &ca so that for the present look upon myself as allmost clear, though I have lost by Willings coming down upwards of Ps.14.000 you ll oblige me by sending the undermentioned articles Vizt.—

2 Reams good writing paper   1 box good red wafers   ½ lb. red sealing wax   1 red Morrocco pockett Book with a compleat set of Instruments & ass skin Leaves on rect. of the same shall pay you their amt....

To ADAM CHRYSTIE, *Pensacola*

Manchac, August 12, 1778

I had the pleasure of writing you the 8th last June (by the Express Mr. Smith) at which time drew on you in favour Mr. Miller for the ballance your acct.—being Ps.57.7½ since which I have not been favoured with any from you[.] Mr. Miller in his of the

9 ulto. acquaints me you had accepted my draft and that you wanted a Copy of your acct.—which I send you here Inclosed—in my former I requested that if you had done with my Books that you would send them to me per Mr. Smith, but it seems you have neglected said Letter or you would have found your acct.—I now request if you have done with the Books please to send them by the Bearer or the first good conveyance that shall offer & you'll oblige . . .

To RICHARD BRADLEY, *Pensacola*

Manchac, August 12, 1778

Hearing that you are not to return to the Mississippi and that you are taking your departure for England, I have taken the Liberty of Inclosing your acct. Currt. by which it appears there is a Ballance due me of Ps.66.5½, which am in hopes you'll find right[.] having paid the ballance due Mess. Arth: Strothers & Co. by a sett of Exchange that goes by this conveyance have valued myself on you in favour Mr. Wm. Weir—wishing you a pleasant Voyage & a happy sight of your Native Country, I am with regard . . .

P.S. when you arrive in England if you find Mr. John Bradley in the Land of the Living please to present my respects to him tell him that his old friend Mons. Duvall of Point Coupie is alive & well—

To MESSRS. MORGAN AND MATHER, *New Orleans*

Spanish Manchac, August 28, 1778

Your esteemed favour of the 11 Inst. I duly recd. by John Wall by which you acknowledge the rect. of the Money you advanced to Jaces for which I again return you my most hearty thanks—I have observed that as yet you have not been able to do any thing in Haywards affair therefore when you do request you will act in it as your own & whatever you do in said affair shall allways be approved of by me as if acted by myself—I have further to request of you if you can find out with whome Thomas Newman Left his affairs as he is in due me per his Bond about 800 dollars as you have allways [been] so obliging to me I have intruded on your good nature so far as to Inclose you Richard Bacons Note for Ps. 26.2 as the Interest on Do. is 1.6 which ought to have been paid last October and as he is with you if you ll receive the same & pass it to my Credit I shall be further obliged to you—Mr. Edward

Taylor is in due me Dr.51.1 informs me he can't pay me as he has no Money but waits for an answer from you before he will give an order on you for the same[.] to be plain with you I have no great opinion of Mr. Taylor therefore request you'll favour me with your answer if I get said order whether it will be acceptable to you or not. . . .

P.S. I have made enquiry about the Negroes can't hear any thing about them if they should come this way & I hear of it you may depend I shall do the needfull & inform you of the same—

To MONSIEUR DARCHUTTE, *St. Louis*

Spanish Manchac, September 1, 1778

The last time I had the Honor of seeing you here, you was so obliging as to offer me your service, if I had any commands in your parts from your obliging offer I gave you an order to receive Messrs. Dubriel & Papins joint Note from Mons: Depearness to whom I had delivered it some time before your arrival here to procure me the payment, but I have been informed that the Commander Mons. Libas has got said obligation into his hands,[37] by what manner cannott say as he had no orders from me on that subject and as you have not favoured me with a Line can't tell how to act in the affair (I have taken the Liberty once more from your wonted goodness so often experienced by me) to Inclose to your care the following papers Vizt. John Franks Note and his acct. Currt.—a small order on Mons: Du Volsey and Winston & Kennedy's Bond—this John Franks was heretofore a Hunter when I supplyed him with sundry Goods as you will see by his Acct. Currt. upwards of 4½ years agoe, and which Debt he has never endeavoured to discharge (though he has had it often in his power) therefore request as he is an Inhabitant of your Village that you will not spare him but put him to all the Expence your Country Law will allow of the Ballance due per his Note is for Money I paid one Jacob Winfire of the Natchez for the Negro Man he has now with him, so that if you are obliged to have his Negro seized on you may do it as my property as he has never discharged the same also make him pay the Interest, as I look on it as much my right as the Principal having been obliged to pay Money myself for the Negro & other things he had from said Jacob Winfire tuo Months after the Effects was delived to the Amount of 436 dolls. as per the acct.—I have wrote Mons: Valley a Letter on the subject in case you are obliged to carry him before his Tribunal for to recover the payment—Mons. Du Volsey's acct.

---

[37]/When Don Pedro José Piernas, lieutenant-governor of upper Louisiana, passed through Manchac on his way up the river, he made friends with Fitzpatrick, who entrusted him with a draft for 329 pesos and 6 reales on Dubrieul, a resident of St. Louis, so that Piernas might collect it for him. Within four days of leaving Manchac, Piernas sold the draft for the price of five kegs of rum and a barrel of gunpowder, then arranged a more profitable sale and tried to cancel the first one. In the argument that followed, Don Fernando de Leyba, commandant of St. Louis, learned of the affair and took possession of the draft, so that he might arrange for Fitzpatrick to be paid. See Fernando de Leyba to Gálvez, July 11, 1778, in Kinnaird (ed.), *Spain in the Mississippi Valley*, I, 295–96.

I am well assured he will discharge with pleasure—& as for Winstons & Kennedys Bond for Ps.898.7Rs I shall leave the whole management to yourself and whatever settlement you shall be able to make with them be assured it shall allways be approved of by me—I say nothing to you about Commissions for your trouble in said affairs[.] be you assured that shall be settled to our satisfaction at our first meeting or deduct it from the sums you may receive—you will please to observe that all these papers are payable in dollars and not in Skins; but as they are not the currency of your part of the Country you will be obliged to take skins in that case you will take them on such Conditions that I will not be a sufferer—for the price of your Country scraped skins is only 25 sols per lb. and Skins in the hair 40 sols this is for your Government in your own affairs but the bearer of the present can inform you much better as I have not been in Town since you left it—we have nothing new with us all things remain in the same situation as when you left this, therefore have nothing further to add...

P.S. you will please to observe to Mr. Winston that the order on Isaac Johnson of the Natchez he never would agree to pay excepting that Mr. Winston will accept of Messrs. Winstons & Kennedys order on him without which he never will agree to pay the amt. of his receipt—further I have Inclosed you the bill of Liberty of his Negro woman & her Children in which he acknowledges that at the time he gave them their Liberty he did it with no Intention to defraud his Creditors in the least this he attests on Oath, therefore request you will not deliver the bill of Liberty to him on any acct.—Excepting he discharges his acct. to the last sol—

To MONSIEUR VALLÉ[38]

Spanish Manchac, September 1, 1778

After a long silence of some years since I had the pleasure of writing you from N: Orleans the present is in the first place to assure you and Madam Valley of my most humble respects, secondly to acquaint you that Madam Villiar & your youngest Son honored me with their Company for a few minutes in their way to N: Orleans they both told me that you & Madam Valley still Enjoyed a very good state of health may the same blessing long continue is my most hearty wish.—Having been informed from a Number of Gentlemen of your part of the Country that you Occupy the place of chief Judge in all Civill affairs and as I have an affair

38/Probably Francisco Vallé, first Spanish commandant of Ste. Geneviève and the wealthiest man in Spanish Illinois. Vallé came from Canada to Kaskaskia, then moved to Ste. Geneviève when the eastern Illinois country was ceded to Britain. His only daughter married Louis DuBruil de Villars. Vallé died in 1783. See Houck (ed.), *The Spanish Regime in Missouri*, **I**, 54 n 4.

with an Inhabitant of your district named John Franks, heretofore an Hunter an account of which with his Note I have sent per this conveyance to Mons: Darchute not chusing to give you so much Trouble in affairs that was contracted under another Goverment or should have addressed myself to you. my only request is that if the said John Franks should offer to evade paying his just Debts & that Mons: Darchute should be under the disagreeable necessity of bringing him before your Tribunal of Justice that you will render me the Justice that the uprightness of my cause demands[.] therefore Sir I flatter myself you will not refuse me, & nothing further do I request of any Man—Having Nothing further to add only once more to return you & Madam Valley my most hearty thanks for the many favours recd. from your hands when in your Country . . .

the above Letters translated into french & sent per [blank]

To JOHN MILLER, Pensacola

Spanish Manchac, September 14, 1778
I have been favoured with your tuo Letters the first of the 15 May & the second of the 9 July the Contents of which have duly observed[.] I was sorry to find by your last that Governor Chester would not discharge my just demand without putting me to further trouble about my Money the one half of which I paid in Cash out of my pockett to the hands that helped up with the Provisions on the arrival of the Troops but since he has refused it I am determined it shall go with the Money due me for the hire of my House which they refuse to pay also[,] all which I have given up all hopes of receiving anything of Excepting there is a new Governour comes to your province—I am sorry that it was not in my power to discharge the remaining Ballance due on my Bond ere Mr. Swanson left this. I have done all in my power for the present[.] the remainder shall be paid ere long in the mean time request you will Insist on Mr. Smith discharging his Note in your hands when he is at your place for here I can't get any thing from him but promises[.] I have sent you Mr. Taylors & Rowleys acct. attested therefore they can have nothing further to alledge against paying them, Mr. Taylor I am apt to think has a great mind to humbug all those that he has ever had any dealings with this way if it was in his power therefore recommend him to your care for the amount of his acct.—having nothing further to add . . .

To WILLIAM WEIR, *Pensacola*

Spanish Manchac, September 16, 1778

I had the pleasure of writing you the 12th ulto. which hope you have recd. ere this in which I Inclosed you a small order on Richd: Bradley for Ps.66.5½ which am well assured will be honoured on demand[.] I now Inclose you according to my former promise the following Bills Vizt.—

Captn. Frans. Miller my favour at 60 days sight for . .	172.2
Lieut. Grahams Certificate payable by Govr. Chester .	226.1
	398.3
With my order on Mr. Bradley . . . for . . .	66.5 ½
makes	Ps.465.—½

which request you'll Indorse on my Note when they have met with the proper acceptance after which you will oblige me by sending the Note to some Gentleman of your acquaintance in these parts to receive the balance that may remain due thereon[.] my reasons for requesting this that I am on the point of finishing all my former connections in your parts, therefore should be glad to have the Note at hand to take it up when I have it in my power which I am well assured will not be long—

I am sorry to acquaint you that the military force sent here for the protection of the remaining Inhabitants heretofore English (but now obliged to turn Spaniards) is so different from what they had a right to have expected that very few have returned to their former possessions for in the first place the Gentleman that has the command in chief carries so high a hand over all those that has not his hat decorated with a Cockade that there is no such thing as living under his arbitrary Government without one has a mind to put up with the appellation of Villan, Rascall, & Rebel[.][39] for my own part I have great reason to Complain for in the first place when they came I delivered up my House the Long Store & all the out Houses &c that belonged to me for which I was to have recd. 12 Dolls. per Mo. that House that was formerly Banks 5 Drs. per Mo. and lastly I got up all their provisions from the forks on their arrival all which amounts to 365 Drs. and when I made a Demand of my payment I was answered that I might hold myself happy if ever I got the sixth part thereof—this Sir is the reason added to the arbitrary way of proceeding of the said Gentleman which has obliged me as well as many others to accept of that generous offer made us by his Excellency Don Galvez of taking protection under his Banner since unhaplly for us we cannott enjoy it under that, that was formerly so dear to us. I have nothing further to add only to assure you that although I have

39 / Captain William Barker arrived at Manchac with a force of one hundred men in May, 1778, with instructions to begin construction on a new fortification. Barker remained in command of the Manchac garrison until the arrival of Lieutenant Colonel Alexander Dickson early in March, 1779. See Starr, "Tories, Dons, and Rebels," 199; Haynes, *The Natchez District and the American Revolution*, 177.

taken a Determination of becoming a subject to another prince & Throwing up all further claim to my Houses & the Large Improvements I have made at a very great expense it will allways give me pleasure to render you all the service in my power therefore shall conclude . . .

P.S. Since my writing the above your favr. of 4 May came to hand have not time to Answer it now as Mr. Swanson is Just going of but will write to you per first opportunity—

Part Four
1779–1790

To ROBERT MONTGOMERY, *Pensacola*

Manchac, February 17, 1779

By Captain Smiths being hurried away in so Precipitate a manner and the necessity [?] that I am in myself in getting my Effects Transported over to the English side, has realy prevented me from being able to make out a proper Memorandum of Such things as will be Sealable at this place, but as I am in hopes that these Throubles will be Soon over and that I shall have liesure time by the Next Conveyance shall write you more fully releative to the Conversation we had when in pensacola, In the Intrim I having Given Captain Smith a note of some small things which are realy in demand and Request that they may be forwared by the first Conveyance &c—

Your Negroe boy Seems well pleased with this part of the province and Talk no more of about his being a Free Man, had he not been Indowed with the Faculty of speaking so many Languages I should have been able to have Sold him for the Sum of 300 drs. But I am in hopes Ere long to get that sum for him, Till such time as an Appertunity offers I shall keep him Employed in the Kings Works with my Own having nothing more to add . . .

The above is a Coppy of my Former letter

Dr. Sir

Since my Writing the above Captain Smith has returned with the Troops to this place, the hurry still Continues, we poor Inhabitants of this place are Kept out of our houses what is still worse we have not as yet Received one dollar for them to Innable us to rebuild; As for my own part I am Determined to go to no further Expence in the Buildg. way till such times I know whether the Main Fort is to be here or at Baton Rouge, this is fifteen Miles up the River—The Memorandum I gave Mr. Smith, are plenty of goods [*illegible*] once, which can be Renewed if found wanted— I have a very great Talk here Among us [?] that the Americans will be down this Spring if so God only knows,[1] for God Sake do

---

1/ About the middle of July, 1778, the commander of the Spanish fort on the Arkansas reported to Governor Gálvez that a boat manned by twenty-five Americans was descending the Mississippi with supplies for Willing's force. When the Americans learned of the presence of British forces on the lower Mississippi they returned to Fort Pitt, but Gálvez immediately spread a rumor that a force of two thousand Americans was about to descend the river to take all British forts in West Florida. In order to insure the wide circulation of this tale and encourage fear among the British, Gálvez communicated it to the commanders of all Spanish posts in lower Louisiana. See Kathryn T. Abbey, "Spanish Projects for the Reoccupation of the Floridas During the American Revolution," *Hispanic American Historical Review*, IX (1929), 273.

not fail if possible to send the hinges and Stock Locks, on their Arrival the[y] are all Sold, and that for Ready Cash, to the Spanish Commandant at Galvez Town the Amount shall be Remitted back in the same Vessell That Brings them. . . .

P.S. your Boy Jack is to work for the King and Shall keep him in that Employ till find a good Opportunity to dispose of him to advantage.
11th March 1779

To JOHN MILLER, *Pensacola*

Manchac, March 11, 1779

You have here Inclosed the Memorandum you requested I would send you for the Sundrie Goods that I shall want, for the Insuing year; and as things no[w] appears I am in hopes they will Come to a good Market, Especially shoud the Troops Remain in our Neighbourhood and that Tranquility Rains on the River,—But shoud this not be the Case I shall take proper Care to give you timily Notice so that your Gentlemen and Self shall run no Risque—I request you will Acquaint Messrs. Clark & Milligan; or any Other Gentlemen with Whome you Correspond in London; that are the Shippers, that they are as particular as possible in the Choise and Quality of the Articles for on this depends in a great Measure the Quick sale of the Cargo; and which will Inable me the Sooner to make you the proper Remittance, I also must beg that you will have the Mem. Compleated, Allthough it may amount to a few hundred pounds more than my former order did, I am the more anchious to have it full filled as there is, and in all appearce. will be much greater demand for Goods than there has been Sinc I have been up the Mississippi and without a Compleat asortment (though a small one) it will be not worth my while doing any thing in that way—

I have been very Spearing as to the Indian Goods Being fully Determined never more to dow anything with them or hunters—I further Request that all may be Insured to this place; as there is almost as many Dangers on the Coast between here and pensacola as there is from England to your place (the Enemy only Excepted) lastly that you order that all that will admit of it may be packed in Flat Trunks; about 3 foot 4 Inches &cc having nothing further to Say for the present only request you will favour me with your Answer, that I may know what I have to depend on. . . .

To JAMES FAIRLIE

Manchac, March 11, 1779

As you ware so obliging as to offer to Send me from time to time the few goods I may want (after the Arrival of your Ship) I have thought it advisable to give you the following Memorandum which Request you will Ship per the first Conveyance that shall offer after your Arrival in pensacola—
Vizs:

    10 pieces ¾ Linen Check
    4 pieces of yard wid[e] Cotton ditto
    4 pieces of German Oznabourghs
    10 pieces of Linin the first cost not to Exceed 15 or 18 d per yard
    1 piece of Course Cambrick
    12 dozen of Table Knives and forks
    12 ditto of pewter Spoons
    2 ditto of Good pen knives
    2 ditto of Black Silk hankerchiefs
    1 piece of Red Silk Pollock Romalls
    2 pieces of 9/8 Cotton Strip ⎱ the Strips to be light Blue
    2 ditto of 5/4 Ditto— ⎰
    12 ditto of Nankeen with Trimmens for the Same
    2 dozen of pair Mens Strong Shoes
    2 dozen pair of Womens black Ever lasting
    2 dozen papers of pins
    1 dozen of Good fine Castor Hatts
    50 pair of Hooks & Hinges: 50 p. Hs. and 100 Stock locks
        the hooks & hinges 15 Inches & the Hs. Eight Inches

This Sir Are the things I shall want for the present, and Request you will send them as Soon as possible, as for the Remittance the[y] shall be made as follows, in Cash, Bills or the Country produce once as least Every three Months from the time the Goods Arrives at the forks of the Amitt[.] You will I Expect be as favourable as possibble with me on the advance on the Goods —Having nothing further to add only to wish you a pleasant passage ...

To WILLIAM STROTHER, *New Orleans*

Manchac, March 12, 1779

As You have always been so obliging; to me on all Occasions, I have taken the Liberty to Inclose You the following Notes of Hand belonging to the following Gentleman lately from the Illinois, and are now in Orleans they Called on me in there way down & requested that I would send them to some one in Town to receive there Amount—Viz—

Monsieur Darchutes Note for	Ps.190.5
Do ... Receipt for Messrs. Dubriel & Papin do	329.—
which Money is in Monsr. Connons Hands—	
Messrs. Reneaux & Rasi Note for	67.6
Mr. Charle Charleville's Note for	93.2
Which Money is in Mr. Faugeaux hands	
Monsr. La Chances Note for	108.5
	Ps.780.2

Which Sums if you Receive You will oblige me by Keeping them in your hands till such Times You hear further from me, having nothing further to add...

To JOHN MILLER, *Pensacola*

Manchac, March 25, 1779

I did myself the Pleasure of writing You the 11th Instant in which I inclosed You my memorandum for Sundry Goods I shall want for the ensuing Year. Since my return from your Place; I have not had it in my Power to Pay Mr. Swanson more than I have done, on account of Messrs. McGillivray, Struthers & Co. an Account of which You have here inclosed[.] On Mr. Taylors Return to this Place I requested he wou'd Pay me the Amt. of his Account he told me he had Settled it with You according to my Order if so very well if not Let me hear per the Next, I am in hopes Mr. McPherson did not leave your Place without Paying the Ballance of his Acct. with me Ps.49.6½ according to his Promise to me in your House

I now inclose You according to Request Captn. Alexander McIntosh for Ps.150 and Earl Douglass Note for Ps.187.6½ with 5 Months Interest on the same is 6/2 & is in all Ps.344.0½ which Captn. McIntosh promised me he wou'd Settle when at Pensacola, provided he cou'd Settle his Affairs there, and as I am no ways of that as they all Lay with Colo. McGillivray it will be the same to him, to keep so much in his hands on my Acct.—this added to the former Sum will make Ps.607.2. this with former Sums You may have received for me at your Place You will add together and indorse on my Bond although I left Mr. Swanson an Order on Mr. Ward for the Balle. of his Acct. Ps.298 odd Bills[.] When I left this for your Place [*illegible*] have never been able to get one Dollar as yet from him[.] he always says he will pay but God knows when[.] Nothing further to Add...

To WILLIAM STROTHER, *New Orleans*

Manchac, March 25, 1779

I did myself the Pleasure of writing You the 20th instant by Mr. Tounoir and inclosed You Mr. Maxents Bon for 210 Dollars which hope You have received e'er this[.] In my former I made a Mistake in Regard to Mr. Weir Account for I only mention'd 541 Drs. and it is 644 Drs. for which I have given him an Order on You which You will oblige me in Paying out of the Moneys You may have received for me, then Pay Yourself & Pay the Remainder to Mr. Thomas Booker in so doing You will much oblige . . .

To WILLIAM STROTHER, *New Orleans*

Manchac, March 28, 1779

I had the Pleasure of writing You the 20 & 25th Instant the last per Mr. Tounoir & the other per Mr. William Weir; in the former Inclosed You Monsieur Moxants Bon for 210 Dollars. Both which I hope You have received e'er this[.] Since my last I am favoured with Yours of the 23d by Mess. Watkins & Rapalji when arrived here last Night, I am really Sorry to find by yours that Monsur Dachute is disappointed in his Expectation as to his Bills but he ought to remember at the same time, that when I delivered him my Effects, I never expected, but I shou'd have been paid according to agreement as he was always accustomed to do with me; as to his Receipt for Debrieul & Papins Note it is Nothing more than to get the Note from him according [to] Monsr. Maisons Request I have inclosed You his Acct. Current, as for what he says about Ps.160 for Negroes sold him I know Nothing of it as I never sold him a Negro in my Life this is a Ballance due me of Ps.64.6¾ as per Acct. Currt. which I am in hopes he will find right[.] I have given an Order at the Foot of it in Your Favour if [re]cover will always be so much But I am afraid this will meet with the same Reception as the Notes But we must always hope for the best. . . .

NB. This not Sent—

To WILLIAM STROTHER, *New Orleans*

Manchac, March 28, 1779

I had the Pleasure of writing You the 20th & 25th instant the first per Monsr. Tounoir & the other by William Weir in the former inclosed Monsr. Moxants Bon for Ps.210—Both which I hope

Merchant of Manchac

You have received e'er this. Since which I am favoured with Your's of 23d by Messrs. Watkins & Rapaleji which came to hand last Night the Contents of which was alarming to me[.] I am really sorry to find that Monsr. Darchute is disappointed in his Expectation but he ought at the same time to Remember that when I deliver'd him my Effects I never expected but I should have been paid according to agreement as he was always accosstomed to do with me & one which I much depended on as to his Receipt for Debruiel & Papins Note is Nothing more than to get the Note from him and when You have apply to Monsr. Cannon for the Money, who has it in his Hands since the 12th Octr. last per his Letter of that date here inclosed[.] As for Messrs. Le Chance & Plasé I really might have expected they wou'd have taken up their Notes as they took down Flower with them which from the Present want of that Article in To[wn] must Suppose they have sold it well, Be You Assured I wou'd be Sorry to press them But I am really pressed, myself on all Sides and from what I told them here when a going down might I think induce them to stretch a Point in regard of me, the more so, as I made them acquainted with my Intentions and for what Reason I was under the necessity of so doing they then Promised they would do all in their Power for me But they have not been so good as their word (French Man like) as for myself meeting with such Disappointments, it's nothing being this long Time accustomed to Nothing else from all quarters insomuch that they are partly become customary to me. But the Gentlemen to whom I am in due there Patience will be worn out, & what the Consequence will be is unknown, but certainly they cannot be the most agreeable ones to me, as there is nothing gives me more uneasiness than to think Mr. Weir's meeting with a Disappointment as he is going out of the Province, therefore if You have received Ps.210 from Mr. Moxant give them to him, in part for if he was paid I shou'd be really happy But I still flatter myself that the Illinois Gentlemen, that are in due me, will pay some part of there obligations, if they cant discharge the whole e'er they leave Orleans which will enable me to pay Mr. Weir, But shou'd this Glair of Hope be frustrated I Request [you] acquaint Mr. Weir I am really Sorry for his Disappointment, that it is not my fault and that for whatever Ballance that may remain due on the Draft, Let him leave it with any one he shall please, and he may be Assured I will Discharge it e'er Long. According to Mr. Maisons Request I have sent You his Acct. Currt. with me, By which it appears he is indue me Ps.64.6¾ and which I am in hopes he will find right, which Ballc. if You receive will always be so much, But at the Time I am giving the Order the Ballance may be paid to You I am afraid it will meet with the same Reception as the Notes have met with But we must always hope for the best as for what Mr. Mason says about Ps.60 for Negro or Negroes, I know nothing of it as I never sold him a Negro in my Life. . . .

To WILLIAM SWANSON, *New Orleans*

Manchac, March 28, 1779

Since Your Departure from this I have received a Letter from Mr. William Strother, informing me that the French Men from the Illinois, has not paid him one Dollar on my Acct. as they have been disappointed in the Payment of the Bills they brought down this is really hard on me the more so as Mr. Weir will meet with a Disappointment and it is what I never had the least Suspition of Till I Recieved the above Letter, if You can be of any Service to Mr. Strother in Recovering any Part (if your own Business will Permit of it) I shall be much obliged [to] You for the Trouble. I have inclosed You Mr. McCormacks Receipt for 540 Carrots of Tobacco; and have left the Letters open for Mr. Miller for your perusal. You will [be] so obliging when at Pensacola to acquaint Mr. Pinhorn it is not that I have not forgot him about the Tobacco but as it is for himself I would not send him the Point Coupee; being allways very bad. I am in dayly expectation of some from the Natchitoches when it comes shall send him the amt. of his acct. say Ps.67.4 worth of it this he may depend on. You can tell him what You have seen Your Self and how much I had Damaged of that I had here, this with my good Wishes for your Voyage and same Return is the Needfull . . .

To JOHN MILLER, *Pensacola*

Manchac, May 9, 1779

I had the Pleasure of writing You the 11th of Last March; Since which I have not been favoured with any of Yours, I have been informed by Messrs. Ross & Campble that all the Expences that Government has been at on the Mississippi are to be paid without further Delay if so I am in Hopes my Houses will be paid for when at your Place I gave into the Governor a Petition requesting he wou'd appoint Two Gentlemen of this Place to have a Survey on my Houses and Improvements with an Acct. of what they cost me which Petition and Accts. was delivered into the General and when I had the Honour of waiting on him he told me that when he come to Manthac I shou'd be paid to the last Farthing, Since which I have heard nothing further about it; I have often Spoke to Colo. Dickson, to Know if he had any Orders Relative thereunto, but he always tells me he has not, Now as the Improvements are daily going to Destruction and no Survey has been Ordered I am much afraid they have determined [?] to deprive me of my Property without paying me for them, for which reason I have inclosed I have inclosed [sic] You a Copy of the Amount of what they cost me this taken from my Books[.] I request You will get Mr. Morrison or some other Person to make me out another Petition to Present the General in my Name that he will Order a Survey thereon that I may be paid for the same according to his Promise to me and which I am in hopes he will fullfill when he is put in mind of it again. I have further to Request You that You send me the following Small Articles for my own use Viz—

    1 Ps. of Oznabrigs
    2 Ps. common blue Romalls
    1 Ps. blue Strouds
    25 lb. Gun Powder
    100 lb. Small Shot No. 5 or 4
    4 or 5 Setts of Desk furniture for Mr. Carpenter

For the Amount I will Remit You a Bill By the return of the Vessel that brings them that is a Bill of the board of Ordinance, You will Please mention in your next if You have sent Home my Memorandum or not[.] We have nothing New with us all things remain as heretofore, therefore have Nothing further to add . . .

To JAMES FAIRLIE, *Pensacola*

Manchac, May 9, 1779

Your Favour of 18th ultimo I have duly received it is now before me The Contents of which have duly observed, I am Sorry to find that your Ship is not yet arrived but am in hopes eer this comes to hand she will be if so expect You will send me the Articles mentioned in the Memorandum I gave You if not Request You will acquaint me per next Conveyance. We have Nothing New with us from Illinois as yet We have not been able to Learn any thing from Major Hamilton that was at Port St. Vincent. Clark has left the Illinois where he is gone is to us unknown. Having Nothing further to Add . . .

N.B. if You can't send all the Hinges & Locks mentioned let that be no hindrance of your sending the other Articles—

To ROBERT MONTGOMERY, *Pensacola*

Manchac, May 9, 1779

Your much Esteemed favour of 19th Ultimo is now before me the Contents of which have duly observed I am Sorry to hear of the Disappointment You have met with in your having your Vessel taken, But am in hopes You will not be a Sufferer (which certainly must be the Case if not properly insured) But this are Disadvantage's that all Gentlemen in Trade labour under in these Troublesom Times. I observe well what You mention in Regard to your Negro Jack. Be Assured I have done all in my Power to Dispose of him e'er Captn. Smith's Arivel But am Sorry to acquaint You it was not in my Power to do unless I had given him on Credit which I would not without your Positive Order for so doing Since I could not do otherwise I have kept him to work and he has now coming to You for his Work 25/4rs which will be paid eer Long and for which I shall be accountable on Demand when I get the Vouchers for the Work done by him and my Negroes, further if You will accept of 250 Dollars for him payable in Six Months from the Date of this I will take him for my Account if not agreable to to [sic] You shall send him back with the Amount of what he shall have earned by the Return of Captn. Smith[.]

I am Sorry to acquaint You that of the 18,00 Carrots of Tobacco I had on hands when at your Place I have Lost 12,00 By the overflowing of the Mississippi in one Night's Time that added to the Total Loss of all my Cattle will amount to upwards of 900 Dollars but is to be hoped I shall be more Lucky another Time according to your Request I have sent You Doctor Thomas's Draft in my favour on David Holmes for Ps.100 which I am in hopes will meet with due Honour when due[.] If I have not been of further Service to our Friend Captn. Smith in Settling his Affairs with Mr. French, Be Assured it was not in my Power as it has been an impossibility of getting out of his Hands a proper Acct. Sales till such Times as that is Effected there is no such thing as to bring him to a Settlement[.] hereafter if I can be of any Service to You or any of your Friends in this Place must Request You will favour me with your Commands having nothing further to add...

To WILLIAM WEIR, *Pensacola*

Manchac, May 9, 1779

I am favour'd with both Yours of the 9th & 13 ultimo from New Orleans and am really Sorry to hear of the Disappointment You met with it is well known to your Self that it was not owing to any Neglect in me for I had nothing more at Heart than that You shou'd be paid e'er You Left the Province, You Request I would Remit You the Ballc. to Pensacola as soon as possible[.] Be You Assured it shall be done but for the Present it is really out of my Power occasioned from the many Disappointments I have met with of Late in recovering Moneys that have been a long time due me, but this I can Assure You that I shall have coming to me e'er Long 260 Dollars from the Board of Ordinance for Sundries supplied them and for which I shall get a good Bill to Send by the next conveyance, which when I get shall Remit to your Friend Mr. Amoss to receive for You in Case of your having left the Province and if Possible I shall at the Same Time Remit the Balle. with it if in my Power & will with Pleasure Pay You such Interest as shall be required till fully discharged[.] Having Nothing further to add . . .

To CAPTAIN JOHN DAVIS, *New Orleans*

Manchac, May 16, 1779

Your much Esteemed favour of the first Instant I Received Last Night, from Mr. David Ross the Contents of which have duly observed[.] I am Sorry to hear that the Negroes Back was in such a way on your Account But be Assured he deserved all he got if not more. I accept of your Offer though much under the Fellows Value, for be you assu'd if it had not been for his Late Action I would not have taken Ps.500 for him therefore send me your Obligation for 325 Dollars with Lawfull Interest as you propose in your Letter it being the Price he cost me, and this shall be your Voucher for the Same, the first Time I have the Pleasure of seeing You I will give You a proper Bill of Sale, Having Nothing further to Add only to Wish more Contentment with the Negro than I have had with Him . . .

To JOHN MILLER, *Pensacola*

Manchac, May 25, 1779

I had the Pleasure of writing You the 9th Instant which hope You have received e'er this, Since which Mr. Thomas James has been here with one from whom I had Reason to have Expected the Amount of his Account in Cash, but on his Return from New Orleans to my great Disappointment, he had Nothing to give me but the inclosed Bills amounting to Ps.112.6¼ which he requested I wou'd send to You for to Receive their Amounts; which if You do You will please to Place to my Credit with You in Account for the Trifles I Demanded in my Last, if the least Difficulty shou'd arise about the Payment Request You will remit them to me per first Conveyance that I may acquaint him of the Same & that he may find out some other Method to Settle his Accts. Mr. Lyman of the Natchez sent me Word some time ago that he had payed or Left in your Hands about 52 Dollars that he is indue me this three Years, if so Request You will let me hear[.] By the Last Accounts that we have from the Illinois & Point Couppee, Mentions that there is 1500 Americans coming Down e'er Long, if so although the great Expence Government has been at already that is if they Pay the Bills for Work done I Assure You we are really in a very poor State of Defence, should this be the Case I am much afraid we shall be obliged to seek Protection a Second Time from Don Galvaiz, But all our Gentlemen, seems to Imagin it is only french News (if so God be thanked) for if obliged to push again we may all take up Budgets and go aBegging, having Nothing further to Add only to Assure You—I am always &c—

Dr. Sir—Since my writing what I have mentioned above Captn. Halley has arrived here from New Orleans, and has brought with him a Paragraph taken from a Letter of Daniel Murrays at the Illinois to his Brother William, the Date of the Letter is 29 April in which full mention is made of Major Hamilton, and his small party of 75 Men of the hard Defence they made for 18 Hours against Colo. Clark and the 750 Men under his Command, but was obliged to Surrender after the Small fort of Post St. Vincent was almost battered down about his Earrs, so that brave Hamilton, and what of his Men that remained alive is e'er now all Prisoners, with Colo. Clark whom they Say uses them in a most humane Manner Possible it is further Reported that Colo. Clark will Continue up the River Waubash with an Intent to Join a Large Party that are going from Fort Pitt to Detroit, to Lay Siege to that Place and if Possible to Cut off all Communication with Canada & the Upper Countries &c it is further mentioned in the Paragraph, that a Party from Fort Pitt has Cut off and destroyed the greatest Part of the Mingoes—those are of the Six Nations that belongs to Johnson's Department & that Lived about 200 Miles from Fort Pitt, if all this is true I am much afraid we shall have them a Second Time among us[2]—I have Nothing further to Add . . .

To LIEUTENANT J. J. GRAHAM, *Pensacola*

Manchac, May 25, 1779

I am favoured with Both your Letters of this Month, the Contents of which have duly observed. I am really Glad the Money

2/George Rogers Clark and his troops were active in the Ohio Valley in the late 1770s. He failed to reach Detroit, but in 1778 his forces occupied the French towns in the Illinois country and captured a British force under Lieutenant Governor Henry Hamilton early in 1779, after a desperate march to Vincennes. See John Richard Alden, *The American Revolution, 1775–1783* (New York, 1962), 211–12.

You received for my Negroes work was any way Serviceable to You, I only wish it had been something more for your Sake, there I have charged You with drs. 58.1r. I have not as Yet Signed the Paylist, as Mr. Gower told me that there was Something omitted in the forms & that other Copys must be made out when they come to hand shall Sign them with Pleasure. I observe what You say in Regard of John Skinner's Account with me, and my coming down to your Place to endeavour to Settle that Matter, for the Present it is quite out of my Power to go down being Daily employed with a Young Man, that is now here with me in bringing up my Books, that are many Months back; and till Such Times they are finally finished it will not be Possible for me to Leave this, thought at the Same Time I have send You here inclosed a Copy of his Account, properly attested, by which You will see that the Ballc. then due me was Ps.239.2¾ since I have paid for him 9/4 so that the Ballance is Ps.248.6¾ so that if You can be of any Service to me in recovering any part thereof I shall be much obliged and which You will please to keep in your hands, if nothing else is paid me for the Work Done by him I am in hopes Government can't be against Paying me for the Tools, Iron Steel Grinstone & the Cash I advanced him to Pay the Hands that brought the Effects to Manchac when at Point Couppee he gave me from under his hand before Monsr. Grand Prée[3] that the Tools, Iron & Steel &c, was my Property and not his—as he acknowledges he had not payed for them, I have inclosed to You a small acct. of Ps.19.6½ against William Queys now in Your Employ which Request You will receive from him and place to my Credit with You[.] The Acct. Current, that Skinner gave me against You Last fall by which it appeared there was a small Ballance due him if right at that Time I omitted another Small Acct. for Ps.4, which I now inclose, should there not be Sufficient to authorize You to see me paid, I Request You will send me back all the Accounts. Having Nothing further to add . . .

To CALEB KING, *Natchez*

Manchac, May 25, 1779

Yours of the 2d Ultimo came to hand the 12th of last Month am very Sorry to hear by your Letter that You have not recieved your Money from Captn. Jackson but at same Time can't help informing You that when I Deliver'd You my Goods You told me You had the Money at Home & that You would remit it to me per the first Conveyance after Your Arrival at the Natchez. This with many other Disappointments of the like Nature are great Moths

3/Don Carlos de Grand Pré, Spanish commandant at Pointe Coupée.

to me as daily I meet with such from the Inhabitants of your Settlement[.] Was it not that I have Money to Pay myself I should be quite easy but in my present Situation I must earnestly request that You may immediately Pay Mr. Stephen Shakespear[4] the Amt. of your Note otherwise think noways hard if Mr. Shakespear shou'd take such Steps as I have authorized him to do. Which must, tho' Necessity requires but in force such disagreable Methods of recovering my outstanding debts, but hope You will with Chearfulness prevent in doing of which You will much oblige...

To ANTHONY HUTCHINS, *Natchez*

Manchac, May 25, 1779

My Friend Mr. Shakespear is going to your Parts to Settle some Business he has their, he has been so obliging as to offer me his Service which accepted with with [*sic*] Pleasure, therefore have taken the Liberty of drawing on You for the Ballance of your Small Account with me Say Ps.70 had it been otherwise with me than it really is I should have waited with Pleasure till convenient for Your Self but really I am much Necessated being hard pushed by the Gentlemen I am in due therefore flatter myself my Draft will meet with due Honour. I formerly remitted You an attested Acct. against the Estate of Jesse Lum which You were pleased to tell me had never been paid if not yet paid you Request You will Deliver it to Mr. Shakespear that he may Recover its Amount from the Administrator[.] having Nothing further to Add...

P.S. My Best Respects to Mrs. Hutchins & Children NB We have Nothing New with us that can be depended on

To JOHN FALCONER, *Pensacola*

Manchac, May 29, 1779

By the Cato Captn. Benjamin Watson You will receive Six Boxes of Candles, Marked IF which were to have gone by the Packet Captn. Smith, but it was impossible to get them down to the Amitt before her Departure as the Captn. of the Schooner has not been here, I have not been able to get a proper Receipt for their being Shipped but as no Price is agreed upon, You will pay the Customary freight and Charge the Same to Account of Mr. Richard Carpenter & oblige...

4/Manchac merchant and planter.

324 Merchant of Manchac

To JOHN McGILLIVRAY, *Pensacola*

Manchac, [May] 29, [1779]

The last Time I had the Pleasure of seeing You at Pensacola I made You acquainted with my having given in to the Governour a Petition requesting that he would Order a proper Survey on my buildings at Same Time gave him in an Account of what they Cost me in Expectation that he would have order'd said Survey, and that Since they were retained for the Good of the Service I might have received what they should be esteemed to be worth, which could not be less than what they cost me, He told me as the General[5] was then arrived he could do Nothing in the Affair himself but should lay it before the General the first Time he saw him—which he did for when I had the Honour of seeing the General he was pleased to Shew me the Petition & Account and was so good as to Prommse me I should be paid as soon as he came to Manchac, and that he would have them valued such a Promise gave me Hopes that my Grievances would soon have met with a Redress equitable to the Justness of my Demands—And as his Honour has been prevented from coming this Way, owing to the disagreable Situation we have all been in this Three Months Passed, there has Nothing been done in the Survey[.] I have often mentioned the Affair to Colo. Dickson[6] whom has as often told me had not received any Orders relative thereunto, so that till such Times He the Commanding Officer receives said Orders I need not expect the least Redress tho' at the same Time the Buildings are Daily going to Destruction[.] His Honour, omitting having sent said Order I am apt to imagine has slipped his Memory owing to the Multiplicity of Business of more Consequence than my small Request, though at the Same Time the Amount of which I have a right to expect for my Improvements &c, Deprives me for the Present of the Satisfaction I Promised my Self I should have enjoyed, as it would in the first Place have enabled me to Discharge with Honour allmost all my Remaining Debts and secondly it would have Left me at Liberty to have kept together my Negroes which will be not long the Case if not Redress in a short Time, this I Mention to You for your Government in the Affair and from your wanted Goodness which I have Experienced on so many Occasions heretofore gives me Reason to hope that if their is any thing in your Power, in which You can serve me in the Affair You will do it, in a Letter I wrote Your Mr. Miller the 9th Instant I requested he would get Mr. Morrison or some other Gentleman to make out a Petition in my Name and Lay it before his Honour, Should this not have been done e'er this Comes to

---

5/Brigadier General John Campbell arrived in West Florida in 1779 with military reinforcements for the province. He coordinated the defense of the colony until he surrendered it to Gálvez in 1781.

6/Lieutenant Colonel Alexander Dickson, British commander at Manchac and director of British defenses on the lower Mississippi.

Hand I am in hopes You will second Mr. Millers endeavours in seeing me wrighted, Having Nothing further to Add . . .
   P.S. Mrs. Fitzpatrick Joins with her best Respects—

To DON FRANCISCO COLLELL, *Gálveztown*[7]

Manchac, June 9, 1779

From an Advertisement now up at Mr. Hickeys I learn that all the Creditors of Thomas Wescoatt lately deceased at your Port are requisted to send in their Respective accounts properly attested, I being one amongst the Number I have taken the Liberty of inclosing mine to You by which You will see his Estate is indue me Ps.58.3 and that You may be a better Judge in the Affair, I have sent You a Copy of it in french, further the Deceased Mr. Wescoatt, was Administrator to the Estate of the Deceased William & Elizabeth Cantey who were indue Thomas Bentley as per his Acct. a Ballance of Ps.44.7½ this Sum the Deceased Wescoatt was to have paid Mr. Swanson attorney for said Bentley last fall by Order of Messrs. Delavillbouver & Dedisnee, but never did it, therefore if there is wherewith I am in hopes from your just Manner of Proceedings amongst You on such occasions that Mr. Bentley will receive the Ballance of his Account so long due, either from Estate of the Administrator or from the Estate of the Deceased William & Elizabeth Cantey, I further think it adviseable to make You acquainted that a Part of the Negroes which the Deceased Wescoatt took with him over to your Port, were mortgaged to Mr. John Miller of Pensacola, that is when Mr. Miller sold him the Negroes he wou'd not Let them go on any other Conditions than this, He let him have the Negroes at Nine or Twelve Months Credit which of the Two I am not really sure of, but one of the Two was their Agreement, and if then paid Mr. Miller was to have given up the Mortgage, otherwise it was to remain in full Force (which has been the Case, as the Negroes have not been paid for) when his Excellency Don Galvaiz, was here last Fall, Mr. Swanson (Attorney for Mr. Miller) applyed to his Excellency for Justice requesting that his Excellency wou'd give an Order that the Deceas'd Wescoatt shou'd either deliver up the sd. Negroes or Pay for them[.] His Excellency according to his wonted good Nature, did not want that any of the Inhabitants of his New Town should be distressed, the more so as they gave him their Words, if let alone for five or Six Months at a Number of Publick Works were carrying on at your Place, undertaking a Part of which wou'd enable them to discharge with

7/Spanish commandant at Gálveztown. Born in Catalonia about 1740, Collell had served in the Louisiana regiment since 1762. The village of Gálveztown was established about 1778 on the right bank of the Amite River immediately below the confluence of the Iberville River, mainly to guard that part of the "Island of Orleans" against British encroachments. Sponsored by Governor Gálvez, the settlement was founded and named by British refugees who fled West Florida following the depredations of Willing's raiders. Colonists from the Canary Islands were sent there to bolster the population, which comprised about two or three dozen English families and about three dozen Spanish families. As the unrest of the American Revolution spread, other families came to Gálveztown until the population reached about four hundred people in 1779. The town lost its strategic importance after the Spanish occupied the British posts along the Mississippi River and eventually disappeared. For a detailed history of the settlement, see V. M. Scramuzza, "Gálveztown, a Spanish Settlement of Colonial Louisiana," *Louisiana Historical Quarterly*, XIII (1930), 553–609. Archivo General de Simancas, sección de Guerra Moderna, Legajo 7291, Cuaderno I. Regimento de Infanterio fixo de la Luysiana, December, 1787, p. 4.

Honour what Money they were due on this Side on these Conditions & no other His Excellency prevailed with Mr. Swanson to allow them said Term of Time which he did His Excellency promising Mr. Swanson that if not paid in that Time he would see him paid. Now as Mr. Swanson is not here himself I have thought it adviseable to make you acquainted with forementioned Circumstances for your Government[.] If Opportunity shou'd soon offer You will Please favour me with your Answer in Order that I may be able to embrace the earliest Opportunity of informing Messrs. Miller & Swanson what they may expect relative to said Debt. Having Nothing further to Add . . .

To JAMES FAIRLIE, *Pensacola*

Manchac, June 15, 1779

I am favoured with Yours of 20th Ultimo which came to hand the 8th Instant the Contents of which have duly observed. I am really Glad to hear of your having received certain Accounts of Your Ships Safe Arrival at Jaimaca, therefor Suppose her now at your Place[.] Should this be the Case Request You will embrace the first Opportunity bound to the Amitt to Ship the Sundries mentioned in the Small Order for should they come when the Waters are Low the Expences that I shall be at to get them up will greatly Augment their Prices[.] I shall be much obliged to You if in Stead of 10 Ps. Irish Linen mentioned in the Order, You will Send me 3 or 4 Rheams of Paper 1000 fish Hooks 4 or 6 doz. of fishing Lines sorted & another Ps. of Cambrick a Box or Cask of short Pipes, 1 Kett of Salmon & one half Ferkin of Butter if You have any out in half Firkins if not a whole one, my Reason for requesting the Change is that Messrs. Rosses have brought here a Quantity of Linens which I have in the House to Dispose of for their Accounts, & as I would want Nothing but things that will meet with Quick Sales so as to enable me to make You the Remittance as heretofore agreed on Having Nothing further to Add . . .

To CAPTAIN JAMES CRAIG

Manchac, June 16, 1779

Yours of the 15th Instant with the Receipt for the Ps.48.2 I have now before me, You may rest Assured that when the remaining Part of your Goods are Sold, I shall pay the Cash into Mess. David Ross & Co.'s Hands, that is if You are not soon back Yourself—I have sent You 75 lb. of very fine inferior Indigo that Cost

4½r this Money per lb. & 12 lb. very good in a small Bag at 7rs per lb. this I request You will Dispose of for my Acct. when at Pensacola & Credit me with Same—I am Sorry to acquaint You that the Notice You sent me was too Short to have got You any Potatoes as we have to Send for them 18 Miles up the River[.] I have made Inquiry if there was any in Town for Sale, But there was not or should have sent You some these that Jacqueau Delivers You for Messrs. Fairlie & Mitchell, have been got by Mr. Gower some Days ago, Having Nothing further to Add only wish You a Pleasent Voyage . . .

To ROBERT MONTGOMERY, *Pensacola*

Manchac, July 2, 1779

Your favour of 12th Ultimo, is now before me the Contents of which have duly observed, the Remains of your fellow Jack, I have delivered to Mr. McPhersons as per his Receipt here inclosed, I say the Remains as the fellow has been always sick since the 15th May last & has never done me one Days Work, I was much afraid I shou'd have been the looser but the Prior Sale You made of him e'er my Letter of 10th May last came to hand, has saved the Ps.250 & for which I return You my most hearty Thanks it may be that as Mr. McPherson is a going to the Natchez where the Lands are much higher & of course more healthy the Fellow may recover but this is a Quarey to me whether he will[.] From the Expectation that my Proposals would have met with your Approbation & for your Interest till Such Times I had your Answer, I Spared no Pains or Expences to recover him, but shall Charge Your Account with Nothing more than what I Paid the Doctor Ps.8.4—All my Trouble & attendance I give up with Pleasure. I acquainted Doctor Thomas with that Part of your Letter in which You mention Mr. Holmes not accepting his Draft for which he is no ways Pleased as he really looks upon it that Mr. Holmes had no right to have refused it as having Money of his in his Hands. He is much obliged as well as myself to You for not protesting the Order but as he writes You himself Refer You to his Letter for further Information on the Subject[.] As I am not Sure of the Amount of my small Account You with You [*sic*] request You will favour me with it per next Conveyance on the Receipt of which will Remitt You the Ballance, till which I am with Esteem . . .

P.S. Please to inform Mr. Smith on his Return that I have never been able to do any thing in Settlement of his Affairs not being able to obtain any Acots. nor Accts. Sales—

To JAMES FAIRLIE, *Pensacola*

Manchac, July 2, 1779

Since my writing You the 15th Ultimo to which I refer You, Your esteemed Favour of 7th Came to hand, inclosed a Bill of Parcells of Sundries Amounting to Drs.194.9r, which is to your Credit with me[.] I am Sorry in one Respect that You had not wherewith to Compleat the Small Order Yourself without Your having applyed to any one else, The Gentleman that You Spoke to do it & his Refusal is no ways Surprizing to me, the more so as I never had any Dealings with him Though I have had some Accounts with his House which have Paid, but never intend any thing further that Way, Secondly I am really glad that the whole Amount did not come as there will not be any Possibility of getting any thing up from the Upper Forks for a Month or Six Weeks to come by Land[.] The Navigation is obstructed in the Bayou by Loggs in Such a Manner that there is no such thing as Passing in Boats. In my former Letter I requested a few small Things merely for my own use which Request You will if not already done send me per first Conveyance as I really am in want of them[.] I observe what You say in Regard of the High Prices that all Goods are at with You, as for their Quality I can say Nothing as they are still at the Amitt, & will be this Some time to Come, You have here inclosed an Order on Henry Stuart Esqr. & accepted by him Payable 20 Days after his Arrival at Your Place where he is to be very soon for 99 Ps. which when You receive You'll Place to my Credit with You the remaining Part, You may expect by the Return of the Vessell that goes for your Place, a Month after this[.] Having Nothing further to Add . . .

P.S. when at your Place last Feby. I left with Mr. Soymon a pair of Gold Sleeve buttons to have them mended if done request You will pay his Demands & send them by first good Conveyance

To JOHN MILLER, *Pensacola*

Manchac, July 10, 1779

Both Your Esteemed favours of the 16th & 25th last May have come to hand in due Time, The Contents of which I have duly observed in Yours of the 16 last You mention Your not having sent Home the Memorandum sent You per Mr. Swanson, as in the first Place, You say it wou'd have amounted to a much larger Sum than I thought at first. Secondly as You cou'd not get a General Consent of your Gentlemen for so doing. Thirdly as You are determined to have done with the Mississippi Trade till Such

Times Peace is reEstablished all this Added together is more than a Sufficient Reason, for not Complying with my Demand[.] for my own Part, must return You my most hearty Thanks, for not sending it Home, as Things in this Place does not seem to go in the right Channell at all, when they will is to me unknown for be Assured that I look upon our Present Situation if we were attacked much worse than when we were left intirely to our selves[.] they will tell You we are protected this I acknowledge we are, but how long can we depend on the Protection as more or less of the Men are daily deserting to our Neighbours the Spaniards The Number the Spaniards have now in their Service is 96. I am much obliged to You for your generous offer of an Assortment out of your own Cargo. The Sum You are pleased to mention will be full enough for this Place at a Time and more I wou'd not request had I the Money in hand to Pay for it, in Your's of 25th came Bill of Parcells of the same things You were pleased to send me Amounting to Ps.89, which is to the Credit of McMinn, Miller & Co. with me & which I request You will Pay Your Self out of the Ps.112.6½r Sent You the 25th May & the remainder Place to my Credit with McGillivray, Struthers & Co. Since my writing You last, Thomas Wescoat parted this Life on my hearing of it I immediately wrote a Letter to the Gentlemen commanding at Galvaz Town, setting forth to them the Circumstances of your Affair with said Wescoat as You will see by a Copy of it here inclosed as also that Gentlemans Answer this Sir is all I cou'd do in the Affair had I been able to have done more, be Assured I would have done it. further I can tell You that although I had acquainted the Commander as before mentioned he has sufferd the Negroes to be sold at Publick Vendue, this for your Government as You have always been so obliging to me. I have one favour more to Request that You will if to be had to send me the following small Articles Viz—

- 400 fish Hooks sorted
- 2 doz fish Lines Do.
- 2 lb. Green Tea
- 1 White hatt bound which with You Cost 6 or 7 Drs. & not more
- 6 Extra Sockett Spade

Without which I shall not be able to perform a Work that I have partly undertaken, To wit the making a new Levie round this Place The want of which will be a great Detriment to me as I have no other Employment for my Negroes[.] We have had Sundry Boats from the upper Country with Family's from the Norward all which agree in their News, they Say we shall have a second attack [?] from them Parts, but as it has been long talked of & no Appearance of them Our Gentlemen don't imagine they will come this Way[.] For God Sake Let no Opportunity slip in Speaking to the General about my Houses and request he will Let me know what I am to expect at once. Having Nothing further at this Present to Add . . .

To CAPTAIN JOHN DAVIS, *New Orleans*

Manchac, July 12, 1779

Since my writing You the Commencement of this Month, Mr. Fitzgerald has arrived here and acquaints me that You have some good old Jamaica Rum for Sale, he could not tell the exact Price You would take per Gallon by the Puncheon, if so & that You will send me 3 or 4 Puncheons at 1 Ps. per Gallon I Paying all Expences, from your Place here, You may Send them, if the following Propositions shou'd meet with your Approbation, Viz. every Month after the Receipt of the Rum I will remitt You in Cash or Sterling Bills, the Amount of one Puncheon, if more sold in that Time will remitt it also but at the utmost only request three Months from the Day of its Arrival to Pay the whole[.] I have to acquaint You that I Presented Mr. Campble with his Account & the Bill, The Account he put in his Pocket to Examine it but as for the Ballance remaining due on the Bill he said Nothing about[,] this Suppose is because he had not looked over the Acct. He is now at Batton Rouge, when he comes to Town again Expect he will settle the Matter to your Satisfaction if so or not shall advise You of the same—

The Captain of the Waldeckers[8] has been with me this Morning & requested I wou'd write You or some other Gentleman at Orleans for the following Articles for his Use. Viz—

    3 doz. of French Plates (say Boan)
    1 Small Tureen—for 4 Persons
    4 Galls. Orange Juice, this very good
    1 doz french Spoons—of the best Sort
    1 doz knives & forks—if to be had
    1000 Corks & ½ doz Mulberry Chairs at about 6 or 7r per Chair

for which he will Pay the Cash in hand on their Arrival, Should Mr. Lewis Rose be still with You to whom I should have wrote myself if it was not that I imagine he is on the Way eer this You will endeavour to Ship them with him or any good Conveyance for this Place Also the Rum if You think Proper to send it, You will Please to acquaint Mr. Rose that I have this Morning Wrote Monsieur Borrée [?] of Point Coopee to bring down the Tobacco

---

8/ After the emergency created by Willing's raid, the British colonial administration decided to reinforce the military establishment in West Florida. Among the troops which left New York in October, 1778, were 695 Waldeckers, German mercenary soldiers from the province of Waldeck, who arrived in Pensacola in January, 1779. In the early spring, Lieutenant Colonel Dickson was sent to Manchac with about 300 men, including troops from the Waldecker Regiment. Another detachment of Waldeckers was sent to Manchac the following August. See Starr, "Tories, Dons, and Rebels," 225–28, 260; Haynes, *The Natchez District and the American Revolution*, 114.

& if he cou'd not do it himself requested he wou'd employ some other Person if they wou'd do it for the Ps.200, as Mr. Rose Offered—We have nothing new with us though Mr. Blommart arrived here last Night from the Natchez All things remain as heretofore. This being the Needfull . . .

To MESSRS. MORGAN AND MATHER, *New Orleans*

Manchac, July 24, 1779

Some Days ago a Gentleman from the Nachitosh passed by this Place of the Name of Monsr. Boujeau & although he stopped here I knew nothing of his being here till the next Morning & although he had a Letter for me, he did not think proper to deliver it himself which was owing I suppose he was afraid I should have made a demand of Money due me this thirty Months[.] he has served me in this manner twice before for which reason Gentlemen I have taken the Liberty to inclose You his Note for Ps.145.6 with 30 Months interest thereon is at 8 pCt is Ps.29.1½, the whole Ps.174.7½ which if You receive request You will pass to my Credit[.] if he shou'd want to put it off longer desire You will Put it into a Lawyers Hand and oblige him to pay it e'er he leaves the Town for if he is permitted to [*rest of page illegible*]

. . . made bold to take 10 Bushels of Corn out of your Boat for which I shall with Pleasure pay You any Price You shall think proper to Charge (and request You will Let me know the Price per the first conveyance and shall remitt its Amount) I should not have [been] so bold but that I am now engaged in making the Road to the Amitt and cant leave it one Day before it's finished & had not one Bushell for myself or Negroes which Reason I am in hopes will plead my Excuse with You for so doing[.] Having Nothing further to add . . .

To JAMES FAIRLIE, *Pensacola*

Manchac, August 6, 1779

Since my writing You the 2d ultimo, I have not been favoured with any of Your's, I now according to my former Promise inclose You the Ballance remaining due You, in Ensign John Kennedy's Draft on Humphry Grant Esqr. at Ten Days Sight for Ps. 120, which make no doubt but it will meet with due Honour [*illegible*] for part of his Pay, the more so as Mr. Grant is his Attorney, and is properly authorized to receive all Moneys due him from

Time to Time, if Paid there will be a small Ballance due me which request You will keep in your Hands, on Account of the Articles I wrote for in my last, which if You have not as yet sent, beg You will per the first conveyance as I am much in want of them. Don't forget my buttons & to them to Add if any in your Place 6 pr. of 8 Inch H Hinges & four Six Inch Iron Rimm'd Locks, which I want for my own use being obliged to build again. I have the Pleasure of acquainting You that we have certain Accounts from the Illinois and other Places up the River that all the Rebels that was in them Parts under the Command of Colo. Clarke have been countermanded it is further said that instead of their coming down this Way they are gone against Fort Detroit. But it is the General Oppinion that they are all ordered back to their own Country to endeavour to defend it against the Brittish Troops, This is the News we have at present. P.S. Since my writing what is mentioned above I have been favoured with Your's of 6 Ultimo the Contents of which have observed, and in Answer have only to return You my most hearty Thanks for your kind offer. For the Present the Linens will not Answer at the Prices You mention as I have yet on Hand upwards of 10 ps. of much such prized Linens belonging to Messrs. David Ross & Co. & can't dispose of them to Advantage, for which Reason it wou'd be useless to have a larger Quantity of that Article on Hand till such Times the Demands are greater than at Present—Although You have had out no Ironmongerry Your Self if You can procure me the small Articles I mentioned for my own Use You will greatly oblige me, as I am much distressed [?] for them, this with the other small Articles formerly mentioned will be quite enough at a Time. . . .

To JOHN MILLER, *Pensacola*

Manchac, August 19, 1779

Since my last of the 10th Ulto. your esteem'd favor of 20th June came to hand, the Contents of which have duly observed. As yet have not settled with Henry Smith for the Balance remaining due, but the first time he comes this way shall settle it and the Expences due thereon Ps. 19:7—I will be much obliged to you to mention in your next the whole Amount paid Mr. Bay on my account that the same may be passed to your Credit.—Mr. Alexr. McIntosh is still here & has been this some time past but as yet has said nothing to me about his Account which I suppose is owing to the trouble he is at, in getting up his Goods from the

Forks, should he neglect it himself I shall desire a Settlement e'er he leaves this & shall acquaint you of the same [in] my next. Be assured his Cargo will be an advantageous one to him as Goods now sell on the Mississippi if Peace & Tranquillity continue of which we have no reason to doubt at present from the Advice We have received since my last by a Batteau from the Illinois.—I return you many Thanks for the continued Favors shewed me on all occasions to advance my Interest & be assured they shall not be forgotten but shall be always recent in my remembrance, and since you have thought proper to send home my Order, am much obliged to you for having put in Clause of a Spanish War. I have nothing further to add only to request you will not fail of sending me the Spades let them cost what they will, as I cannot do without them[.] This being the Needful . . .

P.S. All the Articles you sent the Messrs: Ross's I have delivered. Should you have any Turlington please to send me four large bottles.

To WILLIAM EASON, *Natchez*

Manchac, August 19, 1779

Since your departure from hence, Mr. Swanson is arrived from Pensacola & brings an account that Mr. Humphry Grant has sailed for England, Some days e'er he left that place, so that if I sent the Bills You gave me they would without doubt meet with a Protest from his Attorney this added to the information given me by Mr. Samuel Moore lately from your place say that e'er he set off to Come down, there had a number of Bills drawn by your Gentlemen on Mr. Grant, come back under Protest from the afore mentioned Cases, I have thot. it adviseable to make you acquainted with all the Circumstances that you may have your Recourse in due time on the Drawer as you are all acquainted how my small Affairs now stand, and that I shall to pay the amount of the rum on Settlement for that will be shortly, having finished all the Sales, belonging to David Ross & Co. and as I cannot with any propriety send a Bill to a Gentleman that I am in due that I am well assured will come back under a Protest, and which will be attended with Expence to us both which will serve no end as I am well assured You will have it in your Power, I request You will remit me the Price of the Rum per the first Canoe, and at same time acquaint me what you will have done with the bills, We have nothing new with us, all things remain as when You left this . . .

To JOHN MILLER, *Pensacola*

Merchant of Manchac

Manchac, October 20, 1779

Your last per Captn. Craigg I duly received but the small Parcell which you Sent by the same Conveyance, was taken in the river Amitt. I now take the Liberty a Second time of Inclosing to you the amount of the last of my Improvements at Manchac certified by Six Freeholders of that District[,] Gentlemen who were well acquainted with the Situation & Conditions they were in When the Detachment under the Command of Captn. Barker took Possession of them which was on the 28th Day of May 1778. If Colonel Dixon had thought proper as he had received orders from the General and that Long before the Disturbance happened, he mi might [*sic*] have saved me from the axiety I now Labour with regard to this Matter, I saw him after the Loss of Baton Rouge[9] on his way to this Place, when he was kind Enough to promise me he would have more leisure to Consider of the affair here, he would do every thing in his power to serve me in the matter, although it was Disadvantageous to me at that time to leave home yet I thought it better to do it in order to know What he would do for me, relative thereto not indeed for me alone, but for the benefit of my Friends to whom I am indebted. The Justice of my Demands the Promise he the Colonel had made me, gave me the greatest reason to flatter myself that he would do me every Service he Possibly could, but to my great Sarprize, I find to the Contrary as he will not give me the least Assistance whatever relative thereto, on which Acct. troubled my Friends by requesting them to Certify the account of the Cost of the same, The Colonel is Pleased to intimate that the Buildings are not to be Valued at what they Origionally Cost, but what they might be Worth at the time the Troops first took Possession of them without paying the least regard to the Interest of the Money the Augmentation of the Mens Work & Materials and had a due Estimate been made at that time I am well assured I shoud have been a gainer of above 1000 Dollars, as a proof of which let recourse only be had to the [*illegible*] Store Keepers books & it will fully appear what has been paid for Materials & Workmanship, which will Sufficiently enable the General To Judge whether the Estimation I now Transmit you is out of reason or not, for which reason I flatter myself that the General will have no objection to my being paid the amount of my Account, but Should this not be the Case, I request that you will by the return of the Flag of Truce[10] send me a Coppie of your account Current that I may Settle with Mr. Swanson for the Ballance Remaining Due & Sooner than you Should not be forced to the last farthing [?] eer he leaves this I will Sell my

---

9/Baton Rouge fell to Spanish forces under the command of Governor Gálvez on September 21, 1779. For a description of the campaign, see Introduction to this volume, p. 29.

10/See *ibid.*, p. 9.

Negro's & remit by him, the balance due you tho' this will be hard Seeing I am Deprived of my Property by both Parties. I have only to request of you that if you Should receive the amount of the Inclosed that Voucher of Captn. Barkers that you would be pleased to place the money [?] to my Credit. I beg you would acquaint Mr. Pinhorn that agreeable to his Desire, I have paid the Messrs. Rosses the 60 Dollars for which have taken their receipt, but as that & all my other Papers are at the Governours house Which I cannot get as yet, Prevents my Sending it to him by this Conveyance, but Shall not fail doing of it the first opportunity, & have nothing further to add...

P.S. Should you be so fortunate as to recover the amount of my buildgs. in that Case you will please to pay on my Account as follows

To John Stephenson Esqr. for my Note	300 Ps.
To James Fairlie Ballance of Acct.	100.—
To William Weir	390.—
	Ps.790.—

The remainder please keep in your Possession till such time as you Shall hear further from me on this Matter—

To WILLIAM FERGUSON, *Natchez*

Manchac, February 21, 1780

I had the Pleasure of writing to Mr. McPherson Two letters Since my Return from New Orleans (Last November) But Never Received an answer, which makes me Imagin my Letters Never Came to hand.

Being Informed that he is gone to Pensacola; and that he has left his affairs in your hands to Settle have thought it adviseable to Send you his small account with me; among Sundry others, which I have taken the Liberty to inclose to your Care; which have to Request you will Endeavor to recover for me an Acct. of which you will find here annexed. I must further request that you will not Accept Tobacco if offered in payment for any part thereof as I should not know what to do with that Commodity But Pork in Barrels will be acceptable, provided at a Natchez price well Cured, or if they think Proper to send it Down themselves and pay there Acct. in Cash Still Better, if it should So happen that any of them that are in Due me; Should be Coming down; & will not Settle with you; for there Debt, in that Case you'll oblige Me by sending me there account or Note; that I may have it in my power to oblige them to Settle it hear (always observing Not to send By the person in Due) as Mr. Boles whent with Mr. McPherson, shall be much obliged to you to Inform me if he Left any thing for me at your Place as he was Endue me Money & in his [?] he promised to pay a Long time ago. all Charges attending to the Receipt of any the ball. Notes &c Shall pay with Pleasure & your Compliance Shall be most Greatfully acknowledged...

P.S. if you Can send me 20 Bushells of Shelld Corn at 4/ per Bushell will pay the price But should it Cost more [*illegible*]

A List of the Accounts Notes & a Bond Sent to Mr. Wm. Ferguson of the Natchez to recover for me Vizt. . . . . . .

Timothy Hotichkiss acct. with Interest	37.1
Edward Careless Ditto . . . Do	12.0¾
The Estate of Jesse Lumm Do . . . Do	41.1¼
Donald McPhersons Acct.	23.2
John Watkins's Acct. & Bond Ballance Due thereon	244.7¾
Jean Dunnwan acct. & Note Ballce due thereon	273.6¼
Robert Dunbars Note Do . . . Do	13.0½
Starling Spells Note Do . . . Do	62.2
Caleb Kings Note Do . . . Do	75.4
amount . . . Dollrs.	780.1½

The Notes and the Bond will be Delivered you By Mrs. Bacon & out of the first Money you receive; you'll please to pay Isaac Lewis the amount of a Small Note of mine.

To ANTHONY HUTCHINS, *Natchez*

Manchac, February 26, 1780

This is the Second Letter I did myself the pleasure of Writeing you Since my return from (Orleans) last November) in my former I acquainted You, that I had saved for you a part of a Box of Tools, that was at Mr. Hickeys (it may they are all there as I do not know what was the Contents, at first But I say a part; as I found it Broke open, an Inventory of what found you have hear Inclosed, as allso a Small Scketch of your Account with me, when in Town I applied to Mr. Maxant, a Bout your Mill Stones; either to have them returned, or the payment, he always told me he would Settle it. But was obliged to Come away without affecting any thing for you, had it have been at any other time Should have known what Steps to have taken; but for the Present Must Say Nothing[.] in the year 76 the Damber I delivered you an attested account against the Estate of Jesse Lumm; but as yet

Never heard anything further about it, if Still in your possession Request you will Deliver it to Mr. Willm. Ferguson to whom I have wrote to receive its amount for me; the moreso as; I proposed Leaving the Country if Possible ere the Eight Months is Expired; therefore should be happy of having it in my Power to Settle all my affairs; for which reason; have wrote to the Sundries Gentlemen in due me, and am in hopes they will not fail in remittance of their Ballance of their respective accounts; this being the Needfull . . .

Inventory of the Contents of a Box of Tools Sent to Mr. Anthony Hutchins By Mr. Photts [?] for which he is to pay Ps. [blank] freight Vizt.

 6 Hand saws asorted
 1 Small Broad axe
14 Plain Irons
15 Chizels
 3 frowes
 7 Drawing knives
 4 adzes
11 Different Plain Stock, 6 files Assorted
 5 Augers
 1 Wetstone
 1 oil Ditto
 3 gouges
 4 Rules
 2 Squairs
 1 Tomehawk
 3 gages
 2 old Locks
 2 Spike Gimblets
 1 Bell
 1 Glue Pott
 1 Turn Screw

To JOHN MILLER, *Pensacola*

Manchac, March 2, 1780

I have Been favoured with your Esteemed favour the first of 4 December Last the other of the 2, 3 & 4 Ultimo the Contents of which have Duly observed in your first you were pleased to acquaint me you'll do every thing in your power to receive payment for my Improvements at this Place[.] this I am well assured will be the Case when an Occasion offers, in that of the 2nd Ulto. inclosing my acct. Current as the Occasion is Just going off have not Time to Examin at present But Believe them write only this that you have omitted to Credit me with the amount of Two Bills Sent you 25th of Last May Say Robert McGillivray & Hardy Perrys Draft on [blank] as follows

Fauqeir Bethun Esqr. on Sight for	95.6¼
Joseph Purcells Certificate to Samuel Watkins for	17.0
that is if they are paid	112.6¼

the abatements you have been pleased to make me in the Interest acct. I ashure you shall always be most greatfully remembered as for the Last on Charles Clarks acct. is no ways Surprizing to me; Being this long time aCustomed to many such passes of News from all quarters therefore must put up with it, There being no other remedy left; it only gives me Pain that you Should have been so much Troubled about such trifling affairs; but it often falls out so that we Cannot help being troublesome to our friends sometimes, as we have never had any Courts of Justice heretofore in the District to enable us to Recover our Just Demands; I make no Doubt but the Governor & Generall, are Disgusted with the Inormous Expences Government has been at, on the River But cant help thinking I have a right to be paid; for the house rent; as it was to preserve the Troops from the Inclemmencies of the weather; but as for the payment of my Improvements am in hopes your petition will have the Desired affect if so I should Lay under no Obligation to the Ruleing men heretofore on this River or of your place. Yours of the 3d by Mr. Thomas is Come to hand; But the Gentleman himself is I believe at Orleans Should he Come this way shall do the needfull, your last of the 4th Relative to Mr. Shakespear's affairs Shall Duly observe; and for fear that any one should plead Ignorance Shall put up proper advertisements, at this Place Pointe Couppée & the Natchez, having nothing further to add, only to wish you health happiness & prosperity . . .

P.S. My Compliments to Mr. Pinhorn if with you.

To MESSRS. MATHER AND MORGAN, *New Orleans*

Manchac, March 2, 1780

I have been favour'd with three Letters the first of the 5th of January Containing my Acct. Current with you Balance in your favor Ps.205.2¾ which after Examination found quite right only that you have omitted some small things to my Credit for which I have sent you mine, so that the Ballance is reduced to Ps.188.3¾ which I hope will meet your approbation this Ballance you should have received long ere this had it been in my power but although I have Considerable Sums Still outstanding I am not able to get a Dollar, Interest owing to the indulgence given by the Governour of Orleans to the Inhabitants although many have realy Suffered, there are Numbers that have it in there power if they would; and for forceing them to the rigours of the law I realy Cannot; I have sent you here Inclosed Edmond Connallys Note for Ps.61, which you will receive on Demand Likewise an order on Mr. David Williams for the Balance of his Account Ps.103.2½ which is 164.2½ the remainder say 24.7¼ you shall Receive as soon as Mr. Folley Comes down whom is daily expected from the last accounts and to whom request you will Deliver all my Notes; in yours of 12 Febry. Contained an order for a Cross Cutt Saw, which shall send by Mr. George Mather when he returns your last of 19th Ulto. Informes me that Mr. Stephenson has sent you my Note for Ps.300 payable last may for a negro Bought of him, this it is quite out of my power to Comply with for the present; But shall do every thing in my power to pay it, with the Interest due thereon in six weeks from this date [as] the Illinois Batteaux are Daily Expected Down, in the which there are many Gentlemen that are Considerably in my debt, and as I am well assured they will be able to Discharge my Demands against them, you may rest assured I shall Comply according to my Promise to your Satisfaction[.] In the meantime I am with much respect . . .

P.S. If that Mr. Stephenson Did not receive a bill on Pensacola for 150 Dollrs. on Acct. was not my fault it having been taken which I received afterwards in Orleans after the first flag of truces Departure.

To JOHN DAVIS, *New Orleans*

Manchac, March 2, 1780

Your Esteemed favours of 16th January them of the 21st & 24 Ulto. have Duly received the former should have answered Long ere now But Being in Daily Expectations of Mr. Sturs's return By whom have sent you the amount of your small Account Ps. 13.3 and I return you my Most hearty thanks, in that of the 21st. I observe what you mention, about my acct. with Mr. James Farlie of Ps.198.3 which account is Very Justly Due him; and it is not my fault that he was not paid long ere this for I wrote him the 6th of Last Augt. & sent him a bill of Exchge. for 120 Ps. which was taken in the Amitt By the Spanish armie and which was returned to me when in Town after the Departure of the first of

Truce, I should have sent you the same Bill; But the Drawer & Indorsers are Daily Expected here from the Natchez and as Captn. Willm. McIntosh has Setled the affairs of his Company, will have the Money with him to Discharge his officers accounts, ad to all this the Disapointments I am Daily meeting from the Inhabitants of Baton rouge Pointe Couppee &c whom Embrace the Indulgences of the Governour Gave them of Paying there Debts in 12 Months &c But be assured I will do every thing in my power to Comply with Mr. Fairlies Just Demand as soon as I have it in my Power, which am in hopes is not far off, Yours of 24th of Last month Contained Two orders on a Gentleman Mr. Thomas Dicas for Ps.169.6 which shall acquaint him of by the first Conveyance, but am much afraid shall meet with the same answer from him for you, as he has given me for myself, for money due me since 76, of which I have never been able to get one Dollar; But shall Done all in my power to searve you[.] I have taken the Liberty to Inclose to your Care an Account Currt. and an order given me By Doctr. Thomas for a hundred Dollars which order you will please to Deliver him on his paying the Acct. Sales [?] Indorsed to the Deceased Mr. Mongommary to pay him a Ballance on an account I was in due him, and which was to have been Setled on his arrival, But Death prevented it having the Desired effect, for which reason, & the Disappointment, now Trust [?] with the order I am in hopes it will Ingage the Doctor to Discharge it the sooner. In the mean time I am ...

To DOCTOR EDWIN THOMAS, *New Orleans*

Manchac, March 2, 1780

Your order on Mr. Holmes for 100 Dollrs. my favour is return'd me By Mr. Robert Donald Administrator to Mr. Mongomery, Lately Deceased on his passage to Pensacola, at the same time that Gentleman Demands the Balance of my Acct. with the Estate (which from the Sundry Disappointments Lately Sustained) have it not in my power to Comply with his Just Demand without being under the Disagreeable Necessity of Calling on the Gentlemen indue me; for which reason have remitted the Order & your account Current with me amounting to Ps.85. 1½ to Capt. John Davis, whom will Deliver you your order on paying the amount of your account, which from my present Necessity & the want I am in of making remittance to said Gentleman, (as it is Justly Due) makes me to flatter myself; that you will Strain a point to Comply with my Request, your white hat you would

have had By Mr. John Moor, but he would not give it a passage; having nothing further to add...
   My Compliments to all old Acquaintance.

To CAPTAIN WILLIAM BARKER,
New Orleans

Manchac, March 2, 1780

The Voucher you was pleased to give when last in Town I sent to Mr. John Miller to receive its amount (Say Ps.50), But did not meet with acceptance therefore Came back by the last flag of Truce, if you can be of any farther Service to me in the affair I request you would. Mrs. Fitzpatrick has taken the Liberty of Sending you a Small pot of Butter, and begs your acceptance had she had a Larger pott would have sent it full, She joins me in wishing you a Better State of health; than we hear you have enjoyed this some time past; having Nothing further to add...

To LIEUTENANT J. J. GRAHAM,
New Orleans

Manchac, March 2, 1780

Your Esteemed favour of 16th Ulto. is now before me the Contents of which I have duly observed, I return you my most hearty thanks for your having given Mr. Miller the Necessary Certificates about my Building & the Smiths Tools; which I am in hopes some future day to be able to recover their amount, the more so as Mr. Miller acquaints me that he has wrote home about it, according to your request I have sent you a Copy of your account Current which I am in hopes you will find Right you will please to observe that the articles Marked with an X were omitted in your former Acct. deliverd in at Orleans, By this account there is a Ballance due me of Ps.4.6½ thi[s] you will Deduct from the Money I am Still Indue you, which hope ere long to have it in my power to pay you with honor, but for the present is Impossible; you'll please to acquaint Babée that I recd. 9 Dollrs. from a Spaniard for house Rent, which shou'd have Remitted ere Now But thought it was Better to keep to repair any thing that might be wanting I have repaired the front Levee which is Ps.4.2 and if we are obliged to make an End Levee the 4/6 that remains will Do it[.] I am with much Regard...

To STEPHEN SHAKESPEAR, *New Orleans*

Manchac, March 2, 1780

I had the pleasure of hearing you was Safely arrived to the Bayeau St. Johns; with the other Gentleman; from which reason I flatterd myself I should have been favour'd with a Line from you; & Being quite uncertain whether you Determine to remain at Orleans or return, I thought it adviseable to acquaint you that the order you gave me when in Town Last October to Receive Ps.50 for you the man has not as yet returned from the Natchez (though he has been Expected this Long Time passd) when he Comes shall do the needfull in my Power, the Razors Gimblets & knives you Left to Dispose of for your Acct. are still on hand, when Sold shall account with your order for the amount, having Nothing further to add only to request you will favour me with your Commands (if I can be of any Service to you in these parts) & believe me to be with much regard ...

To WILLIAM STROTHER, *New Orleans*

Manchac, March 6, 1780

All your Esteemed favours Since I had the pleasure of seeing your Self have duly received, and should not have omitted answering them in proper time But have been in continual Expectation of Mr. Sturs's return, whom will pay you the Balance of my small account as it may be some time ere I go down, have taken the liberty to Inclose you a small order on Mr. Alexander Cosalas Lady for 7 Dollars; which am well assured will be paid on demand & for your Government have sent you a Coppy of your account which am in hopes you will find wright [.] As for the affair betw[een] me & Mr. OBrient my objections; Stands as follows

1. It is True that when in Orleans when I first saw him I partly Igaged him at £40 Sterling per annum But on his passage up I found out that he was incapable of the under Taking (as I did not want my Books spoilt) afterwards was the Case with them of Monsr. Monsanto; therefore Never Imployed him a day, But he rem[ained] at my house till the above Gentleman Imployed him— at my E[x]pences. 2d The Letters and accounts; he mentions to have wrote for me in 76 I know nothing of them as yourself was at the House (Exceptg. it be the writing done by your order) & for which I paid him your account P.10 [*illegible*] of which was too much as Can be shewn by the Books in which he wrote. 3 the writing done for me ere my Departure for Pensacola 79 was as

follows Vizt. 2 half Sheets Containing an Estimate of my Improvements at Manchac, 2 half Sheets Containing an Account of my outstanding Debts this with Copies & Origionalls. 4 the making out three Vouchers [?] one of which you have here inclosed he Spoilt the other five he Mentioned in your/his [sic] acct, as he Could not or would not follow a true Coppie Layed Before him and after all [I was] obliged to get them Drawn over again by Mr. French.

5th the Letters wrote after my return from Pensacola to Send [with] Captn. Smith, was as follows a Letter to R. Mongommary another to John Miller Esqr. & the other to Mr. James Fairlie with a small note of some Goods I wanted from that Gentleman each on half Sheets & then Copied into the Letter Book 6th he might have wrote some Letters to send by the Transport, that brought the Troops, But never Copied in the Letter book But I am in doubt of his having wrote any as it was not many Days after my arrivall in Smith by whom I had wrote.—

7 the Memorandum to England Contained only five Sheet 4½ of them of them [sic] was in my way of writing was Imployed & which he reduced to three. 8th. Know of no Writing Done for me since I came over the Boyeau. By him. for He Left this 24 April and did not return from orleans from 22 or 24 May insuing; at which time I had Mr. Whitfield with me till the 2 August so had no need of his assistance[.] 9th An Account Sales for Mr. David Ross on 5 Sides the Coppie on the Same Number
10th This as apears in his Acct. Currt.
11 this as aps. Do. . . Do. . . . Do.
12. this as aps. Do. . . Do. . . Do.
13 & 14 the Money and Order on Mr. Murphy Imployed in hhd. of wine 20 Dollars freight of Ditto 2 Dollrs. the remainder Imployed at Monsr. De forets in Laces gauzes &c for his Woman as per acct. rendered him on my return from Orleans for which reason made no Charge of them in my Books nor are they in his Acct.
15 Short Creditted me on his acct. for ye wine . . . . 4.—
16 Short Ditto on the Barrell of flower . . . . . . 3.—
P.7.0

These Sir are my objections against that infamous & unjust Account, which am well assured he Dare not if in an English Government offer to attest to, without indangering himself to the Recompence, Attending them that are found guilty of such Crimes by Law. it Seems something Verry Surprising to me & am well assured it will to every one that will allow himself one moments reflection to think, how a Man in his Circumstances Should Leave, this in the Month of November 77 and give me his Note for the Balance of my account payable in March 78 for 41.2 without mentioning his Demand again[st me] had he been able to make any appear he would not have given his Note as above mentioned, admit he had made an Omission on his; Leaving this, on his return in 78 when in Captn. Millers Company it is to be supposed he would have had time to have recollected that I was in his debt. The more so as I am well assured; he was often in whant of money, but all this time I never heard of any such debt. in June 79 When his Woman turned him out of Doors and that he had nothing to Subsist upon Except that 2 or 3 Ceggs of Brandy she allowed him to take away and he remained at Mr. Connolleys allmost for Charity sake the Immaginary account was never mentioned to me, when he took his passage with Captn. Craigg for Pensacola I spoke to him about the 50 Dollars I paid Mr. West for him; he told me he had not above 6 Dollrs. in money to take with him But if I would send his note to Pensacola (& if he got into Employ) he would pay it which I really proposed doing but before I had wrote he returned with Mr. Alexander McIntosh for this place; if I Charge him the 54 Dollars it was Intirely owing (finding) that [he] wanted to use me, in the same manner he has all them that have ever done any thing for him since in the Country, to pay them with Ingratitude, But this has allways been his ruling Passion, therefore I am no ways surprised[.] You will see by Mr. Smiths Certificate how much I pay him per Sheet, this I am willing to allow him but this to be Deducted from the 54 Dollars as sunner than have any further Connection if he will pay the Ballance of his acct. give him up his Note & the Account. Should he not Comply with this offer then Leave it to the Persons you may think Proper, if yourself is one of them & that you are able to Compromise matters Between two Irish men. I shall then Really think you are Intitled to one of the first places in any Court of Arbitration; when a Disbute may Arise between any two men of any other Nation[.] having nothing further to add . . .

To JOHN DAVIS, *New Orleans*

Manchac, April 2, 1780

Your Esteemed favour 14 Ulto. I have received, the Contents of which have Duly observed; you Informe me that Mr. Alexander paid you the Ballance due on his Note, as appears by the Coppie of the receipt, By what means Mr. Whitfield obtained orders to Receive any part of it as the Note was in my hands is unknown to me, But have reason to Suppose it has been by an Order of Mr. R. R. when at the Natchez if so alls Wright as the Note was the

Messrs. Ross's property and not mine therefore request you'll account with them for what you have received, on said note and Whitfield must account for the remainder. I have heard you'll be soon Comeing up this way when you are if you'll oblige me so far as to Bring me 20 or 30 lbs of french Soap, (as it is now Cheap to what it has been) I will pay you for the same on receipt of it. Be assured I shall soon have it in my power to pay the amount of Mr. Fairlies account, when it Comes in Shall Lay Hold of the first Conveyance of remitting it you. Till which I am with regard...

P.S. There is Nothing to be got from Mr. Dicas as yet it may be When you come up you will get Something yourself but for me I cant get my own.

To WILLIAM STROTHER, *New Orleans*

Manchac, April 2, 1780

I acknowledge that I have Comitted a mistake in the account sent you of P.31.2, this was Intirely owing to my having lost the blotter, the Ballance was Struck in. But on Examination of my other Books, find it quite Wright; and which you may depend on having it remitted you the first money I receive Till which I am with Regard...

P.S. if OBrien Comes Down from Natchez, please Settle, that affair for me Let it go how it will.—

(The following is the editor's translation from the original French.)

To MONSIEUR [BRION], *New Orleans*

At Mr. Brian's, Manchac, April 7, 1780

I have the honor of greeting you and at the same time of advising you that Monsieur Matard will pay you on my [?] account the sum of 166.5 pesos, as soon as you present him with his note. Herewith enclosed you will find a letter for Monsieur Cannond relative to the amount of Dubreuil and Papin's note for 329 pesos, which you will please request from Monsieur Matard. I believe he is ready to pay the interest since the expiration [?] of the note, which I hope Monsieur Cannond will not oppose. Monsieur La Chance has sent a quantity of flour in Monsieur Cercé's bateau, so the owner, who is charged with the sale, can pay the remainder of his note, 108.5 pesos, with the interest due according to the arrangement made with Monsieur La Chance when he was in Town last year. I am sorry, Sir, to bother you with this, but when I was in Town and had the honor of speaking with you, I believe you said that [I might request your help]. I will pay with much pleasure whatever commission you judge appropriate to charge me for such a recovery, since I am in despair of not having been able to settle sooner, but those who do not receive cannot pay. I beg you to assure Madame of my very humble respect . . .

(The following is the editor's translation from the original French.)

To MONSIEUR CANNOND, *New Orleans*

Manchac, April 7, 1780

Some time ago you wrote me that you had orders from Messieurs Dubreuil and Papin to pay me the balance of their note drawn up on the 24th of June 1777 for the sum of 329 piastre gourdes, but when I sent it to Mr. Strothers to collect this amount, you told him that you had no more funds in your hands belonging to these men. As it is a long time since this note was cashed, I hope that you received some money from these men by the convoy that has just arrived, since either Monsieur Dubreuil or Papin has on Monsieur Corpee's bateau [*illegible*] packet of pelts. This is why I am writing you to ask if you have received the money to pay Monsieur Brion the balance of this note. As it is some time since its expiration [?], I believe it is only just that these men pay the interest for the said sum, which is eight percent, according to the custom of the province. I have nothing else to tell you . . .

(The following is the editor's translation from the original French.)

To MONSIEUR BRION, *New Orleans*

Manchac, April 13, 1780

I had the honor of writing you on the 7th of last May concerning two notes of Monsieur Matard, amounting together to 166.5 pesos, which he promised me he would pay you as soon as he arrived in Town. At the same time I wrote a letter to Monsieur Cannond, which I enclosed with your letter and which I do not doubt he received from you. This letter concerned Messieurs Dubreuil's and Papin's note for the sum of 329 piastres which they ought to have paid me a long time ago, but which I believe Monsieur Cannond will pay since he received some money by the last bateaus. If this note is paid, it will make a sum of 495.5 pesos, which added to the 350 pesos which I paid you in Town by Monsieur Maxant's bond makes a balance of 845.5 pesos, and as my bond is only for 820 pesos, there is a balance of 25.5 pesos in my favor, which I ask [?] you to send by some good opportunity with the remainder of the note in your hands. Of course you will deduct the cost of your trouble. I have nothing else to tell you, except that I beg you to assure Madame of my very humble respect...

(The following is the editor's translation from the original French.)

To MONSIEUR BRION, *New Orleans*

Manchac, May 30, 1780

I had the honor of writing you on the seventh of last month and on the 13th of this month, the last of which Mr. Swanson told me he delivered to you, so I hope you have received the first as well. In each letter you can see how much I was grieved that the balance of the note was not settled sooner, but I hope that this difficulty is removed and that the money I left in your hands was sufficient. Since Monsieur Matard and Monsieur Cannond are in Town, I do not doubt that the first paid you some time ago, as he promised me when he passed by here, and the second I am well assured will not oppose it, since it is a long time since he had orders to pay Messieurs Dubreuil's and Papin's note.

Your letter of the 27th of last March was delivered to me this morning, coming from Baton Rouge. How long it was there, God only knows. I await your response concerning these matters by the first opportunity. I wish you as well as Madame good health...

To CAPTAIN WILLIAM McINTOSH, *Natchez*

Manchac, June 11, 1780

I did myself the Pleasure of writing to you some days ago by Mr. Bacon, which hope you have received ere this, your Esteem'd favour of the 31st Ultimo Came to Hand and is now before me the Contents of which as well as the inclosed have duly observed[.] be assured that the one that was Inclosed gave me great surprise at the first Sight as Comeing from such an infernal Yellow Bitch in which she does not flatter me nor endeavour to Apalliate Matters but tells me in Plain terms that I have Publickly robbed her house to a large amount. the Accusation I possitively deny as false

& Injurous to an Honest Mans Character she talks of living witnesses that Can prove the fact and this she must, as I am determined to leave no Stone Unturned (either by the English Law if yet allowed off,) or them of Spain to see myself Wrighted[.] I have Inclosed to you a Proper State of all her Transactions with me from the first Commencement till this date by which you will see how I have been used by that Strumpet[.] She Produces receipts & accounts to you which she says has not been Indorsed on her Bond Should any such appear and that you do not find them Creditted in her Acct. Currt. then they are Valuable and may be reduced from the Ballance Still due and upon no other terms, as I opserved by your Letter that Several of your Gentlemen acknowledges their Debts but will not pay them without you are properly authorised I have sent you my proper power of Attorney with a Letter to Monsr. De La Ville baveur in which I have fully Explained the Accusation laid against me which after haveing perused You ll Please to seal & deliver him and from his Wonted Manner in rendering Justice to all them that has recourse to his tribunall I am well assured he will do the needfull for me in that Delicate point where my Character is Attacked in so gross a manner and which could be never laid at my door by any Man Since in the Province. I have returned you her last letter which request you will properly Explain to Monsr. La Ville Boeueur, which is a Convincing proof of her Accusation.

She mentions one Mr. Thos. Fry and his wife as her living witnesses of my haveing Committed the Fact[.] I am willing to admit of them as I look upon them both to be Verry Honest People, and does not Immagine that ever [?] one of them would be able to Counterfeit a Jounden or a Fisher (as the saying goes with us) but at the same time, there ought to be added the other Living witnesses that was at the Grand Gulf at the time of my residence there Vizt. Mr. Thomas James & his Wife, Robert Scarce & Jenny Finney with many others. I am well assured that Mr. Thomas James & his Wife can Avouch that on my Arrival at their Landing on the 4th of February 74 in Company with Mr. Alexander McIntosh that she had not neither [a] Peice of Strouds nor 20 Gallons of rum in her House [as she had] not been able to impose upon any body besides me, to get any of that Article which was then Verry scarce in the Country Since the rum she had per me per 5th Bill the 26 of October 73 & then only 120 Galls. it Verry true that Mr. Ladley was at the Natchez Landing at our arriving there & had some rum for sale which McIntosh & self Purchased in behalf of the Company the last that he had, and a Part of which Mr. Thos. James Purchased as there was no rum at the Gulph but What we had and the Same day of my Arrival at Mr. James's She made me acquainted partly with her Situation and told me she had given out the greater Part of my goods that I advanced her upon Credit to the Sauvages & without I could assist her once more she would not be able to withdraw her debts[.] I took Compassion on her and Expecting as I was to be there myself that she would really do something to Extricate herself from the large debt then indue me[.] I let her have a Piece of Strouds and a Gun of the Companies Goods & Charged them to my Private Acct. as Mr. McIntosh would not advance her to the Value of a Dollar[.] I further after advanced her 7¾ yds of Strouds as you will see by the Account Currt. to endeavour to still help her [illegible] was proved abortive as all my former endeavours had done[.] I do not offer to Deny but some time after Mr. McIntoshes Departure to Come down with our Skins, as I then resided at Mr. Barbours Place where she Did I asked her one day in these words Now Nelly as I am here and have not much to do let me have a sight of your books that I may have the Satisfaction to know into whose hands my goods had been given (as she had nothing in the Store as I could see of the large advanced I had made her) and told her I would assist her in Setling her Accounts for you must know at this time I now Mention I had not received out of the amount of her Bond Drew in October 73 for Ballance due me at that time but 249 Ps. 2 rs. this give me great uneasiness Seeing no appearance of further Payment and her Extravagance Daily augmenting, She told me to be under no Concern for that She was in Daily Expectation of a large Party of Savages Comeing in with a quantity of Skins and which I should have to the last on their arrival with this I put up and waited many days always in Expectation of receiving the said Skins but finding no Skins Comeing in nor any likelihoods thereof and the Time of my departure Drawing near I told her in Plain terms that I must see her books when she found that She Could not deceive me any longer She produced me the books but what was my Surprise after a due Examination to find there was hardly Any thing therein and the little that there was in Such Hands that I am well assured to this day She has never received the one third[.] this put me in such a Violent Passion to see myself so Humbugged by such a Strumpet that I Could not help asking her in a verry abrupt manner what have you done with my propirty[.] She answer'd me in that Ville language which she is much Mistress off Damn your Blood I have fucked them away[.] This I Could not bear & therefore Struck her which I am well assured were you or any other man in my Place you would not have put up with it and have done as I did, She Endeavourd to make her Escape but I followed her in a room Where I gave her a Couple of Clouts She then made her

Escape into the Field where I did not follow her[.] it is true I took the Key of her room but returned it instantaniously to Mr. Robert Scarce but never touched to the Valuation of a Sol. I have Wrote to Scarce who is now at New Orleans for a Certificate relative to the said affair and which I am well assured Shall be able to remit you by the Next Conveyance and which I'm in hopes you'll make proper use of for I should I be obliged to sell to the last of my Negroes I am Determin'd to have Justice.

I have the following Objections against her Account Exclusive of what she mentions about rum or Strouds in the first place she Charges me 30 Dollars for a Balleasey built boat this is the same she had Credit on 7th April 74 as per Agreement 16 Ps. nor will I allow her more for the Particulars about Said Mr. Alexander McIntosh can inform you as it was he took her down with our Skins. 2ndly. She Charges me 17 Dollrs. for House rent which I will not pay her but if I am to pay it Shall Settle it with pleasure with the Proprietor of the Plantation & the Houses thereon, whom is Mr. Phillip Barbour, 3dly You'll please to observe that I have Credited her Account with 43 Ps. 4 rs being Mens Wages Provisions a Tarpolian oars And me & my Mans Maintainance while at the House (tho' by the by I had a Plenty of Provisions for my self which She Cooked & that was all. 4thly Youll Please to observe that in a former Account Sent her I had Creditted her with 60 Dollars for a small Barge she Sold me as her property but in reallity was not for Mr. Barbour after his return from the Nchz. acquainted me in the presence of Mr. James that the Barge was his & had only Left it with her to take Care of till his return, and in consequence of which would insist upon being paid and which affair I setled with him to his Satisfaction. therefore if she Cannot produce or make it appear that she had a right to Dispose of said Barge by Certifycate or Letter or some paper from under his hands She must not Expect that I will allow it, but Should she be able to produce either of the above mentioned Vouchers in that Case I am Willing to allow it in account as either of them will enable me to recover the amount from Mr. Barbour. 5thly You will find in her acct. Current that I have Charged her with Ps. 39.4 that being the Amount of Roger Rosses Note which she gave to me as a payment at the time that the said Ross gave his Note to me for her Acct. he said then that he was not indue her that Sum & had her receipts in full of all Demands but not then with him, & before he would Concent to Sign Said Note he requested of me in her behalf a Certificate that if he produced the said receipts the Note Should be Null'd, Which he has fully as you'll see by my Letter to Mr. McPherson & his Answer here inclosed[.] I am Sorry to have been so verry Tedious in troubleing you with so long a letter on a So Disagreeable a Subject, but Since you are so obliging as to offer me your Service & my Being Distant from your District, has obliged me to give you an Idea of the Whole Process Without which if there is any thing to be recovered from Nelly you [*illegible*] might not have been able to have done it, What you have have [*sic*] done with Mr. Alston is verry well; but be assured that the money would have been much better, being greatly necessiated therefore request if you are able to recover any part for me of the amt. in yr. Hand you will please to Convey it to me by first Safe Oppertunity. I have nothing further to add only to request my Compliment to Mrs. McIntosh & the Family . . .

To WILLIAM FERGUSON, *Natchez*

Manchac, June 11, 1780

Your Esteem'd favour of the 31st Ulto. I have duly received and note the Contents[.] my having wrote to you by Captn. McIntosh to deliver up the Papers then in your Hands was entirly owing to my being informed you were soon to depart for Pensacola & as there was nobody in your district with whom I had the least acquaintance I thought it more advisable better [*sic*] as he was to remain on the Spot and might get in some part from time to time that they should be in his hands sooner than you should remit them to me here and I really hope that he will do the needfull As far as lays in his power.

I have now one favour to request that is if your own business will Permit of it, that you will assist Captn. McIntosh in the Affairs as far as you Can, either in Examineing the Account of Nelly Price as well as looking over my long letter to him on that Disagreeable Subject, which trouble I will willingly Pay any thing you may Demand in reason.

According to your desire Mr. Blommart spoke to me about the Ballance Still due me[.] I told him it was verry well and offerd to produce the Accounts but he told Me that he had not the money, on that head I put up the said Account again and told him that as I was not acquainted with suivelling that Mr. Ferguson was as good to me as for that sum as Mr. Blommart on which we Parted, but always good friends[.] I have nothing further to add only to to [*sic*] assure you that if in Case there is any thing this way in which I can serve you you will freely Command . . .

Mrs. Fitzpatrick presents her Compliments to you

(The following is the editor's translation from the original French.)

To MONSIEUR BLONDAIN

Manchac, June 12, 1780

It is more than a year since I entrusted you with my goods, and your obligation ought to have been paid some months ago. I assure you that I have always believed that you would have had some regard [for me], as you cannot be unaware of all the losses I have had since I had the honor of seeing you. I was hoping until the present to receive either the remittance which is due to me or a letter from you. That is why I have not written you sooner. So as soon as the present is delivered to you, please have the goodness to send me the balance of your obligation by the first good opportunity that comes down from your place, and you will infinitely oblige . . .

(The following is the editor's translation from the original French.)

To JUAN DE LA VILLEBEUVRE, *Natchez*[11]

Manchac, June 12, 1780

After a long silence on my part, caused by my having nothing worth the bother of writing you about, I am now obliged to have recourse to your justice against a free mulattress of your district named Nelly Price. Having no doubt that you will give me the justice that I deserve, it suffices to tell you that this mulattress has owed me a very considerable sum for six years, according to her account current and obligation now in the hands of Captain William McIntosh, without which I cannot arrange to be paid in entirety or in part. Not content with seeking the most fraudulent means of depriving me of my money, she is trying to destroy my reputation with the public by means of the most vile manner ever practiced in the world, and which I believe is the most distressing to an honest man. She writes that when I was at Grand Gulf in 1774, in order to collect the payment that she owed me, I took by force a piece of Limbourg and 100 gallons of rum from her house. At the time that she claims to have lost these goods, it is easy to prove to you, by Mr. Thomas James and his wife who were then resident in the same place, that this evil woman had not a single piece of Limbourg nor twenty gallons of rum in her house until I advanced her a piece of Limbourg to help her credit in the hope of collecting some part of the great sum that was owed me. The particulars of this matter as well as her letter accusing

11/Juan de la Villebeuvre became commandant at Natchez after the settlement capitulated to the Spanish in September, 1779.

me are in the hands of Mr. McIntosh, who will explain to you the article that I have not mentioned here, as the explanation would make my letter too long. This is why, Sir, I have recourse to your tribunal, so that this mulattress may be arrested, first for the debt that she owes me, second so that she will be obliged to prove the accusations that she has advanced, in consequence of which I am ready to place in the hands of whomever you judge proper the sum of one or two thousand pesos until the time that this matter is decided and my innocence is proved. But, on the other hand, if she cannot prove her accusations, as I am well assured she cannot find any people evil enough to wish to support them, I hope she will be punished according to the law. I have nothing else to tell you, except that my wife and I present you our very humble respects, and I beg you to oblige me by presenting our very humble respects to Monsieur and Madame De Lacosta...

(The following is the editor's translation from the original French.)

To MONSIEUR DEVERGES, *New Orleans*

Manchac, June 14, 1780

William Inrufty, the American hunter, has left in my hands his power of attorney and your receipt of the 22nd of last month for the sum of 163 pesos and 25 sols that he placed in your hands before leaving New Orleans, occasioned by the complaints which have been carried to you by James Carter, formerly employed by Inrufty and his partner, James Ferguson, who is not at present in this area but in the upper part of the White River. Settling this matter may be impossible, since all the receipts for money paid to their various employees in 1777 when Ferguson came down with their pelts are with him and not among their papers which are here. But here are the circumstances which seem to me to be for all intents and purposes convincing proof, but this I leave to your justice and superior acquaintance with such affairs.

First, James Carter swore in your presence that Inrufty and Ferguson still owed him for the balance of his wages and a rifle the sum of 188 pesos 25 sols, but that you found it appropriate to deduct 25 piastres, so there still remained 163.2 pesos, of which he swore he never received a sol on account. Secondly, when he left their service here in Manchac at the time I went down to New Orleans, he came to hire on with me for the trip, and all the time we were on the trip, which was about twenty days, I never heard him say that he was really broke, that I should advance him some money before it was earned, or that Inrufty and Ferguson were still in debt to him. Thirdly, the account books of Samuel Ferguson, formerly in business at this post but at present a prisoner in England, are in the hands of our commandant, who states that Samuel Ferguson was paid by James Ferguson 19.2 pesos for Carter, and there is even his receipt for this sum. Fourth, Stephen Hayward's account books, which are in my hands, record that Inrufty and Ferguson paid on Carter's account 21 pesos on the 31st of March 1775 and then 5 pesos 6 sols on the 16th of March 1776, which makes 26 pesos 6 sols. However, he says he received nothing. Fifth, furthermore, Mr. Blommart, who is now in Town, can prove that Ferguson paid him some money on Carter's account, but I do not know the exact amount. Sixth, since the money was placed in your hands and Inrufty was obliged to come down to Town (believing that Monsieur Rosamond had sent down the papers belonging to him and his partner) thinking he would find the receipt which Carter gave Ferguson when he paid him in 1777. Knowing that this man in fact had nothing, I wrote to Mr. French at his suggestion to ask him if he would be so kind as to ask Monsieur Rosamond for the papers which were supposed to have come down and to take out Carter's account in order to show it to you. But what do you say, Sir, to a man who would be capable of making a proposition like he made to Mr. French. He told him in these words—I know that you ought to examine Inrufty's and Ferguson's papers; if you should find some paper of mine or a note by which it appears that I gave him a receipt, if you would destroy [?] it, which you can do without anyone knowing, I will pay you well and when I receive my money I will give you 40 pesos. All these reasons and several others Mr. French states in his letter of the 2nd of this month. If these reasons put together are a proof for Inrufty and you judge proper, remit the money to Mr. Davis, to whom I send the power of attorney with your voucher and a receipt. I shall be very obliged to you. I have nothing else to tell you . . .

To DAVID ROSS, *New Orleans*

Manchac, June 14, 1780

Some time about the Comencement of Febry. 77 I wrote to Mr. Jacques Rapalje In behalf of Messrs. John & Thomas Comyng hunters whom I had fitted out for their hunt that if he had any Beaver traps Still for Sale; to Let them have Some, & if they were not able to pay for them in Hand if he thought proper to Credit them; as I Believed them to be verry Honest Man, that if they did not pay him; in Twelve Months I would become paymaster for said Traps; Now you must Know that in May 1775 When Mr. Jacques Left the Province he was in due me a Ballance of Ps.68.5½ Which Mr. Garret Rapalje Senr. assum'd to me from the Time I wrote my Letter as above Till of our Settlement, he never so much as made Mention to me, he had Supply'd them, with any Traps Nor did I ever Know any thing of it, till some time last December, when Mr. George told me of the affair, which gave me some surprize. If the Said Some was not paid Long ere this, it is intirely owing to the Messrs. Rapalje Never have made me acquainted that they had Charged it to my Acct. if they had, I had where with in my hands to have paid them for in 1777 they sent me doun by George Williams a quantity of Skins; that amounted to Ps.436 & they were only indue me per their Note 280 Ps. with 27 Ps. for the Interest made 307 Ps. so that there was a Ballance in my hands of Ps.129, which I paid them as per their Receipt the 10th Oct 1778, Now as the whole fault of not being paid; is intirely owing to Mr. Jacques; or Mr. Garret, not makeing me acquad. long ere they did & that I have Nothing further in my hands, But they owe me as per their Note 84 Ps. for sundries advancd them after paying the Ps.129. I do not think that I can be the Looser & if the some is lost them Gentlemen; must be the Loosers; and if the Sum is Lost, But if to End all Disputes; Mr. George Proposed Leaving it to your Judgement & what ever your pleas'd to pronou[nce] on the Affair Shall be a Law for Dr. Sir Yours . . .

To CAPTAIN JOHN DAVIS, *New Orleans*

Manchac, June 14, 1780

Your Esteem'd favour per Mr. Hiron I Duly received the Contents of which have duly observed; I am in hopes ere this that Doctr. Thomas has paid the amount of his account (what gives me reason to Suppose it) is that we are inform'd all the English Gentlemen & officers, are to be paid off. On the Arrivall of the first Money (which by hear Say) is Come to town some time ago. I am well assured Monsr. Maxant Junr. has paid you nothing as yet, he is now our Commander therefore I am in hopes he will settle ere he Leaves this as he is Superceeded.[12] I have Taken the Liberty to Inclose to your care a Lettr. for Mr. Deverges the Civil Judge, which please to deliver him after yr having perused & sealled, also his rect. for 163 Ps. 2r Deposited in his hands by William Inrufty on Account of Charge Brot. agt. him and his partner by James Carter, the said Carter has sworn before Monsr.

12/Antonio de St. Maxent, son of New Orleans merchant Gilbert de St. Maxent, was born in New Orleans about 1760. He entered military service in 1775 and was placed in command of a Spanish garrison at Fort Bute from the time of its capture by the Spanish until he was assigned to the command of the Spanish post at Gálveztown in July, 1781. Archivo General de Simancas, Sección de Guerra Moderna, Legajo 7291, Cuaderno 1, Regimento de Infanterio fixo de la Luysiana, December, 1787, p. 41.

Deverges that there was Still due him for his Wages Ps.188.2 from which Mr. Deverges Deducted Ps.25 So there only remains a ballance of 165 Ps.2 as Specified By said receipt which Mr. Deverges was to Keep in his hands for one Mon[th ?] till such Time as the man Could produce the proper proofs, for you must Know that Carter swore that he never had received any part thereof & Inrufty was sure he had, which has realy been the Case for in the first place, I find in Samuel Fergusons Books 19.2 paid by Inruftys Partner for him with his own acceptance 2dly in Steph. Haywards Books 36.6 paid him by sd. partner his acct. 3dly Mr. Blommart has something his Books against Carter which was paid him by said Partners, Lastly the Most Convincing proof is Mr. Frenches Letter of 2 Inst. here inClos'd[.] therefore Look upon all this a Convincing proof. if Mr. Deverges pays you the Money after Deducting his fees from the same you'll retain in your Hands the amount of Mr. Jas. Fairlie's acct. Say 98 Ps.6r which request you'll deduct as also your own small acct. Say Ps.11.2 & if you Can and have received any thing from the Doctor in that Case you'll keep in your hands 95 Ps.0¾ for acct. of Mr. Robert Donald Mercht. in Pensacola to remit him per first Conveyance; But should you not have been so fortunate as to receive the Doctrs. Amt. you'll only Keep the 110 Ps. & remit me the remainder as I have been obligd. to be his Security here, ere he Cou'd depart for 40 Ps. that is if said Money is recover'd, shou'd you want Mr. French in the affair as he is well acquted. with the Circamstance, pay out of it his demand[.] I am Sorry I cou'd not have [*illegible*] Letter but when Law is in the Case every Circumstance must be explain'd[.] I hope to have [*rest of line illegible*] . . .

To BERNARD LINTOT, *Tickfaw River*[13]

Manchac, July 10, 1780

As you have been so obligeing as to offer me your Service in Pensacola the Present is to request that you will pay into the Hands of Mr. Robert Donald the Attorney or Attorny, or administrator to the Estate of the Late Mr. Montgommery or any other person properly authorised to receive the said Money the Sum of Ps.95.1, that Being the Ballance due said Estate as per Mr. Donalds Letter of the 1st of February last, Should Interest be requested (though I am in hopes it will not) as it has not been owing to any neglect in me that the Money was not paid long ere this but through the Sun of Misfortunes[.] pay it, takeing a receipt for the same for the reimbursement of which, if Mrs. Lintot

13/Bernard Lintot, originally from Connecticut, left after the beginning of the Revolution to seek asylum as a loyalist in West Florida. In 1775 he applied to the West Florida Council for a grant of 1000 acres on the Tickfaw River, and in 1776 he applied for 950 additional acres, which were also granted. See Petition to Council, November 15, 1776, PRO, CO 5/593, p. 215.

wants it to Day let her send for 50 ps. & the rest when she shall think proper to call for them, having nothing further to add only to wish you a pleasant Voyage & a Safe return . . .

To JOHN DAVIS, *New Orleans*

Manchac, July 11, 1780

Your Esteem'd favour of 25 Ultmo. I have duly received and note the Contents. I was really glad to find that you received the money of Mr. Deverges on acct. of Mr. Inrufty but am sorry to see by your Letter that their is no such a thing as getting any thing out of the Hands of Doctor Thomas, to whom request you'll Deliver the Inclosed Letter after perusal & sealing it, and if nothing then to be got I am determined to make him a Compliment of it, for I cannot help thinking that, that's what he wants, in my former letter I mentioned to you if you'd received Moneys for me, to remit to Mr. Donald 95 Ps. ¾rs my account, but now I have Setled the matter with Mr. Lintot who is to pay the said Money therefore shall not trouble you for the future on said Subject. Having nothing further to add . . .

P.S. If you Could Conveniently send me by the return of the Boat 24 Ells of Oznabrigs, I'll be much Obliged to you, its amount if not Detained it in your Hands shall remit, it to you per first Convayance[.]

To LIEUTENANT J. J. GRAHAM, *Pensacola*

Manchac, July 13, 1780

In my Letter which I did myself the Pleasure of writeing you the 2nd of Last March in which was in clos'd your account Current with me in which was included all our Gameing Accounts (Excepting the 50 Dollars which you won from me at Mr. Hickeys in presence of Mr. Wilson, on which account there was a Ballance due me of 4 Ps. 6½rs this is to be deducted from Said 50 Ps. there remain'd a Ballance in your favour of 45 Ps. 1½ rs [.] on the Morning of my Departure for Pensacola, the 11th Jany. 1779 you delivered me in your account Current of 645 Ps. which is to your Credit as per Account remitted you, Since which have been favour'd by a Letter from you by Mr. Walker in which you make Mention that you wou'd soon depart for England & wou'd be glad of havg. all small affairs setled ere your departure[.] I embrace the first opportunity that offered for New Orleans and wrote you in which I requested that you would draw upon me for said Ballance 45 Ps. 1½ which if said Letter never Come to hand I am not to be Blamed for it, since which your surprising Letter of the 5th Instant Came to hand with a Memorandum to Mr. Monsantoe requesting me to settle with him at the same time he produced me a Memorandum of yours for 385 Ps. in which there is a Mistake of 180 Ps. for you say that I lost 75, 80 & 50 which added together only makes 205 Ps. Give me leave to assure you that I never had the Honour of playing a game with you Since my return from Pensacola but twice the first at Mr. Hickeys in March 79 when I lost the last Mention'd 50 Ps. & Secondly on Sunday the 3d of last September in the same house where you won nothing from me therefore must be verry plain in telling you that this last Account has certainly been a mistake Committed inadvertantly and which I never will pay. Since your Letter Come to hand Mr. Wm. Quays has presented me your refers which I have paid say Ps.19.6½ this deducted from the 45.1½ remains Ps.25.3 in your favour & for which you may draw on Sight in favour of whom you please & it shall be paid on demand, In your last favour you Intimate that you have no inclination of Distressing me. I shou'd be verry sorry if you had it in your power for if you had you wou'd be one of the first that ever had since on the River, though have been in due many Thousand without ever being Distressed for it was always a general rule with me to pay when I could, tho' I have been deprived of my right this long time past without redress & if I am for the present moment under the Clouds its intirely owing to the unparalled proceedings of some of our noble Commanders heretofore. I have nothing further to add only to wish you a pleasant Voyage . . .

P.S. In a former letter, Requested you'd desire Babie to remit me my french Books lent her when a going to the River Amitt, but as yet have heard Nothing of them, I have 4 Ps.6 of hers in my hands which will remit her on sending me my books as ther's no Levee to be made at the Ends—

To THOMAS BENTLEY, *Kaskaskia*

Manchac, August 1, 1780

The Letter you was pleased to write to Mr. Swanson of 20th of Last June I received from Monsr. Dupray 21st Ulto. & Being properly authorised By Mr. Swanson, open'd the same the Contents of which have observed; I am sorry to acquaint you that Mr. Swanson had left this for to go to Pensacola four days ere yours Come to hand; on Reading the same; I found it would be to your advantage that you should have an answer to them by the first Conveyance, & as no one Could do it but Mr. Swanson for which reason I forwarded the same to N/ Orleans, in hopes they would have overtaken him there, which I am afraid they did not for he does not mention it in his last Letter from thence; on the Eve of his Embarking for Pensacola. therefore I have taken the Liberty to answer your Letter in some parts, Vizt. in the first place it is out of my Power to give you any account how your Accounts stands with the House of M M & Co. as I have heard Mr. Swanson say Nothing on that Head,—[illegible] all the Peltrys that you sent down that are Not mentioned [illegible] were on Hands when Willing & his party Came here & was taken out of your House By himself & Early, to a Large amount, the Real Value of which for my part Cannot Rightly acquaint you with. What they have done with Mrs. Cantey Ellis Elliot & Lum & Cos. I Believe is as follows. all Mrs. Canteys Lands were Sold at Pensacola to make good the Money due you & [illegible] forfeit of the Ps.1000. that is as far as they would go, but for how much they sold for Cannot say, as Mrs. Cantey in her life Time By the advice of Mr. Phillip Livingston would never make the titles over. Elliot I believe has paid, but for Ellis & Lum & Co. I Cannot pretend to say how far they may have Setled for your acct. But this I am well assured off, they are still largely indue the House[.] as for Barbers Refusing to pay on Account of Bacon I cannot assure you his reasons for so doing But they are both in these parts Still. It is true your house was Burnt By willings party, but not by their puting fire to it themselves; But they might as well have done it—for Willings part he was not hear; But at Orleans, the party was under the Command of Lieut. McIntyer, whom after he had Drove all the Cattle over the Boyeaux and Taken Every thing he Could find from the place he then set fire to all the Staves then hear Say abt. 40,000 of which there was about 20,000 Before your place [?] just over the Levee [.] the wind was verry Strong at N.W. which is right over the house; So that are the Staves were half Consumed, the whole house was in flame; allthough when first Discover'd by us at the Spanish fort to which place had all with drawn, we Run; but alass, all to no effect; for it was no Sooner on fire then it was out of the power of man to Stop it, all the old Buildings adjoining Suffered the same fate; your Cows & horses were Still in WestCoats, hands, At the time Willing & his party Came down, Though Wescoat had left your plantation at the forks some time before then without giving Mr. Swanson timely Notice thereof; to go on one of Mr. Bowkers & whil[e] Mr. Swanson was endeavouring to Bring him to a Settlement, the affairs happened and then there was Nothing further to be done for that Moment; Wescat moved over to the New Settlement on the Island of Orleans, which now Goes by the Name of Galvez Town, & took over your Cattle & Horses &c the latter with the waggon has been since sold by Mr. Swanson for your Account But the former God only Knows what has become of them all, for since Wescoatts Death there is no such thing as geting any proper account from his Executors[.] Mr. Swanson a few days ere his departure found out that James Nicholson had bought a Part of them, but from whom cannot pretend to say But this will be Known in time. 2 or 3 others of them are now hear under my Care as for anything else of yours that Remain at this Place I Know of not (Your desk & Papers Excepted) which are all safe, you'll receive here Inclosed 3 Letters for you, which has been here this some years left with me by Mr. Swanson to be forwarded by the first Conveyance, which is the Present. I am sorry to acquaint you, that Collins is with Mr. Swanson to whom he now belongs at Present, whether he will be willing to part [with] him Cannot say. But this I have often heard him mention, That he only Bought him to have it in his power to Return him to you on your Reimbursing him his Money with Interest &c. the Negro Damon was Sold some time ago By order of Mr. John Stephenson as one of the Attorneys to Messrs. Bradley & Harrisson &c. In the postcript of your letter you mention having sent me some Notes and accounts to Recover for you[.] Be assured I was never able to recover one Dollar on thim; & when I found that to be the Case I deliver'd them to Mr. Swanson, whom had the Care of all your other Effects. I am in hopes by the next Bateaux you will have a full account; of all your affairs from Miller & Swanson (that is if your Letters gets safe to hand in time) in which I make no doubt they will send you all the proper Vouchers you request—having answer'd your Letter as far as I am able; it is now time; for me to say Something to you on my own Account. Be assured you have not Been the only one that has Been the sport of fortune since the war Begun, we have all had our part of it in this quarter not one Excepted, but has felt his share of the Effects of the [*illegible*] troubles[.] for my part I lost about 12,000 Dollars By willing & his party; Next the kings troops took possession of my Improvements [and] I have not been paid so that I may say there is another dead loss of Ps. 2700. Lastly on the Spaniards Takeing this place the 7th of last Septr. I then lost abt. 1800 Dollrs. more, having been made Prisoner & robbed by the Indians, almost all my Cattle Killed before my face yet Could Say Nothing; so that in my present Low Circumstances if you Could remit me the Amount of your note so long due it will be a great assistance to me in my Present Situation; your Compliance shall be greatfully Acknowledged by . . .

To MESSRS. MORGAN AND MATHER, *New Orleans*

Manchac, August 8, 1780

Since my writeing to you the 2nd of Last march In which I inclosed your account Current Ballance in your favour Ps.188.5 & at which time Remitted you Ps.164.2½ in Mr. William's Account & Connely['s] Note both which hope have been paid long ere this, there remain'd then a Ballance your favour of Ps.24.1¼ which Mr. Patrick Foley promised me he wou'd pay & take up my notes in your hands But whether so or not am Ignorent as I have not been favour'd with an Answer from you, nor have I either seen Mr. Williams or Forley in their way up, as they did not stop here. But if they have paid as I am in hopes they have from your Silence in that Case request you will send me my Notes in your hands[.] I dont mean the [*rest of page illegible*] had that Villain paid you According to his promise to me when here in his way down I might have taken up Mr. Stephensons Note But it shall not be long ere I will effect it till which I am Gentlemen . . .

To WILLIAM SWANSON, *Pensacola*

Manchac, September 4, 1780

Since your Departure from hence I have not been able to Recover for you One Dollar of yr small Accots. you intrusted me with therefore have not any thing worth mentioning to you about your affairs[.] Some days after you went off I received 2 Letters from Mr. Bentley which forwarded to you at Orleans per the first Conveyance though it seems they did not overtake you there[.] I am in hopes you have Received them ere this, as they were Directed to the Care of Mr. William Strothers, on my finding that you had not Received them, I wrote Mr. Bentley an answer a Copy of which you have hear Inclosed for your Government & forwarded the three Letters you left me for him. if you received my Letter that I wrote you Concerning Sundry small Trifles for my Family's use & mine if you have received it hope if Possible youll not fail to send them as they are not [?] to be had hear for love nor money. Please to let me here from you Per [first ?] Conveyance let me know if you have been [*illegible*] Paid for my Improvements or whether I am to Loose from them [*illegible*] I have taken the Liberty of Inclosing to your Care the following accounts orders & Notes, as the Persons indue me them are at your Place and maybe youll be able to recover some part thereof if so I may say it is so much out of the flame Vizt.

George Thorntons 9 Notes with 3 years Interest thereon	402.1
Ps.412.1 received on account 10 Dollrs. Remains due	
John Pomroys Note for	39.7½
Captn. William Barkers Voucher for	50.—
my order on George Bowles for Ballce of h/a . . .	57.1½
Mr. McPhersons acct. 23 Ps.2r. Benjn. Pettys do. 3/6 . .	27.—
	576.2

Your Wench is Still on her legs little Jack has been verry poorly ever since you left this; But is to be hoped he will soon get the better of it as the Cold weather is coming on. Mr. Down I made leave the house, as she took much of the Lady on herself, when she found the Wench alone. McCoy says he will pay you 50 Dollrs. as I have threatned him to turn him off the Plantation, poor William OBrient was drowned in Crossing the Boyeaux above the Fort of Baton Rouge, going to settle with Mr. Campbell. Doctor Flowers has lost his youngest Son, your Negro, damon remains Still the same dunce of a fellow he always was; it is with pain he will do any thing But I spur him up now & then, he is quite Naked & if you Cannot send something to Cloath him God Knows how he will pass the Winter. we have had a mighty Rainy weather almost ever Since your departure[,] our small Crops will fall much Short of our Expectations owing to a violent gail of wind & rain which happened on 24 Ulto. which I am much afraid has Caused great Destruction in many parts, But as yet we have not been informed of the Particulars of the Melancholly effects of its source. Mrs. Fitzpatrick Joins me in wishing you a better State of health than you had at Orleans[.] She desires you'll not forget her 3 Pr. of Shoes, having nothing further to add . . .

P.S. I have wrote to Mr. Miller Per this Conveyance.

To JOHN MILLER, *Pensacola*

Manchac, September 6, 1780

Since my writing to you the 2nd of last March I have not been favour'd with a line from you, although there has been Sundry occasions to Orleans this I suppose is owing to your great hurry of Business and your not haveing as yet received any Account of the Situation [*illegible*] about my Improvements.

In your last you desired to know if Mr. Henry Smith had finished paying the amt. of his Account. I can only mention that I never received one Dollar only what has been paid to yourself. Not having an opportunity of seeing him since the troubles Commenced, But as he is Still in good pay & has it in his Power to Discharge it I have sent you a Copy of his Account But hope you'll have no trouble in Recovering the Ballance (still due) as I have not heard any thing from you this Long time. I am still Ignorant about the Fate of the two bills sent you the 25th May 1779 for Ps.112.6¼ Say Robert McGillivrays for 95.6¼ & Joseph Purcells Certificate for Ps.17, which Request you will favour me so far as to mention in your next, if I did not write you by Mr. Swansons Convoie it was no ways owing to any Neglect in me but as he was agoing to your Place himself Could give you as true a Description of my affairs as if I had wrote myself, having nothing particular to mention had I wrote. Should you receive any favourable account of my Petition hope You'll Let me hear per the first Convoie, having Nothing further to add . . .

P.S. Mrs. Fitzpatrick desires her Compliments to you & Mr. Pinhorn if Still with you.

To MESSRS. MORGAN AND MATHER,
New Orleans

Manchac, September 6, 1780

Your favour of the 11th Ulto. by Captn. Davis is now before me, the Contents of which I have Duly observed, But Cannot without Some Concern think, on the manner Messrs. Williams & Foley, Treated me after their giving me their promise that they would pay the amount of their Accounts to you, if Mr. Foley had not Comply'd I should not have thought so much of it, though there is a Ballance in my favour of Ps.36 or Ps.38. But as for Mr. Williams if he had not paid the wholle of his Account he ought in gratitude have paid the 63.0½ which I settled with Mr. Ward Last October, soonner than he should be troubled by Mr. Ward, whom was determined he should not leave Orleans till such times it was paid having been of a long Standing, this I did to oblige him. when you sent me the Account you did not send me the acceptance, which Request you'll by some Safe Conveyance, for without it I shall not be able to Carry him before the Commander & since he has used me in the manner he has I shall leave no Stone unturned to Reduce him to settle his Account. Be assured I am really as uneasy about the payment of Mr. Stephensons Money as you may be; if so much had Come in since you have had the Note it should have been paid long ere this, But all them that are indue me put me off till the Crop. how it will turn out God only Knows. But this I will Assure you off, that if I han't it soon in my power sooner than Mr. Stephenson shou'd wait longer I will Dispose of a Negro but he shall be paid[.] As to the Order Capt. Conner Left with you for Ps.83.9 a part of which I shall not be against paying, when in my power Say a part for in the first place there is 2 hundred of Pickets furnish'd him for his Yard Ps.12. Books Lent him which he Never returned though demanded by Mr. Hickey Sundry times for which I shall Charge him Ps.13 more so that the Ballance will be only Ps.58.2 in his favour, and this shall Settle as soon as possible, Till which Believe me to be . . .

P.S. as my Notes to your Proffit & Topham are all paid please send them me by some safe Conveyce.

To CAPTAIN JOHN DAVIS, *New Orleans*

Manchac, September 28, 1780

Your Esteem'd favour of 20th Instant, I have this Moment Received by Captn. Hinson with the 15 lb. of Shott, for which I am much obliged to you[.] I observe the trouble you have had in looking for some Cloathing for my Negroes, but since no such thing is to be had God only Knows how they will pass the Winter if Mr. Swanson does not send me something from Pensacola, But this I am in hopes he will if possible. I further observe what you mention about Doctor Thomas having paid the 70 Dollrs. to Blommart this I was well assured of Long ago, as the Doctr. Told me he had the same afternoon, while Blommart was Still here, when the Gentleman for whom you have the Letters arrives which I am in hopes he is ere this, youll deliver it him, & from the Length of time he is indue it me I flatter myself he will use some means to pay it, at least I have reason to Expect it, so from him, In my former I omitted to send you Mr. John Hendersons Letter in which he acknowledges having received some part of the Money indue me by one Robt. Scarce, & as I am well informed that said Scarce is now in good Employ & will be able to pay the Remainder or if not all at once, you'll receive it as he can pay it in, as it will be much better in your hands than where it now is, as Mr. Henderson has Left Orleans[.] I suppose he has left the Note with Mr. Pollock for which reason I have wrote him the Inclosed Letter to request him to Deliver them to you[.] if you receive this or any other Moneys for me after paying yourself [*illegible*] small things you may send me from time to time & [*illegible*] Remainder I request you will pay into Mr. Mather's [*?*] hands on Account of my Note, which I shall be Glad [*illegible*] I had it paid [*?*] If the flag is not gone ere this Comes to hand youll forward Mr. Swansons Letters with them formerly sent you, my best respects to Mr. Strothers . . .

P.S. as I don't seal either of the Letters Request you will put a Wafer to each after perusal.

To WILLIAM FERGUSON, *Natchez*

Manchac, October 12, 1780

Your much Esteem'd favour of 16th Ulto. Came to hand some days ago, in which you make mention of my having made a mistake respecting your private account[.] all I can say to you on that head is this that Mr. Kennedy & self Examin'd all your & Williams's account from one end to the other, and as we could find no such entry to your debit we Imag'd it had been an Omission in posting therefore Charged your Account with the same[.] But since your letter Came to hand your Mr. William Williams has been here; to whom I mention'd the affair and we together re-Examined the Books & found it Charged to the account of Lum Williams & Co. Remit you the Inclosed account which you'll please to receive for me [and] pay yourself the amount of the Error Committed to your Disadvantage & when in Cash for the same Remit me the Ballance, as it always will give me the same pleasure to pay as to receive, while Mr. Williams was here I inquired if he was going to your place as he goes up[.] he told me not for the present But that he Expects to see you ere Long, in his way down; for it seems Monsr. Mennar is something afraid of the Indians if he went up the River for which reason he goes in his Boat to the falls on the red River from their to the Nachitosh & so on to the Arcansaws, he told me the Occasion of this Voyage is to Settle your Company affairs there, he further told me that when he has the pleasure of seeing you it will be to settle all your Accounts together. In a Letter you wrote to Messrs. Monsanto, which they were pleased to show me, I see that Mr. Mathews makes a demand of Ps.20, for a small Cabbin which he had put up here ere Willings Come down, & which I took down after Mr. Mathews had abandoned it, but as I medled with it I had it apprased by 2 men whom Vallued it at Ps.13 as there was but 210 Indifferent Clabboards in the whole with 2 [?] upright Posts[,] Round plates &c., all put put [sic] together in a very indifferent manner, I told them, that since I had an Occasion for it immediately as all my effects was then Exposed to the weather; on the Spanish side I would pay him 14 Ps. instead of 13 Ps. this I acquainted Mr. Mathews with on my way from Orleans when I saw him at the homma Village [*rest of page illegible*]

... May 1778 on the 16th of June following Madam Cantey Executors knowing that this money was Still in my hands applied & got an Order from the Civil Commander Monsieur Dutince to pay them that some, on Acct. of Ps.20 indue the Deceased for her attendance of Mr. Mathews while sick at her house. I therefore paid it as per receipt but for my paying it again, or more than I have already paid is a thing I am Determined not to Comply with, as I will not be imposed on, he may think himself well off; for if I had not taken it away as I did he would have had a verry flemmish Account of it when the Troops come, as you are so obliging as to offer me your Service, I'll take it as a Particular favour, if you Can assist Captn. William McIntosh in anything about my affairs that you'll do it, as I am really in great Want of all the Moneys indue me; to enable me to discharge some debts I am still indue[.] Your Compliance shall be most gratefully acknowledged by . . .

P.S. After writing the above [*illegible*] I omitted to mention to you that I had inclosed you [*illegible*] Notes to Henry Lefleur, for 16 Ps. & indorsed by said Lefleur [*illegible*] I would request that youd make him make good his endorsement

To JOHN DAVIS, *New Orleans*

Manchac, October 14, 1780

Your Esteem'd favour of 7 Instant, with the Inclosed Note I received From Mr. Lintot whom (& God be thanked) is Safely arrived with his family, I am glad to hear Monsieur Valler is Returned, and hope he will be as good as his word, ere you pay any money for me to Mr. Mather Reduct your Commission; then request him [to send] me all my Obligations (I mean them Concerning their house & to Mr. Proffit & Topham, as they are paid it is but right I should have them [sent ?] up also. Request he will either send me David Williams's Acceptance for Ps.63.0½ that I may be able to recover it here or pass it to my Credit and the Note to Mr. Stephenson[.] your Compliance will oblige . . .

To BENJAMIN WARD, *Natchez*

Manchac, October 22, 1780

I did myself the pleasure of writing you Last August by Monsr. Poidrass, But whether it Came to hand or not, am uncertain as I have not been favour'd with an answer, in my former I took the Liberty of Informing you that I was much pressed for money that I am indue, & which, I am not able to Discharge without having recourse to the Gentlemen; that are indue me and as you are one of the Number, (and that your Debt has been for some years Standing) I flatter myself you will endeavour to Discharge the same; without obliging me to wait longer, which if you do not be assured it will be verry detrimental to my Interest. I should be sorry to be troublesome but at the same time Consider that I am necessiated therefore have given your Acct. Current By which you'll see there is a Ballance Still due me of Ps.264.4¾ which I am in hopes you'll find Right to Mr. David Ross, as also an order for the Money due his Sales. your paying the same to him will oblige & be in full of all demands from . . .

To CAPTAIN WILLIAM McINTOSH, *Natchez*

Manchac, October 22, 1780

Since my writeing you the 11th of Last June I have not been favour'd with any of yours, this I suppose has been owing to the hurry in your own affairs; and your Indisposition for I heard some time ago that you are confined to your Room which I am in hopes is removed ere this and that you enjoy your former good state of health; I know not what to say to you about my small Concerns that are under your Care as I am quite Ignorant what you have been able to do for me since your last. I formerly drew a small order on you in favour of Mr. Rapalje for Ps.20 [?] whether you were pleased to accept it or not is unknown to me and as he is now going up to Settle a plantation in your District, as he may be in need of Sundry articles, which he may be able to procure from some of the persons indue me, which they can easier supply him with than get the Money to Discharge their accounts or Notes, I have given him an order on you for such notes or Accts. as he shall think proper to receive as payment. If he should find any among them in your hands that he will Take as Real payment, you may let him have to the amount of Ps.287.0¾ that being the Ballance I am still indue his Sales for Since our Setling the 9th Instant I have Accounted with him for Ps.238.5 which makes the Ballance as it stands in the account say Ps.525.5¾ & should you have been so happy as to have received so much for my Account please to pay it him, in either Case you'll please to observe to take his receipt, in full of all Demands, on account of said Sales. There is Still some outstanding debts due the Sales they are to be Accepted, as I am not accountable for them till they are Recover'd, and this in some measure will Diminish the trouble you may have with them. I have heard with a great deal of pleasure, that all your accounts that you left unsetled at Pensacola have been honourably paid on which I make you my Compliments. If the three Vouchers I gave you the 8th of May 1779 for the amount of Skinners account for work done for your Company was Included you'll please to pass their amount to my Credit, with you Say Ps.35.2½ which I Believe will Ballance all private accounts between us. If not Included please to remit them me by the first Conveyance that I may have it in my power to Imbrace the first Occasion of sending them to Mr. Miller [?]. when [illegible] will get in their hands if your health & affairs will permit you. I request you'll favour me so far as to let me hear from you By the first opportunity after the Receipt of this, mention in it what I have to Expect from your quarter as to payments, as I am really in want which them indue me ought to Consider, Being so long due as I should be glad to Leave the Country as soon as my affairs would permit me so to do, your Compliance will greatly oblige ...

To GEORGE RAPALJE, Natchez[14]

Manchac, October 22, 1780

Instead of a Power of Attorney which I dont think proper to give till such times as I have some Accounts from Captn. McIntosh of what he has been able to do for me, you have my order here incloasd on him for any notes or Accounts which you shall think proper to receive, or which you may think may turn to account, for the Ballce. Still remaining due you, say Ps.287.0¾. if this is not agreeable have Requested him the first Money he may receive for my account to pay you with same as I should be sorry you should meet with any Disappointment that I can Remove, you'll please to observe that the Ps.17 for Isaac Monsanto is not indicated, Being almost assured you had Corn from him at sundry times the first in 1774, and the last in 1775. But this matter will be soon Setled when Mr. Jacob Comes from town, whom promised me he would Look over their [?] Books; whether or not we shall always settle the affair to your Satisfaction, when we have further Information. the Letters for Messrs. McIntosh & Ferguson I request you'll deliver them yourself. I have [illegible] remitted, which are to your credit & having nothing further to add only to wish you a pleasant Voyage ...

P.S. The Shoe maker has not done your shoes, or should have sent them—he says it is impossible to promise you 4 pr. more as he has promised work which he is not able to finish

Copy of the order sent to Mr. Rapalje Drawn on Captn. William McIntosh
Sir
   You'll please to Deliver to Mr. George Rapalje or his order any Notes or accounts which he may think proper to accept you may have of mine, the amount of Two hundred & Eighty seven Dol-

---

14/George Rapalje, a relative and possibly son of Garrett Rapalje of Baton Rouge, was an officer in the Royal Provincials and came to West Florida from New York after it was ceded to Britain. He married Jane Farrar, of a distinguished Mississippi family, and owned a large plantation near Ellis's Cliffs. He also apparently kept a store on the Big Black, probably on land owned by Garrett Rapalje. See Claiborne, *Mississippi*, 163; George Rapalje Notebook, Department of Archives and Manuscripts, Louisiana State University; Confirmation, October 3, 1805, Ellis-Farar Papers, Department of Archives and Manuscripts, Louisiana State University.

lars, three quarters of a Ryal, Taking his Receipt for the same, as per advised and this shall be your discharge for the same & oblige

     Sir
      Yours &c.
To Captn. William McIntosh at the Natchez

To CAPTAIN WILLIAM McINTOSH, *Natchez*

Manchac, November 22, 1780

I did myself the pleasure of writeing you the 22nd Ulto. which Youll now Receive, & to which Refer you intending it should have gone by Mr. George Rapalji, But he had set off ere my letter got to Baton [Rouge] Since which your Esteemed favour of the 28th of last month Came to hand the Contents of which have observed. I Return you my most hearty thanks for your attention to my small affairs in your hands. be assured any thing that you can recover for me will be a great assistance to me at Present having Moneys to pay or shall be obliged to sell my Negroes, if not able to Recover some of my outstanding debts to inable me to Discharge them, or should not be so troublesome. What you have been pleased to do for me in the Recovering way give me great Satisfaction and had I been there myself dont think I could have done so much, as for Nelly [Price] she is a verry bad Woman, & if I cannot get my Money I am determined to get proper Satisfaction when in my power to put the Law in force against her Infamous Slander. I am Glad Mr. Johnson has paid for they say he is Generally Long winded. Mr. Vousdin has merited being put to Some Expence, as it is his own Seeking. Mr. James is good for Hogscases [?]. when King pays you, give the money to Mr. Rapalji; as mentioned in my former, with any Notes to the amount of my order, take his receipt as Before mention'd. I shall be really glad to see Mr. Watkins this way, But am more so to receive the money so long due, I am in hopes you'll bring Mr. Alston to his proper Bareings, as I am of an Opinion he never [?] intended to pay any man, which he Can avoid. What ever you shall think proper to do with Madam Jean for the Receipt [?] of the Money will be agreeable if you have Any Commands this way [*illegible*] them[.] we have nothing new with us excepting Account of the Governor Galvez's having Left the havanna the 16 Ultimo with 7 Ships of the Line 4 Frigates & 4500 Land fources in an Expedition against Pensacola.[15] But as yet no further accounts whether arrived or not, having Nothing further to add only to request my best respects to Mrs. McIntosh . . .

15/See Introduction to this volume, p. 29.

To CAPTAIN JOHN DAVIS, *New Orleans*

Manchac, November 25, 1780

Both your Esteem'd favours are now before me the first of 9 Ulto. and the other of 14 Inst. the Contents of which have observed[.] In your former you mention your having sent my Letter for Pensacola I pray [?] they may arrive safe, & that Monsieur Valier had paid you on account Ps.117 with his note for the Ballance payable in 2 months but [he] would not allow any Interest, Since he would not allow what is law full for me to Expect, Be assured; he will never make any other [adv]ance, therefore think myself happy that you have Brought it near a Close, for with such Shavers they must take what they can get [in] these troublesome times. if you have not ere this waited on the Father ask [?] you do it so that I may know if that some is another dead Loss, Is Doctr. Thomas still with you does he seem any ways inclined if in his power to pay his debts [?] In your last I observe that Mr. Scarce paid into the hands of Messrs. Pollock & Henderson on account of Ps.115. I am Glad to hear it. But should be much more so if once in your hands, I am something surprised at Mr. Scarce for Expecting I should pay 25 Ps. on account of Mr. Boles, is it because he was in my employ that I am to be answerable for his debts & ones I never assumed or did I Know anything of Boles Being in his Debt for the thing was never mentioned to me when Mr. Boles lived with me[.] he Bought a Horse from Mr. Scarce in August 1778 the only one Scarce ever had at this place and paid him for it in Cash Ps.17 of which I advanced him [?] at the time of the purchase. But supposing Boles had bought this Horse I never became Security in any ways for the payment for Mr. Boles left my Employ he remained with Captn. McIntosh [*illegible*] at this place. Mr. Scarce was then hear/ why did he not settle it himself, as he was daily [*illegible*] of seeing him. Further [*illegible*] Mr. Boles left this he never so much as mention'd any such thing to me therefore will never Consent to any such Demands—Let him only remember the Money he is indue me not for Goods on which I had an advance, but for my being his Security & which I have been obliged to pay a long time ago, with Interest & there has been no interest Charged him for 14 Months past, therefore shall Expect he will finish paying the Ballance as soon as possible, for Gods sake press Mr. Pollock till you get the Money Note & Account from him.

In my former of the 14 Ultmo. I request you wou'd speak to Mr. Mather about Delivering you my Obligations in his hands, as they are all paid, also to request he will either Credit my Note to Mr. Stephenson with the amount of David Williams's Acceptance for 63.0½ Ps. or send it me that I may recover its amount, One or the other I have a right to Expect. Please pay him all the Moneys you receive my Account till such time Mr. Stephenson is paid, but see the Sum Indorsed on the Note, if you have not had time ere this please dont omit Demanding them when you have, You are pleased to Mention in Your last that there are Vessels in the River with Cloathing[.] I am Still in want, but should [?] not trouble you till such times I have the Money to send for them which I am in hopes to have ere all is sold off, as I am determined to do without every thing that I can Possibly avoid, till such times Mr. Stephenson is paid. if you can send me 4 lbs of Gun Powder & 50 lb. of Sugar if at the old price will be all requested for the Present[.] I have nothing further to add . . .

To GREGORY FRENCH, *New Orleans* [?]

Manchac, December 9, 1780

In looking over some papers the other day, I found Your favor of 21 Decemr. 1777 from the Apelases, in which you make mention of your having presented, the order I gave you on Mr. Granding of whom you say acknowledg'd it right (yet never have heard anything further abt. it) as I have never been favor'd with any of yours since the Commencemt. of the troubles, I shall be much obligd to you if you did or not receive the amount of Monsieur Silvester's note, you'll let me hear when any opportunity offers for this place, there is yet a small account subsisting between us, on which side the Ballce. lies cannot for the present pretend to say but should it be in yr favor; after the Recpt. of yours, it shall be sent you per first safe conveyance[.] Your black Gauze was all sold at 4/ per Ell how much there was of it when receiv'd, really cannot say, therefore must leave that to yourself. having nothing further to add . . .

To DANIEL HICKY, *Baton Rouge* [?]

Manchac, December 9, 1780

Since my last to you by Mr. Watts, I have not been favor'd with any of yours, I have now to acquaint you that Madm. Tessier has sent me word she shall not come to Manchac, so that I might sell the House, if any opportunity offer'd, in consequence of which, Doct. Flower is now in it since the Commencemt. of this month, he says it is only for 10 or 15 days longer as he is to have the house Mr. Watts is in, who has purchasd. that place, that was formerly Mitchells, from Paul Sharp, for 500 Dollars (a sweet bargain indeed) on which he proposes making Timber, but I am well assur'd it will be in it these three months if not longer, therefore shall charge him 8 Ps. a Month. Swanson's black Cattle are all in the Kitchen. I say black Cattle, for the Wench has had 2 Children at a birth, both as black as the ace of Spades, one of which is still alive, the other Died e'er the Doctr. moved. I put up all your front fence anew, (the House put up for Mr. Steward, —fence [?] is entirely gone, therefore I had to make up your Garden fence put up Gate-posts &c so that all is in good order, the Oven has had a new Coat & covering also, I am still putting things to rights[.] I have the house I am in all anew, a new Store 20 by 16[,] new Negro houses 30 by 14[,] a sleeping Room 18 by 14, Dug a fine Well, have a good Garden, put up all the fence round the Lott anew (for whom all this God only knows) for my own part I have been for some Weeks pass'd very unwell which still seem to continue, all my Cloaths have outgrown my Body, so that if I put any of them off for 6 or 8 days & want to make use of them Mrs. Fitzpatrick is oblig'd to take a reef in them, I keep [to] the house more than ever I han't been so far as Heindsens these 6 months, nor have I been at Watts or Monsanto's above twine in that time, & now that Mr. Lintot has left this; as he has bought the Doctor's Plantation in the Accadian Coast, it may be a Month or two e'er I go the length of my Garden, on the late bought of Escott; which I always keep in good order, in hopes that one day they will bring me something, I should be much oblig'd to you for my accot. of the sundries had from you since the last settlemt. in Novr. 1778 I find a charge of sundries against you in my Books. I shall be glad to have [an opportunity] to put all things to rights as I have nothing else to do at present, having nothing further to add, only to wish you Mrs. Hickey & Children [?] health . . .

To CAPTAIN JOHN DAVIS, *New Orleans*

Manchac, December 14, 1780

This is to acknowledge the receipt of your esteem'd favor (by Mr. Dunbar) the contents of which have duly observ'd. Mr. Mather is now here, but as yet has said nothing to me about my papers, which I suppose he will e'er he leaves this, if not shall speak to him about them myself. I have given him an order on David Williams for Ps.77.3½, which if he receives is to be put to the Cr of my note to Mr. Stephenson, which will always be something whether or not shall advise you by his return, I am glad to hear you are likely to get the money from Mr. Pollock, for it seems he does not disburse freely in many matters[.] what you mention abt. getting Doctor Thomas's note for the amot. of my Accot. say Ps.85.5½ do in the affair whatever you shall think proper, for whatever you do in the sd. affair it shall meet with my approbation. The powder you were pleas'd to send me never came to hand, being left by mistake at Mr. George Mathers, when it will come up God only knows, Mr. Proffitt let me have the Sugar, so that I am stock'd for some time (by the occasion of Mr. James Mather) I shall take the liberty of sending you a Barrell of Poatatoes & Turnips, of my own raising which request you'll accept[.] I remain with much regard . . .

To CAPTAIN JOHN DAVIS, *New Orleans*

Manchac, December 28, 1780

Your esteem'd favour of the 16th Inst. with the Linnen handfs. I duly receiv'd from Mr. Alexander, the amot. of which you will deduct from the Inclos'd draft on Mr. Jno. Gordon who will pay you the amot. on his selling any one of his Negro's, but should it happen that he can't get away or that he does not find a proper Price for his Negro's in that case it may not suit him to pay you more than the Ps.23 for the last things sent me, take it, & write it on the Draft. I am no ways surpriz'd at the Fathers refusing to pay the paultry sum of Ps.16.4 as maybe he looks upon it, as so much taken from the hereticks, therefore God bless him with it[.] I am glad you have got the money from Mr. Pollock, & from what you mention am in hopes that Scarce will pay the remainder without my being oblig'd to force him to it. Mr. Joseph Carpenter returns you his most hearty thanks, & wishes to have it in his power to return the Complimt. as Mr. Mather is not come down can say nothing to you abt the order I gave him, therefore defer saying on that head till I see himself[,] which will be in a day or two, therefore have nothing further to add only request my Complits. to Mr. Strothers . . .

To CAPTAIN JOHN DAVIS, *New Orleans*

Manchac, January 1, 1781

I wrote you 28th last month by Mr. Gordon Inclosing you my Draft on him for Ps.71.1, which he promis'd me he would pay you on his disposing of any one of his Negro's, which hope has come to hand e'er this[.] in the same I promis'd to write, by Mr. Mather, but his stay here was so very short I had not time to make out the Inclos'd Accots. In that of Messrs. Morgans & Mather you'll see there is a Ballce. still due them of Ps.200, that is if they don't charge Interest on the Note, which if I am oblig'd to pay will be hard (as the Laws of the Country will not oblige any one to pay it to me) but pay it to the last Farthing & then the Ballce. will be 238 dol: for 19 months Interest on 300 Dol from May 1779 to Decemr. 1780 will make the 38 dol more. I have wrote Mr. Mather a few lines about his allowing me the amot. of Mr. Foleys Accot, which I am in hopes he will, for whilst he was here I really omitted it, should you receive [Mr.] Gordons money & that Mr. Mather will allow Mr. Foleys accot. when you are taking up my note to Mr. Stephenson, request Mr. Mather to deliver you my other Notes, which he told me here he had not time to look for them, but would deliver them you to send me, after all this is over pay yourself for Comissions trouble &c and for sundries sent me from time to time, if enough remains in your hands please send me 4 or 5 such pieces Linnin as you sent Mr. Carpenter(if still to be had at the same price) but should you not have sufficient in your hands, dont send them, for I really cannot tell when I could pay you as I am not able to recover a Dollar from them that [are] indebted to me. In a Ltre I receiv'd from Mr. Ward some time since he promis'd he would be up here in 20 days & then he would pay me the Ballce. of his accot. two hundred & odd Dol: but as yet have heard nothing further of his leaving Town, if he has please mention it in your next & oblige . . .

To WILLIAM FERGUSON, *Natchez*

Manchac, January 26, 1781

Your esteem'd favor of 10th Inst. inclosing Mr. Rapalje's respects [?] & your small memorandum came to hand last night [the] Contents of which have duly observed & Inclosed you my most hearty thanks [for] your kind offer of serving me, which I am so well assur'd of from the many [*illegible*] that have no reason for Doubt that [*illegible*] only wish for an opportunity to acknowledge them all in some more particular manner, I am sorry to acquaint you, that the articles you stand in need of are not to be had at Manchac; nor do I believe you would find them all in Orleans, owing to the great scarcity of Goods, for my own part I have not any thing for Sale, nor have I had for some months pass'd, except a few Augers, falling Axes &c. I carrie'd your note to Messrs. Monsantos. Mr. Jacob told me should his Brother Emanuel (who is now at Orleans) bring any such Goods he would send them, on his arrival, shall see what he has & if only part of them, they shall be sent you by first conveyance (as you have not paid Mr. Blommart, request you will not, as he will shortly be down & I will settle it with himself, please enquire if Mr. Blommart has reciev'd anything from Mr. Easton on my accot. for I gave him accots. & notes to the amot. Ps.362.2 to recover for me, but since his departure from this I have never heard from him, the Letters I mentiond to you in my former have since come to light[.] I have nothing further to add . . .

To GEORGE RAPALJE, *Natchez*
Manchac, January 26, 1781

I am favor'd with yours of 7th Inst. the Contents of which have duly observ'd; you acknowledge having receiv'd from Mr. McIntosh Mr. Kings note with Interest due thereon amot. Ps.79.5 this is right also Ps. 84.1 from Mr. Ferguson by an order on Mr. Hutchins which sums amot. to Ps.161.6 and this being deducted from the Dr'ft in your favor for Ps.287.¾ leave a Ballance still due your Fathers Sales of Ps.125.2¾, exclusive of outstanding Debts not yet recover'd, & the little Interest due on the draft, which Ballce. with the Interest have requested Mr. McIntosh to pay you on receipt of my Letter, by this conveyance you'll please to observe, I have not accepted your Draft in favor of Messrs. Monsanto's nor can I accept any other you may think proper to draw, on account of the foregoing ballance still remaing. till such time as the Drafts already given you (for that purpose) comes back under a proper protest, which I am well assur'd will not be the case, as Mr. McIntosh has receiv'd on my accot. since the date of your Letter, the amount of Mr. Phillip Alston's Note from John Farqhuar, who acquainted me with the same in his way down therefore request you will apply for the same. as for the Dol.17 of Isaac Monsanto [*illegible*] Mr. John Davis who is daily expected here, & to whom Mr. Strothers has given the proper state as it stands in the deceas'd Books. be assur'd I have often spoke to the Shoemaker since your departure, but have not been able to procure any Shoes for you or would have sent them, I have nothing further to add . . .

To CAPTAIN WILLIAM McINTOSH, *Natchez*
Manchac, January 26, 1781

Your much esteemd favor of 15th Inst. Inclosing Mr. Rapaljes recpt. & Mr. James note I have duly receiv'd & noted the contents, you'll please observe Mr. Rapaljes receipt is for more money than he got for Mr. Kings note was only for Ps.68.2 with 25 months Intert. the sum at 8 pCt is dol.11.3 so that the whole amot. is no more than 79.5 instead of Ps.82.2 therefore request you'll rectify the Error with him say Ps.4.5[.] Mr. Rapalje has also rec'd from Mr. Ferguson on my accot. Ps.82.1 this added to Ps.79.5 is Ps.161.6 & these sums deducted from the amot. of my draft on you in his favor for Ps.287.¾ will leave a ballance still due him of Ps.125.2¾ which am in hopes you have paid e'er this as Mr. Farqhuar is his way down told me he had paid you the Amot. of Mr. Alstons Note, which if you have not paid request you will on recpt. of this, there will be some Interest due him pay it also, taking his recpt. as mention'd in my former Letter, for I should be sorry he should suffer any disappointmt. as he seems to Intimate will be the case in his Letter of 7th Inst. in not receivg the full amot. of the Draft, but this Letter of his was dated I presume e'er you had got Alstons money. I have nothing further to add . . .

To PHILIP BARBER, *Grand Gulf*

Manchac, February 3, 1781

When going up on your Voyage to the Ilinois, you was pleas'd to promis'd me, that on your return you would pay the Ballce. of your accot. as also the remaing Ballce. due me by the Deceas'd Capt. Harrison for which reason have Inclos'd the accots. to Mr. Jennings (which am in hopes you'll find right, & if convenient for you to discharge he will give a proper receipt for me, therefore if you can be assur'd it will greatly oblige me . . .

To CAPTAIN JOHN DAVIS, *New Orleans*

Manchac, February 22, 1781

Your favor of the 14th Inst. with all my papers that were in the hands of Messrs. Morgan & Mather, & your Accot. currt. came safe to hand, In examing. the accot. I find you have committd. some errors to my disadvantage thrô mistake for which reason thought proper to send you the Copys of your own Accots. & mine which after proper examination, I am in hopes you'll find right, for in the first place you'll please to observe you have debited me in each account with the Ps.11.2 being the amot. of the Soap sent me by Mr. Alexander, nor do you in either give me Credit for Ps.11.2 paid you on my account by Mr. Strother, as by his Letter

4th Augt. 1780, therefore these sums leaves an error of Ps.22.4, secondly the 20½ lbs Steel you sent by Jacques makes another of Ps.15, having never requested you to send me any such thing, therefore imagine it to have been a mistake & intended for some other, & for which reason return it, these two makes Ps.37.4[,] thirdly you'll observe by the accot. that I have not creditted you with the Ballce. paid Mr. Strother for the Barrl. of Sugar, sent me by Mr. Harman [?] as I have mislay'd the accot. & cannot for the present find it, but this I remember it was abt. 30 Dols, for the exact Sum Mr. Strothers can inform you, & when added to the afore mention'd Ps.37.4 I believe will make the Ballce. as struck in my accot. or within a few bits[.] I observe what you say abot. your not being able to get Monsr Valler to allow anything for the Interst. (with such Men I may think myself happy if I get the principal, thô at least I think if he acted like a Man of honour, he ought to allow somthing, you say nothing whether Mr. Strother has paid you the Ps.6 for Mr. Barber or allow's me the Ballce. of Aickmans Accot. this you'll please mention in your next[.] further in looking over Messrs. Morgan & Mathers accot. I find they have not allow'd me the amot. of Mr. Foleys accot. if he is still in Town please speak to him abt. it, tell him the 10 Bushells of Corn taken out of his Barge Mr. Mather has charg'd me with, therefore he will have to pay them 10 Dollars more than the Ballce. struck in his accot. as it is not right I shou'd allow it him & pay Messrs. Morgan & Mather, whom have charg'd me 5 Dol: more for the same Corn than the Corn sold for here, therefore request he will bring me the receipt which will be good. I am sorry I have it not in my power to send you by this opportunity the Potatoes, you request not having them myself[.] I have wrote to Mr. David Ross to get me a Barrell if any for sale in his settlement which if he sends I shall forward them by the first occasion. I will be much oblig'd to you, if in your next you will let me hear wether the papers sent you for Mr. Swanson, have return'd as the Gentlemen that left Orleans for Pensacola; did not perform their Voyage[.] your Complyance will oblige . . .

To CAPTAIN WILLIAM McINTOSH,
Natchez

Manchac, February 23, 1781

In my last of the 2d Inst. I acknowlg. the receipt of your favor of 22 Ulto. inclosg. your Accot. Currt. against me, which since have examind & found right (excepting the following omissions) the first is the error in Mr. Rapaljis receipt say Ps.4/5 which I have put to right, in my account here Inclos'd, the next is your have not given me Credit for the Ps.25 paid John Craven, for your note to him for that sum, & the amount of your order on me in favor of the Carpenter, for Ps.23 which sums makes Ps.48, these ōmissions leave a Ballce. in my favor of Ps.38.7 as by the Accot. & which I am in hopes after examination you'll find right, if not please to note it in your next, In your accot. I observe you have omitted to charge your Comissions, this I request you'll do for give me leave to tell you I cannot expect it from any Gentleman for nothing, & knowing the trouble you have given yourself with my affairs, therefore request you'll charge it in your next, I once more repeat my former request of your taking up my Draft from Mr. Rapalje, which I flatter myself is done e'er this—The Bearer will deliver you four Bottles of T[?] that I mentiond in my last & that Harley would not take in, We have nothing new only that Mr. John Moor & Mr. Tho: Comyns are arriv'd. . . .

To JOHN BLOMMART, *Natchez*

Manchac, February 27, 1781

Since your departure from this I have always been in expectation, from the promise you were pleas'd to give me of hearing of your having done something for me with Mr. Eason, but seeing so many occasions from your place, & having no accot. occasions me to imagine, you have entirely forgot me thrô a hurry of your own business, for which reason I have inclos'd your receipt for the sundry papers delived you, to Capt. Will McIntosh to whom I request you'll deliver them, there is a small Ballce. still due you (as Mr. Ferguson did allow the accot. it being an error committed thrô mistake of abt. 30 Dol. which if you shall think proper to Indorse it on the Note or account e'er you deliver them it will if not shall settle it with you myself when I shall have the pleasure of seeing you[.] I have nothing further to add . . .

To CAPTAIN WILLIAM McINTOSH, *Natchez*

Manchac, February 28, 1781

I did myself the pleasure of writing you the 23d Inst. to which refer you, I now take the liberty once more of troubling you by inclosing to your care Mr. Jno. Blommarts recpt. for sundry papers deliverd him last August against Mr. Wm Eason amountg as by account thereof & his receipt to Ps.362.2 which have always been in expectation Mr. Blommart would have done somthing for me therein till now, but wether owing to his hurry of business or otherwise I have never been favor'd with a line from him on that subject since his departure, tho so many occasions has offer'd from your place,—I have wrote him by this conveyance requesting he will deliver them to you & e'er you give him up the upper Receipt, get my receipt to Mr. Eason for the ballance of the sitt of Exchange as therein mention'd, when once in your possession if you think Eason has werewith push him for the payment without giving him further Linety, but should it be otherwise it is not worthwhile to throw good money after bad, thô I must say he really deserves not such treatment from me, therefore whatever you shall think proper to do in the affair shall meet with my approbation, Mr. James in his way down did not call here for which reason I have thought it advisable to send my Accot. Currt. against him, with the note to Capt. Davis to recover for me as the Gentlemen who go to Town with their produce, hardly ever remember they are indebted elsewhere, so that in their way up, their answr. is we really forgot it, but we will send it you by first Canoe, these promises are generally attended with twice more longer time, this has been so often the case with myself that [illegible] as abovementioned. Please mention in your next if you have [illegible] thing from that Loutt Mathews. . . .

To CAPTAIN JOHN DAVIS, *New Orleans*

Manchac, March 4, 1781

I did myself the pleasure of writing you some days ago by Mr. Prein from the Natchez, & inclos'd you Mr. Jame's account Ballce. in my favor Ps.65.2 which hope you will be able to receive from e'er he leaves Town, but should this not be the case request you'll send them me by first conveyance, so that I may have it in my power to give him a talk here on yt. head[.] Since which yours of 16 Ulto. came to hand in which you mention, youre not able to lay your hand on my Letter abt. sending me Iron, be assur'd that since I have had the honor of your Correspondence I never wrote for either Iron or Steel, having no occasn. for either, nor can I find by looking over the Copys of all my former Letters, any such thing so much as mention'd, therefore must imagine it must have been for some other of your Correspondents up this way. the Hat you sent up by Jaccau I sent it down by Mr. Duvall, which hope you have been able to return to Mr. Dejean as you ment. in your last, in my last I told you I had sent up to Mr. Ross & at the same time sent money with Doctr. Flower to get you a Barrl. of Potatoes, but alas it was too late for all that was in that Settlement for sale had been sent to Town, some time ago & any that remaind unsold was planted e'er your Ltre came to hand, so that for the present it is not in my power to send you any, but in all appearance if them I have planted turns out any ways good I shall be able to supply you with aplenty[.] Should Mr. Strother apply to you for the Ballce. of Mrs. Bacons Note, if in Cash for me please pay it—if not do it with the first money you may receive on my Account[.] I am in hopes Monsr. Valler has paid you e'er he set off & if Scarce will he will soon finish paying the small remainder due on his Note, should Mr. Gordon be still with you please present him with Mrs. Fitzpatricks & my best respects, tell him each time I take a drink of Grog his health is drunk in it which shall be always continued till such time as I hear he's out of the Land of Egypt, having nothing further to add ...

To WILLIAM STROTHER, *New Orleans*

Manchac, March 4, 1781

Your favor by Mrs. Bacon, came to hand the other day, the contents of which have obser'v, & according to the promise she gave you, will pay the Ballce. of her Note with pleasure, for which you'll please to apply to Capt. Davis, whom if in Cash for my account will I am assurd take up the Note; if not have to request he will the first money he may receive for me. I have taken the liberty of Inclosing to your care a note of sundry papers left in the hands of Monsr. Briant as a security for the amot. of my note for Ps.820 payable to the bearer & as I have been informd that he has been able to recover all them you'll see mark'd paid there be a sum [?] of Ps.25.5 in my favor, provided he does not charge Commission for receiving this (I don't think he will) besides Notes to the amount of Ps.535.6 which with that of mine for Ps.820 Request you'll send me up by first good opportunity that shall offer, for should there be a further change in affairs to our disadvantage I am determin'd on the first account of it, to sell off all, settle the remaing part of my affairs & leave the Country, by the first occasion, the note of Monsieur Lafonds if you will present it to Monsr. Borée perhaps he will pay it should that be the case you'll please to observe there is Interest on it from the date (as far as I can remember) I should not have troubled you with this affair but as Capt. Davis does not understand the french so well as you do I flatter myself you'll do me this small piece of service, which will be conferring another favor to the many already received ...

To WILLIAM STROTHER, *New Orleans*

Manchac, March 10, 1781

I did myself the pleasure of writing you the 4th Inst. inclosing to your care a note of sundry papers left in the hands of Monsieur Briant which hope you have been able to [*blank*] with my obligatn. &c since which Monsr. Repickeau has been here in his way to Orleans & offer'd to pay me the amot. of Monsr Lafond's note, I told him he would find it in your hands, therefore request you'll call on him for the money, should he want to evade the payment of the Interest, give him a recpt. for the money he will pay you on account of the note, & indorse the same on the note &c without delivering it up, thô I am in hopes he will pay the whole without further delay[.] from what he told me e'er leaving this, Monsr. Darchatt the bearer of the present will pay you the amot. of his Note with the Interest due thereon, which when you have receiv'd please send me up, by the first good conveyance, (as I am really in wants of a little Cash) with all my Papers, you'll not forget to deduct your Comission & if the Ballce. of Mrs. Bacons Note has not been paid keep it also[.] your complyance will oblige ...

To JOHN BLOMMART, *Natchez*

Manchac, April 4, 1781

I did myself the pleasure of writing you the 27th Feby. last, but as yet have not been favor'd with any answer thereonto thô there have been plenty [?] opportunitys from your place nor should I have known [*illegible*] been for Capt. Wm. McIntoshs Letter of 29th Ulto. the reason of this detention after demanding is a matter of surprize to me for since you'll not act yourself, according to the most solemn promises you gave me whilst here of doing the needfull, why will you detain my papers longer since I have authoriz'd another that I am assur'd will recover their amot. if it is to be had, I have only to add, that I again request that you'll without further detention deliver up my papers to Mr. McIntosh whom will return you, your receipt, or their reason why; I have requested that the case may be laid before the Cammandt. if no other way will oblige you to deliver them up[.] Be assur'd Sir that this is what I am sorry to be oblig'd too, but it is your own seeking and not mine, as necessity knows no Law....

To CAPTAIN WILLIAM McINTOSH, *Natchez*

Manchac, April 4, 1781

Your esteem'd favor of the 24th Ulto. came to hand last night the Contents have duly observ'd—In the first part you say you have paid Mr. Rapalje, the ballance due him on the Draft for which I return you my most hearty thanks, as I shall now have it in my power of calling on that Gentleman for a proper security, for the monies paid him on account of his Father (as it is now well known, that he has no power from the old Gentleman, to settle his affairs in these parts) secondly you mention Farqhuar having told me a lie. I am sorry he shou'd have committed so gross an error (which by the by) I should not have given Credit too had it not been for your own Letter of 22d Jany 1781 mentiong your having got it out of Alstons hands (by what you are pleased to call Civilities), a turn that I am not [?] well acquainted with, but if he has erred, that is not my fault nor should it be laid at my Door, thirdly you say I have made a mistake in Kings affair in that I can only ansr. I am not infallible & may have committed the error you mention, but as you only speak of Intert. due on that note (without saying anything of expences, if any was on it) I say the Interest was rightly calculated, therefore request nothing further from the Man, but for the future shall have nothing further to say in any matter that you shall think proper to settle, if you think proper to keep my Papers in your hands thô from what you are pleas'd to mention in y'rs in desiring me to look out for some other person who is more able and willing than yourself to finish my small concerns in your parts[.] In ansr. to this request I have only to say I should be sorry to be any ways troublesome to any Gentleman nor would I wish that any man should put himself to any inconvenience to serve me, without he will charge for his trouble as is customary in this Country for transacting Business for others, therefore request that you will when convenient to yourself furnish me with your account, charge your Comissions & all other expences, you may have put yourself too on my account[,] rectify the omissions you say I have made in the accot. renderd in to your own satisfaction; stop in yr. own hands the amot. of my Certificate to Douglass (so that he may have his note & if afterwards there is anything coming to me, remit it me by some safe conveyance, but should there be a ballce. in your favor draw for it in [the amount ?] you think proper & it shall be paid, on their delivering me the remaining papers with John Skinners accot. & the three vouchers for havg. receiv'd the amount of said accot. from you (but which you say now has not been paid) which if not return'd look upon it that I have a right to charge it to your account, with the same Justice, thô shall leave the whole to yourself, & you would not do it yourself if in my place; (if you say no all's well).

As Pensacola is in all appearance on the point of being taken (if so) I propose myself for that place, on receivg. the first accounts, so that I may have it in my power to settle all my concerns in that Quarter e'er a general seperation takes place, if you will send me the certificate & accot. before mention'd, I will endeavr. to recover its amot. with my other demands against Governmt. whatever you shall think to do with Mr. Blommart abt. the recovery of my papers shall meet my approbation, I have wrote him myself on that subject, which request you'll seal after perusal & deliver; I am sorry there is no such thing in this quarter as a Dutch Oven for sale, or be assurd it should have been sent you, by this conveyance, if hereafter I shall be able to meet with one, you may depend I will get it, having nothing further to add . . .

To CAPTAIN JOHN DAVIS, *New Orleans*

Manchac, April 12, 1781

This serves to acknowledge the receipt of your favor of 24th Ulto. with your Accot. Currt. which after examination find fully right[.] there is a small error of 7¾ this is owing to your having credited my accot. with only Ps.36.6 instead of Ps.37.6 which was the amot. of Mr. James Note as you'll see by the Copy of your account Currt. here Inclos'd, further you'll observe that I have credited your Accot. with the Ps.11.2 that Mr. Strothers mentions in his Letter of 4 Augt. 80, to have paid you my accot. therefore debit him with the Ps.14 he receiv'd from Allem for 2 lbs. green Tea[.] I have not receiv'd any part thereof. I observe what you say abt. his not having paid you the six dollars for Barwell, nor the Ballce. of Aickmans Accot. (it is all the same) I shall settle them with himself when I shall have the pleasure of seeing him (which I am assur'd will be shortly) I am sorry you did not Thomas's [*sic*] Note instead of Bills on Morgan & Mather, as it was well known that them Gentlemen had no property of his in their hands, as I make no doubt but you settld your own affairs with him in the same manner, whate'er you shall think proper to do with your own, let mine share the same fate thô I shall be sorry to throw good money after bad, in my former to you I requested you would let me know, something abt. the paper you sent forward to Mr. Swanson, as the Gentlemen to whom they were delivr'd did not proceed on the Voyage....

To GREGORY FRENCH, *New Orleans* [?]

Manchac, June 22, 1781

The bearer of the present Mr. David Ross will pay you the Ps.19 that I am indue Mr. Manuel for the piece of Destik [?] Cord for which I return both my most hearty thanks, the money should have been sent to me but for want of a proper opportunity[.] should you or Mr. Manuel have any good fresh Brittanias in your Store, please chuse me out 4 pieces of the best of them as they are for my own use, which you'll please send me by the first good Conveyance with a Bill of their Amot. which you may depend I will [pay by the first] occasion that shall offer after yours comes to hand[.] should you hear of any Gentle[man] that wants to purchase a pretty assortment of English Books, to the Amot. of 250 dol you'll oblige me by letting me know & I will send you a list of them, with their price affix'd, the reason that I have for disposing of them as well as all my Negr[oes] & houshold Furniture &c is that I am going to leave the Province in the month of Septmr. or Octobr. next with a number of our English Gentlemen, provided we shall be able to get a flag, & this we are not much affraid but we shall obtain[.] all my outstandg Debts shall leave in the hands of some friend, if any is recoverd it may be that I shall get them some future day, if not I must only place them to account with the many other losses already sustain'd since the commencmt of the troubles on the Mississippi....

To CAPTAIN WILLIAM McINTOSH, *Natchez*

Manchac, June 28, 1781

The troubles, that have subsisted for this some time pass'd in your Districk, has prevented me from having the pleasure of writing you e'er this, but as this is the first safe opportunity that has offer'd I embrace it with pleasure—I make no doubt from the Revolution that has happend, at your place,[16] but all expectation of payment are now at an end (at least for some time to come) for which reason have to request when opportunity shall offer & that

16/Early in 1781, British sympathizers in the Natchez district joined a scheme to overthrow Spanish authority in the area. Although the instigators, John and Philip Alston and John Turner, intended eventually to annex the district to the United States, they led their supporters to believe that Britain would regain control. Led by John Blommart, a force of 200 settlers and Indians set siege to the fort on April 22, 1781, and on May 4 Spanish commandant de la Villebeuvre surrendered Fort Panmure and the Natchez district to Captain Blommart. Blommart seized control of the rebel leadership and effectively eliminated the American sympathizers from any role in the new government. After the fall of Pensacola, the Spanish reoccupied Natchez and the rebel leaders were arrested. For a full account of this incident, see Haynes, *The Natchez District and the American Revolution*, 134–43.

you have time, that you'll remitt me a state of my small concerns in your care, with any accounts Notes or Bonds that you have not been able to recover, so that I may know with more exactness how my affairs Stands[.] my reason for requestg them to be sent me is that I am now disposing of all my remaing Effects, so as to be able to leave the Country in company with the rest of the English Setlers, who all propose going off in the month of Octor or Novr ensug. I believe that our destination will be to Charles Town....

To BENJAMIN WARD, *New Orleans*

Manchac, June 28, 1781

On my arrival here from Town according to promise I sent you by Monsr. Padrass (he being the first occasion I found) six Nutmegs which hope you have receiv'd long e'er this, but have never heard wether or no, by the opportunity of Mr. Jacob Monsanto the bearer of the prest. you'll receive, your Barrl. of Sugar, as I have never been able to dispose of one pound of nor has it been open'd only to give Mr. Foley the 41 lbs as by his receipt deliver'd you, when last in Town, the Cask of Salt is still on hand but have not [*illegible*] it may happen that I can dispose of it e'er I am leaving this place if not shall bring it down with me, here inclos'd you'll find a Copy of your account Currt. with an accot. of sundries sold for you, by which it appears there is still a Ballance in my favor of Ps.189.5 which on examing. hope you'll find right & if convenient shall be glad you'll pay it either into the hands of Mr. David Ross or Mr. Wm Strother having affairs with them both which I must settle e'er I leave the Province (which I expect to do in all the month of Novembr. or Decemr. ensuing without fail) as I am daily selling of[f] my Effects for that end. I flatter myself you'll use your endeavors, you'll please observe I have neither charg'd you Commissions on the Sales, or Interest on your accot. since last December thô have been obligd to pay the latter myself....

To DANIEL HICKY

Manchac, October 21, 1781

In all my former Letters for this some time pass'd I omitted to put you in mind of the Seal I sent you by Mr. Ross to get mended for me, if you have not had it done, please sent it me in the same Condition for I would not loose the stone for 20 Dol. being a present from a Countryman in the year 1758. Apropost. in your last you say the draft the Doctor gave you, for your house Rent, was not accepted[.] do you intend letting him remain in it and have it [?] for the same price, you must remember your fences will soon want new [illegible] as he has never put up one pailing since he has been in it; it is true he has had the House white wash'd & that is all, your oven I put a new Coat on it, & put a good Shed over it, but since I had nothing to say to it, all is almost demolished, I hope you'll not take these general hints to you as Compliments it is only to give you a proper Idea, how things stands, for at present I see no manner of prospect of being able to sell your house for you. I have the pleasure of acquaintg. you, that the fever has left me since the 17th Inst. so that I am daily getting better, if you have any news of our friend Jno. Moor please mention it in your next. . . .

P.S. Mr. Macnamarra has quite forgot me.

To BENJAMIN WARD, *New Orleans* [?]

Manchac, October 21, 1781

I did myself the pleasure of writing you the 28th last July & then remitted you your accot. of Sales of the sundry small things you left with me for sale, whether or no they meet with your approbation cannot say; as you have never thought it worth your while to answer my Letter, at the same time [I] transmitted you, your accot. Currt. Ballce. still in my favor Ps.189.5 which I requested you would pay to Mr. Wm. Strother or David Ross as I had affairs to settle with both them gentlemen, but you have not comply'd with either. I have now to advise you that I [illegible] Twenty Gallons of Salt for 7 Dol. so that the Ballce. is Ps.182.5 for which I shall draw in favor Mr. David Ross, or his order, & hope that you'll comply as an account commenc'd in May 1776, will not admit of a longer standing, the more so as I am under an absolute necessity of paying the Ballce. of my Accot. to a Gentlen. who is on the point of leaving the Country, therefore your Complyance will oblige . . .

To JOHN GORDON, *Pensacola* [?]

Manchac, November 1, 1781

Your favr. of the 22 Ulto. with the Soap & Osnabrigs I have duly receiv'd, but you have omitted sending 2 lbs Gun powdr, and

3⅓ yd. Bath Coatg. (but it is all the same) now you need not mind them as I have wrote to Mr. Moore for somthing to make me a Coat,—The Bearer of the present Mr. Charles Bordman will deliver you Ps.34.1 of which you'll take [?] for the Debt due by Mr. Russ to Mr. Wier Ps.21.7 the other Ps.12.2 you'll pay Mr. Connolly & take his Recpt. for the same, which please forward in yr. next, as for the other money due Mr. Wier it is out of my power to get ym. in, therefore think it advisable to Inclose you the accots. as you are about to leave the Province, have heard Mr. Patrick Foley is shortly to be down, with Pork, Butter & Cheese, I have thought proper to Indorse his note for Ps.44 to Messrs. Morgan & Mather, which them Gentlemen will pass to my Credit when paid, as for the Staves that was in Mr. Lintots yard the Commandt. claims them as belonging to the King, the greatest part he has burn'd so that the remainder are not worth regarding, or should do it with pleasure. . . .

To WILLIAM STROTHER, *New Orleans*

Manchac, November 22, 1781

Your favor of 1st Inst. came to hand this moment, (by Mr. Ellis) which somthing surpriz'd me, as I don't know of any thing that I am due Mr. Brion, for if you'll only be pleas'd to remember what I mention'd you in my Ltre of 4th of last March, in which I requested you would withdraw out of his hands my Note for Ps.820 and the other notes left with him as a security for the payment of the aforesd. Note, having been inform'd that a part of them was paid insomuch that there was a small Ballce. in my favor of Ps. 25.1. what pass'd between you & him when you took up my Note, is to me unknown, but when last in Town you gave me up my Note & others which he delivr'd you up to the amount of Ps.535.6 without ever mentiong. to me that there was any [*last line of page illegible*] spoke to himself & askd him if he was contented with the Settlement, he told me all was well & that all was settl'd only that Monsr. Maxant had not paid his Bond for Ps.350, but as he had taken it as a paymt. & Indors'd it on my note, he must only wait for it, had he then said any thing to me about Langlois Note not being paid, it was in my power at that time to have got the money as Mr. Langlois; had then Ilinois Flour selling in Town, by one Monsieur Richard, who came down with his Batteau, but his silence & your delivering me my note, with all my other Papers, left me no room to doubt, there was a ballance remaing. due him, therefore know not of any Remittance, I have to make him on that account & as for anything else I am sure there is none, for the Ps.25/1 if not recover'd from him, when you have mention'd this Circumstance, I will take proper care that you shall be paid —But it's more than I will promise you, for the money indue you, by the Este. of James Banks, as I shall be a sufferer by the said Este. upwards of Ps.350 of which I never expect to recover one Farthing. . . .

To CAPTAIN JOHN DAVIS, *New Orleans*

Manchac, November 23, 1781

I am sorry to be under the disagreable necessity of beging your assistance, once more, the distance I am from Town & the expence attending a voyage obliges me thereunto, therefore hope your forgivness for all the trouble I give you, there is a small affair between Mr. Henry Alexander Junr. & me which we have agreed to leave to the decission of four English Gentlemen, & I have taken the Liberty of chusing you & Mr. Farlie (if still with you) but if gone & that Mr. Campbell will be the other I shall be much oblig'd to him for his compliance (Mr. Alexander will chuse for himself) Now this is the case[:] in Augt. 1779 Mr. Alexander gave me a set of Vouchers sign'd by Capt. Barker & Lieut. Graham, payable by Governmt. for £46.4.2 sterlg. being for his services in the Kings works, for which I gave him an accountble. Receipt, to be answerable to him or his orders, when I receiv'd advise of their being accepted or paid (& if I am not mistaken) thô I really dont remember, if neither accepted or paid to return the said Vouchers, this youll see by my Recpt. some days after I gave them in paymt. to David Ross & Co. as by Receipt there inclos'd, they sent the two first by one of the Vessells that was taken, either in the Amit or on the Lakes, the third Mr. David Ross left with Mr. Strother to forward by the first opportunity, & he sent it by one of the Flags, but unfortunately this also miscarri'd so that the three Vouchers are lost, the question now is which of the two Gentlemen am I liable too for the amot. of the Vouchers; Mr. Ross is a party concern'd & he will be in Town in four [?] Days hence, I request he may be made acquainted, with the time the Gentlemen assemble to give their opinions, so that he may be present, should this small affair be of any hindrance, in your own concerns, I beg that you'll make it convenient to yourself, for I should be really sorry, if it should detain you one moment from business, when I wrote you the other day I thought the Doctr. would have gone down with his Raft, but he is getting Staves & will be shortly down with them. . . .

P.S. Messrs. Ross receipt you'll please return [when] you favor me with a few lines[.]

To WILLIAM VOUSDAN, *Natchez*

Manchac, December 3, 1781

According to your request I have sent you a hundred wt. of Sugar & as my Coffee was all sold, have only been able to send you 20 lbs (for which I paid 3 ry Cash) sooner than you should be without it. I am sorry to hear of the many misfortunes, that you have sustain'd since you were sent from the Natchez, but as for the Villainy of the Persons to whom your affairs were intrusted, that part of your Ltre is now ways surprizing to me, nor to anyone that has been on the River these two Years past, that them we look'd upon formerly as honest Men, chang'd their principals when the Country chang'd masters, all which I am in hopes will soon meet with their Deserts, as for News I shall say nothing to you abt. any, but this I can assure you, that there is nothing against us, I am very glad to hear that Monsr. Grand Pré was so much your friend, & it may be in your power one day to return the Compliment. I shall not forget your Complimts. to Monsr. Palao & family, when in your power come down yourself as I shall be glad to see you[.] Mrs. Fitzpatrick joins me with her best respects, says she will be glad to see you when you will do us that pleasure & we will settle all matters about the Boat. . . .

To JOHN GORDON, *New Orleans*

Manchac, December 8, 1781

By return of Mr. Chas. Bordman you omitted to send me a receipt for the money sent you to pay Mr. Connolly, this I request you'll send by first opportunity. I beg that you'll oblige me so far as to present the Inclosd order for Ps.42/2½ to Mr. Mather for acceptance, which if he accepts he will pass to my Cr. in settling with Mr. Dicas for his Rank [?], but should there not be sufficient to pay me in Mr. Mather's hands, in that case Mr. Dicas must pay the [*illegible*] Town. . . .

To STEPHEN HAYWARD, *New Orleans*

Manchac, December 8, 1781

Sundry persons told me that you were return'd to New Orleans, but from your former misfortune there I was doubtfull if it was you or no, till such time Mr. Campbell assur'd me you were there, for which reason I have thought it advisable to acqut. you that I have a Book of accounts & a parcell of Notes of yours, which was put into my hands by Mr. Evan Jones, by order of Messrs. Morgan & Mather & for which I gave a receipt, & as they are no manner of account to me, (nor do I believe them to be to any body but yourself) I should be glad to have up my Receipt & if you can get permission to go up the River you might get in some part of their amount, which in some manner would help you to discharge the moneys you are Indebted. Be assur'd that the money you are Indue me, if I had it; would have put me in a condition to leave the Country with the other English Inhabitants, but it & the many other losses that I have sustain'd, are the only thing that keeps me here, for instead of doing any thing I am daily going down hill, & yet cannot get away; for want of wherewith to discharge money's that I am indue; therefore use your best endeavours to get a permission & come up, take your Papers & see what you can do to help me, in my present situation, which will greatly oblige . . .

To CAPTAIN JOHN DAVIS, *New Orleans*

Manchac, December 9, 1781

Your favor of 23d Ulto. by Mr. Campbell came to hand some days ago the Contents of which have duly observd. I am sorry to hear Monsr Valler has given you so much trouble & that he has not paid the Ballce. but this is like the Man, for when in Pensacola he told Mr. Miller, that he had paid me the whole amot. of Miller's Accot. & my own, at a time that there was this Ballce. due, so that in every respect he makes himself a Liar, if you are so happy as to recover the Ballce. I shall be glad. Mr. Scarce I think may discharge the small Ballce. that remains due, if he has a mind, for he cannot complain of being shorted but has had time enough, the Doctr. is to be at your place with his Staves, abt. the end of the month, then if you can stop the amot. of the accot. from him I shall be glad, for here I am [not] able to oblige either of them to pay me the amot. of their private accounts, out of the first money you receive for my account you'll please pay yourself the money I am indue you & for your Commissions, whatever may be over you'll please pay Mr. David Ross, taking his receipt for the same, for which reason Inclose you a scetch of our Account. Mrs. Fitzpatrick is much obliged to you for your kind remembrance, joins in respects with . . .

To JOHN STEPHENSON, *Pensacola*

Manchac, January 10, 1782

In Januy. 1777 I had the pleasure of informg. you, that I had receiv'd from the Illinois; a parcell of Deer Skins in part of Monsr. Maxants Debt to Mr. Wm Barrow & requested to know from you, if you had any power from that Gentleman or his Attorneys; to receive the Effects from me—your answer of 17th Feby. following was that you had not, but to oblige him you would request Mr. Will: Strother (at New Orleans) to receive them from me & that you wou'd give a sterling Bill for their amot, which I comply'd with & the skins were sold to Messrs. David Ross & Co for thirteen hundred & fifty one Dollars which money I suppose to have been remitted to you, by the Sales & the Bills given as before mention'd and which was paid to Mr. Barrow or to some of his friends in England, but of which I have never heard any advice, this I suppose has been owing to the troubles (& as I have yet all Mr. Barrows affairs in my hands) which I almost dispair of ever being able to finally settle, with Monsr Maxant (or if ever, not till there is a Peace) & as it is not in my power to leave this Country till then, owing to the many losses, that I have sustain'd since Februy 1778, the money still due me which I am not able to recover, the money I am indue which I am not able to pay; (if I dont dispose of my Negro's) without being able to receive, put it quite out of my power to leave the Country for some time to come; had Government only paid me (as they have done every one else) for my Improvemts. taken for his Majesty's use, that cost me Ps. 2627.7 three months Rent e'er they agreed to build the Fort abt. them at Ps. 62 per month is 186 Dol. a set of Blacksmiths Tools & Iron supply'd a Blacksmith with by Mr. Grahams request cost Ps. 244.4[,] 311 Gallons Jamaica Rum (bot. of me by Mr. Robt Ross) for the use of the Troops by request of Colonel Dickson at 10 ry per Gallon is Ps.386.6[.] the Rum was then in the store & was taken there when this place was taken, & as Mr. Ross left the Country, without giving me a Certificate I could never get a Voucher for it or my Improvements from Col: Dickson, for the Smiths tools I have a Letter from Mr. Graham in which he mentions having given Mr. Miller a Certificate for them; but as Mr. Miller does not mention anything of it to me, it is a doubt with me whether it was ever given. I say had I been paid I should have been able to leave the Country; & should have done it e'er now, but you see Sir what detains me, from the reasons heretofore mention'd. I will take it as a particular favor done me, if e'er you leave the Province you'll oblige me with a small acknowledgemt.

of your having remittd. that money to Mr. Barrow or to his Corrospondt. for his account (as I never had any such thing from Mr. Strother,) which will inable me to settle with him, or some Attorny. from him; in some future day. having nothing further to add only to wish you & Mrs. Stephenson the Complimts. of the Season, a happy return of many more & your safe arrival in the land of Liberty...

To JOHN STEPHENSON, *Pensacola*

Manchac, February 16, 1782

As you have been so very obliging as to offer me, your services relative to my House, Store & other Improvemts. taken by Capt. Wm. Barker of the 16th Regmt. for the use of his Majistys Troops under his command 28th May 1778, Iron & Smith tools supply'd Lieut. John Jas Graham (acting Engineer) & 3 puncheons Rum &c I have taken the liberty of inclosing the proper Certificates with a petition & letter of Attory. to your care which request you'll lay before the Lords of the Treasury as soon as opportunity shall offer, after your arrival in England, the whole amountg to 3502 Dollars which I flatter myself their Lordships will pay when they are made acquaintd. with the particulars from yourself, when the sd. Improvmts. were taken possession off, I apply'd to Capt. Barker for the proper Certificates, but was put off, from time to time by him alledging for his reasons that he was in expectation of receivg. orders from Govr. Chester, to have them valued, & as I could not obtain the proper Certificates or Vouchers, from that Gentlemen, I went to Pensacola in Jany 1779 & laid in a petition to his Excelly. Govr Chester, requesting redress, his Excelly. told me could do nothing in the affair then as the command had devolv'd on General Campbell, to whom I must apply when I mention'd the matter to his Excelly. General Campbell, he told me that I should have proper satisfaction, & that he should be soon on the banks of the Mississippi, himself & have a proper survey of them taken & that then I should be paid, sometime after my return to this place Lieut. Col. Alex: Dickson, of the aforesaid Regmt. came to the command of Manchac, to him I also apply'd for the Certificates, but was put of in the same manner, till such time as the place was taken by the Spanish Troops under the command of his Excelly. Don Bernardo De Galvez in Septemr. 1779 after the reduction of Baton Rouge I apply'd again to the Lieut. Col: Dickson, for the aforesaid Certificates, but was refus'd them except I would give a full discharge on my account

Certificates &c for the sum of Four hundred pounds sterling, this I possitively refus'd to comply with, telling him I was determin'd to have all or none at all, these Sir, are the most particular circumstances that I can remember abt. the whole. should their Lordships, think proper to order me payd for said Improvmts. I have to request you'll pay the sums, hereafter [*illegible*] that I am indue to the following Gentlemen, taking their Recpts. for the same a Copy of which you'll please to forward me, under cover to Mess. Morgan and Mather—Vizt.

To the house of Comyns & Dunnithorn	879.5¼
To any of the house of McGilivrey Strothrs. & Co. . .	260.2¾
To Mr. Wm. Strother for accot. of the Este. of James Banks	32.—
	1189.4

the remainder you'll please hold in your hands, till further advice, but shou'd a Peace take place (& the Colony should return to its former Government) in that case you'll please Ship me, by some Vessell that shall come this way, such Goods as you may Judge to suit this place, but taking care to have proper Insurances made thereon, which you'll address to the aforesaid Gentlemen[.] having nothing further to add only to wish you & family a safe & happy passage to your native Country . . .

To CAPTAIN WILLIAM McINTOSH, *Natchez*

Manchac, February 27, 1782

Since your departure from this, this is the third Letter I have had the pleasure of writing you, without so much as receivg a Line from you, I have once more to beg of you, that you will please to remember, that I am much distress'd, owing to my being oblig'd to pay Mr. David Ross & Co the Ballce. due them Gentlemen, also to pay him as Attory. for McGillivrey Struthers & Co the Ballce. of all former accots. which has laid me under the necessity of taking money on very high Interest to dischge. the said demands & therefore have to beg of you, that you will remit me the money you have of mine in your hands as soon as any good opportunity shall offer for this place, out of which deduct the Ps.53 with the Interest due thereon till such time you are in Cash for my account of Earl Douglass[.] it is not worth while to send you a Copy of your accot. again as I did it in my last. . . .

To RICHARD BACON

Manchac, March 4, 1782

I have been in expectation for this some time past, that you would have remember'd, you are Indue me a small accot. for things had from myself & that I became your security to Mr. Wm Strother for the Ballce. of your Wifes Accot. say Ps.46.5 which have been oblig'd to pay[.] Now Sir as my present circumstances will not admit of my laying out of the money paid for yr. accot. any longer I flatter myself, that on recpt. of this, that youll remit [me] the amount of yr. accot. here Inclosd for yr. Governmt. 55 Ps. as I am much in [*illegible*] youll oblige . . .

To GEROME LA CHAPELLE, *New Orleans*

Manchac, March 20, 1782

Youll receive here inclos'd a Bill of one hundred Dollars, which you'll please to Indorse on my note, to morrow or the next day, I shall send you, by Mr. Mayo Gray, the remaing ballance of my note, should your Brig or the Balander bring in any Goods, which you think will suit this way, please reserve for me about four hundred Dollars worth of them, such as you shall think the most saleable, or such as I shall send you a note of in my next. . . .

To JOHN STEPHENSON, *Pensacola*

Manchac, March 26, 1782

Since writing you the 16th Ulto. to which I refer you, I have found out on examination sundry errors, that have been committed in my accot. Currt. with McGillivrey Struthers & Co (which suppose have occur'd, by mistake of entrys with their different Fermes, which being corrected reduces the Ballce. due to Ps.160.3¾ as by accot. here Inclos'd for your governmt. therefore instead of paying to any of them Gentlemen that you shall find in London the Ps.260.3¾ mention'd in my former only pay them the Ballce. due as per accot. out of the first money you shall be able to recover from Governmt. on my account, taking the same precation as mention'd in my former, should Mr. Robt. Ross be in London if wanted I am well assur'd he will oblige me so far as to attest the accot. of the Rum as he was the person Col: Dickson sent to me to engage it for the use of his Majistys Troops, having entirely omitted in my former to say anything abt. Mr.

Wm Barrow, I have now to request, that if you hear of his being in England, that you'll oblige me so far as to acquaint him that I have never been able to reduce Monsr Maxant to a finall settlement as have I ever got anything from him on his accot. but the Skins that I deliver'd to Mr Wm Strother at New Orleans in April 1777 by yr. request &c but as I am oblig'd to remain in the Country for some time longer, to endeavr. to recover some part of my outstanding Debts & as Monsr Maxant is appointed Governor, for this Province & soon expected out to take possession I may stand some chance of being paid for him, if not you may assure him my endeavors shall not be wanting, as have they ever been for his Interest, as is well known to many, but I am sorry to say that my best endeavors have not been so successful as I could have wish'd, had I taken any other methods, that would have occur'd any expence for Mr. Barrow he wou'd not have been any thing the nearer his money, for all them that have remains to this day unpaid[.] this you are well assurd of yourself from yr. knowledge of the Country, should Governmt. think proper to pay my just demands, which I flatter myself they will not refuse, when the affair is properly represented by you, you'll please to discharge the different sums mention'd in my former & the remainder to hold in yr hands till I have the honor of hearing from you, that is if Peace is not reestablish'd & the Province does not return to its former Governmt. (but should this be the case, I beg you'll follow my former request, in employing it in such Goods as you know will suit this Markt. &c to which you'll please to add the Histy of the present War, a set of good accompt Books, say, a Journal & Ledger, in Calf; letterd on the back, both to be rul'd for Dollars & bits so as to keep Dr. and Cr. on one side of the Ledger. I have nothing new to acqt. you with only that we all remain in quiet possession of our small remains [?], under the protection of that worthy Gentleman Monsr Mirro[17] in the same manner as when you left us, when any opportunity shall offer & that if you are at leasure I beg you'll favor me with a line from you[.] it now only remains with me, to wish you & Mrs Stephenson one continual scence of happiness in your native Country, in recompence for the many dangers you have both experienc'd in this I say in your native Country as it is the only one, that I know off where the Goddess of Freedom has ruled her Throne, this being & shall always remain the sincere wish of him who seeks the honor to subscribe himself, Yours . . .

P.S. if there is not a probability of yr. succeedg in my affairs please not to omit sendg me the Histy of prest War, if it can be done with safety[.] I will remit the amot. by Mr Mather, or your order.

17/Esteban Miró was appointed governor of Louisiana in 1785. He had arrived in the colony in 1778 and served as Gálvez's aide-de-camp; in 1781 he had organized the recapture of Natchez from British rebels, and in 1782 was named interim governor during Gálvez's absence in Havana. He served as governor until 1791.

To PETER SWANSON, *London*

Manchac, March 26, 1782

Your much esteemd favor of 14th of last June, came to hand the first of Augt followg & after it the small Case contg sundry small articles, pack'd up by yr. deceas'd Brothr. was deliver'd me by Mr. Ross in good order, their Amot. is to the credit of his Estate's account which I thought was more advisable than to have given them to the Wench Sukey, as she has turn'd out an abandon'd Strumpt. for when your Brother left this, he thought she was with Child, by him but behold when deliver'd she had two fine Negro's one of which only liv'd [*illegible*] Days but the other is still with her, as for little Jack, I have him wherewh. for Shirts & Gowns, out of them I had charg'd myself with, with all the small things that came for him. I observe your having recev'd my Letter to yr Brother of the 4th of Sept. 1780 by way Mobille in February followg containg sundry Notes & accots. (apart of their amot. you acknowledge having rcievd, but you say nothing abt Capt Henry Smiths accot Currt. ballce. in my favor Ps.96.3¾ (his note was in Mr Millers hands since June 1776) but this omission I suppose has been owing to your hurry at the time you wrote[.] from what you mention abt Thornton I am in hopes you have been able to recover the Ballce. due on his Note, say Dol 302/1 on his arrival at Charles Town. I am really sorry to hear that you shou'd have had so much trouble, abt. my small concerns as you have had, in some future day it may so happen that I may have it in my power to return the Compliment, which be assur'd when the occasion shall offer, shall with sincerity be acknowledged. Mr David Ross your Atty here presented my accot Currt. with Messrs McGillivrey Struthers & Co dated at Pensacola 31 May 1781, by which it appeard that I was still indue that ferme Ps.1590.8¾ (cut money) some after the presentg the first accot. a second Accot Currt. came to hand dated at Charles Town 4th Sept. 1781, with an augmentation in the Ballce. of Dol 159/1, how this augmentatn. could occur is to me unknown, as I have had nothing from either of your houses since August 1779, this put me on examg all our former transactions, which after having properly done, I avouch that both the accots sent Mr Ross are very erroneous in many respects, this may for a moment appear to you a Parodox, but will not I flatter myself be of long duration (when I tell you that these mistakes & wrong Entries must have occur'd thrô your number of Fermes, that is if your own Letters, your former accot. renderd in; with your Reciepts have their proper wieght in settling our accots.—I say yr. two last accots. Currt. are erroneous, for which reason I thought proper to draw out a proper state of all our Concerns, with your different fermes, under their respective heads since my settlemt. with Col McGillivrey 8th Augt. 1778, which delivered to Mr. Ross; to be forwarded to you, & which I flatter myself on a proper examination you'll find right (if not they are all signd errors & omissions excepted) in the price of the Skins deliver'd to Messrs McIntosh & Miller at New Orleans in March 1774 (as by their Recpt) is no more than what I have a right to expect, it being your own offer, in all your Letters from the 28th July to 25 Decemr. 1773, when in Mobille in August 1774. I told yourself in the Store one day, that this was a point I should never think of giving up, further when I settled with Col: McGillivrey here in Augt. 1778 I told him [the] same & shew'd him all your Letters, relative thereunto, this may seem hard to you, but at the same time be pleas'd to remember that every pound of them Skins cost me 28 Sols per lb three hundred miles up the River & should you allow the price agreed for in your Ltres say 30 Sols per lb it will not more than pay me their real Cost & charges thereon till they were deliver'd. I shall be always ready & willing to leave the affair to the arbitration of Merchts. when time & opportunity shall offer (which God send may be soon) then if given against me, shall pay with pleasure, but till such a decission shall take place, shall always think I have right on my side, as I have been charg'd Interest on all Ballce. remaing due on Bonds &c I think it no more than just that the Ps.419.6, that being the Difference in the price agreed for, & the price you allow me in your Accot Currt. of 28 July 1774 (we'll admit of the same Increase) this will bring it to Ps.667.3½ as it now stands to your Debit in the Accot Currt. furnish'd Mr Ross it may so happen that you may think that my present situation occasions my making the aforemention'd charge, Disabuse yourself of that way of thinking (I beg of you) for be assur'd; that I am still the same John Fitzpatrick, that had the honor of being known to your Houses fifteen years ago! for it is not the length of time, the distance we are seperated from each other, or the change in the Governmt. we live under, that shall ever aleniate me from what is right to all Men, & when time & opportunity shall offer, as before mention'd (if it is given against me) will pay it with pleasure (but not till then) there is some other Charges in the accot. one is an error of Ps.25.4 overpaid Col: McGillivray when I took up my Bond to McGillivrey and Strothers, it occurd in making out the Interest accot. on the Bond for instead of having deducted Ps.319.4 paid Mr Miller 20 June 1777, as per his Recpt. I was charg'd 12 Months Intt. for the whole sum of Ps.2481.2 this Error leaves the difference of Ps.25.4 in my favor as above mention'd, next is a small Accot. against Findley McGillivrey of Ps.9

Merchant of Manchac

delivd. Mr Miller 25 June 1777, (as by his Recpt.) which was omitted on settlemt. with the Col: which when I mention'd it to him he desir'd me to place it to the Debit of McGillivrey Struthers & Co. as I have done, but on all yr. accots. sent me you have omitted it to my Cr after which follows Robt. McGillivery's & Hardy Perrys Draft on Farqhuar Bethun Esqr for Horses sold him for Ps.95/6½ for his Majistys service, with Mr Joseph Purcells Certificate for Ps.17 in favor of Saml. Waths, is in all Ps. 112.6¼ remitted Mr Miller 25th May, 1779 & which he acknowledges the recept of in his Letter of 5th August following, these also are to your Debit, as there's no further mention made of them, or have they been return'd, therefore suppose them to have been paid & have been omitted in the accot fournish'd[.] the next charge is the full sum of the moneys reciev'd from Messr. Boles McPherson & Thornton say Ps.171.4½ as you have only Creditd my accot. with Ps.50, & lastly the Interest you allow me for moneys, receiv'd from sundries my accot. since my Settlement with Col: McGillivrey in 1778 Ps.144.4½ every thing else in the accot. with McGillivrey Struthers & Co agreeable to your own acknowledgments in my possessions on the reverse side of said account you'll see the following Credits Vizt. my assumption for Monsr. Pavée 24 Dollars, the ballce. due on settlemt. as by accot. given in Ps.1964.5¼, the 180 Dollars paid Will. Swanson out of Col: McGillivreys order on me, in favor of Joseph Maison for Ps.400—14 Dollars short (that Mr Miller in his accot. of 4th Feby 1780, says he was never able to recover for the deceased Charles black, lastly the Ps. 496.7¼ Interest due on my account dated 31 May 1781, althô it is erroneous, as shall be here after mention'd, now by your adding the Debits & Credits, you'll find there is a difference of Ps.628.3¼ say Ballce. due McGillivrey Struthers & Co. which have transferr'd to the credit of your general accot Currt. with the Ps.174 due Miller Swanson & Co by that [*illegible*] Mr. Valler, who told your Mr Miller when in Pensacola, that the money had been paid me long e're then, but Mr. Ross, to whom I refer you, the the [*sic*] remainder was only paid 10th ulto. when I was in Town, next is the Ps.50.2 due Miller McIntosh & Co on an exchange account this when added together makes up the sum Total of the general Accot. Ps.852.5¼ against which I have placed to your Debit Ps.22.7¼ due me by Jno. McGillivrey & Co Ps.14.0½ due me by McMinn Miller & Co. the 184.2¾ due me by the Estate of William Swanson, as by my attested account delivered your Attorney, these sums being deducted from the Dol.852.5¼ leaves a Ballce. due to all your fermes of Ps.631.4¾ as by account sign'd 10th of Novemr. Ulto. since which I have drawn out a new accot. which you have here

Enclos'd that reduces the Ballance still due to all your Gentlemen to Ps.160.3¾ this Ballance I have requested Mr Jno. Stephenson, who I have appointed my sole Attorney, to pay to any of your Gentlemen, that he may find in London out of the first money he shall recover from Governmt. for my account, which I flatter myself he will be able to recover, it now remains with me to say somthing in regard to your Brothers affair & mine, in the first place you'll please to remember [?], that the Note given him in March 1779 for Dol 1100 was for so much he had recover'd [?] for me & won at Gaming e'er the date of the Note, as for Goods or any [illegible] of Merchandize, he had no such thing here at that time, but it was put [illegible] own consent, after his return from Pensacola (in august 1779) we often gamed it again in which I won back from him at sundry times Ps.1041. so that there was only a Ballce. due on the note of Ps.59, as by account delivered him e'er he left this in July 1780, a Copy of which you have here inclos'd, on my giving him the sd. account I requested, that we might come to a general Settlemt. e'er he set off, but he told me we must defer it till his return which he said would be in Novemr. ensuing, & for a further reason told me my note was at Pensacola, all which I consented too (little imagining that was to be our last meeting herebelow) what surprizes me the most; is to find he never Indors'd any thing on the Note, further that he shou'd have omitted to credit my accot. Currt. with the following Sums Vizt. 57 Dol paid Mr Maxant his account[,] 34 Dollars paid Mr Wm Bay, 150 Dol: detain'd in his hands by order of the Commandt from Alexander McIntosh of the Natchez, till such time as the affair between McIntosh & me was decided by arbitration, 50 Dol: Cash paid him in the presence of Mr Bernard Lintot, the day e'er he left this, with sundry other articles supply'd him at sundry times, since our last Settlement in august 1778, for the 9 mo. boarding I suppose he meant to put it off, till his return here again, (but seeing there has been nothing of either of these done, I can only suppose it arose from his continual Illness from the time he left Orleans) till he departed this Life[.] the whole of our Transactions here may seem somthing Irregular to you but be assur'd they are only represented in their true light, as they really happd. & should I be the sufferer, I shall only have to place it to the Debit of my having had too much Confidence in any one when Interest was at Stake, But this I hope will not be the case with you; when you shall have a proper Idea of the whole, I have nothing further to trouble you with, only to observe to you that it is somthing surprizing to me, that you should have sent my Bond to Mr. Ross without having Indorsed, the moneys you have recev'd from time to time on my accot. as by your own Letters &c or have authoriz'd him to have Indors'd them, which he would not do, it now only remains with me to assure you, that I shall always retain a most gratefull acknowledgmt for all pass'd favors & if Peace & tranquillity was once more reestablish'd I trust the province should return to its old Master & that you should be so dispos'd to settle in it again; of having further dealings together (after all our affairs [?] shall be settled to our joint Satisfaction....

P.S. [*illegible*] will soon be with me[.] he is now at Mr. Ross's Plantation[.] I have in [*rest of line illegible*]

To WILLIAM SMITH, *New Orleans*

Manchac, April 1, 1782

The Bearer of the present Monsr Jacqueau will deliver you a small pot of Butter a Round of our Manchac Beef & a small pocket Ledger, which will serve you instead of a pocket Book, which I remember you told me, when in Town, you were in wants of therefore beg your acceptance of them. having been inform'd that Capt. Harrison is shortly expected down from the Natchez, it may so happen that he may pass in the night & I not see him[.] I have thought it advisable to inclose you Capt. Phillip Barbers Accot Currt. with his Letter as a proof of his being indue me the sum mention'd in said accot. say Dol 101.3½ that you may have it in your power to demand it of him, as Mr. Barbers attorney, you'll please to remember on settling with him, you must put another Years Interest on Ps.43.5½ as that time has expir'd since he acknowledg'd the justness of my demand[.] from the last Illinois Batteaus I hear Monsr Motard, is to be shortly down, to leave the Province, in that case you'll know how to handle that Gentleman, as for the others Monsieur Paul Due told me he did not know when they would be down, Mr Paul Due told me he would take up Mr Charlevilles Note, if he will do it & allow the Interest due thereon, if he has not the money to pay in hand you may exchange Charlevilles Note for that of Mr. Paul Due's payable in the run of the present Year, but if he objects against the Interest, keep the one you now have, as we shall be able to make him pay it another Day....

To CAPTAIN JOHN DAVIS, *New Orleans*

Manchac, April 12, 1782

I shall be much oblig'd to you when any good opportunity shall offer, that you send me David Ross & Co's receipt; with the award of the arbitration abt Alexanders vouchers, from what you told me when in Town, I put into Mr Henry Alexanders hands, Monsr. Darchusts note of Ps.185 as a security to him, since which on settling accounts with Mr David Ross for himself and the Company, he has made me pay it a second time, without his returning the Vouchers, not leaving me any hopes, of my ever being able to get it repaid, he promis'd when in England that he would use his best endeavors, that I should not be the looser, but that [is] only [a] promise for should he not succeed, I must loose them. I heard you are shortly expected up this way, if, bring them yourself if not please send them, if you have heard any thing of Mr Hickey since I was in Town, please let me hear, and oblige . . .

To GEROME LA CHAPELLE, *New Orleans*

Manchac, April 16, 1782

I had the pleasure of writing you the 20th Ulto. by Mr Mayo Gray, to which refer, by which I acquainted you that he was to pay, you the Ballce. due on my Note which flatter myself he has done, but whether so or not I cannot say, as I've not seen him since his return from Town, nor have I been favor'd with an answer from you on that subject. In my former I mention'd to you, that I should want a few more Goods, on the arrival of one of your Vessells, now as Mr Wilkins informs me, that your Balander is safely arrived, I have taken the Liberty of Inclosing you a small memorandum of the things I shall want which if you'll oblige me so far, as to lay by for me, & acquaint me with the same, on the recpt. of which I will go down for them, for the amount I must acqt. you I am not able to pay you the money on the taking of the Goods, but shall expect three or four months time to pay it in but should I be able sooner you may depend on my complying with my engagement. If through a hurry of Business you have not time to ansr my Letter, I beg you'll tell Mr. Proffitt to do it for you. . . .

Memorandum of the Goods I shall want Vizt.

    2 pieces of Brain but if there is no Brain 2 ps of good osnabgs. will ansr
   12 pieces of Brittanias
    3 pieces of white coarse Irish or french Linnin
    4 Dozen Silesia Handkfs.
    2 doz blue Cotton Roun Ditto
    4 lbs fille de Rain
    6 pieces of Province Callico or any others that is not fine with large red flowers for the Indians,

6 pieces ¾ Linnin Check french or English
2 pieces ⅞ French Cottonade
200 lbs Coffee
25 lbs Gunpowder (say french)
50 lbs small Shot
1 Ream of writing Paper.

To DAVID ROSS, *New Orleans*

Manchac, April 20, 1782

You have here inclos'd a Letter for Mr. Peter Swanson, which have left open for your reading which when done please put a Wafer, also all Mr Priests accounts, by which you'll see there is a Ballce. remaining due him, which I am sorry it is not in my power for the prest, to come on[.] should do it with pleasure, but it shall not be long e'er it shall be paid to the person you shall appoint your Attorney e'er you go off, that is if I am able to recover any part of the moneys due me from sundries, I beg you'll not forget me when in England, but if in your power get me 198 Dollars for the Vouchers which if you shall be able to recover, you'll please pay it to one of Mr Priests Corrospondents in London, it will be always so much on accot. having nothing further to add, only to wish you a pleasant Voyage & a happy sight of your native country . . .

N.B. Mr Watson paid Mrs Fitzpatrick dol.4.6 for the Butter, therefore repay him[.]

To [JOHN STEPHENSON, *London*]

Manchac, May 30, 1783

Your much Esteemed favour of the 16th of Last October Came to hand the 15 Ulto. it is now before me; its Contents have duly Obsarved; It give me real pleasur to hear of your having had the good Luck to Shack off so Sune as you did the Epidimacal Complaint that accosted you so Villently on your arivall in England. This am apte to Suppose is in Sume measure owing to the Sudden change of Clements [climate]; which I flater myself will not be atended with further relapeces once you are a Littel Time accustomed to your Native aire.

Parmitte me Dr Sir to retourn you my most Sincer, thank for all the Trouble and pains you have allrady Given yourself on my account; and which you are pleased to tell me you'll Continue to dou for my Interest, Thaugh from one part of your Letter I am af[r]aid, it will not be attended with that Suckcess the justices of my Case Desarves (from Govrement) for Should I not get payement for my houses and othere Improvements; Taken for its use; I am much afraid my friends will Suffer by me, owing to the many former Losses I have Sustaind in my fourtune; Since the Commincement of the Troubles on the Mississippi, for I may Say with much Saftey that I have been; the Sport of fourtune, and a verry Considrable Louser, by each of the three Cont[end]ing powers; that have been on the river Since Febraury 1778. But as these things, are Suff[ic]iently Known to you alrady, Shall say Nothing further to you on that head.—relative to my Demands against Goverement; I have no further Vouchers to add to them (allrady in your hands) to prove my Clame, Therefore Leave the wholl to your; hands [?] in the affer as you shall think the most advisable; we are told that peasce is restablished between all the Contending powers; that have [been] at ware so long; and that there is 18 months allowed for the Emigration and Setteling thear affears, which Terme of Time I Shall be obliged to remain where I now am; to Indever to get in Some part of the moneys due me in this Country, for Should I go without them; I have nothing remaining to Support me in another. Therefor Shall take it as a further Continuation of your wonted Kindness; if you'll Lett me hear from you, from time to time, Either by the way of Jamaica, or Directly from the River, This with my most Sin[c]er wishes for yours; Madam Stephenson and familly, for thir health, and prosperity are the real Sentiments of him that is with much respact Dear Sir . . .

P.S. If there is anything in these parts in which I Can Searve you; I flater myself you'll honour me with your Commands.

To DANIEL HICKY, *New Orleans*

Manchac, September 22, 1783

Your much Esteemed favour of the 16th Instant with your Jar; is this moment Come to hand; had it only came two hours Sunner you would have receved it by Mr Charles Gerome whome was then hear; but this is the first that has offered—in my Last I promised to have the butter ready; so as to Embrass the first Convayance that should offer, I am realy sorry the jar was not Some thing larger then it is; as it only hold a lb which I am afraid will not be anoufe for your Voige (Please to Obsarve the Jar when delivred me was brack in the same manr. as you'll receve it.—

Mrs. Fitz. and self are hapy to find the Jar of butter Sent Mrs. Limcocks meets with her approbation[.] She may Depend on always having it as will put up, It may be She will have bether, as the wether is geting much more favrable; as we advance in the autumn[.]

I requst you'll present our best respacts to Mr. & Madam Limcocks, assure him from me; that his Present was verry acceptable; and for which I beg Leve to retourn him Thanks.—

I Dont write him by this Convayance, but Shall in a few days hence, and then shall send him down the other Jarfull. I might have Sent it now, but defer it that it may be filled with buter just from the Churne—you'll find hear Inclosed a recept of Mr. John Blommarts for Dr.363.2r the amount of Sundries papers Delivred him, to receve for me at the Natchez their amount, which after he had them in his hands about 14 Months without ever so much; as acquanting me with what he had been able to do for me in the affere (though I offen wrote him on the Subjit) requsting him either to retourn the papers or remitte me there amount; which from the Latte Captn. William McIntosh's Letter hear inclosed, I have all the reason in the wo[r]ld to think he had recoved there amont for when Captn. McIntosh maid a demand of the papers; as my Attorney; Blommart would neither detean [?] the papers, or thear amount, from his not Complying with mine, or my attorneys requst (so offen maid) I am will assured the affear was Setteled in Such a manner; as Mr Eason has got up his note and account Current with my receipt to it, and Blommart the amount thereof Long e'er this, But the Troubles Coming on as they did in the Natchez and his Misfourtune and Confinement; that attended him since; has put it out of my power to do anything in the affer till he Left the Country. the present is to request you'll take it with you to Jamaica; and if Blommart is Still there; it may be that he will discharge the Same (if at all) any part of it; as he must be Sencable how much he distrasses me by Carr[y]ing of[f] such a Sum; in my present Sutuation; or with out so much as Writing me a Line from Orleans; after he was out of Confinement, —although Mr. David Williams; as my friend Spock to him on the Subjit by my requst. Dow with it therefore as if it was your own and if any thing to be got; it will be (as I may say) as things now Stand so much out of the fire.—I have nothing further to add only to wish to see what you are pleased to mention about your being again my neighbour fullfilled; for at Present I am only Surrounded with apostets and Jannens.—A Dieu dear Hickey; Mrs. Fitzpatrick joins me with her good wisches for your safe arivall and Speedy retourn beleave me to be with Esteem & regard ...

To WILLIAM SMITH, *Natchez*

Manchac, October 8, 1783

Since your passing by hear, I have been under the disagrable necesity of giving a morgage, on two negros, say finne Slave; to Mr. Samuel Steir, to rease only $340; which he advanced me at 10 pCent Interest; payable in January Ensuing. Neither of which Slaves I would part with for 400 drs. (this I mention to you; to Shew how much; I am Cramped in my affers; owing Interly to the base Tratement that I have receavd; and daily Continue to receve from them that are indue me so long; and whom simes to think from there manner of proceedince; that I have now no right to demand my just due,—Now Dr Smith having maid you fully acquanted how maters Stands with me at present; I have to beg of you once more for Gods Saik, if you have Hayward with you; not to let him Leave the Natchez; to go for more horses; (as he may say) are you have Secured all you Cane; if the moneys for the horses that he has Sold; in the Settelment is not paid him yeat; and that he offers to make that any Excuse if the peopel that are indue are to your Licking; Oblige him to Indorse the notes, Dow with him as if the affere was your own, But if you Let him live [leave] the Natchez; once with out your geting all he is able to pay; if only 6 or 7 hundred Dollers; either in money or notes; if as before mentioned, for be assured now that he Knows that you have his Bond; and other Obligtions he will neaver retourn to your part with horses for Sale, this I am Confident of from his former Tratement of me, [*page torn*] and beg of you; to Secure for me all you Can; whill you have him in your power, for without some such a supply; from him; or Some one Eles of my Creditors; I am well assureded I Shall not be able to prevent; at the Time of payement, the foreclosing of the Morgage on the two Slaves.—As for the amount of my account agint Mr. Phillip Barbour; and the Latte Captain Harrison's note; with the Interest due thereon; I flater myself that Mr. Richard Harrison, as attorney to the former; will pay them without any further Trouble; after your having let him See Mr. Barbour's Letter. If you have not had Time Since your arivell; to have Spock to Mr. Ferguson; about what I mentioned to you; in your way up, I requst that you'll the first Time you See him; after the recipt of this. that you'd ask him if he has answered my Last Letter; if he has or will do it als well, If not by the next Convayance shall send you a Copy of his and Company's accots. so as that you have them Setteled.—We have nothing new with us, Since your passing; all things remain as when you Left town, or at least we have them so with us. only that Charles Bordeman is marred to Mrs. Battsey

Carpenter; By Mr. Dunbar, the 2d Instent, its said he has got a good Bargen; & if nothing Els the C——— and her C——— God Blass you both[.] make mine & Mrs. Fitzpatricks Compliments to Mrs. Smith and to your Sister Salley; and belive me to be with Sincrety . . .

P.S. what ever you Shall be able to receve from Hayward; do not Indose it on the Bond, Let that remain as it now is; without it may be so much over paid for the Other artils Sent him by his Barge; the money paid Dutton; and the ballance of the Interest and any thing above there amounts you may Indorse on the bond—

To WILLIAM SMITH, *Natchez*

Manchac, February 27, 1784

Your Esteemed favour of the 8th Instant, was handed me yesterday by Mr. Castills, in his way to Town, the Contents of which have duly obsarved; But am a good deal Surprized at the meads you have taken to Settel the account with Mr. Hayward. If nothing Eles Could not have been don with him; I should not have been aginst allowing him a delay (provided he had given Segurity) But to alow him Seven years longer for the Last payement; is the [same] as giving up all that sum; for real loss; the more so as things are Lickly to tourn out; any how in a Case of such Consciquence; as I was so neare; parmitte me; Dear Smith; to till you that I aught to have been maid acquanted; with his proposelles; are you had finished with him finnilly; as it seems to me [*illegible*] Account Current Sent me, to Know if I had Committed the Error you mention, by that manner of proceeding I Shall have had it in my power to have Cleared up; that Erroneas; and I say notorios Charge of $316.2¼ that he brings aginst me, and that you have admitted of with out my Knowledge (But which I beg you'll rember that I'll not; nor Cannot allow of) for the following reasons Vizt. In the first place; you have I think his Letter to me of the 9th January 1775; that will show how many Skins was Sent me by his Barge, which when Compar'd; with the account of there weight and number of them; Sent him in my Letter of the 28th of the Same month (a Copy of which you have hear inclosed for your Goverement) I Say when Compaireded you'll find that 961 good Skins, Weight 2420 lb; and 79 Light and Damaged Wt 88, that they will Compleat the number Sent me by the Barge. If any distortions was maid in the accot. it was owing to this; Thomas Hamman; Mr. Hayward's patron, told me that Mr. Hayward receved a number of them Skins; from his hunters as the barge was just Comming off; and the he [*sic*] requstd that I should be particular, as to the weight and number of Each man's Skins according to their marks; so as that Mr. Hayward might account with them for there amounts, as I receved them from him. This Dr Sir; and nothing eles occationed my making menching Charles Howard's Skins by them Salves; But the wholl amount of the Skins then receved say for $619.1½r was passed to his Credit; this I am willing and reddy to Depose on oath; and which I am will assured that he Knows to be the Case, you'll See by the Said Copy of my Letter before mentioned, that I would not Keep the Beaver on my own account, but would Dispose of it for him to the Beast advantage (as the Beaver was much pattered) although much buf had been taken off alrady. no one would give more for it hear than 5 r per lb; this I would not take; and as I Could not go to Town then myself, I Delivred it to Mr. John Blommart (to whom Hayward was indue money; this you'll See is the first; by his receipt of the 4th February 1775 for the same, (a Copy of which you have hear also inclosed) of this Mr. Hayward was maid acquanted with what I had don for him by James Donnoldson; to whom I Showed the receipt; and am fully assured, that Blommart accounted with him for the amount the beaver sold for in Town, for had that not been the Case, as I Sent him Sundries Copys of his accot Current with me he would have menchened Long are this of my having omitted to Credite his account with the $255—I retourn you Mr. Elliotts Indorsement with which I'll have nuthing to do, for the reasons hereafter menchioned; I[t] Can be maid apeer; that Mr. Hayward is indue to Messrs. Robertson & Carter's Estate's; for Sundries goods Bought of them in there way up the river; in the Summer of 1774, and as they both were Killed; the moneys due for said goods was never paid, this I am but too well assured off, as it was from me they had the goods; and by there Deaths I louse the amount of there notes for Dr.504; For a further proof of the affer in November 1774; when Mr. Hayward gave me his bond for Dr.2012.2r Mr. Elliott then sold him there note and account Current for 61 Drs. this money I paid Mr. Elliott for Mr. Hayward; accot. by his requst; as at that Time there was no accounts of the poor men's Deaths and as he was Indue them the moneys; he would have got by the Bargon Dr.21.2½r[.] This I can make apeir to be the case by my books; of having paid the 61 Dr. for said papers.—A Still further proof; is had Mr. Elliott been indue him that Sum so long; Why did he not Settel it himself; at the Time they were both in New Orleans together in the Spring of 1778. (this you Know yourself was the Case) any how let Mr. Hayward, receve such outstanding Debts himself; for Sunner then to have anything to do with a thing that I Know to be so

Erronous I would rether Louse its amount; and this you'll find to be the Case; when Mr. Elliott retourns to this Country. I have therefore to request that you'll Oblige him to rembors these Sums, and I flater myself; that the Commandent (to whom I am so much obliged too for his Kind asitence to you in the affer alrady) when he Comes to Know of the peice of Villiney that he has maid use of; to rob me of the $399.1¼r But that, he will oblige him to Discharge the same off of hand; any how do not Don him Longer, Time for the payement of it then till December insuing; and get sequoirty (and this only) if nothing Eles can be got from him now,—If you are, or that I am so misfourtunet, as to be nonsulted, in the Case of Barbour & Harrison; in so just a cause; it is high time to leave a Country; where one man Cannot oblige another to pay his just Debts; therefore having nothing further to add only to assure you and Mrs. Smith that I remain with Esteem ...

P.S. you have a young man in your District of the name of John Croom [?], formely a soldier; in Captn. William McIntosh's Company; tow him I paid in May 1780 by Captn. McIntosh request 25 Drs. & as I am a friend I have left the receipt he gave me on the back of the Captains note to him for that Sum (as I cannot find it among my papers) and as I am on the point of Commincing a Sute aginst the Estate; for moneys due me; and which Mrs. Mcintosh only thinks of paying at the nixt Crop; and then not my wholl Dimand; thought upwrds of 2 years due, apart Moneys Sent him in his way to Town; the last moneys [*illegible*] by my power of attorney; Join them that was indue me at the Natchez[.] I shall take it as a particuler favour, if you hear he is still in your districk; that you'll get him to give me his acknowledgement of having receved the said money from me; on and for account of Captain McIntosh; which when you have got it; you'll oblige me by sending it me by the first Oppertunity; that shall offer, as I only whant it for it and Some other papers Delivered Mr. FitzGearld to go to town & Commince the Sute &c—NB if I rember right you were present when I paid the Money; the fellow whill hear Lived with old Paggy.—

To LAURENT ERMANTINGER, *Montreal*

Manchac, March 8, 1784

Some time in last January; when at New Orleans, a Gentleman from the Illionis of the name of Monsr. Cerée; Presented me an account Current; Signed and atested by you; aganst me and Indorsed in favour of Mr. Marischaux; or to his order, amounting to £7487.16 Soles, Such an Erroneous; charge put me on Examinging the particuler of said account, & to my Verry great surprize, found that your verry first charge against me of the [illegible] august 1762, for £80.16.5 New york Cry. or £1212.6 Sols to be Erroneous; should be paid for my bill in favour of Mr. Bonavanture Augé, a man with whom I never had to the Value of one Doller Dellings with in all my Life on my own account, there fore if you paid him moneys on any order or Bill from me, it aught to have been pleased to the Debte of Messrs. Oakes & Godderd; in whose Imploye I then was; with Mr. Augé; and for whom I then acted, & never for myself, and if paid him; it is to be supposed it was for his wa[ges ?] as he really left the Imploye of them gentlemen about that Time you Debt my account with that I [illegible]

Nothing more of the affer then this; that I am fully assured neaver to have had any account with Mr. Augé; that might have occationd my giving him a draft on you; on my own account, Therefore am fully Determined never to account to you for one Sol on that head, further; for if so had been the case; Why was it not mentioned to me in December 1764, after my retourn from Captivtée; of your having paid such a bill or order on my accot. which if it had been dun allthough it was 28 months; before the Time I am now Speaking off—I say had you mentioned to me I should have been able to have Cleared up the affer to your satisfaction as then all them Transactions were frash in my rembrance; that are now intirly forgotten by the Length of Time—I am really Sorry to Say I saw your atistation to so Erroneous a Charge, which with the 17 years Interest thereon at 6 pCent will mak an abattement in the amount of £2448:16.16d, This Sir is really to much—Your Second Charge is £87.4.8½d which you Say is Dr. 1744.14 Sols But I say not, as £87.4.8½ your Currency at Dr. 2/4r per pound is only $218.0¾ of a reayel, which at the Exchange at 6 Livers per Doller will only make lb.1308.9 Sols. this will occation another Error of lb.436.5 Sols add to that the 17 years Interest; will make it amount to lb.811.4.6d. These mistakes I flater myself you'll see rectifye in your books. As to the £87.4.8½ I Cannot pretend to say if realy right; as you have Committed two such Capital Errors to my Disadvantage alrady; a third may also have been Committed in this; which is not in my power to rectifye now; as I Left your bill of parcells; in my way to the Illionis in Septmr. 1765. therefore requst that you'll furnish one; and mention the particulers (which parmitte me to say aught to have Acompan'd [illegible] account) according to the Common mode of Proceeding.—Your Third Charge I belive to be right, and if I am not verry much mistaken I gave you a promisary note for the beaver, this (if so) I have a right to see also, as I really

Merchant of Manchac

thought it had been paid you many years ago, for on my Leaving the Illionis to Come down hear I Left every thing that I found with my partener Francis Lavaring; belonging to us; which he told me amounted to £4500 in palterys; in his hands in order to pay off any Demands that might remain against us at Michillimakina and to remitt you the balance [?] of my note. This I Can make yeat apear to have been the Case; by his receipt of 24th Novemr 1765 Dated at St. Louis—But if not Complyed with and my note is Sent me; I shall make it good; as sune as it is in my power, To all which charges; I have only the following reasons to Alledge; that had your account of the things you Supplyed me after my retourn to Montreall; in December 1764, and my note for the watch; if they had been sent hear many years ago (if the Latter was not paid; as before mentioned) I should have paid them with pleasur—As I then had it in my power; and was always Willing (which is not the case now) owing to the many Losses I have Sustained Since the Commencmt. of the Troubles in this parts. I have wrote you Sundries Letters; Since my Setteling hear; the Last of them by Mr. Garrett Rapalje; a Gentleman of New York; in august 1775, In all of them I acquanted you that I had it in my power; and would pay any Lawfull Demand you had aGanst me, to Send your account; and order to whom it should be paid, But was never favoured with an answer, to any of them, Which I suppose have been owing that they have all miscarred; Since then I have never wrote you; Imaging; as I had never hard from you that you were either Deceased or that you had Left Canada; on account of the Calamities, that always atends on Sivill wares, But now that I find that nither of them is the Case I embrass these occation with pleasur In the first place to mention to you the Losses I have suffered by the Calamities of the three Contending parteys that have effected this Countery Since the Trouble first Comminced; in February 1778 a party of amiaricans; or Rether a banditti under the Command of one James Willing & McInter; Robed me of $14,600—In the month of may following a Captain William Barker of the 16th regiment, with a Command of British Troops from Pensacola; Came and took possession of my dw[ell]ing house Stores and houses & all my other Improvements, I had hear to the amount of $3546. for his Majestys use (and for which I have never as yeat receved one Dollar) and Bueilte a fort abought them, which was Taken by the Spanish Troops; under the Command of Don Barnardo De Galvez; on the mor[n]ing of the 7th Septemr 1779, at which Time I again Lost (as the place was Taiken by Surprize) Dr. 3400 In Negros Sum Cash; Marchandize, Cattel; and all my household fournitour; to this I may add $1400 that was due me by Sundries inhibitance of the Settelment of the Natchez, that revolted from the Spanards in April 1781 under the Command of one John Blommart, whom when there Chife was Taiken; and that the Spanard retook possession of the fort & Settelment; they Disparsed them Selves into the Different Colonies of North america; so that I may say that [they] are also Lost for me; this will make the wholl amount to $22,946, of which as things now Stand, I have no Expectation; of ever being able to recover a Doller, But that; that is due me by the British government for Captain Barkers Vouchers; which Certifyes his having Taiken them for the use of Goverement.—If I am so happy as to receive this; which is so justly due me, I shall have it in my power; to pay off the Principall of all my remaining Dibts; of which yours is by much the Largest of any one, But shall not be able to pay any Interest; as Goverement will not allow it to me; for the moneys of mine it has in its hands now almost six years. I Say I shall be happy if I get the Princepall; there fore Send your just account; of the things had after my retourn to Montreal; and my note for the watch; which if your account of £87.4.8½ is right you'll find will only amount to lb.2058.9 Sols or $343.0½; this and nothing further will I Consent to pay; as Sune as I have receved the moneys due me by the British goverement; or Sunner if in my power, But should this mode of proceedings; not meet with your aprobation; in that Case you must, Trow in your accounts I now acknowladge to be just (and shall always acknowladge what if realy so;) But nothing further; with the accounts of my othere Craditors; and receve your Devidant; when said Vouchers are paid.—Or I'll with pleasur give up the receipt of the Gentleman; by whom I sent them home to Demand the payement; this Sir is all that now remains with me; to offer; out of a Verry prettey fourtune I was master off; Six years ago. I have nothing further to add to so many Disagrable Subjits allrady mentioned in the Course of this Long Letter; only to assure you that I am with much respect . . .

NB: this etter Sent per Via of the Illionis & Michillimackinas favd. by Mr. Marishiaux.

To MONSIEUR MARISCHAUX, *Illinois*

Manchac, March 8, 1784

Some Time in Last January; your friend Monsr Cerée;[18] of the Illionis; presented me an account Current, Signed and Indosed in your favour by Mr. Laurent Ermantinger of Montreal, amounting to £7487.16 Sols, which Erroneous Sum; parmitte me to Tell you is verry Erroneous; in so much that I'll have nothing to say

18/Gabriel Cerré was born in Montreal in 1734. By early 1755 he was established in Kaskaskia, where he became wealthy in the fur trade. His open attachment to the British cause made his life uncomfortable after the Americans occupied Kaskasia in 1778, and he left the settlement some time in 1779 to settle in St. Louis. He became one of the most influential citizens of that town and died there in 1805. See Alvord and Carter (eds.), *Cahokia Records*, 1778–1790, xx.

to; I am Trully sorry for Mr. Ermantingers; saik to see his attestation to such an Erroneuos an affer, I shall always acknowladge to ow him some money; but belive; when a proper State of things is maid out; about the one quart of the sum he mentiones in the account sent by you; will pay him off. I have wrote him fully in the Letter; hear Inclosed on the Subjit, & Till such Times I have his account, I shall not agree to pay anything; therefore requst that if you do not retourn yourself this Spring; that you'll forward the Inclosed by some Safe Convayence; having Nothing further to add ...

Sent by Monsieur Cerré

To MANUEL MONSANTO, *New Orleans*

Manchac, June 5, 1784

This Searves to acknoladge the receipt of the soap that you sent me by Mr. Profitt [?]; for which am verry much obliged to you; as I was verry much in want of it; when it come to hand; the 31 Ulto. I sent Doctor Dow [?] a pott of Butter Weight 22 lb Nett and recomanded it to your care; which hope he has receved are this; and in the same good order it left hear, Its amount 11 Dollers you'll please to pass to my Credite with you, If Mr. Netare paid you the amount of the beaver (which I flater myself he has Long are now) I requst you'll Send me up the note I requsted you to pay Mr. Probanit [?]; and a smaller note of my account with your house; as I am in whant of Some other small artites from you. But will not Send for them Till the old account is paid off. Therefore beg that when you have a Littel Time; you'll favour me with the aforesaid memorandum, for my govnement, having nothing to add ...

To MANUEL MONSANTO, *New Orleans*

Manchac, June 23, 1784

I wrote you the 5th of this month per Mr. Carpenter; which suppose you have receved are this; Since which I have receved your favour of the 10th Instent; In which you mention, that Mr. Netare had paid you moneys on my account, and that the amount of my accot. with your house was Cleered off; and that the Surplus you had paid to Monsr. Chabaut for me, I am sorry you did not Say how much had been paid that Gentleman, on my accot. that I might Know, how much I am Still indue him,—Neither have you mentioned if Mr. [illegible] had paid you the Dr.6.4r on my account; or whether you had recovered the Jarr of butter Sent Madam Dow [?]; the 31st of last month, Say 22 lb. this particullars I suppose you have not mentioned owing to a hurry in Business; if so, May it Long Continue in that Chanell; is my Sincere wish—From Mr. Netar's, manner of proceeding with me; in the wholl affer I have great reason to believe he has really *humbouged me*; for the first place he makes [illegible] 14 lb. Beaver above, as mention'd to you in a former Letter, and then [?] gave me 30 pounds of Light & damagd. So much for puting it in his power to use me in that manner;—

I have given Mr. Rowille [?] the moneys to pay the Ballance due on my note to Monsr [illegible]; I will Take it as a particular favour done me; if you'll make him and his good Lady my Compliments, Tell him I am realy much oblig'd to him for his Confidance.—

If all my fourmer accounts with you are [paid]; I Shall be much obliged to you, if you'll send me by some safe Convayance the small artils mentioned in the memorandum; hear inclosed; they shall be paid for; as Sune as in my power; but any how, you may depend on there amount [illegible], and the New Year; If that late[.] I have nothing further to add . . .

To LOUIS [illegible], *New Orleans*

Manchac, June 23, 1784

Your favour of Last Saturday Came to hand this afternoon, and an order to your requst oppened your Pocketbook; and found there in 14 Spanish bills in all amounting to Dr.190.1¼r; and 3 others Small ones that I receved from the Commandant amounting to 10 rayeaux is in all Dr. 191.3½, as per the account hear in inclosed, out of which I Paid for Sundries as per Said account Dr. 20.5r so that there remains Dr.170.6½ which I hope you'll find right.

I am Sorry that we had not the pleasur of seeing you once more are you left the Country; as in all appearces I shall not, as I Cannot go to town, till the fall (if Monsier MacCartey's Vessells [illegible] arrive) are you go out, Mrs. Fitzpatrick; has taken the Liberty of making a Saisure of your five Bottels of [illegible] that was in Simons box; with which she proposes drinking your health; and safe arivell in the country from whence it came. This she flaters her self you'll forgive her for—The remainder of your things I have delivered to Simon, and has recomended him to make all heast to town; that he posibly Can he will leave this to morrow morning [?], as he has to make meal of his Corn; as I had no Price to give him; I have nothing to add only to wish you health; happiness & a Plesant voige ...

To CAPTAIN MATTHEW WHITE

Manchac, July 30, 1784

I am sorry for your saik; that I have not had it in my power; to send out you; your mulatress [?], as I Know you are in whant of her Sarviss; But be you assured it was not owing to any neglect of mine; for I have applyed to the ow[n]ers of every boat that has passed hear for your place to get her a passage; Since she has been able to under take the voige; But nown would take her in till this. I flater myself that she is now parfictly recoverd of her former Complaint; and must assure you that Doctor Flowers; was verry atentive all the Time she was in danger; which was from the Time you left her; till about the 10th of may; you have hear in inclosed his account; amounting to Dr.20; which I think you'll say is not unreasonable; also you have mine amounting to Dr.27.1r so that leaves a ballance of Dr.2.7r in your favr. and which I have paid to the Doctor in part for your account.

Should you think making charge for her mintaince for 45 days is any thing out of the [?] way, only mention it, and it shall be call off. Since the first of June, till now I Charge nothing for her mintance; as I only Supplyed her with such provisions as I gave my own negroes corn and milk, Your Barrell of Salte is still on hand; therefore hold it at your order. having nothing further to add ...

To CAPTAIN JOHN DAVIS, New Orleans

Manchac, March 28, 1785

Having hard by the last boat from Town, that you were not yeat gon; I have Taken the liberty of Inclosing; you tow Letters; the one for Mr. Supaidess Senr. and the other for Mr. Alexander Offitt; that Came by Doctor Flowers from New York, and as I understand he is now Settled in Kingstown have further to requst of you if it will not be to much for you, to do to bring me from Jamaica 6 pieces [?] holland Bath coating, with the binding and proper buttins; for making it up into a [illegible] and Vest, what ever the par of exchange may be at the time of your arivill; I'll pay with pleasur, as it may so happen that I shall be able to pay for it in indigo—I Should not Trouble you with such a Commission; if there was any to be had in the Country, or was it that I had proper winter Clothing for the insuing winter, But I realy have nothing but a blanckt Coat—Mr. McPherson for whom you have the Letter is to be found on an Estate Called [*blank*] having nothing further to add . . .

To MR. SUPAIDESS, SENIOR, *Kingston, Jamaica*

Manchac, March 28, 1785

The Present I hope will find you in the Same State of good health; as when I had the pleasur of seeing you last at New Orleans, and my most sincer wishes are that you found Madam Supaidess and the rest of your familly so on your arrivill at Jamaica. I Lay hold of this occation of puting you in mind; that you were pleased to promise to get me a Small Box of towles, now if it so happen, that you do not retourn to this Country this fall, Please send the box by Captin Davis; to our good friend Mr. Manuel Monsanto, with the bill of its Cost. Please let it be Such a one as might have Cost in England about £3.10 or £4. Sterling, its amount shall pay to your friend either in indigo Tobacco or Paper money at the advance the exchange may be at on its arivill—we have nothing new all things remain in the Same Sutuation with us as when you were hear. this beeing the needfull . . .

To MONSIEUR CHABAUT, *New Orleans*

Manchac, April 18, 1785

The bearer of the present, Mr. Hindson, will pay you the balance of my note, which I ask you to return when you are satisfied. Permit me, Sir, to thank you very humbly for the confidence you had in me. If you would like to continue it and can send me by the same bearer a quarter of Havana sugar, like that I had the last time, and a quarter or two hundred pounds of coffee, I shall be very obliged to you. As for their payment, it will not be possible for me to pay sooner than next September, unless the sale is made sooner, but in that case you will have the money before September. Having nothing else to tell you for the present, except that I beg you to assure Madame Chabaut and Mademoiselle your daughter of my very humble respect . . .

To DOCTOR ROBERT DOW, New Orleans

Manchac, May 23, 1785

Having hard from Mr. Dunbar; whom was hear with me the last night; that you were agoing home in Mr. McCarteys Vessell; I have Taken the Liberty of inclosing to your care a Letter for Mr. John Stephenson, which beg that you'll be so obliging as to forward him on your arivill in London; by the first safe Convayance as it Concerns me much, as its Contents are about my Dimand against Goverement for my houses &c.—In his Last Letter to me he Disires me to Direct my Letters for him to the care of Mr. Arthur Strother[,] Carolia Coffé house Birchin Lane London; as he was agoing to live in the Country. Now as Mr. Strother is daily expected out to Pensacola I am at a Loss; where to Direct the Letter too, the more so, as he he [*sic*] has not made mention to what part he was going to Settel in—Therefore when you are in London; you'll have an oppertunitty of seeing some one of the Gentlemen; that was formilly of Pensacola; whom will informe you where he resides. then I flater myself you'll oblige me so far as to put the remaing part of Instruction [*?*] on the letter, and forward it. I have nothing further to add only to wish you a plesant pasage, Great Success in your undertaking, and a Safe retourn to your familley[,] with these Sentiments I remain . . .

To JOHN STEPHENSON, London

Manchac, May 23, 1785

Your must Esteemed favour of 30th December 83 was handed me the 21st august last, Since which Time there has not been any Oppertunitty of answering it from these parts; till the present which I imbrass with Pleasur. I am Sorry to find by your's that all your indevours for me; have not meet with that Success I had a right to have expected from the British Goverement (But as you Verry justly Obsarve; that Country is no longer what it has been) I therefore must put up with the Loss.—which in the end will be my total runnen, as I have not being doing anything for these six years passed in the mercanttil way; for whant of a Small Capitall to begin with again, and always flattered myself that this would have come Sunner or later to my asitance, which I hope may yeat be the case, the more so as you seem to have some hopes yourself Still; that if General Campbell was to go home; you might do somthing with him for me, What ever you think proper to do; in the affer; will always be agrable to to [*sic*] me, (for this I am will assured off, that if you are not able to do anything in it, I have no occation to give myself any further Concearn about the mater, but look upon it as So much Lost.—

This last fall I made a trip up to the Natchez; wher I reecoverd sundries old outstanding Debts to the amount of $1400, this was in Tobacco's which I unfourtunly Shiped in a flate of Mr. John Ellise's for New Orleans; But on the 23d December; intirly owing to mismanagement the flate sunk above the Settelment of Point Coupée with 14,000 Carretts on bord, by which accident I am a louser of $1257, having only been able to save to the Value [?] of 243 out of the wholl I had on board; you alsow are a louser by this accident; for there was a Barrell of Peucans on board for you which In the hurry and Confusion of unloading and throwing things aShore got Stove; and were all lost, Since which I have not been able to procour another; although I have offered $16 for one, the reason is this, they are so verry Scarce; is the last year was not there bearing year; but this is, and this fall there will be no whant of them, & then you may Depand on receiving one by the retourn of Mr. Mathew's Vessell; or by the first that shall live the river for England.—

In answer to your request about the Nigar Diamond; he was the property of Messrs. Bradley & Harrison; Left by Mr. John Bradley with Messrs. Bentley & George Harrison; in Feby 71 as Attorneys hear for the former Gentlemen, in 72 on Bentley's retourn from England; as poor Harrison was no more; he then became there Sole Attorney; and Keept the boy always about his house—in 74 (when Bentley whent first to the Illionois) he left the boy diamond, and another negro named James, (the property also of Messrs. Bradley & Harrison) With the Latte Thomas Wescoatt, with whom Bentley was in partnership; for Selling a plantation on the Ibbervill & Transporting goods from the forks to there place; and by their agreement (to which I was a Witness) Bentley was to fournish the waggon and horses; with two negros; and as he had occation for his own, to go up with him, he left them of Bradley's & Harrisons with Instructions to Said Wescoatt; in case of Mr. Bradly or any one from him Coming out on there business, to deliver them up. The Negro James was lost in the woods the december following & was neaver hard of more, and Diamond always remained with Wescoatt, although Bentley Came twist [twice] down; in 75 and in 76 he never offered to take the boy away; but left him hear to be Delivered when any demand was made, as before mentioned—and he remained with Wescoatt till in august 78; then as Wescoatt had left Bentley's Plantation; on the Ibbervill and Setteled at Galvez town the Latte William Swanson; as Bentley's attorney hear Demanded the negro; which Wescoatt would not Del[i]ver without going to the

Spanish Commandent (Monsieur Collille) whom obliged Wescoatt to Deliver the negro up to Mr. Swanson; this is all I Know about the negro; and which if required I Shall be Willing to atest too.—

As it Comes in the way; to speek about Bradley & Harrison, and of the property, These Gentlemen are indue me $113.0½ Since the 10th Febry 1771 [?] it being a ballance remaining due after Mr. Bradly gave me the Sett of exchange for £95.10 Sterling, which bills I remitted to you, Bentley was to have paid the Said ballance, But the Apostet, has not only Carred that off with him but near 500 Dr he is indue me as per his note for the Balla[n]ce of his previous [?] account, to the Norward where he now lives. If these Gentlemen are yeat in being I flater myself; they would not that I should louse it (though no demand has been made of it; so long as it has been due) as I always had hopes that Bentley would have paid it, But now there are no longer any such hopes remaining with me. If it Comes in your way; please to speak to Mr. Bradly when you see him, and when you think proper to answer this please mention what he says on the Subjit; I Should have inclosed a Copy of there account Current; but am uncertin if either of them are Still in the land of the living—Please present my most humble respects to Madam Stephenson and to the Chilldren, tell her I am much obliged to her for her Kind rembrance; this with assuring you that I am allways most respactfully ...

P.S. the five English that Still remain in the Country, are trated with great indulgence and Sivillity by the goverement, and as things now stand with us; if we had only a free head in to the river; I do not Know where we Could go to Better ourselves.— Pray is John Blommart in England or Can you inform me wher he is. he Carred off from me 360 Dollars as per his recept for notes put into his hands to recover ther amount [rest of line illegible]

To GEORGE FITZGERALD, Natchez

Manchac, August 21, 1785

Both your Esteemed favours; the first per Mr. Wall, containing the pannce, and your last of the 8th Ulto. came safe to hand; there contents have duly obsarved, I am much obliged to Captin Breedin for Kind remberance; you'll please to till him (as I have not Time to write to himself, as the damed favair is now Coming on again; that I have accepted of his present in part, that is, the small [illegible] and the piece of sole Leather, but the side of neats leather; the black grained deer Skin; that I shall dispose of them for his account; when an oppertunitity shall offer;—or Retourn them by some safe Convayance; and for my so doing I hope he will not take it amiss; as I realy do not Know what to do with if I was to Keep them. It may be that Norton; will take them if he had only sole Leather; to work them up; of which he is quit[e] out. If he Can send him; five or Six sides of his own Taning (But not Spanish; on any account) he will be much obliged to him. he may depend on reciving the amount; by the first occation that shall offer after the Leather Comes to hand.—I have Sent my Country man; a Small jarr of Butter, and beg his acceptance of the same, the jarr, is the property of Madam Limcocks, which when imtey requst it may be delivred her, you have hear Inclosed 3 Dollars Indue you for the millk pans; with many thanks for your Compiance; for [illegible] for your money. I have at Last receved a Letter from Mr. John Stephenson of 30th of Last December; and you'll see by it what he says on the Subjit of my Demands against Goverement; he says that I have no longer any reason to expect; that ever the British Court will ever pay a farthing of my account against it (so much for being a Subjit) I have nothing further therefore Conclude . . .

To DAVID ROSS, *New Orleans*

Manchac, October 22, 1785

As you were so obliging; as to offer to bring me any Littel thing I might whant from Jamaica, I am in whant of many, but Cannot think of asking you; to Lay out Silver; and not have it in my power to retourn the same; the only things; I shall make boald to ask for; and them if they can be brought without any Danger to your other property; are the two following, beeing both; or would be both verry Usefull to me hear, the first a Small Box of medcines; with the Instructions, to cost about 2 or £2/10 Sterling the first Cost.—the second a Small box of Joyners Towles; such as you might have seen many off in the Country some years ago for Sale, to Cost about 3 £ Sterling the first Cost.—Now if either of them or both; should fall in your way; & that you find it Convinnent to bring them, me; If I have it not in my power; to get you Either the hard money or Indigo; to pay there amount; I'll with thanks make good the Differen[ce] there shall be in the exchange.—I have nothing further to add only to wish you; a pleasent and profitable Voige; & a Safe retourn; this beeing the needfull . . .

To ARTHUR STROTHER, *New Orleans*

Manchac, June 4, 1786

This moring I had the pleasur; of receiving a Letter from Mr. William Barrow, of the 4th March 1785, In which he acquaints me, of his having apointed you his attorney, to indevr to Settel his affer with Monsieur Maxant (which, for his sake, I realy wish you may be able to effect, but of which I am much in doubt;) He requsts that having dun all in my power to bring him to a Setlemen many year ago but to now affet—I give you all the insight in my power about the affer; thise I shall do with real satifation, as Sune as I am able to overhall my papers; that may any way be relative thereonto, (Though I am some what afraid; there are Some of them wanting; if so they were Lost; with maney of my own; the the [*sic*] moring of the 7th Septr. 1779, when this place was Taken; for then all mine; were taken; and Sent to New Orleans; and in the october following I recovered a part of them, from Monsr Duforest at Monsr. Navars; By an order of Monsur De Galvez. But to my misfourtune found that there were many of them wanting, But a loss there was owing to the fourtune of war—What of them I may have among mine remaing Shall forward to you by Som Safe Convayence; as Sune as shall be able to make out the accounts; that will be requst for you to have also, so as to inable you; to Settel the affer; if you are so succesfull as to bring him to Consent to have it finished, all which shall be dun as Sune; as posible; or that I have a Littel time; & that I Know you are not gon for England; for from what Mr. Fitzgerald told me; I have reason to think that this will not find you at orleans; But if it dus, on the receipt of a Line from you; or any one acting for you in your ass[i]stance, Shall be able are then to have them ready &c. for the presents I have nothing further to trouble you with; as I have given over all thoughts; of Troubling you or any Gentleman; with anything further about my just Demand, against the British Goverement; as that worthey Gentleman; Mr. Stephenson has not been able to effect anything in my favour; as he mentions to me in his Last Letter; which Came by yourself.—

It only remains with me to Carve your wonted indulgence; for a little time longer; then the time mentioned in my note for the payment of its amount; for as yeat I have not sold of the things taken from your Store for $30, & having been Disapointed in not receiving Sume moneys due me by this new accidens [*i.e.*, Acadians] for Provisions that I supplyed them with; have not as yeat been able to recover; from them; owing as they say to the Largnest of the Bills that the Goverment has sent up to pay them (& which Cannot be Changed hear) therefor if you'll oblige me; to wait till the fall; I'll with thank pay you the Common interest that is going in the province; and shall always most Greatfully acknowladge the favour. having nothing further for the present . . .

A True Coppy—
Copy of a letter from Mr. Fitzpatrick to Arthur Strother 4 June 1786

To ADAM BINGAMAN, *Natchez*

Manchac, November 10, 1786

I have taken the Liberty of Inclosing to your Care; sundries notes, and accounts; amounting to $522.5¾ as per List with them; which is due me in your District; the wholl payable this fall (and some of them ought to have been paid, many years ago). Which if your own business; will admitte of your reciving for me; Ill pay you a Commission; and all other expences you Shall be at on my accot. with Thanks, If it so happens that it is not Convenent for you to recive them; pleas Oblige me so fare; as to put them into the hands of Sume one that you Know will do the needfull.—If it is yourself or another I requst; that if payement Cannot be uptained when applyd for; that you'll; without giving yourself; or the person you give them too, any further trouble; put them all in Sute, I say all, excepting that of Captin Harrison's; and that of Stephen Hayward's; the former I am will assured he will pay when due; and the Latter I would not wish to Distrass if he seems willing to pay. Therefore if he Dus not pay the note when due; Send it me down by some safe Convayence after you have dun all that you Can without Shuing. This I have mentioned to each of them would be the Case; in the Letters I have wrote themsalves; which I requst you'll forward by the first occation so as they may not protend Igneress; I am sorry to be under the Disagrable necessitty so to do, But my affers will not parmitt my laying out of my money any Longer—Having; Since I had the pleasur of Seeing you Last [?] A Letter from Mr. John Stephenson; informing me that the British Goverement will not pay for my houses taken from me; in May 1778 for His Majesteys Use, this is another dead Loss to me of $4764.—

I should have had the pleasur of seeing; you at at [sic] your place this fall; had not maters tourned out with me as they have; which puts it quit out of my power for this year. Owing to my having a new Livee to make in frunt of my plantation; from the one end to the other, this has obliged me to get more hands; which I have now at work on verry hight wages. But when once don; it will be a Livee to the place for my lifetime. When Col. Hutchins whent up, I sent Mr. Fitzgerald some good Garden seeds; a part of which was for Madam Bingiman—according to promise; which I hope She received in due time and; that they tourned out to her Sitifation; Should she Stand in whant of any more for the Insuing year, please Let her make me acquanted With it in time; and if I have them not all myself; I will procur them from others for her—We have nothing new with us; all things remain in the greatest Tranquillity; as to apperence, But in truth it is now a Long time Since we have had any Europing News; for which reason I have nothing further to add only to assure you; and Madam Bingiman that I am with much respect; to which Mrs. Fitzpatrick joins her most sincer wishes for Both your prosperity; with this Sentiment I remain . . .

P.S. I requst that you'll not receive anything Eles in payment But Cash or Tobacco; as nothing Ells will Sute hear—

To GABRIEL CERRÉ, *Illinois*

Manchac, May 21, 1790

Your much Esteemed favour of the 11th of Last month; I recieved from Monsr. Pratt at new Orleans the 29th of the Same, Wheare I then was on Some Business; Its Contents have duly obsarved; and it was my Intent are your Letter Came to hand to have paid the [a]mount of my note; and the Interest due there on; in to the hands of Monsr. Suored [?] are I Left Town, Provided I had maid Sale of my Crop, For I maid the Last Season; a Crop; of Tobacco, & Indigo Seed; which ought to have Brought me in, 2400 Dollers But by having the wholl of my tobacco refused at the Kings Stores; and the Indigo Seed falling from 35 Dollers per Barrell to 10 Dollers; so that out of the wholl; I have not maid 500 Dollers, which was a great Disapointement to myself and friends, But yett for all this you may rest assured; that you; nor any other Gentleman; that has obliged me heartofore; shall not Louse one Sols by his Confindance,—For I have at Last, aptained Gegiment aginst Mr. Stephen Hayward of the Natchez; for the Sume of 2236, Dollers that he is indue me since November 1774, which money is to be paid me in all the month of Dicember Insuing, which of its Self will be much more then will discharge all my Debts; Besids which I have a fine prospect of a fine Crop on my Plantation.—But Should, Both this fall; I have Still remaining 11 Good Slaves, a fine Stock of Cattels; and a plantation in good order; which of itself is much more then will discharge me; if obliged to Dispose of it of all my Intrallements; and this you may

Depend I Shall due this Insuing fall Sunner then you or any other
Gentleman that has obliged in the manner you have don; Shall be
Capt Longer out of their money then the Insuing fall; and then
you Shall be paid Both prancipill and the Interest due thereon,—
Having nothing further to add...

Montreal 1762

Monsieur John Fitzpatrick owes Laurent Ermantinger—

August 28
    For your draft on me in favor of Monsieur Bonaventure
    Augé for £80.16.5 . . . . or   £1212.6

1765
May 20
    For merchandise and money advanced to you during your
    illness when you were here, according to the account
    furnished you, £87.4.8½ in the currency of the
    province . . . . or   1744.4
    For 100 pounds of beaver that you owe Madame Ermantinger
    for a gold watch, which was worth 7/10 per pound . .   750.—
                                                         3707.—
    For interest due from the 1st of September 1766 until
    the 1st of September 1783, 17 years at 6 percent . . .   3780.16
                                                         £7487.16

A True Copy Taken from Mr. Ermantinger's account; maid over
to Mr. Marischaux—

N.B. Verry Erroneous as per my Letter to him—J. Fitzpatrick

Appendix I
THE SUCCESSION OF JOHN FITZPATRICK

WHEN JOHN FITZPATRICK died on March 20, 1791, his property was immediately sealed by Lieutenant Francisco Rivas, commandant of Fort Bute and therefore acting local civil authority, until an inventory could be made of it. Because the inventory provides so detailed a description of Fitzpatrick's material standing at the time of his death, as well as some insight into his interests and tastes, it has been included here. The following account is extracted from Lieutenant Rivas' reports in the Spanish West Florida Records.[1]

... just now, at about seven PM, a negress belonging to John Fitzpatrick has informed me that her master has just died at his house, which is next to the fort, leaving as his heir his wife, Maria Nivet, and as it appears that he has many debts, for the security of the property I went to the house, and there I saw a man lying down in bed, who was apparently dead and who was being prepared for burial. I affixed seals to two paper containers, two trunks, and a chest, and I took possession of four keys given to me by Maria Nivet, wife of the deceased....

On May 4, 1791, Lieutenant Rivas began the inventory and appraisal of Fitzpatrick's estate. Phillipe Englehardt and Josef Mir were appointed as appraisers, and Simon Daigre and Paul Daigre served as witnesses. The inventory was completed on May 11. Following is the list of Fitzpatrick's property, with the appraised value of each item:

	Pesos	*Reales*
Eight mahogany chairs of English make, used, in the living room	12	
A large mahogany table of English make, used	8	
A small mahogany table, broken, of English make	6	
A used cypress table	1	
A mirror, two feet long and sixteen inches wide, used	4	
A walnut bed, a feather mattress, a pair of sheets of Russian cloth, two woolen blankets, and two feather pillows	21	4
A pair of andirons, a shovel, and a pair of tongs, all used	7	

[1] The translation of the Spanish West Florida Records prepared by the Survey of Federal Archives contains numerous errors and omissions. The following material is extracted from the original records, held in the office of the Clerk of Court, East Baton Rouge Parish, Baton Rouge.

Appendix I

	Pesos	Reales
Two coffee pots, one sugar bowl, three pitchers, three coffee cups and saucers	2	
A flask, a pitcher, two small bottles, two glass salt cellars	2	
Six wine cups, twelve liquor cups, all of glass, and four small wine glasses	3	4
Four maps, very old	1	
In the room where Fitzpatrick died, a small cypress table, very old		4
A used long-sighted field glass, and a bottle case with twelve empty glass bottles	4	
In one of the sealed chests, seven sheets, six of them made of Russian material, and the other one used	12	
Three large damask tablecloths, two of them rat-eaten, and two napkins, all used	6	
A cotton quilt, used	4	
Four Holland cloth shirts, used	4	
Two pairs of long trousers, one pair of drawers, and one pair of stockings, all of linen	2	
In one of the drawers of the chest, a box containing a razor, a whetstone for the razor, and a mirror . .	2	4
A little box with two pairs of silver shirt buttons, broken	1	
A package of Indian trinkets, and two pair of silk stockings, used	1	
A package containing eleven augers of different sizes, a set of two lancets, and some skeins of thread for making buttonholes	4	
A small box containing scales and weights for weighing medicines, and some medicines . . .	6	
A pair of silver shoe buckles	6	
The said chest, made of mahogany, used . . .	15	
Six tin plates, part of a table service	6	
Two platters and an inkwell, made of chinaware	2	
A copper coffee pot	1	4
A mousetrap, a funnel, and a strainer	1	
Four pair of somewhat used shoes	4	
A used hat, and a hammer		4
A large empty chest, without keys, used	1	
A second chest in the same room, containing papers and books	10	
A somewhat used mahogany couch without a back	6	
Two iron cooking pots, one with four or five holes and the other with two, both broken, two copper candelabra, and a pair of snuffers	4	
In the warehouse, a stone for filtering water, with a cypress frame, used	8	

	Pesos	Reales
Three glass jugs and a chinaware container of varnish	3	
A large tin pitcher for storing gunpowder, a large funnel of the same material, and a used cypress chest without keys	2	
Nine platters of different sizes, and two English china mixing bowls	4	
Fifteen chinaware plates, of English make . . .	1	4
Two lots of land, upon which was constructed the wooden house where Fitzpatrick died, which was twenty-two feet long and thirty feet deep, with two galleries, a warehouse, and a kitchen, all quite old	40	
In the warehouse on Fitzpatrick's plantation, about two and one-quarter leagues from the fort, a large cypress clothes press, with copper trimmings, in good condition	14	
Three small cypress tables, old	2	
Three old chairs with backs	1	4
Two old chairs with backs	1	1
A cypress bottle case with copper trimmings, and four glass flasks	7	
A carbine	4	
An English shotgun, with two powderhorns and a bag for ammunition	4	
Seventy-eight cords for tying tobacco, used . . .	15	
Six hoes, four in good condition and two in bad condition	6	
Four good hoes	4	
Nine shovels, seven in good condition and two broken	7	
Five used axes	3	4
A carpenter's iron	2	
Two iron presses, and a hoe for cutting roots, used	1	4
A used ox plow	10	
A somewhat used horse plow	6	
Another rather used horse plow	6	
Four horse collars, with harness for plowing horses, and two old bridles	3	
One old hide, a somewhat used building axe, a hammer, two chisels, four large and small augers, all carpenter's instruments, used	3	2
A handsaw	3	
A used saw, six and a half feet long	5	
Another saw, six feet long	8	
Another saw, six and a half feet long	5	
Six scythes, all in good condition	2	

The Succession

Appendix I

	Pesos	Reales
A small knife for splitting shingles, somewhat used, and two small iron rings	1	4
Twelve fathoms of new cord, one inch thick	2	4
Two collars for plowing horses, with new harness	4	
A riding saddle and bridle, somewhat used	7	
About seventy or eighty pounds of new nails	15	
A box containing old scrap iron and some old nails	5	
A glass jug, some bits for English bridles, and a bell for livestock	1	4
Two large kitchen grindstones	9	
Four iron cooking pots, one large, three medium size	5	4
Four cracked iron cooking pots, an old copper cauldron, an iron coffee pot in good condition, and an old funnel	3	
A skillet and a griddle, somewhat used	2	6
In the warehouse, a grindstone with iron handles, almost new	5	
Eight ox hides	6	
Two large tubs, two small ones, four buckets, a crock for making butter, all somewhat used	8	4
Three dozen empty bottles	3	
Four irons for pressing cloths	1	4
Six large earthenware basins and four small ones, two of which are cracked	3	6
Two ordinary earthenware soup bowls, four platters, two of medium size and two small, and eighteen plates, all of English chinaware	4	
Six small platters, and two large cups, all of English chinaware	2	6
A medium-size china cup, four small coffee cups with saucers, and four chocolate cups with saucers, all of English chinaware	2	4
Five small glasses, and three glass salt cellars		5
Six table knives, eleven English forks, fourteen spoons, eight small spoons for coffee, all old	2	
One large silver spoon	6	
A scale with seven and a half pounds of copper weights, and twelve pounds of lead weights, English weight	6	
Two hand saws, one very fine, both in good condition	6	
Two finishing axes and two hatchets, used	3	4
An English instrument for making holes, with twenty augers, and a small hammer	6	
A knife, and a mason's trowel, all used	1	

	Pesos	Reales
Five augers, ranging in size from one-half inch to one and one-half inch, in good condition	4	4
Seven small augers of different sizes		6
Four used chisels and one jackknife		6
Four curved chisels and an English tool . . .	1	2
Two two-handed knives, old	11	4
A shotgun spring, two pairs of pliers, and five iron cutting instruments, all used	6	
Six files, three for wood and three for iron . . .	5	
A vise	4	
Two old caulking instruments	1	4
A lock and two hoes	2	4
Three carpenter's galleys and a carpenter's plane, one without a knife and the others in good condition	3	
Three carpenter's planes for moldings	3	
A pair of small shackles and a piece of chain two and one-half feet long	2	
A pine chest, without keys		6
A coat and sleeveless vest of fine material in a stained pearl color	6	
Two cotton frills, used, and two pairs of cheap cotton pants, torn	5	
An old overcoat, and two old sleeveless waistcoats	1	
A waistcoat, and a ragged old vest of a dark color	2	
Three striped waistcoats, two quite used and one slightly used	2	4
Three striped cotton vests, slightly used, and four pairs of patched trousers of the same material . .	6	
Six pairs of long trousers, three in good condition and three used, and three undershirts, one in good condition and the other two used	6	4
Seven ornamented shirts, in good condition . . .	14	
Eight old shirts	8	
Six ordinary muslin bow ties	3	
Six pairs of stockings, very old	1	
Three old sheets, one old window curtain, and three napkins in good condition	3	4
A somewhat used hat	2	
A trunk, without a key	1	
A chinaware bottle, with some quinine and some other medicine	3	
Fourteen files of different sizes	2	
A trunk, with key	1	
Fifty barrels of corn, mostly on the cob	50	
Two barrels of English potatoes	6	

	Pesos	Reales
Two branding irons	1	4
A sickle, and some scrap iron		4
A cypress pirogue, thirty-four feet long and three and one-half wide, used and damaged . . .	16	
Another cypress pirogue, twenty-four feet long and two and one-half wide	6	
Three cart horses, two old	70	
Fourteen cows with calves, each pair appraised at twelve pesos	168	
Thirty-one pregnant cows, each appraised at ten pesos	310	
Eight untamed oxen, each appraised at twelve pesos and four reales	100	
Three bulls, appraised at twelve pesos each . . .	36	
Twenty-eight heifers, ranging in age from one to two years, appraised at four pesos each . . .	112	
Eleven sows, six of which have thirty-six piglets, those with litters appraised with the litters at twenty-six pesos and the other five appraised at fifteen pesos	41	
Thirty-six hogs of all ages	33	
A Negro named Manchak, of Senegal nationality, about forty-eight to fifty years old, field hand, occasionally afflicted with kidney trouble	200	
A Negress named Ana, of Dunba nationality, thirty-eight to forty years old, field hand	240	
A Negro named Pedro, a native of this province, fifteen years old, son of Ana	350	
A Negro girl named Maria Luisa, a native of this province, fourteen years old, daughter of Ana . .	280	
A little Negro girl named Francisca, a native of this province, nine or ten years old, daughter of Ana .	210	
Another Negro girl named Angela, a native of this province, about seven years old, daughter of Ana .	150	
A Negro named Teodoro, of Senegal nationality, about thirty-eight to forty years old, a laborer and handyman who can also work skillfully with carpenter's tools	400	
A Negress named Mariana, of Temene nationality, about forty-four or forty-six years old, who can, wash, iron, and cook a little bit	250	
A Negress named Juliana, a native of this province, sixteen years old, daughter of Mariana, has worked as a maid, knows how to sew and wash	300	
A Negro named Santiago, of Papa nationality, about seventy or seventy-five years old, field hand . . .	140	

	Pesos	Reales
A Negress named Teresa, of Coranco nationality, fifty-five or sixty years old, field hand, afflicted with an unknown disease	70	
A plantation containing eleven arpents in front with the usual depth of forty arpents, bounded on one side by the land of Zachary Norton and on the other by that of Louis Toutant Beauregard, the plantation covering about sixty arpents in area of cleared land, with an English cypress fence and some other cypress fences; a good warehouse twenty-seven feet long and eighteen wide, with porches in the front and back nine feet wide, with pillars in the ground, all made of cypress; a house, only partly finished, thirty feet long and fifteen wide, with a porch eight feet wide; a chicken house resting on piles, ten feet long and nine feet wide; four Negro cabins; a horse stable built of cypress, in good condition	2,000	
A history of Mr "Guipte," written in English, four volumes	4	
Another history in English, titled "Peregrine Pickle," in four volumes	4	
Four volumes in English by Alexander Pope . .	4	
Four volumes in English by "Chrysal"	4	
Two volumes, "Roderick Random"	1	
A history of different nations, in eight volumes, by Rollin	8	
"The Spectator" in eight volumes	10	
"Works of Alexander Pope" in six volumes . . .	6	
Two arithmetic books by William Gordon . . .	2	
Two books titled "Commercial Law" by T. Cunningham	2	
"Works of Milton" in two volumes	2	
A book of instructions for gardeners	4	
A "Gazetteer"		4
"Works of Junius" in two volumes	1	
"Fables of John Gay"		4
A universal history in one volume	15	
A history of England in two volumes, unbound, by William Henry Montague	8	
A French and English dictionary by Boyer . . .	3	
An English dictionary for merchants by Beawes	2	
A history of the Turkish empire in one volume . .		4
The works of Jonathan Swift in fourteen volumes, lacking volumes one, two, seven, eight, ten and thirteen	3	

	Pesos	Reales
A history of England in four volumes by Catherine McCauley, lacking volume three	2	
A history of Persia in three volumes, in French .	1	4
"Philosophy of Politics" by Abbé Raynal in ten volumes	4	

Among Fitzpatrick's papers was found a relation of credits in his favor, written December 14, 1790, describing debts owed to him amounting to 3,192 pesos. Another paper, written the same day, described his debts, amounting to 2,262 pesos and 7 reales.

Appendix II
GLOSSARY OF EIGHTEENTH-CENTURY MERCANTILE TERMS[1]

Baise (*bayes*): a coarse woolen cloth used mainly to make work clothes.
Batiste: fine white linen fabric of French or Flemish manufacture.
Bengal: a thin, light cloth made of skin and hair, manufactured in India.
Bill of exchange: a written order by which the drawer obliges the addressed person (drawee) to pay a specific sum at a given date to the drawer or a third party.
Bit: See *dollar*.
Blanket: any thick, heavy wool, cotton or combination fabric with a short nap on both sides; sometimes used for clothing.
Bombazine: a dress fabric made of silk or a combination of silk and cotton.
Bon, bond: a type of mortgage, by which an individual gives a deed binding him to pay a specified sum of money by a certain date.
Brig: a two-masted, square-rigged vessel.
Broadcloth: a soft, smooth-surfaced fabric made of wool, cotton or silk.
Brunswicks: a twilled fabric originally produced in Brunswick, Germany.
Buckram: a coarse, stiffened linen used for linings.
Calendered cloth: fabric pressed with a roller designed to smooth or glaze it or give it a wavy appearance.
Calico: cotton fabrics imported from Calicut, India, and usually printed with various patterns and colors in England.
Callamanco: woolen fabric of Flemish or English manufacture, sometimes containing silk or goat hair.
Cambric: a thin, fine white linen or cotton fabric.
Cape, The: Cap François on the island of Hispaniola.
Carrot: in Louisiana usage, a bundle of tobacco leaves rolled lengthwise into the shape of a large cigar and dried, usually weighing about ten pounds.
Castor (*caster*) *hats*: hats made from beaver fur or any imitation of beaver fur.
Check: any fabric woven in a checked pattern.
Clayed sugar: a nearly white refined sugar, produced by a process employing clay.
Corduroy: a coarse cotton fabric used for work clothes.
Dimity (*dimothy*): a heavy cotton fabric with woven stripes or figures, used for garments, upholstery, and hangings.
Do: ditto.

1/Some of the definitions in this glossary are derived from Philip L. White (ed.), *The Beekman Mercantile Papers, 1746–1799* (New York, 1956), III, 645–55.

Dollar: the English name for the Spanish peso, often broken into bits of one to seven reales. Two bits equalled a quarter of a dollar.
Duck: a strong, untwilled linen or cotton fabric, used for clothing or small sails.
Duffels: a coarse, napped woolen cloth.
Ell: in English usage, 45 inches.
Fustians: a coarse cloth of cotton or cotton and flax, sometimes with a short nap.
Garlits: a type of linen produced in Silesia.
Gauze: a thin, transparent fabric made of silk, cotton, or linen.
Grosgrain: a coarse fabric, often stiffened with gum, made of silk, wool, or a combination of the two; a heavy taffeta.
Guinea: an English coin worth 21 shillings.
Half Joe: popular name for a Portuguese gold coin (johannes) worth about 36 shillings.
Headright: the right by which the head of a family could apply for a land grant. In British West Florida, the head of a family could receive one hundred acres. By "family right," he could request fifty acres for his wife and each child, slave, or indentured servant.
Hogshead: a large barrel containing up to 140 gallons.
Holland: a closely woven white linen fabric, mainly used for shirts and bed linen.
L.: common abbreviation for the French *livre*, monetary unit equal to twenty sols.
Muslin: a type of finely woven cotton fabric most often used for dresses and curtains.
Myrtle wax: a candle wax made from the berries of a species of myrtle tree.
Nankeen: a sturdy cotton cloth, originally produced at Nanking, China, of a yellow variety of cotton, or any imitation of this fabric made of cotton or wool.
Osnaburg (osnabrig): a heavy, coarse linen fabric originally made in Osnaburg, Germany.
Pettyauger: a corrupt spelling of *piragua* or *pirogue*, referring to an open canoe or an open, flat-bottomed sailing vessel.
Pistole: a Spanish gold coin worth slightly less than one British pound sterling.
Polonese: the fabric used in the construction of a *polonaise*, a female garment worn in the late eighteenth century consisting of a bodice with the skirt open from the waist downwards.
Porterage: charge for the services of a porter.
Prussians (prusianas): a type of fabric produced in Prussia.
Puncheon: a large cask usually containing from 80 to 100 gallons.
Quarter: a measure of capacity for grain and other commodities. The British imperial quarter equalled 8 bushels, but there were a number of local variations. The term was also used to refer to the quarter part of a hundredweight, which equalled 28 pounds.
Romall: a thin silk or cotton fabric, or a handkerchief or neckerchief made from such a fabric.
S.: abbreviation for shilling or sol, depending on the context.
Schooner: a fore-and-aft rigged sailing vessel carrying two, three, or four masts.

Silesias: a thin, coarse linen or cotton fabric, originally made in Silesia, used in garment construction.
Sloop: a small, fore-and-aft rigged sailing vessel carrying one mast.
Stroud: a blanket manufactured especially for the Indian trade, usually made of wool and often having a striped design.
Stuff: any woven textile, but especially used to refer to woolen fabrics without a nap.
Taffia: a rum-like distilled alcohol derived from low-grade molasses or refuse brown sugar.
Turbit (*turpeth*): a cathartic or purgative drug.
Turlington's balsam: a medicinal preparation, probably applied externally for healing wounds or soothing pain.
Worsted: a high-quality woolen fabric.

BIBLIOGRAPHY

SPECIAL GUIDES

Doyle, Elisabeth Joan, comp. *A Guide to Archival Materials Held by the Catholic Diocese of Baton Rouge, Department of History and Archives.* Baton Rouge, 1964.
Hill, Roscoe R. *Descriptive Catalogue of the Documents Relating to the History of the United States in the Papeles Procedentes de Cuba.* Washington, D.C., 1916.
Holmes, Jack D. L. *A Guide to Spanish Louisiana, 1762–1806.* New Orleans, 1970.
Peña y Camara, José de la, et al. *Catalogo de documentos del Archivo General de Indias, Sección V, Gobierno, Audiencia de Santo Domingo.* 2 vols. Madrid, 1968.
Porteous, Laura L. "Index to the Spanish Judicial Records of Louisiana." *Louisiana Historical Quarterly,* VIII (1925)–XXXI (1948).

PRIMARY SOURCES

Archives

Archivo General de Indias, Seville.
    Audiencia de Santo Domingo, Legajo 80.
    Papeles Procedentes de Cuba, Legajos 1232, 2351.
Archivo General de Simancas.
    Sección de Gueura Moderna, Legajo 7291 (Hojas de Servicios Militares de América).
British Museum, London.
    General Frederick Haldimand Papers, Additional Manuscripts 21729.
    Ps.8/15276.
Catholic Life Center, Baton Rouge. Department of History and Archives.
    Registres mortuaires des blancs, 1785 à 1856. St. Gabriel Church Records.
East Baton Rouge Parish Clerk of Court's Office, Baton Rouge.
    Spanish West Florida Records.
Louisiana State Land Office, Baton Rouge.
    Acts of Congress Pertaining to Louisiana.
    Greensburg District Claim Papers, Book #25, Section 45: Plat of Louis Beauregard, A–N 255.

Greensburg District Claim Papers, "Old Plats," TS 85, R 1E (April 15, 1831).
Louisiana State Museum, New Orleans. Archives and Manuscripts Collections
 New Orleans Superior Council Records.
 Spanish Manuscripts, Mississippi Valley.
 Spanish Judicial Records.
Louisiana State University, Baton Rouge. Department of Archives and Manuscripts.
 Baton Rouge Census Document.
 Luke Collins Documents.
 Ellis-Farar Papers.
 Daniel and Philip Hicky Papers.
 Morgan Family Papers.
 George Rapalje Notebook.
 Reggio Family Papers.
 Henry Wilson Papers.
New Orleans Notarial Archives.
 Acts of Joseph Fernandez.
 Acts of Jean B. Garic.
 Acts of Pedro Pedesclaux.
New Orleans Public Library. Louisiana Division.
 Documents concerning the estate and succession of Don Gilberto Antonio de St. Maxent.
 Inventory of the notarial office of Charles Ximenes, 1768–1770.
 Inventory of the notarial office of Pedro Pedesclaux.
Public Record Office, London.
 Colonial Office, Series 5. Vols. 574–622.

Printed Documents and Contemporary Works

Alvord, Clarence W., and Clarence E. Carter, eds. *Cahokia Records, 1778–1790.* Collections of the Illinois State Historical Library, II. Springfield, Ill., 1907.
———. *The New Regime, 1765–1767.* Collections of the Illinois State Historical Library, XI. Springfield, Ill., 1916.
American State Papers. Public Lands, II. Washington, D.C., 1834.
Bartram, William, *Travels through North & South Carolina, Georgia, East & West Florida, the Cherokee Country, the Extensive Territories of the Muscogulges, or Creek Confederacy, and the Country of the Chactaws.* Edited by Francis Harper. New Haven, 1958.
Bates, Albert C., ed. *The Two Putnams, Israel and Rufus, in the Havana Expedition 1762 and in the Mississippi River Exploration 1772–73 with some account of The Company of Military Adventurers.* Hartford, Conn., 1931.
Carpenter, W. M. "The Mississippi River in the Olden Time, a Genuine Account of the Present State of the River Mississippi and of the Land on its Banks to the River Yasous, 1776." *Debow's Review,* III (1847), 115–123.
Dart, Henry P., ed. "British Proclamation of October 7, 1763, Cre-

ating the Government of West Florida." *Louisiana Historical Quarterly*, XIII (1930), 610–16.

———. "Cabildo Archives." *Louisiana Historical Quarterly*, II (1920).

De Ville, Winston, ed. *Colonial Louisiana Marriage Contracts. Post of Pointe Coupée, 1736–1803*. Baton Rouge, 1962.

Gianelloni, Mrs. S. J. "Louisiana's Spanish West Florida Records." *Louisiana Genealogical Register*, XVII (1970), 1–14.

Houck, Louis, ed. *The Spanish Regime in Missouri*. 2 vols. Chicago, 1909.

Hutchins, Thomas. *An Historical Narrative and Topographical Description of Louisiana, and West-Florida*. Facsimile edition, edited by Joseph G. Tregle, Jr. Gainesville, Fla., 1968.

Kinnaird, Lawrence, ed. *Spain in the Mississippi Valley, 1765–1794: Translations of Materials from the Spanish Archives in the Bancroft Library*. Annual Report of the American Historical Association for the Year 1945. 3 vols. Washington, D.C., 1946–49.

Lewis, Anna, ed. "Fort Panmure, 1779, as Related by Juan Delavillebeuvre to Barnardo de Galvez." *Mississippi Valley Historical Review*, XVIII (1931–32), 541–48.

Maduell, Charles R., Jr., comp. *Marriage Contracts, Wills and Testaments of the Spanish Colonial Period in New Orleans, 1770–1804*. New Orleans, 1969.

Phelps, Matthew. *Memoirs and Adventures of Captain Matthew Phelps, Particularly in two voyages from Connecticut to the River Mississippi, 1773–1780*. Bennington, Vt., 1802.

Pittman, Philip. *The Present State of the European Settlements on the Mississippi; With a Geographical Description of that River, illustrated by Plans and Draughts*. Edited by Frank Heywood Hodder. Cleveland, 1906.

Robichaux, Albert J., Jr. *Louisiana Census and Militia Lists 1770–1789*. Vol. I. *German Coast, New Orleans, Below New Orleans and Lafourche*. Harvey, La., 1973.

Rogers, Robert. *Journals of Major Robert Rogers*. Ann Arbor, 1966.

Romans, Bernard. *A Concise Natural History of East and West Florida*. New York, 1775.

———. "Part of the Province of East Florida" [Map of Florida, 1774]. New York, 1774.

Rowland, Eron, ed. *Life, Letters and Papers of William Dunbar of Elgin, Morayshire, Scotland, and Natchez, Mississippi*. Jackson, Miss., 1930.

Scott, Kenneth, ed. "Britain Loses Natchez, 1779: An Unpublished Letter." *Journal of Mississippi History*, XXVI (1964), 45–46.

Serrano y Sanz, Manuel. *Documentos históricos de la Florida y la Luisiana, siglos XVI al XVIII*. Madrid, 1912.

Survey of Federal Archives. *Confidential Despatches of Don Bernardo de Gálvez to His Uncle Don José de Gálvez*. Baton Rouge, 1938.

———. *Archives of the Spanish Government of West Florida*. 18 vols. Baton Rouge, 1937.

Wilton, William. "Part of the River Mississippi From Manchac up to the River Yazous." Photographic copy prepared by the Survey of Federal Archives. Baton Rouge, 1937.

SECONDARY SOURCES

Books

Alden, John Richard. *John Stuart and the Southern Colonial Frontier: A Study of Indian Relations, War, Trade, and Land Problems in the Southern Wilderness, 1754–1775.* Ann Arbor, 1944.

Alvord, Clarence W. *The Illinois Country, 1637–1818.* Springfield, Ill., 1920.

———. *The Mississippi Valley in British Politics: A Study of the Trade, Land Speculation, and Experiments in Imperialism culminating in the American Revolution.* 2 vols. Cleveland, 1917.

Baudier, Roger. *The Catholic Church in Louisiana.* New Orleans, 1939.

Bolton, Herbert Eugene. *Athanase de Mézières and the Louisiana-Texas Frontier, 1768–1780.* 2 vols. Cleveland, 1914.

Caruso, John Anthony. *The Mississippi Valley Frontier: The Age of French Exploration and Settlement.* New York, 1966.

Caughey, John W. *Bernardo de Gálvez in Louisiana: 1776–1783.* Berkeley, 1934.

Claiborne, J. F. H. *Mississippi, As a Province, Territory and State, with Biographical Notices of Eminent Citizens.* Jackson, Miss., 1880.

Clark, John G. *New Orleans, 1718–1812: An Economic History.* Baton Rouge, 1970.

Clayton, James D. *Antebellum Natchez.* Baton Rouge, 1968.

Coleman, James Julian, Jr. *Gilbert Antoine de St. Maxent: The Spanish Frenchman of New Orleans.* New Orleans, 1968.

Cuneo, John R. *Robert Rogers of the Rangers.* New York, 1959.

De Ville, Winston. *First Settlers of Pointe Coupée. A Study, based on Early Louisiana Church Records, 1737–1750.* New Orleans, 1974.

———. *Opelousas: The History of a French and Spanish Military Post in America, 1716–1803.* Cottonport, La., 1973.

De Vorsey, Louis, Jr. *The Indian Boundary in the Southern Colonies, 1763–1775.* Chapel Hill, 1961.

Fortier, Alcée. *A History of Louisiana.* 2nd ed. Baton Rouge, 1972.

Gillis, Norman E. *Early Inhabitants of the Natchez District.* Baton Rouge, 1963.

Giraud, Marcel. *L'Histoire de la Louisiane française.* 4 vols. to date. Paris, 1953– .

Hamilton, Peter J. *Colonial Mobile: An Historical Study.* Boston, 1910.

Hardin, J. Fair. *The Presidio and Mission of Los Adaes, For Fifty Years the Capital of the Spanish Province of Texas, And the Spaniards in Northwest Louisiana.* Privately printed, n.d.

Haynes, Robert V. *The Natchez District and the American Revolution.* Jackson, Miss., 1976.

Hodge, Frederick Webb, ed. *Handbook of American Indians North of Mexico.* 2 vols. New York, 1959.

Holmes, Jack D. L. *Honor and Fidelity: The Louisiana Infantry Regiment and the Louisiana Militia Companies, 1776–1821.* Birmingham, Ala., 1965.

Howard, Clinton N. *British Development of West Florida, 1763–1769.* Berkeley and Los Angeles, 1947.
James, James Alton. *Oliver Pollock: The Life and Times of an Unknown Patriot.* New York, 1937.
Johnson, Cecil. *British West Florida, 1763–1783.* New Haven, 1943.
Kinnaird, Lawrence, ed. *New Spain and the Anglo-American West. Historical Contributions presented to Herbert Eugene Bolton.* Los Angeles, 1932.
Korn, Bertram Wallace. *The Early Jews of New Orleans.* Waltham, Mass., 1969.
Marchand, Sidney, Sr. *An Attempt to Re-Assemble the Old Settlers in Family Groups.* Baton Rouge, 1965.
Martin, François-Xavier. *The History of Louisiana from the Earliest Period.* New Orleans, 1882.
Meyers, Rose. *A History of Baton Rouge, 1699–1812.* Baton Rouge, 1976.
Moore, Edith Wyatt. *Natchez Under-the-Hill.* Natchez, 1958.
Moore, John Preston. *Revolt in Louisiana: The Spanish Occupation, 1766–1770.* Baton Rouge, 1976.
Nasatir, Abraham P., and James R. Mills. *Commerce and Contraband in New Orleans during the French and Indian War. A Documentary Study of the Texel and Three Brothers Affairs.* Cincinnati, 1968.
Phillips, Paul Chrisler. *The Fur Trade.* 2 vols. Norman, Okla., 1961.
Proctor, Samuel, ed. *Eighteenth-Century Florida and Its Borderlands.* Gainesville, Fla., 1975.
Savelle, Max. *George Morgan, Colony Builder.* New York, 1932.
———. *A History of Colonial America.* Rev. ed. New York, 1964.
Surrey, Nancy M. Miller. *The Commerce of Louisiana During the French Regime, 1699–1763.* New York, 1916.
Sydnor, Charles S. *A Gentleman of the Old Natchez Region: Benjamin L. C. Wailes.* Durham, N.C., 1938.

Articles

Abbey, Kathryn T. "Peter Chester's Defense of the Mississippi After the Willing Raid." *Mississippi Valley Historical Review,* XXII (1935), 17–32.
———. "Spanish Projects for the Reoccupation of the Floridas During the American Revolution." *Hispanic American Historical Review,* IX (1929), 265–85.
Bjork, David K. "Documents Regarding Indian Affairs in the Lower Mississippi Valley, 1771–1772." *Mississippi Valley Historical Review,* XIII (1926), 398–410.
Born, John D. "Governor Johnstone and Trade in British West Florida, 1764–1767." *Wichita State University Bulletin, University Studies,* No. 75. Wichita, 1968.
———. "John Fitzpatrick of Manchac: A Scottish Merchant in the Lower Mississippi." *Journal of Mississippi History,* XXXII (1970), 117–34.
Brown, Douglas Stewart. "The Iberville Canal Project: Its Relation to Anglo-French Commercial Rivalry in the Mississippi Valley,

1763–1775." *Mississippi Valley Historical Review,* XXXII (1946), 491–516.

Carter, Clarence E. "The Beginnings of British West Florida." *Mississippi Valley Historical Review,* IV (1917), 314–41.

Caughey, John W. "Bernardo de Gálvez and the English Smugglers on the Mississippi, 1777." *Hispanic American Historical Review,* XII (1932), 46–58.

———. "The Natchez Rebellion of 1781 and Its Aftermath." *Louisiana Historical Quarterly,* XVI (1933), 57–83.

———. "Willing's Expedition Down the Mississippi, 1778." *Louisiana Historical Quarterly,* XV (1932), 5–36.

Coker, William S. "Luke Collins Senior and Family: An Overview." *Louisiana History,* XIV (1973), 137–55.

Cusachs, Gaspar, trans. "Bernardo de Gálvez Diary of the Operations against Pensacola." *Louisiana Historical Quarterly,* I (1917), 44–84.

Din, Gilbert C. "Proposals and Plans for Colonization in Spanish Louisiana, 1787–1790." *Louisiana History,* XI (1970), 197–213.

Ellis, Frederick Stephen. "American Activity in Louisiana and West Florida during the Revolutionary War." *The St. Tammany Historical Society Gazette,* I (1975), 3–19.

Faye, Stanley. "The Arkansas Post of Louisiana. French Domination," *Louisiana Historical Quarterly,* XVI (1943), 633–721.

———. "The Arkansas Post of Louisiana: Spanish Domination." *Louisiana Historical Quarterly,* XXVII (1944), 629–716.

Haarmann, Albert W. "The Spanish Conquest of British West Florida, 1779–1781." *Florida Historical Quarterly,* XXXIX (1960), 107–34.

Hanson, Marcus L. "The Population of the American Outlying Regions in 1790." *Annual Report of the American Historical Association for the Year 1931,* I (1932), 398–408.

Haynes, Robert V. "James Willing and the Planters of Natchez: The American Revolution Comes to the Southwest." *Journal of Mississippi History,* XXXVII (1975), 1–40.

Holmes, Jack D. L. "Indigo in Colonial Louisiana and the Floridas." *Louisiana History,* VIII (1967), 329–49.

———. "Juan de la Villebeuvre: Spain's Commandant of Natchez During the American Revolution." *Journal of Mississippi History,* XXXVII (1975), 97–129.

———. "Some Economic Problems of the Spanish Governors of Louisiana." *Hispanic American Historical Review,* XLII (1962), 521–43.

Howard, C. N. "Colonial Natchez: The Early British Period." *Journal of Mississippi History,* VII (1945), 156–70.

James, James Alton. "Oliver Pollock, Financier of the Revolution in the West." *Mississippi Valley Historical Review,* XVI (1929–30), 67–80

———. "Oliver Pollock and the Free Navigation of the Mississippi River." *Mississippi Valley Historical Review,* XIX (1932), 331–47.

Johnson, Cecil. "Expansion in West Florida, 1770–1779." *Mississippi Valley Historical Review,* XX (1934), 481–96.

Kniffen, Fred B. "Bayou Manchac: A Physiographic Interpretation." *Geographical Review*, XXV (1935), 462–66.
Matthews, Richard Ira. "The New Orleans Revolution of 1768: A Reappraisal." *Louisiana Studies*, IV (1965), 124–67.
Moore, John Preston. "Antonio de Ulloa: A Profile of the First Spanish Governor of Louisiana." *Louisiana History*, VIII (1967), 189–218.
Morgan, Madel Jacobs. "Sarah Truly, A Mississippi Tory." *Journal of Mississippi History*, XXXVIII (1975), 87–95.
Peterson, Mary A. "British West Florida: Abstracts of Land Petitions." *Louisiana Genealogical Register*, XVIII (1971), 318–77.
Rea, Robert A. "Redcoats and Redskins on the Lower Mississippi, 1763–1776: The Career of Lt. John Thomas." *Louisiana History*, XI (1970), 5–35.
Scramuzza, V. M. "Gálveztown, a Spanish Settlement of Colonial Louisiana." *Louisiana Historical Quarterly*, XIII (1930), 553–609.
Siebert, Wilbur H. "The Loyalists in West Florida and the Natchez District." *Mississippi Valley Historical Review*, II (1916), 465–83.
Sumner, William G. "The Spanish Dollar and the Colonial Shilling." *American Historical Review*, III (1898), 607–19.
Taylor, Garland. "Colonial Settlement and Early Revolutionary Activity in West Florida up to 1779." *Mississippi Valley Historical Review*, XXII (1935), 351–60.
Tyler, Bruce. "The Mississippi River Trade, 1784–1788." *Louisiana History*, XII (1971), 225–67.
Wells, Gordon M. "British Land Grants—William Wilton Map, 1774." *Journal of Mississippi History*, XXVIII (1966), 152–60.
Whitaker, Arthur P. "Alexander McGillivray, 1789–1793." *North Carolina Historical Review*, V (1928), 181–203.

Unpublished theses and dissertations

De Ville, Winston. "The Opelousas Post, from the Earliest Settlement to 1803." M.A. thesis, Louisiana State University, 1963.
McKenna, John Reilly, Jr. "The Role of Water Transportation in the Settlement of Bayou Manchac and the Amite River, Louisiana." M.A. thesis, Louisiana State University, 1975.
Miller, Wilbert James. "The Spanish Commandant of Baton Rouge, 1779–1795." M.A. thesis, Louisiana State University, 1965.
Quattrocchi, Anna Margaret. "Thomas Hutchins, 1730–1789." Ph.D. dissertation, University of Pittsburgh, 1944.
Starr, Joseph Barton. "Tories, Dons, and Rebels: The American Revolution in British West Florida." Ph.D. dissertation, Florida State University, 1971.
Texada, David Ker. "The Administration of Alejandro O'Reilly as Governor of Louisiana, 1769–1770." Ph.D. dissertation, Louisiana State University, 1968.

INDEX

Acadians, 148, 148n, 166, 420
Alston, Philip: letter to, 259; mentioned, 351, 369, 376, 382, 384n
American merchants: trade with Louisiana, 31, 39, 54, 139, 170
American Revolution: origins, 181, 184; in the Northeast, 256, 258, 268, 270, 271; in Illinois, 204, 231, 266, 268, 318, 321; in the Southwest, 278, 289, 293, 311, 311n, 321, 329–30; impact of on Mississippi trade, 192, 218, 296, 302, 319, 328–29
Amite River, 6, 13, 19, 29, 162
Amoss, James: letters to, 37, 74; mentioned, 320
Arkansas, 83n–84n, 194, 229, 266, 269, 269n, 365
Arkansas Post, 5, 24, 212, 235, 237
Arkansas River, 20
Attakapas, 287
Aubry, Charles Philippe: identified, 42n; mentioned, 42, 62, 63

Bacon, Richard: letter to, 394
Balize, 6, 64, 115
Banks, James, 307
Barber, Philip: letter to, 376; mentioned, 349, 350
Barber, Thomas, 20
Barber, William, 40
Barker, Captain William: identified, 307n; letter to, 341; mentioned, 307, 334, 345, 392
Barrow, Robert: identified, 73n; letter to, 73
Barrow, William: identified, 49n; letter to, 92–93; mentioned, 49, 50, 51, 54, 58, 67, 71, 74, 85, 91, 95, 98, 101, 117, 162–63, 225, 227, 241, 261–62, 391–92, 395, 420
Bartram, William, 14
Baton Rouge, 6, 19, 29, 31, 87, 204, 252, 311, 330, 334, 392
Bay, Elihu Hall: identified, 278; letter to, 278–79; mentioned, 291–93

Baynton, Wharton and Morgan: identified, 73n; letters to, 73, 109; mentioned, 78n, 125
Bayou Manchac: description of, 11–12; clearing project, 12; mentioned, 6, 13–15, 127, 139, 148, 157, 230, 326, 328
Bayou St. John, 6, 52, 52n, 53, 139
Bayou Sara, 19
Bentley, Thomas: identified, 102n; letter to, 358–60; mentioned, 13, 18, 102, 103, 122, 142, 152, 155–56, 167, 193, 294, 325, 361, 417–18
Bingaman, Adam: letter to, 421–22
Blain, Madame. See Fitzpatrick, Marie Nivet Blain
Blanchard, Charles: identified, 205n; letter to, 205–206; mentioned, 18, 248, 253
Blommart, John: identified, 83n–84n; letters to, 378, 381–82; mentioned, 20, 83, 143, 148, 191, 209, 290, 291n, 331, 351, 354, 356, 364, 375, 379, 383, 384n, 404, 407, 411, 418
Boisdoré, Louis, 45, 52, 55
Booker, Thomas: letters to, 275, 283–84, 292–93, 296; mentioned, 300
Bordman, Charles, 405–406
Bradley, John: identified, 47n; letters to, 56–57, 75, 78–79; mentioned, 13, 47, 84, 87, 92, 94, 95, 96, 101, 103, 104, 105, 106, 118, 303, 417–18
Bradley, Richard: letters to, 281, 303; mentioned, 302, 307
Brion, Monsieur: letters to, 345–46, 346–47
British West Florida: trade with Louisiana, 7–8, 9, 11, 17, 18, 68–69, 72, 77; new towns in, 15–16, 91, 91n, 98, 127–28, 131, 192, 194; lack of local courts in, 195, 210, 220, 255–56, 278, 279, 338; during American Revolution, 23–24, 26–29, 289, 290, 293, 324, 330, 383

Browne, Montfort: identified, 128n; visits Manchac, 177, 191, 194; mentioned, 15, 79, 87, 128, 207–208

Campbell, Lt. James, 12
Campbell, John: identified, 102n; letters to, 223, 242; mentioned, 102, 244n
Campbell, Gen. John, 27–28, 30, 324, 324n, 330, 334, 392
Cannond, Monsieur: letter to, 346; mentioned, 347
Cap François, St. Domingue: trade with Louisiana, 42, 116, 175, 197, 252
Caresse, Pierre, 43, 43n, 53, 65, 69, 72, 93, 93n
Carpenter, Richard: identified, 214n; letter to, 214
Carr, Richard: letter to, 217
Cerré, Gabriel: identified, 411n; letter to, 422–23; mentioned, 408, 411
Chester, Peter, 23, 112, 306, 317–18, 392
Chrystie, Adam: identified, 231n; letters to, 231, 293, 302–303; mentioned, 26, 211, 215, 290, 291n
Clark, Daniel, 194, 226
Clark, George Rogers, 321, 332
Collell, Francisco: identified, 325n; letter to, 325–26; mentioned, 329, 418
Collins, Luke: identified, 160n; letter to, 160–61
Comite River, 19
Commercial Decree of 1768, p. 11
Comyn, Phillips: identified, 64n; letters to, 64, 68, 75, 230–31, 232–33, 238; death and estate of, 260, 277
Comyn, Valens Stephen: identified, 46n; letters to, 46, 50–51, 60, 62–63, 67, 70
Concord, 20, 25
Continental Congress, 23, 181, 181n
Corn, 6, 37, 52, 87, 95, 104, 196
Craig, Capt. James: letter to 326–27

Darchutte, Monsieur: letter to, 304–305; mentioned, 306, 314, 315, 316
Datchurut, Jean: identified, 260n; letter to, 260–61
Davis, Capt. John: letters to, 320, 330–31, 339–40, 344–45, 355–56, 357, 364, 366, 370–71, 372–74, 376–77, 379–80, 383–84, 388–89, 390, 400, 414–15; mentioned, 340, 379, 380, 415

Descoudreaux, Charles: identified, 118n; mentioned, 118, 147, 148, 160, 163, 179
Dessalles, Luis, 263, 263n, 282, 283, 286–88
Deverges, Monsieur: letter to, 353–54; mentioned, 355–56, 357
Dicas, Thomas: identified, 276n; letter to, 276; mentioned, 340, 345
Dickson, Col. Alexander, 27, 29, 244n, 318, 324, 324n, 330n, 334, 392, 394
Dow, Dr. Robert: letter to, 416
DuForrest, Joseph: letters to, 286–88, 299, 300; mentioned, 283, 298, 420
Dunbar, William, 204n, 406, 416
Duralde brothers, 43, 43n
Durnford, Elias: identified, 79n; letter to, 102; mentioned, 76, 79, 84, 85, 122, 123, 126, 128, 143, 147, 148, 150, 155, 205, 265

Eason, William: letter to, 333; mentioned, 274, 404
Ellis, John, 417
Ermantinger, Laurent: letters to, 196, 408–11; mentioned, 4, 411–12, 423

Fairlie, James: letters to, 313, 318, 326, 328, 331, 332; mentioned, 340, 345
Falconer, John: identified, 48n; letters to, 48–49, 54, 74, 210, 323; mentioned, 53
Farmar, Maj. Robert, 12
Ferguson, William: letters to, 335–36, 351, 365–66, 374–75; mentioned, 337
Fitzgerald, George: letter to, 418–19; mentioned, 422
Fitzpatrick, John: early life, 3, 4, 93, 96, 209, 409–10; Indian captivity of, 4, 59, 64, 66, 111, 209; moves to Manchac, 74, 76–79, 83; petitions for land, 19, 91, 91n, 98, 209–10, 219, 225, 241–42; health of, 113, 262, 264, 274, 372, 386, 418; financial losses of during American Revolution, 360, 390, 391, 403, 410, 416; becomes a Spanish subject, 308; plantation of, 421–22, 431; death of, 32, 425
Fitzpatrick, Marie Nivet Blain: identified, 76n; mentioned, 22–23, 32, 76, 78, 137, 154, 170, 209, 212, 217, 229, 258, 264, 270, 274, 278, 283, 288, 325, 341, 351, 362, 372, 380, 389, 390, 402, 404, 406, 413, 422, 425
Flags of truce, 9, 9n, 334, 399, 341, 384

Floating warehouses, 41n
Flour: shortages of, 39, 53, 316; regulation of quality by Spanish government in Louisiana, 69, 71; from New York, 38n, 177; from Illinois, 186; from France, 161; mentioned, 44, 45, 96, 109, 121, 125, 132, 149, 161, 218, 227, 255, 387
Flowers, Dr. Samuel, 29, 181, 204n, 362, 371, 414
Fort Bute: established, 12–13; abandoned by British, 13, 15; mentioned, 14, 16, 17, 18, 27, 49n
France: relations with Britain, 241: relations with Spain, 241; administration of Louisiana, 9–10; trade with Spanish Louisiana, 9, 25, 39, 42, 42n, 43, 87, 161, 230, 230n; in Illinois fur trade, 57, 61
Francis, John, 110
Frank, John, 304, 306
Fraser, Lt. Alexander, 40
French, Gregory: letters to, 371, 384; mentioned, 22, 87, 88, 89, 91, 95, 97, 98, 99, 101, 115, 116, 117, 343, 354, 356
Fry, Thomas, 348
Fur trade: organization of, 4–5; mentioned, 13, 15, 31, 39, 43, 44, 49, 54, 55, 57, 58, 59, 61–62, 69, 90, 93, 94, 96–97, 99, 100, 107, 108–109, 110, 112, 114, 119, 120–21, 126, 133–34, 140, 145, 151, 159, 164–65, 168, 169, 170, 176, 179, 181, 189, 195, 208–209, 224, 225, 226–27, 229, 237, 239, 259–60, 270, 277, 305, 406–407

Gage, Gen. Thomas, 12
Gálvez, Bernardo de, 21, 24–30, 41n, 230n, 236, 236n, 244, 244n, 245, 283, 307, 311n, 321, 325–26, 339, 340, 369, 392, 420
Gálvestown, 30–31, 49n, 312, 325, 325n, 329, 355n, 360, 417
Garig, Jean B., 245, 245n
Gibson, Capt. George, 24, 218
Godley and Raincock: identified, 40n; letters to, 49–50, 51, 53–54, 57–58, 66–67, 70–71, 91, 95, 98, 101–102, 129–30, 162–63; mentioned, 40, 225
Gordon, John: letters to, 386–87, 389
Gradenigo, John, 62, 62n, 63, 64, 67
Graham, Lt. J. J.: letters to, 321–22, 341, 357–58; mentioned, 294, 307
Grand Gulf, 20, 111, 166, 167, 168, 171, 180, 234, 254, 287, 348, 352
Grand Pré, Carlos, 29, 322, 389

Hamilton, Henry, 321, 321n
Hardy, Thomas: identified, 64n; letter to, 64
Harrison, George, 18, 106, 106n, 118, 417–18
Harrison, Reuben: identified, 221n; letter to, 221
Hayward, Stephen: identified, 181n–82n; letters to, 181–82, 185, 187–88, 208–209, 270, 273, 389–90; mentioned, 269, 300, 303, 354, 356, 405, 406–407, 421, 422
Hicky, Daniel: identified, 47n; letters to, 47–48, 371–72, 385–86, 403–404; mentioned, 212, 275, 283–84, 325, 336, 357–58, 401
Hodge, David: letters to, 162, 195–96; mentioned, 225
Holmes, David, 327, 340
Hoopock, Michael: letters to, 236–37, 247–48, 256–57, 271, 173–74, 295–96; mentioned, 212, 213, 216, 236, 274
Hoopock and Stampley: letters to, 201, 202–203, 233–34; mentioned, 235, 269
Hutchins, Anthony: letters to, 224, 323, 336–37, 422; mentioned, 25, 422
Hutchins, Thomas: identified, 109n–110n; letter to, 125–26; mentioned, 14, 27, 109, 208

Illinois: trade with Louisiana, 109; American Revolution in, 332, 333; mentioned, 3–4, 7, 20, 94, 95, 111, 112, 174n, 260, 305, 305n, 306, 318, 321, 339
Immigration: from Louisiana to British West Florida, 12, 15, 58; from Atlantic colonies to British West Florida, 20, 23; from British West Florida to Louisiana, 26–27, 29, 307, 308, 325n, 329
Indians: attacks by, 47, 143, 144, 144n, 266, 269, 269n; trade with, 49n, 83n, 97, 102, 118, 134, 312, 349; mentioned, 3, 12, 16–18, 94, 111, 114, 138, 194, 321, 365
Indigo, 5–6, 20, 31, 32, 42, 91, 118, 194, 196, 217, 263, 281, 326–27, 422
Inrufty, William, 353, 354, 355–56, 357

James, Thomas: letter to, 162; mentioned, 171, 179, 185, 320, 348, 352
Jennings, John: identified, 251n; letter to, 251–52
Johnson, Isaac: identified, 180n; letters to, 180–81, 222; mentioned, 305
Johnstone, George, 7–8, 12
Jones, Evan and James: identified, 121n–122n; letters to, 121, 124–

447
Index

25, 132, 149, 154, 158; mentioned, 194
Jones, James: identified, 121n; letter to, 155–56; mentioned, 15, 21, 121

Kennedy, John: letter to, 269–70; mentioned, 270–71, 273–74
Kennedy, Patrick: letter to, 247
King, Caleb: letter to, 322–23

La Chapelle, Gerome: letters to, 394, 401–402
Lafitte, Jean: identified, 77n; letters to, 77–78, 79, 156, 177; mentioned, 78
Lafitte, Jean, Junior: letters to, 133–35, 280–81
Land: policy of British government, 18–19; sales of, in Manchac, 183
Lavering, Francis, 4, 410
Lefleur, Henry: identified, 59n; letters to, 72, 108–109, 112, 113; mentioned, 59, 65, 73, 366
Levees, 14, 32, 329, 341, 358, 421–22
Leyba, Fernando de, 304, 304n
Linn, Lt. William, 24
Lintot, Bernard: identified, 356n; letter to, 356–57; mentioned, 357, 366, 372, 377
Livingston, Philip, Junior: identified, 116n; letters to, 116, 234, 258–59; mentioned, 18, 156, 278, 359
Los Adaes, 87, 87n, 88
Lum, Jesse: identified, 130n; letters to, 130–31, 161; mentioned, 142, 147, 148, 150, 151, 152, 163, 167, 172, 323, 336
Lumber, 6, 19, 38, 39, 112, 213, 285, 372, 390

McGillivray, Daniel: letter to, 184
McGillivray, John: letters to, 55, 170–71, 189–90, 219–21, 324–25; mentioned, 27, 147, 148, 152, 314
McGillivray and Struthers: identified, 38n; letters to, 43, 47, 53, 55–56, 58–59, 62, 65–66, 68–70, 71–72, 83–84, 86–89, 90–91, 93–94, 96–97, 99–100, 100–101, 102–103, 107–108, 109–110, 111–14, 114–16, 119–20, 121–22, 123–24, 126, 129, 133, 135–37, 139–40, 141–42, 145–46, 150, 151–52, 153, 158–59, 159–60, 164–65, 167, 168–69, 176, 178–79, 190, 289; mentioned, 38, 45, 155, 302
McIntosh, Alexander: identified, 58n; letters to, 73, 76, 169, 245–46, 258, 274–75; mentioned, 25, 58, 65, 66, 84, 88, 90, 91, 94, 99, 117, 123, 128, 139, 142, 145, 148, 150, 151, 152, 154, 165, 167, 168, 173–74, 182, 189, 240–47, 256, 314, 332, 348, 349, 350, 399
McIntosh, Daniel: letter to, 131
McIntosh, William: letter to, 347–51, 367–68, 369, 375–76, 377–78, 378–79, 382–83, 384–85, 393; mentioned, 27, 301, 340, 351, 352, 366, 370, 378, 381, 404, 408
McMinn, Captain, 45, 54, 78, 79, 84, 89, 90, 97, 99, 100, 108, 112, 135–36, 168
Macnamara, Bartholomew: identified, 78n; letters to, 78, 177; mentioned, 84, 87, 89, 92, 121, 125
McPherson, Donald: letters to, 231–32, 238, 239–40, 242, 246–47, 255–56, 264–65, 267–68, 285; mentioned, 335, 336
Maison, Joseph, 38
Manchac: description of, 14, 127; effects of Willing's Raid on, 26–28, 289, 290, 359–60; occupied by British troops, 294, 306, 307, 307n, 311, 312, 324, 329, 334, 338; under Spanish occupation, 28–29, 30–31, 355, 360, 392; mentioned, 11, 13, 15, 16–18, 39n, 74, 83, 84, 87, 182–83, 371
Marshall, William: identified, 79n; letter to, 79; mentioned, 11
Mexico: trade with Louisiana, 31, 97
Miller, Francis: letter to, 217; mentioned, 265, 307
Miller, John: identified, 118n; letters to, 118, 120–21, 123, 146–47, 153, 155, 160, 163, 166–67, 171, 172, 177, 182–83, 184–85, 263–64, 265–66, 268, 277–78, 294–95, 306, 312, 314, 317–18, 320–21, 328–30, 332–33, 334–35, 337–38, 362–63; mentioned, 115, 179, 195
Miró, Esteban, 19, 395, 395n
Mississippi River: flooding of, 127, 139, 170–71, 319
Mobile, 19, 29, 76 79
Monsanto, Benjamin, 39n
Monsanto, Isaac: identified, 39n; mentioned, 13, 39, 41, 43, 46, 51, 53, 55, 56, 57, 58, 59, 62, 65, 72, 94, 103, 166, 368
Monsanto, Jacob, 18, 149, 368, 374, 385
Monsanto, Manuel: letter to, 412–13; mentioned, 18, 39n, 141, 141n, 163, 164, 211, 214, 231, 281, 285, 374, 384, 415
Montgomery, Robert: letters to, 311, 319, 327; mentioned, 340, 356
Moore, Capt. William, 38, 40n, 77, 78, 79

Morgan, George: identified, 66*n*; letter to, 95–96; mentioned, 66, 67, 73, 77, 78, 79, 109, 126, 266, 297
Morgan, Patrick: letter to, 286; mentioned, 129, 129*n*; 244*n*
Morgan and Mather: identified, 240*n*; letters to, 240, 243–44, 250–51, 254–55, 260, 281–82, 284, 285, 297, 300, 303–304, 331, 338–39, 361, 363–64; mentioned, 211, 212, 221, 239, 244, 245, 246, 282, 374, 377, 383
Murphy, Francis: letter to, 248
Murphy, Patrick: letter to, 166
Murray, John, 111

Natchez: early settlement of, 13; attacked by Indians, 84, 84*n*; attacked by James Willing, 25; rebellion against Spanish rule, 384, 384*n*, 411; mentioned, 6, 19, 20, 29, 31, 47, 83*n*, 161, 210, 248, 263*n*, 291*n*, 323, 327, 417, 421
Natchitoches, 5, 31, 42, 51, 87, 116, 317, 365
New Orleans: description of, 4–5; economic conditions in, 9–10, 12, 42, 48, 49, 75; British merchants in, 9, 11, 20, 244, 244*n*, 245–46; in the American Revolution, 24, 26
New Orleans Superior Council, 4, 22, 43–44, 50, 53

Oakes and Goddard, 409
O'Connor, Capt. Fitzmorice: letter to, 175–76
O'Conor, Hugo: identified, 87*n*; mentioned, 87, 88
O'Keefe, Thomas: letters to, 212, 238–39, 240, 243, 249, 252–53, 272, 291–92, 295, 297–98, 299; mentioned, 296
Opelousas, 281, 284, 371
O'Reilly, Alexander: identified, 62*n*; mentioned, 4, 9–11, 40*n*, 62, 63, 65–69, 72–76, 83–84, 87, 91–93, 96
Overseer: hire of, 217

Page, Joseph, 49–50, 50*n*, 93
Pavie, Joseph, 18
Pearis, Capt. Richard, 26, 290, 293
Pecans, 138, 171, 219
Pensacola: attacked by Spanish, 29–30, 369, 383; mentioned, 15, 19, 296, 324
Piernas, Pedro José, 304, 304*n*
Pinhorn, Joseph: identified, 228*n*; letters, 228–29, 263; mentioned, 229, 317, 335, 338
Pittman, Philip, 12
Pointe Coupée, 20, 39*n*, 77, 111, 134, 138, 144, 147–48, 166, 211, 213, 215–17, 222, 263–64, 295, 317
Pollock, Oliver: identified, 125*n*; letters to, 197, 213–14, 228, 234–35, 249–50, 251, 267, 271–72, 276, 292; mentioned, 24–26, 125, 141, 142, 156, 177, 181, 191, 209, 212, 218*n*, 234, 239, 242, 249, 291, 298, 299, 370, 373
Pollock, Thomas, 213
Poupet, Pierre, 43, 43*n*
Poussett, Francois: identified, 139*n*; letters to, 141, 214, 242; mentioned, 32, 139, 204*n*, 229, 245, 286
Price, Eleanor (Nelly), 162, 180–81, 267, 347–53, 369
Priest, John: identified, 221*n*; letters to, 221, 262–63, 275; mentioned, 275, 402
Putnam, Rufus, 14

Ranson, Louis, 90, 90*n*, 91, 92, 100, 106, 110, 115, 116, 117, 119, 127, 156
Rapalje, Garrett: identified, 186*n*; letter to, 186; mentioned, 196, 204*n*, 224, 355, 410
Rapalje, George: identified, 368*n*; letters to, 368–69, 375; mentioned, 355, 367, 369, 374, 376, 382
Rapalje, Jacques: identified, 158*n*; mentioned, 158, 161, 354–55
Rebellion of 1768, pp. 10, 40*n*, 43*n*, 45, 45*n*, 46, 69
Red River, 365
Reggio, François Marie, 21
Rice, 6, 19
Ritson, John: identified, 40*n*; letters to, 40, 47, 50, 52, 60–61, 61–62, 63–64, 65, 66, 71, 75, 80, 83, 85–86, 101, 103–106, 124; mentioned, 51, 62, 64, 113, 128, 157, 168, 183
Roads: in Louisiana, 6; along Bayou Manchac, 13, 15, 32, 148, 150, 162, 165, 178, 331
Rochon, Pierre, 122, 126, 133
Rogers, Robert, 4, 209
Ross, David: identified, 41*n*; letters to, 196, 216–17, 221–23, 224, 229, 235–36, 237, 250, 252, 255, 259–60, 297, 298–99, 301–302, 354–55, 402, 419; mentioned, 204*n*, 225, 228, 244*n*, 245, 326
Ross, Robert: identified, 41*n*; letters to, 41–42, 276, 290; mentioned, 291*n*, 350, 391, 394
Rum, 55–56, 103, 122, 149, 166, 186, 216, 231, 276, 330, 348, 391, 394

St. Domingue, 11
St. Louis, 304, 304*n*
St. Maxent, Antonio de, 355, 355*n*

St. Maxent, Gilbert Antoine de, 49, 49n, 57, 67, 70, 71, 85, 90n, 91, 92, 95, 96, 98, 101, 117, 225, 227, 262, 315, 316, 336, 347, 387, 391, 395, 399, 420

St. Pé, Pierre, 44, 44n, 54, 62, 69

San Gabriel de Manchack, 14, 26, 118, 138, 147, 153, 179, 263, 263n, 280, 281, 294, 359

Santa Rosa Island, 122, 133

Sarpy, Jean Baptiste: identified, 51n; letters to, 85, 117, 261–62; mentioned, 51, 66–67, 92, 95, 129, 162, 225, 227

Scarce, Robert, 348, 350, 364, 370, 373, 380, 390

Shakespear, Stephen: letter to, 342; mentioned, 252, 253, 323, 338

Shipwrecks, 76–77, 78, 121–22, 133, 417

Slaves: conspiracy of, 204, 204n; runaway, 111, 131–32, 235, 245, 291–92, 304; hired, 123, 311, 312, 322, 329; sales, 39, 45, 46, 51, 67, 84, 147, 215, 292, 304, 315, 317, 329, 335, 339, 350; mentioned, 12, 20, 23, 31, 32, 60, 62–63, 88, 89, 101, 112, 149, 181, 209, 213, 221n, 262, 293, 294, 295, 297, 298, 305, 311, 319, 320, 324, 325, 327, 360, 362, 363, 364, 369, 372, 373, 396, 405, 414, 417–18, 422, 425, 430–31

Smith, William: letters to, 400, 405–406, 406–408

Smuggling: as a branch of intercolonial commerce, 8–9; in Louisiana, 8–9, 11; from British West Florida into Louisiana, 13, 20; by British merchants on the Mississippi River, 20–21; mentioned, 17, 24–25, 31, 41n, 244n

Spain: establishes control of Louisiana, 63–71; and commercial regulation of Louisiana, 25, 120, 120n, 121, 122, 136–37, 221n, 235, 236; supports American Revolution, 24, 210, 218–19, 237; and occupation and administration of British West Florida, 334, 339, 340, 348, 360, 410, 418, 420; grants asylum to British refugees, 307, 321, 359

Spanish Manchac: *See* San Gabriel de Manchack

Specie: shortage of, in French Louisiana, 9–10, 11; shortage of, in New Orleans, 37, 38, 39, 41, 46, 48n, 52, 54, 55, 71, 72, 169; shipments of, from Cuba, 65, 70, 74; shortage of, at Manchac, 106, 109

Stampley, Henry, 235, 236, 248, 257

Stephenson, John: identified, 38n; letters to, 38–39, 39–40, 41, 42–43, 46, 51, 124, 127–28, 130, 138–39, 157–58, 168, 171, 175, 183, 191–92, 204, 205, 207–208, 209–210, 218–19, 225–26, 237, 241–42, 244, 391–92, 392–93, 394–95, 402–403, 416–18; mentioned, 19, 40, 47, 50, 85, 86, 103, 104, 105, 106, 124, 244n, 254, 339, 363, 370–71, 372, 399, 416, 419, 420, 421

Strother, William: letters to, 210–12, 213, 215–16, 226–28, 301, 313–14, 315–17, 342–44, 345, 380–81, 387–88; mentioned, 225–26, 299, 300, 317, 346

Strothers, Arthur: identified, 63n; letters to, 63, 68, 75, 76–77, 300–301, 420–21; mentioned, 303, 416

Stuart, Charles: identified, 59n; letters to, 118, 132, 137–38, 143–44, 146, 194–95; mentioned, 59, 72

Stuart, Henry: letter to, 301; mentioned, 18

Stuart, John: identified, 115n; letters to, 115, 118; mentioned, 18

Stuart's Rangers, 290

Sugar, 6, 100, 103, 156

Sutton, James: identified, 57n; letter to, 57

Swanson, Peter: identified, 44n; letters to, 44–45, 52–53, 89, 94–95, 97–98, 98–99, 110–11, 114, 116–17, 122–123, 128, 30, 131–32, 137, 144–45, 148, 150–51, 152–53, 159, 164, 165, 172–73, 176–77, 178, 189, 195, 396–400

Swanson, William: letters to, 317, 361–62; mentioned, 118, 172, 176, 178, 188, 294, 308, 325–26, 333, 358–60, 363, 364, 372, 377, 396, 398, 399, 417–18

Taffia, 56, 56n, 96, 141, 276

Tangipahoa, 94

Terry, Jeremiah, 44, 44n, 69

Thomas, Dr. Edwin: letter to, 340–41; mentioned, 327, 340, 355, 357, 364, 370, 373

Thomas, Lt. John, 16–19, 22, 112, 115–20, 122, 130, 138, 143, 144n

Thompson's Creek, 19, 29

Tobacco: Spanish royal monopoly of, 422; mentioned, 6, 20, 31, 32, 42, 42n, 84, 87–90, 94–95, 97–99, 114, 145, 152, 156, 159, 220–21, 251, 317, 319, 330, 335, 417

Topham, Thomas: identified, 224n; letter to, 224; mentioned, 18

Trade conditions: in New Orleans, 42, 48, 49, 75; at Manchac, 110,

374; on the Mississippi River, 328–29; mentioned, 96, 128–31, 133, 136–39; 143–44, 150, 167, 170, 182, 192, 194, 218, 220, 229–30, 263, 294, 302, 333
Trist, Nicholas, 277, 284
Truly, Sarah: identified, 256n; mentioned, 239, 256, 264–65

Ulloa, Antonio de, 10, 41n, 45n
Unzaga, Luis de, 18, 24

Vallé, Francisco: identified, 305n; letter to, 305–306, mentioned, 304
Vallière, Monsieur: letter to, 282–83; mentioned, 286–88, 299, 300
Van Horn, Capt. Cornelius: letter to, 215
Vaughn, Capt. John, 120, 121, 126
Villaescusa, Don Lucas: identified, 41n; mentioned, 41
Villebeuvre, Juan de la: identified, 263n; letter to, 352–53; mentioned, 29, 263, 266, 282, 325, 348, 384n
Villiers, Balthazar de: identified, 212n; mentioned, 212, 269, 269n
Viviat, Louis: identified, 61n; letter to, 202; mentioned, 61, 64, 64n, 66
Vousdan, William: letter to, 389

Waldecker Regiment: stationed at Manchac, 330, 330n
Walker, David: letter to, 253
Walnut Hills, 20, 25
Walters, Thomas: letter to, 265; mentioned, 266
Ward, Banjamin: letters to, 366–67, 385, 386; mentioned, 263, 374
Ward, Daniel: identified, 45–46n; letters to, 45–46, 159; mentioned, 47, 48, 52
Watts, Stephen, 29, 204n, 278, 279, 371, 372
Waugh, Capt. John: identified, 175n; letters to, 175, 178, 235, 243, 248; death of, 271; mentioned, 139, 142, 168, 244, 245, 249
Weir, William: identified, 271n; letters to, 271, 289, 302, 307–308, 319–20; mentioned, 303, 316, 317, 387
Wescott, Thomas, 293, 300, 325, 329, 359–60, 417
West, Nathaniel, 165
West Florida (British sloop), 26
White, Matthew: letter to, 414
Williams, David: identified, 253n; letter to, 253; mentioned, 181
Williams, William, 209
Williams and Ferguson: letter to, 273
Willing, James: identified, 125n–26n; letters to, 141, 191; raid on British West Florida, 25–26, 289, 291n, 294, 295, 302, 359, 360, 365; mentioned, 20, 125, 129, 130n, 141, 142, 156, 161, 181, 209, 221n, 253, 410
Wilton, William: letters to, 183, 187, 188, 229–30; mentioned, 123–24, 126, 225
Wine, 39, 44, 48, 52, 56, 59, 61, 63, 88, 89, 97, 100–101, 114 116, 156, 211, 231, 245, 258
Winston, Richard: identified, 174n; letter to, 174–75
Winston and Kennedy: letters to, 186, 192–93, 204; mentioned, 186, 260, 304, 305

{451

Index